edited by
Jim Obelkevich
Lyndal Roper
Raphael Samuel

Disciplines of Faith

Studies in Religion, Politics and Patriarchy

First published in 1987 by
Routledge & Kegan Paul Ltd
11 New Fetter Lane, London EC4P 4EE

Published in the USA by
Routledge & Kegan Paul Inc.
in association with Methuen Inc.
29 West 35th Street, New York, NY 10001

Set in 10/11pt Bembo
by Columns of Reading
and printed in Great Britain
by T.J. Press (Padstow) Ltd
Padstow, Cornwall

Library of Congress Cataloging in Publication Data

Disciplines of faith.

(History workshop series)
1. Religion and sociology.   2. Religion and
politics.   3. Sex role—Religious aspects.
I. Obelkevich, Jim.   II. Roper, Lyndal.   III. Samuel,
Raphael.   IV. Series.
BL60.D57   1987   291.1'7   86–15416

British Library CIP Data also available

ISBN 0–7102–0750–6 (c)
        0–7102–0993–2 (p)

To John Walsh

Contents

Contributors

Henry Abelove is Associate Professor of History at Wesleyan University, Middletown, Conn.

Luisa Accati is one of the editors of *Quaderni Storici*.

James Ault, a sociologist, is Associate of the Five Colleges, Amherst, Mass.

Eileen Barker, Dean of Undergraduate Studies and Senior Lecturer in Sociology at the London School of Economics, has written *The Making of a Moonie* (1984) and numerous other works on new religious movements.

Stephen Barton is Tutor in Biblical Studies, Salisbury and Wells Theological College, Salisbury.

Guy Boanas is completing a study of fifteenth-century Rome.

John Bukowczyk is Associate Professor of History at Wayne State University, Detroit.

Rickie Burman is Curator of the Museum of the Jewish East End and Research Centre, London.

E. Ellis Cashmore lectures in Sociology in the University of Hong Kong.

Inga Clendinnen teaches history at La Trobe University, Bundoora, Victoria, Australia.

Robert Colls, Lecturer in the Department of Adult Education, University of Leicester, has written *The Collier's Rant* (1977) and co-edited *Englishness: Culture and Politics 1880–1920* (1986).

Tom Gallagher lectures in the Department of Peace Studies, University of Bradford.

Sheridan Gilley teaches church history in the Department of Theology at the University of Durham and is co-editor of *The Irish in the Victorian City* (1986).

Christopher Hill was formerly Master of Balliol College, Oxford, and has written numerous works on seventeenth-century religion and society.

Michael Lynch, Lecturer in the Department of Scottish History at the University of Edinburgh, has written *Edinburgh and the Reformation* (1981).

Phyllis Mack teaches European and women's history at Rutgers University, New Brunswick, N.J., and is completing a book on women visionaries in seventeenth-century England.

Hugh McLeod lectures in the Department of Theology, University of Birmingham, and has written *Class and Religion in the Late Victorian City* (1974) and *Religion and the People of Western Europe* (1981).

Roger Magraw teaches history at the University of Warwick and has written *France 1815–1914: The Bourgeois Century* (1983).

Gail Malmgreen has written *Silk Town: Industry and Culture in Macclesfield 1750–1835* (1985) and is Associate Editor of the Papers of Elizabeth Cady Stanton and Susan B. Anthony, University of Massachusetts, Amherst.

Alison Milbank is completing a study on Victorian fiction at the University of Lancaster.

Jim Obelkevich has written *Religion and Rural Society: South Lindsey 1825–1875* (1976) and lectures at the Centre for the Study of Social History, University of Warwick.

David Ormrod is Lecturer in Economic and Social History at the University of Kent at Canterbury and is an active Christian socialist.

Alex Owen is completing a book on women and spiritualism and is Research Associate and Visiting Lecturer at the Harvard Divinity School.

Tristan Platt, an anthropologist by training, spent some ten years in Bolivia and is now writing in a cottage in Wales.

John Pollard is lecturer at Cambridgeshire College of Arts and Technology, Cambridge and has written *The Vatican and Italian Fascism 1929–1932* (1985).

Terence Ranger is Professor of History at the University of Manchester, a member of the editorial board of *Past and Present*, and a former chairman of the Ecclesiastical History Society.

Chris Read is Lecturer in the Department of History, University of Warwick, and has written *Religion, Revolution and the Russian Intelligentsia 1900–1912* (1979).

Franco Rizzi teaches history at the University of Rome-La Sapienza and is the author of numerous works on the history of the peasantry.

Lyndal Roper lectures in history at King's College, London, and is an editor of *History Workshop Journal*.

Raphael Samuel is Tutor at Ruskin College, Oxford, and an editor of *History Workshop Journal*.

Bob Scribner lectures on history at the University of Cambridge, has written *For the Sake of Simple Folk: Popular Propaganda for the German Reformation* (1981) and is on the editorial board of *Social History*.

Angelo Torre is a historian at the University of Turin.

Christopher B. Turner, a historian of Welsh Nonconformity, is Assistant Registrar at the University College of Wales, Aberystwyth.

Cornelie Usborne teaches in the Open University.

Merry Wiesner is in the Department of History, University of Wisconsin at Milwaukee.

Eileen Yeo teaches history at the University of Sussex, has co-edited *Popular Culture and Class Conflict 1590–1914* (1981) and is a member of the executive committee of the Society for the Study of Labour History.

Acknowledgments

This volume has its remote origins in the 'Religion and Society' group – one of the feeders for 'History Workshop' – which began meeting at Nuffield College Oxford in 1965. The Group, which contained a number of people who were to become 'History Workshop' editors and contributors, began from a radical dissatisfaction at the exclusion of religion, as a central subject for enquiry, from the Oxford history course. (Members of the group were Peter Burke, Roderick Flood, Brian Harrison, Patricia Hollis, Tim Mason, Raphael Samuel, Gareth Stedman Jones, Gillian Sutherland.) It was a homespun way of trying to make good the deficiency. Each week we took a text – starting with Pascal's *Pensées*, going on to Wilberforce's *Practical View*, and making some first navigations of nineteenth-century Evangelicalism. John Walsh was the one senior member of the university who encouraged us, who came loyally to our meetings, and who also, by his particular combination of passionate commitment (he is a son of the Manse) and ecumenical curiosity, provided us with a model which over the years we have tried to live up to. What was true of the original Workshop group was also true of numbers of those who took part in the organization of the 'Religion and Society' workshop in July 1983 – people who had benefited from John Walsh's friendship or his help in the apprentice stages of their work. So the dedication of this volume is more than a formal one.

The Workshop from which this volume is drawn covered three days and involved a vast range of papers, only a fraction of which are included here. The project has accumulated many other debts: to Friends House, who provided us with an ideal venue for the Workshop; to the many American scholars who came over for the Workshop, and who have made this volume in some sort a Transatlantic project; to Peter Burke who solicited our Italian contributions and to Guy Boanas who translated them; to David Blackbourn who obtained overflow premises for us at Birkbeck College; to Anna Davin who at a late stage in the Workshop preparations made feminism central to it; to David Ormrod, Judith Herrin, Liz Mason and Hugh McLeod, members of the core organising group; to Chloe Chand, Dagmar Engel, Judy Loach, Sarah Lambert and Jay Dixon who ran the organization of the three-day workshop.

Phyllis Mack's article, 'Feminine symbolism and feminine behaviour in radical religious movements: Franciscans, Quakers and the followers of Gandhi', has appeared in the *Journal of Women in Culture and Society*, 11, no. 3 (Spring 1986).

The illustration 'The meeting of a family in heaven' by William Blake is reproduced by Courtesy of the Trustees of the British Museum.

1 Introduction

1
Introduction

JIM OBELKEVICH, LYNDAL ROPER, RAPHAEL SAMUEL

I

That Religion and Society should be the theme of a volume associated with the Left may seem surprising. Hostility to organized religion is – or at least was, until very recently – a leitmotif of the socialist movement, as of the various forms of popular radicalism from which it drew its original strength. As the child, albeit a rebellious one, of the eighteenth-century Enlightenment, socialism took its stand on the side of reason against revelation, science against superstition, and it was only too ready to equate religion with 'mysticism', 'obscurantism' and backwardness of all kinds. Socialists followed their radical forebears in championing freedom of thought; in equating priestcraft with feudal and monarchical tyranny, and in looking to education as the great engine of emancipation. In Catholic Europe, anticlericalism was a major component of the socialist idea, down to the 1914 war and beyond. A startling late example of this would be the burning of the monasteries during the Spanish Rising of 1931. In the Protestant countries of northern Europe relations between socialism and Christianity were more ambiguous, but taking a tilt at the clergy – or even, as readers of *The Ragged Trousered Philanthropist* will know, the 'shining light' chapels of the small-town bourgeoisie – was a stock in trade of socialist advocacy.

These hostilities were reciprocated. For Robert Owen's clerical opponents of the 1830s and 1840s, 'socialist' and 'atheist' were interchangeable terms; while the 'godlessness' of socialism was the prime target of those Christian-Social movements which, in the 1880s and 1890s, were one of reaction's principal weapons against the rising socialist movements of Central Europe.

In the 1920s and 1930s – as the articles on Italy and Spain in this volume may remind us – anticlericalism was given a new lease of life by the open way in which Catholicism allied itself with reaction in resisting the revolutionary tide, while the leading role of the Vatican and of Christian democracy in the building of an anti-communist alliance in the Cold War inflamed historic suspicions of the Church as an international conspiracy against progress in Labour and Communist movements.

3

Yet socialism, as a doctrine, is closely wedded to religious modes of thought, espousing a secular version of millenarianism and promising a world in which all things will be made anew. The reappearance of impossibilism in the post-1968 feminist and socialist movements has made for a much greater receptivity to the proto-religious elements in early socialism. Recent historians such as Barbara Taylor have enabled us to recognize not only socialism's debt to religious paradigms and values, but also the broad range of early socialist interests, encompassing not only material relations, but also questions such as the division of labour between men and women, and the reorganization of domestic life. These religious influences should not be regarded as a deformation of a true, secular socialism; nor should early socialism's broad range of preoccupations be seen as diversionary. Socialism, after all, was utopian before it was scientific.

As a political movement, socialism has been only too apt to mobilize its supporters behind ritualized sets of beliefs, while its advocates, whether evolutionists or revolutionists, utopian or scientific, have commonly conceived themselves as an aristocracy of the Spirit, carrying light into dark places, and enjoying privileged access to the higher truths. The socialist idea first made its appearance, in the 1830s and 1840s, as a secular religion – what Saint Simon called the 'new Christianity', and Weitling 'Christian Communism'. The *Communist Manifesto*, when Marx and Engels began drafting it for the workers of the German diaspora, was initially cast in the form of a catechism, and at every point in the nineteenth century when socialism touched a popular constituency, its message was typically cast in religious or proto-religious forms. Pamphlets took the form of tracts; and in the period when socialism emerged as a mass movement in the Italian countryside of the 1890s, arguments were often advanced in the form of parables, speeches and addresses, concerned to paint word-pictures of the socialist future.

When in the 1880s, socialism revived in Britain, it quickly took on the character of a 'religion of socialism', whose converts entered a 'new life', indeed found a new purpose in life, serving their fellow men and women, joining in comradeship with other socialists, experiencing some of the joy and fulfilment that awaited all mankind with the advent of socialism. For some, socialism was the practical application of their existing Christian faith (Anglican as well as Nonconformist); for others, sceptical of the traditional faiths, it was a new religion in itself. And it was not only the 'soft Left' of the ILP that had a religious character, but the hard Left of the SDF, where the educated few preserved the faith in its purity, like the early Church, in the face of indifference and persecution. In its period of greatest dynamism and vitality, British socialism was religious.

In Germany, the Social Democrats of the 1890s and 1900s, and later the Communists, set themselves up as a kind of anti-Church, offering their followers a whole range of counter-religious ceremonial and an alternative mental universe in which to live. 'Cosmic mooning', as E.P. Thompson has sarcastically named it – or the idea of socialism as a new life – was a fundamental component of the socialist appeal to its followers: the 'gleam of socialism', owing more to Christian eschatology than to a more secular reformism, was the stock in trade of the platform orators.

This close, if unofficial, engagement with religion, is nowhere more apparent than in socialist writings on history. The Primitive Church was a subject of fascinated attention of the early socialists – like Primitive Communism, another favourite object of historical reflection, it provided socialism with a historical pedigree. Belfort Bax's three-decker *The Social Side of the German Reformation* – an account of the Anabaptists – is the first English-language work of historical writing in a Marxist tradition, and it prefigured what was to be a major theme of later work by socialist historians, most famously in Tawney's *Religion and the Rise of Capitalism* and more recently in the writings of Christopher Hill. Later socialist historians, taking their cue from Eric Hobsbawm's *Primitive Rebels* – a work itself much indebted to the anthropology of religion – have been no less concerned with popular messianism (a riveting chapter in E.P. Thompson's *Making of the English Working Class* is the rescue of the Southcottians from the 'enormous condescension' of posterity), or with the place of ritual in labour movements. Similarly, and most recently, a fascinated attention to the magical underpinning of scientific experiment and of the millennial components of 'rationalist' thought is emerging as a leitmotif of contemporary socialist work in the history of ideas (Logie Barrow's *History Workshop* volume on plebeian spiritualism is a case in point).

II

The Religion and Society History Workshop started out from a recognition of the power of religion as a shaping force of politics in the contemporary world. Such an acknowledgment is uncomfortable for socialists who have traditionally anticipated the eventual triumph of reason over superstition, as it is for sociologists with their paradigms of secularization and rationalization, allegedly characteristic of the modern world. The power and extraordinary destiny of the Revolution in Iran; the bitterness of the war in Northern Ireland; the disturbing transformations effected by Jewish identity and consciousness in Israel; the role of the Catholic church in the solidarity movements in Poland; all show the inadequacy of such firmly held convictions as the commonplace that the modern world belongs to a post-religious epoch. (Speculatively, the hesitations of the British labour and trade union movement in welcoming Solidarity and the Polish October came from an unease at the salience of a Catholic faith amongst insurgent Polish workers: photographs of Gdansk shipyard workers kneeling to the Madonna and taking communion were disturbing images for anyone brought up either in Protestant or in free thought traditions, and they fitted with none of the iconographies of proletarian struggle.) Even in the heart of the most advanced capitalist economy in the world, the United States of America, we are confronted by the recrudescence of the moral majority and the political mobilization of born-again Christianity. James Ault's 'The Shawmut Valley Baptist Church' in this volume analyses that political presence at local level, and points, too, to its roots in family needs and disturbance. Yet what these and other examples suggest is that the role of religion in contemporary political struggle is no simple one: if it is reactionary it is also sometimes progressive, and often a mixture of the two. The churches' recent interventions in British politics are another reminder.

But it is changes in Roman Catholicism which have done most to affect the Left's views on religion. The liberalization of the Catholic church initiated by Vatican II, the rise of radical and sometimes revolutionary movements among Catholics, notably Liberation Theology in Latin America, the role of Catholics in peace movements, the Christian-Marxist dialogue, and the shift in its centre of gravity from Europe and North America to the third World, have all made it increasingly difficult to conceive of the Church as a monolithic bloc; while the renewed vitality of the Catholic church has made it impossible to go on regarding it – in the manner of freethought propaganda no less than that of Protestant bigotry – as a survival of feudal barbarism. Nearer home, the influx of ex-Catholics into the feminist and student movements of the 1960s and 1970s has made Catholicism a less alien phenomenon to the British Left, if not necessarily a more sympathetic one.

When we started planning for this workshop, our first thought was deliberately to confront work drawn from the study of

Catholic religious practice and Catholic cultural formation with a more traditional English left-wing preoccupation with radical nonconformity. The Workshop was intended to subvert – or at any rate to question – the routine anti-Catholicism of the British Left and an unarticulated but essentially Protestant 'common sense' which had underpinned the work of British Marxist and radical historians. Indeed, it has arguably coloured the character and ideals of both British socialism and the Labour movement. In Britain, socialist historians have historically been peculiarly uninterested in Catholicism, either abroad or as the practice of a minority in Britain. This inattention is all the more strange since the Catholic minority in Britain is largely both working-class and Irish – and among the most consistent supporters of the Labour Party. In Scotland, Catholics are more pro-Labour than Protestants at every level of society.

III

The cultural revolution of the 1960s has perhaps made socialists more ready to admit the power and autonomy of the imaginary, to consider belief systems as a *primum mobile* which structure and constitute action rather than passively reflecting it. It has made us more sensitive to the ways in which belief acts, not so much as a reflection of material interests, but as an independent cultural force.

More disturbing to either Marxist or social historical categories of explanation and inquiry are the areas of fantasy, desire, myth, fear – what might be termed the domain of the psychic. The preoccupation with this territory is clearly one of the shaping influences in our volume, and we believe it raises questions which any study of religion must confront. It cannot be subsumed under the study of 'collective mentalities' which have long enjoyed a legitimacy in social history, nor can it be marginalized as a study of the exotic and safely anthropologically distant. It reaches beyond, to subjectivity and individual experience, something which has never formed part of the province of the historian. The dialectics here, whether between the conscious and the unconscious; society and self; masculine and feminine; ideal and real – are not those with which social historians, Marxist or otherwise, have been particularly well equipped to deal. They evidently fall short of or transcend the line of class. One of the most uncomfortable questions raised by these essays, especially the feminist contributions, is to what extent this is historical terrain, both because of its intractability and because of the apparent persistence of the phenomena it describes. It is not easy to see how the psychic can be sited in a specific temporal and material context; yet without tackling these problems, we shall be unable to even guess at the emotional, psychic and imaginative force of religious thought, action or language. Here, the exciting article by Luisa Accati on the cult of the Madonna in Catholic and Protestant Europe, which seeks to site psychic and familial patterns in the structures of devotional themes, breaks new paths.

But the most important influence on the historical study of religion for this workshop has been feminism. For post-1960s feminists, perhaps even more than for socialists, religion has often appeared as a prime and undifferentiated force of oppression; and it has been the more important to identify it as such because of the insidiousness of its hold over our non-conscious imagination. While feminists have felt on sure ground in attacking the institutional Church, with its usually male clerical face, and its frequently expressed opposition to abortion, contraception, or (on occasion) its espousal of the most rigid model of appropriate womanly role, the question of the gendered nature of religious imagery – most obviously, the masculinity of God in traditional Christian and Jewish faiths – has proved a far more troubling issue. At least in part this stems from the centrality of such gendered symbolism to our own cultural traditions; and just how resistant to mere reform or counter-balancing these can be has been brought home to feminists in the cult of the Virgin Mary. The mere existence of a female presence in religious cults cannot guarantee an affirmation of real women: indeed, the contradiction of virgin motherhood can work to make earthly womanhood appear irreducibly corrupt. Yet none of this can really engage with the actual power and attraction which the image of the Madonna can exercise, even subliminally, as it provides the cultural backdrop against which we imagine and desire perfect mothers.

For feminists studying religion in the past, a point of departure has been the common assumption that women are by nature more spiritual than men, essentially more religious. Feminist historians have been engaged in deconstructing this naturalization of feminine religiosity, showing, in the process, how women's devotional expressions can subvert and undermine the social order – how they can subtly exploit the contradictions of gender relations. As Alex Owen's essay on women and spiritualism in this volume shows, it was the very perceptions of women as more closely linked to the emotions and more open to external forces – the very factors which underpinned the conception of women as domestic beings – that were also thought to make women better spiritual mediums.

When we originally planned the Workshop on religion, and decided to conclude with a plenary session on Women and Christianity today, we were making what we thought was an appropriately contemporary recognition of the importance the questions of gender, sexuality and family had acquired in our own approaches to the study of religion. To link the study of feminine piety, the question of the sexual division of religious labour, or the nature of religious authority in the past, with discussion of developments in feminist theology and debates about the admission of women to the priesthood in the Catholic and Anglican churches today, seemed a simple and obvious recognition of a connection. We were wrong.

The plenary session released a great deal of anger, most of which centred upon the very idea that there could be a feminist Christianity, with the room literally as well as figuratively divided between those who were thought to 'believe' and those who rejected the terms of the debate itself. Indeed, as we were forced to recognize, a dispassionate liberal curiosity about the progress of feminism in the churches is possible only when there is nothing at stake. The force of religion is still very much alive, as was nowhere more evident than in the anger of women against a reactionary Church; and against a religion which cannot easily be exorcized.

Jim Obelkevich, Lyndal Roper, Raphael Samuel

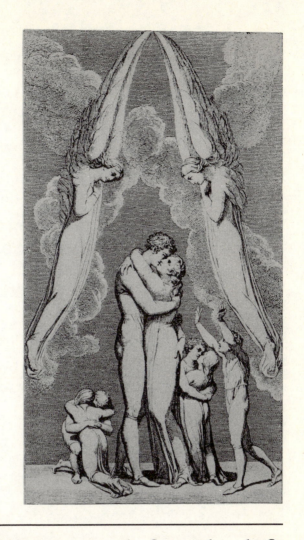

Religion and family life

2

*Family and fundamentalism: The Shawmut Valley Baptist Church**

JAMES AULT

This ethnographic sketch of a fundamentalist Baptist church community in the United States stems from a broader inquiry into the social bases of popular support for the conservative 'pro-family' movement. That inquiry involved field work also among right-to-lifers, parents campaigning against sex education and conservative Catholics running their own 'home school'. This report was written four months after I began field research in the Shawmut Valley Baptist Church. Although this research continued over the next three years, subsequent findings have not led me to change, in the main, any of the impressions set down here.

Some Christian readers may see in this report an implicit secularism. Since it is addressed initially to a social scientific community, it is framed in terms of human, rather than extra-human, agency – particularly, given my concerns as a sociologist, in terms of the way human action is shaped by the creation of concerted human life: small group cohesion, faction fights, trust, kinship, and the like. Whatever truth such an account may hold, it does not preclude a Christian reader from seeing in these social arrangements the Lord's design for, say, how a local New Testament church should work. While some would think this beside the point, it is not our task here to pose or resolve such differences.

Protestant fundamentalism has continued to enjoy an astonishingly rapid growth in the United States, despite contrary trends toward secularism and despite the predictions of scholars, who, ever since its rise to national prominence in the 1920s, have anticipated its imminent demise.[1] Such a misreading of fundamentalism's fate in the modern world suggests a fresh consideration, based on first-hand observation, of some elementary questions. How does such a Protestant fundamentalist community work? What does it accomplish for its members?

Answering these questions is a necessary first step toward understanding why such communities sustain popular support for a constellation of 'new right' enthusiasms: abortion, the ERA, school prayer, sex education, creationism, school busing, military preparedness, capital punishment, and so on. In 1965, Richard

13

Hofstadter had to lament that, despite the historic prominence of fundamentalist ministers in conservative movements and the 'fundamentalist style of mind' prevalent among right-wing political leaders, 'We know more about the role of fundamentalist leaders in right-wing groups than we do about fundamentalism among the mass following.'[2] Almost twenty years later the same can be said. Yet the task seems increasingly urgent given fundamentalism's continued growth and the unprecedented impact of the 'new Christian right' on contemporary American politics. Behind the mushrooming empire of the TV evangelist, behind the smooth machinery of the Moral Majority's direct-mail politics, and behind the nationwide impact of NCPAC in recent elections, stand millions of supporters whose commitments are galvanized in church communities like the Shawmut Valley Baptist Church (SVBC).[3] It has been estimated that there are more Baptist ministers in the state of Texas than there are Catholic priests in the United States at large.

This is a study, then, of one of the elementary units of Protestant fundamentalism and popular conservatism, a unit whose internal organization has historically generated support for a strikingly stable ensemble of attitudes and enthusiasms. When seen against the background of the biographies of members of the SVBC, this inquiry into its internal organization also reveals something about those more general structures of family and community life which have routinely nourished such church-building efforts.

The SVBC is set back off a road on the outskirts of an industrial city in central Massachusetts, where the suburban housing of postwar development blends with that of older farm communities and long-stagnant mill towns characteristic of the New England industrial hinterland. The area has a somewhat eclectic appearance. Proper suburban homes with neatly trimmed lawns sit alongside self-built ones whose idiosyncrasies reveal their piecemeal construction. Commercial vans parked in driveways, derelict pieces of machinery in the yard, and hand-written signs – 'Sewing Done' or 'Curios 'n' Things' – reveal the presence of family-based business. In the short commercial strips laid out on what have become the more important thoroughfares, the common installations of mass society – MacDonalds, Bonanza, an outlet for electronic banking – sit brashly next to establishments like 'Kenny's Lounge', the 'Valley Bait Shop', or 'Papa Roc's Diner'. Papa Roc's advertises 'Home Cooked Meals' and, given the personableness of the old Greek couple working it, serves as 'home' for truckers and young working men in the area.

It is from this area that the SVBC has drawn many of its members in the four and a half years of its existence. Its founder and pastor, the Reverend Frank Marchetti, an Italian and ex-Catholic, grew up in one of these towns, where his wife, Angie, and he were high-school sweethearts. He tells his congregation: 'I was born and raised in this town and our past sins are known. Not so much Angie's – she was a good kid – but mine. Just to know me had her pegged.' During combat duty in Vietnam two anti-personnel rockets exploded next to him, riddling him with shrapnel and tearing off part of his scalp and nose. He was not expected to live. He now has a wooden leg, needs braces on both legs to walk, and requires an operation annually to relieve the pain in an ear damaged by the explosion. He still has pieces of shrapnel working their way out of his body.

After being 'born again' and eventually graduating from Jerry Falwell's Liberty Baptist College in Lynchburg, Virginia, Marchetti and his wider family worked to build the SVBC. Its growth has been impressive. From 14 members meeting first at home and then in a defunct social club in town, it grew to a congregation of about 150 at its peak. They meet for worship three times a week in a stone and mortar building which looks as little like a church as the bakery it was in earlier years. Behind it looms the newly built 'gymnatorium' in the spare, box-like style characteristic of larger, newly built fundamentalist churches. When complete it will convert easily from a gym to a sanctuary much larger than the room they now use. Hidden behind it, a chain of trailer classrooms stretches out to the woods behind. They house the church's 'Christian Academy' covering kindergarten through twelfth grade for some 70 students.

When first I announced my intention to attend Sunday worship, Reverend Marchetti asked, 'Do you have a Bible, Jim?'

'Yes, I do. . . . It's on one of my bookshelves, I think.'

'Well, bring it with you,' he continued, 'because true scriptural Christians all bring their Bibles to church.' It was helpful advice. Every adult carries a Bible to church. It is a badge of membership making visible the distinctive nature of membership in a fundamentalist religious community: the acceptance of, and submission to, the Bible as the divinely inspired and inerrant word of God. It provides, as several members put it, 'our handbook for life'. In their view it offers a set of unchanging and absolute standards by which they can order their lives.

Much attention is given to reading the Bible, both collectively and individually. I was impressed with how many couples spoke of reading not only as their principal means of moral and political enlightenment, but also as a way, by reading together, of becoming either reunited, or for the first time strongly united, in their marriages. It seems that many members of the SVBC never learned to read in a critical way – that is, to study. Several men, including the pastor, confess quite publicly they never read before they were born again. Both adult Sunday school and Wednesday night service are given over largely to instruction in Bible reading. The pastor leads the congregation in the study of an assigned passage. The result is much like a college seminar, provoking spirited responses and concentrated effort by any academic standard.

> – Pastor Marchetti asks, 'What do you do as soon as you see the word "wheretofore"?' A plump woman in a worn overcoat promptly raises her hand and, as others are raised, he calls on her.
> 'It means all that he just said before.'
> 'Right. It refers to all those things he just talked about. So what he's saying here is. . . .'
> – He interjects at one point, drawing on previous lessons, 'Always remember the Biblical meaning of "perfect" is "mature". Man cannot be perfect.'
> – 'What's the Biblical definition of "wrath" again?' he asks. 'Who wants to define "wrath"?'

The pastor seems to show good judgment in posing questions and fielding answers while leading members to a point he has in mind. He draws heavily on personal and public knowledge of individuals to encourage the shy, cajole the tentative and deflect the irrelevant or unuseful comment. After four years of practice, he is a fairly skilled teacher, quite apart from the content of what he teaches. (All this, I might add, from someone who describes himself as having graduated from high school 'functionally illiterate' [sic].)

In this way, techniques of reading scripture are developed by building up knowledge of a specific lexicon, which, like all jargon, has a technical aura associated with its mastery, and by teaching certain rudimentary methods of reading such as the attention to paragraph organization and 'thesis sentences' as guides to understanding the meaning of particular passages. In addition to studying the assigned text, some members have even struggled with an approved fundamentalist concordance.

Whatever the substantive educational consequences of this process, it serves to build confidence in the group's independent basis for an authoritative reading of a text they believe contains absolute standards by which to govern their lives. It is seen to be quite explicitly independent of, and truer than, those interpretations prevalent in established 'liberal' churches and in the intelligentsia at large. Efforts at revised interpretation, either through scholarship or revelation, are openly derided: 'How can you correct the word of God? How silly.' If, then, as the pastor impressed on his congregation during adult Sunday school, 'We've lost the art of defining the terms of our own soul,' this discourse can be seen as an effort to recover it.

Given the remarkable fact that well over half of this independent Baptist congregation are ex-Catholics, the emphasis on reading the Bible involves, in certain senses, a recapitulation of the Reformation. The Catholic church is, in fact, excoriated from the pulpit, and by individual ex-Catholics in private, for inhibiting believers' access to 'the word'. But the study of God's word is not limited to fundamentalist Protestant churches. I found it practised and lauded by Catholic activists in the right-to-life and conservative home school movement, and they openly acknowledged their debt approvingly to the fundamentalist Protestant tradition. Some Catholic women even attended largely Protestant Bible study groups. Others sent their children to Baptist Sunday schools to receive appropriate instruction in scripture. It is a form of religiosity, then, made use of by a number of activists in the conservative 'pro-family' movement regardless of their specific denominational backgrounds or affiliations.

If the Bible is looked to as a 'handbook for life', it soon becomes clear that it is not looked to primarily for guidance on how, say, to organize the national economy or run one's business. Instead, it is looked to, above all, for moral standards to govern family and personal life. Sermons abound with commentary on family life, from personal disclosures of the consequence of sin in the preacher's own life to issues of public controversy and public policy. Reverend Marchetti denounces the 'cultish' character of the United States government, which, in seeking to sit in the place of God, has 'legalized murder' by legalizing abortion. He notes that a law before Congress would permit a child to sue his or her parents, at public expense no less. Such an outrage he and the congregation feel needs no further comment. The ERA is said to threaten catastrophe by abrogating God's order of the family, and homosexuality is likewise condemned:

> 'The greatest wrath of God, the Bible tells us, came down on who? The Sodomites. Take away the 's' 'o' and you have what they are? "Dumbites" (laughter). . . . Did you ever see any group speaking out like homosexuals today? . . . They've been out of the closets for a long time. They're growin' and you can't increase your numbers in the closet (laughter). . . . It's the most filthy thing.'

These are not central themes, however. Nor is the emphasis so much on urging members to take public action on these matters, even though the pastor's extended family has been active in local campaigns against sex education. Rather, they are referred to as so many dangerous features of an environment threatening the creation of a Godly order of family life in members' own lives. This is of central concern. According to members, everything that interferes with 'God's plan for the family' – feminism, liberal sex education, homosexuality or abortion – is bound to have disastrous consequences.

Many of the preacher's themes can be seen as part of a theological and biblically based diagnosis of family problems and means for remedying them. He is quite aware that his major appeal to young couples in their twenties and thirties, who are the critical recruits to his congregation, is his ability to speak effectively to their problems in marriage and family life, drawing directly on his own experience. 'I do most of my counselling from the pulpit,' he comments (that is, not privately, it is significant to note). Topics are readily translated into the domestic domain. The virtue of 'meekness in receiving God's word', for example, becomes discussed principally in relation to the need to listen to one's spouse. The dictum 'be slow to anger' is discussed in relation to marital fights, the pastor drawing freely, as he usually does, on his own personal life. Under the formula that falling out of fellowship with a spouse is a consequence and sign of being out of fellowship with God, virtually every kind of marital problem can be discussed in these terms.

But the importance of finding an order for family life is more prominent in members' own stories of how they came to be saved and what its consequences have been in the conduct of their lives. All of the couples I interviewed at length characterized their marriages prior to conversion as being paralysed by endemic conflict, disorder and meaninglessness. While there is some degree of formularization in their presentations, the concreteness of detail and confirmation from their close relatives lend credence to their accounts. For example, Ann Jones, a woman in her mid-thirties and a mother of four, characterized in the following way the period prior to her and her husband's being born again:

> 'There were no guidelines for my marriage. As far as it went, I had likes and dislikes and Ricky did his thing and, if I didn't like it, what could I do? . . . There was no common denominator. There was nothing you could bring it to. And it would, then become a battle of will. Whose will is stronger and whose will is going to survive. . . . It was chaos.'

Though she often acquiesced to his demands, she continued to fight, they both agreed, by withdrawing co-operation and emotional support. Others told similar stories revealing domestic realities aptly expressed by a metaphor the pastor used to describe to me his own marriage before his wife and he were saved:

> 'How would you like to play a football game or a basketball game without referees and . . . without a rule book. All you got is the field marked off.'
> Q 'Is that what your family life was like?'
> A 'That's what it was. . . . Everybody's playin' by their own rules. . . . A stupid, idiotic way of living, right straight out of the pits of hell is *that* kind of living.'

It is partly against the background of such experiences of conflict and anomie in domestic life that the appeal of fundamentalism in these cases is to be understood. Through their faith members feel they have found a way out of chaos, disorder and meaninglessness by ordering their lives in accordance with the Bible, or what Ann Jones's husband, Rick, called 'our rulebook for life'. The pastor went even farther, in a strikingly Durkheimian formulation, to say, 'God is the medium, the center point, the rules.' For Ann Jones it provides the medium through which husband and wife, as two naturally different kinds of persons not able fully to understand each other, can unite, very much, as she explains it, as fractions with different denominators can be added only by reducing them to one common denominator. 'That common denominator,' she explains, 'is Christ.'

By submitting to God's plan for the family members feel they have found 'a way out' of chaos to peace, order and meaning in their lives. It is an order they see as fixed and transcendent, the 'plan' of an omniscient and infinitely wise God. It stands above and beyond the individual wills of husband and wife; under it, many stressed, 'both have rights'. Being born again and submitting to God's word in this way leads, they and their relatives recount, to dramatic changes in the conduct of their lives. These changes are most evident, it is curious to note (a point to which we will return), in the conduct of men, who mention, among other things, coming to love their wives more, finding new harmony with their in-laws and learning how to discipline their children correctly. However, those changes singled out as the most dramatic signs of the behavioural consequences of being saved are how easily they were able to give up 'bad language' and drinking.

Readers may well wonder what blueprint for family life scripture makes so clear. Little more would need be said, in fact, if the Bible bore the same kind of relationship to family life as, say, the rulebook for football – which most football players have never seen let alone read – bears to playing football. In fact, recognizing the considerable latitude possible in interpreting the moral implications of scripture for daily life (its potential contradictions and inconsistencies are legion), many readers might find it puzzling – if not, for critics, either blind or hypocritical – to assert its absolute character.

It is undoubtedly such latitude that led Catholic theologians faced with Luther to raise the spectre of social chaos if individuals were permitted their own reading and interpretation of scripture. That such chaos does not, in fact, ultimately prevail within contemporary fundamentalism, points to a question of considerable importance: how is it that an orthodox and uniform reading of the Bible's moral implications for family and personal life is achieved? Such a question is, to be sure, out of keeping with members' beliefs. When I attributed one informant's changed behaviour towards his wife and in-laws to his *own* reading of the Bible, he immediately corrected me by interjecting, 'No, that is the *Bible's* reading of the Bible.'

What members arrive at as the Bible's rules for personal life corresponds, generally speaking, to what is taken as traditional morality. More specifically, it corresponds to the traditional morality within which informants were raised. Speaking of 'God's directions for how to make a good marriage', one husband remarked, 'If there isn't the order in the family, if I don't take on the position of the father image and do the things a father is required to do, as far as provide for the family and give discipline when necessary and do the other things, right? . . . I throw it out of order.' In their most general formulation of God's 'plan' members describe, drawing on Ephesians Chapter 6, a chain of command in which, just as husbands are subject to God, so, too, wives are subject to their husbands, as head of household. Wives are enjoined to love their husbands. And husbands are required to love their wives 'as Christ loved the church'. More specific kinds of guidance can readily assume the form of the following illustration offered by Rick Jones:

> 'Suppose I'm driving down the street and pass a girl in a tight sweater. Now, I might want to turn around and get a better look. And the next thing, I might be tempted to talk with her or something. Now, the Bible teaches you not to do the first thing. It's these "superfluities of naughtiness" that lead to greater sin.'

What the Bible provides, then, is absolute sanction for what believers already know as the traditional way to order family and personal life. The content of this morality is not to be discovered in the text itself. The text provides, rather, a set of handy tags and labels bearing the imprimatur of the sacred. Hence, the relatively limited concern with a rationally defensible clarification of the meaning of the text in favour of drawing selectively from it a set of phrases, dicta and formulae to be used repeatedly in their original language. Outsiders often see this practice as the narrow literal-mindedness of fundamentalists' readings of the Bible. But this simply is a consequence of the uses to which their reading is put within a traditionalist machinery for creating social order.

In fact, the authority of scripture as a handbook for life seems warranted in the eyes of some members precisely because of the elements of traditional folklore they find in its pages. An older Italian man confessed how astounded and impressed he was, upon his first reading the Bible as an ex-Catholic, by all the wisdom it contained. 'You know the saying "If man will not work, neither shall he eat"? Well that's from the Bible, Proverbs I think . . . and lots of other things. You'd be surprised what's in that book!' This is one of the advantages of fundamentalists' distinct preference for the King James Version, it would seem. In addition to its venerability, it abounds with such maxims, sayings and phrases which, cast in the memorable language of believers' childhoods, have the hypnotic ring, and carry the aura, of eternal verities.

Fundamentalism, as distinct from the more general category of evangelical Christianity, has always represented, above all, a defence of traditionalism in the face of the rationalization of social life. It has been identified, in terms of its pervasiveness and influence, as a distinctly American phenomenon ever since its emergence at the turn of the century and its effervescence in the 1920s when it was associated, it is significant to note, with the 'red scare', nativism, the attack on progressives in public schools, and the controversy over evolution culminating in the Scopes trial.

The pastor himself attributes the rapid growth of the church to the simple fact that, 'When people see you have a handle on life they don't have, they want it.' But why this particular handle? What accounts for the particular appeal of a small, independent Baptist church, of a biblically based traditionalism in which the horrors of homosexuality, sex education, abortion and secular humanism are regularly preached and the traditional model of patriarchal authority routinely asserted?

Born-again experiences in the fundamentalist Baptist tradition are often elaborated along chains of kin. All of the fourteen original members of the church, for example, were related by blood or marriage to the pastor. In this case it was his mother- and father-in-law who were first saved and then brought his wife to Christ. Several months later he followed and eventually his own parents (both ex-Catholics), his wife's sister-in-law, and his wife's younger sister and her husband all became active members.

This not the only, or even the largest, assemblage of kin in the small congregation of 80–90 adults. Four extended families furnish well over half of the adults who attend regularly.

But the church not only incorporates existing kinship ties among adults, it also gives them privileged place in its symbolic order. Members are collectively addressed, for example, as 'Brother Jo' or 'Aunt Kate' regardless of actual blood ties. (Aunt Kate is a widow whose own siblings are dead and whose children have moved far from the area.) This is not, in symbolic terms, a 'Society of Friends' in the Quaker formulation, but rather a community of kin. Assimilating the all-important relations among fellow believers to the idiom of kinship rather than friendship serves to valorize such obligations in categorical terms above and beyond other kinds of relationships, while at the same time lending weight to the relations they establish through their faith. It serves to make the church community more family-like and members readily describe the church as 'family'.

In keeping with tradition, deference is accorded older members of the congregation. During one Sunday service the oldest woman, whom everyone calls 'Granny' ('She's really just Kathy's grandmother,' a person sitting next to me explained with laughter) was singled out for special attention. At a particularly telling point in his sermon the pastor paused to ask, 'Am I right or wrong, Granny?' as if to seek her stamp of approval for an accepted truth he had just enunciated.

The presence of kin, both actually and metaphorically, is part and parcel of the familiar and informal atmosphere that prevails in all activities of the church. Even on the most formal occasion, Sunday worship, the pastor encourages exchanges with the congregation. Calling on 'Brother Jo Slazik' for the prayer of invocation, he asks, 'Is that an Italian name, Jo?' (Laughs.) (Ethnic jokes, including those about Yankees, are common. When done freely and reciprocally among those who have ethnic attachments, as do many members, such jokes serve, by releasing possible tension, to knit together solidary relations in the congregation.[4]) Introducing visitors in Sunday worship, he mentions their relation to members of the congregation ('She came with Betty and is her brother's sister-in-law, aren't you?'), asks them about their work ('Am I right that you work with her at Scooby's [a fast food place in town]?'), and often finds some way to joke with the person in question ('I know you. You're a sister-in-law of Mike's aren't you? You have a tangled mess of relations over there [he gestures to that section of the sanctuary] but I'm gettin' it straight.').

But such give and take seems reserved in comparison to the informality of Wednesday night services which are, for that reason, spoken of with special fondness. They are attended by a smaller number of people (somewhat over half the Sunday turnout), what one called, significantly, 'the old home crowd'. One might term them the core of church membership, namely those who attend all three services in the week, are most involved in the entire range of church activities, and who, therefore, see each other quite regularly. Throughout the Wednesday night service the pastor addresses individuals and jokes with them personally, and they respond in kind.

  – 'What do you think of that, Mary?' he asked his mother-in-law, referring to what one man in front of her had just said. 'You don't have to mind his beard,' he added.
  'I shaved mine off this morning,' she retorted to general laughter, before she offered her comment.
  – Commenting on an unusually long anthem sung by the music director, he quipped appreciatively, 'I'd rather hear Mike sing than eat . . . I've heard him eat.'

By the end of the service he has personally recognized close to half of those present. Such an atmosphere of 'at homeness' is also evident in the spontaneous and informal character of socializing taking place among members. It would not be uncommon, as one member characterized it, for one to say to others after a service or meeting, 'Let's go get some dinner, chew the fat, and have some fun and talk about our problems.' After Sunday service members might spontaneously invite others over to eat or agree to meet at a local restaurant. All those with formal positions in the church – those on the payroll, on the Board of Directors or Board of Finance, the Deacons, choir members and teachers in the Christian Academy (in sum, at least half the congregation) – are required, as part of church discipline, to attend all three weekly worship services in addition to their other meetings (including Bible Study Groups). In addition, many see each other while picking up their children at school every day or simply by dropping in at each others' homes either to talk with someone about being saved or just to 'chew the fat'. In these ways core members become involved in a dense pattern of activities through which they come to see and know the same people in common, which for many includes close kin.

This all-encompassing, integrating character of the church community is strengthened by the regime of abstinence required of core members. That they cannot drink, dance or swear and that they must always be giving 'good testimony' in the presence of others makes it hard to sustain ties outside the church. Such behaviours tend to make others uncomfortable. In that way the community's inner cohesion and, therefore, its power to place demands on its members is strengthened.

There are obviously limits to the scale on which such a community is viable and members are quite aware of these constraints. Several commented, based on their experience in churches of a similar kind, on what they saw as the ideal size for a 'nice church'. That was about 100 and certainly no more than 150. The number of members in this congregation had, in fact, been depleted considerably, by about 40, the previous spring when a split had occurred, a not uncommon feature of such churches. Still obviously shaken by this experience, the pastor, in his more generous words, attributed it to what he called 'church psychology':

'When you're small, it's hard to get people to join your fellowship. What happens is that in the beginning you get people with a pioneering spirit who get in there and fight to make things work and they become a clique. Then you grow, new people come and when it gets to 100 they feel the pastor doesn't have time for me. They take it as a personal insult. . . . It's kind of like a family. . . . When a church reaches 100 to 150 there is a faction that develops that doesn't want it to grow. They like that close-knit stuff. . . . When you hit certain plateaus church psychology says you're going to have certain problems.'[5]

While we will want to return later to some of the political realities underlying this split, the point here is that these comments testify to the fundamental importance of the 'close-knit stuff' in this community for members' commitments to it.

The close-knittedness of this community lends it certain capacities. The rapid development of its material infra-structure over a four-year period would have been impossible, for example, without the pooling of volunteered efforts and resources, from the use of construction equipment to labour involving an array of different skills. That individuals' contributions come to be publicly known by all and contribute to his or her reputation in the community provides incentives to contribute in this way. In addition, a good standing in the church carries the probability that, when in need, a member will, in turn, find support and help. This represents what the pastor referred to as the third phase of church development, 'the interaction within the fellowship where people do things for people.' Not leaving things solely to the Spirit – 'God expects us to do things, not just sit and wait,' as several members insisted – the pastor made a point, for example, after one Wednesday night service, of introducing a new member, a young self-employed plasterer, to an older member of the congregation who owned a small insulation business, raising the possibility that the latter might be able to help him in some way.

Herein lies, from one point of view, the power of prayer in a closely knit community of this kind. Members testify again and again to the ways God has answered their prayers. Quite apart from the peace of mind it affords, they testify to the concrete and material ways He responds. For example, one man had had the misfortune of having an automobile accident when his car registration and, hence, his insurance had temporarily lapsed. On the $6700 salary he was paid for teaching in the church's school (one third of what he previously made as a foreman in a local wire mill) he could not afford either the repairs or the $200 fine. He prayed and entrusted the matter to God, as he, nevertheless, continued to look for solutions.

'And what happened?' he said. 'I came up with the $200 and God provided money for rent and a number of other things.'

'In what way?' I asked.

'Oh food and . . . just people being good to us. Sometimes people don't know that God uses them, but he does.'

'Who were these people?'

'Oh, people who weren't even saved, my family . . . her [his wife's] father, a number of people around the church who knew us.'

To understand the efficacy of prayer, it is crucial to note that such prayers rarely remain private matters. At every service the pastor encourages members to bring to him anything they want him to pray about with them, always adding the assurance, 'I will not embarrass you in any way,' signifying, I believe, that he will treat the matter with accepted standards of discretion. (He does not say he will keep it private.) Prayers are also done collectively in Bible study groups and in the pastor's study before each service. In some churches, I am told, the congregation divides up in small groups of four or five at Wednesday night prayer meeting and members take turns praying aloud to others in their group. And, in addition, individuals often ask family members or friends to pray with them about a particular problem. Thus, the problems that give rise to prayer soon become, in a multiplicity of ways, matters of common knowledge and public concern in a close-knit community of this kind in which everyone knows and sees everyone else regularly.

Furthermore, by publicizing a need in this way, prayer serves also to publicize in advance the act of Christian charity which ultimately will meet that need. And, although members stress the desire for anonymity in giving – recounting stories of finding envelopes with money in their car to cover a medical bill they could not pay, or finding groceries at their door each week – they often come to know, in fact, who is responsible for such clandestine acts and, more generally, claim to have firm knowledge of who is generous and who tight-fisted in the congregation. However, that is not spoken of openly, but rather in the kind of hushed whisper that bespeaks the gravity of the matter, while sustaining the pretence of secrecy.

It would be difficult to trace the actual communicative work whereby prayer, as a collective and individual meditation on a person's problems or needs, might eventually lead others to offer consolation, emotional support and material solutions to those problems. But it is not difficult to imagine how that might routinely occur.

In response to a call for prayer requests at the beginning of one Wednesday night service, for example, Erv raised his hand and said, 'My wife is ill and my mother-in-law is looking for an apartment.' The pastor repeated the request for the whole congregation to hear. He couldn't resist adding, 'You're sure it's not the other way around, Erv?' provoking good-natured laughter throughout the congregation, since everyone knew he and his wife had been struggling for sometime with marital problems. This prayer request would, then, join Erv's marital problems on members' prayer lists. Over subsequent weeks these problems would be meditated upon by member in a more or less regular fashion. And sometime or other someone would mention, for example, in conversation or in prayer, that Crystal needed help moving out of her old apartment, which had grown too small for her and her three children. Since Erv's mother-in-law would be in the minds of many, some listener would readily recall her need for an apartment. And soon need and resource would be providentially brought together.

If, as informants put it, 'God has a way of bringing things into effect,' and 'God always works through people,' this is one of the ways that people carry out those effects or enact the will of God in answering prayers of the faithful. It represents, from believers' standpoint, the materialization of God's will in the world. This reality is reflected in members' accounts of how they gradually learn to feel God's presence in the world by His answering their prayers in immediately apprehensible ways and by thus encouraging them to entrust more of their problems to Him through prayer. Many recounted their having learned the important lesson that there is no problem too small to be of concern to the Lord, even, as one recalled, finding a parking place.

As is the case with any community, the degree it can do something *for* you provides some measure of what it can do *against* you and, therefore, exact from you its demands. It is the ever-present sense of both potential benefit and potential injury that mediates members' commitments to community standards of conduct. A community of this kind is rife with gossip and rumour which stand to unleash irksome, fearful and, at times, overwhelming consequences. Apart from the multitude of beneficial or adverse effects that come from having either a good or bad standing in the church, members can be removed from positions and, in extreme cases, expelled from the community altogether for not keeping its discipline. That includes, at the formal level, not drinking, smoking, dancing or attending 'Hollywood movies', and, at the informal level, even such things as 'fighting too much in the family', or, as the pastor described it in the case of a school principal he fired, 'having his family life all out of line'.

Members are always on the lookout for the ever-present possibility of 'backsliding'. The way backsliding is continually identified, testified to publicly, and sanctioned – events heavily shaped by communicative work such as gossip – is a major means by which the community's customary order of family and personal life is controlled. The degradation of a person's reputation may produce such an unbearable sense of shame that he or she must withdraw completely because, as one former fundamentalist put it recalling an experience in another congregation, 'I couldn't hold my head up in church anymore.' The overwhelming character of such public humiliation is brought into clearer focus by bearing in mind that this community includes, for any individual, not only workmates and friends, but also life-long ties to 'family'.

Such publicly humiliating consequences of sin, as organized within the church community, find expression in the dominant image of the judgment day at Christ's second coming. Members prefer to envision it, not as an individual faced with a judgmental Lord and Father, but rather as an individual's sins being read aloud publicly to the entire community including his or her own family. And, according to one former fundamentalist, it is particularly when the dangers of backsliding are most acutely felt in a church that the second coming and the final judgment are vehemently preached.

The strength of communal sanctions finds expression in church theology in other ways as well. The God through whom this community unites is a God of both bountiful love and fearful wrath, both of which rain on his people according to His will, not their individual ones. As one put it:

'God's just like my father. If you have a good father and you do something wrong, you're going to know about it. He doesn't come out, turn me over His knee and spank me. . . . But He lets things happen in my life whereby I know that He is working in my life.'

This theology they contrast, in hostile terms, to that of 'liberal' churches which preach, in the pastor's words,

'a perpetual diet of how to be nice, God is good, God is love, nice to your neighbor, neighbor nice to you. . . . They're preaching half truth. . . . They never come across with the part that says, "It's a fearful thing to fall into the hands of an angry God". . . . They don't ever preach the other side of the coin: the same coin, two sides.'

While 'liberal' theology, in their view, portrays Christian action in this world as a matter of individual moral discretion, members of this church prefer to see it as a matter of their ultimate fate in this world and the next, which they see placed in the hands of a God standing above and beyond their will. Their theology matches the degree they are encompassed by, and dependent upon, their church community. Their willingness to, in the words of a popular fundamentalist hymn, 'Lean on Jesus' is a measure of their willingness to depend on the church community. Just as the upper-middle-class suburban church, as social club and as source of private pastoral counselling, reflects the social organization of the suburban community based on autonomous nuclear families brought together temporarily by their common style of life, so, too, the SVBC reflects the broader social life of its communicants: the mutual dependence in the solution of the problems of day-to-day living of those bound together by long-standing ties to kin and locality, and the consequent public nature of 'sin' in one's personal life.

Some may wonder why women, who comprise well over half the congregation, embrace a regime which explicitly requires them, as a matter of principle, to submit to their husband's authority, and a community which vigorously asserts the model of the traditional patriarchal family? This question poses itself concretely in a striking comment by Ann Jones:

'Men are logical; women are very emotional. You know, they just basically don't see eye to eye. Somebody has to have the final decision, somebody has to be the head. In God's plan it's the man and the wife is to support the decision the man makes. . . . Today we're being taught that the woman has just as much right to her decision as the man. . . . So whoever has the strongest will in that marriage takes over, there's no higher standard. . . . It becomes chaos.'

This affirmation of patriarchal authority needs, however, to be read side-by-side with her diagnosis of that very chaos she saw prevailing in her family prior to accepting God's 'plan' (viz. p.18). This was when she and her husband lived in Florida for a few years and where they had their first two children.

One might suggest that her submission to the patriarchal scheme of the church made available certain moral constraints on her husband's conduct, a 'higher authority', as she goes on to say, to which disagreements could be brought. Such constraints and such an authority refer to a pre-existing order she and her husband see as standing above and beyond them as two individual wills coming together in marriage, the antithesis of those assumptions underlying, say, 'contract marriages' or the practice of spouses' writing their own vows.

I have suggested that the fundamentalist use of scripture as a 'handbook for life' is, in some sense, misleading, for it is generally used to buttress what members already know and take for granted as traditional morality. However much such historically received tradition bridges the gap between the ambiguities of scripture, on the one hand, and the need for moral certainty, on the other, like all forms of traditional legitimation, the curtain of alleged 'timeless truths' always conceals behind it a continuous drama of conflict and change. This is one reason it is mistaken to view fundamentalists' Manichaean presentation of right and wrong as inflexible at the practical level.

This point is necessary to understand why, alongside the SVBC's unwavering commitment to traditionalism in family life, the pastor can, at the same time, preach a sermon on the theme, 'the name of the game is change'. The church does in fact engineer considerable change in the content of tradition. For example, though many members came from families in which mothers were full-time homemakers, the church is on the verge of launching its own day-care programme, called 'cuddlecare', a project initiated by church women. At worship services the pastor earnestly calls on the congregation to pray for its success. This recognition of the fact that many mothers of actual or potential members work outside the home goes hand-in-hand with the frequent insistence, by women even more than men, that housework and child care represent a 'full-time job' and that this is a wife's principal responsibility, just as it is a husband's to provide for the family.

Other departures from the pattern of their childhood are more explicitly recognized in community discussion. Informants often recalled it was unfortunate, though sometimes necessary that their fathers spent so little time with them as children, and it was generally reported that fathers rarely assumed domestic responsibilities. However, current church discussion enjoins men to focus more on family life and, above all, to listen to, and communicate with, their wives (no small change from the silent and withdrawn, yet occasionally explosive, working-class father they at times describe in their biographical accounts). It is in this regard that we should understand the importance attributed to men's renunciation of drinking and 'bad language' as evidence of the 'complete turnaround' being born again is seen to have wrought in their lives. Since these practices are the hallmarks of masculine sociability outside the home in working-class milieux, renouncing them is emblematic of giving up such socializing in favour of focussing more on family life. From several accounts it was clear that being saved meant, for men, turning away from their habitual pattern of 'hanging out with the boys'. The men themselves characterized this as part of becoming more 'mature' than their former friends. In recognition of the greater role fostered by the church for men in family life, the pastor proudly announced recently the commitment of the new day-care programme to have a man present, on a full-time basis, to provide a suitable father figure for the children.

In the evolution of this traditional order there are, then, certain modifications in what for members have been the ideals of masculinity. These are seen in the person of Christ, who provides, for members, the model of masculinity men should strive for. In addition to greater involvement in domestic life, they are to aspire, in relation to their families, to Christ's patient, long-suffering and self-sacrificing example. That such changes in men's behaviour are highly valued is evident in the much greater pre-occupation in church discourse with men's sin than with women's and with what is seen as the difficult matter of involving men in church life. At the close of the last hymn during one Sunday service, for example, the pastor asked all 'the ladies' to sit down for a minute leaving the men standing and then took time to comment:

> 'Where in the church today in America do you see so many men? About a 50 per cent ratio [a slight exaggeration]. You won't see that anywhere! On Sunday morning most churches across America today are filled with women.'

Recruiting men to a religious life in the church is seen, then, as a noteworthy achievement.

In a community like the SVBC it would be tempting to think the power to shape changes in tradition rests in the hands of that person formally recognized as head, namely, the pastor. Independent Baptist churches are notorious for how little formal constraint they tend to place on a pastor's authority. But one must bear in mind how the organization of an independent church substantively limits a pastor's autonomy. There is no larger church organization to which he owes his authority or to which he can turn for support. Despite the arduous and impoverished years it took to build up the church from its small beginnings with a handful of relatives, if his congregation deserts or rebels, he is out of work.

Given their vulnerability in independent Baptist churches of this kind, some pastors respond by taking out what amounts to an informal 'insurance policy'. They put church property in their own name and keep church records among their personal ones. But, whatever they do, suspicions about the church treasury can easily be ignited. And, since concern for worldly things is so morally reprehensible in members' eyes, allegations of financial self-aggrandizement quite often serve as a basis for overthrowing a pastor (in addition to the also frequent scandals of sexual immorality). Indeed, in this particular case, allegations of financial misconduct surfaced from the sea of gossip and rumour and played a critical role in the split that occurred six months earlier. As the pastor explained, 'When the offerings go up from $500 to $2000, then you're talking eight grand a month. They stop trusting you, but they don't say anything to you.' To defuse rumours in advance he now goes so far as to lay out church chequebooks and financial records for inspection and discussion during 'fellowship nights' when members gather for pizza and volleyball.

Measures of this kind cannot insure against a pastor being undone by any faction that shifts the tide of public opinion against him for any reason whatsoever, even, for example, out of disappointment with the waning of personal closeness attending the church's growth. Therefore, he must be careful about creating enemies and must vigilantly scan the sea of public opinion to discern any disturbances beneath its apparent calm. Also, in order to keep his congregation loyal, he must preach the gospel as they 'need' to hear it and this includes generally affirming the customary order of family life they embrace. To go against that would be to court disaster.[6]

If the pastor's freedom to shape what is taken by members to be the moral order of family life is thus circumscribed, who else contributes to its shaping? As far as women's sense of that order is concerned, there is no question about the major source. It comes from routine socializing with other women in a range of sex-segregated activities in the church, from Bible study groups and 'Joy Circles' to day-to-day, informal co-operation with child care. According to informants, it is through these activities that older women come to instruct them in how to be a Christian wife and mother. For some this discourse involves older women kin as well.

One might well ask: is there not a parallel discourse among men which contributes equally to the formation of the traditional order of family life? There are reasons to think not, certainly not to the same degree. Quite simply, where traditional gender roles remain intact, men do not generally discuss, on a collective basis, the details of domestic life in any realistic or sustained way. Their very achievement of adult male status requires that they distance themselves from what are seen as women's affairs.

While men's knowledge of family order tends toward relatively vague 'formulae', women's seems more realistic. The contrast I have in mind appeared in my interview with the Joneses. Rick Jones was under the impression that he got answers about the conduct of life directly from the Bible, referring to times he would call the pastor to get the relevant chapter and verse for a particular item or theme. His wife, Ann, cautioned,

> 'You'll find, though, that most mature Christians, when they argue, it's not something you can open God's word to and say, "OK, dear, God says this, you said this and I said this, so we'll have to do it this way." [Rick looked perplexed.] It's something that 99 per cent of the time that the Christian is out of fellowship with the Lord and, therefore, out of fellowship with her mate. . . . It's more your feelings, and it's something you have to deal with between you and Christ.'

Such a view, it seems to me, represents a more realistic and pragmatic grasp of the malleability of God's 'plan' for the family as it is enacted in this community. (It remains unclear how an individual actually goes about, in her terms, re-establishing fellowship with the Lord or dealing with Christ, but I suspect it would involve her day-to-day fellowship and discourse with other church women.)

Regardless of the relative weight of these various influences giving shape to members' continually evolving sense of God's 'timeless plan' for the family, one thing that is clear is that the SVBC provides organization for a sex-segregated discourse among a collectivity of women which is brought to bear in creating an order of family life in a small, kin-based community of personal relations where informal controls have considerable strength. These women do not face the dilemmas of domestic life in social isolation. Indeed, as an extension of their socially structured role in maintaining diffuse reciprocities among kin, women seem to play a predominate role in knitting together the moral bonds of this community. This role is paralleled, in a familiar scheme, by the fact that all formal positions in the church are deliberately reserved for men, an allocation the pastor explained as part of the effort to enhance the masculine image of the church and, therefore, its appeal to harder-to-win male recruits.

But why within this order are commitments to patriarchal arrangements of family and gender not only sustained but also so resolutely and explicitly affirmed? This requires understanding of the ways in which this order of family life incorporates, and draws sustenance from, a pre-existing customary order and the ways in which the effectiveness of women's collective discourse rests, in a multiplicity of ways, on patriarchal elements within that order. This gestures well beyond what I can argue here and to a discussion developed at length elsewhere.[7] Nevertheless, several observations will indicate what I have in mind.

As we have seen, the church has, in fact, been built up through existing relations among kin. Such relations, it is worthwhile reminding ourselves, owe their definition and the strength of their obligation to the heavily gendered roles articulated within the traditional family. The church depends upon, and gives pride of place to, relations among persons identified as 'mother', 'brother', 'sister', 'aunt', and so on – that is, relations seen as involuntary and 'natural' rather than as matters of individual choice or deliberation. As the archetype for such obligations, those arising from procreation are to be seen not as matters of choice or of individual calculation. Hence, members' antipathy not only to abortion and the 'contraceptive mentality' they feel it embodies, but also, more generally, to the value placed on 'the development of the self' and on 'doing your own thing'. The latter they associate with permissiveness at the expense of discipline, rights to the exclusion of obligations, and pleasure as opposed to sacrifice.

The privileged place of women's discourse in regulating relations of this kind, and relations in the domestic domain in general, depends upon members' commitments to a radically dimorphic view of gender which allocates that domain to women by the very same stroke it requires men to seek the family's livelihood in the public sphere. The sex-segregated character of activities and discourse in the church rests on this same rationale. Men and women join separate Bible study groups and prayer groups. In the eyes of most members women share common understandings that they cannot, and should not expect to, share with men. As fundamentally different types of beings, they 'enjoy' (as members insist) different types of rights and responsibilities.

In fact, it bears pointing out that it is precisely men's routine achievement of adult male status, which requires they avoid being tainted by the devalued sphere of women's affairs and hence judged 'fags', that contributes to preserving the integrity and privileged place of women's discourse within the specific domain of family and kinship. It is the very status that gives the pater familias's *individual* voice unquestioned authority in his own household which, at the same time, underwrites women's *collective* voice in elaborating the traditional order (or 'higher authority') of that domain, in general. Finally, if women are seen as the custodians of such traditional morality and men the most likely backsliders against it, that is only consistent with the time-honoured assumptions underlying the 'double standard'.

In these ways, then, the effectiveness of women's discourse in shaping and deploying a moral order of family life in a small-scale church community is built up upon the structures and cultural premises of the patriarchal family. That is to say it exists not despite the traditional family, but in and through it; not by challenging traditional gender roles, but by subscribing to them; not by rejecting patriarchal authority, but by affirming it. (This does not mean women do not try to limit the exercise of that authority even while they affirm it as principle. Many assert they certainly won't be subservient or a 'door mat'. At the same time they hold that a husband should have the last word and, hence, ultimate responsibility for decisions.)

The homology I am suggesting between the machinery for ordering family life in the fundamentalist church community, on the one hand, and the more generalized pattern of traditionalism found in communities based on dense, kin-based and highly localized networks, on the other, is not simply the result of a 'cultural lag' or the manipulation of a nostalgic model of the patriarchal family – though such idealizations are surely involved in this process. Instead, it is a result of members' efforts to reconstruct, or reconstitute, patterns of family and community life just as well-known to them as they are generally unfamiliar to the middle-class intelligentsia.

Most have continued to be heavily involved with kin on a regular, if not daily, basis. If they did not grow up in one of the immediate townships, they were from the wider metropolitan area itself, where many, if not most, of their relatives still live. Their own families were established and took shape in that context. If they attended college, it was a local junior college and they did not leave home to attend. Even once married it was common for them to spend considerable time in the early years living with relatives. This represents not only their own experience, but even more important, that of people they knew, which furnishes them with the general expectations they hold for what family life 'is' and should be. Such expectations are the lens through which they see the world around them. They take such a pattern so much for granted that they assumed, even after months of association with me, that, since I was not married, I must still be living 'at home' – that is, with my parents. Virtually all the single men and women in the church, whether in their 20s or 30s, continue to live 'at home'.

The unbroken co-operation and intimacy among women kin, which this pattern sustains, was evident in Angie Marchetti's reflections on the shock she experienced when, in her early thirties and as a mother of two, she moved to Lynchburg, Virginia, while her husband attended Liberty Baptist College:

> 'Frank and I were on our own for the first time. It was great . . . and it was bad. The first couple of weeks I remember going around and crying . . . "I want my Mom!" [She mimics a child's whine.] You know, just really so sad. I didn't think my little heart was goin' to make it. . . . I went through this traumatic experience of not having any friends, not having Mom and seeing all these girls out with their mom's and enjoying it. Just the typical thing.'

The forms of sociability in this pattern of family life – including the intensive and continuous involvement in a kin-based community at the expense of individual autonomy – have furnished members historically with familiar and emotionally satisfying means for creating security and meaning in life. Their church represents, to begin with, an extension or reconstruction of an order of family life to which they were accustomed. But, on top of this, its discourses provide absolute sanction for this order and invest living life according to it with absolute meaning. There can be nothing more valued or desirable to the believer – no professional success and recognition, no living the good life of fine foods, pleasant vacations and 'educational experiences', no personal growth or self-understanding, no enjoyment of the paraphernalia or substance of power or prestige as displayed in the mass media – than fulfilling this order according to God's word.

While this does not begin to exhaust all that fundamentalist Baptist church communities do for their members, it does point to the foundation upon which their conservative politics of the family is built. All of its elements – from the ERA to school prayer and from abortion to military preparedness – can be rightly seen to serve the moral defence of traditionalist family-based communities in the face of secular, middle-class culture. How that is the case and why some people in certain times and places make use of these social forms to serve these, as well as other, ends will be discussed in later reports of this research.[8]

Notes

*   I would like to thank both the American Council of Learned Societies and the Pembroke Center for Teaching and Research on Women for fellowship support under which this research was begun. I am grateful to Karen Fields and Nancy Jay for sharing their insights in the sociology of religion over many years of colleagueship. For comments on an earlier draft I would like to thank, in addition to Professors Fields and Jay, Karen Johnson, Stephen Arons, Faye Dudden, Robert Liebman and members of the Pembroke Center seminar on 'Gender Representation and Politics'. To the pastor and members of the Shawmut Valley Baptist Church I extend my heartfelt thanks for their trust, patience and kindness during my several years of work with them.

1   Ernest R. Sandeen, *The Roots of Fundamentalism: British and American Millenarianism, 1800–1930* (Chicago: University of Chicago Press, 1970), p.ix.

2   Richard Hofstadter, 'Pseudo-Conservatism Revisited – 1965', in his *The Paranoid Style in American Politics* (NY: Alfred A. Knopf, 1965), p.75.

3   In accord with my initial understanding with informants I have protected their anonymity by using fictitious names for both the church and its members.

4   Cf. William Kornblum, *Blue Collar Community* (Chicago: University of Chicago Press, 1974), pp.41ff.

5   Anthropologists may recall here Victor Turner's discussion, in *Schism and Continuity in an African Society* (Manchester: Manchester University Press, 1957), of problems of scale that regularly lead to faction fights and eventually fission in village communities among the Ndembu.

6   For a revealing account of the nature of such struggles between a pastor and conservatives in this congregation see James Street's novel, *The Gauntlet* (Garden City, NY: Doubleday, Doran, 1945).

7   See my 'Class Differences in Family Structure and the Social Bases of Modern Feminism' (Doctoral dissertation, Department of Sociology, Brandeis University, 1981), especially Chapter 6, 'Gossip and Customary Controls Over Family and Community Life'.

8   A fuller presentation of findings gained over three years of field research, and their implications for understanding the conservative 'pro-family' movement in general, will appear both in a documentary film on the church (co-produced by James Ault and Michael Camerini) to be released in 1987 and a book now in preparation.

Women in Jewish religious life: Manchester 1880–1930

RICKIE BURMAN

This paper will suggest that in the period between 1880 and 1930 an important change took place in the centrality of women's domestic practices to Jewish religious life. Whereas in Eastern Europe, in the nineteenth century, women's religious activities within the home were viewed as relatively peripheral to the fundamental concerns of Jewish religion, a shift took place in twentieth-century Britain, so that these same activities developed as core reference-points in the form and maintenance of Jewish identity.

Consideration will be given to the role and importance of Jewish women's religious practices in three specific situations:

1   in the *shtetls* of Eastern Europe, small towns with predominantly Jewish populations, from which many thousands of immigrants came to England in the late nineteenth and early twentieth centuries;
2   in the existing Anglo-Jewish community, already well established before this major influx of Eastern European immigrants;
3   in the immigrant community which developed in Britain as a result of this migration. Here, particular reference will be made to Manchester, where some 300 oral history interviews have been recorded with Jewish immigrants and their children.[1]

Discussions of the role of Jewish women have often tended to take an ahistorical view of their subject. On the one hand, some feminists have blamed Judaism for the birth of patriarchy, without due regard to the context in which its laws were formulated and developed; and, on the other, Orthodox apologists have emphasized the progressive aspects of early Jewish law, giving little consideration to the dynamism of women's role. Both viewpoints have found in the Talmud, the post-Biblical teachings of the Rabbis, ample support for their own particular stance.

Yet this paper will show that, far from remaining static, the role of Jewish women in religious life has changed in subtle but important ways. For most women, this change has occurred not at the level of formal religious laws, but rather in the content and significance of their actual domestic practices.

Women in the Eastern European *shtetl*

Jewish settlement in Eastern Europe was characterized by a distinctive pattern of social and cultural life centred upon the *shtetl* communities, which began to emerge in sixteenth-century Poland-Lithuania and crystallized following the partitions of the eighteenth century. Whilst in areas under Habsburg rule, communities were scattered through provinces such as Galicia and Hungary, Jewish residence within the Russian Empire was restricted to the 'Pale of Settlement', which extended from the Black Sea to the Baltic. Within that area further restrictions were imposed, and in the nineteenth century a series of laws was passed expelling Jews from residence in rural areas.

In this context, *shtetl* culture developed partly in isolation, partly in opposition to the wider society. This account of women's role will be confined to the more traditional environment of the *shtetl*, which represented the background of many of the respondents interviewed as part of our research project in Manchester.[2] However, it should be noted that the nineteenth century saw an increasing trend to urbanization and industrialization in Russia (Mendelsohn, 1970), and it is therefore likely that developments parallel to those to be noted in Britain had also been set in motion in the cities of Eastern Europe, with possible ramifying effects on the smaller *shtetl* communities.

Within the *shtetl*, the major arenas of religion practice, the synagogue and study-house, were essentially the preserve of men. Male status was closely bound up with religious scholarship, which represented a primary avenue to social recognition and an important source of political influence. As an immigrant from Yashliske in Galicia explained,

> 'A man could be wealthy, but he wouldn't be held in high regard because he had all his money. But being descended from a family of saints or scholars would confer status which was sought after. It was sort of an aristocracy of learning' (J99).

A major distinction was drawn between the 'unlearned', common people and those who were well-versed in religious law, this division often, but not invariably, coinciding with divisions based on class (Burman, 1982). Where wealth had been acquired, but religious legitimation was lacking, the daughter of a wealthy man would often be married to a promising scholar, who would bring *yichus*, prestige and status, to his father-in-law and descendants. A recently published autobiography shows marriage-brokers jostling to make matches between 'the boys of poor families but learned in Torah' and 'the daughters of the profiteering rich' (Marsden, 1983, p.28). In the case of such a match, the marriage contract would often include an undertaking by the father-in-law to support his son-in-law for several years, while he continued his religious studies (Burman, 1982, p.34).

Although women could thus serve as a channel through which male status could be attained, they had little religious status in their own right. According to traditional Jewish law (Meiselman, 1978; Hyman, 1976), they were excluded from the obligation to participate in communal prayer and thus not counted in a *minyan*, the quorum of ten adult men required for a religious service to take place. They were not allowed to lead or play any public role in communal prayer, and if they chose to attend synagogue had to sit in a separate area, screened from view, so as not to distract male worshippers from their prayers (Abrahams, 1932, pp.39–40).

Whereas, on the death of a parent, a man was enjoined to say *kaddish*, the mourner's prayer, every day for eleven months, and every year on the anniversary of the death, a woman was not qualified to do so, even in the absence of a close male relative. Anzia Yezierska, who grew up in Russia in the 1880s, wrote that 'a boy could say prayers after his father's death – that kept the father's soul alive for ever', whereas, 'the prayers of his daughters didn't count because God didn't listen to women' (Yezierska, 1975, pp.9–10). Small wonder, then, that the birth of a son, a *kaddishel*, was often greeted with more enthusiasm than that of a daughter. A boy brought the possibility of increased social prestige and religious recognition, and a daughter the burden of a dowry (Feldman, 1917). The difference in religious status was epitomized in the blessings included for men and women in the daily morning service: while men thanked God for 'not making me a woman', the women gave thanks to God for 'making me according to thy will'.

Women were said to be relieved of the privilege and obligation of observing 'time-bound' religious commandments (which tended to relate to public worship), so as to be free to fulfil their primary domestic functions. In the *shtetl*, these activities were sometimes extended to include breadwinning, women attending to the material concerns, while their husbands engaged in more spiritual pursuits. Thus an interviewee, born in Manchester in 1910, notes that her grandmother ran a little grocery shop in Lithuania, which 'more or less kept the family going', while her husband 'prayed all day' in synagogue (J219). In other cases, the material/spiritual division was maintained, even when a woman's material role required her to travel away from home on business (Burman, 1982, p.35). A woman could assume an active economic role, but was still dependent on her husband for religious status.

To underline their responsibilities within the domestic sphere, three specific *mizvot* (religious duties) were assigned to women: the lighting of the sabbath candles, the setting apart of a small portion of dough when baking bread, as a gift to God, and the observance of the laws of *niddah*, which entailed abstinence from sexual intercourse for at least twelve days during and after menstruation, and purification in the ritual bath, or *mikveh*. In addition, as a routine part of their housekeeping role, women were responsible for the maintenance of *kashrut*, the Jewish dietary laws, and for the housework and cooking necessary to celebrate sabbaths and festivals in the appropriate spirit. These activities were taken for granted as part of the very rhythm of domestic life, and not seen in themselves as essentially religious acts.

The marginalization of women was increased by the accentuated demarcation of gender divisions, which was legitimated by an emphasis on their sexuality. The prohibition on physical contact with a woman during menstruation was generalized into a constant prohibition on physical contact between the sexes in day-to-day life, and, according to some authorities, after the birth of a daughter, a woman was regarded as unclean for double the length of time specified in the case of a son (Feldman, 1917, p.186). Women were seen as a constant source of temptation to men, distracting them from lofty, spiritual thoughts, and, to limit their attractiveness to men other than their husbands, they were expected to cut their hair on marriage and cover it with a *sheitel*, or wig (Abrahams, 1932, pp.303–4).

Although, technically, Jewish women were not actually forbidden to participate in religious study and worship, nor even to don the major ritual accessories, the *tallit* (fringed prayer shawl) and *tefillin* (phylacteries), with very rare exceptions these activities were effectively prohibited.[3] Women were often actively discouraged, and even prevented, from learning the sacred language of Hebrew and studying religious texts. The authoress, Kreitman, gives a poignant account of her longing to achieve significance through religious study.[4] Women were generally literate only in Yiddish, and were expected to gain their religious insights from devotional and mythological literature, such as the *Tsenna urenna*, a sixteenth-century paraphrase of the Pentateuch, intermingled with tales, interpretive comment and romantic fiction. As a result of this lack of learning, women tended to be associated with unthinking superstition, and in Yiddish literature they are depicted seeking out amulets and other magical forms to protect against barrenness and the evil eye (Singer, 1980, pp.166–7).

The positive image of the *shtetl* woman as a 'woman of valour' (Proverbs 31 : 10–31), charitable and energetic, deriving satisfaction from her worldly activities carried out for the good of husband and children, coexisted with a negative image of a subversive, uncontrollable woman, who rejects the constraints upon her, becoming possessed by a spirit or *dybbuk* (Emanuel, 1976). The characteristics of one such *dybbuk*, reported in Lithuania, are significant:

> Ordinarily she was a quiet girl, but suddenly she would begin to howl like a dog, and to speak with a man's voice. Then she sang like a cantor, and her voice was as powerful as the roar of a lion. She knew all the prayers by heart (Singer, 1980, p.123).

It is likely that the majority of *shtetl* women accepted their secondary role and sometimes managed to create for themselves a position of informal influence within their own sphere (Zborowski and Herzog, 1952, pp.124–41). But the incidence of spirit possession suggests the deep-felt need of some women to challenge constraints which they found intolerable and from which they could find no other escape (Emanuel, 1976). Although accounts of *dybbuks* tend to have a somewhat mythological flavour, the personal account of Singer's own sister (Kreitman, 1983), highlights, albeit in a less dramatic way, the severe tensions which women's marginal position in the major sphere of religion could induce.

Her account suggests too that, although by the late nineteenth century the *shtetl* was undergoing considerable socioeconomic change, the sexual demarcation in religious life remained substantially unchanged. This is also indicated by interviews carried out in Manchester.

Women in the Anglo-Jewish community

The Anglo-Jewish community was already well established and well integrated into English society by the time the influx of Eastern European immigrants reached its height in the period between 1880 and 1914. This was a strongly middle-class community,[5] dominated by a small number of inter-related families, who had been in England for several generations and combined an attachment to communal affairs with an equal dedication to English life and institutions (Bermant, 1971;

Gartner, 1960, p.21). In contrast to the *shtetl*, which had developed its social values partly in opposition to those of the wider society, ideas in this community were closely influenced by those prevalent among the English middle classes.[6] As in Eastern Europe, a major distinction was drawn between the natural qualities and appropriate spheres of activities for men and women, and the latter's essential domesticity was stressed. But whereas, in the *shtetl*, a primary division was drawn between the spheres of the sacred and profane, women being relegated to the latter, in England, as in gentile society (Davidoff, 1979; Davidoff *et al.*, 1976), the major separation was between public and private spheres, the workplace and the home. Occupational status and prestige in the eyes of the wider society, rather than religious scholarship, represented the primary avenues to social recognition.

In this context, following the precepts of the domestic ideology current in the nineteenth century (Hall, 1979), women were not viewed, as in the *shtetl*, as material providers supporting the activities of men. Rather, breadwinning was seen as a male prerogative and responsibility, and a woman's involvement in paid work would have cast a dark shadow on her husband's integrity and social standing. In the same way, direct involvement in practical domestic activities was out of the question, the employment of domestic servants being another indicator of social status. This resulted in a striking inversion of the gender roles traditional in the *shtetl*. In nineteenth-century England it was seen as the task of men to engage in secular, worldly pursuits, whilst women were assigned the role of spiritual guardians of the home, a source of inspiration and refreshment to men weighed down by the worldly pressures of public life. Women were seen not as material providers but as spiritual helpmeets, and the home as a secure and sacred haven, rather than a source of worldly distraction.

Earlier in the century, Grace Aguilar had written eloquently on the vocation of the Jewish woman in England:[7]

> The ordinances and commands of our holy faith interfere much less with woman's retired path of domestic pursuits and pleasures than with the more public and more ambitious career of man. Her duty is to make home happy; her mission, to *influence* man, alike in her relative duties of mother to her son, wife to her husband, sister to her brother, and, in her own person, to upraise the holy cause of religion. . . . To obtain this superiority is to become more spiritual; for in that single word every feminine grace and Jewish requisite is comprised (Aguilar, 1886, pp.570–1).

She argues that spirituality is:

> so peculiarly woman's attribute, that without it her loveliest charms, her highest intellect, appears imperfect. By man it is unattainable . . . unless infused by the influence of woman (*ibid.*, pp.573–4).

This view of woman's innate spirituality is still evident at the turn of the century. A report on the Conference of Jewish Women, held in 1902, speaks of a 'tremendous revelation to the community of its latent spiritual forces' (*Jewish Chronical*, 16 May 1902). In a contrast drawn between the women's conference and a Conference of British Congregations, held at the same time and regarded as 'a similar movement in the purely masculine sphere', it is stated that,

> The activities of the Ladies' conference will centre round the religious and educational needs of our people; the efforts of the 'Conference of British Congregations' will be addressed to matters of more secular concern. The division of labour is not unnatural (*Jewish Chronicle*, 25 April 1902).

Despite this emphasis on their spirituality, women continued to be excluded from active participation in communal worship and synagogue affairs. These limitations were underlined by Rev. A.A. Green in a paper read before the fashionable Hampstead Synagogue Guild in 1899:

> It must be confessed that looking around the community the opportunity and the influences of the Jewish woman cannot be said to present entirely satisfactory features. . . . Still the daily prayer provides for the Jewish man the words which make him bless and praise the Almighty who has not made him a woman. Still the authority of the Jewish Synagogue system recognises as a congregant a boy of thirteen, while it ignores the contribution to the formation of *minyan* of that child's mother, though she may be a saintly woman. Still the Barmitzvah is reserved for the boy for whom the doors of the congregation are opened wide, while his sisters pass unnoticed as though it were of more consequence how a boy should grow into a man than how a girl should approach the dawning duties of womanhood. Still the women sit unnoticed in the gallery, while the so-called honours of the synagogue go one and all to men; and still the laws of the United Synagogue give a voice in the synagogue management to 'male persons above the age of 21 years occupying seats in the body of the synagogue'. We might perhaps have less to regret today if in the constitution and

management of our synagogue affairs there was less said about that 'body of the synagogue' and a little more thought about its soul (*Jewish Chronicle*, 20 October 1899).

Most women accepted their indirect role in religion, seeking to achieve a sense of self-worth within the limits imposed. Thus, Miss Raphael, headmistress of the Manchester Jews School, speaking at the 1902 conference, records the ideals held out to working girls at weekly sabbath services:

> They learnt that the future of our race will depend on the goodness of the women, and that while all cannot be clever and beautiful, each one can improve the world by cultivating gentleness, piety, firmness and graciousness. Women may not take an active part in the public functions of our religion, but it is the mother, sister or wife of the man who helps him in some way to produce each religious observance (*Jewish Chronicle*, 25 July 1902).

A decade later, however, it became evident that a number of influential women were growing dissatisfied with the contradiction between the spiritual role assigned to them and their exclusion from communal religious life (De Bruin, 1913; Spielmann, 1913). These were well educated women, who had gained confidence and experience through their work in philanthropy, a branch of public life now perceived as a natural extension of their domestic role, and in keeping with their spiritual vocation. At a time when declining church attendance figures had become a matter of general concern, it was apparent that, whereas women provided the main support of the Church of England, the proportion of women attending synagogue services was markedly lower.[8] It was feared that some anglicized women were drifting away from a religion from which they felt excluded (Montagu, 1943). As early as 1899, attempts were made to secure for at least widows and single women the vote in synagogue elections (*Jewish Chronicle*, 17 November 1899; 26 April 1901). However, although not oblivious to feminist demands (Bayme, 1982, p.63), the United Synagogue (the association of Ashkenazi Congregations in London under the religious authority of the Chief Rabbi) remained obdurate.

The failure of the institutions of Orthodox Judaism to accommodate to the needs of women was an important contributory factory in the development of Liberal Judaism. Lily Montagu, a distinguished communal worker and founder of the Jewish Religious Union (1902), which developed into the movement of Liberal Judaism (c.1911), drew a direct connection between her rejection of the traditional role of women in religion and her interest in reform (Bayme, 1982, p.68). From the inception of the movement, it was determined that men and women should be equal in their congregational privileges, boys and girls both receiving 'confirmation', men and women sitting together, and women holding seats and voting rights on the synagogue council as a matter of course, although the privileges of leading a service and delivering sermons were not granted to women until after the First World War (Montagu, 1943, pp.38–42).

The emergence of the Liberal Movement may, however, have strengthened the conservatism of mainstream Judaism, opposed to this schism (Bayme, 1982, p.67). In 1912 further efforts were made to improve the position of women with the establishment of the Jewish League for Women's Suffrage (*Jewish Chronicle*, 8 November 1912). Although a concerted campaign by the League for the 'enfranchisement of women seat-holders' met with some success in individual synagogues (J.L.W.S., 1913–14), it was not until 1954 that female members of the United Synagogue were finally granted voting rights (Newman, 1977, p.197).

The immigrant community in England

The immigrants arriving in England from Eastern Europe in the late nineteenth and early twentieth centuries differed from the established Anglo-Jewish community in class, culture and religious values. They settled in different areas and established their own patterns of communal life, founding the *chevras*, *cheders* and other institutions which had characterized religious life in the *shtetl*.[9] Whilst the established community took an active interest in the development of immigrant life, seeking to discourage the continuance of 'alien' customs and institutions in England, there was little interaction between the two groups at an individual level.

Within the immigrant community, the change in the centrality of women's religious observances resulted more from a shift in the relative importance of their activities than a change in their aspirations or practices. This is suggested by a detailed analysis of 150 of the interviews conducted with Jewish immigrants and children of immigrants in Manchester. These show that most immigrant women continued to play a minimal role in formal religious life, even in the most orthodox families generally attending synagogue only on the High Holydays. Many of the small immigrant congregations met in the attics or upper storeys of private houses, and those few women who did attend the sabbath services often had to listen from a separate room, or in the case of the Solela Chevra in Manchester, from the bedroom of the house next door (J87).

Most immigrant women were illiterate in Hebrew, and where a woman could '*daven* (pray) like a man' (J192), she was seen as quite exceptional. This was the case with Mrs Singer, who was descended from a 'high rabbinical family', as her daughter related:

'On Purim . . . about ten women used to come in and they used to sit round my mother and she used to say the Book of Esther in Hebrew, and they all used to say it after her, because none of them had been taught anything . . . she was a very well learned woman' (J104).[10]

Although immigrant parents were prepared to make considerable sacrifices to send their sons to religious classes, or *cheder*, to quote one interviewee, 'the old-fashioned people didn't believe in girls going to *cheder*, they didn't. . . . There was a certain taboo about girls going to *cheder*' (J98). Another interviewee, born into a very religious family, contrasted his own education with that received by his sisters:

'Religion, learning, *chumash* (the Pentateuch), and things like that wasn't stressed for girls. In fact, it was looked upon almost a little askance. Well, a girl doesn't need to learn . . ., a girl needs to know her *dinim* (laws), whatever she needs to know, *dinim shabbos* (laws pertaining to the sabbath) and so on, but it was left to the male members of the family to learn.'

There were exceptions to this pattern, however, as was shown by the daughter of Mrs Singer:

'Me and me sister went to *cheder* like a boy . . . not many girls went in those days. . . . We went four days a week. . . . I had to go and give the sixpence which my mother could ill-afford, but she was determined we had to learn Hebrew' (J104).

The only formal religious tuition received by the majority of girls was that provided by the Anglo-Jewish community in the Manchester Jews School and two Board Schools with substantial Jewish populations. This instruction seems to have had little impact, one interviewee commenting that many girls reached the top class of the Jews School without having learnt any Hebrew (J49).

Although some women discarded the *sheitel* (wig), often under pressure from their children who saw it as ugly, foreign and old-fashioned (Livshin, 1982, pp.250–4), the majority remained conscientious in their domestic observances, at pains to observe the dietary laws and travelling long distances, if necessary, to consult a rabbi if doubtful whether a hen they had opened was properly *kosher* (i.e. fit for consumption according to Jewish dietary law). The following extract gives a vivid impression of the work entailed in the annual changeover of foods and utensils for the festival of Passover:

> 'Everything had to be changed . . . we had big cellars and all your pots had to be changed, and we had two big tea chests, that had all the Passover pots inside, that you only used for Passover. All the pots we had in the back kitchen . . . had to be taken down and washed and put away in a box and taken into the cellar, and all the tables and cupboards had to be washed down, fresh white paper put inside. . . . We had a red rug in the back kitchen that had to be red raggled and the yard had to be whitewashed. . . . The oven had to be whitewashed inside, because we'd cooked ordinary food during the year' (J228).

Less extensive, but still time-consuming, preparations were made on a weekly basis for the sabbath, which was ushered in as women lit the sabbath candles on the Friday evening. On the following day, a gentile, or *'shabbos goy'*, was commonly employed to light the fire and stoke it up, actions prohibited to Jews on the sabbath.

The religious observances of immigrant women in England were thus characterized by a strong continuity. Among the Anglo-Jewish women, the practical duties of maintaining a *kosher* home and preparing for sabbaths and festivals had become of less direct importance, being observed with less rigour or carried out through the agency of domestic servants, but for the immigrant women they constituted an integral part of their daily household labours. Their concern was directed not to the spiritual sphere, which the more anglicized women now saw as their province, but to the practical management of the material world. They accepted as their lot the sexual division of labour, familiar from the *shtetl*.

Despite this continuity in role expectations, a major disjuncture was evident in the sphere of male observance. In the new, urban environment, religious scholarship and piety no longer provided major avenues to status and respect. The son of an immigrant tailor expressed contempt, rather than admiration, for a pious uncle who prayed three times a day and refused to work on the sabbath, 'To me, he didn't bring his children up right. All that he worried was *davening* (praying), *davening*, *davening*. There was other principles in life, . . . which he didn't uphold' (J142). His scrupulous observance left him little time to provide for his wife and children, who consequently 'had a poor life'.

The erosion of traditional religious values, consequent upon the immigrants' more open interaction with the wider society in England, was reinforced by the policies of anglicization adopted by the Anglo-Jewish establishment. The negative view which the latter took of the immigrant religious institutions has been well documented for Manchester (Livshin, 1982). In 1881, an English-born minister explained to an immigrant audience that,

> England was not famous for its *Yeshibot* (religious colleges) because Hebrew learning did not pay in this commercial country, and therefore it was incumbent upon them to do something more than educate their children solely in Hebrew and Rabbinical teachings (Rev. A.L. Green, *Jewish Chronicle*, 1 April 1881).

On a more practical level, synagogue attendance and religious study did not combine well with the economic demands and opportunities in England. An 'ethical sermon delivered to the working classes' by a senior religious authority observed that back in Eastern Europe 'it is easy to be pious and it is no great matter to observe and uphold the Divine Commandments. But here, in this country, it is a great thing and a very great test' (Spiers, 1901, p.11). It was estimated that more than half the Jews of London went to work on the sabbath, although the observance of festivals was more general (Gartner, 1960, p.195).

These observations are borne out by respondents in Manchester (Williams, 1979). Here, an immigrant recalls his sadness on first going to work on the sabbath: 'I just put up with it, but . . . I hated it. . . . I remember the first day, it's a *shabbos* . . . I was broken-hearted. . . . Yes, they used to work *shabbos* them days, tailors' (J29). For small traders, Saturday was the critical day of the week. An immigrant market draper explained succinctly, 'We thought, "It's a necessity". That's how it was. You couldn't make a living if you didn't work on a Saturday in England' (J218).

In some cases, liberation from the restrictions of orthodox observance was welcomed by immigrants (Gartner, 1960, p.195) but even those who retained an active interest in religious prayer and study had little success in communicating that enthusiasm to their children (J242). Whilst most Jews retained a nominal affiliation to a synagogue, and attended on the High Holydays, in general the synagogue and its related institutions lost their dominance of the central stage of mainstream communal life, remaining the core preoccupation only for an attenuated minority (Gartner, 1960, p.268).

In this context, women's traditional domestic practices acquired a new significance. What had previously been merely an accepted part of daily life, the observance of Jewish dietary laws and the preparations for sabbaths and festivals, now assumed a greater prominence as religious acts, which served to define the Jewish identity of the household, and to distinguish the homes of Jewish families from their neighbours. Many interviewees described how, although their fathers worked on the sabbath, their mothers continued to uphold their own practices and create a special sabbath atmosphere. The child of a credit draper in Stockport recalled,

'We were told what dad had to do for the business. That was our living and our bread and butter, it couldn't be helped, but we weren't allowed to do anything. We had a fire *goy* (gentile) who came in to do the fires and my mother didn't do any cooking on the sabbath' (J202).

Although Jewish children often mixed freely with their non-Jewish neighbours in the street, and sometimes visited their homes, the warning not to eat non-*kosher* foods, as well as the different dishes cooked in gentile homes, gave them an early consciousness of their Jewishness (J28). Thus, for many of the immigrants' children, their sense of identity as Jews was closely linked to early memories of their home environment. Interviewees' most vivid recollections, related with most enthusiasm, are often of their mothers preparing for the sabbath, cooking traditional dishes and scrubbing the house clean; or of the Friday night meal with the family assembled before the glowing candles in their newly washed and pressed clothes (J104, J254, J273).

In a major recent study of patterns of acculturation amongst the children of immigrant Jews, Rosalyn Livshin has shown that, although many of these children drifted away from regular synagogue worship and sabbath observance, and although many went dancing or courting with non-Jews, very few took the ultimate step towards assimilation – that of marrying a non-Jew (Livshin, 1982, pp.277–84). It was not the dictates of formal, public religion which held them back, but rather concern for their parents and the association of Jewishness with their early life in the home. An interviewee stressed that, although he went out with a non-Jewish girl, for him, intermarriage 'was impossible. I would never have dreamt of it . . . because you've been brought up in a Jewish atmosphere . . . fancy sitting down on a Friday night without *lockshen* soup . . ., the candles not lit, things like that' (J71). Such homely details should not be dismissed as mere nostalgia. They clearly had the power to create a strong impact on children, constituting part of the fabric of their lives, and at the same time something special which set them apart.

Although an affective identification with Judaism was maintained in the second generation, by the 1920s it was becoming recognized that many of the children of immigrants had only a shallow knowledge of their own religious laws and history. A new impetus developed to improve teaching methods and establish study circles at a higher level (Livshin, 1982, pp.208–20). Partly in recognition of women's importance in the transmission of religion (*Jewish Chronicle*, 24 February 1922), and partly in keeping with general attitudes to girls' education and the concern of some prominent Anglo-Jewish women with religious education, girls were included in these efforts. In Manchester this was marked in 1930 by the inauguration of the 'Ivriah School for Girls', the first of several measures taken to increase the provision of Jewish education for girls (Slotki, 1950, p.71).

The patterns developed in the immigrant community can still be discerned at the present time. A recent survey of the London Borough of Redbridge, one of the densest areas of Jewish settlement in Britain, revealed a low participation in the predominantly male sphere of public worship, but a strikingly high level of home observance (Kosmin and Levy, 1983). Whereas in 70.2 per cent of households women lit the sabbath candles, only 9.7 per cent of the adult population attended synagogue on a regular basis, the majority of these being male. Men's observance of home rituals was also more lax than women's: the high proportion of women lighting candles contrasts with the lower proportion (26.4 per cent) of men reciting *Kiddush* (the customary blessings over wine and bread) on Friday evenings. Associated with this pattern of strong domestic observance, was a low rate of intermarriage (*ibid.*, p.39),[11] and a high degree of commitment among women to the transmission and preservation of Judaism. Whilst women in every age group had received a lower average Jewish education than men, a consistent improvement in their access to education had occurred since the Second World War.

It thus appears that, among the descendants of the immigrants, the gender-based division of labour within religious practice has been maintained: public religion has remained a predominantly male arena, and domestic observances the responsibility of women. Yet, whilst the actual practices of women have undergone relatively little alteration, the significance of these activities has changed. Once regarded as mere adjuncts to the major sphere of male religion, in twentieth-century Britain they have assumed a greater importance.

Conclusion

In the three situations compared in this paper, Jewish women have been subject to the same formal religious laws. Yet we have seen that, in effect, both the content and the significance of their role in religious life have differed markedly in important ways. In all three situations, women's domesticity was stressed, but with different results. In the *shtetl*, the profane associations of the domestic sphere strengthened the barriers excluding women from the recognized spheres of religious endeavour, but gave some scope for their involvement in independent economic activities. In contrast, the association of domesticity and spirituality in the Anglo-Jewish community, although providing a justification for women to engage in philanthropic work, excluded them from the economic sphere and gave them little effective power in mainstream religious life. In the immigrant community, formal religion and spiritual endeavours continued to be seen as more properly the preserve of men, but their declining relevance to daily life, combined with economic pressures and opportunities, gave women's domestic practices a new centrality. Formerly regarded as peripheral, they now developed as key components in the transmission of a sense of Jewish identification and attachment.

The shift in the centrality of women's domestic observances was thus closely related to a major change in the nature of Jewish identification. For many Jews, the migration from East to West marked a transition from a society where Jewish status was primary, automatic and non-negotiable, defined according to external structural constraints and a cohesive internal ideology, to one in which the status of individuals was no longer necessarily subsumed by their Jewishness (see Epstein, 1978, pp.101–2; Wallman, 1978). Active identification with the group became more open to personal choice, and, as Gartner has noted, it became possible to retain a stake in 'Jewishness', a consciousness of being Jewish, without fulfilling the formal dictates of 'Judaism' (Gartner, 1960, p.273). With the development of this more optional ethnicity, the significance of women's religious practices moved from periphery to core.

Ironically, the limitations imposed on women's religious role in Eastern Europe, in a new context, became a source of strength. It was the very fact that they were rooted in the material world and integrated with the routine, practical tasks of the domestic environment, which gave to women's observances their power of continuity and affective valency. Yet, despite some improvements in their status, the increased centrality of their role in religion did not result in a corresponding increase in communal stature or authority. For religion no longer represented a major avenue to social status, and the focus of male aspirations had changed.

Notes

I would like to thank Judith Emanuel, Wendy Flanagan, Riva Krut, Rosalyn Livshin, Daniel Miller, Sheila Saunders and Bill Williams for help and comments on this paper.

1 For general historical accounts of Jewish life in Eastern Europe, see Mahler (1971) and Baron (1964). A useful compilation of source materials is given in Roskies and Roskies (1979), and a more idealized view of *shtetl* life in Zborowski and Herzog (1952). For the process of industrialization and urbanization in Eastern Europe, see Mendelsohn (1970).

2 These interviews were recorded by Bill Williams, Rosalyn Livshin and myself as part of a wider research project into the history of Manchester's Jewish community, based at the Manchester Studies Unit, Manchester Polytechnic. The majority of the interviewees were born between 1890 and 1910. The numbers prefixed by the letter 'J' indicate the tape reference number within the Manchester Studies archive.

3 A notable exception was Hannah Rachel, the 'Rebbe' of Lodomir in the Ukraine (1805–92), who prayed with ecstatic emotion and studied advanced rabbinical texts. After experiencing a vision, in which she received a 'new and sublime soul', she began to observe the religious duties of males, donning *tallit* and *tefillin* when she prayed, and eventually established a religious following (Rabinowicz, 1970).

4 In her recently republished autobiographical novel, Kreitman shows that, although her mother was highly educated, her father disapproved of such erudition in a woman and determined not to make the same 'mistake' in her own case (Kreitman, 1983, p.6). It is interesting to compare Kreitman's account with the memoirs of her better-known brother (Singer, 1980). In some cases, women's exclusion from religious instruction and more open interaction with the wider society gave them more opportunity to learn the local vernacular (Burman, 1982).

5 It was estimated that, by 1980, 14.6 per cent of London's Jewish population was upper- or upper-middle-class, with incomes over

£1,000 per annum, and 42.2 per cent were middle-class, with incomes between £200 and £1,000 per annum (Lipman, 1970, p.47).

6   For the integration of these families into English life, see Bermant (1971), Lipman (1961) and, for Manchester, Williams (1976).

7   Aguilar lived from 1816 to 1847, and wrote a number of novels directed to women, such as *Home Influence*, *The Mother's Recompense* and *Women's Friendship*.

8   'The empty benches and how to fill them' represented a theme of some concern in the *Jewish Chronicle* (e.g. I. Spielmann in *Jewish Chronicle*, 3 May 1899). The 1903 survey of church attendance showed the proportion of women attending church to be higher than the proportion of men, except in the borough of Stepney, where synagogues were largely attended by men (McLeod, 1974, p.30).

9   See Gartner (1960) for an account of immigrant life in London and Williams (1976, pp.268–97), for the development of the immigrant community in Manchester.

10 The name 'Singer' is a pseudonym. Purim is the 'Feast of Lots', when the Book of Esther is read.

11 The survey indicated 3.4 per cent cases of mixed marriages, with 88.8 per cent parents opposed to any potential outmarriage. This contrasted with a survey in Los Angeles, which showed that 74 per cent of the sample would accept their children's marriage to a non-Jew. In Los Angeles, the sabbath candles were lit in only 18 per cent of the households surveyed.

References

Abrahams, I. (1932), *Jewish Life in the Middle Ages*, London, Goldston.

Aguilar, G. (1886), *The Women of Israel*, London, Groombridge.

Baron, S. (1964), *The Russian Jew under Tsars and Soviets*, London, Macmillan.

Bayme, S. (1982), 'Claude Montefiore, Lily Montagu and the origins of the Jewish Religious Union', *Transactions of the Jewish Historical Society of England*, vol. 27, pp.61–71.

Bermant, C. (1971), *The Cousinhood: the Anglo-Jewish Gentry*, London, Eyre & Spottiswoode.

Burman, R. (1982), 'The Jewish women as breadwinner: the changing value of women's work in a Manchester immigrant community', *Oral History*, vol. 10, no. 2, pp.27–39.

Davidoff, L. (1979), 'The separation of home and work? Landladies and lodgers in nineteenth and twentieth century England', in S. Burman (ed.), *Fit Work for Women*, London, Croom Helm, pp.64–97.

Davidoff, L., L'Esperance, J. and Newby, H. (1976), 'Landscape with figures: home and community in English society', in A. Oakley and J.

Mitchell (eds), *The Rights and Wrongs of Women*, Harmondsworth, Penguin Books, pp.139–75.

De Bruin, E. (1913), 'Judaism and womanhood', *Westminster Review*, pp.124–30.

Emanuel, J. (1976), 'The elite mind and the common body: a study of ecstacy and spirit possession among Jews in Eastern European ghetto communities', unpublished B.A. dissertation, Sussex University.

Epstein, A.L. (1978), *Ethos and Identity*, London, Tavistock.

Feldman, W.M. (1917), *The Jewish Child*, London, Balliere, Tindall & Cox.

Gartner, L. (1960), *The Jewish Immigrant in England 1870–1914*, London, Simon.

Hall, C. (1979), 'The early formation of the Victorian domestic ideology', in S. Burman (ed.), *Fit Work for Women*, London, Croom Helm, pp.15–32.

Hyman, P. (1976), 'The other half: women in the Jewish tradition', in E. Koltun (ed.), *The Jewish Woman*, New York, Schocken, pp.105–13.

Jewish League for Women's Suffrage (1913–14), *First Annual Report*, available in the Fawcett Library, London.

Kosmin, B. and Levy, C. (1983), *Jewish Identity in an Anglo-Jewish Community*, London, Research Unit of the Board of Deputies of British Jews.

Kreitman, E. (1983), *Deborah*, London, Virago (first published 1946).

Lipman, V.D. (1961), 'The age of emancipation 1815–1880', in V.D. Lipman (ed.), *Three Centuries of Anglo-Jewish History*, Cambridge, Heffer.

Lipman V.D. (1970), 'The development of London Jewry', in S. Levin (ed.), *A Century of Anglo-Jewish Life*, London, United Synagogue.

Livshin, R. (1982), 'Aspects of the acculturation of the children of immigrant Jews in Manchester 1890–1930', M.Ed. thesis, Manchester University.

McLeod, H. (1974), *Class and Religion in the Late Victorian City*, London, Croom Helm.

Mahler, R. (1971), *A History of Modern Jewry, 1780–1815*, London, Vallentine, Mitchell.

Marsden, N. (1983), *A Jewish Life under the Tsars: the Autobiography of Chaim Aronson, 1825–1888*, New Jersey, Allanheld, Osmun.

Meiselman, M. (1978), *Jewish Woman in Jewish Law*, New York, Ktav.

Mendelsohn, E. (1970), *Class Struggle in the Pale: the Formative Years of the Jewish Workers' Movement in Tsarist Russia*, Cambridge, University Press.

Montagu, L. (1943), *The Faith of a Jewish Woman*, London, Simpkin Marshall.

Newman, A. (1977), *The United Synagogue 1870–1970*, London, Routledge & Kegan Paul.

Rabinowicz, H. (1970), *World of Hasidism*, London, Vallentine, Mitchell.

Roskies, D.K. and Roskies, D.G. (1979), *The Shtetl Book*, New York, Ktav.

Singer, I.B. (1980), *In my Father's Court: A Memoir*, Harmondsworth, Penguin Books.

Slotki, I.W. (1950), *Seventy Years of Hebrew Education 1880–1950*, Manchester Central Board for Hebrew Education.

Spielmann, G. (1913), 'Woman's place in the synagogue', *Jewish Review*, vol. 4, pp.24–35.

Spiers, B. (1901), *Dibrey Debash. Part 1. Eighteen ethical sermons delivered to the working classes*, London.

Wallman, S. (1978), 'The boundaries of "race": processes of ethnicity in England', *Man*, vol. 13, no. 2, pp.200–17.

Williams, B. (1976), *The Making of Manchester Jewry 1740–1875*, Manchester, University Press.

Williams, B. (1979), 'The Jewish immigrant in Manchester: the contribution of oral history', *Oral History*, vol. 7, no. 1, pp.43–53.

Yezierska, A. (1975), *Breadgivers*, New York, Brazillier (first published 1925).

Zborowski, M. and Herzog, E. (1952), *Life is with People*, New York, Schocken.

4

Domestic discords: Women and the family in East Cheshire Methodism, 1750–1830

GAIL MALMGREEN

While on a visit to a remote country town William Hazlitt once observed a procession of Methodists coming to attend the consecration of a new chapel nearby. He described them with contempt:

> Never was there such a set of scarecrows. Melancholy tailors, consumptive hairdressers, squinting coblers, women with child or in the ague, made up the forlorn hope of this pious cavalcade. The pastor of this half-starved flock, we confess, came riding after, with a more goodly aspect. . . . He had in

truth lately married a thriving widow, and been pampered with hot suppers to strengthen the flesh and the spirit.[1]

Hazlitt may have loathed Methodists, but he was an acute observer, and he touches here on some salient features of the early Methodist societies. There were indeed numerous converts from the artisan and shopkeeper classes, and a sizable female contingent. He even hints at the special appeal of evangelical religion to those facing the hazards of pregnancy or illness. Finally, he recognizes that influential figure in many a provincial chapel – the widow of independent means.

A hundred and seventy-five years or so after Hazlitt historians are only just beginning to give these social dimensions of the evangelical revival the closer scrutiny they deserve. It is rather surprising that students of women's history and historians of religion have been rather slow to venture into each other's territory. Church history has been preoccupied with clerical heroes and with matters of governance and doctrine – all of which naturally results in a male bias. Yet it would not be unreasonable to say that, in modern Western cultures, religion has been a predominantly female sphere. In nearly every sect and denomination of Christianity, though men monopolized the positions of authority, women had the superior numbers. Recent pioneering work by historians of American religion has shown how some precision may be given to this general notion. Mary Maples Dunn, Nancy Cott, and Mary Ryan, among others, have collected data indicating that in America from the late seventeenth to the mid-nineteenth centuries 60 to 75 per cent of church members and of those responding to revivalist 'awakenings' were women. These social historians have looked at religion in its local context, and concerned themselves with the motivation and experience of rank-and-file lay members. Only in this way can we hope to recapture the spiritual lives of ordinary women, and in the process we will have to recast our broader notions about the role of religion in society.

For the British historian anxious to follow these leads Methodism is a logical choice of subject. As the first mass evangelical movement in modern Britain, it was, both chronologically and geographically, the spiritual accompaniment to the demographic and economic revolutions of the eighteenth century. Unfortunately Methodist historians have not been very minutely concerned with the social history of their churches; the 'official' histories of Wesleyan Methodism barely mention women.[2] The special category of denominational literature that does deal with women has concentrated heavily on the awe-inspiring figure of Susannah Wesley, or enshrined the memory of other exceptional women: the inner circle of Wesley's female disciples, the women preachers, and the wives of the most prominent ministers.[3] Such accounts cannot fully explain why women, and men, of the factory towns, mining communities, and rural villages gathered so eagerly in open fields, cottage parlours, and rented meeting-rooms to hear Wesley's message. But the study of provincial centres of Methodism, the first seed-beds of the revival, can.

East Cheshire is just such a place; it became, and remained a flourishing centre of the new faith. Wesley found a tremendous response there and returned to the region again and again from the mid-1740s on. The area was prosperous, with an advanced agricultural economy specializing in dairy farming and market gardening for the urban markets of Liverpool, Manchester, and London. By 1750 there was also a developing industrial economy in East Cheshire, based on local coal mines and large-scale cotton and silk spinning mills powered by the fast-flowing streams of the Pennine foothills. Artisan workshops multiplied around the mills – carrying on dyeing, handloom weaving, hat-making, and other skilled crafts. East Cheshire market towns took on a new identity and vitality, luring population from the rural hinterlands. The town of Macclesfield became the cultural and financial centre for the region, and by the end of the century its silk mills and weaving shops were drawing immigrants from as far away as Dublin and London. A demanding new culture was being superimposed on a well-established old one – in a civic atmosphere unusually free from the interference of either aristocracy or Anglican episcopacy. In the vast Diocese of Chester the Established Church was in a generally decayed state, and the sprawling parishes of East Cheshire suffered very much from clerical pluralism and absenteeism, inadequate finance, and insufficient accommodation in churches and chapels.[4] In such conditions there was fertile ground for a new religious movement with broad popular appeal.

Women were at the forefront of the Wesleyan revival in East Cheshire from the beginning. The first patron whose name is recorded was Miss Mary Aldersley of Hurdsfield, who invited a number of itinerant evangelical preachers, including Wesley, to speak in her farmhouse sitting-room.[5] The first Quarterly Meeting of the Manchester Circuit, which then included East Cheshire, was held in 1752 in the village of Booth Bank at the home of Alice Cross. This forceful woman organized a small local society, of which she was Class Leader; she had a pulpit erected in

her largest room, which was used for many years as a place of
worhip.[6] Elizabeth Clulow, called 'the mother of Macclesfield
Methodism', was a generous contributor to the new Society there.
She co-signed the lease of the first meeting-room the Methodists
rented in the town, directed the renovation of the premises, and
paid all the workmen's expenses when a new chapel was built in
1764.[7] Her husband, a prosperous baker, neither shared nor
impeded her religious interests. Two widows of Macclesfield
textile manufacturers, Mrs Ryle and Mrs Daintry, brought part of
their husbands' fortunes and many of their younger relatives into
the chapel. Mrs Ryle's son, John, became the town's first
Methodist mayor in 1774.

Methodism attracted women of all ages and conditions, and
clearly it had a special appeal to the young, but everywhere the
most prominent female converts tended to be those who were in
some sense independent: affluent spinsters or widows, or married
women whose husbands were unusually sympathetic or com-
plaisant.[8]

John Wesley was a warm admirer of women, but it cannot be
said that he began with very high expectations for women as
evangelists. Rather, he approached the 'woman question' as he
approached many other doctrinal problems, in a spirit of brilliant
pragmatism. The enthusiasm of women for his teaching and their
success as proselytizers took him by surprise, and he slowly
revised his initially conservative views. By the 1760s he was
encouraging his most talented female followers to speak out about
their own spiritual experiences and to read in public from his own
sermons or other devotional writings – but he continued to
caution against going 'too far' in public exhortation.[9] In 1771 he
sent his oft-quoted letter of advice to a female friend who was
attracting hundreds to her prayer meetings:

> I think the strength of the cause rests there: on your having an
> extraordinary call. So, I am persuaded, has every one of our lay
> preachers; otherwise, I could not countenance his preaching at
> all. It is plain to me that the whole work of God termed
> Methodism is an extraordinary dispensation of His providence.
> Therefore I do not wonder if several things occur therein which
> do not fall under ordinary rules of discipline.[10]

Thus, the very singularity and ambiguity of the Methodist
position, functioning within and yet apart from the Established
Church, opened the doors wider for women. Wesley could argue
that Methodist meetings were not church services and that he
ordained no ministers, and consequently the public speaking of

Methodist women did not strictly contravene the Biblical prohibition against women preaching in church. Women continued to travel widely as unlicensed itinerant preachers until some years after Wesley's death in 1791. Two of the most famous, Sarah Crosby and Ann Cutler, made several tours in East Cheshire during the 1780s and 90s. Still, it apparently never became common practice in the local chapels of the north-west for women to address large gatherings.

In remote districts women sometimes took office when there was a shortage of suitable or willing men. We know, for example, that women occasionally served as chapel trustees and stewards in Lancashire and Cheshire in the 1750s – but these offices were soon to become a male preserve. To the extent that women were given substantial responsibility in the local Societies their opportunities were the result of exceptional circumstances rather than of conscious egalitarian impulses.

Revivalism found its strongest response among adolescents and young adults. In both men and women the conversion experience seems to have occurred most commonly between the ages of twelve and twenty-one. The religious awakening was closely associated with the passage into adulthood, with questions of education, apprenticeship, and the choice of a trade or profession, as well as with matters of inheritance, awakening sexuality, the death of a parent, or separation from the family home. For the rootless, whether families who had recently migrated to the region or young single adults living in lodgings and working in the textile mills, the Methodist chapel could provide a new form of community, a structured intimacy, even a surrogate family.[11]

The main vehicle for binding the local membership together was the weekly class meeting, in which a dozen or so individuals met with a leader chosen from their ranks, who cross-examined them closely on the 'state of their souls'. Class meetings were open both to the converted and to those who were struggling and seeking for a sign from God – and non-Anglicans were welcome to attend. Members were encouraged to speak freely of any matters, religious or personal, which troubled them during the past week. Those who sought a more frequent and intense exchange of spiritual experiences were separated out into smaller units called 'bands'. Here only the converted were admitted, and the proceedings were entirely private. To ensure a close communion of shared understanding and concern, bands were segregated according to sex and marital status.[12] Although exceptional women, like Elizabeth Clulow and Hester Ann Roe, became respected Class Leaders, it was unusual for a woman to direct a mixed-sex class. It is not clear to what extent the all-female bands may have taken advice or direct supervision from male clergy or preachers. But in many provincial areas, where the over-worked itinerants would have little time for weekly band-meetings, the women's bands must have been a significant base for autonomous female activity. Bands themselves declined steadily in importance within the Society as a whole in the nineteenth century, with the spread of large chapels and the new emphasis on more centralized, impersonal forms of worship under the leadership of a professional clergy.

The work of identifying the earliest local converts to Methodism, from scattered membership lists and fragmentary chapel and circuit record-books, has only just begun. A preliminary survey of some early lists from East Cheshire indicates about 55 per cent female membership, on average.[13] This figure, in contrast to American data showing 60–70 per cent female membership as typical, closely matches the sex ratio of the population as a whole in textile manufacturing centres like Macclesfield. Early nineteenth-century lists from Stockport and Manchester show a higher proportion of female members, indicating that in England, as in America, urbanization brought a 'feminization' of the churches.

A remarkable feature of the early membership lists is the information they yield on marital status of members. In most societies female members were far more likely to be unmarried than were male members. In Congleton (1759) one fourth of the male members were unmarried, whereas nearly half the female membership was unmarried or widowed. In Macclesfield (1794) only one sixth of male members were unmarried (including 11 widowers), and again nearly half the female members were unmarried (including 39 widows). Both lists indicate that the majority of male members participated along with female relatives, whilst most women, both married and unmarried, were not joined in the Society by male relatives. One is tempted to see here evidence of differing motivational patterns for male and female members. For men, joining the Society apparently formed part of a 'settling down' process, whereas for women, religious commitment may more often have represented an act of independence, part of a prelude, or postlude, to marriage and family responsibilities.

When we take note of the imbalance between unmarried women and unmarried men in some local Societies, it becomes easy to understand why early Methodist diaries and letters reflect so much concern, even agony, over the problem of finding a suitable marriage partner. John Wesley himself was deeply troubled about the danger of female members making 'unequal marriages', that is, marriages outside the Connection. He frequently had occasion to warn his female friends against marriage and devoted considerable part of his correspondence to promoting female friendship and support networks within the movement.[14]

Not all of Wesley's followers, of course, were anxious to marry. It is clear that for some women (and men) religion became a means of avoiding or delaying marriage, and even after marriage the call to preaching or missionary or philanthropic work could become the excuse for long separations and other unconventional domestic arrangements. Young women of 'good' family, like Hester Ann Roe of Macclesfield, daughter of an Anglican clergyman and niece of Charles Roe, the town's wealthiest industrialist, used religious arguments to resist her relatives' pressure to make an advantageous match. Miss Roe recorded in her journal the fate of a friend, Ann B., who had the misfortune to fall in love with and marry an irreligious man: 'in consequence she lost much of her spirituality of mind. But the Lord loved her, and sent a lingering affliction. – slew the body but saved the soul!'[15] Another melancholy case is that of Ellen Stangers, a young Macclesfield working woman courted by an acquaintance of her employer. She received this man's addresses for fear of offending her master, but had 'no partiality for him'. Sinking into despair, she could neither eat nor sleep and contemplated suicide. On a friend's suggestion she attended a Methodist meeting, where the minister urged her to turn to Christ and cry to Him for deliverance. Twelve members of the Society gathered to pray with her the next day, until,

> hope dawned in her soul. . . . All pain and sorrow fled away, and she was entirely healed, both body and mind. . . . The perplexity concerning her relation to her suitor was solved by Divine Providence. She was not spared to become a wife. . . . The Heavenly Bridegroom called her . . . she died full of faith and love.[16]

As these examples indicate, the spiritual 'family' could offer comfort and consolation to those wrestling with both personal and public anxieties and conflicts. Renewals of piety were periodically stimulated by natural disasters and epidemics. During the 1780s and 90s in East Cheshire an earthquake, outbreaks of typhoid and cholera, and several serious accidents in the textile mills became the occasions for local revivals and flurries of conversions. Women especially were the caretakers of the sick and dying, and many turned to religion out of an awareness of the near presence of death. The best known example is that of Hester Ann Roe, who experienced conversion at the age of seventeen, at a time when she believed herself to be dying of consumption. She describes her acute sense of her own sinfulness, her terror of dying unsaved, and the culmination of a long inner struggle:

> I was instantly filled with such humbling depths of love to God,
> and union with Him, with such discoveries of my own
> nothingness, as wholly swallowed up my soul in gratitude and
> praise. . . . I cried, This is what I wanted: I am emptied of self
> and filled with God.[17]

Her case is far from unique. One is struck by the high proportion of those memorialized in tracts and sermons who died in their teens or as young adults, many within a year or so of their conversion.[18]

But we must not lose sight of the equally strong positive motivations for becoming part of the rapidly expanding Methodist circle. There was a kind of centrifugal force within the Connection, legitimating travel and new experiences, and breaking down the narrowness of provincial life. Ordinary members, as well as local preachers and itinerants, walked many miles to meet with neighbouring Societies, to attend chapel anniversaries and Love Feasts, or to hear famous metropolitan preachers. Letters and diaries, such as those of John Bennet, Samuel Bardsley of Manchester, and John Birchinall of Macclesfield (all in the Methodist Archives, Rylands Library) make it clear that female members travelled and participated widely, though they usually did so in the company of male friends or under the protection of family members.

For many young converts the association with Methodism was clearly part of a general effort to better themselves. Hence the extraordinary popularity of the evangelical Sunday School movement of the 1790s. Female students may well have benefited from this new educational venture more directly than did the males, as the general level of female education in the eighteenth century was appallingly low. National figures on levels of literacy, as measured by the ability to sign the marriage register, show the male rate remaining constant at about 68 per cent literacy between 1780 and 1840. During the same period the female rate improved from about 39 per cent to 52 per cent.[19] At a time when most women were lucky to have a year or two of dame school, the Methodists were offering free instruction in reading and writing –

and sometimes in arithmetic and more advanced subjects.

Macclesfield Sunday School was originally an ecumenical venture, but soon came to be dominated by the Methodists and some Independents. An imposing institution enrolling about 2,000 children by the turn of the century, it seems to have attracted roughly equal numbers of male and female pupils. We find no record of women teaching Sunday School in East Cheshire in the early days, but the numbers of female teachers steadily increased as a pool of competent former students was built up. Yet even in the 1820s and 30s no women are listed as Sunday School superintendents or as members of the elaborate committees which administered the affairs of the schools. Again, it was in the more out-of-the-way places that women could take unconventional initiatives. In about 1810 a Miss Bradford was teaching Sunday classes in the kitchen of her uncle's farmhouse at Smallwood, a village so remote that the itinerant preachers rarely came there.[20] Such private ventures were always a possibility, for those who could afford them and who could escape chapel authority.

Throughout the history of Christianity there has existed a certain tension between the demands of the biological family and the allegiance exacted by the fellowship of worshippers. To some extent Methodism was the beneficiary of the breakdown of certain familial, or quasi-familial, institutions, for example the traditional domestic economy and the system of apprenticeship. It may be, as Lawrence Stone has argued, that new bonds of family connection and affection were being forged among the upper and upper-middle classes in eighteenth-century England. But farther down on the social scale, in the wide band extending from the master craftsmen to the poorest labourers, the family unit was being subjected to alarming pressures and strains. In prosperous times migration and new sources of employment for the young threatened family solidarity. In hard times, poverty and its attendant curses – alcoholism, violence, disease and early death – took an even heavier toll. Methodism, with its emphasis on the virtues of temperance, industry and neighbourly assistance, offered an alternative and a refuge. E.P. Thompson and other critics of early Methodism have highlighted the emotionally overheated, sometimes bizarrely erotic imagery of its popular literature – charged as it often is with guilt and self-loathing. But equally common is a less extravagent form of language, in which the repentant sinner addresses God, or Christ, or Wesley himself, as a child addressing a benevolent parent. The daily life of the chapel, with its 'brothers and sisters in Christ', its Love Feasts, and its regular visits to the poor and suffering often simply extended the family metaphor. People came to the chapel to find God, and also to find friends and sweethearts. After the first generation or two there emerged a new social structure in the chapels, a tightly intermarried network of Methodist families which soon came to form an inner circle or elite.

The 'official' accounts of family relationships among early converts have it that sweetness and light prevailed. One Methodist historian has written, 'Many of the early Societies grew rapidly because the living experience was communicated from father to son, from brother to sister.' (He might more properly have written, 'from mother to son, from sister to brother'.) He continues, 'Children could not but admire such parents and seek to know the secret of their courage and their joy.'[21] This is a cosy picture, and some families did join *en masse*; but at least as far as Cheshire is concerned, there is abundant evidence that the younger generation more often led the way, and that children often found salvation in open defiance of their parents and guardians.

We hear of parents who beat and threatened their children to keep them from the Methodists – fearing the social stigma and possible loss of worldly prospects which might follow from association with the disreputable 'enthusiasts'. Sometimes it was the young person's employer who objected, as in the case of Mary Kirk, a farm labourer whose master first threatened her and then offered her 2s 6d for each time she stayed away from chapel.[22]

In a number of households pious, strong-willed mothers or elder sisters were the dominant influence, vying openly with husbands or father for control of the younger family members. Local preacher Adam Rushton recalled how his mother went to live apart from her husband, a farmworker in the Pennine uplands who did not share her faith. She took her children to live in Hurdsfield, to be nearer the chapel and Sunday school. Elizabeth Clulow exercised complete control over the upbringing of her two sons. The elder, William, was exemplary; he studied law, joined the chapel, and became one of John Wesley's attorneys in London. The younger, John, was a black sheep, a gambler and brawler. When he was eighteen his despairing mother sent him on a round of the Macclesfield Circuit in the company of a blameless young preacher, in hopes of reforming him. But John soon eluded his keeper and turned up drunk in a tavern, surrounded by disreputable cronies. John Clulow later became Town Clerk of Macclesfield, and a thoroughly worldly fellow; but he stood by the Methodists, serving them as a lawyer and contributing generously to the chapel he never attended, in his mother's memory.[23]

Another instance of virtual matriarchy was the home of Hannah Swindells, who became a popular Sunday School teacher in the 1820s. She strongly identified with her mother, a devout woman who, we are told, 'possessed a vigorous understanding and . . . devoted a considerable portion of her time and attention to the intellectual and spiritual improvement of her daughter'. Young Hannah was converted by her mother at age thirteen in 1794, and she in turn converted her father, a man who had 'lived without God' and was a source of 'domestic uneasiness'.[24]

Others turned to religion without the support of either parent. Rachel Bower of Macclesfield, born in 1747, spent the years from age twelve to twenty in more or less constant battle with her widowed mother, a God-fearing woman who had heard reports of the Methodists as 'the filth and offscourings of all things', ignorant people misled by 'illiterate and designing' preachers.[25]

Hester Ann Roe defied both male and female relatives. Her mother once threatened to disinherit her for her Methodist activities, and her uncle Charles Roe declared that his niece was 'the ruin of his family' through her religious influence on his sons and daughters.[26] Hester Ann was convinced that her rebellion was divinely sanctioned, and the result was an odd sort of stiff-necked, arrogant humility. As she recounted it in her journal,

> I now reasoned with my mother, and entreated her not to confine me any more; telling her in humility, and yet plainness, I must seek the salvation of my soul, whatever the consequences . . . I am therefore determined to leave you and go to be a servant rather than be kept from the Methodists.

Understandably, Hester Ann's exasperated mother pronounced her 'incorrigibly pious'.[27]

In many ways the situations of individual families mirrored the progress of Methodism itself as a domestic discord within the Established Church. Wesley's revolt within and yet against Anglicanism was characterized by all the rancour and stubbornness typical of intra-familial disputes. There is an irony in the reflection that he created his own unchallenged patriarchal regime within Methodism, and that under this regime women were offered religious opportunities they had never enjoyed under the Establishment.

Numbers are only one standard of success, but even by that measure Methodism did very well indeed in East Cheshire.

Between 1790 and 1830 Methodist membership in the Macclesfield area more than quadrupled, at a very conservative estimate, while the population tripled.[28] In these years the Connection was evolving steadily toward full, independent denominational status. A by-product of this development was to be a marked change both in attitudes towards women and in the possibilities open to them within the movement. The increasing formalization of chapel government, the emergence of a paid Wesleyan clergy, and the enhanced role of clergy-dominated regional and national assemblies in church governance all tended to drive women farther from the centre of affairs. On the local level they turned more and more to auxiliary tasks such as sick-visiting, organizing teas and fund-raising bazaars, teaching the youngest children, and providing hospitality for visiting ministers. Women no longer appear as trustees or stewards, although the financial contributions of wealthy widows continue to be welcome. As in other spheres of life where women have been excluded from the direct exercise of power, indirect influence, usually dependent on social prominence and personal access to male leaders, became women's chief recourse. Within the local chapels there was an emerging parallel hierarchy of women, wherein fine gradations of social status, with appropriate niceties of dress and manner, counted for much. George Slater, whose memoirs present a shrewd and vivid portrait of Cheshire Methodism in the first half of the nineteenth century, comments on the elevation of Miss Maclardie of Macclesfield by her fortunate marriage to the great Jabez Bunting, soon to be known as 'the pope of Methodism'. As Slater put it,

> There is an old saying that a wife shines through the medium of her husband. . . . Mrs Jabez Bunting was regarded as the queen of Methodist Society. . . . All [the ministers' wives] were expected to observe religious propriety, especially in public, but they were nevertheless human, and some of them were very human indeed. Mrs Bunting was a capital talker and enjoyed great latitude. Her words sometimes tasted of a little pepper.[29]

In 1803 the Annual Conference passed a resolution declaring that women should not be encouraged to preach – giving as justification the fact that there were already a sufficient number of male clergy. The Conference further decreed that if a woman felt an 'extraordinary call' to speak she should address only those of her own sex, speak only outside her own circuit, and secure written permission from both her own superintendent and the superintendent of the circuit she wished to visit. Naturally these restrictions had a crushing effect on women's public activity, though some continued to preach under the guise of 'teaching' or 'praying'. There seems, as always, to have been some latitude in local situations, away from the eye of authority. Some clergy wives seem to have addressed their husbands' congregations regularly as unofficial 'assistant preachers', but we have no record of such practices in East Cheshire.[30] It is possible that some of the most discontented and ambitious women left Wesleyanism to join the Primitive Methodists or other denominations and sects where female preaching was more welcome.

In a society where the roles of women were severely restricted religion provided virtually the only acceptable sphere of public activity. When the range of religious opportunities suddenly expanded dramatically, as it did in the early decades of the Methodist revival, women were quick to take advantage, even at the expense of family harmony. When male domination reasserted itself in the early nineteenth century, women retreated, but without withdrawing. They continued to serve as they could, and organized philanthropy, including both domestic and foreign missions, was soon to provide new wedges for forcing admission to all-male committees and conferences.

Mary Maples Dunn has argued that the 'feminization' of Christianity over the past three centuries should be seen as one aspect of a larger process of separation of church and state. Increasingly, she says, 'To be a good woman was to be a good Christian. But to be a good man was to be a good citizen.'[31] In eighteenth-century England the long-term development was accelerated by the notorious feebleness of the Anglican Establishment, particularly in the large poorly-served parishes of the north. Against such a backdrop, new religious forms, bypassing the clerical apparatus in favour of a simpler 'religion of the heart', were sure to win support. Women rallied to the evangelical movements with their emphasis on traditionally 'feminine' virtues of submission and service. But when a professional clergy was created in Methodism, women were excluded from it, and as the hierarchy of lay positions within the chapels became more elaborate women were relegated to the lowest niches.

The American historian Donald Mathews, in a recent review essay, poses the question of whether female religious activists were more often dutiful wives and daughters or 'courageous if mild dissenters who entered the church for support and self-esteem.'[32] One of the reasons for Methodism's initial success was that it made room for both types. For women who followed conventional domestic careers, the chapel could provide inspiration, comfort and companionship. For those who had left their families behind, whose homes were broken, or who rejected marriage, the religious life offered an alternative form of kinship and shelter, and new outlets for female enterprise. None the less, from Wesley to Bunting, and beyond, everything that was done by and for women in Methodism was done without overturning the fundamental and traditional imbalance of power between the sexes.

Notes

1   William Hazlitt, 'On the Causes of Methodism'. *Collected Works of Hazlitt* (London: J.M. Dent, 1902), I: 59.

2   See W.J. Townsend *et al.*, *A New History of Methodism*, 2 vols (London: Hodder & Stoughton, 1909); Rupert Davies and Gordon Rupp, eds, *A History of the Methodist Church of Great Britain* (London: Epworth Press), vol. I, 1965; vol. II, 1978; and Rupert E. Davies, *Methodism* (Harmondsworth: Penguin Books, 1963).

3   The 'great woman' approach, though with a less hagiographical bent, persists. See, for instance, Leslie F. Church, *More About the Early Methodist People* (London: Epworth Press, 1949), chap. 4; and Maldwyn Edwards, *My Dear Sister: The Story of John Wesley and the Women in His Life* (Manchester: Penworks Ltd, [1981?]).

4   See R.B. Walker, 'Religious Changes in Cheshire, 1750–1850', *Journal of Ecclesiastical History*, XVII (1966): 77–84.

5   As E.A. Rose has pointed out, the ground was well prepared for Wesley by the earlier efforts of local evangelists, notably John Bennet of Chinley in Derbyshire. Rose, 'Methodism in Cheshire to 1800', *Transactions of the Lancashire and Cheshire Antiquarian Society*, LXXVIII (1975): 22–4. Bennet was an attractive and susceptible young man; the complexities of his relationships with women, before his marriage to Wesley's beloved Grace Murray in 1749, are detailed in his ms. diaries in the Methodist Archives, John Rylands Library, Manchester.

6   James Everett, *Methodism in Manchester and Its Vicinity* (Manchester, 1827), pp.63–5.

7   Benjamin Smith, *Methodism in Macclesfield* (London: Wesleyan Conference Office, 1875), pp.46, 59, 74.

8   *Ibid*, p.17; Joan Alcock, *Methodism in Congleton* (n.p., [1968]); and Howard Hodson, *The Old Community: A Portrait of Wilmslow* (Wilmslow: Hampsfell Press, 1975), pp.103–4.

9   See John Wesley to Sarah Crosby, 14 February 1761, quoted in John S. Simon, *John Wesley, The Master-Builder* (London: Epworth Press 1955), p.293; JW to Sarah Crosby, 18 March 1769, in *The Letters of the Rev. John Wesley, A.M.*, ed. John Telford (London: Epworth

Press, 1931), V: 130 [hereafter cited as *Letters*]; and JW to Grace Walton, 8 September 1761, *Letters*, IV: 164.

10   JW to [Mary Bosanquet], 13 June 1771, *Letters*, V: 257.

11   Adam Rushton's *My Life as Farmer's Boy, Factory Lad, Teacher and Preacher, 1821–1909* (Manchester: S. Clarke, 1909) is a vivid account of the suffering of a country child set to work in a Macclesfield textile mill, and the solace he found in Methodism.

12   In the larger urban societies classes, too, were often segregated by sex. But in the provinces people seem to have preferred to meet with their own friends and neighbours, regardless of gender.

13   See, e.g., John Rylands Library, MAW/LHB 44.2, Manchester Circuit membership list, 1759; and Cheshire CRO, EMC 1/4, Macclesfield membership list, 1794.

14   See, for example, JW to Hester Ann Roe, 3 May and 2 June 1776, in *Letters*, VI: 217, 222; and JW to Ann Bolton, 13 February and 7 April 1768, in *Letters*, V: 80–1, 86.

15   *The Experience and Spiritual Letters of Mrs. Hester Ann Rogers* (Manchester: Samuel Johnson & Son, 1845), p.63.

16   B. Smith, *Methodism in Macclesfield*, p.92; see also pp.88–91.

17   *The Experience of HAR*, p.108. See also memoirs of Rachel Bowers (*Methodist Magazine*, XXX [1807]: 323) and Hannah Swindells (*Methodist Magazine*, LXVI [1842]: 192).

18   See the brief sketches for funeral sermons in Cheshire CRO, EMC 1/13/1, 'Memorial Book of the Rev. T. Hardy'; and 'A Record of Happy Deaths', a series of pamphlets issued annually by the Macclesfield Society for several years, to commemorate the deaths of Sunday School scholars and teachers.

19   Thomas W. Laqueur, *Religion and Respectability: Sunday Schools and Working Class Culture, 1780–1850* (New Haven: Yale University Press, 1976), pp.90–1. Literacy figures are from R.S. Schofield, 'Dimensions of Literacy, 1750–1850', *Explorations in Economic History*, X (1973): 442–5.

20   J. Alcock, *Methodism in Congleton*, p.32.

21   Leslie F. Church, *The Early Methodist People* (London: Epworth Press, 1948), p.222.

22   Obituary in *Methodist Magazine*, LIV (1831): 576–7.

23   A. Rushton, *My Life*; and B. Smith, *Methodism in Macclesfield*, pp.124–7.

24   A.S., 'Memoir of Mrs. Swindells of Macclesfield', *Methodist Magazine*, LXVI (1842): 191–7.

25   John Ryles, 'A Memoir of Rachel Bower of Macclesfield', *Methodist Magazine*, XXX (1807): 323–6.

26   For the tumultuous story of Hester Ann Roe's influence on the family of Charles Roe, see, 'The Experience of Mr. Robert Roe',

Arminian Magazine, 1783, pp.521–4, 580–2, 638–41.

27 *The Experience of HAR*, pp.27–8; 224.

28 Cheshire CRO, EDV 7/2/103, (Bishop's) Visitation: Articles of Inquiry, 1789; and CRO, QDR (Constable's) Returns of Non-conformists, 1829.

29 George Slater, *Chronicles of Life and Religion in Cheshire* (London: Andrew Crombie, 1891), p.83.

30 See Wesley F. Swift, 'Women Preachers of Early Methodism, Part I', *Proceedings of the Wesley Historical Society*, XXVIII (1952): 90–1. Jabez Bunting utterly rejected women's right to preach and dismissed the claim of an extraordinary call as 'every fanatic's plea', *ibid.*, p.92.

31 In J. James, ed., *Women in American Religion* (Philadelphia: University of Pennsylvania Press, 1980), p.39.

32 In Thomas and Keller, eds, *Women in New Worlds* (Nashville, Tenn.: Abingdon Press, 1981), vol. I, p.42.

Further reading

Brown, Earl Kent, *Women of Mr. Wesley's Methodism* (Lewiston, N.Y.: Edwin Mellen, 1984).

Butler, H.M., 'The "pious sisterhood": a study of women's roles in English Methodism, *c.*1740–*c.*1840', BA thesis, La Trobe University, 1978.

Cott, Nancy F., 'Young Women in the Second Great Awakening', *Feminist Studies*, III (1975): 14–29.

Davis, Sidney Thomas, 'Women's Work in the Methodist Church', PhD thesis, University of Pittsburgh, 1963.

James, Janet W., ed., *Women in American Religion* (Philadelphia: University of Pennsylvania Press, 1980).

Thomas, Hilah F. and Rosemary Skinner, eds, *Women in New Worlds*, 2 vols (Nashville, Tenn.: Abingdon Press, 1981, 1983).

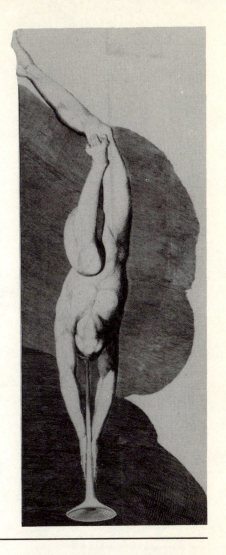

Sexuality

5

The larceny of desire: The Madonna in seventeenth-century Catholic Europe

LUISA ACCATI

In this article, I shall try to unravel the complex mesh of maternity and desire. I shall try to show that even where the elements which compose the family remain the same, simply changing the way in which they are combined radically changes the construction of sexuality.

I

I think it will be useful to start off by examining Christiane Olivier's justly acclaimed book, *Les Enfants de Jocaste* (1980).

As Olivier reminds us, Freud argued that a child's sexuality is awakened and developed by maternal care: the child's first love-object is an incestuous one. Now, if we bear in mind the fact that the mothers who bring up children of both sexes are *women*, it follows that they must find their love-object in their *sons* – these sons, then, will be love-objects for the mother while her daughters will not be. Conversely, while the little boy is provided with an appropriate sex object right from birth in the shape of his mother, the little girl's only appropriate sex object is the father – and he does not concern himself with her.

For the little boy, the satisfaction of his needs is thus accompanied by sexual desire; but such desire is absent in the relationship between mother and daughter. The little girl must wait until she becomes adult and is desired as a woman before she can discover satisfaction.

With her son, the mother has a unique chance to see herself in a masculine form, the chance to believe in the old myth of the bisexual androgyne. But the boy child is not her and is not even hers. Even if she were able – just for a moment – to believe she could possess the other sex, her son will soon rid her of her illusions as he grows up. The boy's struggle will be the more violent and persistent the more prolonged and intense is the mother's conviction of her oneness with her son.

The little boy must overcome an additional hurdle which the little girl does not face (one which Freud did not describe) because he must escape from the Oedipal complex against his mother's will: she does not want him to grow distant from her or leave her. From this moment on, the little boy is at war with female desire. At first, this war is directed against the mother. Bed-wetting, nappy-soiling and the tensions of growing up spring from his being, as it were, chained by maternal love – a love of which he will always be afraid, in the shape of fearing domination by women. Misogyny is the terror of being caught in the love-symbiosis-prison of the mother. Even with his lover, he will avoid tenderness, for it might remind him of his mother.

As the person who cares for the son, the mother is unique and special for him; while for the mother, her son is the one man who stays with her. The father is absent from the child's upbringing and the husband ignores or abandons his wife. A woman whose husband holds her at a distance attaches herself particularly strongly to her son – thus training him to hold his future woman at a distance. One woman sows the misogyny which the next woman reaps. In this way, it is carved into men's identity to reject women as equals. There is a sort of terrible circle in which the woman who has not been desired as a child searches, as an adult, for the desire and approval of men. Men, for their part, take advantage of their position of strength to settle accounts with their mothers. So, the woman who is searching for love from a man which will make good her previous emptiness ends up by falling into a love which castrates her – love of a man who sees an attempt at domination in every manifestation of a woman's affection, and who has decided once and for all that She will never rule again.

The route to a greater autonomy and a freer development of personality for women must therefore lie through the desacralization of the Mother, whose reign has generated misogyny in man and jealousy in woman. If we are to construct another family, we must do so by means of a different form of upbringing, a different division of parental tasks and of social roles more generally – one which allows the child right from birth to have a reference model of the same sex and a complement of the opposite sex (the first as a basis for identification, the second as a basis for Oedipal development and the formation of identity) (Olivier, 1980).

The objective which Olivier proposes to us is certainly desirable, and it could be attained – provided, however, that we are fully aware of the cultural roots and the elements which make the mother a *social and cultural* symbol. The shaping of the maternal role is, in any case, only partially in the hands of individual mothers. Few figures are so loaded with symbolism as the mother. The behaviour of a woman who is a mother is magnified, distorted and dislocated by the meanings with which she is encrusted, whatever the intentions of the particular woman who takes up the role.

The inhibition of desire has deep roots and is a complex interweaving of social, historical, psychological and cultural facts.

I should like to develop a few of the points which Olivier raises. She tells us that the archetypal model of the possessive mother appears to be the Madonna. All those figures of Virgin and child hold their sons with expressions of pride, fulfilment and self-satisfaction. The Madonnas thus sing a eulogy to the mother-woman who finds happiness and self-fulfilment outside the father. He is reduced to a myth: God the Father. This is a male religion, constructed by men who recognize in women only the womb which carried them. It is an intensely Oedipal religion since it makes the father disappear and gives the mother centre stage.

I do not want to suggest for a moment that this is not an Oedipal religion (it is Oedipal, one might remark, not only because it sets the father aside in favour of the mother, but also because of its exclusion of the existence of brothers or sisters); nor would I deny that the centre of the Holy Family is the male child. But what we are dealing with is not so much a religion constructed by men in general, but the creation of a particular hegemonic group of men – priests – whose prime function is to control other men. Both the representation of Mary and the cult and liturgy must keep to strict rules established by the church; and there can be no free expressions of devotion, for either men or women.

God the Father is set aside in favour of the Mother, but who is this Mother if not holy mother Church? Could it be that the wish to keep the son tied and fixated on the Mother, never allowing him to become adult, corresponds to a desire for domination which is not unique to Mothers? Is it not possible that protectiveness and care are forms of power which require non-responsible subjects?

If the son is to remain fixated on the mother, it is essential that he should not love his father. Since the Virgin-Mother does not desire her husband, jealousy is not produced in the son and hence he is not impelled to take the father's place – the propulsive factor of rivalry is missing. Being surrounded by a love which is unconditional, having his wants satisfied even before he can formulate them, he is not able to become conscious of his needs and desires in a way which would enable him to resolve them, but remains instead eternally desiring (Montefoschi, 1977). We must ask ourselves how much of this pattern can be attributed to mothers and how much to powers which use this bond with the mother as an instrument of control.

The Madonna is what Turner calls a dominant symbol. A dominant symbol occupies a central position within the whole cultural system. It has the function of condensing meanings, unifying disparate meanings in one single form and organizing them around two extreme poles which reinforce each other – the physical or tangible referent and the normative or normal referent (Turner, 1967).

Although the Madonna is a dominant symbol for the whole Catholic world, not all Madonnas are the same. Even though the Madonna is always at the centre of the holy Family, her influence on the internal equilibria of the numerous different types of family found in the Catholic countries is different. One can begin to grasp this diversity by considering the different emphasis placed on the normative pole of the symbol in worship as compared with the physical pole – the complex balance between Virgin and Mother.

Whoever has control over a symbol (as the Church does in this case) has to choose the physical support of that symbol carefully. It cannot ignore the real social structure of the subject population from which the symbol draws its inspiration, lest the efficacy of the symbol itself be diminished. We can be sure, then, that the spread of Christianity in general and of the cult of the Madonna in particular will find fertile soil where mother-women are prominent in the social fabric. In a stratified society, moreover, the dominant symbol must be general enough to be of relevance to everyone and rich enough in meanings to be adapted to the different needs of the various social strata.

Finally, the two contradictory attributes of the Madonna – Virgin and Mother – are intimately connected with female sexuality. We must therefore remember that the symbol of the Madonna will have a different significance depending on whether it is men or women who are worshipping her.

II

To illustrate the important role of the Church in the construction of this symbol, I will refer to material on people living in the Friulian countryside in the seventeenth century, taken from the archepiscopal archive of Udine. I have used the Inquisition trial for evidence about love sorcery and peasant magic.

(a) Love sorcery

Women of all social strata frequently made use of magic to prevent their husbands abandoning them. In 1655, one of these women said, 'So that my husband should love no one but me, I had to take some of my menstrual blood and give it to my husband in his food and drink, so that then he would love me alone' (Trial 282 bis).

All the love-magic trials have an identical structure: the women are goaded into action by the nagging fear of being abandoned. Since they lack a social identity of their own, without a husband they risk falling into that category which is most likely to attract the dangerous accusations of witchcraft – the category of orphans, widows and deserted women. Their need is for social-juridical protection, while affection seems to be, for them, the acceptable and positive element of this dependence on husbands.

Women enjoyed great autonomy in the field of magic and regarded their blood as a positive instrument for their use (Accati, 1979). The Inquisitor and other men, by contrast, saw this blood as a powerful and dangerous poison which women might use at any time to enslave men or even drive them to death.

Men, on the other hand, have a social identity and social autonomy which are not dependent upon women. One finds no traces of love bewitchment trials (trials *ad amorem*) of men who want to prevent their wives leaving them. Instead, many men go to the Inquisitor because they believe themselves to have been 'bewitched' by their wives or by other women. Typical is the case of Lorenzo della Negra who declared in 1659 that for three months he had been unable to eat or rest, and that he had felt almost compelled to go at night to the house of Caterina, with whom he felt 'wildly in love'. Having rejected the hypothesis that this was a psychological phenomenon, Lorenzo went to the doctor, who confirmed his suspicion that he had been the victim of witchcraft and told him 'this love is nothing other than a supernatural effect'. Lorenzo then went to the Inquisitor and denounced Caterina, saying that she must have made him drink some of her menstrual blood in order to keep him tied to her.

Not being brought up in a position of social dependence as women are, men are amazed and in unfamiliar territory when faced with emotional dependence, and they flee from it as a magical phenomenon. Besides, they have no counter-poisons to oppose it with; their bodies are not magical in themselves. In *their* sorcery, they have to rely on instruments, books and formulae.

The emotional dependence on a loved person which character-izes love relationships harmonizes with the upbringing and social destiny of women – indeed, it is almost a logical consequence of it – whereas emotional dependence seems to cause explosions within men. ('I feel my heart burst,' a young man from Udine says to the Inquisitor.) Love is a contradiction for men. It goes against the grain of all the upbringing and destiny which is reserved for men, in which self-affirmation and independence from others are so crucially important.

The Church transforms menstrual blood from a positive love force into a negative, maleficent power. At a stroke, it takes over male fears and transmutes women's initiative: women who use their blood are wicked and must be made to repent.

(b) Fertility sorcery

Another particularly clear example of the clergy transforming what, for women, was a positive power of the female body into a negative characteristic is fertility sorcery. Around the middle of the seventeenth century, a large number of women went to don Polidoro Frattina and revealed that there was a *preento* (a spell) which had been passed down from mother to daughter for driving away the weevils which destroy the harvest in the fields. A young virgin must go naked through the fields astride a kind of barrel on wheels, saying, 'Fui, fui ruie che il mio con ti mangiuie' (Get away, get away weevils, my cunt is coming to eat you) (Accati, 1979).

For these women, virginity was an active quality, a power which asserts itself. The moment of maximum female fertility, it has nothing to do with modesty and chasteness. It seems to be the threshold from which life expands. Yet it is impossible to believe that in the Virginity of the Madonna as propagated by the Church there is anything of this affirmation of physical potency.

Indeed, the Madonna's Virginity has much more in common with the male idea of female virginity. For men, women's virginity is a relational concept – a virgin is a woman who has never known a man, who is intact. Virginity is thus an obstacle, a test to be overcome. All the warrior imagery of the Conquest, connected with the problem of virile potency, is catalysed around this virginity (Flachaire, 1957). The virgin resists the assaults, courtship is a siege, virtue is like a fortress and it falls, capitulates, yields, and so on. The discourse surrounding female virtue is one continuous military metaphor of the male sex act. The aggressiveness betrays the fear of impotence. And the resistance and intactness of the virgin serve to forestall the possibility of a checkmate.

It is this idea of Virginity which is taken up by the Church, and which reappears among women in the form of shame, modesty and the *denying of desire*. Here again, the Church adopts the male vision of female virginity and transforms virginity from a positive to a negative state, from something active into something passive. It is in this perspective that we must view the Inquisition's attitude to women's magic, love sorcery and field magic.

III

The accentuation of the normative aspect of the Madonna symbol corresponds to a political requirement of the Church. In the mid-sixteenth century, Christianity divided and two reference models of the family were formed. In one, the Madonna dominates and St Joseph and the baby and God the Father are in the background; in the other, the Madonna is cast down from her role as symbol and has left the scene, leaving a model composed exclusively of God the Father and the adult Christ (Leach, 1969).

In the Protestant world, the old priesthood and the superiority of the unmarried man disappear together with the Madonna. The Protestants accused Catholics of praying to the Madonna as if she were a pagan goddess, forgetting that her Son, not she, was God. For them, worship of the Madonna amounted to idolatry (Bertetto, 1957). Mary is certainly a mother worthy of reverence, but she gave birth to the Son in order that we might believe in Him. We ought not to worship her as a Mother – rather, it is she who has rendered us an act of service (Luther).

The theological controversy between Catholics and Protestants brings out the connection between the priest and the Madonna (Olier, 1676). The power of priests is closely bound up with the mediation between divine and human, between that which can be explained and that which remains mysterious. The Madonna is precisely that figure who, while being human, brings God into the world (Leach, 1969). Her miraculous parturition celebrates and augments the mystery of life: the passage from non-being to existence is via the maternal womb. But priests too put themselves forward as mediators between God and men. Thus they have a dual interest with respect to female sexuality: on the one hand, they must keep its value high; on the other, they must ensure that it is under their control.

Protestantism took a logical consistent line and denied priests powers superior to those of other men. It insisted there could be no mediators between God and men: to assert otherwise was blasphemy. There were no human means for bringing us closer to God, for this depended on His will alone. Neither Madonna nor priest could intercede – each individual, man or woman, clergy or lay, was equally and directly responsible. As Natalie Zemon Davis (1975) argued:

> Certainly it is true that the Reformed solution did promote a certain desexualization of society, a certain neutralizing of forms of communication and of certain religious places so that they became acceptable for women. These were important gains, bringing new tools to women and new experience to both sexes. But the assimilationist solution brought losses, too. This-worldly asceticism denied laymen and laywomen much of the shared recreational and festive life allowed them by Catholicism. It closed off an institutionalized and respectable alternative to private family life: the communal living of the monastery. By destroying the female saints as exemplars for both sexes, it cut off a wide range of affect and activity. And by eliminating a separate identity and separate organization for women in religious life, it may have made them a little more vulnerable to subjection in all spheres.

The elimination of women from the ideal model of the family meant the denial of their special moral status. In the Catholic world, the subordination of women to the hegemonic group of priests guarantees them a certain margin of autonomy in relation to the family, father and husband. Yet, as we have seen, the Church confronts problems of shoring up its power and increasing its effectiveness; and thus, more than ever, it must ensure the control of women.

In the course of the seventeenth century, then, there is a general deterioration in the social position of women in both Catholic and Protestant areas (Zemon Davis, 1975). But the question which we need to address is not to determine which zone saw the greater deterioration, but rather to analyse the *different* way in which it happened.

During the seventeenth century, the Church set out to absorb any and every magical phenomenon into the ecclesiastical-religious category of the sacred. The capacity to intervene in life and death is a part both of the sphere of magic and of that of the sacred. In women, priests have their most potent allies, but also their most potent rivals. The protection which the clergy provides for women is full of ambivalence, and women's fervent faith is no less so. Eternal life and the salvation of the soul are a splendid promise, but life on earth and sin are realities which offer their own pleasures. Women, with their capacity to bestow earthly life, are *de facto* irreducible antagonists of the priests. In the uncertain battle between body and soul, they can always intervene authoritatively on the side of the body. The Church promises salvation of the soul: women promise nothing, but they do possess the manifest capacity to give bodily life.

During the seventeenth century, priests steal from women their self-desire, their pride in the potency of their bodies, compensating them with social protection and respectability in the eyes of the community and the family.

The ways in which this expropriation took place are symptomatic of the equilibrium between clergy and civil power, and are the fruit of deep conflicts within the Church itself.

To help understand these tensions, we can distinguish two types of Madonna which the Church hierarchy presented to the faithful: an imposing Mother-Madonna whom the Son loves with respect and admiration; and a humble servant-like Madonna whose sole reason for living is to take care of the Son.

(a) The Mother-Madonna

Let us now examine briefly the first type of Madonna, prominent in areas where the threat from Protestantism is more remote. The Jesuits and St Francis de Sales no longer restrained popular fantasy – all the most unashamedly sentimental forms of devotion to Mary were encouraged. The Madonnas become young and extraordinarily tender, the Jesuses become babies who abandon themselves to their mother's embrace. The prayers and the cult of the Madonna take their inspiration from the mystic tradition and borrow their language from that of love:

> This kiss so long denied and delayed, was at last granted to this
> holy lover, Our Lady, who, more than any other woman,
> deserves the title of bride and lover. It was vouchsafed to her by
> the heavenly bridegroom on the day of the Annunciation,
> which we celebrate today, at the moment when she gave a deep
> sigh of love. Oh! that he might kiss me with a kiss from his
> lips! (St Francis de Sales, 1621)

In this kind of structure, there is a continual web of connections between Mary and Jesus: sometimes Jesus is Mary's betrothed, sometimes her son; now she smiles at him like a lover, now she gazes at him contemplatively like a mother. Everything which is forbidden in real life becomes permitted in this fantasy form of the cult: the baby is God, just as his Father in heaven is God, and just as the Holy Spirit, author of the conception, is God. The baby is thus the son of himself, and he is the husband and lover of his mother.

The aim is to dominate men through their love object; the effect is symbiosis, and symbiosis with the mother is just a prelude to symbiosis with the wife. Where the mother is a holy *domina* (a great and powerful lady) the wife is no less holy than she. She is certainly not held at a distance, and she does not have to rely on men to confirm her identity. Bringing a baby into the world and nourishing it are acts so extraordinarily divine as to be prized for themselves. The mother is not dependent on the son; on the contrary, the son must prove himself deserving of such grace. She asks nothing; but he is indebted to her for life – the endless profane gifts which he could give her can never equal the sacred gift which she has given him. Symmetrically, the wife is always 'the mother of my children' and thus continues to perpetuate the cycle of unrepayable debt.

As Olivier rightly remarks, the mother certainly does not feel desire for the female child; but from the moment of birth, she awards her a very high value which is different from the social-juridical value conferred on her brothers. To the daughter, her brother's social and legal privileges may even seem to be given as a compensation for the fact that they do not share the esteem which she enjoys. This is an excellent starting-point for the development of her narcissism (albeit one different from that of her brothers). The father is not responsible for her physical care, but neither is he absent: she comes into contact with him since he spends a substantial part of his time controlling and supervising the mother, and very soon his possessive attention will be turned on her too. Now, jealousy may limit a person's freedom, imprison them in a role, and create serious, complex problems, but it certainly does not depress self-esteem. The sacred character of female sexuality compensates her for her social and legal inferiority and the representations of the family flatter the figure of the woman to the point of awarding her the principal role in the sphere of the affections. In this context, therefore, the female figure shares in the construction of the super-ego. Via this route, male children are able to take on aspects of behaviour and principles of the maternal figure even in spite of the rigidity of the division between male and female roles. Legal and social power may lie exclusively in the hands of men, but the emotional measure of power – its prestige – consists above all in the ability to protect, as can be seen from the relationships of patronage and mafia so widespread in Catholic countries. To have a large number of clients is gratifying in the same way as having many sons: the powerful man is an intermediary.

This structure fosters the expression of very intense maternal feelings and creates a space for their expression through pain and sorrow. Indeed, the mother's body expresses its potency, in sublimated form, through its capacity for suffering. The gracious *mater dolorosa* who offers her suffering up to God (the figure of the *juxta crucem*, that of the *Pieta* or the Madonna with the pierced heart which becomes widespread at a later period), who is constantly willing to be the suffering mother, is doing precisely this – translating pleasure in herself into a highly dramatic, hyperbolic form of pain. Our Lady 'is a living martyr: for her, everything was a Calvary, every day was a Good Friday, her life was one perpetual Passion and every day her heart was crucified at the hands of love (which bring death just as much as the hands of death itself)' (Binet, 1624).

The suffering mother asks nothing, her self-abnegation is a *will* to submit even before her husband or son think of attacking her. Since she is incapable of punishing anyone, and since the conditions for forgiveness are therefore absent, she makes herself into a monument for other people's guilt. Her suffering renders her husbands and sons guilty, and her resignation places them at the mercy of the priests who control the path to a submissive pardon. She tirelessly multiplies guilt and remorse to the greater glory of God and his ministers and to the confusion of men.

A woman who conforms to this model can draw enjoyment from her body so long as she knows how to invert desire completely, in every area of her life. Lust must be translated into shame, satisfaction in fullness into vomit, childbirth into death:

> 'When Vito was born I cannot tell you how much I suffered. I was laid out on the bed – faint and white – and I had stopped breathing. Everyone was crying. It was evening, the time for vespers, and a friend of mine went to the church and said to the priest: "Don Raffaele, ring the bells, Amalia is dead" and I lay there, unable to move, and I heard the bells ring!'

The focus of the picture is the deathly pale body of the woman in childbed. All around are the dark tones of evening and anxiety. All the other characters are in shadow; the baby is invisible. 'You have problems, we were Martyrs' – concludes the woman narrating the story. The baroque birth is the mother's death.

(b) The servant-like Madonna

The second Madonna, on the other hand, is an instrument of the holy Father, and her reason for existence is her relationship with her son. With her, the Church pushes the normative pole of the symbol to the point where the physical pole disappears. This

Madonna hardly acts as mediator between the Father and the Son – she is rather the instrument of both. In the Holy Family this Madonna does not have specific functions of her own and she is not an active protagonist, either in the love relationship with the Father or in that with the Son. Of the one she is the handmaid, of the other, the adorer.

This is the Madonna of the gallican church which Bossuet (1627–1704) described so well. Mary is our advocate, we can turn to her; but we must not surrender ourselves to forms of worship which make us forget that the prayers are directed towards God.

In other words, both the Madonna and the figure of the mother are diminished by the downgrading of birth – as it becomes less magical, less sacred and less sought-after. The mother who is presented here as a socially approved model is not sacred enough to constitute part of the super-ego, nor profane enough to be considered the equal of her husband before God. Like the other mother-madonna, she too is a prisoner of her role as mother, but in addition she sees this role lose value. At this point, the desire for the son is *a priori* altered by the frustration inherent in the situation. She comes not to desire him as the fruit of her womb but as a consolation for her own insignificance – to heal her wounded self-esteem, to make up for the lack of recognition or appreciation of her sex which in this case has no compensations: 'there is no doubt that, just as Jesus surpassed Mary in everything else, so he was a better Son than she was Mother' (Bossuet, 1767).

Only this second Madonna provides the basis for the syndrome described by Olivier. For if motherhood has value in itself, the children must prove themselves worthy of the gift received. If, on the other hand, the mother is simply an instrument of the Father, her motherhood will be valued only if the son to whom she has given birth is a man of value; and similarly, the daughter to whom she gives birth will have to wait for confirmation and recognition of herself: during her childhood, she will have no significance.

In terms of emotional relations, the shift in emphasis from Mother to Son deprives the Mother of her function of mediation and places Father and Son directly face to face. In *this* situation, the *mater dolorosa* does not involve either the Father or the Son in her sufferings. Like childbirth, her suffering is simply a service which she renders, and this infinite capacity for suffering is merely a symptom – of no great merit – of her humility and purity:

Ordinary intercourse induces a ferment of impurity in our bodies, thus it is evident that progeny germinated from virginal

stock will draw from this root a marvellous purity. . . .
Besides, it is obvious that the flesh of the Saviour had to shine
with the brightness of a virgin's blood, *so that it would be worthy
of being united with the Word and being offered to the Father* as a
living victim in expiation of our sins. (Bossuet, 1767)

The mother who must conform to this model cannot have
desires of any kind. A devout, well brought-up woman will not
have yearnings of desire either in the prohibited form of pleasure,
nor in the permitted form of suffering: she is emotionally sterile.
As Bossuet notes, given these premises, no one was more fitted to
attest the divine pregnancy of the Virgin than Saint Elizabeth – a
sterile woman made fertile by a miracle (Bossuet, 1767).

It seems plausible that (when this type of socialization succeeds)
a man who is the son of a profoundly devout mother will tend to
be distant from his wife and incapable of tenderness, since he has
never been truly desired and has never experienced anything but
distant emotions. Stereotypical emotions may *appear* very intense,
but even this intensity is part of the formula. The condition for
real intensity – self-love – has been stolen from his mother.

Translated by Michael Eve and Lyndal Roper

References

L. Accati, 'Lo spirito della fornicazione: virtù dell'anima e virtù del
corpo in Friuli, fra '600 e '700', in *Quaderni storici*, XIV, May–August
1979, pp.644–72.

D. Bertetto, *Maria e i protestanti*, Rome, 1957.

P. Binet (1569–1639), *Le Grand Chef-d'oeuvre de Dieu ou les perfections de la
Sainte Vierge*, Paris, 1624.

J.B. Bossuet (1627–1704), *Oeuvres*, Liège, 1767.

L. Carli, *Maria S.S. Madre e prototipo della Chiesa*, Rome, 1965.

C. Flachaire, *La Dévotion à la Vierge dans la litterature catholique au
commencement du XVIIe siècle*, Paris, 1957.

Francis de Sales, *Oeuvres complètes*, in particular *Sermons* (1595–1622),
Paris, 1821.

E. Leach, *Genesis as Myth and Other Essays*, London, 1969.

M. Luther, *Werke*, vol. 11.

M. Luther, *Scritti religiosi*, Turin, 1978, see in particular the commentary
on the *Magnificat* (1521).

S. Montefoschi, *L'uno e l'altro, interdipendenza e intersoggettività nel rapporto
psicoanalitico*, Milan, 1977.

J.J. Olier (1608–75), *Traité des saints Ordres*, Paris, 1676.

C. Olivier, *Les Enfants de Jocaste*, Paris, 1980.
V. Turner, *The Forest of Symbols*, Cornell, 1967.
N. Zemon Davis, *Culture and Society in Early Modern France*, Stanford, 1975.

6
The sexual politics of early Wesleyan Methodism[1]

HENRY ABELOVE

John Wesley wanted the Methodists who were converted to refrain if they could from marrying, and he told them so repeatedly, both in print and in exhortation.

He first published his views on the subject in 1743, early in his career, in the pamphlet *Thoughts on Marriage and a Single Life*. Here he said that he had often been asked which was to be 'preferr'd', a 'Married State, or a Single Life', and that he had decided to write out an answer. It was that the 'Single Life' was better, at least for believers, and in fact was required of them.

This answer Wesley grounded on Scripture, particularly on the passage in the Gospel of Matthew where Jesus says: 'and there be eunuchs which have made themselves eunuchs for the kingdom of heaven's sake. He that is able to receive it, let him receive it.' Wesley thought that the meaning of the passage was clear: that 'eunuchs which have made themselves eunuchs' meant persons who 'have abstain'd from Marriage all their Lives, have remain'd Single 'till Death'; that 'he who is able to receive it' meant 'Every believer in Christ'; and that 'let him receive it' was a plain order, a command. So the passage was to be understood as commanding that every believer stay single and celibate.

Wesley acknowledged that his reading of the passage was more rigorous even than that of the 'Romish writers'. They said that Jesus was not commanding celibacy there but rather counselling it, and that although everybody was supposed to keep His commands, His counsels were not obligatory. But according to Wesley nothing in the text justified a distinction between counsels and commands. Such a distinction had 'no place' anywhere in Scripture, least of all in that particular passage in Matthew. After all, the words were not, 'He may receive it, if he will', but instead: 'Let him receive it.' These words were certainly a command. 'How,' Wesley asked, 'could a Command be more clearly exprest?'

It was a command addressed, moreover, to all converts, all justified persons. For they were the ones 'able to receive it', the ones who had the gift of continence. That gift they had got at the time of their 'Redemption'. At that moment, 'lust' had vanished, and so long as they kept themselves in the faith, praying, and looking to Jesus day and night, lust would 'never return'.

But what if the convert were at the time of his 'Redemption' already married? In that case he should continue to be married, continue willingly to satisfy the sexual wants of his partner. 'Support' would come to him 'therein' from God. All other converts should be eunuchs for the sake of heaven. It was at once their privilege and their duty. If, however they faltered in faith, then they might lose the gift of continence and become 'weak again', like ordinary people. In that situation, they should marry, unless they felt sure that they could recover the lost gift 'soon'. For without that gift they might easily slide into the sin of fornication, and marriage was of course preferable to fornication.

Wesley also warned that nobody should forbid marriage or despise it or foster divorce. Still, he made clear that marriage was second-best. Celibacy was what Jesus wanted, and he wanted it of all those who were born again, so long as they stayed faithful, and unless they happened to be married already.

This view was not absolutely unique to Wesley. There were at least two other revivalists during the great mid-eighteenth-century revival who put a comparably high value on celibacy, both obscure, both based in the North American colonies – Shadrach Ireland, who led a small sect in Harvard, Massachusetts, and Johann Konrad Beissel, who founded a quasi-monastic community at Ephrata, Pennsylvania.[2] Although not unique, Wesley's view was nevertheless highly unusual, and it was not held by his helpers and clerical sympathizers. In fact they opposed it, and forcefully enough to persuade him to modify it a little. When he published a second time on the same subject, in 1765, his argument showed some signs of their influence.

He called his new pamphlet *Thoughts on a Single Life*, and here he again maintained that the single life was preferable for the converted. But he no longer said, as he had before, that it was required of them. He also acknowledged that the gift of continence, which every justified person got at the time of his conversion, did not 'continue long' with most. It was in fact usually withdrawn, perhaps on account of some 'Fault' in the convert. Then marriage was called for, and Wesley said something about it especially positive. In the previous pamphlet he had said that nobody should forbid it or despise it. Now he went a step further and said that 'persons may be as holy in a married as it is possible to be in a single State'.

That was certainly a concession to his colleagues, and almost as though to counterbalance it, he included a fervent listing of the advantages enjoyed exclusively by those who stayed single. They alone could serve God without distraction. They alone were safe from 'the greatest of all Intanglements, the Loving one Creature above all others'. And, they alone need accumulate no wealth. They could give all their earnings to God.

Having listed these advantages, Wesley went on to urge that single people 'prize' them and 'keep' them and 'use' them. He also gave a few prudential warnings. He said that single people who were trying to hold onto the gift of continence they had got at their conversion would be well-advised to converse often with 'like-minded' persons of their own sex and to avoid 'all needless Conversation, much more all Intimacy', with 'those of the Other Sex'. They should also refrain from masturbating ('Satan will not cast out Satan,' Wesley explained), and they should live hard, eschewing 'self-indulgence' and 'softness', exercising as much as their strength allowed, and spending as little time in bed as possible.

Wesley expressed his preference for celibacy not only in these pamphlets on the subject but also in his pastoral conduct and arrangements. First of all, he exhorted. He told the unmarried to stay as they were. Especially in the bigger societies, where there were sizeable groups of young, still single persons, Wesley would from time to time meet with them, men and women separately, and encourage them, tell them how 'good' it was to remain single, urge them 'to consider, to prize, and to improve' their advantages.

Wesley also opposed the institution of mixed-sex seating in family-pews, something that was then usual both in the churches of the Establishment and the chapels of Dissent. No doubt he disliked the ostentation that often went along with these pews. In many chapels, they were virtually closed-off rooms, resembling parlours, lined with baize and covered by curtains. No doubt he disliked also the use of reserved seats. He wanted the Methodist preaching-houses to be open to anybody who might want to enter them. But Wesley's chief objection was neither to ostentation nor to reserved seating. For he did not willingly permit family-pews

that were unostentatious, nor did he want families to sit together
even on seats that were unreserved. His chief objection was to the
mixing of the sexes. He ordered that the seating in the Methodist
preaching-houses be entirely segregated by sex, the women on
one side, the men on the other, and a rail between.

Wesley even tried to arrange that Methodist meetings for
fellowship be segregated by sex. From the very start of his career
as a travelling evangelist, he divided the flock who were already
converted into bands. These were small groups, whose members
met regularly for mutual edification and guidance. Naturally the
meetings produced a kind of intimacy, and because the bands
were constituted as all-male or all-female, the intimacy was kept
guardedly intrasexual. Alongside the bands Wesley established
also another sort of group for fellowship, the select-bands. These
were smaller and fewer than the bands and included just the
Methodists who were already Perfected, or who were pressing on
to Perfection. Here the purposes of meeting were also mutual
edification and guidance, and the intimacy was intenser even than
in the bands. For there was a special rule that nothing said in
select-band could ever be repeated to anybody else. These groups
as well were segregated by sex.

Finally, Wesley made his preference for celibacy vividly clear by
his attitude towards marriage ceremonies. He disliked the work of
performing them, and he chose to perform very few. From 1738
until 1791, throughout the whole length of his career as a
travelling evangelist, he mentioned in his Journal only four
marriages that he had officiated at or assisted at. Of these four,
one was a family affair that he could hardly have escaped, the
marriage of his brother Charles. During that same period, he
mentioned on the other hand 104 funerals that he had officiated at
or assisted at or preached at. His reluctance to perform marriages
may even have been one of the private motives behind his public
decision to make his career as an itinerant rather than as a parish
clergyman. If he had taken a parish in the usual way, he would
have been canonically obliged to perform marriages – lots of
them.

Did the Methodists do as Wesley taught and stay single and
celibate? All indications are that they did not. They deferred to
Wesley, and they loved him, too; but one of the chief
consequences of their attachment to him, as he himself often
remarked, was that they came to be closely united with each other
as well. In that union they discovered shared needs and views.
Among the needs was heterosexual desire, and among the views,
a strongly favourable outlook on marriage, which had come

down to them from their Puritan forebears particularly and from the Protestant tradition generally. In union they resisted Wesley's preference for celibacy, resisted also the pastoral arrangements which he made to enforce it, and refused to let him be what perhaps he wanted to be – the only marrying Methodist.

Extra-marital intercourse they disapproved as strongly as Wesley could have wished. That they saw as definitely a sin. One Methodist, a London man, called it, perhaps with just a touch of complacency, his 'reigning sin',[3] but that it *was* a sin he simply took for granted. Pre-marital intercourse they also regarded generally as wrong, and a young Lancashire man, who spent a whole night together with his woman-friend, would feel the need to explain even to his own diary that he had never taken his 'Cloaths' off, that he had in no way 'Brought Condemnation' on his 'soul' by the 'Nights Proceeding'.[4] But towards marriage they felt differently, positively. It is true that very occasionally they hesitated about it on religious grounds,[5] and one small group of Methodist men at Tetney actually made for themselves the sort of quasi-monastic community that Wesley most approved. Ordinarily, though, they kept firmly to a position favouring marriage, and if a young society member was hesitating, scrupling about his own sexual wishes, he might be advised by an older, fellow-Methodist, as one young Yorkshireman was: 'he gave me to understand that I'd often taken that for lust which was rather an innocent Natural Effect and had sometimes wish'd that destroying [sic] in me without which I could not long subsist'.[6] Probably they stood ready even to accept a certain measure of sexual intimacy between those who were engaged or near-engaged. A Methodist man could write to his fiancée, who lived in another town than his, and ask that she arrange to have a private room available for a meeting between them, where they could spend some time together undisturbed, either 'at Mr. Atkinsons or at Mr. Smiths', both Methodist households, on the day he was planning to come for a visit.

Such numerical evidence as may now be found tends to confirm that the Methodists resisted Wesley's pro-celibacy stance. For instance, a list is still extant, in Wesley's own handwriting, of the members of a society typical in many ways of Methodism generally, the Kingswood society. This list is dated 1757. It therefore shows what the society was after it had been under his pastoral oversight for about a generation. After each member's name, Wesley indicated her or his marital status. Altogether there were 172 members in the society that year. Only 31 of them were not, and had never been, married.[7] Of these 31, some were probably just children. There was no bar to admitting children to full membership in Methodism, and in fact they were encouraged to join. If some were children, the number who were physically prepared to marry but had not done so was smaller even than 31, maybe much smaller. This was all the result that Wesley had of preaching and teaching celibacy at Kingswood for nearly a generation.

As for the pastoral arrangements that Wesley made for keeping the sexes apart, the Methodist resisted them, too. His rule requiring separate seating for men and women at worship provoked much grumbling and at least two open showdowns, one between him and the Manchester society, the other between him and the London society. But in his commitment to this rule Wesley was immovable. He won the showdown with the London society in what he called a 'calm and loving consultation', and he prevailed at Manchester by issuing his ultimate threat. He said: 'by jumbling men and women together you would shut me out of the house; for if I should come into a Methodist preaching house when this is the case, I must immediately go out again.' If in resisting separate seating the Methodists were beaten back, they were more successful in resisting the bands and select-bands, the meetings for fellowship, segregated by sex, that Wesley had also arranged for them. A seating-plan was something tangible, visible, controllable. Wesley could see that it was as he wished or order that it be redone. But the popularity of institutions like the bands and select-bands, the measure of emotional energy that went into them, was something intangible and diffuse, something that even Wesley could not control. Gradually, the Methodists let the bands and select-bands atrophy.

These institutions did not disappear entirely. During Wesley's lifetime, anyway, they continued to exist here and there. But even the relatively few bands and select-bands that lasted were by no means so closed as Wesley wanted. They generated intimacy and secrets, but they could not always contain what they generated. For the members were typically thinking also of persons excluded from the group, persons of the opposite sex. Sometimes the members would have preferred to include these outsiders, and told them about what was discussed inside. One Macclesfield woman, for instance, found that her fellow select-band-members had revealed her secrets to a man. As she wrote in her diary: 'the Girls have been treacherous . . . are these they, whom I have Loved as my own Soul, to whom I have open'd the secrets of my heart? – Ah My God – *Where* is Sincerity to be found? Where is Xtian friendship?'[8]

In fact the institution for 'Xtian friendship' the Methodists generally preferred, gave their energy to, and came to trust in, was the one they had devised themselves in the early 1740s, the class. Unlike the band and select-band, the class was ordinarily sexually mixed. It was based on neighbourhood, and it was made up of a group of people who happened to live near to each other, including of course whole households and families. Every local society was divided into classes, and every class met weekly. Here at the class-meetings, advice and reproof were exchanged, and spiritual experiences were discussed, just as at the meetings of the bands and select-bands, but in a format the Methodists were willing to favour and support: men and women together.

As for Wesley's obvious reluctance to perform marriages, this the Methodists simply accepted. They could get their marriages done by their parish clergymen anyway. It was understood that their 'good old Father' would be absent from the ceremony, even if he were travelling in the vicinity; and they did not hope for his participation, as they hoped that when they died, he might be there to bury them.

Although the Methodists resisted Wesley's pro-celibacy teaching, it still made an impact on them. They heard it, attended to it, and if they did not accept it they may have found sanction in it for doing something quite different from what that teaching directly conveyed. To sum up the matter briefly, there is some evidence to show that they found sanction in what Wesley said for de-valuing and even breaking the family ties that troubled them; for releasing homosexual feeling; and possibly also for practising abstinence, within marriage, at the wife's insistence, as a means of birth control.

It should perhaps be added immediately that Wesley did not say that he approved of the de-valuing and breaking of family ties, did not say that he approved of the release of homosexual feeling, did not say that he approved of birth control based on abstinence. On the contrary he condemned all these practices. But he did present marriage as a second-best option, and by so doing he gave an implied assent to what he otherwise explicitly opposed. The de-valuing and breaking of family ties, homosexuality, the refusal at the wife's insistence of marital sex: these were alternatives to a close marriage as then conventionally established. His followers understood him as they wished, as they needed to, and they heard his implied assent far more distinctly than his explicit condemnation.

For women particularly, Methodism presented a unique

opportunity to modify the family obligations that they felt to be oppressive. First, there was the continuous call to meetings: prayer-meetings, class-meetings, love-feasts, watch-nights. All these meetings took time, and to attend them was at the very least to escape from household drudgery. But the meetings might provide far more than escape. They might provide a choice of new emotional commitments which might partly or even largely replace those at home that felt burdensome. Along with this choice, and making it especially available, was the sanction provided by Wesley's implicit devaluation of marriage and of family.

What frightened contemporaries about Methodism, as much as anything else, was the opening it provided to women. In the polemics against Methodism the issue came up often. As the *Gentleman's Magazine* reported, with outrage, 'Many silly women', from among the ranks of the poor, were attending Methodist meetings 'every Morning', and were leaving 'their children in Bed till their Return, which sometimes is not til nine o'Clock . . . without any Regard to the grand Inconveniences, to which they are exposed by such neglect, contrary to the Laws of Nature.' Similarly, the riot against the Methodists at Wednesbury in Staffordshire, perhaps the most destructive of all the anti-Methodist riots of the eighteenth-century, was sparked by a woman's temporary disappearance. 'The wife of a certain Collier', the chronicler of the riot explained, 'was missing from his House about a Week, without any Difference between him and her, and was found by him at one of the Class-houses.'

Methodist women were admonished, then, with stern talk about 'the Laws of Nature' and on occasion faced with riot. Sometimes they also got personal letters of counsel, half-solicitous, half-menacing. One Chester girl, young, still unmarried and living with her parents, got such a letter from the vicar of the parish. Her mother had told the vicar that the girl had been attending Methodist meetings when she ought to have been doing household chores. He wrote: 'You must allow me to tell you, that I was very much shocked and surprized with the account I had from your good mother yesterday.' He added that the Methodists never failed to bring 'confusion and disorder among families'. He warned her that the chores and the bonds she was escaping from were ordained for her of God, and then he threatened her. He said that if she should 'desert the duties of that state of life' to which God had called her, then he, as vicar of the parish, would 'recommend it strongly' to her mother to throw her out of the house altogether.

Despite appeals to the laws of nature, the danger of riot, and threats, women continued to find scope in Methodism, as Wesley led it, for de-valuing and breaking the ties they disliked. They could re-orient their lives away from the household, could get away, to some extent physically, and perhaps to a greater extent emotionally, from what one Methodist woman called a 'cruel husband'[9] or from parents who were what another called 'God's enemies'. If women particularly found such an escape in Methodism, men found it there as well. They were less bound, of course, to the household and felt less need to escape from it physically. But Wesley's tacit undercutting of marriage and family freed them, too, and enabled them to turn away emotionally from their families as they wished. They found sanction for saying, and feeling, as one Cornishman put it: 'They that love the Lord are nearer to me than my carnal relations.'[10]

From the very start of the movement, even in the days when Methodism was still just a club at Oxford, the Methodists had shown a quick and unconventional sympathy with homosexuality. They had then, in 1732, rather ostentatiously taken the part of a man named Blair, who had been convicted of sodomy. Their support for this man had apparently raised eyebrows throughout the university. As one non-Methodist clerical observer had commented, 'Whether the man is innocent or no they were not proper judges, it was better he should suffer than such a scandal given on countenancing a man whom the whole town think guilty of such an enormous crime.' Then he added, 'Whatever good design they pretend it was highly imprudent and has given the occasion of terrible reflections.'[11]

Presumably the 'terrible reflections' were that homosexual intercourse was a Methodist practice, too. If that was the guess that the Oxonians were making, they may have been wrong. It is now probably impossible to know. On the one hand, there is no verbal evidence of homosexual intercourse in any of the early Methodists' confessional diaries, journals, or letters, thousands of which are still extant. On the other hand, a Methodist who was practising homosexual intercourse would have had good reason to keep the matter quiet. What is clear is that the conditions of Methodist group-life provided an opening for some homosexual feeling, and at the same time Wesley's undercutting of family and marriage provided a sanction. In fact the Methodists came to be unusually tender, men with men, women with women, and their interest in Blair could well have been based on a fellow-feeling warmer than charity.

Their physical demonstrativeness with those of their own sex certainly included kissing. They kissed at highly wrought religious scenes, as for instance, at the big revival at Everton, when the newly converted went around the room, kissing 'all of their own sex'. But their tenderness was probably prompted less by experiences like that, which were occasional, than by the ongoing pastoral arrangements that Wesley had made for them. These arrangements – separate seating at worship, bands and select-bands, the continuous exhorting to stay single – they resisted, but they also lived with. They found themselves often thrown together intimately, men with men, women with women, and they responded to each other. It was easy to respond, too. As one Methodist said of the men-friends with whom he met in band, 'Their experience answered to mine as face to face in a glass.'

Sometimes they not only responded but actually fell in love. These love-affairs were sweet but also painful and awkward, and they typically produced sharp jealousies, maybe because they were unrequited. One Macclesfield woman, Mrs Stonehewer, fell in love with her neighbour and fellow-Methodist, Hester Roe, and almost immediately began to suffer from the fear that Hester cared more for her sister, also a Methodist, than for herself. Hester's diary is the source of our knowledge of the affair. The scene opens with Hester's noting that she had just got a message from Mrs Stonehewer, saying that, 'She was so Unhappy lest I thD Love her sister more than her that she had no rest.' Hester sent back a message, she says in the diary, assuring Mrs Stonehewer of friendship, yet warning her against expecting in the creature what alone is to be found in God. When the diary passage about the relationship closes, Mrs Stonehewer is talking of suicide and Hester is responding by dealing 'freely and plainly wTH her yet affectionately'.[12]

Men as well as women fell into these loves. One man named John Hutchinson, in his early twenties apparently, fell in love with Charles Wesley. Since John lived in Leeds, and Charles at that time in Bristol, John wrote him letters. Two are still extant. In the first John wrote:

> O Dear Sir *I cannot describe how I love you*, my Heart is ready to break that Providence hath allotted *me to be So far Separate from* you . . . write to me often and love me more, let *no new Convert be my Rival,* continue your loving kindness unto me and admit *no one to have* a greater share in your affection than your poor unworthy ungrateful Young Man. I have been broken-hearted ever since your Departure.

Then, later in that same letter, he commented on the letter he had lately received from Charles. It struck him as insufficiently warm:

> Upon first Sight of your Letter my Heart leaped for Joy, I have read it over Times without Number, but cannot find your accustomed Manner of writing, (wch was), *dear Johnny, dear Youth* . . . I remember in your three letters to Mr. Shent, you begun with dear William, don't be angry at my Simplicity, it is a weakness I cannot help, (what shall I say) in my own Strength I can promise nothing, but according to the present Situation of my mind, I desire I may cease to breathe when I foresake you, you are dearer to me than myself and you shall never want anything I can do for you only continue *to travel and I will work for your Support.*

That was the first of John's letters. In the second of the two that have survived, written about a year later, he made a new suggestion for bringing the two of them together. Previously he had written of working to support Charles; now he proposed that he go to Charles's house at Bristol and board there. He said that he thought he could never be a good Christian until he was there close to Charles:

> I continue yet very irreligious and think I shall never be better *until I make my abode with you.* I have some Thoughts, as I entirely Dislike to live at Leeds, to come and *live at Bristol* as soon as I can be disengaged from Business wch will not be before the Expiration of 2 Years; if please Good so long to spare me, will you let *me board with you.*[13]

Of these two letters the first bears a superscription in Charles's own handwriting, his commentary on the affair. It is a Latin tag: 'Uno avulso non deficit alter.' This was the motto of the Austrian Imperial house. It referred to the emblem of the house, the two-headed eagle, and it may be translated as: One torn away, another takes its place. What Charles meant by quoting the tag was that John's attitude was nothing very new. Some other man also had lately been in love with him.

Historians now generally agree that family planning by various means was sometimes practised in eighteenth-century England. They usually suppose that the means used were 'coitus interruptus', 'coitus reservatus', abortion, and infanticide or neglect amounting to infanticide.

Among the Methodists another means may possibly have been used, too: long-term conjugal abstinence at the wife's insistence.

Here the evidence is scanty and uncertain. But to say at once what may be true but cannot now be proved, the Methodist women who felt that they had attained what they called Perfection, freedom from all inward sin, may have refused ever after to have sexual intercourse with their husbands.

This hypothesis would make sense of the remark a closely observing non-Methodist made about 'double-ribbed' women among the Methodists.[14] It would also make sense of the rumour that one London Methodist heard concerning 'some women' in the society, that they were refusing 'to sleep with their husbands'. It might even make sense of a certain feature of the seating arrangement at the London Foundery. Throughout most of the room, the seats were plain, backless benches. But in a little area just underneath the pulpit there were a few benches with back-rails. These seats of dignity were evidently intended for holy women, whose holiness was somehow representable by their closeness to the preacher and by their straight backs.

Certainly the Methodist women were as frightened as the Englishwomen of their era generally about the pains and risks of child-bearing. One of them, while pregnant and close to term, confessed to Wesley that she was 'greatly afraid' that she would 'die in labour', and although she did survive, her fear was of course realistic. Another woman, a London Methodist, wrote a full account of her feelings about child-bearing, a rare and moving document: 'I had uncommon Suffering in child-bearing which kept me in continual fear.' Because of her sufferings and fear she eventually thought of aborting one of her pregnancies. This thought struck her as a temptation of the devil.

> The Enemie took advantage of my weakness and when I had conceived of my 5th child (enticed) me to use some means to disappoint God's Providence in bringing it to perfection, and that way free my Self from the Pain I so much dreaded. Sometimes I thought it would be Murder. He answered, No, that as yet there was no life.[15]

In this time of temptation, God, she said, helped her. She overcame and bore the child.

For a woman like this, who 'dreaded' the pains and risks of repeated child-bearing, and whose husband was apparently unwilling to help her by practising 'coitus interruptus' or 'reservatus', abortion was of course an option, and it is no wonder that it occurred to her. But she was close to conventional religious sentiment, and disapproved strongly of her own thought of abortion. In her view it would have been 'Murder'. With that way out blocked, there was very little left for her, if she was determined to keep herself from pregnancy, except abstinence.

It is true that abstinence, at least abstinence at the insistence of just the wife and against the wishes of the husband, was as forbidden religiously as abortion. Here, however, Wesley's preference for celibacy may have helped her. It may have prompted her to think about the possibility of living for the future without intercourse, and it may have felt to her like a sanction for insisting on doing so regardless of what her husband wanted. Besides, she was part of a group, a unified and mutually loving group that included many women who were in a predicament like hers. Their need would have reinforced hers, and she and they together may have taught themselves to understand Wesley in a way that made sense to them, in a way that accorded with their wishes.

Wesley taught celibacy, but the Methodists learned something different. Except for a very few of them, like the small group at Tetney whom he so much approved, there was nothing for them in celibacy, nothing they commonly wanted. Resisting the actual content of his teaching, they married and had sex as English people usually did. Still, they adored Wesley and wanted to do as he asked. His pro-celibacy stand may have been unpalatable, but it may have made an impact on them anyway and may have helped them to feel and act on hard-to-reach desires and wants which they shared. If they followed him, it was in their own way.

Notes

1 This is a drastically abridged version of a paper presented at the History Workshop Conference in July 1983. Much detail has been omitted, and so have most footnotes.
2 The Shakers, who taught celibacy a little later in the century, probably got the idea from Wesley.
3 Ms. letter, Jos. Carter to Charles Wesley, 1741 (Methodist Archive and Research Centre, John Rylands Library, Manchester). Hereafter: J.R.L.,M.
4 Ms. Diary, Samuel Bardsley, 14 August 1766 (J.R.L.,M.).
5 See, for instance, Ms. Diary, Samuel Bardsley, 14 July 1766 (J.R.L.,M.).
6 Ms. Diary transcript, Thomas Illingworth, 18 January 1756 (in the possession of Professor the Rev. Dr Frank Baker, on deposit in the Duke University Divinity School Library, Durham, North Carolina).

7   Ms. Membership list, Kingswood Society, 1757 (Pierpoint Morgan Library, New York).
8   Ms. Diary, Hester Roe Rogers, n.d. (J.R.L.,M.).
9   Ms. letter, Margaret Austin to Charles Wesley, 19 May 1740 (J.R.L.,M.).
10 Ms. Journal, James Chubb, 13 July 1782 (J.R.L.,M.).
11 C.S. Linnell (ed.), *Diaries of Thomas Wilson, D.D.* (London, 1964). p.81.
12 Ms. Diary, Hester Roe Rogers, n.d. (J.R.L.,M.).
13 Ms. letter, John Hutchinson to Charles Wesley, 29 September 1751; Ms. letter, John Hutchinson to Charles Wesley, 10 September 1752 (J.R.L.,M.).
14 Ms. letter, John Cass to Thomas Wride, 23 July 1779 (J.R.L.,M.).
15 Ms. memorandum, Mrs Claggett, 24 July 1738 (J.R.L.,M.). My reading of 'enticed' is uncertain.

7

The Christian churches and the regulation of sexuality in Weimar Germany

CORNELIE USBORNE

The revolution of 9 November 1918 had shocked Catholic and Protestant churches alike because it had swept away the monarchy and brought to power the Social Democrats who threatened to relegate the churches to the level of a private club. Of the two great German denominations the Evangelical Church was the more deeply affected by the overthrow of the monarchy. It was not only by far the largest church, with a membership of nearly 40 million or over 60 per cent of the German population, but it had, before 1918, enjoyed the greatest political privileges. As *summus episcopus* the Kaiser had been the head of the Evangelical Church and had protected her interests. Protestant church leaders tended to be conservative and closely identified with the crown. Even after 1918 they remained monarchist, nationalist and authoritarian. The Catholic Church, by contrast, found it easier to establish a positive relationship to the new republic. During the

Bismarck period Catholics had been pushed into political and cultural isolation which the new constitution promised to reverse. After 1918 Catholics could for the first time enter ministries and hold top administrative positions. Nevertheless, many Catholic leaders had a loyalty to Imperial Germany. Although the Weimar Constitution retained the churches' special corporate status, it did away with important privileges and declared a separation of Church and State. Both churches were anxious to re-establish their influence in public affairs in the New German democracy.

Church leaders held the political revolution responsible for the revolution in manners and morals which had taken place. Central to the churches' concern was the alleged 'dissolution of the family'. Christian marriage was to them not only 'a holy sacrament, a mystery of inner life',[1] it was also the 'basic cell of the *völkisch* state organism'[2] and would, if destroyed, lead to the destruction of German *Volkstum* itself. The Catholic Women's Federation dedicated their 1924 conference entirely to the theme 'Catholic Marriage'. The presidential address expressed 'the greatest concern, even shock that the roots of community life are threatened. The values of marriage and family life are no longer upheld but regarded as trivial and often even despised.'[3]

Although the churches conceded that the 'erosion of family life' was partly due to 'political and social chaos' and the economic crisis, they nevertheless considered the main cause to be general 'moral corruption' (*Entsittlichung*).[4] Free love, promiscuity and experiments like 'companionate marriages' (sexual unions between men and women who lived openly together without intending to have children) were widely discussed in the contemporary press, novels and films. Although such practices were almost entirely confined to avant-garde circles in Berlin, the churches felt obliged to pronounce on these matters. The churches were resolutely opposed to birth control, seeing it as a violation of divine will and the natural order. *Menschenökonomie* (family planning) was in their eyes the first step towards *Heidentum* (paganism). Yet after the revolution hundreds of businesses, large and small, were exploiting the confusion which surrounded the pornography laws and produced and distributed all types of contraceptives. Newspapers and journals were inundated with advertisements for birth control. There were reports of pedlars selling 'hygienic' goods outside factory gates and from door to door even in the remotest rural villages.

The rise in the rate of criminal abortion was for church leaders another indication of 'moral laxity'. It is difficult to arrive at an accurate figure of the total number of abortions in Germany since termination of pregnancy was a crime punishable by sentences of up to five years' penal servitude.[5] Nevertheless, there can be little doubt that there had been a dramatic increase in the number of illegal abortions. According to one report by the Prussian Health Authority, the annual rate of criminal abortion which had been around 100,000 in 1914, trebled by 1919. By 1925 it was thought to be half a million and by the onset of the depression in 1929 a figure of a million was usually quoted.[6]

The rising divorce rate was also seen as a sign of the instability of family relationships. In 1913 there had been 15.2 divorces per 10,000 marriages, but in 1921 this figure had risen to 33. Even though the rate had levelled out to around 28 by 1925 and was to some extent offset by the increase in the marriage rate immediately after the war, it was still alarming. The illegitimacy rate, which was traditionally one of the highest in Europe, also increased during and after the war. In 1914 there were 9.8 children per 100 births born outside marriage, in 1918 13.1, in 1919 11.2, at which mark it stayed with a few fluctuations.[7] In fact in absolute terms the number of illegitimate children born had fallen, in line with the decline in marital fertility. Despite this, church authorities continued to speak of moral depravity and quote, as even more glaring evidence, the increase in prostitution and the accompanying spread of venereal disease. In Berlin alone there were over 6,000 registered prostitutes and an estimated 60,000 girls said to be 'trading in vice'. Hedwig Dransfeld, leader of the Catholic Women's Association, speaking of a 'grave moral disease of the entire nation', urged women to work towards the 'moral regeneration and revival of our nation' and to guard the female body against being exploited as 'a sexual lure'.[8] From their annual conference in Fulda in January 1925 the Catholic episcopacy issued a set of guidelines for moral behaviour to counteract what they considered to be the exaggerated importance which modern society placed on the body. It recommended segregation of the sexes for physical education and condemned *Nacktkultur* (the cult of the body), modern dance, pornographic publications, films and plays, and immodest dress.[9] In the same year the Evangelical Women's Federation organized a series of conferences on moral questions as part of their crusade against pornography and immorality.

The churches' anxieties increased when the left-wing parties attempted to introduce into parliament a number of legislative changes which, would, in the churches' view, make the new 'sexual laxity' respectable and legal. There were proposals to replace police control of prostitutes by social welfare supervision,[10] to lift the ban on contraceptive advertising, to raise the status of unmarried mothers and their children, to facilitate divorce and, last but not least, to legalize abortion on demand.

The churches were not alone in condemning the left-wing proposals. Conservative political parties regarded the attack on marriage and the conventional norms of morality as a direct threat to the birthrate, which at the time was taken as a barometer of a nation's power and significance. The German birthrate had fallen dramatically from one of the highest in Europe in 1876 to one of the lowest in 1912, and the population question had become a central concern for governments intent on expanding Germany's role both in Europe and overseas. As part of an ambitious programme 'to combat the declining birthrate' the government sponsored three bills during the First World War to increase the size of German families by prohibiting contraception, sterilization and abortion. The three bills were never codified because the revolution interrupted their progress during the final legislative stages. The churches in the 1920s returned to these themes. The strength of their feeling is well represented by a petition sent to the Minister of the Interior from the President of the German Catholic episcopacy from their conference in May 1924. In this the President puts pressure on the government to resist any attempts at abortion reform and stresses in the strongest possible terms that the Church regards abortion as 'one of the most terrible crimes against divine and natural law' which if allowed to continue will bring 'untold sorrow to future generations and ruin to the nation'.[11] Throughout the Weimar period both churches found the population argument a useful strategy to employ since population growth was at that time considered to be vital for the future of the nation. However, towards the end of the period eugenic theories gradually superseded the earlier simplistic pro-natalism.

The only truly denominational political party in Weimar Germany was the Centre Party. Closely linked to and dominated by the Catholic Church, it considered itself to have a holy duty to protect 'the immutable moral norms of . . . civic laws'.[12] Its role in German politics was considerable in that it provided the only real continuity in the many coalition governments from 1920 to 1932. In the Weimar Republic it filled the post of Chancellor nine times.

By contrast, the Evangelical Church had traditionally been reluctant to get involved in politics, but its views were represented in parliament by the German National People's Party (DNVP) which had been formed after the war. This was a mixture of conservatives, national liberals and other right-wing adherents, and consequently lacked the unity of the Centre Party.

In the 1920s the impact of both the Centre Party and DNVP on the passage of the various bills regulating sexuality was enormous. It was almost entirely due to the Centre's intransigent opposition and its boycott of the committee stage that the divorce law reform was never enacted, despite support by liberals and socialists. It also put pressure on the Chancellor to delay any future debate of the bill and greeted the bill's final demise as a great victory for Catholicism.[13] Both DNVP and Centre successfully opposed the more controversial clauses in the bill 'to combat VD and prostitution'. In 1923 the bill was nearly lost altogether when the Catholic-controlled Bavarian delegation in the Upper House, the Reichsrat, took the unusual action of vetoing a bill already passed in the Reichstag.

By their united opposition both parties prevented any improvement in the legal status of unmarried mothers and their children, and helped to bring about the defeat of the radical motions by the socialists to permit abortion on demand and free of charge. When the amended abortion law, which only changed the degree of punishment, was passed in 1926, it was still opposed by the DNVP and Centre.

On the issue of contraception there was no such common front. Contraception had traditionally been classed with fornication or adultery and this assumption formed the basis of the clause in the German penal code outlawing the display of objects intended for 'indecent' use, i.e. contraception. In Christian terms contraception covered both 'coitus interruptus' and the use of mechanical, chemical or pharmaceutical devices. Germany was one of the leading innovators in contraceptive techniques and by the 1920s all the major methods of birth control were in use, except for the precise definition of the 'safe' period and the contraceptive pill.

The official Catholic doctrine was forcefully propounded at Fulda in 1913 when contraception was condemned as 'a very serious sin, by whatever means and in whatever way it occurs'.[14] Only if there were very strong reasons were Catholics allowed to practise family limitations, and then by abstinence alone.

The Protestant clergy were in agreement with the Catholic, but were less categorical. The Prussian Synod issued a formal statement in 1920 disapproving of the practice of birth control, which they saw as a sign of weakening religious beliefs rather than the consequence of 'higher prices, housing shortage and the rise of female labour'.[15] The German Evangelical Church Council in a petition to the Prussian Minister of the Interior in November 1920 called 'children a blessing and a divine gift' and protested against the spread of contraception and abortion. The Evangelical organization 'Women's Aid of Potsdam' described contraception as 'an offence against the creative right of God and a danger to family life and population strength (*Volkskraft*)'.[16]

In parliament both DNVP and Centre pressed unsuccessfully for the tightening of legislation to prevent the spread of birth control. A similar motion originating from the Bavarian People's Party, the Centre's sister party in Bavaria, failed to get a majority when it reached the Reichstag. It was, however, the issue of venereal disease which finally forced the churches to change their attitude towards contraception. Unlike any other campaign at the time, the fight against VD united all the disparate forces and pressure groups throughout Germany. The spread of the disease amongst the troops during the war and later amongst the civilian population was deemed so alarming that it became *the* symbol of moral corruption. To right-wing circles it represented the worst side of *Sexualbolschewismus*, the wilful destruction of the family by subversive revolutionaries who modelled their ideas on those of Soviet Russia. To the pro-natalists and eugenicists it was one of the most serious threats to the genetic health (*Erbgut*) of the nation. Women's organizations and socialists were enthusiastic supporters of a proposed anti-VD bill which would remove the 'double standard' by which only women were penalized for having the disease. It also promised to abolish police regulations of prostitution for which feminists had been fighting since the end of the nineteenth century. Because of the pressure of public opinion the 'bill to combat VD' was given precedence over all parliamentary commitments concerning sexual policy.

This bill presented the churches with a considerable dilemma. It contained clauses for compulsory examination and treatment for sufferers from the disease and a penalty of up to three years' imprisonment for any infected person who had sexual intercourse, even within marriage. But it did not deal with the issue of prophylactics. The problem for the churches was whether to allow proper prophylaxis and thereby seem to be condoning promiscuity, or simply to urge sexual restraint at the risk of allowing the disease to spread. The ban on the public display and advertising of objects 'intended for indecent use' covered all contraceptives including those, such as the condom, which acted as prophylactics. There was evidence, however, that the distribution of free condoms by some military authorities during the war had had a beneficial effect. In addition continued pressure from the influential German Society for the Suppression of

Venereal Disease led to the inclusion of a clause in the bill permitting the 'public display, advertising and distribution of all preventative methods and devices' provided this was done in an 'inoffensive' manner.[17] The socialist parties wanted this clause to be widened to include all types of contraceptives and to make sex education compulsory in schools for children over fourteen years of age. This again placed the churches in a difficult position as they had traditionally discouraged sex instruction and the discussion of delicate moral issues.

The debates in parliament were acrimonious. Initially both DNVP and Centre Party maintained that the public display of prophylactics would lead to 'moral devastation' and 'reduce women to sex objects for the unrestrained sexual gratification of the male'.[18] Self restraint was, they repeated, the best protection. Nevertheless, the bill allowing prophylactics to be advertised in an inoffensive manner was finally passed in early 1927 with the support of both DNVP and Centre Party. The spokesman for the Centre Party justified his support of the bill on the grounds that it was a useful means of combating the VD epidemic. The impact which the bill made can be judged from the number of condom vending machines which were installed as early as 1928 in the public conveniences of most major railway stations. At least one official committee recommended the open sale of condoms in ladies' washrooms, dance halls, hotels, factories and barracks. After 1927 posters about VD prophylactics appeared in public places in all major cities and condoms were freely displayed in shop windows and underground stations. The police could not and did not intervene.

Even though the clause in the 1927 VD law which permitted advertising of those contraceptives which also acted as prophylactics did not officially replace Article 184 Section 3 of the penal code (which prohibited advertising of all contraceptives with a penalty of imprisonment of up to one year and/or fine), in practice most law courts were reluctant to convict anybody on the grounds of birth control propaganda after 1927. With the quickly expanding network of birth control advice centres from the mid-1920s onwards, some private, some run by local sickness insurance funds, birth control clearly became more widely acceptable, particularly as it was the most effective method of preventing a growing number of abortions.[19] In 1930 Hitler's National Socialist party attempted in vain to introduce a bill in the Reichstag outlawing birth control altogether.[20]

By the middle of the 1920s the Evangelical Church no longer issued any official condemnation of contraception. This silence was taken by many as a sign of tacit approval. The Catholic gynaecologist Albert Niedermeyer later wrote: 'The tendency of the Evangelical Church to make concessions to the *Zeitgeist* became clearer and clearer to me. It was apparent in the question of . . . abortion, sterilization and especially contraception.'[21] With no guidelines from their Church Council many individual Protestant pastors and laymen took their own initiative in working out new rules of conduct. In 1926 a conference on sexual ethics was organized by a group of clergy and laity from both denominations. Its aim was to clarify some of the moral issues and try to provide answers now that the old authorities of law, morality, family and church 'had utterly failed' to bring order to the 'immense chaos' of social life.[22] The leaders of both churches came in for sharp criticism, but it was the group of Evangelical members who demanded an unequivocal endorsement of family limitation in cases of economic hardship and illness. Clergymen, they maintained, should be well informed about birth control lest they lost the goodwill of their parishioners. There was a re-appraisal of the whole question at a special conference held by the United Evangelical Women's Federation at Eisenach in 1928. This organization, which was not renowned for its libertarian outlook, nevertheless published a statement which all but contradicted official dogma. In characteristic Protestant manner, it put radical beliefs into timid words. The Federation were not ready to go as far as separating the sexual act from procreation, but at the same time they could not accept that the sole purpose of coitus was reproduction. Their objection to 'unrestrained and unlimited procreation without conscious and personal responsibility' was a clear reference to dysgenic breeding by the socially inferior. They recommended family limitation where it was necessary to protect the health of the mother, in the interest of existing children, if there was economic hardship and 'to protect the nation against hereditary disease'. Although they favoured abstinence, they were aware that this was often unrealistic and even detrimental to happy marriage, and they conceded that artificial methods of birth control were necessary, even though they constituted 'an intervention in the natural and divine law'. Responsibility lay with the individual, but the individual also had a 'duty towards the *Volk* and state' and should produce at least three to five children 'to secure the normal development of our people'.[23]

The concept that ultimate responsibility lay not with the Evangelical Church but with the individual was also the basic argument in *Guidelines for an Evangelical Sexual Ethic* published in 1930. This was a useful document in that it removed from theologians the onus of having to condemn or to condone family limitation. Gradually, without openly admitting it, the Evangelical Church withdrew its opposition to birth control because it was already too widely practised and also because leading Protestants became increasingly interested in eugenics. The debate about VD had drawn to the attention of a nation struggling to survive a disastrous war the problem of hereditary disease. The opinion grew that public health could be just as significantly improved by the selective limitation of population growth as by social reform. There were various proposals to prevent the mentally subnormal and those suffering from inherited diseases from producing children. These included a certificate of health before marriage, voluntary sterilization and forcible institutionalization of all those who suffered from severe forms of inheritable ailments. But contraception seemed to be the most acceptable method of preventing 'degenerate' stock. Hans Harmsen, who was medical adviser to the Inner Mission, the charitable trust of the Evangelical Church, and secretary of the influential, Protestant-controlled 'Working Group for Public Health and Morality' emerged as one of the chief proponents of eugenic contraception and voluntary sterilization. His views reached a wider audience at an international conference on population held in Rome in September 1931.[24]

Despite being described as having 'remained strong, unperturbed by changing attitudes of the day and able to enlist much enthusiasm by her very firmness', the Catholic Church began to suffer from discord amongst its ranks. From 1928 onwards, beginning with Dietrich von Hildebrand's *In Defence of Purity* and Herbert Dom's *The Meaning of Marriage*, a new theory of marriage rejected the doctrine that coitus was only justified if procreation was intended. In his book, Hildebrand, who was Professor of Moral Theology at Munich, celebrates sex in poetic and mystical language as 'the voice from the depths, the utterance of something basic and of the utmost significance'. 'To overlook the union between physical sex and love and to recognize only the purely utilitarian bond between sex and the propagation of the race is to demean human beings and to be blind to the meaning and value of this mysterious domain.'[25] This theory created a considerable stir within Catholic circles in Germany and encouraged others to explore new approaches to sex and marriage. In the summer of 1930 an article signed by Matthias Laros, a Catholic theologian and later a leading member of the *Una-Sancta* movement, appeared in the influential Catholic periodical *Hochland*. It provoked at once a bitter argument within the Church. In his article, Laros defended the revolt by young Germans against the existing morality and doctrine of the Church. He argued that it was not sufficient to quote Christ, the Apostles and the old scholastics because they were no longer an accepted authority for the majority of Germans. 'What is needed,' he wrote, 'is a radical re-appraisal of the old principles . . . the courage to discuss . . . the difficulties of the marital relationship.' Quoting as precedent Lindner's *Usus matrimonii* which had shown that the Church's pronouncement on intercourse during pregnancy was reversible, Laros pressed for a change of doctrine in cases where coitus 'has to be consummated without an intention of procreation, for whatever reasons'.[26] John T. Noonan has asserted that Laros's article was partly responsible for the official clarification of the Catholic Church's view of sexuality issued by Pope Pius XI on 31 December 1930 in his encyclical *Casti Conubii*.[27]

Much has been written about the failure of both churches to put a stop to National Socialism and they have even been accused of sympathizing with its bio-social programme. It is true that both Protestants and Catholics were dedicated to the idea of a spiritual and physical revival of the German *Volk*. Many welcomed the advances made in genetics, or, as it was called in Germany, race hygiene, as a new method of social reform. This was not really surprising since eugenics were considered progressive and humanitarian. Such ideas were current in most industrialized nations and attracted the support of people of all political complexions. In England as early as 1910 there was a thriving eugenics pressure group which devised policies to increase the fertility of 'valuable stock' and stop the 'unfit' from breeding. The United States were the first to introduce compulsory eugenic sterilization (Indiana, in 1907, followed subsequently by fourteen other states). Between 1907 and 1921 over 3,000 cases of sterilization were reported of which 2,700 were allegedly 'insane', 403 'mentally subnormal' and 130 'criminals'.[28] In the 1920s several Swiss cantons introduced voluntary eugenic sterilization, and Sweden, Norway and Denmark prohibited marriages in cases where one or both partners suffered from VD, epilepsy or feeble-mindedness. By comparison Germany's measures of 'negative' eugenics were few and timid. They consisted of a law, introduced in 1920, which compelled every registry officer to hand out a leaflet to marriage candidates warning them of the hereditary risks of VD and suggesting a medical examination before the wedding. In 1926 Prussia encouraged the setting up of eugenic marriage advice centres which proved to be a failure or else made nonsense of the original intention by providing contraceptive and abortion advice. There had been, since about 1925, repeated proposals for eugenic fertility control. Both eugenic abortion and voluntary sterilization were discussed by a wider public but not until 1932, when the Prussian Medical Advisory Committee adopted the draft of a bill for voluntary sterilization, was there any likelihood of a law reaching the statute books.

There was support for a qualitative population programme by both churches from about 1927 onwards. Within the Evangelical Church the medical adviser to the 'Inner Mission', the Evangelical charitable trust, welcomed race hygienist measures, as did the population panel of the 'Society for Public Hygiene', which was in theory inter-denominational but in practice dominated by Protestants. Some pastors even advocated voluntary eugenic sterilization and abortion but they were in the minority.

It is perhaps more surprising to find evidence of official Catholic support. But it was Cardinal Bertram himself who responded to the Prussian programme of eugenic marriage advice centres. He urged and achieved the founding of Catholic centres to counterbalance the influence of the state. These centres were designed to warn the faithful about birth control and abortion, but also 'to prevent the degeneration of our people'.[29] One official memorandum drawn up by the Catholic 'Caritas' organization advocated the introduction of eugenic marriage prohibition and compulsory health certificates before marriage, but this was not approved of by the hierarchy. The most prominent supporter of negative eugenics within the Catholic Church was the Jesuit and former professor of theology, Dr Hermann Muckermann. From 1927, he headed the Department of Human Genetics at the influential Kaiser-Wilhelm-Institute in Berlin, a post he lost in 1933. During the 1920s he advocated segregation in order to prevent procreation of the 'unfit' but in 1932 he came out as a staunch supporter of voluntary eugenic sterilization. This caused an uproar in church circles, not least because the encyclical *Casti Conubii* had specifically condemned all forms of sterilization the previous year. Muckermann defended the decision of the Prussian Medical Advisory Committee (of which he was a member) to permit voluntary eugenic sterilization on the grounds that the bill provided adequate safeguards against any abuse and that delay might result in the introduction of compulsory sterilization.[30] Muckermann was, to his credit, adamantly opposed to this even after 1933 when such a bill was in fact introduced. When the true exent of the crude racialism of the Nazi government became apparent, Muckermann became a convinced opponent of Hitler's eugenic programme.

While it is clearly misleading to see the change in clerical views on family policy as automatically leading to Nazi ideology, it is true to say that few church leaders foresaw that the 'national regeneration' which they had so welcomed would be the beginning of genocide and a period of terrible suffering for both denominations. By assigning to the state the right to interfere in the personal sphere of reproduction however, the churches had failed to safeguard basic human rights and had helped to open the door to a government that assumed total control over the bodies of its subjects.

Notes

I wish to thank Richard Bessel, Pat Thane, Doris Kaufmann, David Blackbourn, Margaret Chester, Thomas Usborne and Jenny Willis for help and critical suggestions. This article is based on research carried out for a PhD thesis on the politics of fertility control in Weimar Germany. I am grateful for the grant by the Open University and the German Historical Institute.

1 Dr Maria Schlüter-Hermkes, 'Das katholische Ideal der heiligen Ehe', *Katholische Ehe*. Vorträge gehalten auf der Delegiertenversammlung des Katholischen Deutschen Frauenbundes in Hildesheim, Oktober 1924, Cologne, 1925; p.35.
2 M. von Tilling, 'Die völkische Idee als Forderung an uns', *Nachrichtenblatt der Vereinigung evangelischer Frauenverbände Deutschlands*, IV, 7, 1925, p.40.
3 Dr Gerta Krabbel, 'Zum Geleit', *Katholische Ehe, op. cit.*, p.III.
4 *Ibid.*, p.III.
5 In 1926 the abortion law was modified and the punishment for women who had aborted reduced to imprisonment.
6 Bundesarchiv Koblenz, R 86, Rep 319, 2379, vol. 3, *Bericht über die Sitzung des Ausschusses des Landesgesundheitsrats für Bevölkerungswesen und Rassenhygiene am 31.11.1925*, p.9.
7 *Statistisches Jahrbuch für das Deutsche Reich*, ed. Statistisches Reichsamt, Berlin, 1930, pp.14, 32. For the divorce rates see also *Wirtschaft und Statistik*, 1927.
8 Hedwig Dransfeld, 'Sittliche Erschütterungen unseres Volkes', *Die Christliche Frau*, XIX, 1921, p.3.
9 Archiv des Deutschen Caritasverbands, D II 2, Die deutschen Bischöfe der Fuldaer Bischofskonferenz, *Katholische Leitsätze und Weisungen zu verschiedenen modernen Sittlichkeitsfragen*, January 1925.
10 This had been the aim of the German Abolitionist movement for some time; see R.J. Evans, *The Feminist Movement in Germany, 1894–1933*, London and Beverly Hills, 1976, pp.40–5.

11   Archive of the Deutscher Caritasverband, XIIIa, 35. The president of the German episcopacy at their conference at Fulda, Cardinal A. Bertram to the German Minister of the Interior, 24.5.1924, *Sorge um Verhütung von Verbrechen gegen das keimende Leben.*

12   'Das Zentrum – eine Gesinnungsgemeinschaft: Programmatische Aussagen' in J. Flemming *et al.* (eds), *Die Republik von Weimar*, vol. 1, Königstein, 1979, p.25.

13   See Helen L. Boak, 'The Status of Women in the Weimar Republic', unpublished PhD thesis, Manchester University, 1982.

14   'Hirtenbrief der deutschen Bischöfe, Fuldaer Bischofkonferenz 1913', in Dr M. Fassbender (ed.), *Des deutschen Volkes Wille zum Leben*, Freiburg, 1917.

15   Zentrales Staatsarchiv Potsdam, Reichsministerium des Innern, 9347, 7th Prussian Synod, 20.4.1920.

16   *Ibid.*, 9352, vol. 1 Bl. 10, petition dated 15.11.1920, and petition by Evangelical Women's Aid dated 1.12.1920.

17   Reichstag Printed material no. 3523, 1920/23.

18   Report of the 14th committee of the Reichstag, no. 5801, 9.5.1923, p.12.

19   Many official medical bodies continued, however, to regard professional birth control advice as undesirable.

20   Reichstag Printed materials no. 1741, 13.3.1930, *Law for the protection of the nation.* This failed bill provided for a punishment of penal servitude for anybody who 'undertakes to limit the natural fertility of the German *Volk*' or who would promote this action, or anybody who 'contributes or attempts to contribute to racial degeneration . . . by mixing with members of the Jewish or a coloured race'.

21   A. Niedermeyer, *Wahn, Wissenschaft und Wahrheit*, Salzburg/Leipzig, 1934, p.124.

22   F. Siegmund-Schultze (ed.), *Um ein neues Sexualethos*, Berlin, 1927, p.3.

23   'Über Fragen der Ehe und Mutterschaft', *Archiv für Bevölkerungspolitik, Sexualethik und Familienkunde*, 1932, I, pp.25–32.

24   Hans Harmsen, *Geburtenregelung: das europäische Bevölkerungsproblem*, Berlin, 1928, p.11; the same, 'Geburtenregelung', *Die Medizinische Welt*, no. 21, Berlin, 1931.

25   D. von Hildebrand, *In Defence of Purity*, London, 1931, pp.14, 20, 24.

26   Matthias Laros, 'Revolutionierung der Ehe', *Hochland*, 27, 1931, pp.193–207.

27   John T. Noonan, *Contraception: A History of its Treatment by the Catholic Theologians and Canonists*, Cambridge, Mass., 1966, p.424. The other causes were according to this author: 'reaction to the Lambeth Conference vote of August 15, 1930 . . . and a growing uneasiness

among Roman theologians that in practice priests were not enforcing the teaching'.

28 'Eugenische Gesetzgebung im Ausland', *Archiv für Soziale Hygiene und Demographie*, I, 1926, pp.275ff. Harry Hamilton Laughlin, *Eugenical Sterilization in the United States*, Chicago, 1922, pp.52–97; for a discussion of the English eugenic movement see R.O. Soloway, *Birth Control and the Population Question in England 1877–1930*, London, 1982, and for the most comprehensive analysis of the Nazi policies of compulsory sterilization see Gisela Bock, *Zwangssterilisation in Nationalsozialismus. Studien zur Rassenpolitik and Frauenpolitik*, Opladen, 1986.

29 Archive of the *Deutscher Caritasverband*, 349.4, letter by Cardinal Bertram to the Prussian Minister of Public Welfare, 11.1.1927; by 1933 there were such Catholic centres in 50 towns, some of which survived the Nazi takeover.

30 Archive of the *Deutscher Caritasverband*, XIII a/38 A; Hermann Muckermann, 'Zwangssterilisierung?', *Kölnische Volkszeitung*, 12.5.33.

Feminism

8

Feminine symbolism and feminine behaviour in radical religious movements: Franciscans, Quakers and the followers of Gandhi

PHYLLIS MACK

I

The first Franciscans, the early Quakers, and the followers of Gandhi: here are three radical religious movements, widely separated in time and place, but sharing elements which their adherents identified as 'feminine'. We are all familiar with the images of gentleness and domesticity of Francis preaching to the birds and Gandhi spinning. So familiar, in fact, that it would be difficult to describe the personal style of these leaders and their closest followers and *avoid* feminine associations. One thinks immediately of Francis plucking the juiciest grapes to encourage a sick brother to eat, of Gandhi fussing over his family's diet, dispensing garlic to those he decided needed it, and of the 'Mothers in Israel' who were the earliest Quaker missionaries. One of Gandhi's adopted children wrote a biography of him which she called *Bapu – My Mother*. Margaret Fell called George Fox 'our dear nursing father'. The most intimate term which the Franciscan brothers used to address the founder was 'mother'.

The reaction of many modern observers has been to dismiss such stories as anachronistic at best and, at worst, as a crass distortion of spiritual truth: trite, cloying images of great men which obscure their essence, cheapen their memory, and turn the stuff of religious genius into material for children's legends, mass entertainment or plastic figurines to hang from a rearview mirror. A recent biography of Francis tells us that 'the truth lies deeper, in his hard character, and the abrasion of that character on his times'.[1] Current Quaker scholarship stresses the hard, Puritan core of early Quakerism against its softer, mystical aspect. A recent newspaper article on Gandhi reminds New York movie-goers that Gandhi was not simply a nice man with fine ideals but a remote, oriental ascetic. 'Feminine' behaviour has also been discussed as an aspect of the neurotic underside of the leader's personality (Gandhi's ambivalence about his sexuality or his compulsion to dominate the personal lives of his disciples), and as evidence that the movement is culture or time-bound and hence irrelevant for us. So Francis's sense of immanence with nature is charming but 'medieval', the early Quakers who emphasized prophetic dreams over knowledge and nakedness over status and power are courageous but 'primitive', and Gandhi's doctrines of non-violence and self-sacrifice are inspiring but fundamentally 'Indian'. Some would also point out that healing is the activity of doctors and scientists as well as nurses, and that in their tender care of the afflicted Francis and George Fox were, after all, imitating the *man* Jesus.

A more creative critical response to this type of religious phenomenon is that of the anthropologist Victor Turner, who analysed certain social movements according to a typology of structure and *communitas*. Turner wrote about liminality and *communitas* in dialogue with structure: 'for individuals and groups, social life is a type of dialectical process that involves successive experience of high and low, communitas and structure, homogeneity and differentiation, equality and inequality.'[2] *Communitas* affirms the similarity and connectedness of whole human beings, ignoring differences of status, wealth, power or even gender. Such movements, says Turner, occur at historical moments 'when major groups or social categories are passing from one cultural state to another'.[3]

Describing the customs of a patrilineal African tribe, Turner observed a double affinity between structure and masculinity, *communitas* and feminity. Even more revealing of Turner's views on the relationship of gender and society is this general description of the dialectic of *communitas* and structure: 'spontaneous communitas is (not) merely "nature." Spontaneous communitas is nature in dialogue with structure, married to it as a woman is married to a man. Together they make up one stream of life, the one affluent supplying power, the other alluvial fertility.'[4]

I don't know how pleased Turner would be to find himself in the company of feminist theoreticians, but there is clearly an affinity between his own typology and that of Sherry Ortner, who discusses culture and nature in terms of structure and anti-structure, and who views women as occupying an intermediate and ambiguous position between the two. In the remainder of this essay, I want to explore some aspects of feminine symbolism and behaviour in the movements led by Francis, Fox and Gandhi by relating them to the paradigm of culture and nature, or structure and anti-structure. I also hope to build on the theoretical work of anthropologists and historians by re-defining the feminine qualities embodied in these three men and their followers, and by suggesting a different model of feminine attitude and activity which might be used creatively in our own social and political life.

II

Turner actually mentioned Francis and Gandhi as examples of *communitas*; in fact, his typology seems to work neatly as a framework for analysing all three movements. All occurred at historical moments when social and political structures were in a state of flux or of open conflict: conflict between the papacy, the German princes and the independent towns in twelfth-century Italy; between king and parliament, Anglican and Puritan, aristocracy and labourer in seventeenth-century England; between upholders of caste and social reformers, British imperialists and partisans of home rule in twentieth-century India. All set themselves against social and political structures and parties, all were non-violent and, to different degrees, all preached poverty.

Francis, Fox and Gandhi were also aware of a pervading cultural symbolism in which authority, and the absence of authority, were often expressed in terms of gender. On the one hand, they saw masculine figures of political and spiritual power, whether pope, king or viceroy. On the other hand, they and their contemporaries saw feminine figures which were commonly used to convey a sense of liminality, that twilight zone where generation and decay, order and chaos meet. Francis knew the polarity of Mary and Eve. Gandhi understood the double visage of the goddess Kali, the mother and devourer of all life, and he surely knew of the attainments of Ramakrishna, the nineteenth-century Indian mystic who overcame the illusion of personal identity by dressing and behaving like a woman, so much so that he was thought to be able to menstruate by having periodic discharges of blood through the pores of his skin. Fox recorded in his *Journal* the contemporary belief that women had no souls, and he may have also been aware that men sometimes dressed as women during riots – living symbols of disorder – just as Quaker women visionaries were often perceived as living vessels of divine energy.

Given this cultural context, it is not surprising that when Francis, Fox and Gandhi characterized the condition of the true believer by the symbol of nakedness, they chose to associate this nakedness with aspects of femininity. Francis believed that unity with God was contingent on freedom from possessions. He instructed the brothers to live without hoarding, and to follow only the most insecure occupations. Francis also preached a poverty of intellectual attainment; the friars were to live not only without buildings but without books. He spoke of a learned postulant 'in a certain fashion resigning his learning so that he may offer himself naked to the arms of the crucified one.'[5] Finally, Francis denied the reality of status in the world and within his own Order. The brothers were to rejoice when they found themselves among mean and despised persons, and no one was to take on the office of preacher or minister, 'but at whatever hour the command may be given him, he should lay down his office without any contradiction.'[6]

Francis expressed all of this not as elements of an abstract economic and social doctrine, but in the concrete, feminine image of Lady Poverty, whom his followers came to identify with himself. Appropriately enough, this crusade in the service of Lady Poverty, undermined by many of Francis's contemporaries and by most of his successors, was most vigorously upheld by a woman. Indeed his disciple, Clare, almost outdid Francis by sleeping on vine twigs with a rock for a pillow. Even after Francis's death, she continued to battle with the pope for the right of her Order, called 'The Order of the Poor Ladies', to remain poor. As he became less human and more saintly, the persona of Francis himself assumed more strikingly feminine attributes; toward the end of his life he even acquired stigmata, a mark of sanctity usually attained by women.

The Quakers believed in a philosophy of the Inner Light, a state of inner fulfilment which exalted the unity of the spiritual community of believers and denigrated the outward distinctions of wealth, rank and political power. As such they were less militant than contemporary sects like the Levellers, but they were no less egalitarian. The Quakers met in private houses or in fields. Not only did they abandon the clothing of their rank, which was often considerable; they often abandoned clothing altogether, going naked as a sign. They counselled against the hoarding of goods. They repudiated formal social etiquette, so much so that many converts were reluctant to embrace the Quakers because of their reputation as a despised sect. Although they often cited Scripture to buttress their arguments, the Quakers also repudiated formal learning as a means of attaining grace.

One way the Quakers expressed this sense of social and intellectual nullity was by casting visionary women as living symbols of christian nakedness or foolishness, arguing that women should prophesy not because they were the equals of men, but because 'God makes use of the weak'. Quakers who attained a state of salvation, or who had acquired 'the inner light', sometimes spoke as though they had shed the attributes of gender altogether; women declared that they stood before Christ as men, and men declared, metaphorically at least, that they had become women.

When Gandhi died he owned a loin cloth, a pair of sandals, a book, a replica of the three monkeys, and almost nothing else. He advocated a kind of economic populism based on village agriculture and the domestic production of homespun or *khadi*. He spent much energy considering the uses of human excrement as fertilizer. He opposed formal education, refusing to give his sons training for any profession. He dramatized his negation of caste structure by degrading acts – cleaning latrines and treating Untouchables – by his own nakedness, and by the feminine activity of spinning, which he made his followers practise every day. He articulated these activities and programmes as part of a campaign against both the caste system and British rule. But he also insisted that his primary goal was apolitical and spiritual; the negation of all personal desire and the practice of *ahimsa*, 'a positive state of love, of doing good even to the evil-doer.'[7] He also believed that he could attain this universality by becoming physically and spiritually more like a woman:

> Their love was selfless and motherly, stemming from the demands of childbearing and childrearing. They were more virtuous than men, because they had a greater capacity for suffering, for faith, and for renunciation – in fact, for non-violence. They were therefore better qualified than men to preach the art of peace to the warring world.[8]

Gandhi believed that once he had attained the practice of true *ahimsa* or non-violence, even his sexual organs would change their appearance and come to resemble those of a woman.

The condition of outward and inward nakedness which was associated with these movements of *communitas* had another, more positive dimension: the image of salvation as a return to the bliss of infancy. By their capacity for simplicity and playfulness, Francis and Gandhi were prototypes of the worshipper as a naked, erring child, wrapped in the loving motherhood of God. By their capacity for nurture and for healing, all three men gave their adherents a foretaste of God's limitless maternal care. Clare once had a vision that she was walking toward Francis:

> When she reached Saint Francis, he bared his breast saying: 'Come, take and drink,' . . . which doing what she sucked was so sweet and delightful that she could in no way describe it.

And having sucked, that roundness, or the mouth of the pap from which the milk flowed remained in the mouth of the blessed Clare; and if taken in the hand what had remained in her mouth seemed something bright and shining in which all could be seen as in a mirror, in which she saw her own reflection.[9]

For Francis, Fox and Gandhi, the safety of total immersion in God could be experienced only as the culmination of a process of self-annihilation and the negation of all earthly structures; political, social, mental, even anatomical. Such a radical conception of human nakedness must have been a threatening concept on many levels. And since both the soul's homelessness and the sheltering haven of God's love were embodied, for all three men, by symbols of Womanhood, it is not surprising that their attitudes toward actual women were ambivalent. True, all three men affirmed the equality of the sexes in 'real' life. Francis defied canon law in order to establish the Order of the Poor Ladies, led by Clare, and he maintained relations with Clare's convent in opposition to many of the brothers. He even revered Clare herself as a healer, and sent patients to her to be touched. Fox defended the right of Quaker women to preach and to hold independent meetings even against many of *his* own followers; over 200 women were active as missionaries or prophets during the latter half of the seventeenth century. Gandhi supported the right of women to work and to enter politics; his advocacy of the validity of Indian marriages in South Africa in 1913 brought women into the political arena for the first time. And he inveighed against the evil of child marriage with as much vehemence as he denounced the evils of caste.

But all three men buttressed their support of women by a faith in their own ability to transcend desire and by the belief that women, by their humility and chastity, would help them do it. Francis's relationship with Clare was conducted in an atmosphere of complete, out-of-the-body ecstasy. Gandhi bowed to the superior humility and chastity of women, but his relations with them were still marked by *his* absolute control; witness his practice of sleeping with naked girls and quizzing them on their reactions to his seventy-seven-year-old presence. The Quakers were accused of sexual immorality by their contemporaries, but one precondition of women's eminence in the movement was the ability of both men and women to contain their own sexuality. Although the Quakers married, it was their policy for couples to preach separately, ministers travelling with others of the same sex.

In short, while each man affirmed the equality of women – or, more properly, the irrelevance of gender – and while each felt a rich appreciation, even awe, at what he took to be the feminine spirit, all three men believed that they had to sustain a balance of spiritual intensity and emotional distance in their relations with actual women. So it should not surprise us that their contemporaries often felt incapable of such fancy emotional footwork. Many Franciscan brothers opposed Francis's visits to Clare during his lifetime, and the convent was eventually forced to accept a papal rule which made the sisters completely enclosed nuns. Many male Quakers opposed Fox's establishment of women's meetings – focussing, significantly, on the authority of women over whom they married. Quaker women continued to preach during the eighteenth century, but without the institutional buttress of an independent meeting and without access to the meeting for business. And whereas seventeenth-century women visionaries were often described as young, or as mothers of young children, eighteenth-century preachers tended to be middle-aged widows and grandmothers.

Looking at the Franciscans, the Quakers and the followers of Gandhi as expressions of *communitas*, it is easy to see why Turner called them movements of transition:

> Spontaneous communitas is a phase, . . . a moment, not a permanent condition. . . . In practice, of course, the impetus soon becomes exhausted, and the 'movement' becomes itself one institution among other institutions – often one more fanatical and militant than the rest, for the reason that it feels itself to be the unique bearer of universal human truths.[10]

By extension we can also see why women are transitional figures in many radical movements, coming to prominence in the early stages of egalitarian fervour, receding into obscurity with the re-emergence of structure. One can even understand why Turner disparages liminal movements, while asserting the dialectical nature of their relationship to social structure:

> The moment a digging stick is set in the earth, a colt broken in, a pack of wolves defended against, or a human enemy set by his heels, we have the germs of a social structure. This is not merely the set of chains in which men everywhere are, but the very cultural means that preserve the dignity and liberty, as well as the bodily existence, of every man, woman and child. . . . Since the beginnings of prehistory, the evidence suggests that such means are what makes man most evidently man.[11]

In other words, Turner seems to say, cultures need periodic, invigorating doses of *communitas*, momentary affirmations of universal human dignity and oneness as distinct from particular humans with cultural identities and political relationships; but in the last analysis it is the wheel – not love – that makes the world go round. In this context, feminine symbolism might be seen as a kind of reserve ideology, put on ice and treated simply as myth or folklore during some periods, put into practice as a model for human activity in others. And religious women themselves might be viewed as a kind of reserve army of spiritual labour, brought in to affirm egalitarian principles and accomplish dangerous ascetic practices and missionary work, laid off when these activities are no longer timely. In England, that would have been when the development of patriarchal theory and practice made communal models and female public authority both irrelevant and dangerous. Perhaps this is how we should understand one Mary Starbuck, who was responsible for starting the Quaker meeting on the island of Nantucket. She and some other women sustained Quakerism on the island during the years when the men were gone whaling. Yet when the meeting finally got official recognition it was established as a men's business meeting. Modern historical accounts refer to the heroic leadership and self-sacrifice of Starbuck and many other women, and then go on to describe the men who were the 'real' founders of Quakerism in the American colonies.

III

This way of thinking about movements of *communitas* and the place of feminine elements within them has the virtue of being clear-cut, even bracing, in its cynicism. But it is also one-sided; indeed it *has* to be, given the categories of Turner's typology. Turner speaks of individuals, rituals, even whole movements as being either structured or formless, hierarchical or egalitarian, aggressive or pacific. The early Franciscans, Quakers and Gandhians *must*, in this typology, be movements of anti-structure in contrast to their goal-oriented contemporaries, the Dominicans (organized to combat heresy), the Puritans (organized to make England a city of god), or the Congress Party (organized to reform Indian politics and expel the British).

Not only does the paradigm of structure/anti-structure (or culture/nature) encourage a one-sided interpretation of the material; it may also be sexist in its implications. By defining femininity in negative terms (as a symbol associated with movements which reject prevailing structures), or in terms of global collectivity (as in movements which espouse universal equality and love), it implies that the real driving force in any movement – the organization, the vital energy of the leader, the actual plan for reform of society or spirit – must be associated with symbols of masculinity. And it implies that when movements of *communitas* fail, they do so because of their feminine elements.

But the fact is that none of the three movements I have been discussing failed. Of course they rejected conventional modes of exercising authority and limiting personal contact. But one of the most arresting things about Franciscans, Quakers and Gandhians is their worldly effectiveness – the competence and vigour with which these avowedly a-political, other-worldly, even whimsical people took on the worldly Establishment and sustained the life of their communities. For in fact, Francis, Fox and Gandhi did not reject goals or programmes in favour of a formless, impractical and cathartic love-in. Instead, they and their followers sought spiritual salvation and social reform by focussing on domestic virtues and personal relationships rather than on formal public authority, church organization or monastic rule, and by adhering to a fluid strategy of negotiation and self-sacrifice rather than an abstract policy which was aggressive, inflexible and potentially violent. All three groups steered a middle course between the elitism of a revolutionary vanguard and the democracy of a world turned upside down. They cared less about ramifications of doctrine than techniques of communication: Francis, through public preaching and the establishment of a third Order; Quakers, through a system of double meetings ('threshing' meetings for the public, silent meetings for Friends); Gandhi, through popular journalism and public demonstrations of *satyagraha* (truth-force). We might say, indeed their adherents *did* say, that they raised the principle of the inter-relatedness of all people to a higher level, in that they succeeded in projecting the personal, affective relationships of everyday existence into the public sphere. We need a typology for a kind of political and social behaviour which is disordered only in relation to a specific notion of order; one that encompasses the Quakers' skill at providing for their material *needs* alongside their rejection of material *wealth*, and Gandhi's orchestration of peaceful political demonstrations alongside his rejection of party politics. Perhaps we should formulate the difference between, say, Puritans and Quakers by a typology of groups which emphasize the pursuit of fixed goals through formal organizations that are more or less militant, and groups which perceive Truth and social harmony as extensions of concrete, personal experience, tending to equate ends with means.

Moderate theorists have argued that modes of moral thinking which emphasize relationship and concrete circumstance over logic and principle are predominantly feminine. I want to argue that this feminine element of Franciscans, Quakers and Gandhians is of great relevance for our own political life; greater, perhaps, than their use of traditional feminine religious symbolism or their relatively liberated attitudes toward women. And I want to focus on one aspect of this feminine moral thinking as a way of grasping their highly creative political style; a typology of thinking and behaviour associated, in our own time, with active parenthood.

By 'active parenthood' I am not referring to the traditional feminine symbolism of God as Mother – 'Mother' being one who gives unmediated, unquestioning love and nurturance, cutting across the barriers created by ethical standards or social hierarchies. Francis, Fox and Gandhi, were, as we have seen, powerful preachers of God as Mother. But this traditional image of God, and of motherhood itself as a source of pure and unending nurturance, was no more the whole essence of Francis, Fox or Gandhi's truth than it is of any modern parent's. I would like to define parenthood not only as a way of feeling but as a way of thinking; and not only as a state of being but as an active discipline. Such a parent might be described as one who strives to be both reliable and flexible, combining both nurture and judgment. A parent follows a rhythm of feeling and action that shifts from minute to minute, tracking the unpredictable needs and moods of children; but she also seeks to shape and direct that rhythm, and to integrate these domestic and teaching activities with her own strictly adult, or public concerns. More than most educators or psychologists, our archetypal parent is profoundly humble; she recognizes that the most vigilant solicitude and the most advanced theory of child-rearing cannot guarantee against emotional or physical catastrophe, nor can they fully explain the catastrophe when it happens. More than most politicians or public leaders, a parent lives with the ambiguity of benevolent authority. In her daily relations with her child – particularly a young child – she is both master and slave. She experiences an awareness of physical power almost continually held in check, and learns the resilience that comes from all the blows that are contemplated but not given. She also learns the futility of being the undisputed winner over her child in a battle of wills or of bodies. She controls and coerces one whom she also cherishes, and works to set free.

A far more sophisticated typology of maternal thinking has been developed by the philosopher Sara Ruddick. She writes,

For me 'maternal' is a social category: Although maternal
thinking arises out of actual child-caring practices, biological
parenting is neither necessary nor sufficient. Many women and
some men express maternal thinking in various kinds of
working caring with others. And some biological mothers . . .
take a fearful, defensive distance from their own mothering and
the maternal lives of any women.[12]

Such a parent was Gandhi, whose relations with his biological
children were unsuccessful by any standard. Yet Gandhi's
behaviour toward both his intimate followers and the wider
public corresponded to that of our hypothetical parent in at least
two ways: his integration of personal, domestic activity with the
rhythm of his wider political life, and his self-abnegating but
persuasive, even humorous posture toward those in authority.
Gandhi elevated the tasks of daily life to a holy discipline. He did
not leave the cares of the household in order to contemplate
higher things, as most other other Indian ascetics – indeed most
revolutionaries – do. For Gandhi and his spiritual family, truth
emerged out of the mundane activities of eating, cleaning,
sleeping, even defecation. Days of silent contemplation alternated
with periods of domestic business. The practice of physical
restraint flourished in an atmosphere of total physical intimacy.
Personal choices had political significance; hence Gandhi's policy
of blessing only those marriages which crossed class lines.

Gandhi's relations with Indian party leaders and the British
showed a combination of pragmatism and intransigence that
confounded everybody, including his own supporters. He and his
followers deliberately sought martyrdom, while simultaneously
negotiating with the authorities. They ignored laws which they
repudiated on moral grounds, while affirming their loyalty to the
state. They sought positions of strength only to refrain from using it:

Satyagraha was at its height when those who practiced it were
in a position, as they often were, to use violence effectively but
refrained from doing so and invited suffering upon themselves.
. . . (This) element of non-violence in satyagraha is inseparable
from a view of Truth which takes as its criterion the needs of
man.[13]

Gandhi's priority – to respond to particular human needs rather
than to the dictates of an abstract programme of spiritual growth
or political reform – is evident in his ability to work with
opponents who disagreed with him:

In the quest for . . . truth, and in its propagation, it is . . . not possible . . . to inflict harm on others. In so behaving, truth itself would lose its meaning. He who claims a different version of truth from the satyagrahi's must be converted by gentleness. Meanwhile, the satyagrahi must re-examine continuously his own position – for his opponent may be closer to the truth than he is. . . . The objective . . . is to win the victory over the conflict situation – to discover further truths and to persuade the opponent, not to triumph over him.[14]

Now the Quakers: In 1665 Joan Whitrowe, a Quaker preacher living in London, was commanded by God to go to Bristol and call the people to repentance. She went on foot, wearing sackcloth and ashes, and returned the next day to her husband and family, including a year-old baby who was still nursing. The fact that Joan Whitrowe, and many other Quakers, chose to record and publish these personal aspects of their experience indicates that for them, daily life was not merely something to be transcended in martyrdom or in an ecstatic trance. On the contrary; the Quakers, like the followers of Gandhi, placed great stress on the integrity and emotional warmth of their personal relationships, both as a reflection of the harmony that flowed from the presence of the Inner Light, and as a message to the wider community. Hence the importance of providing for the economic needs of poor Friends, and the importance which Fox placed on the institution of marriage – giving the women's meeting authority to determine the spiritual readiness for marriage of every couple among the Quakers who was so inclined.

Hence also the importance of friendship in the early Society of Friends. In a testimony to Elizabeth Stirredge, a male Quaker wrote,

> It was her lot many times when she came to our meeting to lodge at my house, my dear mother . . . and she being very intimate friends, and heartily loving each other's company which I also loved, for it was pleasant, and her discourse was edifying to me.[15]

Quaker prophecy itself was, in many respects, a co-operative and collective effort. Many writings, often done in prison, were composed and signed by several people. Numerous accounts of sufferings mention a friend who accompanied a prophet to prison, although she had felt no inward call to speak herself.

It is important to understand that, while these collective experiences were certainly emotional and cathartic, they were not undisciplined or unconscious. The Quakers evolved highly successful methods of determining what they called the 'sense of the meeting' in order to achieve true consensus – the resolution of a problem with no winners and no losers – and these methods are still in use today. The Quakers also evolved strategies for collecting and dispensing charity, and for negotiating for the release of prisoners. More important, they displayed an unusual and very successful combination of humility and assertiveness toward those in power. The Quakers were avowedly apolitical, but they ignored laws which offended their principles. They preached non-violence, but they also aggressively courted martyrdom, and tried to fill the prisons with their adherents. They also exhibited a fine sense of the power of propaganda, establishing a meeting for sufferings which collected and published details of outrages perpetrated by the government on Quaker victims. Alongside all this energetic pacifism, the meeting began a programme of legal education, recruiting lawyers to negotiate with the magistrates for the release of prisoners.

We find a similar integration of personal and public life, although less fully articulated, in the career of Francis. Francis hated money and status not only as barriers to spiritual freedom, but as obstacles to brotherhood; obstacles which he overcame for himself when he kissed a leper – the ultimate outcast. Although drawn to a life of asceticism and isolation, Francis decided, after God had spoken to him through Clare, to live in the world and preach. He also established the Order of the Penitents, to accommodate those whose family commitments obliged them to live in the world, but who aspired to the ideals of Franciscan poverty. In his dealings with worldly authorities he was at once meek and stubborn. He appealed to the Pope for permission to start his own Order by describing a poor woman in the desert who was very beautiful, and who married a king. When her sons arrive at court, the king told them that he would provide for all the sons which she had borne. 'Very holy father,' added Francis, 'I am this poor woman whom God in his love has deigned to make beautiful, and of whom he has been pleased to have lawful sons. the King of Kings has told me that he will provide for all the sons which he may have of me, for if he sustains bastards, how much more his legitimate sons.'[16] Just so did Francis assure the Pope of the Order's obedience, *and* of his insistence that the Order be independent, subject to Francis's own Rule. And in fact, the Franciscans were the only radical group of the period to avoid prosecution for heresy.

Surely part of the appeal of Francis, Fox and Gandhi to their disciples was based on their ability to be simultaneously figures of authority and of intimate association. And surely the public achievements of all three men stemmed from their ability to present a model of behaviour toward those in power that was both pliant and heroic. I have suggested that the model of structure and *communitas*, or Nature and Culture, is less helpful in appreciating these qualities than the model of parenthood, because a successful parent has to be both hard and soft; she integrates the most minute, even degrading details of daily life into an overall conception of adulthood toward which both she and her child must strive. Consciously or not, a parent synthesizes both nature *and* culture, *communitas and* structure, as she experiences the trials and pleasures of a single day.

All of this is not an argument for biological determinism, nor is it a discussion of the family or of parenting as social institutions. If anything, the Lutherans and Puritans put the family more at the centre of their theology than the Quakers did, Luther emphasizing the spiritual importance of marriage, Calvin the importance of the patriarchal father as the family emissary to God. But it is also true that women have traditionally been associated with child-rearing, and that the bulk of the historical literature on the family quotes men, not women. It is therefore impossible to say, at this point, what elements of child-care are unique to the modern, middle-class family and what elements were shared by the cultures of medieval or early modern Europe, or of India. It would be more accurate to say that Francis and Fox prefigured certain types of behaviour which have become generally true of modern, middle-class parents in the West.

It seems appropriate and satisfying to attempt to bring domestic habits of thought and behaviour into the intellectual sphere, as Francis, Fox and Gandhi brought them into the sphere of social life and politics. It is also gratifying to resurrect these particular movements; indeed, *any* movement which challenges structures of authority and advocates egalitarian behaviour is bound to attract women, who have never really shared in creating those structures. It may also be that at this historical moment, when conflicts bred by the structures of nation or class seem likely to threaten our very existence, many of us might be especially receptive to movements which devalue structure and hierarchy and offer creative techniques of non-confrontational public behaviour. The problem for contemporary feminists or peace activists is not that we are too bourgeois to comprehend or imitate the achievements of these radical men and women of the past, but that we are too secular. We tend to overlook or discount the fact that the energy and inner self-assurance of Francis or Clare or Gandhi as they confronted those in power sprang from their submission to an even *higher* power – that of God; and that their ability to sustain unformalized relationships among their adherents – even for one lifetime – sprang from their faith in the existence of a spiritual realm that transcended time itself. Those of us who reject the traditional male model of the narrow-minded, rigid, loveless revolutionary may try to co-opt their political style without reference to their religious faith. In doing so we still face a problem of authority: the problem of sustaining co-operation and unity of purpose when our deepest convictions make us critical of power vested in others – even when those others are our heroes – and distrustful of power vested in ourselves.

Parents, especially those in modern, middle-class, permissive households, confront this problem of authority every day of their lives, whether or not they choose to think about it, and regardless of whether or not they are successful in solving it. I think that the ordinary, unheroic experience of parenthood may have much to offer as a source of insight in thinking about our public behaviour, at a time in our history when it seems particularly urgent to consider forms of political interaction which work to mediate, rather than escalate, conflict. All of this is not to espouse the sanctity of motherhood, or to resurrect those Victorian feminists who tried to turn the whole world into a living room, or even to imply that parents have a monopoly on compassion. Just the opposite: the behaviour of Francis, Fox and Gandhi – only one of whom was a biological parent, and a bad one at that – suggests that 'feminine' domestic habits of thought and activity may be transposed into the public sphere by both women and men; one might even speculate that these feminine modes of behaviour gained moral and political credibility for Francis, Fox and Gandhi just *because* they were being used creatively by men. In any case, I suggest that we would do well to contemplate the virtues of these partisans of non-violent public behaviour, and that we can find affinities with their compassionate activism very close to home, as we move to embrace our own political and spiritual struggles.

Notes

1 John Holland Smith, *Francis of Assisi* (New York: Charles Scribner's Sons, 1972), p.1.
2 Victor Turner, *The Ritual Process: Structure and Anti-Structure* (Ithaca, N.Y.: Cornell University Press, 1977), p.95.
3 *Ibid.*, pp.111–12.
4 *Ibid.*, p.140.

5   Malcolm D. Lambert, *Franciscan Poverty* (London: Allenson, 1961), p.65.
6   *Ibid.*, p.150.
7   Ved Mehta, *Mahatma Gandhi and His Apostles* (New York: The Viking Press, 1976), p.183.
8   *Ibid.*, p.182.
9   Joan Mowat Erikson, *St Francis et His Four Ladies* (New York: W.W. Norton, 1970), p.90.
10 Turner, *op. cit.*, p.112.
11 *Ibid.*, p.140.
12 Sara Ruddick, 'Maternal Thinking', *Feminist Studies*, vol. 6, no. 2, Summer 1980, p.346.
13 Joan V. Bondurant, *Conquest of Violence. The Gandhian Philosophy of Conflict* (Princeton: Princeton University Press, 1958), pp.27–8.
14 *Ibid.*, p.33.
15 *Life of Elizabeth Stirredge, The Friends Library: Comprising Journals . . . the Members of the Religious Society of Friends, Vol. 2* (Philadelphia, 1838), p.201.
16 Paul Sabatier, *Life of St Francis of Assisi*, tr. Louise Seymour Houghton (New York: Charles Scribner's Sons, 1935), p.98.

For a full list of works cited and consulted, see an expanded version of this essay in *Signs: Journal of Women in Culture and Society*, 1986, vol. 11, no. 3, pp.457–77.

9

Women and nineteenth-century spiritualism: Strategies in the subversion of femininity

ALEX OWEN

Modern Spiritualism, a belief in the survival of the spirits of the dead and in their ability to communicate with the living, was still in its infancy when it made its way across the Atlantic during the early 1850s. Originating with the two young Fox sisters who were to become leading Spriritualist mediums, spirit-rapping found ready converts in America and was enthusiastically received in England. In fact it became all the rage, one English woman writing to her husband in 1853:

> The great talk now is Mrs Stowe and spirit-rapping, both of which have arrived in England. The universality of the phenomena renders it a curious study. A feeling seems pervading all classes, all sects, that the world stands upon the eve of some great spiritual revelation. It meets one in books, in newspapers, on the lips of members of the Church of England, Unitarians, even Free-thinkers. Poor old Robert Owen, the philanthropist, has been converted, and made a declaration of faith in the public papers.[1]

Spiritualism certainly attracted both Christian and Secular adherents, the former experiencing it as an extension and enhancement of personal religious devotion and the latter as material proof of the survival of the spirit. Although there was no strict divide along class lines working-class believers tended to be more inclined towards Secularism than their middle-class counterparts, and sought to explain their beliefs within a framework of quantifiable fluids and forces.[2] But middle-class Spiritualists were often those who had become disillusioned with the aridity of orthodox Christianity and who regarded the Church as a wasteland of dogma and ritual. They sought in the Spiritualist seance a direct experience of Divinity and the immortality of the soul.

Despite class differences commonly-held Spiritualist beliefs tended to have an homogenizing affect which was invariably strong enough to overcome the uneasiness with which, for example, middle-class sitters sometimes regarded working-class mediums. All Spiritualists were united in the comfort and consolation derived from communication with lost loved ones at a time when bereavement was still a feature of everyday life, and personal recollections often dealt movingly with the joy experienced at the reconciliation with dead infants and children. But there was also common interest in campaigns and platforms concerned with freedom from the bondage of authority, just as Spiritualistic practice dispensed with establishment theology and intervention. Spiritualists regarded monopolies like the medical profession with deep suspicion, supported a change in the law relating to women's rights, and contributed to the causes of abolition and prison and lunacy reform. A preoccupation with topics like vegetarianism, homoeopathy, natural healing, and temperance reflected a concern with the purification of mind and body in preparation for heightened spirituality, as well as a desire for personal control over health and well-being. If such interests have a remarkably contemporary ring about them it is also relevant to note that they had roots which stretched back through Swedenborgianism, Primitive Methodism, Owenism and Chartism.[3] The cultural elements of former movements fed into Spiritualism with as much tenacity as their intellectual or theoretical underpinnings, and the vigorous and popular elements of that movement were to be found elsewhere long after the passage of the golden years of the 1870s and 1880s.

Spiritualists were concerned with questions relating to the rights and position of women although there was a moderation in the tenor of the discussion in the English Spiritualist press which was absent from its more radical American counterpart. Both men and women on the public lecture circuit were ready to discuss gender relations and some were prepared to pronounce upon the immorality of sexual guilt and ignorance. But these aspects of Spiritualists' concerns did not gather momentum until the late 1860s, and initially Spiritualism remained a more isolated and private affair based around the small family circle. Here, however, what was clear from the outset was that women were central to its practice, and this was because they were thought to make particularly effective sitters and mediums. Believers laid great stress upon what they termed the 'negative' or 'passive' temperament, one which was associated with femininity but which men could cultivate. This yielding and receptive attribute in women was thought to be especially conducive to the harmony of the seance circle and to the reception of spirit, and women were highly valued members of any group. Although this clearly has to do with the reinforcement of a theory of immutable sex differences it nevertheless enabled women to accede to positions of spiritual power which might otherwise have been denied them. Through the controlled and ritualized vehicle of the seance women were encouraged to assume their spiritual inheritance, and the spirits themselves were not slow to voice their preference in the matter.

The majority of seance circles began fairly lightheartedly with a group of friends meeting regularly to see if they could produce some evidence of spirit presence. Men and women would be placed alternately around a table, positive (male) and negative (female) complementing each other, and would wait in dim light or total darkness for a 'sign'. The time was spent in singing or pleasant conversation until the sensation of a cool breeze was felt wafting over the hands of the sitters followed by the involuntary twitching of hands or limbs. These signs heralded the arrival of the spirits and one person would then take charge of the seance by inviting spirit communication. A verbal question would be asked to which a spirit would respond by making raps on the table; one rap or tilt for No, three for Yes, and two to express doubt or uncertainty. During this initial period of investigation one person would usually emerge as the most gifted of the sitters in this exchange, and women were noted for developing more quickly and confidently than men. As the powers of the medium increased so also did the seance phenomena which often progressed from raps to the playing of musical instruments by unseen hands, 'apports' of flowers and gifts into the room, and finally manifestations like the levitation of the medium's body.

By the 1870s the production of spirit shapes in the darkness, or parts of a form like a disembodied hand or face, were common and any medium mindful of her reputation was endeavouring to produce them. Many of the phenomena were produced whilst in a mediumistic trance and a good medium could also take on the voice, facial expression, and personality of a spirit which could then communicate directly with the sitters. But the acme of a medium's powers was undoubtedly the full-form materialization of a spirit complete with suitable spirit garb. This form was produced whilst the medium lay secreted, and supposedly in trance, behind the thick curtain of a cabinet − a simple box-like construction in which the medium sat, or it could even be an alcove across which a curtain had been draped. A good materialization medium was able to produce a fully-clothed spirit who emerged from the cabinet to walk amongst the sitters, touching and also sometimes speaking to them. Meanwhile, behind the curtain, the medium sat in a comatose state, sometimes bound hand and foot to rule out trickery on her part, and often audibly moaning. This was what Spiritualists and non−Spiritualists alike thronged to see; it was the most valued of all phenomena and one at which women excelled.

Women, then, were among the forerunners of skilled mediumship but the level of acceptance of female spirituality was closely linked to the already established ideal of women as purveyors of religious values and guardians of home and hearth. The Evangelical movement of the first half of the century had lain great emphasis on the home and domestic sphere in which the family was nurtured and protected by the morally regenerative influence of wife and mother. This idealization of the sacred hearth reached its peak during the mid-nineteenth century, the moment of Spiritualism's arrival, and emphasized the private sphere as women's rightful domain.[4] The establishment of this 'separate spheres' philosophy made for a more ready acceptance of Spiritualist women's power specifically because it helped to define feminine religious influence as a cohesive force rather than as a threat to male superiority. This enabled men to accede to female directives without loss of face, and to defer to women without appearing to jeopardize their own patriarchal position.[5] Recent work on the Owenite women has also shown that a moral mission ideology could be transformed to become the basis for a self-consciously feminist endeavour, whilst beneath the urbane surface of Victorian separate spheres philosophy ran the tradition of women's involvement in radical millenarian movements. There was already ample precedent for women entering the political and feminist fray through the vehicle of religion and the language of heresy.[6]

Those women, usually working- or lower middle-class, who made their way into the public life of professional (paid) mediumship, were certainly offered a degree of autonomy unusual for this period. The most successful were courted by the wealthy whilst those who could put on a good platform display of clairvoyance, mesmerism, or healing had an enthusiastic following. The career of the gifted Emma Hardinge Britten who was a renowned platform speaker, giving unprepared inspirational addresses at the behest of the spirits, was evidence of the way in which a theme of spiritual equality could be readily conflated with a demand for temporal rights. But for these mediums, just as for those who remained at home and operated only within a private home circle, a species of moral influence still pertained. The Spiritualist press spoke glowingly of those who embodied the womanly and domestic virtues and great emphasis was laid upon charm and manner. However, what I now want to consider at length is the way in which Spiritualist women were able to oppose contemporary definitions of womanhood, and to look more closely at the way in which the language and behaviour of women mediums effectively subverted the normative feminine ideal.

Women were considered to be good trance mediums because of their ability to surrender to Spirit, a characteristic attributed to the so-called innate passivity which was so much a part of the construction of the meaning of femininity during the nineteenth century. The notion of womanliness in this period was intrinsically tied to female biology and was assumed as an unproblematic constant from which women's place and function naturally followed. Three of the other major constructs of femininity were illness, silence, and functional (de-eroticized) sexuality, each of which were deeply inscribed within female consciousness. This social construction of a sexual identity (with many concomitant implications for the psyche) was reproduced in the language and behaviour expected of Victorian women. However, resistance to prescriptive femininity – not necessarily as a conscious endeavour – also spoke through language and behaviour, and in a variety of ways which disclosed unconscious ideas, desires and represent-ations. In order to identify a species of this resistance it is necessary to turn to the pivotal device of Spiritualistic practice, the mediumistic trance.

The value placed on women within Spiritualism centred around the figure of the good trance medium who relinquished her own personality in order to become the temporary vehicle for the spirit of a dead person. Certainly there were degrees of trance or inspiration and a materialization medium was hidden from view, but in essence the fact remained that after a certain point in the seance the medium let go of her conscious personality and invited spirit possession. The remainder of the sitters, whether seated in front of the closed curtain or around the table, were prepared for the signs which announced the onset of trance. These were usually twitching of the body and limbs, moaning, restless movement, and changes in posture or facial expression. Spiritualists knew what to expect and had an intellectual framework within which to fit the events of the seance.

But for non-Spiritualists a variety of explanations for the reported phenomena spring to mind. It is possible that the medium was completely conscious and was perpetrating a deception for any one of a variety of motives. Again, it was possible that she had begun by having a genuine convulsive or numinous experience and had then sought to reproduce it without recognizing her actions as fraudulent. Equally, what had begun as fraud could become so habitual that she ended up fully believing in her own powers.[7] Fraud was a constant bone of contention for Spiritualists and astute believers were alert to the possibilities presented by a darkened seance room, although even when a medium was caught in the most flagrant of spirit impersonations she was usually thought to have been mislead by an evil spirit. Apart from fraud in its various guises, though, there remains the fact that as far as the medium and her sitters were concerned a genuinely supernatural event had taken place. This raises the thorny problem of the nature of the real and the question of the community of belief, both of which lie beyond the scope of this paper, but it must be said that it is important to remain sensitive to the authenticity of the experience for those involved and to 'let those who believe in spirits speak for themselves'.[8]

There remains a final major category of explanation and it is the one that I want to take up here; this is that the medium had indeed fallen into trance and that in this sleep-like state of dissociation the unconscious in some form was permitted to speak.[9] Explanations involving the use of concepts or techniques appropriated from psychoanalytic theory tend to be contentious in both historical and feminist circles, and certainly a blanket mapping of this culturally specific discourse onto historical material is not necessarily helpful or appropriate. But without seeking to privilege the psychic level of analysis, or to postulate a devout species of Freudianism, what I want to suggest is that there is a case for moving beyond a methodology bounded by empiricism where the so-called measurable event must always be taken as stock in trade. What I hope to achieve here is a more open and porous reading of the material which takes into account what is being occluded by certain language or behaviour, or representation of an event, in order to reveal what lies submerged beneath the surface. In the context of feminist historiography this facilitates a shift from emphasizing, for example, formulated radical conscious-ness and action to a more careful cognisance of the fractured and contradictory nature of women's resistance to patriarchal structures and systems of meaning. It allows for an analysis of a resistance which might not yet have reached articulation but which is nevertheless present in the language of behaviour or the symptomatic act.[10] This is perhaps most obvious in the appearance of non-pathological illness; the tongue is silent but the body speaks. Assuming for the moment, then, the existence of an active unconscious which contains repressed or hidden thoughts and impulses, one which is hidden and yet not hidden, let us consider what was permitted to emerge in the guise of spirit communication. However, before doing so I should like to turn briefly to the function of illness within Spiritualism and its importance as a forerunner of psychic power.

Part of the orthodox construction of femininity involved the definition of woman as ill and as a kind of permanent invalid. The vulnerability of women to the exigencies of a precarious biology was thought to make them prone to both physiological and psychological disorders, which in turn rendered them unfit for public life. The standard norm of health was basically a male one, and the medical profession was quick to reinforce this view with an armoury of scientific evidence. Menstruation reduced woman to the status of 'an invalid. Such she emphatically is, as compared with man',[11] whilst the tyranny of the reproductive system made it virtually impossible to escape the pitfalls of female destiny. But in Spiritualism illness took on a different meaning which had nothing to do with either the headlong flight of the hysteric or the inescapable biological destiny of women. Illness was interpreted as a cleansing of the temple in preparation for psychic gifts, and was thus an accepted and acceptable route to powerful mediumship.

Andrew Jackson Davis, a leading American Spiritualist, commented that all illness was spiritual in origin and disease 'the effort of the spirit to clear its tenement of morbid obstructions',[12] whilst women mediums in particular laid stress on illness as a dominant factor in their early lives. These childhood 'beds of sickness' gave their young occupants the opportunity to wander at leisure in fairy lands of their own making, but they also seemed to mark an initiation into the unknown world of the spirit. It was only in later years that mediums realized the degree to which their earlier fantasy lives had, in fact, been glimpses of the Spiritualist Summerland – hints of the 'other side'. Florence Theobald, a middle-class private medium, felt that the long years of adult ill-health that had necessitated a withdrawal from the world had been an important contributory factor in the development of her own powers. The seclusion of illness and the suffering entailed in it were all aspects in the attainment of mediumship, and spirits referred to their own easy passage in terms of a soul prepared by the weary hours of illness. For Florence, the long sojourns in Hastings during the winter months were conducive to her spiritual life:

> I do not think the volume of spirit-teachings which I have received would or ever could have been given to me, but for the seclusion necessitated by this illness. . . . I also think still more decidedly that but for this rapport, so strongly established between me and my spirit-guides, I should have passed away at that time.[13]

The sick and invalid woman leading a lonely and empty life found herself blessed with the consolation of spiritual power, and this drew like-minded seekers to her door. Florence became the centre of a circle when she was away from home just as she had been the initiator of one within her own family.

Many Spiritualists preferred alternative methods of treatment to those offered by the orthodox medical profession, and women mediums often discovered in themselves the healing gift. This appeared to commence without any startling display and would usually involve a simple laying on of hands or a process of passing the hands down the sufferer's body. Some claimed the ability to see into the body, thus isolating the cause of illness, whilst others passed into trance and took the symptoms upon themselves using the help of the spirit to then absolve themselves of the complaint. Bessie Fitzgerald worked in this way and was used in a diagnostic capacity by a male healer, Doctor Mack:

> She would be ensconced in a corner of his waiting-room and tell him the exact disease of each patient that entered. She told me she could see the inside of everybody as perfectly as though they were made of glass. This gift, however, induced her to take on a reflection (as it were) of the disease she diagnosed, and after a while her failing strength compelled her to give it up.[14]

Physical exhaustion was a well-known hazard of mediumship and when powers began to fail or the medium fell prey to bad experiences she had to stop work and have a complete rest. For Bessie Fitzgerald, struggling to bring up two tiny children on her own, the possibility of a rest cure must have been remote. But despite these difficulties Spiritualist women were able to adopt a much more positive attitude towards illness than was usual during this period. As healers they confronted and dealt with illness in others, and as sufferers were able to present it in the positive light of heralding an advance in spiritual development.

The medical profession, with its high investment in the lucrative field of women's disorders, was less than enthusiastic about alternative healers and disliked Spiritualists. As swiftly as women shook off the negative and 'sick' construction of themselves medicine sought ever more firmly to reinstate them as patients. This led to a series of confrontations between Spiritualists and the profession during the 1870s and 1880s, especially over the issue of Spiritualism and insanity in which the incarceration of women was a major factor. But at least within Spiritualist circles illness as confirming female inferiority was implicitly trounced; it could be the forerunner of profound powers which in turn could help combat sickness in others. Whilst this was not the result of direct resistance to prescriptive femininity on the part of women believers it had the effect of providing a framework within which illness took on a positive value, and for mediums was considered to be an almost obligatory *rite de passage*. It was also a valorization which escaped some of the connotations of nineteenth-century notions of religious salvation through suffering, although for some Christian Spiritualists there undoubtedly was an element of this. Illness was the gateway to higher powers, and if women tended to be more sickly than men then – lo! – the obverse was also true. They were more powerful.

Just as illness had negative connotations for femininity in the dominant ideology of the nineteenth century so, too, did passivity. Women were defined as passive by nature but medically this was associated with a lack of vital will-power which in turn was connected with loss of volition and a tendency to insanity. Spiritualists, however, thought differently. They upheld the attribute of passivity, although still maintaining that it was essentially a feminine one, and sought to cultivate it. The more passive the medium, the more powerful the manifestations. A trance state of supreme surrender allowed total possession, and out of the medium's passivity a very different kind of activity was born. A new personality emerged which was at complete variance with the medium's normal waking state and this could be engagingly child-like, or assertive and aggressive, masculine in persona, or overtly sexual. But what was frequently dispensed with was behaviour becoming to a young lady, as passivity gave way to an activity of an extraordinary nature.

This was most noticeable with the materialization mediums who specialized in the production of specific spirits who would become as familiar with sitters as members of their own family. Young working-class mediums like Miss Fairlamb and Miss Wood were able to produce several such familiars at one sitting and these ranged from the child-sprites 'Cissie' and 'Pocha', through beautiful young women like 'Minnie', to the athletic and often belligerent 'George', 'Bennie' and 'Sam'. At one of Miss Fairlamb's Newcastle seances the sitters reported hearing the medium being slapped about the face as she sat in the cabinet, and then:

> out came a form with broad shoulders, black beard, and large arms and hands. The latter aroused my curiosity particularly, and I asked him to let me feel his hand, which request was immediately granted by his hitting me, in not a very gentle manner on one side of my face . . ., I said, 'It's all right' and 'we take all in good part', when he rubbed his hands and nodded his head, seeming to enjoy it. [15]

Later, at the same seance, 'Minnie' appeared:

> with all that grace and saint-like appearance which is characteristic of her . . . her beautiful arms quite bare, her right hand holding the roses and her snowy white garments reflecting like the silvery rays from some hidden sun. [16]

At another of Miss Fairlamb's seances the curtains parted to reveal a man of extremely dark complexion, complete with beard and moustache, wearing a striped flannel shirt, calico drawers, and a handkerchief tied around his head. He began to flex his muscles and perform gymnastic movements in front of the sitters, but when one of them inquired whether or not he was 'Willie':

> the man, or rather the materialised form, stepped nimbly up to him and, in answer to his question, dealt him a ringing blow on the side of his head with the palm of his right hand, and continued dealing similar blows in answer to questions, until Mr Armstrong hit upon the right name, 'Sam', when he – the form – politely bowed an acknowledgment.[17]

A short while later Mr Armstrong was again suffering at the hand of the pugilistic gentleman, and was clearly held in some disfavour by the 'spirit'. The observer on this occasion also came in for some attention from 'Sam', and twice noted that he was dealt blows with the palm of the hand and not with a clenched fist, but failed to note that 'Sam's' style was that usually associated with women. He did, however, remark that this same aggressive individual was all gallantry when it came to dealing with the women.

Miss Wood was renowned for the production of the tiny black spirit, 'Pocha', whose colour was certainly a source of titillation for certain sitters. She was a mischievous imp who delighted in stealing money and small articles from her audience, and enjoyed sitting on the laps of gentleman sitters whom she kissed and teased by pulling their whiskers. Most reports agreed that she was about three feet tall and if this was indeed Miss Wood on her knees, in whatever state of consciousness, then it was undoubtedly skilfully done.

At times the effect of all this activity on the medium was so powerful that she would be discovered after the seance in a state of serious depletion, and sometimes in a state bordering on derangement. At times like these she would be walked constantly around a room or garden until she became calmer and would then be given hot tea and something to eat. Miss Showers, a private medium who produced manifestations for select audiences, gave life to a spirit form called 'Lenore' who had a profound effect on medium and sitters alike. Observers found the spirit unnerving and unpleasant because she brought with her the smell of the charnel-house, similar to that of a corpse that had been buried for a few weeks and then dug up again. But she also severely exhausted her young medium who had all the appearances of having lost a great deal of weight so that her dress hung loosely on her body, whilst the overall impression she gave was that of a 'mummy of a girl of four or six years of age'.[18] Other materialization mediums were recorded as having lost weight after a seance and Spiritualists believed that some of the energy expended by them could never be wholly replaced. So intense was the actual process thought to be that Spiritualists warned against physical contact with the spirit unless specifically invited in case it mortally injured the medium responsible for its production. The mysterious link that bound medium and spirit might easily be snapped if there was any kind of sudden disturbance, and this could put the life of the medium in danger. When Miss Showers was discovered during a private seance standing on a chair wearing a ghostly head-dress and operating 'spirit hands', a general commotion broke out during which attempts were made to seize and expose her. At this point some of those present shouted that the medium would be killed if the spirit was manhandled despite the fact that it was apparently Miss Showers who stood on the chair before them. Calm was restored by one gentleman leading the sitters in communal song, albeit of a popular type, and Miss Showers was brought round whilst her supporters declared it to be a case of 'unconscious somnambulism'.

Whatever the explanation for the materializations they were produced by an extraordinary feat of skilled activity on the medium's part and she instigated a kind of activity that would have hardly been thought proper in any other setting. What emerged in the guise of masculine spirits complete with full set of whiskers and risqué repartee, or sensual beauties who enjoyed the caresses of their male admirers, might well have been figurative representations of unconscious ideas, conflicts or wishes within the medium herself. But what is ultimately relevant is that such symbolic behaviour, if such it was, could be enacted within the safety of a circle of believers who were ideologically prepared to accept the persona at face value. A spirit was not a medium and the behaviour of one was not interpreted as the actions of the other. When a spirit got seriously out of hand the sitters would hasten to restore harmony through singing or prayer, and the lights would be raised, but in the end the unacceptable was made acceptable because the medium was not held to be responsible. The trance medium, this ultimate exponent of the art of passivity, was able to engage in unorthodox activity because she knew that ultimately it would be condoned. She was safe in the knowledge that she was not herself.

In contrast to much trance behaviour the notion of the

'womanly woman' was associated with a modesty of demeanour and limitation of expression which both contained and controlled her access to speech. A dutiful woman was one who remembered Mrs Ellis's advice to the unhappily married to 'suffer and be still'.[19] During the seance, though, it was a woman who became the centre and instigator of all activity, and the communicator and interpreter of speech. Utterance was central to the business of mediumship. However, as Freud noted during the 1880s when he was working with Charcot, writing could also operate vicariously in the place of speech, and hysterical patients were able to write 'more fluently, quicker, and better than others did or than they themselves had done previously'.[20]

Passive writing was a practice much beloved by Spiritualists, mediums and non-mediums alike. The technique was simple and involved the writer in adopting a meditative frame of mind whilst holding a pen above a blank sheet of paper. If the conditions were harmonious, and the writer sufficiently 'passive', a spirit would then communicate by causing the writer's hand to move across the paper. Once again, women Spiritualists were particularly adept at this and Florence Theobald recalled how she was granted the gift of passive writing after a long period of trial and error:

> God fulfilled his promise. . . . Hundreds of pages of deep
> wisdom and of marvellous beauty were poured through my
> hands . . . and so rapidly was page after page written, that what
> was given in ten minutes by the spirit-writing, would take me
> an hour or more to copy.[21]

Florence had discovered that her pen almost flew across the page as she wrote, and her anxieties about the source of the communication were assuaged by the realization that she wrote in a kind of trance state, the sentences seeming to be formed without her conscious volition. Her spirit guide, communicating with her through the writing, also assured her that if she accepted 'prayerfully and passively' whatever came that her mind would not interfere with the process.[22]

Professional mediums also often began as gifted passive writers who were able to contact dead relatives of their sitters or lofty spirits who sought to explain the secrets of the universe. Adepts quickly learned to distinguish between different spirits' scripts and could tell immediately if a new spirit was in possession of the pen. Madame d'Esperance began her career as a valued passive writer:

> Sometimes my hand would write quickly and steadily for two
> hours at a stretch, while I kept watch on the paper as it was

gradually covered with the small close character of Stafford, or
the large bold writing of Walter, and supplying with my left
hand fresh sheets as required. . . . My arm and shoulder at such
times would ache till I felt sick with the discomfort and almost
faint with pain, but I was beginning to value these
communications too much not to bear these trifles patiently,
even gladly.[23]

However, passive writers were also aware that at times the
recorded messages seemed far from God-sent, and when the script
began to grow large and unwieldly it was taken as a sign that an
undesirable spirit was in control and the work was hastily
stopped. They knew from experience that if they did not stop
something shocking might emerge, although the exact nature of
such unfortunate missives was not enlarged upon by the writers
themselves.

Giving voice to the unutterable was a feature of this type of
Spiritualist activity, although there were attempted safeguards,
and observers were not slow to point out the unsavoury character
of some of the writing. They warned of the possibility of evil
spirits gaining control of the writer's mind through her constant
cultivation of 'mind passivity', a condition which might easily
erode her will. One member of the Society for Psychical Research
spoke of the moral dangers 'necessarily attending such a condition
of helplessness and of loss of self-control',[24] and it was
acknowledged that passive writing could take on an overtly sexual
nature. Sometimes, though, the communications expressed ideas
or fantasies which would probably not have been seen as sexual
by their writers or readers, but which we might interpret as such.
One unhappily married Spiritualist woman, Louisa Lowe, engaged
in lengthy dialogues with her spirit-guide during the height of her
marital troubles and sought from him an explanation for the
behaviour of her husband whom she suspected of infidelity:

SPIRIT: My poor weary child, the spirits have not all lied, thy
husband was on the roof in and out of the chimney half the
night.

LOUISA: Father, though saidst Satan helped him to slip in and
out like an eel. Who my friend and comforter, doubles him
like an opera hat; but how can a great six-feet man get in and
out a chimney like this?

SPIRIT: My child, no one doubled him up; he unbuilt the upper
part of the chimney, and built it up again.

LOUISA: Holy Father, I did hear, as Thou knowest, queer noises
in the chimney all night, but he is no mason; how did he

manage to build it up again, and where did he get his mortar?
SPIRIT: My child, he had no mortar. The chimney will be
rebuilt properly tomorrow, by Withingstone's order.[25]

This kind of writing, later used against Louisa as evidence of her insanity, used what we might take to be explicitly sexual imagery and was tied up with her conviction of her husband's illicit 'night rides'. However, the slippery eel, expandable opera hat, chimney, and night noises meant little to the medical practitioners of the 1870s. They were far more concerned with a written dialogue with a communicant who seemed to be uncomfortably close to God in Louisa's mind, and with her expressed intention to divorce her husband. After all, her accusations were levelled at a man of the cloth who presented as a spotless member of the community, whatever the nature of his behaviour in his own home. But for Louisa the writing expressed her most intimate concerns and reinforced her worst suspicions, and her spirit-guides were eventually to support her in her endeavour to leave home.

The search for independence and autonomy was also a recurrent theme in Louisa's writing, and other aspiring mediums found that their spirit communications gave them a new sense of validity and purpose. Louisa, the wife of a servant of the Church of England, now refuted much of the Church's orthodox teaching and preferred her new-found wisdom. She accepted, after lengthy theological debates with the spirits, that Christ had not been divine (an unusual stance for one of her class), that Satan was a principle rather than an entity, and the doctrines of karma and reincarnation as more meaningful than the Christian notion of heaven. Freedom of thought and belief were considered by her to be the greatest gift bestowed upon her by the spirits, and she continually acknowledged this debt to spirit communication. These intimate and swiftly-penned dialogues with the unseen could prove devastatingly subversive in content, questioning the right of man's authority over woman and courting resistance to the established order. But more than that they facilitated the expression of the inexpressible, and constituted a space within which silence could be broken. The trance speaker on the platform, the medium leading a seance, the passive writer in her sitting room – each were given access to speech, either directly or vicariously.

The idea of substitute activity in relation to the practice of Spiritualism is perhaps most interesting and evident in the area of sexuality. Amongst the middle and upper classes stiff and formalized relations between the sexes effectively tabooed any real intimacy beyond that allowable by marriage. Even in the married state female sexuality was safely de-eroticized by its close identification with the maternal role, and this view of the 'wife as mother' was reinforced by the medical profession. A common view was that the 'woman who disdains motherhood out of self-regarding interests, and the wife who, cultivating barrenness, is satisfied to be the mistress of her husband, frustrate their natural function and full being'.[26] Feminine sexuality was only acceptable when it was aligned with the ties of marriage, motherhood, and this was an excellent device for maintaining respectable limits to erotic pleasure.

Sexual norms were thus strictly controlled and maintained but Spiritualists, operating within the context of their own ritualized practice, were able to flout convention in a variety of ways. The seance circle was itself built upon a conception of male/female harmony which allowed for a fair degree of physical intimacy, the sexes sitting alternately and linking arms or holding hands as a matter of course. This physical contact was important to the maintenance of power within the circle, and was also used as a device to limit the chances of fraudulent acivity. The spirits, too, favoured the stimulus of touch and their presence was often heralded by gentle breezes which caressed the hands and faces of the sitters. There were occasions when sitters were manhandled by ugly spirits and were struck about the head or body, whilst it was not unknown for articles of clothing to be removed or damaged. Because so much of spirit activity took place within a darkened room the senses were especially alert to the stimuli of touch and sound and, unless it was a materialization seance, participants could only judge the phenomena by what they could feel or hear. The tinkling of a musical instrument on the far side of the room or the brush of a spirit hand across the cheek took on a greatly heightened significance and importance when it was impossible to see what was happening, and it is not difficult to surmise the part that imagination must have played during these proceedings. Even during materialization seances, when the sitters could see the spirit, touch played its part and one sitter recalled that when the beautiful 'Meggie' appeared at a Barrow-in-Furness seance she stroked his cheek with 'a touch which spoke'.[27]

The 'speaking touch' was also evident during the rituals of spiritual and mesmeric healing when the hands were passed down (or held slightly above) the body of the sufferer. Healer and patient alike were made aware of a tingling sensation as power passed from one to the other and sessions were accompanied by expressions of pleasure and gratitude. Georgiana Houghton, middle-aged and unmarried, clearly found the activity of healing sensually pleasurable and described it as 'if I were a stringed instrument, and as if every fibre in my body were vibrating under a delicate touch'.[28] Although Georgiana was a gentlewoman, and was not ostensibly a healing medium, it was perfectly permissible for her to be stroking the hand of the Reverend John Murray Spear and for him to express his pleasure by telling her that she was putting him 'in tune'. Such pleasurable tactile sensation was acceptable because it was carried out within a Spiritualistic framework of belief and practice, and this element is still present in contemporary healing activity where the 'words, movements and sounds are suggestive of a woman about to reach climax' as the healer initiates this tender exchange.[29]

The motif of touch was transferred to the realm of the spiritual world during materialization seances, and here pleasure associated with looking was also manifested. During the seance the medium was hidden from view behind the curtain and was invariably tied to her chair by a complex web of twine and knots in order to rule out the possibility of fraud. It would often be a male volunteer who completed these arrangements to his own satisfaction, and as the seance progressed the attention of the sitters was fixed upon the notion of the medium, bound and unconscious, behind the curtain. The degree of sexual fantasy involved in this bizarre procedure was never made explicit although some voices were raised in protest against what they took to be a degrading and inhuman treatment of the young women concerned. If a medium was to maintain her credibility, however, she had to agree to these measures otherwise her sitters might suspect her of trickery. It was customary, then, for the medium to enter the confines of the cabinet in her everyday clothing, to be bound to her chair, and to prepare herself for a state of deep trance. The sitters, ranged in front of the curtain, could hear her moans and movements as she became unconscious, and every eye became fixed upon the curtain in the expectation of the spirit's appearance.

After the tension caused by the waiting, and the uncertainty as to which spirit would make its entrance, the atmosphere in the seance room had become electric by the time the curtain finally parted. This moment had a highly theatrical quality and was greeted with some emotion by the assembled company who now gazed upon the materialized form. Because of the miraculous nature of such manifestations a great deal of curiosity was focused on the spirit's body and hints as to shape, structure, and corporeality were gleaned from a careful scrutiny of the spirit's movements. This intense perusal of the body, albeit an unearthly one, was an activity scarcely becoming to a person of breeding in the usual way of things but it was quite normal during this type of seance. The sight of a materialized form was the pinnacle of Spiritualist experience and the looking that was involved on such occasions, particularly when the spirit was a lovely young woman, was a blend of curiosity and pleasure that was heightened by her determination to keep her body hidden. Flowing white robes were an essential prerequisite of a female spirit's wardrobe and it hardly needs a Freud to explain that 'concealment of the body which goes along with civilization keeps sexual curiosity awake. This curiosity seeks to complete the sexual object by revealing its hidden parts.'[30]

Certain privileged and trusted sitters were allowed to feel the spirit's body and 'Katie King', produced by the young medium Florence Cook, was both confident and impudent enough to ask the gentlemen whether or not they squeezed. William Crookes, the scientist who conducted experiments with 'Katie', was publically permitted to touch the whole of her body, a performance which at least one observer found distasteful and improper.[31] Some of the touching was explained on the grounds that it was necessary to ascertain whether or not the form was wearing stays, something that believers felt would not be compatible with spirit existence and which would indicate fraud. Creaking corsets and rumbling stomachs led to the direst suspicion but Spiritualists tried to prevent fraudulent masquerades by having the medium searched prior to the onset of the seance. This disrobing by some of the female sitters became a frequent feature of seance procedure but it was still not enough to stem accusations of a medium stuffing the necessary props down her drawers, and it seemed that these were not removed.

Miss Florence Marryat, an ardent believer, was perhaps the only sitter to claim to see and feel the naked body of a spirit, and this occurred at the final appearance of 'Katie King'. She reported:

> When she summoned me in my turn to say a few words to her behind the curtain I again saw and touched the warm breathing body of Florence Cook lying on the floor, and then stood upright by the side of Katie, who desired me to place my hands inside the loose single garment which she wore and feel her nude body. I did so thoroughly. I felt her heart beating rapidly beneath my hand; and passed my fingers through her long hair to satisfy myself that it grew from her head, and can testify that if ever she be 'of psychic force', psychic force is very like a woman.[32]

Although this was the only recorded encounter with a naked spirit body it was not unusual for spirits to engage in endearing or seductive behaviour. Henry Burton recounted his experience at one of Miss Wood's seances after the little black sprite, 'Pocha', had materialized. He asked if he could kiss her and she agreed:

> so I got upon my knees, and she took my glasses off, and then presented a little black face for me to receive her favour. That the face was black, to me, was beyond a doubt, and that they were palpably sensible warm lips I kissed, I positively know. She afterwards shewed [sic] a plump little black arm and hand, dispensed a few more favours, and retired.[33]

The iconology of the plump, black girl-child dispensing her 'favours' to white Victorian gentlemen is both fascinating and complex. The fantasy element is a heady blend of innocence and exotica, child and lover, sexual provocation and submission. The symbolic use of blacks in European painting has been tellingly illustrated elsewhere, but the pictorial message is one of nubility, bondage, submission, service . . . slavery.[34]

The incidence of radiant young female spirits who apparently also unstintingly distributed their favours was high, and it is notable that even those Spiritualists who denounced any hint of debased behaviour in mediums could accept a pronounced degree of eroticism in spirits. James Burns, the editor of a leading Spiritualist newspaper and severe critic of immorality in any form, gave the following report of one of his visits to a Newcastle seance:

> The gentleman to my right asked her ['Minnie'] to favour him with a kiss. She did so, seemingly desirous of adding to the pleasure and spiritual convictions of all. She then stood opposite to me in a hesitating manner . . . advanced a little, stooped down slightly, our lips met firmly, a fervent kiss was recorded on the surrounding atmosphere. I was distinctly conscious of two impressions: the peculiar thrill of affection which passed through me, and the physical conformation of 'Minnie's' lips.[35]

The theme of seduction ran through many of the contemporary seance reports but was never explicitly recognized as such. It was a matter of seeing and experiencing the phenomena within the context of Spiritualist beliefs and however beautiful the spirit's body might be it was still considered to be 'of psychic force'. This put the spirit, and spirit–sitter interaction, safely beyond the realm of flesh and blood sexuality without actually diminishing the pleasure of any exchange. It is interesting that spirit behaviour fell firmly within the domain of accepted gender roles, male spirits making up to the women and flaunting their masculinity whilst female spirits turned their attention to the men. But beneath this ostensible behaviour, of course, lay the fact that it was women mediums who were responsible for the 'production' of male spirits and who were in some degree initiating the pugilistic attacks on men and the sexual attention towards the women.

It seems almost certain that there were undercurrents of sexual intrigue within Spiritualist circles which had nothing to do with the behaviour of spirits, although Florence Cook's husband either boasted or complained that 'Katie' used to materialize at night in order to accompany Florence to bed, and that he was often not sure which of the two was his wife.[36] Florence herself was not above suspicion and years later allegations were made to the effect that she had admitted to an affair with William Crookes prior to her marriage, the implication being that the scientist's steadfast avowal of her was the result of his infatuation either with her or with 'Katie'. Certainly Crookes himself was aware that he was 'getting the reputation of a Don Juan', and that scandalous rumours about him were being spread during 1875. As the source of these seemed to be the mother of Mary Rosina Showers, the materialization medium and friend of Florence, it is possible that Crookes was guilty of more than one dalliance.[37] The sexual underworld of Spiritualist circles was hinted at from a variety of quarters, and a letter received by the medium D.D. Home in 1876 stated that the well-known Mrs Guppy used her seances solely for facilitating illicit assignations and to allow certain undesirable persons to 'further carry out their lewd propensities'.[38]

Whatever the morality of Florence Cook and other young mediums, the medical profession was in no doubt as to the innate immorality of the Spiritualistic trance. Medical psychologists equated ecstatic and abandoned possession with morbid and degenerative pathology, a perverse moral sense, and delinquent sexuality. Indeed, such spiritual states were seen as little more than vicarious orgasm:

> Every experienced physician must have met with instances of single and childless women who have devoted themselves with extraordinary zeal to habitual religious exercises, and who, having gone insane as a culmination of their emotional fervour, have straightway exhibited the saddest mixture of religious and erotic symptoms – a boiling over of lust in voice, face, gestures, under the pitiful degradation of disease.[39]

Doctors like Henry Maudsley maintained a clear connection

between religious transport and sexual expression but, and this was the fatal point, they interpreted it as evidence of illness – usually insanity. These associations with states that were common to trance mediums ensured the pejorative treatment of women Spiritualists by male physicians, just as they raised the old question of hysteria and rampant erotic desire.

Spiritualists, whilst fully accepting that seances could go badly wrong and the medium become uncontrollable, did not equate this with sickness. They accepted that sometimes they had to 'contend with what we called evil controls, when the most stubborn aspect of human nature was exhibited, combined with low, reckless manners', but invariably produced a spirit-based explanation or excused the medium on the grounds of exhaustion.[40] Unregulated or erotic behaviour, usually referred to as 'unsuitable' or 'low', was not welcomed but neither was the medium blamed or chastised for its appearance. There was no question of degeneracy or erosion of the moral sense, and a degree of accepted (if unspoken) sexuality remained a constituent element of Spiritualist practice. Sexuality was tacitly on the agenda and women mediums who were 'entered', 'seized', 'possessed' and 'ravaged' by spirits remained the focus for it. If behind the acceptable face of Spiritualist ritual there lay another dimension of sexual intrigue and involvement, this would undoubtedly not have been acceptable to the majority of believers, and it remained a matter of rumour and innuendo. What is sure is that a definition of female sexuality purely in terms of the maternal function was undermined by the behaviour of women mediums, and that Spiritualist practice allowed for an unusual degree of legitimate intimacy between the sexes.

What I have tried to suggest here is that Spiritualism permitted an element of freedom of language and behaviour, particularly for women, which would have been difficult to achieve outside the circle of believers, and which elsewhere might have been construed as evidence of mental disorder. Accounts left by both mediums and sitters indicate that many Spiritualistic phenomena were produced whilst the medium was in a deep trance state, or in a condition not related to normal consciousness, and I am proposing that what emerged on such occasions was a formulation of unconscious desires and impulses. Even the high degree of fraudulence does not alter the fact that seance conditions permitted the reproduction of a type of activity which would have been impermissible elsewhere, and that mediums were at liberty to express themselves in any way they chose. Within the safety of the Spiritualist circle women also acquired an awareness of themselves as powerful individuals which surmounted notions of Victorian gentility and frailty. They were able to subvert, transpose, and re-situate normative femininity which was based on an assumption of immutable sex difference, and which relied upon the constructs of illness, passivity, silence and functional sexuality. But they often did so without an overt, or perhaps even conscious, awareness that this constituted a deep-seated challenge to the patriarchal order. Some Spiritualists were feminists by design, but I would suggest that others were speaking and acting an unconscious resistance to an order which sought to define and control women in an effort to subdue them. The Spiritualist medium attained power because of qualities which were associated with her femininity, but such power allowed her to move beyond the confines of prescriptive behaviour and into forbidden territory.

Notes

1   Mary Howitt to her husband, cited by Hester Burton, *Barbara Bodichon, 1827–1891*, London 1949, p.44.

2   For a discussion of nineteenth-century working-class Spiritualism see Logie Barrow, 'Socialism in Eternity: The Ideology of Plebeian Spiritualists, 1853–1913', *History Workshop Journal*, 9, Spring 1980, pp.37–69. The mesmeric tradition had already paved the way for a rationalist explanation of the spirit's survival, and this was based upon the notion of a mysterious force which emanated from the body but which could survive death.

3   I am grateful for this point to an unpublished BA thesis by Robert Kent Donovan, 'The Ultraviolet World: Spiritualism in Great Britain, 1852–1898', 1954, held in the Harvard University archives.

4   See Catherine Hall, 'The Early Formation of Victorian Domestic Ideology', *Fit Work for Women*, London 1979, pp.15–32.

5   These ideas have cross-cultural parallels. See, for example, I.M. Lewis, *Ecstatic Religion: An Anthropological Study of Spirit Possession and Shamanism*, London 1978, p.86.

6   See Barbara Taylor, 'The Woman-Power: Religious Heresy and Feminism in Early English Socialism', *Tearing the Veil: Essays on Femininity*, Susan Lipshitz (ed.), London 1978, for elaboration of these points. John F.C. Harrison, *The Second Coming: Popular Millenarianism 1780–1850*, London 1979, p.31ff., has a discussion of the role of women within millenarian movements.

7   The findings of social anthropologists tend to confirm that this is

often the case and that it is as though a kind of double consciousness exists which allows the medium to both commit fraudulent acts, and to believe in them. See Claude Lévi-Strauss, *Structural Anthropology*, vol. 1, 1958, London 1968, pp.172–82.

8 Lewis, *op. cit.*, p.29.

9 I am using the term 'unconscious' in its widest application to include and 'connote all those contents not present in the field of consciousness at a given moment', J. Laplanche and J.-B. Pontalis, The Language of Psycho-Analysis, London 1980, p.474. I intend to avoid a lengthy discussion of the variety of psychological explanations of the mechanics of the trance state: dissociated personality, hysterical dissociation, secondary or multiple personalities, etc. Interesting though these are, they are not strictly relevant to the point I am making here.

10 This is behaviour which represents an unconscious process, for example, a slip of the tongue or a particular compulsion. The concern with symptomatic acts as symptoms is one of the problems with psychoanalytic theory. Its formulation on a medical model means that any behaviour which deviates from a cultural norm can be interpreted as a symptom of illness and as a suitable case for professional medical intervention.

11 James MacGrigor Allan, addressing the Anthropology Society of London 1869. See *Anthropological Review*, 1869, cxcviii-cxcix. Cited by Elaine and English Showalter, 'Victorian Women and Menstruation', *Suffer and Be Still: Women in the Victorian Age*, M. Vicinus (ed.), London 1980, p.40.

12 Cited by James Burns, *Medium and Daybreak*, 30 November 1877, p.753.

13 F.J.T., *Homes and Work in the Future Life*, Part 2, London 1885, p.48.

14 Florence Marryat, *There is no Death*, London 1891, p.220.

15 *Medium and Daybreak*, 17 August 1877, p.522.

16 *Ibid.*

17 *Ibid.*, 5 October 1877, pp.626–7.

18 Marryat, *op. cit.*, p.150.

19 Mrs Ellis, *The Daughters of England*, London 1845, p.73. Cited by Vicinus (ed.), *op. cit.*, p.x.

20 Sigmund Freud, 'Fragment of an Analysis of a Case of Hysteria ("Dora")', *The Pelican Freud Library*, vol. 8, London 1980, pp.72–2.

21 F.J.T., *Heaven Opened; or Messages for the Bereaved from Our Little Ones in Glory*, London 1870, pp.3–4.

22 F.J.T., *op. cit.*, p.49.

23 E. d'Esperance, *Shadow Land, or Light From The Other Side*, London 1897, p.145.

24 J. Godfrey Raupert, *Modern Spiritism: A Critical Examination of Its Phenomena, Character, and Teaching, in the Light of the Known Facts*,

London 2nd ed., 1909, p.77.

25 Evidence given before the 1877 Select Committee on the Operation of the Lunacy Law, question 7279. In order to make the nature of the dialogue clearer I have not presented it in its origiñl prose form.

26 Henry Maudsley, *Organic to Human, Psychological and Sociological*, London 1916, pp.28–9. This was particularly revealing coming, as it did, from a man whose marriage had been childless.

27 *Medium and Daybreak*, 6 July 1877, p.420.

28 Georgiana Houghton, *Evenings at Home in Spiritual Seance*, London 1881, pp. 77–9.

29 Vieda Skultans, 'A Study of Women's Ideas Relating to Traditional Feminine Roles, Spiritualism and Reproductive Fuctions', DPhil thesis, University of Swansea, 1971, pp. 75–6.

30 Sigmund Freud, 'Three Essays on the Theory of Sexuality', (1905), *Pelican Freud Library*, vol. 7, London 1981, p.69.

31 Rev. Charles Maurice Davies, *Mystic London: or, Phases of Occult Life in the Metropolis*, London 1875, pp.317–19. The observer on this occasion felt that Professor Crookes' espousal of Florence Cook was 'with prejudice scarcely becoming an F.R.S.'.

32 *The Spiritualist*, 29 May 1874, p.259.

33 *Light*, 6 August 1881, p.243.

34 See John Berger, *Ways of Seeing*, New York 1972, pp.114–7.

35 *Medium and Daybreak*, 7 June 1878, p.362.

36 Marryat, *op. cit.*, p.193.

37 The allegations regarding Florence Cook and Crookes were revealed by Trevor H. Hall, *The Spiritualists. The Story of Florence Cook and William Crookes*, New York 1962, but were first made by Francis Anderson in 1922. He claimed to have had an affair with Florence Cook in the early 1890s, during which she apparently admitted to the earlier affair with Crookes. *The Spiritualists* caused a considerable stir at the time of its publication because it slighted one of the foremost Victorian mediums and an eminent scientist and psychical researcher. There have been several subsequent contributions to the discussion and perhaps the most comprehensive is that by Mr R.G. Medhurst and Mrs K.M. Goldney, *Proceedings of the Society for Physical Research*, vol. LIV, March 1964. Dr E.J. Dingwall revealed the controversy, drawing on the work of Medhurst and Goldney, in a privately printed work, *The Critics' Dilemma*, E.J. Dingwall, The Stanley Press Ltd., 1966.

38 Medhurst and Goldney, *op. cit.*, p.59. Cited by E.J. Dingwall, *op. cit.*, p.144.

39 Henry Maudsley, *The Pathology of Mind*, London 1879, p.144.

40 *Medium and Daybreak*, 16 October 1877, pp.674–6.

10

Josephine Butler: Christianity, feminism and social action

ALISON MILBANK

To write about Josephine Butler at present is to enter a minefield. Her rediscovery by feminists has put her at the centre of debates about male and female sexuality, and the feminist stance on prostitution. Attitudes to her tend to be of three kinds. First feminist writers such as Judith Walkowitz[1] and Rosalind Delmar[2] praise her for her feminist opposition to the Contagious Diseases Acts while blaming her for helping to create a climate of sexual puritanism. The religious element in her thinking is regarded, even by Jenny Uglow[3] who views Butler with some sympathy, as totally unacceptable. Second, almost single-handed, the redoubtable Joseph Williamson,[4] an East London priest who himself worked with prostitutes, has campaigned for the recognition of Butler as a Saint and she is now remembered in the Anglican Calendar on 30 December. Despite his rather Victorian style, Williamson's presentation of Butler is quite fair, although he underplays the radicalism of her feminist ideas.

A third evaluation of her is that of the writers of several modern male secular studies of nineteenth-century prostitution like Michael Pearson,[5] who regards Butler as an histrionic exhibitionist, her chief value to her cause being her undoubted sexual attraction.

All three groups of writers show some unease in placing Butler: She does not fit neatly into any categories. This article aims to show the actual coherence of her ideas by looking at the religious categories in which she worked, and it is hoped that by addressing the usual feminist criticisms of Butler also to shed some light on the methodology of her detractors.

Foucault has pointed out how the Victorians, far from hiding sex, delighted in codifying it and detailing it as clearly as possible. Walkowitz rightly sees the Contagious Diseases Acts, in which VD among the armed forces was to be eliminated by the forcible examination and treatment of those considered prostitutes in military or naval areas, as one more extension of this principle. It was legislation regarded by many as logical and progressive, supported by doctors and clerics. Organized opposition to the Acts was of three main kinds. There were male radicals in London who opposed the loss of civil rights involved, provincial nonconformist liberals, already disturbed by the large amount of prostitution and by the immorality of the aristocracy, particularly the Prince of Wales's set, who deplored the implied state regulation of prostitution, and lastly middle- and upper-class feminists, particularly of Quaker origin. Butler of course belonged to the third group,[6] which formed its own organization and campaigned on moral, constitutional and feminist grounds. Butler was President and influential speaker, activist and thinker. From her letters to other women supporters and their own writings, it seems that this Christian Feminist critique of the Acts was common to a group. Butler in her writing was addressing a real audience. Her theological ideas often chime in too with those of F.D. Maurice, who was well known to her, and sometimes her social ideas are similar to those of certain Owenite socialists. This latter similarity may be accidental but it is worth noting that Maurice took many of his notions of socialism from the Owenites. Butler's own social origins were in the Northumbrian gentry; her father was a radical agriculturalist and supporter of all sorts of social reforms.

The authority of an outsider

Writers have often referred to Butler's sense of divine mission (something she shared with other feminists such as Anne Clough). What has generally been ignored has been the basis for her vocation: Butler's belief that she received direct visions of God's presence. These experiences are both hinted at and openly acknowledged throughout her writings;[7] she was a mystic. The significance of her experience is two-fold; it gave her unassailable authority, cutting across the hierarchy of male structures of authority, and it also kept her outside those structures. All her life Butler, a worshipping Anglican and wife of a cleric, held loosely to denominational divides, regarding inter-church disputes with some detachment.

Despite her direct religious experience and her lack of desire to participate in the church power structures, Butler needed some means of reassurance of the validity of her ideas. She found this on a personal level in the absolute support of her husband, who lost chances of preferment because of his wife's activities, but on an intellectual level she appealed to models in the Christian tradition, to Christ himself and to Catherine of Siena, the medieval mystic and reformer.

Gladstone noted, perhaps quizzically, in his preface to Butler's biography of Catherine,[8] how close were the 'veins of sympathy' between author and subject. Catherine was for Butler justification and model, inspiration and reassurance. Like Butler a feminist pioneer, she too cut sideways into the public life of her time, gaining personal authority over the Pope himself and as an outsider she approached the problems of the time on her own terms. Butler too, despite her concern for women's economic independence, the suffrage and equal educational opportunities, gloried in her outsider status, almost in the manner of Virginia Woolf in *Three Guineas*.

Another model that Butler found meaningful is that of the prophet. A role justified for women in scripture, involving personal rather than institutional authority, it links the private and the social spheres, without the need to accept the terms of the latter. Indeed prophecy is the expression of mysticism in practice, which precludes compromise, referring always to its own inner validation.

Butler's constant references to scripture in even the most official report were a means of emphasizing her authority, although she was no biblical fundamentalist. Her approach was hermeneutical as she tested her ideas against the text and allowed the text to mediate reality to her. She treated the Bible very much as an open text and so the interpretative process was her norm, providing her with a flexibility of response in the face of different situations and audiences. Her rhetoric had itself evolved in a hermeneutic activity.

Scripture also provided her with an interpretative tool for analysing society. She brought to this analysis a liberal upbringing, a strong sense of evil and a firm belief in the value and potential of each individual. It is interesting that the analysis she found in scripture was collective, although allowing for the personal contribution of individual human beings. This analytical tool was apocalyptic: not the simple millenarian belief that God will end time and humanity can do nothing, but a radical critique of secular values in which the whole of life, social and personal, is under judgment and in which human beings have a role in working towards hastening the coming of the kingdom. For the Christian or humanist such a model allows for the evil in humanity while still preserving an optimistic picture. For the nineteenth-century liberal it provides a way of extending morality into the social and political spheres. These considerations were no doubt important in the evolution of eschatological ideas among many socialists of the period, for example certain Owenites, many of whom were Christian in background.[9]

Feminist writers have ignored the importance of Butler's eschatology, although it was her primary tool from the beginning. Indeed it is apocalyptic that provides a framework for judging prostitution, Butler's style becoming ecstatic as she writes of the liberation of all prostitutes that will take place on the last day. In such a model of enslavement and deliverance, prostitutes are objectively victims; it does not matter if they succeed in the trade or not. They are victims in terms of power relations. Butler was well aware, despite Uglow's and Walkowitz's denials, of the varieties of prostitutes' experience, as her letters show, but she concentrates in her rhetoric on the abuse of class power, the poor girl victim/rich seducer model as the clearest picture of the power relationships involved. Prostitution and much modern pornography are still to feminists clear images of the much more subtle structures of power imposed on women by men. So clear was this image to Butler that she used the terminology of sexual power to describe and analyse other political and social questions such as the Boer War and Irish Home Rule.[10]

Like some American contemporaries and certain Owenite women, Butler found in both Old and New Testaments evidence of the equality of the sexes, especially in the teaching and actions of Christ, for each meeting of Christ with a woman was accompanied, she believed, by an act of liberation, releasing the woman from the bonds of tradition, or unpleasant menstrual disease, or from male judgment and violence. Butler also had the model of good male/female relationships with a liberated father, husband, and friends. Allowed to a great extent to be herself, like Octavia Hill and Florence Nightingale she greatly appreciated feminine values and the role of motherhood. Uglow accuses Butler here of 'arguing from an accepted view of women as guardians of domestic virtue to the extension of this "special influence" which would come if women were involved in public life'.[11] Butler rigorously refuted this view of women by men[12] as a device by which men were freed of any moral responsibility but she believed that women, because of their continued oppression had preserved values lost to their oppressors. However, unlike Hill and Nightingale Butler believed that if feminine values were good, then they should be applied to men as well, who could be mothers in role if not in biology.

Motherhood in Butler is viewed by feminist writers as a political device, but her writings and life show that this is wishful thinking, although Butler would naturally appeal to an audience of mothers through their children – as she also appealed to one of fathers! For Butler, as for her two contemporaries mentioned above, the family was the model for society in reaction to the misguided application of Lady Bountiful philanthropy and to the evils of manipulative Utilitarianism. Unlike Hill and Nightingale, Butler puts great stress on the need for family life to be 'redeemed', from its selfishness, exclusivity and lack of equality between the sexes. Butler hates any kind of coercion and sees the redeemed family as a space for freedom, mutual sympathy and mutual dependence. Vitorian society claimed the family as the preferred model for personal relationships: why then should its principles be relegated to that sphere alone? As with motherhood, Butler takes a Victorian convention and pushes it to its logical conclusion, thus revealing its ideological basis.

Butler is often criticized for her romantic view of prostitutes as Magdalenes. She certainly did regard them, at least potentially, in this way, but not on the usual Magdalene/Madonna axis. If the Madonna figure is used by Butler, it is either as an example of a male device to clothe their contempt of women by presenting her as a vapid, insipid Madonna or else Butler shows Mary as a sister to Mary Magdalene in proclaiming liberation. The Magdalene image with which Butler works is either an example of suffering womanhood oppressed by men or the Magdalene who witnesses the resurrection appearance of Christ. In this latter role the Magdalene, human values reversed, is evangelist of the gospel of liberation and bearer of spiritual insight.

Despite this weighty role that the prostitute carries for her, Butler did not idealize individual prostitutes. She recognized that although it need not be wrong to becme a prostitute, in that the women concerned had no effective choice, yet being a prostitute was not conducive to one's liberation. The prostitute too, must have some moral responsibility for her actions or else she ceased to be a person at all. It was the hardening effect of a life of prostitution that was wrong, the sin of prostitution was that of the men who ordered the system. Butler treated prostitutes she met with love and courtesy, following the teaching of Christ. Her refuges were comfortable, flower-filled homes, not reformatories. Recognizing the economic basis of prostitution, Butler saw no need for penance on the part of her guests.

Butler's treatment of prostitutes as equals is challenged by feminists who allude to her use of mother imagery to describe her relationship to young prostitutes. They see this as implying a hierarchical relationship.[13] However, 'mother' imagery in Butler is far less common that 'sister'. 'Mother' imagery relates to her grief for her dead daughter Eva, whom she found again in finding and rescuing girl prostitutes. 'Sister' imagery was basic to her strategy both in Christian terms and in her belief that women are *solidaire*; and while some women are prostitutes all women are in bonds.

This accusation against Butler for accepting a hierarchical relationship between older and young women surfaces in discussion about the raising of the age of consent in 1885. Butler supported the new legislation as a protection against male harassment and a prevention of child prostitution. Walkowitz[14] is critical of her stance, seeing in the new rights of a mother as well as a father to 'control sexual access' to their daughter, a validation of a 'hierarchical custodial relationship' between mother and daughter. Unless one takes an extremely liberal view about childhood exercise of sexuality (which would be both anachronistic and also inadequate as dependent children can be so easily exploited, not having grown into the possible exercise of freedom as adults have) it is difficult to see how, in the context of the time, the legislation could have been regarded as sinister. First it recognized the parental role of the mother (a great advance!), second it extended the age at which young people were thought to need protection, and third it encouraged the idea that children were not just appendages of their parents, to be disposed of as they saw fit, but individuals with rights of their own. The evidence for child prostitution at the time is very confusing and one cannot pretend to any certain knowledge. However, just taking into account the sexual pathology of the Victorian male, his use of the child/woman as erotic focus in art and literature and in many a work of contemporary pornography,[15] it seems likely that there was a ready market for child prostitution. Also, in evaluating the amount of 'repression' involved in the 1885 legislation one needs to take into account the physical development of working-class girls of the period, which owing to a poor diet was often late.

An objective view of prostitution

As was mentioned above, Butler's critique of prostitution was economic. She saw it as a totally male-created entity, justified by the equally socially constructed double standard. Men denied women independent employment, then divided them into a double workforce, one part to minister to their domestic comfort, the other to their 'need' for lust without responsibility. Butler sees both sets of women as slaves, their interests set against each other. She found her tools for such an analysis in the Old Testament prophets, quotations for whom are so prevalent in her writings that it is often difficult to distinguish the radical nature of her opinions. The prophets gave her objective categories of power, of the social dimension of sin, of the relationship of power and control of production. They see God's message to the oppressed as one of liberation from unjust structures. Also within the prophetic writings there is a critique of idolatry which Butler applies to patriarchy.

It is interesting that Uglow finds Butler inconsistent in her analysis of women's subordination precisely because Butler believes it to be both a function of patriarchy and also the function of a materialist society that defines all relationships in economic terms.[16] The value of Butler's ideas rests precisely in her ability to combine the economic and patriarchal elements in her analysis. Through her appropriation of the Hebrew prophets she came closest to anything resembling a Marxist analysis. That is also why the poor girl/rich seducer model was so important to her rhetoric as it is objectively true. To Walkowitz and others the existence of a large working-class clientele negates both the objectivity of this view and the oppressive nature of the system. However, the combination of ale-house as employment exchange and pay office (in large coins, that had to be changed by buying drinks) and pick-up place for prostitutes was solely of value to the brewer and the employer. When one adds to the situation a prematurely aged wife/lover working at home, too worried about the economic consequences of another child to have frequent intercourse, one has a complex picure of oppression. Another argument used to attack Butler's analysis is the fact of the comfortably-off mistress or even the well-married courtesan. That these received some advantages from the system is undeniable but their attraction for men was very much the total power that could be exercised over them. They had literally been bought, bringing no money or birth to equalize the relationship. Similarly female servants were sexually attractive not just because of their close proximity to young men of the house but also because of their inferior status and economic dependency. To empathize with the subject of one's concern, as do feminist historians of prostitution, should entail seeing them in their social and economic context. This Butler did, being well aware of the working-class use of prostitutes and understanding the exploitation by big business involved (this was very much the motivation behind her alignment with the temperance movement). She described the objective economic situation with its class as well as its gender elements, and also admitted her own class guilt in contributing to the system.

Despite her positive and objective approach to the subject of prostitution, Butler, was continually haunted by the evils and injustices of the world, which made Christian faith hard for her. This seems to have been separate from her belief in the redemption of every soul and she had a difficult balance to keep. The resolution of these ideas in her liberation theology and use of apocalyptic are obvious, and the two approaches encouraged her to separate sin and sinner. (She was much relieved to discover, late in life, that it was at last thought possible for orthodox Christians to deny the doctrine of eternal punishment.) She was correspondingly pessimistic in her approach to social structures, which she saw as often evil and manipulative. For this reason, despite her friendship with individual socialists, she was critical of the socialist philosophy as she understood it to entail a coercive, centralized state. In 1895, however, she read the *Christian Socialist* magazine with pleasure finding its ideas to agree with her own.[17] She also made use of Chartist rhetoric in her addresses to working men, invoking Magna Carta and Wat Tyler. Her defence of the home as a model for society was based on its non-coercive nature. As mentioned above, she criticized the family as the Owenites did for its selfishness, hoping to see in her 'redeemed' families an acceptance into them of sick or needy people and others who are not blood relations. The only authority in a family, she believed, was love just as that was the only authority of 'the divine energy of maternal love' of the Mother/Father God.[18] When she wrote of the home influence being extended into society, she did not work out the power relations but was mounting an attack on the depersonalizing of human beings in institutions like the work-house. This was a limitation. Butler's feminist and independent religious outlook made her suspicious of the increasing codification and extension of power structures in society and led her to look for new models of power. Although she formulated an effective critique of present power relations and found some criteria, such as non-coercion, to use in finding something to replace the present system, she never took her ideas further. Like other feminists of her time, she expected huge changes when women received the vote.

Butler and current debates

In identifying the religious categories that motivated Butler, this article has attempted to explicate her social and feminist activities and draw attention to the coherence of her independent ideology. This has entailed some criticism of feminist historians who have done important work in helping us to see nineteenth-century prostitutes in their own terms. It is hoped that the criticisms made of their responses have something to say about feminist scholarship generally. It is exciting and a valuable exercise for women to reclaim and celebrate their foremothers and for them to understand past groups of women's experience of oppression. To understand, however, involves analysis as well as empathy and to comprehend a 'deviant' group like prostitutes involves more than trying to prove the inherent rationality of their actions. One needs to see their experience of oppression by analysing their function, economic and social, in the society of their time.[19] This article has argued that Butler did just this in her activism and writings. 'From Sympathy to Theory' is the title of Uglow's article about Butler. As modern feminists we need to make that connection too.

This article has not attempted to enter the 'social purity' debate in which Butler is often presented as someone who, despite her own wishes but because of her rhetoric, helped to create a climate of sexual repression. This development is then used to warn feminists today of the dangers in taking critical stances on pornography, etc. The reason for the silence in this article has been that the more one studies these purity movements, the more complex the picture becomes. Today feminists are on the horns of a dilemma, unsure whether to support the implied puritanism of the Angry Women in attacking sex shops or to accept the criteria of *laissez faire* liberalism. If we have anything to learn from Butler it is that as feminists we must apply our own coherent and prophetic analysis that will cut across the poles of the debate. Butler was opposed to the state's manipulation of sexual behaviour but was also aware that sexuality is not a totally innocent category but is itself nearly always linked to power and manipulation. There is a sense in which the puritan element is a valid part of her rhetoric. Butler also, beginning to analyse male/female relations, went on to analyse society generally. This is something that feminists today must also attempt and the example of the women's peace camps is important here. We need to deepen and extend the dialogue with socialism and to examine critically our present liberal philosophical assumptions such as the use of a personal rights model. Most of all we need a *critical* engagement with our own feminist history that does not try to read our foremothers as modern-day liberal feminists but is sensitive to their own philosophical and political assumptions. We usually think that the Victorian feminists were necessarily liberal and individualistic in comparison to our own more analytical stances. We need to be aware that sometimes the reverse is true.

Notes

1   J.R. Walkowitz: (a) *Prostitution and Victorian Society*, Cambridge University Press, 1980; (b) 'Male Vice and Feminist Virtue', *History Workshop*, 13, Spring 1982, chapter 4; (c) 'The Making of an Outcast Group', *A Widening Sphere*, ed. M. Vicinus, Indiana University Press, 1977.

2   R. Delmar, 'Liberation 1880s style', *The Guardian*, 16 September 1982.

3   J. Uglow, 'Josephine Butler: From Sympathy to Theory', *Feminist Theorists*, ed. D. Spender, The Women's Press, 1983.

4   J. Williamson: *The Forgotten Saint*, Faith Press, 1977; *In Honour Bound*, J. Williamson, 1971.

5   M. Pearson, *The Age of Consent: Victorian Prostitution and its Enemies*, David & Charles, 1972. See also G. Petrie, *A Singular Iniquity*, Macmillan, 1971, p.63 where Butler is not even considered to be a feminist.

6   Walkowitz, *op. cit.*, has a detailed and helpful analysis of the sociological make-up of the repealers.

7   See letter to B. Jowett 1858 and to Mrs Stead 12 July 1893 in Fawcett Library Collection for open remarks on this subject.

8   J. Butler, *Catherine of Siena: a Biography*, Dyer Bros, 1875.

9   See B. Taylor, *Eve and the New Jerusalem*, Virago, 1983, p.158 for a discussion of eschatology among socialists.

10   J. Butler, *Our Christianity Tested by the Irish Question*, Fisher Unwin, 1887, and *The Native Races and the War*, Gay & Bird, 1900.

11   Uglow, *op. cit.*, p.157.

12   J. Butler, *Sursum Corda*, Annual Address to the Ladies' National Association, 1871, p.35:
> You must make us good and keep us good, you . . . must forgive our impurities and wash them away by your own secret tears . . . and for our reward you shall be called angels, in many a pretty poem and essay; you must minister to us in our dying moments. Smooth our pillow and speak soft in our ear and somehow you must, you *absolutely must* get us into heaven at last. You know how! We leave it to you; but remember you are responsible for this!

13   *Ibid.*, Walkowitz, *op. cit.*, (a), p.117.

14   *Ibid.*

15   Walter, *My Secret Life*, abbreviated version edited by G. Grimley, Panther, 1972, gives details of hundreds of sexual encounters with children and young girls.

16   Uglow, *op. cit.*, p.152.

17   Letter from Butler to G.B. Johnson quoted in N. Boyd, *Josephine*

Butler, Octavia Hill and Florence Nightingale, Macmillan, 1982, p.20.

18   Butler, *The Lady of Shunem*, Marshall, 1894, p.3.

19   G. McLennan, *Marxism and the Methodologies of History*, Verso, 1982, p.119f. has an interesting critique of feminist historical methodology.

Popular piety

11

Paul, religion and society

STEPHEN BARTON

In a recent article entitled 'The Social Identity of the First Christians: A Question of Method in Religious History', E.A. Judge argues against defining early Christianity as a 'religion'. He says:

> Only the establishment of Christendom in the fourth century created the conditions which make the typical modern use of the word historically realistic. It was of course a Roman word before that. But it is hard to see how anyone could seriously have related the phenomenon of Christianity to the practice of religion in its first century sense. From the social point of view, the talkative, passionate and sometimes quarrelsome circles that met to read Paul's letters over their evening meal in private houses, or the pre-dawn conclaves of ethical rigorists that alarmed Pliny, were a disconcerting novelty. Without temple, cult statue or ritual, they lacked the time-honoured and reassuring routine of sacrifice that would have been necessary to link them with religion.[1]

Now, there is always value in reminding historians of the dangers of anachronism and of hidden agendas in their work. It is likely, for example, that the self-conscious counterpointing of the abstract nouns 'religion' and 'society' would have appeared strange to Paul and his contemporaries for whom heaven and earth were intimately and supernaturally related. We must beware, therefore, of reductionist possibilities in our accounts of both religion and society in the time of Paul. But this need not lead us to deny the appropriateness, even the inevitability, of evaluating Paul in modern terms: 'What a text (or other phenomenon) "means" depends at least in some important degree on what the interpreter wants to know.'[2]

Apart from the category question, there is good reason to doubt that, even on his own terms, Judge's description of the activities and ethos of the Pauline and other early Christian groups is adequate. There may have been neither temple nor shrine but was there no sense of sacred space?[3] There may have been no festivals but were there not sacred meals commemorating their founder's death, resurrection and promised return in messianic glory? If they had stopped participating in cultic sacrifice does this mean that the idea of sacrifice was repugnant to them? If they were without ritual how are we to describe their practice of baptizing converts (not to mention baptism of the living on behalf of the dead: 1 Cor. 15:29!) and their incorporation into 'the body of Christ' through the regular eating of his body and drinking of his blood (1 Cor. 11:17–34)? If, as Judge says, they were 'ethical rigorists', what was their motivation if not religious, steeped in the traditions of Jewish monotheism and apocalyptic eschatology? If they were 'talkative . . . and sometimes quarrelsome', what were they talking about if not Scripture and its interpretation in the Messianic Age? If their meetings appeared to outsiders as some kind of convivial debating society, why do Pliny, Tacitus and Suetonius all describe Christianity as a *superstitio* – which is a negative way of categorizing it as a *religio*?

In short, Judge's position is a *tour de force*. He wants to maintain the novelty and distinctiveness of the 'style of life' of Paul and his followers by subordinating the principle of analogy along with its systematic application in the social sciences. Yet without analogies and the ability to decode cultural items it is impossible to evaluate any degree of novelty or claim to distinctiveness. This is especially the case with regard to phenomena which, in both first- and twentieth-century terms, may be described as 'religious'.

In what follows, therefore, I wish to sketch some aspects of the ethos of Pauline Christinity – to suggest what it felt like to belong to one of Paul's groups – and to show how this ethos resulted from the highly creative interplay between the beliefs and practices of early Christianity as mediated by Paul and the common culture and social system which Paul shared with his contemporaries.

One of the growth points in recent attempts to give a social description of early Christianity has been the discovery of the importance of social ecology. Gerd Theissen has shown that the Jesus movement in Palestine was one of a number of religiously inspired renewal movements whose diverse aims and identities were reflected in their relationship to the environment:

> We can no more imagine the Zealots without their mountain hideouts than the Qumran community without the desert oasis of the Ain Feshka or the baptist movement without the river Jordan. One characteristic of the Jesus movement is its being rooted in the rural world (or better, hinterland) of settled Palestine.[4]

The antagonism of these groups to the Temple expressed itself in antagonism towards the city as well; and this feeling was reciprocated. It was, after all, the Temple authorities and the Roman administrators in Jerusalem who were responsible for Jesus' crucifixion.

The Pauline movement, on the other hand, was entirely urban; and this socio-ecological and socio-cultural transfer from rural Palestine to the Hellenistic cities of the Roman world was to play a major part in the persistence of the new religion and its eventual triumph under Constantine. At the cost of over-simplification, the change may be characterized thus: (1) It was one of language: from Aramaic to Greek and from parable to *paraenesis* ('advice' or 'counsel') and other forms of Greek rhetoric. (2) It was one of social pattern: from village itinerancy supported by *ad hoc* hospitality and charismatic begging to urban itinerancy along the principle Mediterranean trade-routes and financed by rationalized donations and economic activity. Ronald Hock has suggested recently that, far from being antagonistic to 'rational' economic pursuits, Paul's preaching and teaching frequently took place in the setting of his artisan's workshop, after the manner of certain Cynic philosophers.[5] (3) It was a change of style: from the homelessness of the Son of Man whose disciples were called on to subordinate household ties to groups of urban Christians organized on a household basis.[6] (4) It was a change of constituency: from the economically vulnerable and socially marginal followers of Jesus to the highly stratified and status-conscious city-dwellers who joined Paul's groups. (5) It was a change of message and medium: from Jesus' prophetic announcement to Israel of the imminent 'kingdom of God' by means of parable and miracle to Paul's preaching (and writing) to Jews and Gentiles of Jesus as universal *kurios* ('lord') and to the worship of this *kurios* in small, emotion-charged house-groups.

It is important to emphasize, therefore, that the success of Paul's mission and the life-style of his 'churches' (so-called) were indebted to the ethos, institutions and social patterns of the Hellenistic cities of the Empire.[7] The cities provided a network of transport and communication: hence the mobility of Paul and his 'co-workers' and the rapid spread of the Christian message. Hock estimates that Paul alone travelled 10,000 miles as a Christian apostle.

The cities provided models of association for the meetings and organization of converts: clubs, trade guilds, cult groups, the synagogues, the household and, of course, the autonomous city-state (*politeia*) itself. One cult group in particular shows important analogies to the Christian gatherings.[8] Coming from Philadelphia in Asia Minor, the inscription (dated to the late second century BCE) speaks of the private initiative of one Dionysius in founding a cultic association in honour of a pantheon of Greek gods under the guardianship of the native, Phrygian goddess Agdistis. Access to meetings is extended to 'men and women, slave and free'; the conditions of membership demand moral more than ritual purity and have a strong bias towards sexual ethics; the meetings take place regularly and are located in Dionysius' own *oikos* ('house' or 'shrine'); and the purpose of meetings and membership includes worship, moral improvement and mutual support. It can hardly be doubted that, in some respects at least, the Pauline groups would have appeared to an outsider as not dissimilar to cult groups like this one.

Third, the cities provided institutions which could influence, positively or negatively, the form and function of Paul's mission and his 'churches'. One negative example is instructive. The law-courts at Corinth provided the Christians there with the temptation to have their disputes settled outside the fellowship (1 Cor. 6:1–11). In Paul's eyes, however, such action was shameful. It weakened the authority of the fellowship to govern itself, made private disputes public, and contradicted their self-understanding as 'brothers' of one another and 'saints' who would judge 'the world' at the Last Day. Instead, it is clear that Paul expected the group to appoint arbitrators from 'the wise' amongst its own ranks. In this it would follow the pattern set not only in the synagogue associations but also in clubs like that of the Iobacchi at Athens.

The ethos of the cities also contributed to the identity and self-understanding of these urban Christians. It is impossible to understand the significance of Paul's boast to 'have become all things to all men' (1 Cor. 9:22) outside the context of the pluralism of the Hellenistic city. Nor was this pluralism racial only. The controversies in the Corinthian groups over sexual practice, food taboos, idol worship, and hair-styles all bear witness to the 'cultural potpourri' which influenced their style of life.

Further, the cities were places of opportunity. Their anonymity gave a slave like Onesimus the opportunity to run away. Their public places gave him the opportunity to hear philosophers debate and the apostle preach. Their private voluntary associations, like the Christian meetings, gave him the opportunity to belong to a new household, elsewhere called the 'household of faith' (Gal. 6:10), and in that context to be reconciled to his master Philemon, 'no longer as a slave but more than a slave, as a beloved brother

. . . both in the flesh and in the Lord' (Phmn. 16). Here, Onesimus' rank as a *doulos* remains unchanged but his status has been raised – by his connection with Paul, by his membership of the Christian community, and by his role in maintaining harmony in the partnership relation between Paul and Philemon. But it would be a mistake to omit the most significant of Onesimus' new connections: his being 'in the Lord' (Phmn. 16). For it is this transcendental connection which provides the basis for the re-evaluation of his status both by himself, as a believer, and by his fellows in the community of believers. There can be no doubt that a large measure of the novelty of the ethos in the Pauline groups arose out of this very self-conscious re-evaluation of the status and role of members by virtue of their common belief that they belonged to Christ Jesus, the heavenly *Kurios*. This allowed, ideally anyway, for tensions deriving from differences in social rank, brought into the gatherings from the society-at-large, to be absorbed and transformed by the distinctive ethos of the groups as this was created by worship of their common Lord, participation in a common meal and experiences of boundary-transcending *communitas* and ecstasy.

Another social group who found in the city opportunity for movement up the social scale was women. The 'sexual territoriality'[9] of former times, which confined the woman to the social space of the household, seems to have weakened under the Principate, especially in Rome and the cities of Italy. By various means – advantageous marital alliances, economic enterprise, patronage of civic events and institutions, membership of cult groups, and by exerting influence on the men and women within the orbit of their households – women could win honour in public as well as in private. We should not be surprised then to find that women were attracted to the Christian associations and played a prominent role. They provided hospitality and finance for Paul's mission, hosted church meetings in their houses, contributed to worship by exercising such highly valued gifts as prophecy and prayer (1 Cor. 11:5), and served, with the men, in the governance of the churches. The fact that Paul insists that the Corinthian women not go unveiled when they pray and prophesy (1 Cor. 11:2–16) shows what liberty they felt they had in the meetings as well as Paul's concern that the patriarchal order of the churches and of society-at-large be maintained. The injunction bidding wives to be silent in church (1 Cor. 14:33b–36) implies a similar claim on the part of the wives and a similar concern on the part of Paul (or the interpolator). But the controversy itself is understandable in the context of an urban culture which strongly disapproved of women speaking in public, however much it approved their contributions in other ways. The prohibition by Paul of recourse to prostitutes (1 Cor. 6:12–20) shows that there were limits to his tolerance of the urban ethos. As in the Jewish communities, prostitution was a role forbidden to women and the avoidance of *porneia* ('immorality') of all kinds was a rule for both men and women (e.g. 1 Cor. 5:9–13). There could be no clearer example of Mary Douglas's observation that 'the human body is always treated as an image of society . . . bodily control is an expression of social control'.[10] The sex rule, like the rule about idolatry (1 Cor. 8;10:14–22), distinguished both Christians and Jews from 'the world' about them and reinforced their own sense of being the holy and elect people of God, destined shortly to 'inherit the kingdom of God' (1 Cor. 6:9–10).

In speaking about slaves and women, I have been speaking of social categories, rank, status, honour and shame. And rightly so, for the Hellenistic cities in which Christianity took its rise were highly stratified. Ramsay MacMullen has given us a 'lexicon of snobbery' which indicates the prejudices of the literate upper class of Rome against the lower.[11] He also points out that the overcrowded, public character of the city together with the verticality of the formal distribution of power created an ethos of rivalry, ostentatious display, paternalism, peer loyalty and group and individual perceptions finely-tuned to the social distribution of honour and shame. This situation was replicated in the provincial cities, for Rome set the fashions. The attribution of status depended on many variables. Tony Reekmans, in his study of Juvenal's satirical criticism of social change in Rome, isolates seven social categories each with its own distribution of ranks. The categories are: extraction, nobility, personal liberty, fortune, business, age and sex.[12] One's status reflected the correlation of one's place on the hierarchy of ranks within each of these categories. Traditionally-speaking, one's obligation was to know one's place and to act accordingly (cf. 1 Cor. 7:17–24). But because the cities were places of social and economic opportunity, people's status (or sense of status) was liable to change. Such change often led to experiences of 'status-inconsistency', arising from a lack of fit between (say) income and occupation or between birth and education.

The implications of this model of a socially stratified urban culture for understanding the beliefs, practices and controversies of Paul and his churches are manifold and have been recently explored by Wayne Meeks.[13] The picture which emerges is that Paul's groups were attractive to, and constituted by, a cross-section of urban society apart from those highest and lowest on the social scale. The free artisan or small trader, together with his (or her) dependents, appears to be typical. Such people were often upwardly mobile in social terms. This mobility is likely to have made conversion and church membership attractive both because church provided a new opportunity for extending one's patronage and range of connections and because the meetings provided a symbolic and social context in which one could overcome one's sense of anxiety created by experiences of status-inconsistency in the wider world. As possible examples of status inconsistents in the church, we may cite the converts from the 'household of Caesar' (Phil. 4:22); wealthy women like Lydia who traded in luxury goods, was a pagan adherent of the synagogue at Philippi and headed her own household (Acts 16:12–15); Crispus, who 'believed in the Lord' in spite of his office as 'ruler of the synagogue' (Acts 18:8); Prisca and Aquila, Jewish artisans with Roman names, expelled from Rome under Claudius and with means enough for frequent travel and for hosting Christian gatherings (1 Cor. 16:9; Rom. 16:3–5; Acts 18:2–4); and Paul himself, a converted Pharisee of provincial origins but with education in Jerusalem, Roman citizenship and an artisan's trade, who moved restlessly around the cities of the provinces, preaching the 'gospel' which had been revealed to him in an apocalyptic vision (Gal. 1:11–17).

To such people the Christian message, as interpreted by Paul himself, had much to offer. It offered powerful symbols of unity which could function to integrate men and women, slave and free, Jew, Greek and barbarian. Theissen has rightly described the symbolism of Pauline soteriology as 'sociomorphic',[14] for it bound people together under 'one God', 'one Lord' and 'one Spirit' and incorporated them into 'one body', the 'body of Christ'. The differences of category, rank and status which divided them in 'the world' were overcome by symbolically re-locating them 'in Christ' (Gal. 3:27–28; 1 Cor. 12:13; Rom. 10:12; Col. 3:10–11). This re-location was confirmed ritually: by baptism 'into Christ Jesus' (Rom. 6:3) as the *rite de passage* into group membership; by sharing in the 'Lord's meal' involving rituals which served to re-incorporate members each time they gathered (cf. 1 Cor. 11:17–34); and by the re-affirmation of their shared identity in the practice of worship (cf. 1 Cor. 12;14). Even the 'kiss of peace' (1 Thess. 5:26; 1 Cor. 16:20; Rom. 16:16) played its part as an important, tactile symbol of mutual recognition and of the 'peace' to which believers had been called (1 Thess. 5:13; 1 Cor. 7:15).

Paul's message also offered powerful symbols of change. 'Christ crucified', with its paradoxical juxtaposition of power in humiliation and victory in defeat, offered a theodicy to men and women socially and psychologically at odds with the dominant culture, by inverting its notions of honour and shame, both those of the Romans (based on the quest for personal prestige) and those of the Jews (based on Torah-piety). This symbolic inversion of values created the basis for a new community whose identity, authority pattern, ethics and rituals could all be expressed in terms of the cross. So, in respect of ethical patterns Paul could say: 'And those who belong to Christ have crucified the flesh with its passions and desires' (Gal. 5:24). To encourage the voluntary redistribution of wealth, he says: 'For you know the grace of our Lord Jesus Christ, that though he was rich, yet for your sake he became poor, so that by his poverty you might become rich' (2 Cor. 8:9).

Belief in Christ's resurrection and imminent return could function similarly. It created an ethos of hope and optimism for the future and an expectation of compensation for social dissonance experienced in the present. It provided a model for transformed social relations understood as an anticipation of what was to come: 'And he died for all, that those who live might live no longer for themselves but for him who for their sake died and was raised. From now on, therefore, we regard no one from a human point of view . . . if any one is in Christ, he is a new creation: the old has passed away, behold the new has come' (2 Cor. 5:15–17). Yet again, the apocalyptic belief that time was short and that the New Age had begun already encouraged the possibility of distancing oneself from 'worldly' ties and obligations and of living 'as though' they were no longer important. This could have radicalized social relations; and what Paul says in 1 Cor. 7:25–31 doubtless gave a strong impulse to the development of Christian asceticism. On the whole, however, it is interpreted by Paul in a socially conservative direction. Because 'the form of this world is passing away' (1 Cor. 7:31), the believer's attention is focussed, not on changing the world, but on the need for 'undivided devotion to the Lord' (1 Cor. 7:35).

This devotion expressed itself in an essentially other-regarding ethic, summed up in the term *agapē* ('love'). Paul's words in 1 Cor. 13:4–7 have a particular resonance against the background of a highly stratified and status-conscious urban environment: 'Love is patient and kind: love is not jealous or boastful; it is not arrogant or rude. Love does not insist on its own way; it is not irritable or resentful; it does not rejoice at wrong, but rejoices in the right' (cf. Rom. 13:8–10).

Social differences are largely taken for granted in Pauline Christianity. Indeed, Paul takes advantage of them. Firm government by the political authorities and subordination to them (Rom. 13:1–7) creates an orderly macro-society within which itinerant preachers of the gospel like himself can move freely and with relative safety. Similarly, the patriarchal household structure provides an orderly micro-society within which the new socio-religious vision can be celebrated and practised. However, social differences are also transformed and transcended in Pauline Christianity. This transformation is partly cognitive and psychological, but it is no less 'real' for being that. Paul's apocalyptic doctrine[15] of the impending defeat of 'every rule and every authority and power' by Christ (1 Cor. 15:24) implies a radical contingency in social patterns and in every form of domination (cf. Rom. 8:35–39). His equally apocalyptic doctrine of the coming of the Messianic Age and the end of the period of the Torah (Gal. 3) made possible the unity of Jew and Gentile as 'sons of god' in the 'new creation'. It was a message of 'Paradise regained': 'There is neither Jew nor Greek, there is neither slave nor free, there is neither male nor female; for you are all one in Christ Jesus' (Gal. 3:28). But the transformation was not only cognitive. The mission to the Gentiles; table-fellowship shared by Jew and Gentile, rich and poor; the prominence accorded women as well as men; the radical attachment to an ethic of humility and love: these all demonstrate that the message had social power as well. The persistence of Christianity has to be explained therefore, not only in relation to its urban setting but also in terms of what it offered in that setting: namely, a symbolic and social pattern of integration and solidarity open to men and women from a distinctively wide range of social locations.

I have tried to convey something of the ethos of early Christianity in its Pauline form and to show how this ethos developed out of the interplay between Paul's gospel and the social pattern of the Hellenistic city-state. That Paul's groups were relatively lacking in the normal paraphernalia of first century religion need not surprise us to the extent E.A. Judge expects. The non-participation of believers in the official cults of the Hellenistic cities reflects at least three factors: (a) the roots of the new movement in Judaism, with its abhorrence of idols and its doctrine of election; (b) the roots of the movement in recent history – the crucifixion of the Messiah – an event having its location in only one city, Jerusalem; and (c) the apocalyptic orientation of the movement which generated social stances of separation and itineration legitimated by claims to experiences of divine revelation (*apokalypsis*). The Christian cult was taking place in heaven, not in temple or shrine (cf. Gal. 4:25–27; Phil. 3:19–20; Rom. 8:15–16). To neglect this would be to misunderstand what it meant to belong to Paul's groups.

Notes

1   E.A. Judge, 'The Social Identity of the First Christians: A Question of Method in Religious History', *Journal of Religious History*, 11 (1980), p.212.

2   W.A. Meeks, *The First Urban Christians* (New Haven and London: Yale University Press, 1983), p.4.

3   See S.C. Barton, 'Paul's Sense of Place: An Anthropological Approach to Community-Formation in Corinth', *New Testament Studies*, 32 (1986), pp.225–46.

4   G. Theissen, *The Social Setting of Pauline Christianity* (Edinburgh: T. & T. Clark, 1982), p.31; cf. *idem*, *The First Followers of Jesus* (London: SCM, 1978), pp.47–58.,

5   R.F. Hock, *The Social Context of Paul's Ministry: Tentmaking and Apostleship* (Philadelphia: Fortress Press, 1980), pp.37–42.

6   On discipleship of Jesus, see M. Hengel, *The Charismatic Leader and His Followers* (Edinburgh: T. & T. Clark, 1981); on Paul's 'house churches', see R.J. Banks, *Paul's Idea of Community* (Sydney: Anzea, 1979) and A.J. Malherbe, *Social Aspects of Early Christianity* (Baton Rouge and London: Louisiana State University Press, 1977), pp.60–91.

7   So, E.A. Judge, *The Social Pattern of Christian Groups in the First Century* (London: Tyndale Press, 1960); *idem*, 'St Paul and Classical Society', *Jahrbuch für Antike und Christentum*, 15 (1972), esp. pp.27ff.

8   S.C. Barton and G.H.R. Horsley, 'A Hellenistic Cult Group and the New Testament Churches', *Jahrbuch für Antike und Christentum*, 24 (1981), pp.7–41.

9   R. MacMullen, 'Women in Public in the Roman Empire', *Historia*, 29 (1980), p.208.

10 M. Douglas, *Natural Symbols* (London: Barrie & Jenkins, 1973), pp.98–9; see W.A. Meeks, *Urban Christians*, pp.97ff.

11 R. MacMullen, *Roman Social Relations 50 B.C. to A.D. 284* (New Haven and London: Yale University Press, 1974), pp.138–41.

12 T. Reekmans, 'Juvenal's Views on Social Change', *Ancient Society*, 2 (1971), pp.123–5.

13 W.A. Meeks, 'The Social Context of Pauline Theology', *Interpretation* XXXVII (1982), pp.266–77; *idem*, *Urban Christians*, *passim*. Cf. also J. Gager, *Kingdom and Community* (Englewood Cliffs, N.J.: Prentice-Hall, 1975).

14 G. Theissen, 'Soteriologische Symbolik in den paulinischen Schriften', *Kerygma und Dogma*, 20(1974), esp. pp.284–93.

15 On Paul's general indebtedness to the thought-forms of Jewish apocalyptic, see now J.C. Beker, *Paul the Apostle* (Edinburgh: T. & T. Clark, 1980).

Further reading

S.C. Barton, 'Paul and the Cross: A Sociological Approach', *Theology*, LXXXV(1982), pp.13–19.

F.W. Danker, *Benefactor: Epigraphic Study of a Graeco-Roman and New Testament Semantic Field* (St Louis: Clayton Publishing House, 1982).

N. Gottwald (ed.) *The Bible and Liberation: Political and Social Hermeneutics* (New York: Orbis Books, 1983).

R.M. Grant, *Early Christianity and Society* (San Francisco: Harper & Row, 1977).

L.E. Keck, 'On the Ethos of Early Christians', *Journal of the American Academy of Religion*, XLII(1974), pp.435–52.

H.C. Kee, *Christian Origins in Sociological Perspective* (London: SCM, 1980).

R. MacMullen, *Paganism in the Roman Empire* (New Haven and London: Yale University Press, 1981).

B.J. Malina, *The New Testament World* (London: SCM, 1983).

R.A. Markus, *Christianity in the Roman World* (London: Thames & Hudson, 1974).

J.H. Schütz, 'Ethos of Early Christianity', *Interpreter's Dictionary of the Bible*, Supplementary Volume (1976), pp.289–93.

12
Feminine piety in fifteenth-century Rome: Santa Francesca Romana*

GUY BOANAS and LYNDAL ROPER

Every year in Rome on 9 March, the city's taxi drivers assemble their cars in the space between the Colosseum and the Forum. It is the feast day of Saint Frances of Rome, the patron of drivers and protecting saint of the municipal government. Out from the nearby church of Santa Maria Nova, where Francesca's body is buried, Benedictine monks come to bless the vehicles which then drive off in procession through the city. In another part of Rome, the Tor de' Specchi convent founded by Francesca in 1433 opens its doors to visitors in commemoration of her death.

A visit to the convent is a popular annual outing, for the core of the original fourteenth-century house where Francesca and the women who joined her lived still survives among the later structures. An upper room, used as a chapel, has its walls covered by a series of frescoes done in 1468 commemorating miracles and cures wrought by the saint during her life. People can buy packets of the ointment made – so it is said – according to a recipe used by Francesca. It is the protective and healing powers of the saint that are emphasized today in her cult, and these were certainly prominent in the fifteenth century when interest in Francesca first developed. Yet neither her healing capacities nor her protective abilities provide the full measure of the nature and power of her cult in late medieval Rome; nor can the modern, rather attenuated popular celebrations replicate the potent, emotional and contradictory spirituality of the Francescan world.

Francesca left no writings of her own; and the accounts we have of her visions, her life or the testimonies of others to her sanctity are refracted through clerical institutions controlled by celibate males: Mattiotti her confessor composed a *Life* and recorded her visions; and the other major source, the witnesses' reports gathered shortly after Francesca's death (in 1440, 1443, 1451 and 1453) as part of the ecclesiastical procedures for canonization, are shaped by the questions put to them by church officials and translated into Latin, the ecclesiastical language.

However, though the ecclesiastical structure of the sources renders them problematic, the clerical control is neither total nor does the record transform Francesca into a hagiographical cypher. Even during formal interrogation, the witnesses sometimes answer irrelevantly and their own Italian occasionally breaks into the scribe's Latin. So also, the colour and range of Francesca's spiritual experience still emerges, from the beatific calm of her divine visions to the noise, stench and violence of the demonic visitations. In part, this is secured by the vivid sensory detail of the accounts; in part, by their homeliness and geographic specificity. So, for example, her demonic encounters, elements common to many saints' lives, do not remain on the level of mere *topoi* but are located very specifically in the Ponziani house where she lived with her husband's family. Here she is said to meet evil spirits hiding on the stairs, spirits who try to throw her from the balcony (*Vita*, pp.284, 287). Her guardian angel uses common household implements, like the vine knife in the kitchen, to stab a demonic snake (*Vita*, p.288).

To tease apart the strands of ecclesiastical and popular devotion, however, would be an impossible and misguided project, for popular response to Francesca was partly shaped by church piety, just as Francesca's own spirituality was formed by it. Rather, the impulse behind this essay is to attempt to uncover that fifteenth-century spirituality, to understand what her life and spiritual style meant to her contemporaries, and how it represented a distinctively feminine devotional mode. The Francescan story, with its complexities and ambiguities, illuminates what may often seem to be the undifferentiated monolith of conventional late medieval 'popular piety'; and highlights the peculiarities of the female voice within it.

Francesca Bussa was born in 1384 and when she was only eleven years old, she was married against her will to Lorenzo Ponziani. Both her natal family and that of her husband were part of a group of families who had made their fortunes, just a few decades before, through the intensive farming of large country estates – bought on the cheap from impoverished old noble families or debt-ridden churches and monasteries. Although not as socially prestigious as the baronial families of the countryside, these newly wealthy families – soon accorded the title *nobiles* – rapidly ousted the old aristocracy from political control of the city. Francesca's cult must be situated in this uncertain play of social forces.

Francesca's aversion to an earthly marriage was just one example of the desire to follow a religious life, a desire which she was said to have shown from her earliest years. Despite her position as a noble wife and mother, living in the Ponziani house with her husband, she gathered a group of like-minded women companions around her, and in 1425 they founded a community under the spiritual guidance of the Benedictines. In 1433 ten of these women moved to lead a common life at the Tor de' Speechi site, but Francesca did not join them until three years later, following the death of her husband. There she remained until immediately before her death in 1440. Yet though Francesca's name has survived and a cult had early developed around her (she was not in fact formally canonized until 1608), both the kind of spirituality and the model of the devotional life she pursued were by no means unique in fifteenth-century Rome. Hers was just one of a number of similar groups founded in Rome at this time –

perhaps in compensation for the decreasing number of convents – and links can be seen to have existed between them. Members of the different groups gave support to each other, were patronized by similar families and can even be seen to have consulted some of the same spiritual advisors.

As saint, Francesca's most distinctive characteristic was that, like Margery Kempe, Catherine of Siena and Bridget of Sweden, she was a married woman, offering a model of holy life to those non-virgins who had taken the spiritually lesser path of matrimony. And as healer and mystic, her spirituality was extraordinarily suited to dramatizing the ambivalences surrounding female sexuality, the family and holiness.

Family and maternity

The devotions to Francesca show her to have been the saint of mothers and children. She herself bore at least three children, two of whom died in childhood. The fresco cycles, paintings, statues and the legends surrounding her life feature the child-like guardian angel who first appeared to her after the death of her son Evangelista. Strongly associated with motherliness, Francesca's cult echoes many Marian themes – like the Virgin Mother, Francesca is accompanied by a child who is more than human. The most frequent image of the saint focusses exclusively on the mother-child dyad, not the family grouping, and even the frescoes of 1468 in the convent she founded depict her dressed in Marian blue despite the universal agreement of witnesses that she wore black. Yet while maternity is celebrated, it is a tragic motherhood. By reminding the devotee of Evangelista's death, the angel's presence points to the vulnerability and sorrow of being a mother, elements present in some Marian cults as well.

Yet Francesca remains an unsettling icon to motherhood. Concentration on the mother-child relationship, which seems to contain women within the family and define them as mothers, can also seduce attention away from the family – a seduction which is all the more disturbing when the 'family' involved is, unlike the Holy Family, so very closely rooted in the human, mundane world of fifteenth-century Rome. Further, in Francesca's life story, as in that of many saints, there are elements in which run counter to contemporary conceptions of the family. Thus we learn that from when she was first married, Francesca refused to participate in the wedding celebrations and parties of other Roman noble families or to take part in the rounds of social visits to women of her class, the ritualized festivities which publicly proclaimed the individual's place among family and kin. She saw them as occasions for gossip and displays of vanity; and she criticized those women who spent their time dressing in finery and attending such parties (*Processi*, pp.22–6). When she refused to dress as a Roman matron and display her husband's wealth, rejecting the rich food at family feasts, and would not advance the family fortunes by taking an active part in social life, Francesca robbed the Ponziani of an opportunity to confirm their status amongst the city elite – an opportunity upon which they, as a newly 'arrived' family, were especially reliant. In a sense, Francesca was refusing to assent to the social function of religion: the use of ritual by Roman families as much to cement social relationships as to worship. By unpicking these intertwined uses of ritual, Francesca's words of criticism unravelled familial and personal spiritual needs and interests, making 'family interests' themselves problematic.

Even when Francesca appeared to be acting as an orthodox noble wife and mother – such as, for example, in showing an appropriately wifely interest in the hospital of Maria in Capella, established by the Ponziani and situated near their palace, her participation in the work of the hospital, feeding the inmates and caring for the sick as if they were her own children, was not appropriate behaviour for those of donor rank (*Processi*, pp.33, 234–6). Her maternal charity implied criticism of the kind of familial generosity which would found a hospital, decorate it with a family coat of arms, and leave the charitable work of caring to employees. In a society where to be a patrician *matrona* was to hold a position of social esteem, a status of maturity deriving both from motherhood and rank, Francesca shaped her life so as to divorce motherhood from class.

The same elements can be seen in the stories many of the witnesses recounted about her behaviour as a mistress of the household, supervising her servants: unlike other *matronae* she spoke gently to them and treated them as equals (*Processi*, pp.40–1). At times, expressly choosing another model drawn from relationships in the household, Francesca is said to have described herself as a servant. Here she followed a long tradition of saintly Christian humility, which frequently has an anti-familial strain. And when Francesca was said to have carried wood like a servant, visited poor families rather than her rich kinsfolk, and sat at church doors begging alms until she could exclaim, 'Now we have enough for supper!', her part-playing amounted to a staged repudiation of the family which conferred prestige and power. Though the alternative models on which she drew were private and domestic, contained within the household or (as with begging) defined at its margins, her rejection was acted out in an intensely public fashion. Her disapproving absence from Roman social life was evident, and if the stories insist that she stuck considerately to back streets when she went begging, she did not shrink from greeting – and shaming – any relatives she encountered. She preferred to beg at Roman churches on Indulgence days, when they were most crowded (*Processi*, pp.25, 22–6, 236–7). The family system was the vehicle through which class feeling was transmitted and manifested; the household the place where hierarchies were supposed to divide masters and mistresses from servants. In the stories which surround Francesca's life, there is an unmistakable zest in the way Francesca brought the worlds of rich and poor into collision, overturning household order.

The miracles attributed to her nicely exemplify how the idea of maternity could be used to subvert fifteenth-century familial values. During a terrible famine, witnesses said, Francesca distributed grain from the Ponziani granary and wine from their cellars to the starving. No matter how much she gave away, the supplies were not exhausted (*Processi*, pp.33–6). In this tale, evidently derived from Jesus' own miracles, Francesca becomes a kind of civic mother figure, able to provide nourishment for all Rome's poor (as in the fiercely pro-Roman, civic form her cult still takes today). But the story would also have been understood as an implied attack on the limits of family generosity. For Francesca was flouting the legal limitations of her sex by disposing of the family riches without first having gained her husband's permission. And worse, the suspicion that Ponziani himself had most likely hoarded the grain to sell at great profit would probably not have escaped the minds of contemporaries. Similarly, during the occupation of Rome by King Ladislas of Naples, when the Ponziani family suffered the loss of most of its livestock and grain (the possessions out of which it had built up its power and wealth), Francesca is said to have responded calmly 'the Lord gives and the Lord takes away; blessed be the name of the Lord' (*Processi*, pp.45, 47). Preservation of the family patrimony, the obsessional imperative of the fifteenth-century Roman noblemen, was quite unimportant to the heroine of these stories.

Indeed, even the names of Francesca's children seem to reflect an alienation from the concept of the family as a patriline. Whereas Roman nobles commonly named their children after their forebears (a custom disapproved by the Church, which advocated naming children after the saint on whose day they were born), Francesca's children, Agnese, Evangelista and Battista, had names which appear in neither the Ponziani line nor, so far as we can tell, that of Francesca's natal family. Here too, membership of the kinship of Christian saints appears to be counterposed to that of the worldly, local family. The theme recurs in the witness stories of Francesca's life which tell how Francesca rounded 'like a lion' on any who swore and insulted the name of God (*Processi*, p.40). Here contemporaries would have read the stories in the idiom of male noble reactions to any insult to family honour. Where noblemen were eager to avenge such an injury, understood as an almost physical wound to family reputation, the story has Francesca using the same rhetoric to attack the vice of swearing – thus at once gently puncturing earthly obsessions with family standing, and stressing the holy woman's sense of belonging to a heavenly family.

Indeed, some of the miracles to which witnesses attested involved direct conflicts between Christian ideals and family obligation. Laurentia, daughter of the tailor Domenico, had wanted to remain a virgin but was married against her will, and even after her husband's death, was forbidden to follow her spiritual vocaton. Francesca did not counsel flight but simply advised her to dedicate herself to God, and immediately, Laurentia found that her family 'who formerly had been like wolves, had now become as gentle as lambs' (*Processi*, p.195). In this story, Laurentia's obedience in the face of family opposition ultimately triumphs and she is able to win acknowledgment from her family of her independent spiritual life. The 'miracle' consists of the story's unexpected resolution of the tension between the woman's individual spiritual vocation and her duty to obey her family – a set of conflicts which would have been familiar to many spiritually-minded Roman women. Yet the description of the happy ending as a miracle, a result of supernatural intervention, suggests how irresoluble such conflicts might often be, and makes it clear that even Francesca's cult did not support an unconditional female right to follow the devotional life in the face of family opposition.

Other miracle stories, however, do not display this ambivalence. Angilella di Federico Ciciliani is said to have visited the saint's body when it was on funeral display at the church of S. Maria Nova, and to have slipped a silver ring onto the dead woman's finger. Taking off the ring, she discovered that it possessed healing properties, and moreover, found it would calm her husband's rages (*Processi*, p.131). In this case, the saint's intervention is secured by more materially manipulative means.

But though the tale revolves around the unhappiness of marriage, it remains on the level of popular stereotypes of married life: Angilella wants merely to manipulate her husband's temper, as all women were presumed to, and the saint's aid provides a sort of fairy-tale wish fulfilment, not a serious challenge to the nature of familial or marital authority.

A third miracle story has a clearer outcome and a more subversive logic. Antonia, wife of Coluzzo Bellamoglie, interceded with Francesca when her husband suffered acute knee pains. But she prayed first that he might be brought to repent his sins, for, as the witnesses to the miracle agreed, he was a most sinful man. Coluzzo was moved to repent, gave his wife permission to join a company of religious women, and himself entered the priory of S. Clemente (*Processi*, pp.288–9). Here Antonia's prayer, which is cast in the guise of conventional wifely solicitude, results in the complete dissolution of the marriage in favour of religious duty. Antonia, while not disobeying her husband, has in fact secured through prayer an outcome which frees her from his authority for good.

The contrary pulls of family and religious loyalties are a theme common to many saints' lives. It may have been an especially resonant one for fifteenth-century women who, in a society where family was increasingly defined through the male line and where wealthy folk were beginning to spend considerable time and money constructing (or inventing) their genealogies, were caught between their natal and marital families. They belonged fully to neither. Requiems and family prayers might not always incorporate the womenfolk, and women were not assured of burial in the family vault. Motherhood, especially motherhood of sons, gave them a place of honour within the family as heir-producers – a fact which the desperate barren women who sought Francesca's aid knew well. But that status was predicated on a patriarchal appropriation of the mother's fruit into the family line. Though the mother appeared to be the domestic emotional nexus of the family, she might at times be utterly invisible in the public representations of family identity. Paradoxically, the offspring which anchored her status as *matrona* might also occlude her own sense of family and kin. With its echoes of the Marian cult, the Francescan devotion may have strengthened the imaginative possibility of a powerful maternity, one which could at least counterbalance paternity. Unlike the ambiguous patriline of the Holy Family, Francesca's family group was firmly located in a fifteenth-century patrician Roman patrilineage. As fifteenth-century Roman women meditated on Francesca's life, or discussed her among themselves, they were also thinking on the painful contradictions of motherhood and family identity in their own lives.

The Devil

Francesca's cradling of the Christ child, her encounters with the saints, visions of fountains and streams, take up most space in Mattiotti's account of the saint's spiritual life; and these peaceful motifs and acts of healing dominate the sequence of frescoes in the chapel at Tor de' Specchi. But Mattiotti also devotes a small section of his biography to a more disturbing, darker side of her spiritual life: her battles with evil spirits. And at the convent itself, somewhat bizarrely to the modern visitor, the fifteenth-century frescoes in the old dining room focus on her encounters with demons. Though both these later frescoes and Mattiotti's rather embarrassedly brief accounts of the evil visions present them as a separate, troubling order of spiritual experience – a categorization perhaps replicated in Evelyn Underhill's classification of 'disordered' visions as a lower form of spiritual life – their position in the narrative of the Francescan story show that they form an integrated spiritual logic. By a sort of systematic opposition to the beatific visions, they intensify the qualities of each and confirm the genuineness of the truly beatific. At the same time, the structure of both 'good' and 'evil' visions reveals a consistent agonistic understanding of the spiritual universe – a world where the Devil is ever-present, ever dangerous.

Most frequently, the evil spirits appear as men – sometimes as old men with beards, once as foresters, and even on one occasion as a priest (*Vita*, pp.255, 277). Most often they are merely described as male. Usually they carry weapons – leather whips, batons and knives (*Vita*, pp.266, 277, 278, 285). They may also appear as wolves, lions, and boars, breathing fire and exuding a fearful smell, and are said to be 'maddened', 'snatching', 'horrible', and 'terrible'. Frequently they arrive as the serpents, dragons, asps, vipers and snakes which Francesca hated most – reptiles whose phallic forms echo the very masculine shapes of the male demons in the frescoes (*Vita*, pp.273, 285, 286, 288). The serpent, of course, figures in the biblical story of the Fall, a passage which medieval commentary construed sexually. Mattiotti mentions demons disguised as monkeys, domestic pigs and dogs, animals which can be tamed, and which might have been kept in the stables of a large *palazzo* such as that of the Ponziani. Yet all these animals are experienced as wild, untamed, sexual and vicious – even the domestic pigs have grown long teeth, and are out of place in the house, disrupting the saint's meditations (*Vita*, pp.266, 277, 278, 280). This is a world associated with the masculine principle – yet it is not one of order and civilization, but of nature run wild, seething with lusts. Francesca's demonic visions evoke fear and the threat of defilement. Unlike male saints, whose encounters with the Devil usually involve carnal temptation and are populated by demons in the shape of alluring young girls, Francesca's visions appear at first to present sexuality as utterly repulsive.

Above all, the demons are presented in terms of absolute physical power and potency. The narrative makes their sheer force vivid – we hear how they throw her up into the air, put her on top of wardrobes, trip her, kick her and drag her along the floor (*Vita*, pp.269, 271, 283). Their strength renders her incapable of anything but passive endurance. They are bent on her annihilation: the lions rush to devour her, the demons attempt to cast her on the fire, and nearly succeed in hanging her from a hook attached to the roof beam (*Vita*, pp.289, 275, 278). In Francesca's visions, this absolute physical potency is identified with masculinity – an equation which mirrored the privileges of masculinity in the Italy of her own day, where men were normally armed, feuding was endemic, and the streets considered dangerous for 'respectable' women. Yet the alien 'otherness' of masculinity, its vital power which makes her own existence so precarious, suggests its fearful sexual attraction for her. It entails being consumed and swallowed up by another, one's body under his complete control. To attain spiritual union with Christ, this sexuality, which represents a force setting itself up in opposition to God, must be repudiated.

By contrast, the 'good' visions present an ordered, tranquil, civilized world, far removed from this 'masculine' anarchy. Yet even so, the account of Francesca's relationship to Christ, the true bridegroom, continues to draw on elements of the same polarity of masculinity and femininity and exhibits a similarly masochistic structure. Francesca's own devotional exercises are described as explicitly masochistic: she wore hair shirts and iron girdles which made her bleed in order to draw closer to visionary ecstasy (*Vita*, p.6; *Processi*, pp.16–18, 240).

It is difficult to know how to address this masochistic strain in the Francescan narrative. Perhaps it can be read as a sado-masochistic drama whose implications are best explored in psychoanalytic terms – a project which lies beyond the scope of this essay. In recent argument about the nature of desire and sexual roles, some feminists have wanted to insist on the liberatory potential of sado-masochism, and the impossibility of sanitizing sexuality so that it ceases to be about dominance and submission. Certainly the Francescan account of sexuality is structured around a masochistic axis. It is deeply coloured by images of violence – and the narrative almost revels in the whipping, disgusting smells and physical humiliation it describes, and in its own coded images of the active, penetrating penis.

But in Francesca's story, the most direct consequence of the use of the sexual imagery is not to undermine but rather to joyously affirm feminine submission. Masochism becomes a metaphor for perfect obedience; and throughout his account of her life, Mattiotti draws attention to her docility. Witnesses too describe how, even during her visions, she would respond to the commands of her spiritual advisor Mattiotti, Christ's representative – behaviour which verges on casting Francesca as an almost ridiculous automaton, sitting, standing or walking about in her trance in obedience to his instructions (*Processi*, pp.29–31). In her visions as during her battles with the demons, Francesca's attitude is described as nearly totally passive: all sensation is inflicted on her from without so that obedience merges with total passivity, the body becomes a battleground where victory is only possible through complete physical abnegation.

Yet this immobility is also seen to bestow on her a particular kind of power and authority which could even implicitly undercut her social role as the humble, weak and obedient woman. Several times we are informed that Francesca's husband heard the noise of her battles with the various demons, or the sound of her voice calling upon Jesus to save her. The demons turn upon him on several occasions. His response is invariably described as one of surprise, shock or horror, and he is termed *stupefacto* – a word conveying astonishment but also, in its Latin root, the meaning 'stupefied'. His simple shock forms a humorous counterpoint to Francesca's tribulations, and is contrasted with Francesca's steadfast faith, lack of amazement and knowledge of divine things. In her greater wisdom, she keeps her visions to herself so as not to worry him with them, and tries to ease his mind by denying that it is demons who have disturbed his sleep. She even becomes his protector, shielding him from the demons so that, after the most fearful attack, he is reduced to pleading with her that 'she must never leave him' (*Vita*, pp.270, 273). Despite his position as her 'head', he provides no support or comfort for her during any of her battles with the demons – a description which would have gained piquancy from the well-known facts of her husband's noble rank and career. Rita, Agnese and Giacomella, her particular women confidantes, are well aware of Francesca's struggles however, and knowing at once what is afoot when they hear the sound of beatings and violence, they immediately run to her cell and offer assistance (*Vita*, pp.271, 289–90).

However, although Francesca's sanctity could be seen to blur the conventional understanding of femininity, the model of sainthood open to her story remained double-edged. All saints, male and female, must be obedient to the Church; but the ideology of obedience has a peculiar pointedness for women which it lacks for men, because it coincides with their prescribed feminine role. If it is the male spirits who are wild, uncivilized and closer to nature, this does not lead to an elevation of female images. Closeness to nature rather than culture does not determine gender inferiority in this symbolic universe, even as metaphor. Rather, the concept of masculinity and the masochistic structure of Francesca's visions, both benign and malign, remain locked in the paradigms of her society which ascribed passivity to women and independence and action to men. The description of Francesca's steadfast perseverance veers toward attributing complete immobility to her as if she is finally frozen by the conflicting pressures of her spiritual world.

Indeed, Francesca did not challenge her own exclusion from priestly office and therefore, from the control, assessment and dissemination of her spiritual experience. Though her visions provided her with a directness of access to God which the priest did not have, Francesca always had to reveal and submit them to her father confessor's scrutiny. The ambiguities of these relationships are given expression in one of the miracle stories: Francesca and her sister-in-law Vannozza went to the church of S. Cecilia to receive communion. But the priest, disapproving of what he considered to be an exaggerated feminine eucharistic piety, substituted unconsecrated bread for the Host. Francesca realized at once that she had not received the body of Christ, and informed her confessor, who found her story to be true (*Processi*, pp.83–4).

Because communion was so often the point of entry to the visionary world, receiving the Eucharist was vital to Francesca's piety. She was thus dependent on the priests who were its stewards, just as she was reliant upon them for validation of the mystical experiences which they could not share: were the visions demonic delusions and was the dreamer therefore a witch? This tension gives rise to some of the stranger passages in Mattiotti's *Life*. Mattiotti records an ecstatic journey of Francesca in which she cradled the Christ Child in her arms. He describes how she brought the Christ Child to him, but that he, her unworthy spiritual father, could not see the Child because he did not have his eyeglass by him! (see *Vita*, p.ix). Here, Mattiotti is required to legitimate Francesca's visionary experience but is literally vision-less, comically disabled rather than a figure of confirmatory authority. In parallel fashion, Mattiotti's own devout but rather simple hagiography is a strangely distorting mirror of Francesca's spiritual intelligence, not an authoritative transmission of her visions.

These complexities emerge most clearly in Mattiotti's account of one of Francesca's most bitter battles with the demons. The evil spirit appears disguised as Mattiotti himself, and praising her, he announces that he wants to transcribe 'the great revelations and visions which God gives you'. Even better, he promises to teach her how to write 'a big book' for herself (*Vita*, pp.255–6). This sounds like an essentially unlettered fantasy about the 'big book' – an almost tactile vision of the intellectual *opera* of the *doctores* of the Church far removed from her own spiritual ambitions. But it would not have been an inconceivable accomplishment for a fifteenth-century spiritual woman. St Bridget of Sweden, who had lived in Rome just half a century before, had indeed composed her own book of visions and Francesca's circle would certainly have known of it. The Tempter offers here the power of having the visions treated seriously, the explicit control of how those experiences would be made public; and by implication, the possibility of dispensing with the need for priestly approval of them.

This vision plays on the ambivalences inherent in the relation of priest to pious woman. It makes dramatically real the possibility that a woman might have direct control of the handing on of her spiritual experience with no need of the priestly ghost-writer and assessor: she too might be a spiritually respected talent. But, we are told, Francesca rejected this option as diabolic. When she refused it, however, we are told that the spirit was at once transformed into a particularly cruel demon who threw her about the room and finally threatened, in one of the most vicious of the sequence of battles, to kill first her son and then Francesca herself with a long lance (*Vita*, pp.255–7).

The sheer violence of the episode underlines the sensitivity of these rather contradictory impulses in the Franciscan cult: for while the cult focusses on the silent, obedient *beata* herself and her visions, it can exist only through transmission. At the core of the cult is the teasing relationship of priest and devotee. The cult itself contrasts Francesca's spiritual elevation with the less exalted spiritual experience of the male clergy – or the almost rustically comic persona presented by Mattiotti (see, for example, *Vita*, p.227). Yet the explicit message of the tale is to instruct the devotee of the absolute requirement to submit all visionary experience to the priestly caste for adjudication. For a woman to speak on her own authority about her spiritual encounters is not to speak in a justifiedly prophetic voice, but to commit the sin of pride. Nevertheless, the devotee is implicated in the irony that Francesca has become a spiritual guide and authority. The very dramatic articulation of the contrary forces at play in the relation of priest and devotee is inherently subversive of priestly power.

The body

Another set of metaphors which dominates the accounts of Francesca's spirituality relate to the body. Cast in vividly sensory language, they invoke feelings about filth and pollution and there are often barely concealed references to excrement. Particularly evocative is the concentration on the sense of smell: all the descriptions of the demons draw attention to the spirits' terrible stench so that 'fetid demon' becomes a consistent motif in the tales. The demons are said to roll her in their filth so that she smells of it for hours after and must be washed; they hold her above the cess pit and seek to throw her down it; they roll her in ashes, stuffing charcoal in her mouth and hair so that even her companion Rita finds it hard to recognize her (*Vita*, pp.257, 266, 272). Often they pull off her head-covering – thus symbolically besmirching her respectability, for the modest headdress was a badge of chaste wifehood. For the nun she later became, the nun's wimple stood for her memberhip of the religious community. The demons pollute her visually as well, by forcing her to watch devils copulating with each other, male with female and male with male (*Vita*, p.282). The dirt, darkness and noise of the demons stands in complete conrast to the sweet smells, light, space and calm she experiences in her beatific visions (for example, *Vita*, pp.35–6, 38, 42, 44, 60, 74).

Here too, the fear of pollution is inextricably linked with the images of masculinity and sexuality in the cult: the very presence of the male demons is dirty, sexually charged and contagious. In the stories surrounding Francesca's daily life, the same apprehensions of sexuality and pollution are dramatized. Francesca is said to have covered her hands with a cloth to protect her body from the stain of touching other men and witnesses recount that she smelt the same stench of the demons when she passed men who were sexual sinners (*Processi*, pp.39–40). These elements become sharply focussed in the tales which deal with Francesca's own sexual life. Despite the fact that Francesca mothered three children, witnesses told how she vomited uncontrollably after intercourse, even bringing up blood (*Processi*, p.39). This kind of sexual hyper-morbidity, which represents penetration as pollution (the body seeks to rid itself of the dirty fluid of semen by expelling all that is within it) is at one level simply an enduring commonplace of Christian asceticism. But such stories of sanctity, especially with this kind of dramatic and particularly feminine form, can also work as a critique of male expectations of heterosexuality. The pious devotee learns how Francesca's husband, seeing after many years of married life the great loathing and suffering Francesca experienced in penetration, finally agreed to a chaste marriage. Though the marriage of Francesca and Lorenzo can be a source of comedy in the cult, it is also represented as a 'happy' marriage, and as such, with Francesca's ultimate achievement of a non-sexual marriage and her markedly protective attitude towards her husband, it stands as a rather unconventional model of matrimony, at odds with the lay ideal of the fecund, obedient wife.

Within the metaphor of the body, bodily effluvia, on the other hand, might be regarded as cleansing. In the account of her visions, the pus from Christ's wounds is described as a precious liquid. A wound on her own breast is said to have suppurated continually so that her confidante Rita had to change the wet dressings constantly. Francesca's sore was only healed when, in a vision, she witnessed the birth of Christ, and Mary herself placed some liquid from a fountain directly on Francesca's body (*Processi*, pp.20, 21; *Vita*, p.54). Thus, in contrast to her care to maintain the intactness of the body, clean and covered from the world outside, Francesca's own mystical wounds, her stigmata and the floods of tears she wept when she contemplated Christ's passion, show her entire body opened. The liquids it emits are cleansing and sacred: the nuns at Tor de' Specchi conserved the fluid and kept her rag bandages to use as curative relics (*Processi*, pp.21, 148).

In stories of this kind, the language of Francesca's sexuality can be interpreted as more than a kind of eccentric version of the married life. It is a reappropriation of her physicality from the role in which medieval wifehood placed it. Francesca altered her body to make it Christ's rather than her husband's. The iron girdle she wore destroyed her attractiveness to her husband while marking her as Christ's own. Indeed, the stories that she refused to eat meat (*Processi*, pp.14–16) – another theme common in many accounts of saintly asceticism – had an additional pointedness in her case, for it was through cattle-raising that Lorenzo Ponziani had made his fortune. In this metaphorical logic, nourishment from his labours was rejected as polluting: she will not allow Lorenzo to be the husbandly provider. Whereas both lay and clerical models of early marriage viewed each spouse as owning the body of the other with the woman subject to the rule of her husband, Francesca redirected this imagery to define her body as a vessel of devotion to Christ.

Many mystics, male and female, have used the imagery of Christ as spouse and bridegroom; but it has a special directness in a woman's mouth, for it is not mediated through a male social experience which prescribes the reverse behaviour outside the mystical context. When the woman is married, it cannot be used without powerful implications for her actual wedded life. The language of holy spousehood permitted Francesca to speak outside her position as wife and endowed her with an extra-hierarchical religious authority.

But it was a double-edged language. Even though Francesca appears to be claiming her own bodiliness outside the categories of human heterosexuality, that reappropriation was ultimately trapped in the social notions of masculinity and femininity which she seems to invert. In the Francescan narrative, men are the polluters; women are dirtied by them. Men's sexuality is powerful and aggressive; women's receptive and inactive. Consequently, Francesca is said to have criticized women for their love of luxury and their carnality, delighting in their own bodies (*Processi*, pp.23, 239), while the same stories report Francesca expressing a kind of fatalistic resignation over men's inherently acquisitive sexual natures. Even when her female body is described as providing nourishing, healing fluids, these pour forth from an impassive, vessel-like body which derives its virtues from absolute subjection to the Divine Will. As she perceives Him, Christ too shares these feminine aspects of submission and humility. Yet though masculinity and femininity, such central elements of Francesca's spiritual language, are blurred and realigned in Francesca's religiosity, she does not really challenge their social meanings. Her cult invokes maternity, humility and passivity. None the less, the dynamic of the cult lies in its emotionally raw recreation of the painful ambiguities of being a woman in the fifteenth-century Roman world, living a spiritual life in a framework constructed by a male priesthood. The very forcefulness of the cult's articulation of these dilemmas undercuts the straightforward clerical homilies about femininity, sexuality and family which it strives to celebrate.

Note

* Our thanks to Sarah Beckwith, Pat Connelly, Ian Robertson, Mike Roper, Ailsa Roper and Carol Willock for their help.

Bibliography

Edited sources

P.T. Lugano, *I Processi inediti per Francesca Bussa dei Ponziani (S. Francesca Romana) 1440–1453*, Studi e Testi 120, Vatican City, 1945 (cited as *Processi*).

for the *Life* by Giovanni Mattiotti:

Acta Sanctorum, Martii, tom. II, Venice, 1735, pp.★93–★178.

Mariano Armellini, *Vita di S. Francesca Romana*, Rome, 1882 (cited as *Vita*).

(The Italian version was apparently reworked in Latin. We have chosen to cite from the earlier and more idiomatic Italian.)

Mario Pelaez, 'Visioni di S. Francesca Romana. Testo romanesco del secolo xv', *Archivio della Società romana di storia patria*, 14, 1891, pp.365–409; 15, 1892, pp.251–73.

Other useful works

Arnold Esch, 'Die Zeugenaussagen im Heiligsprechungverfahren für S. Francesca als Quelle zur Sozialgeschichte Roms im frühen Quattrocento', *Quellen und Forschungen aus italienischen Archiven und Bibliotheken*, 53, 1973, pp.93–151.

Richard Kieckhefer, *Unquiet Souls. Fourteenth-Century Saints and Their Religious Milieu*, Chicago, 1984.

Christiane Klapisch-Zuber, *Women, Family, and Ritual in Renaissance Italy*, Chicago, 1985.

P.T. Lugano, *La Nobil Casa delle Oblate di S. Francesca Romana in Tor de' Specchi nel V centenario dalla fondazione*, Vatican City, 1933.

Carole S. Vance (ed.), *Pleasure and Danger. Exploring Female Sexuality*, Boston and London, 1984.

André Vauchez, *La Sainteté en occident aux derniers siècles du Moyen Age, d'après les procés de canonisation et les documents hagiographiques*, Rome, 1981.

Donald Weinstein and Rudolph Bell, *Saints & Society: The Two Worlds of Western Christendom, 1000–1700*, Chicago, 1982.

13

Village ceremonial life and politics in eighteenth-century Piedmont*

ANGELO TORRE

I

This paper seeks to analyse the spread of the new religiosity fostered by the Counter Reformation. It concentrates on one particular area – rural Piedmont – and one particular aspect – ceremonial life in the peasant communities there.[1]

Despite the importance of ceremony in the local political and social structure, historical studies of religion of rural Europe have usually tended to concentrate on identifying a 'popular religion' and exploring its relationship to the official body of belief. Yet it is only by examining ceremonial activity that we can come to see how religious life represents, albeit in symbolic terms, the various groups and divisions that exist within a community. Ceremony is closely linked to ritual, but it possesses an extraordinary ability to adapt to changing situations. It can therefore provide a unique insight into the interconnections between social structure and the system of belief.[2] An analysis of changes in the ceremonial life of these local communities shows how the Counter Reformation came into conflict with pre-existing ceremonial traditions as it attempted to impose new religious practices on the lay population. The eventual success of the Counter Reformation was thus not a defeat for 'popular religion' but only a stage in a far more complex process. The second part of the paper will show how these new customs and practices were exploited for the power and prestige which they offered in the rural communities – as a resource not only within local politics, but also against the new and encroaching power of the Savoy state in the early eighteenth century.

It is the period between 1680 and 1750 which concerns us here, for it was only then that the Counter Reformation met with definite success in Piedmont. As a growing number of local studies is revealing, it was not until the second half of the seventeenth century – long after the Council of Trent in the 1560s – that the dictates of the Church hierarchy finally overcame the resistance of the rural population.[3]

Of the three major areas of reform which were the product of the Council of Trent – control of social life, of sexual customs, and the insistence on the centrality of the parish church in Christian life – only the last achieved initial acceptance.[4] From the early 1660s the parish clergy began to keep full records of births, marriages and deaths and imposed the practice of annual Easter confession and absolution on their congregations. But although the parish succeeded in carrying out its administrative functions and superintending the rites of passage in the community, this did not mean that parishioners themselves participated emotionally in the new religiosity of the Counter Reformation. Even the parish priests were slow to respond; inventories of parish libraries show that what the clergy read did not conform to what the hierarchy authorized until the early eighteenth century.[5]

Still more difficult was the control of sexual custom. Throughout the seventeenth and well into the eighteenth century a significant number of Piedmontese couples would live together as man and wife prior to receiving the priest's benediction. For them the profane celebrations and the creation of links between their respective families meant more than the religious rite.[6]

Attempts at controlling social life met with mixed results. On the one hand, the Piedmontese Church was quick to emphasize that baptism was an individual rather than a kin celebration and it reduced the number of godparents to two. On the other, it continued to recognize that godparenthood was a position of honour and prestige and that the baptismal ceremony functioned as a means of binding family groups together.[7] By contrast, all the Church's attempts to control another aspect of village social life – lay confraternities – met continual resistance. The Council of Trent had ordered that confraternities be supervised and their numbers limited but this provision remained in abeyance until the late 1600s.[8] The strength of this opposition is extremely significant.

Confraternities – voluntary religious associations of lay people – dated from the late middle ages. They were easily recognizable by the badges, banners and distinctive clothing their members wore, and their activities usually centred on an oratory, separate from the parish church. Here, they recited prayers and practised rituals of brotherhood and solidarity, such as Easter banquets (fiercely opposed by the Counter Reformation bishops), funeral and memorial services for dead members, and ritual 'Washing of the Feet' at Easter. From the sixteenth century on, confraternities had established a strong presence in the community's public life by organizing penitential processions, especially during Holy Week and during the harvest period. The Counter Reformation bishops attempted to control the devotional activities of the confraternities, especially trying to limit older penitential elements such as the public self-flagellation often practised by members during these processions. Yet despite this interference the associations proliferated; whereas in the sixteenth century there was usually a confraternty for every parish, by the seventeenth there were two or even three. Their membership grew as well until by the mideighteenth century 100 to 200 members was normal. A product of this popularity was the creation of confraternities for women which, though under the control of the male institutions, came to share the existing oratories, chapels and even the parish church.

As they sought to control already existing confraternities the bishops adopted the strategy of creating similar organizations which were known as parish companies. They had the advantage of operating from within the local church, and they met at the side altars in the nave. More easily controlled by the priest, these companies concerned themselves with the celebration of masses, novenas and three-day prayer sessions, and the religiosity they practised was more akin to that of the ecclesiastical hierarchy. However, these organizations seldom grew beyond a small membership, usually drawn from the important people of the parish.

By the end of the sixteenth century two particular companies – Corpus Domini and the Virgin of the Rosary – were especially popular. Closely involved with the maintenance and upkeep of the parish church, they undertook such duties as supplying the candles for services and the oil for the perpetual flame above the high altar. From the mid-seventeenth century other types of more purely devotional companies spread into the region, linked to cults made popular by preachers. They too erected their own side altars dedicated to intercessors such as the Virgin of Sorrows, protector of souls in Purgatory, or St Joseph, comforter of the dying.

At first glance, the profusion of these companies seems to suggest that the demands of the ecclesiastical hierarchy were accepted by the rural population. The consumption of the Counter Reformation's new devotional practices appears to be a response to popular demand. If, however, we look closely at ceremonial activity the picture becomes more complex, for the activities of all lay organizations began to compete with those of the local parish church. Thus to avoid clashing with celebrations at an oratory and hence cause attendance at Sunday Mass to drop, bishops ordered that the church service be moved forward to dawn. Even so, the most important processions in the year such as Holy Week and those at harvest time were organized by the confraternity, and when the Counter Reformation introduced new rituals, such as solemn benedictions and forty-hour adorations, these too came under confraternity control.

However, it would be wrong to assume that confraternities represented a static popular religion. They were in fact extremely sensitive to changing tastes and demands in religious practice. During this period, the altars of an oratory would make way for new Counter Reformation saints such as St Charles Borromeo and the Virgin of the Rosary. But they put these cults to their own particular and local use. In the eighteenth century, when the confraternity for the Merciful Heart in the town of Canale adopted the recently canonized St John of Nepomuk, rather than venerating him as the church's new champion against heresy, he was honoured as the protector of crops from frost.

Parish companies too, competed against the local clergy. Indeed their rise in the sixteenth century owes less to the initiative of the Church hierarchy than to a genuinely popular movement to 'return to the parish'.[9] It was the companies which enhanced the prestige of their church by maintaining its buildings and furnishings. With the Counter Reformation they rapidly adopted the new devotional consumerism, and this soon led to competition with the parish church. The petition from the parish priest of Piozzo to his bishop in 1688 illustrates a common phenomenon. He complained that the two major religious companies – Corpus Domini and the Rosary – were attracting a large part of the congregation away from Sunday Mass at the High Altar by holding an alternative service in their own side chapel. At Canale the parish company and the priest peacefully shared the church during the entire sixteenth century but in 1601 the company actually occupied the choir of the church and celebrated the office of the Virgin at the same time as the parish Mass. Their disruptive influence can also be seen in the wrangling over the community's one bell. Owned by the company, it became a symbol of their authority over the parish church and its priest. In 1619 they caused chaos by sounding the *angelus* seven times a day instead of once, while in 1626 the incessant pealing of the bell was disrupting parish services completely. Agreement was only reached in 1667: the priest was allowed to use the bell but only with the company's permission and even then he had to preface his call with special chimes so that the population would recognize it as a parish, not company celebration.

II

The success of the Counter Reformation in altering ceremonial life is mirrored in the changing style of furnishings possessed by local churches and associations. Inventories from the first half of the seventeenth century show a marked increase in both the quantity and elaboration of this equipment. Even the poorest parishes now had a greater number of chasubles to cope with the various colours prescribed for the changing liturgical year. The appearance of both parish church and oratory began to change. From the late sixteenth century the bishops had insisted on the dignity of these religious buildings, demanding that fittings no longer officially approved be replaced. Such decrees were ignored at first and it was only in the late seventeenth century that these decrees began to have effect and buildings came increasingly to reflect the new religious aesthetic.

These stylistic changes cannot simply be interpreted as the 'triumph of the Baroque', for in comparison with the rest of Italy this was a much later development in Piedmont. Rather, they were the result of a transformation in the rural communities themselves, accentuated by the Church's new emphasis on public solemnity and grandeur in its dealings with the faithful.[10] The pyx containing the sacraments which the priest took on his visits to the sick exemplifies this change. Not only does it become more costly, like all other religious objects, but it is now taken around the houses in ritual procession.[11] A new object, the Baroque monstrance with its conspicuous halo of silver or golden rays issuing outwards from the host inside, is increasingly preferred to the older monstrance consisting of a casket bordered by a line of miniature columns, which often enough could be modelled from a mere pyx.

So too, rather than concern themselves with church maintenance the companies now came increasingly to concentrate on an annual procession. Thus at Slondello, the curate announced to the congregation at Mass that a new company of the Carmine would be created for the purpose of holding a procession with the new statue of the Virgin. Likewise, the many activities of the company of Christian Doctrine now became channelled into a newly created Trinity Sunday procession organized by local members. Especially popular were funerals and commemorative anniversaries for the dead; and as the purpose of these companies began to merge with those of confraternities so the complexity and splendour of their processions increased. This often involved the total replacement of all their paraphernalia. Traditional objects, such as candelabras, were now created in a new range of variations, each serving a specific moment in the company's activities. Processions gradually lost their penitential significance as the focus of major attention and expense became the *baldacchino*, the canopy used to carry the sacrament through the village streets. Confraternities were also changing. More and more money was spent on chasubles, and on participation in church services. For example, during the seventeenth century the confraternity of the Merciful Heart at Cavallermaggiore was mainly concerned with decorating the altars of its oratory with candelabras and sculpture. In the following century, however, the confraternity came to regard the procession as the highlight of the year. The work it commissioned moved away from the durable, solid style previously favoured to orders for temporary plaster decorations used to embellish the façade of the oratory during processions.

Both confraternities and companies came to place primary importance on ceremonial activity and began themselves to compete for representation in the public sphere. Indeed, the parish church encouraged this development by providing the occasions at which this new religious consumerism could show itself to best advantage. These church-ordained ceremonies soon came to be imbued with political as well as liturgical significance. Thus, at the feast of Corpus Christi in the early 1700s, all the local public bodies participated in a manner which sanctioned their respective positions within the hierarchy. Here, the *baldacchino*, which protected the Holy Sacrament, the most powerful sacred object, could become the point on which their desires for power converged. These conflicting claims manifested the ongoing conflicts and tensions within the community; but they also revealed the possibility of different alignments of power within the community, which could enjoy a measure of popular support. In Corpus Christi processions, sometimes, each of the four poles of the *baldacchino* would be carried by representatives of various public corporations for the entire length of the processions; sometimes particular corporations would be responsible for a segment of the processional route. So in 1738 at Ticineto, a judge tried to prevent a recurrence of the disturbances of previous years by ordering the village notables to share responsibility for carrying the *baldacchino* between the two confraternities of the Annunciation and St Peter Martyr and the two companies of the Rosary and Corpus Domini. Each bearer was to wear a cap displaying the symbol of his association so as to be recognized by his fellow members and the audience. Even this, however, was not enough to banish conflict. The two confraternities, as the more venerable associations, insisted on holding the handles on the ceremonially pre-eminent right-hand side which the judge had assigned to the two parish companies. This incident is just one of a number repeated in other communities of the time. What such cases show us is that even at the height of the Counter Reformation, the old lay associations remained important expressive vehicles, capable both of giving vent to the conflicts which divided a community, and of displaying its hierarchical structures.

III

As confraternities and companies gradually became more alike they no longer represented different options. Both appear as beneficiaries in wills and their governing bodies were in fact interchangeable. The reasons for this blurring of distinctions is obvious: together, these associations provided a coherent scale of all the honourable offices open to the local population. Each was governed by a series of officers – prior and vice-prior, treasurer and council – and there was a number of ceremonial posts as well. These last, particularly numerous in confraternities, ranged from the Master of Novices to the Sergeant charged with overseeing the smooth functioning of processions. At a lower level in the organization were the *massari*, members whose duty it was to make house to house calls for alms. Each association also employed a chaplain recruited from among the local clergy, themselves usually the sons of the village's most important families. The administration of these bodies was open to manipulation. Nothing prevented one person from holding the same office for a sequence of years or from exercising power in a number of associations at the same time. Yet because high office carried with it the obligation to spend one's own money on ceremonies and devotional furnishings, the priors were usually elected from amongst the rich and influential. In this way the associations avoided bankruptcy while the patronage exercised by a few provided for the satisfaction of the many.

The desire for office stemmed from the powers it conferred. As the associations grew in popularity, there was an influx of new members of all social strata but this was accompanied by an accentuation of the associations' pyramidal structure. The large base of poor and middling people was ruled by a small group of prestigious men who were able to share out the important offices amongst themselves. The hierarchies were even expressed through the associations' services – while the literate elite of doctors, nobles and notaries recited the body of prayers which St Charles Borromeo had devised, the large mass of illiterate members confined themselves to a simple recitation of the rosary. Lavish expenditure on these religious bodies and their furnishings increasingly became the yardstick by which a family's or a faction's prestige was measured. This constituted an idiom through which prestige became publicly expressed and re-presented.[12] The growing importance of ceremonial life in turn offered the elite new and greater outlets for local political competition, based as it was on personal and familial prestige.

A common ploy was to monopolize the offices and exploit an organization's name. In 1742 the parish priest of Ticineto Po was beaten up because he had placed his relatives in the key positions of the village's companies and confraternities in order to ensure a favourable diocesan report. The Sotero, a family of notaries from Guarene, behaved in similar fashion. In 1742, the head of the house, Ignazio, was rector of the chapel of St Rock, chancellor of the Congregation of Charity, and a member of the governing body of the confraternity of the Annunciation. His wife Ludovica was prioress of the Humble Sisters, the women's confraternity; and a relative Don Giacinto was a chaplain attached to the parish church, in charge of an altar linked to the patronage of yet another company, that of the Rosary. Giacinto had other duties: he was father confessor in the church, and he was also rector of the company of Mercy for the Suffering. Two other members of the family, Vittorio and another cleric also named Giacinto, further bolstered the power of the Sotero as councillors in the confraternity of St Michael.

These strategies can only be properly understood as attempts to gain a greater monopoly of power within the community. The result, however, was conflict which was inevitably played out on ceremonial occasions. The village of Montaldo Roero, a short distance from Guarene, was the scene of many such events during the 1730s. Here the progressive monopolization of offices by the notary Sacco faltered when he failed to install his brother Don Giuseppe Antonio as the new parish priest. Instead the bishop had brought in an outsider. Violence soon broke out and after having been physically assaulted a number of times, the new priest used the occasion of a service to threaten some members of Sacco's confraternity of St Bernardino with excommunication. The confraternity's members retaliated by besieging the priest's house and forcing him to retract the threat. Not to be intimidated, the priest launched a series of violent sermons against Sacco, accusing him of not having received Easter communion. He then strengthened his position by taking charge of the community's second most important confraternity – the Merciful Heart – and writing off its debts in return for the members' support.

Sacco replied with even more violent attacks and in 1736 two such incidents disturbed ceremonial life. During a funeral, the priest proposed an increase to the annual tax paid by the members of the company of St Joseph. Sacco, who belonged to this association too, interrupted the sermon and helped by other members forced the priest to retract his decision. A funeral a few months later – for a member of the confraternity of St. Bernadino – was the scenario for a fight between the priest and the dead man's friends over the payment of a burial fee. Sacco then persuaded the confraternity's prior (his cousin) to denounce the priest to the bishop of Asti while in the village there was a revolt against the priest because he had forbidden the burial. The following year Sacco denounced the priest's incompetence to the bishop while numerous witnesses swore to the diligence of Sacco's brother Don Giovanni. A few months later the priest retaliated. He hired a lawyer to plead his case against Sacco for assault and pawned the church's pyx to pay for the legal fees. Sacco reacted immediately – he repaid the pledge for the pyx with his own money and publicly denounced the priest's behaviour. Initial proceedings in the courts also went against the priest who, harried night and day, ended by resigning his post to Sacco's brother in return for a small annuity. Yet this was by no means the end of the conflict. Sacco's overt use of his wide-ranging power now prompted attacks on him from within the community. The notary was denounced in his turn by the municipal council for keeping the pyx in his house rather than returning it to the church. The pyx, centre of the ceremonies which the community helped to finance, was to be regarded as the property of all, not of one person alone.

IV

The actions of Sacco the notary show clearly how religious associations and ceremonial activity in the new style of the Counter Reformation could be manipulated by factions as a means of self-advertisement. It is also apparent that ceremonies were indivisible from the conflicts which divided communities. Yet we still need to explain why it was the ceremonial sphere which became the stage for such disputes. The answer lies in the nature of the local elites and the pressures that moulded their forms of political action in the early eighteenth century.[13] What was new in these power struggles was the need to mediate between the various systems of authority such as local feudal lords, the Church hierarchy and the state. Political competition came to be centred on gaining positions in branches of state offices, in the new Church structures and in the administration of landed estates. At the same time, the local impact of supra-communal authorities made control of power both inside and outside the community essential. It was between these two axes of power – local and external – that local elites oscillated in their attempts to manipulate ceremonial activity.

Once again the career of Sacco exemplifies the process. The earliest details of his life show him deliberately aiming to gain power by monopolizing a wide range of offices. Even in his father's day the family had enjoyed considerable influence. By marrying daughters into important families from nearby communities, his father created a network of alliances which helped him to gain the position of tax assessor in the 1690s. Such an office must have brought links with the court and central government, confirmed a few years later when the duke sold to Sacco's family the rights to name the mayor of their community of Montaldo. The family possessed the spare capital to buy such rights – and they made use of their economic muscle to lend large sums to the debt-ridden community, thereby creating another pressure point on local politics.

Sacco himself extended this network inside and outside the community. He undertook services for feudal and ecclesiastical powers: at Turin in 1720 Sacco was procurator for Count Mazzetti of Frinco, in 1724 he was back at Montaldo Roero deputizing for the Marquis of San Tomaso as village governor. Sacco even had prominent links with the Church. The notary was elected by his fellow citizens as their representative at the bishop's court where he was able to make a large number of important contacts. These in turn formed part of a wider circle of relationships at the provincial capital of Asti where the highest state officials could be counted on to defend his family's interests. Sacco's links beyond the community were translated into power within it. Appointments by the state to various financial and judicial offices in his village made it easy for Sacco to seize the land of peasants too poor to afford legal representation. In this, however, he was cunningly selective – he took over only those lands bordering his own!

Yet the very supra-local nature of the elites' power made it crucial for them to control or at least to dominate certain areas of the public arena of the communities in which they lived. In the first half of the eighteenth century this was becoming difficult for just at this moment Victor Amadeus II was introducing reforms to control local politics. When he instituted provincial intendants between 1696 and 1717,[14] Victor gave them jurisdiction over the whole of a community's political life. Two of their prerogatives were particularly intrusive. First, the community's annual budget had to be submitted to the intendants for approval. Since these budgets registered the outlays borne by taxpayers for expenses of public concern – such as the cost of billeting troops or village councillors' travel expenses – they had often been misused by members to write off debts. This now became impossible. Second, the intendents now had the power to control the actual membership of the council. To prevent cliques monopolizing offices a careful scrutiny was to be made to ensure vacant positions did not pass to a council member's kin.

This new state interference provoked an ambivalent response from the local elites. On the one hand the state could offer fresh opportunities to broaden the extent of their activities, but on the other, this new central governmental control over municipal office increased the importance of local patron–client relationships. Indeed, these now became vital, for they could function as a device to cloak the hoarding of offices. Prestige therefore became more necessary than ever if one were to succeed in local politics. To return to the example of Sacco: despite all his power he was unable to get his son Domenico a job in the local administration and only after a number of attempts was he finally placed as a secretary in a neighbouring village. Sacco's hopes then rested on the appointment of his brother as parish priest, but as we have seen, to achieve this he had to intensify his presence in the ceremonial sphere. At the same time he began to pose as the defender of local government against the central government. In 1734 he opposed higher levies by the state and even came to place himself at the head of a local tax revolt. The case of Sacco the notary thus shows how a successful increase in supra-local influence necessarily required an equally effective consolidation of local power.

V

Local elites began to use the new ceremonial activity to block interference by the state bureaucracy. This strategy can be seen at work in the fate of another reform – that of poor relief – attempted by Victor Amadeus. Between 1717 and 1721 a new body called the 'Congregation of Charity' was set up in every parish to help the local poor.[15] Consisting of the local lord, parish priest, mayor and the twelve largest landholders in the community, these new bureaucratic creations were in marked contrast to the idiom of prestige in local politics where the wealthiest individuals were not necessarily the most influential. Moreover, these congregations marked a break with the previous system. Hitherto poor relief had been financed by rents coming from the large holdings known as 'The Lands of the Holy Ghost', administered by a confraternity of the same name whose officials were nominated by the municipal council.

Piedmontese communities countered the Congregation of Charity in a very revealing way: within a few years many of the new foundations withered away in debt, because peasants refused to pay rents to administrative bodies perceived as emanations of the state. Most of all, the Congregation was incorporated into local ceremonial life, as a confraternity – its notables dealing out bread only to those who attended the body's new Sunday procession, or as a company decorating its altar in the parish nave.

These examples are not the only pointers to the fact that the local elites were resorting to ceremonial activities and the idiom of prestige in reaction to an encroaching bureaucratic idiom of politics. The government itself realized this and in an attempt to understand the success of the various devotional associations it undertook a series of censuses. We know of at least three investigations in less than a century. The first two (1676 and 1729) were probably instigated for tax purposes as the authorities were especially concerned with the size of a confraternity's landholdings. This line of enquiry ended in failure – the results showed the 'lay' organizations to possess little land while in 1729 the large estates of the Holy Ghost were overlooked because they belonged to the 'religious' Congregations of Charity – corporations which, however, often existed only on paper. Only in the census of 1766 did the state adopt a new line of approach by registering not just the property but the totality of ceremonial activity in each community. Next to the budgets of the few surviving 'Congregations' were recorded the incomes and expenditures of the companies and confraternities, wayside chapels and rural shrines. The resulting official report – which makes almost comic reading – complains that the community resources committed to the staging of ceremonies far outweighed those controlled by the Congregation of Charity, and laments the rural population's stubborn attachment to liturgy and ritual – an affection with which the state's bureaucratic charity system simply could not compete.

Behind the contemporary analyses of the 1766 census which

saw the issue in terms of a conflict of jurisdictions, it is possible to perceive a significant social process taking place. The strength of the religious associations and of ceremonial activity (what we might call the 'moral politics' of the Piedmontese communities) displayed a marked increase in the first half of the eighteenth century – precisely when the Savoyard state was trying to strengthen its presence at the periphery. What we are witnessing is not only the belated success of the new ceremonial style of the Counter Reformation but also the creation of a distinctive political system. These new religious attitudes worked to transform ceremony and decoration into a political resource that was extraordinarily adaptable to the power struggles of local parish worthies. On closer scrutiny it also appears that the growing power of the bureaucratic state actually accentuated the local elite's involvement in ceremony: through ceremonial activity, the elite attempted to regain control of the internal dynamics of its community; and this despite the fact that the actual roots of the elite's power often derived from outside the community. However, it was *within* the community – in a network of personal bonds, mediated by the relations of prestige – that power was both developed and represented.

Notes

* Translated from the Italian by Guy Boanas and Lyndal Roper.

1 References to the archival sources used here are in A. Barbero, F. Ramella and A. Torre, *Materiali sulla religiositá dei laici. Alba 1698 – Asti 1742*, Turin 1981 and A. Torre, 'Il consumo di devozioni: rituali e potere nelle campagne piemontesi nella prima metà del Settecento', *Quaderni storici*, 58, 1985.

2 On the role of ceremony in peasant communities cf. J. Boissevain, *Saints and Fireworks: Religion and Politics in Rural Malta*, London, 1965; C. Geertz, 'The Balinese Cockfight', in *The Interpretation of Cultures*, New York, 1973. On the distinction between ceremony and ritual cf. M. Gluckman (ed.), *Essays on the Ritual of Social Relations*, Manchester, 1962; V. Turner, *The Ritual Process. Structure and Anti-structure*, Chicago, 1969.

3 See the series of exhibition catalogues published by the Soprintendenza ai Beni Artistici e Storici del Piemonte: e.g. *Vita religiosa a Canale. Documenti e testimonianze*, 1978; *Inventario trinese. Fonti e documenti figurativi*, 1980; *Per i quattrocento anni della Misericordia. 1579–1979*, 1980; *Radiografia di un territorio. Beni culturali a Cuneo e nel cuneese*, 1980; *Valli monregalesi: arte, società, devozioni*, 1985.

4 John Bossy, 'The Counter-Reformation and the People of Catholic Europe', *Past & Present*, 47, 1970.

5   L. Allegra, *Ricerche sulla cultura del clero in Piemonte*, Turin, 1978.
6   S. Cavallo and S. Cerutti, 'Onore femminile e controllo sociale della riproduzione in Piemonte tra Sei a Settecento', *Quaderni storici*, 44, 1980.
7   On the role of godparentship in these communities cf. G. Levi, 'Strutture familiari e rapporti sociali in una comunità piemontese fra Sette e Ottocento', *Storia d'Italia Einaudi: Annali 1*, Turin, 1978.
8   On confraternities cf. G. Lebras, *Etudes de Sociologie religieuse*, Paris, 1955; M. Agulhon, *Pénitents et Francs – Maçons de l'ancienne Provence*, Paris, 1968; R. Weissman, *Ritual Brotherhood in Renaissance Florence*, New York, 1982.
9   E. Grendi, 'Le confraternite liguri in età moderna', in *La Liguria delle casacce*, Genoa, 1982.
10 Cf. exhibition catalogue *Il Barocco piemontese*, Turin, 1963; M. Leone, Arte sacra a Fossano, in F. Bolgiani (ed.), *Strumenti per ricerche sulla religione della classi popolari*, Turin, 1981; see the peculiar chronology of Baroque in Piedmont in R. Whittkower, *Art and Architecture in Italy: 1600 to 1750*, Harmondsworth, 1958.
11 *Concilium Dioecesanum Casalense*, Casale, 1732.
12 Cf. J. Davis, *People of the Mediterranean*, London, 1973.
13 Cf. generally F. Bailey, *Stratagems and Spoils. A Social Anthropology of Politics*, Oxford, 1970; the political structure of local communities is analysed by G. Levi, *L'eredità immateriale. Carriera di un esorcista nel Piemonte del Seicento*, Turin, 1985.
14 G. Quazza, *Le riforme in Piemonte nella prima metà del Settecento*, 2 vols, Modena, 1957: G. Symcox, *Victor Amadeus II. Absolutism in the Savoyard State 1675–1730*, London, 1983.
15 The edict is published in F.C. Duboin and A. Muzio, *Raccolta per ordine di materia delle leggi . . . emanati dai Sovrani della Real Casa di Savoia*, Turin, 1818–79, tome XII, pp.34ff. On the 'Lands of the Holy Ghost' cf. A. Torre, 'Le visite pastorali. Altari, famiglie, devozioni', in *Valli monregalesi*.

Sects

14

Being a Moonie: Identity within an unorthodox orthodoxy[1]

EILEEN BARKER

This paper is concerned with two concepts: orthodoxy and identity. I shall be drawing upon research carried out on the membership of the Unification Church in the West, but the comments have, I suspect, a wider relevance. It will be argued that there are some ways in which what might appear to be a loss of identity within an unorthodox situation can be interpreted as a quest for an identity based on the principles of religious orthodoxy.

As the concepts of both orthodoxy and identity take many different forms and are applied in many different ways, let me start by indicating how they are used in the paper. Orthodoxy literally means straight or upright opinion or dogma. Religious orthodoxy is associated with a particular cluster or bundle of what are thought to be traditionally held beliefs and values of a conservative nature. In the West, these are assumed to have their foundation in a fundamentalist reading of the Bible. Truth and Goodness, Right and Wrong, are perceived as unchanging, unambiguous and absolute principles that transcend both space and time. A translation of these religious truths into secular values tends to lay stress on the importance of the family, the Family of all believers and/or Humanity, rather than on the individual or society. The rhetoric of orthodoxy tends to extol such virtues as duty and service, and to decry the idea of hedonism. Behaviour ought to be controlled at all times – especially in matters sexual.

As for our other key concept, I find it useful to start from Mol's contention that identity is dependent on some sort of knowledge of who or what one is, and of where one is located in 'symbolic social space'.[2]

'Loss of identity' in the Unification Church

It is frequently asserted that by joining the Unification Church, which has been described as one of the most bizarre, strange and unorthodox of the new religious movements, one completely loses one's identity and becomes a faceless, brainwashed zombie – a Moonie robot.

First, it is pointed out (quite correctly) that conversion to the movement usually demands commitment to a life-style that requires giving up one's previously held, and/or expected future identity. One loses one's role, one's status, and one's standing in society. This would appear to be a particularly significant loss since the majority of members are young people in their early twenties who come from middle-class backgrounds, have reached an educational attainment well above the average, and are likely to be giving up 'good career prospects'. It would appear that the new recruits have been 'absorbed into' a movement that exploitively sends its members out all day on the streets to beg, from complete strangers, for funds over which they (the members) will have no control.

Next, it would appear that the members have surrendered their unique position in the family within which they were raised. Instead of being a (possibly favourite) son or daughter, Moonies call the Reverend and Mrs Moon 'True Parents'. They have, to all intents and purposes, become just one of the thousands of 'children', unrecognized, and probably even unheard of by their new Mother and Father.

Cultural identities appear to be negated as the Anglo-Saxon 'sister' is 'matched' with an Oriental or possibly an African 'brother'. The couple may have scarcely met before taking part in one of the mass wedding ceremonies that will tie them together as man and wife. Physical identities would seem to merge as the member joins the band of indistinguishable Moonies, all of whom are dressed in the uniform of dull respectability – the men clean-shaven, with short hair and sober suits; the women in 'principled' clothes that are perfectly designed to deaden any hint of sexuality. All signs of individuality are concealed. Some of their Christian critics have claimed that Moonies, by accepting the mumbo-jumbo of a dogma that is not merely heresy, but a blasphemous denial of truth, have abandoned their souls (and thus, presumably, their spiritual identity) to the Anti-Christ.

Finally, the Moonie is said to have lost his or her personal identity as a free, autonomous human being. Moonies *must* be brainwashed zombies to have given up their conventional role and beliefs, and to have accepted beliefs and a way of life that are so unbelievably bizarre that they could not conceivably be acceptable to people in full command of their senses. To give up one's life-style, one's life-chances, one's position in society, to deny one's religious training and one's family background – to loose one's identity – in such a manner, is not only unorthodox; it is (it is said) unnatural.

At this point, it might be argued that it is ridiculous to suggest that Moonies have abrogated an identity altogether – they have merely found an alternative (albeit unorthodox) identity in their membership of the Unification Church. My purpose in this paper is not, however, concerned primarily with relativisms. What I hope to suggest is, rather, that by using some of the very same criteria of orthodoxy which would be used by those who decry the Unification Church as unorthodox, it is possible to see how the movement presents an unorthodox version of Western orthodoxy. The suggestion is that the movement is providing a structure that allows the orthodox values of society to be expressed in a way that the conventional institutions of the society itself do not always allow. It provides its members with a number of sources of identity that can make Moonies, who are inclined towards orthodox values, feel more 'at home' than they had felt in the 'outside' world.

Religious orthodoxy within the Unification Church

It is fairly clear that Unification theology (which is to be found in the *Divine Principle*)[3] is not orthodox in the sense that it is considered right or true by the population at large. It can, however, be argued that although the actual content of the theology is (by contemporary standards) unorthodox, the values of the religion, with respect to both theological justification and the practices of the believers, can be recognized to be what has traditionally been regarded as orthodox.

The *Divine Principle* does not accept certain orthodox *creeds*, such as the Virgin birth, but it does have a fundamentalist outlook and presentation in that it accepts the inerrancy of Scripture. It is its traditional *interpretation*, not the Bible itself, that Unification theology questions. Unification theology is not a secular, or a liberal, or a modernist theology, but a strictly orthodox one in that it is inexorably tied to the Scriptures. History is dated from the time of Adam and Eve, and is interpreted as God's (and man's) attempts to restore God's creation to its original, pre-Fall condition. The Unification Church is looking forward to getting back. Its interpretation of the Bible explains why we are here, and where we should be going.

When one comes to consider the practices of the movement, it is even easier to recognize the values of orthodox religiosity. The Unification Church provides absolute, not relative values. It is Kantian in its emphasis on duty; it frowns upon Utilitarian hedonism. It advocates strict and unambiguous moral standards, especially in sexual behaviour.

The values of religious orthodoxy require that belief demands a life of dedicated devotion for every minute of every hour of every day: one does not go to church on Sunday and forget about God for the rest of the week. 'If any man will come after me, let him deny himself, and take up his cross, and follow me'[4] is no idle challenge to the orthodox believer – or to Moonies. They are being offered the chance of identifying themselves with the living Messiah in his mission to restore God's Kingdom of Heaven on earth.

Identity within the Unification Church

How might such an identification be related to the identity of individual members? Identity, it will be remembered, has been defined as dependent on some sort of knowledge of who or what one is, and of where one is located in symbolic social space.

The anthropologist Mary Douglas in her book *Natural Symbols*[5] draws a distinction between what she calls grid and group control. The Unification Church provides an excellent example of a movement exerting high group/low grid control over the individual. For those in such a situation, the primary defining characteristic for any individual is whether or not he or she is a member of the group. Within the Unification Church individuals will identify themselves, and others, first and foremost according to whether or not they are members of the movement.

A significant consequence of having an identity which is defined with reference to a group is that it is unthreatened by the discontinuities of time and place. The continuity of the group is not dependent for its persistence on any *particular* members. Individual Moonies may come and individual Moonies may go, but the Unification Church goes on for ever. Rather than being the pivot of a potentially volatile network (grid), members of a stable community (group) are offered security of tenure in their identity.

Once one has become a member of the group, certain other locations within symbolic social space follow. Many of these are of a purely ascriptive nature and are related to the overall conception of the movement as a family – Moonies refer to the movement as The Family and, generically, to themselves as Family members. Men are known as brothers, women as sisters. They will have a spiritual parent (mother or father) who will have introduced them to the movement, and they may have spiritual children (whom they have brought into the fold) – some even speak of spiritual grandchildren. Reverend Moon is called Father,

Mrs Moon Mother. God is referred to as Heavenly Father.

One's location within the symbolic social space of the Unification Church is not merely ascriptive, however. One can achieve certain positions within the structure of the Church by which one can identify oneself more specifically in relation to the other members. Within the overall hierarchy of the group, one may become a leader – another person's 'central figure'. While it is usually necessary to have reached the age of twenty-three, and to have been in the movement for at least three years, before being blessed in marriage, seniority by itself is not sufficient reason to be selected for a Blessing. The achievement of spiritual maturity is also required, at least in principle, and the married couples (in particular those 'blessed' in the earlier ceremonies) do hold a very special status within the Church. The individual member can also create, affirm or receive his or her more specific identity through certain roles, talents or personality attributes. Such identities (which tend to be limited to fairly circumscribed areas) include musician, artist, cook, teacher, jester, successful fund-raiser or recruiter, spiritually open or sacrificial person.

What the Unification Church provides, in large measure through the religiously orthodox aspects of its beliefs and their related demand for total commitment, is an identity of recognizable value and worth through, on the one hand, simply being a member (one of the elect) and, on the other hand, through doing specific types of directed activity that have visible and clearly defined (in some instances even quantitatively calculable) criteria of success – one can, for example, reach specified goals in fund-raising activities or by bringing new members to a centre. Furthermore, the standards of asceticism and self-control, traditionally expected of religious orthodoxy, are met as a daily challenge of self-denial by the ever-zealous members of the movement.

The symbolic social space of the Unification Church does not demand (indeed it makes a virtue of the lack of) commitment to a clear continuity of identity between the immediate present and the millennial promise of the future. One knows where one is located in the short run, and where one will be located in the eventual scheme of things. It is the middle period, which is going to witness the change in symbolic social space itself, that must be left open and flexible in preparation and in preparedness.

The potential Moonie

I do not wish to enter into a detailed description of the sort of people who become Moonies; I have done that elsewhere. I would, however, like to draw attention to some findings that are relevant to the present theme. First, it should be mentioned that well over 90 per cent of those who are initially attracted into attending a workshop weekend in order to learn about the Unification Church and its beliefs do not go on to join the movement. This would seem to imply that the so-called brainwashing techniques are rather inefficient, or at least very highly selective in their application, and the data that I collected suggest that the Unification Church has a special attraction for those from backgrounds liable to foster a preference for an identity compatible with the values of religious orthodoxy.

One discovers, for example, that the parents of those who joined were less likely than the parents of those who attended Unification workshops but did not become members to have been in jobs in which a primary concern was making or dealing with money or commodities (work in the stock exchange, finance, big business or insurance, for example). Moonies' parents were more likely to have been in professional occupations or jobs offering some sort of service either through caring for individuals (such as nursing, medicine, teaching or social work) or serving their country (through, for instance, the colonial services, the armed forces or the police force). Furthermore, although a higher proportion of people from middle-class homes went to the workshops than actually joined, the non-joiners tended to have parents in lower status non-manual jobs that demanded little or no responsibility (such as repetitive clerical or retail work), while those who did join were more likely to have parents doing highly responsible manual labour (such as foreman or supervisory positions that demanded high levels of skill and decision-making). In other words, those who were seriously attracted to the Unification Church were signfiicantly more likely than those who showed only a passing interest to have come from homes in which, more than economic gain or mere social status, the traditional values of service, responsibility and duty were likely to have been present at some taken-for-granted level.

Generally speaking, those who become Moonies have had a happy childhood within a close-knit family atmosphere. The hypothesis that people join the movement in search of a set of family relationships that they never had is not nearly so strongly supported by the evidence as a hypothesis that they are seeking to re-identify themselves in a warm, protective family atmosphere. Moonies are unlikely to have been dragged from the bosom of their family. Most of them will have left home over a year before they met the movement (38 per cent of them will have left over three years previously), but they may well have been not entirely successful in finding an acceptable identity for themselves within the society in which they found themselves.

Moonies tend to have been brought up in homes in which religion and church-going were of above average importance, but in a sizeable proportion of cases (43 per cent) the parents came from different religious traditions (most commonly one was Catholic and the other Protestant). Religion, in other words, will have been valued in the home, and religious questions will have been assumed to be important, but this will have been without one clear set of answers necessarily being taken for granted. Although at the time of joining the movement a not inconsiderable minority of Moonies will have been going to church, their general attitude towards the established churches – an attitude more than echoed by the non-Moonie control group – was that the churches (clergy and congregations) are hypocritical and 'not really Christian'. Of those who attended a Unification workshop, the people most likely to join were those who believed in God and, at some level, accepted traditional religious values, but were uncommitted to any *particular* dogma or church. Those who either did not believe in God or religion, or, conversely, who knew exactly what they did believe, were unlikely to stay in a Unification environment for long.

In some cases those who go to a workshop do so because they are suffering from what could be termed an identity crisis. Like many young adults, they will have been uncertain about who they really were and where they should be going. It must, however, be added that although a slightly higher proportion than average of those who attended workshops had had psychological problems, those with the worst problems tended not to join.

Those who join the Unification Church should not be thought of as drifters. They are not. They tend rather to be 'doers' who will, in many ways, be more determined in outlook, more achievement-orientated and more anxious to contribute than many of their peers. What they will be uncertain of is *what* to do, *how* to be of most service, *which* role they can best play in society – *in what way* they can be of greatest value and worth in their lives.

Perhaps one of the most significant and marked differences between Moonies and non-Moonies was the response given to one of a series of inquiries about the importance of certain ideals. The ideal in question was, curiously enough, ' "something" but do not know what'. Those who were to become Moonies tended to say that this had been very important and that they had been actively involved in searching for it. The other respondents were far more likely to say that it was not at all important, or what a damn silly question it was and what the hell did it mean anyway? It is, of course, difficult to interpret what it *did* mean, but what seemed to emerge by talking to members was that the society in which they found themselves was experienced as having a gaping vacuum – as though there were an absence of some symbolic social space within which they could locate themselves, or, at least, locate themselves according to the principles, hopes and the kind of self-identity that their past experience of society had taught them to value.

It was as though society had prepared them for something, but then, when they came to look for it, they could not find it. One area in which this manifested itself was that of education. Those who were to become Moonies frequently defined themselves in terms of the educational system at an early stage in their lives – they seemed to be all set to climb to the top of the educational ladder and to be given thereby the passport to a secure and worthwhile future identity. At some stage, however, a contradiction or tension had emerged. Either the educational system had rejected them, or they had rejected the system because they felt that it was not leading them in the sort of direction in which they really needed to go. But they were not sure exactly where they did want to go. They were not the sort of people who had been brought up to be happy in the uncertainty of an antinomian counter-culture.

Both Moonies and non-Moonies laid particular stress on the importance of being in control. When asked how much control they felt they actually had, the majority of them said that they had considerable but by no means total control over their own lives, and that they had very little or no power to change the world. The Moonies felt, however, that since they had joined the Unification Church they had far greater control over their own lives, and that their capacity to change the world had increased enormously because, as members of the Unification Church, they were working for God.

One of the most distressing results of the whole study was to be found in responses to a question asked of the non-Moonie control group about what they thought the world would look like in the year 2000. Quite a few merely stated that there was not going to be a year 2000 – we would have blown ourselves off the face of the earth by then. Most of the other responses were extremely pessimistic: the atmosphere would be polluted, resources exhausted; we could expect deformed children and painful deaths for a population exposed to nuclear accidents; third world countries would be taking a horrible revenge upon their erstwhile masters; mass starvation, over-population – every conceivable horror seemed to be about to descend upon the world. The general feeling was one of hopelessness and helplessness about the future – and uncertainty about what the respondents' roles in the future might be. Few believed that there was anything that they could do about the situation – except, that is, for the Moonies.

The Moonie vision of the New Age that is to be heralded in by the Unification Church was in marked contrast to that of most of the non-Moonie respondents. Their pictures conjured up images of children's paintings. Everyone was happy and smiling and full of love for one another. The sun shone all day, and God and man were in perfect harmony.

Discussion

I conclude this paper with a brief appraisal of some of the ways in which modern society might impede, and the Unification Church assist, the realization of four aspects of identity to which certain segments of European and North American youth might aspire: spiritual self-development, self-realization through others, control or self-determination, and continuity or self-perpetuation.

Young people in the West, both from the middle classes and from a sizeable proportion of the working classes, are likely to have had sufficient experience of material comfort to suspect that, by itself, it will be unlikely to bring about a satisfactory state of self-development. Although they may want a sports car or a new motor-bike, it is unlikely that they will believe that this is all they need for self-fulfilment. Man does not live by bread alone. The more educated they are, the more likely they are to believe that they have a spiritual dimension or potential that ought to be developed – and the more likely they are to have had some sort of personal religious or spiritual experience.[6]

At the same time, much of the language and many of the institutions of Western society have become largely secularized. It is frequently difficult to find either the concepts with which or the social context within which to explore this aspect of oneself. A group with orthodox religious values, can, however, provide the religious concepts and social permission that allow the individual to seek a spiritual identity – to locate oneself within a socially acceptable space through religious symbolism.

Identity has to do with one's relationship with others. A location in symbolic social space needs, by definition, to be one that is recognized by or experienced through others if it is to be recognized and experienced by oneself. This is true both at a personal, face-to-face level, and at the more impersonal, societal level. Discovery of oneself through personal relationships has always been a problem for young and old alike, but in some social contexts there exist conditions of constraint which, while not perhaps allowing the full range of self-exploration, do provide a certain degree of protection from some of the more devastating ravages of self-exposure to others. Today young people are likely to have learned, on the one hand, that it is important to be free and not tied down to any institution or person and, on the other hand, that it is very important to have deep, meaningful, open and loving relationships with one's fellow men – and women. Everything can be desired and sought; but nothing should be demanding or binding. The pseudo-security of contemporary psychobabble encourages unprotected explorations of 'in-depth relationships'. But such exposure risks rejection and the feeling that not only one's public presentation of self, but one's whole inner identity has been found wanting.

Within the permissive society, attempts to find, at a physical level, a closeness that has had no time or security to develop at the emotional or spiritual level can leave the individual who is searching for meaningful love utterly lost and confused, wondering whether it would ever be possible to find someone who could accept the 'real me'? It is perhaps interesting that several non-Moonies who were asked how they would react to having their marriage partner chosen for them replied that it might be rather a relief. Certainly the majority of Moonies (many of whom had tried but failed miserably in their attempts to find the right partner) claimed to be overjoyed at the prospect of having the Messiah suggest whom they will marry – on becoming a Family member, it is believed, you can (usually) talk to members of the opposite sex without worrying whether you wanted to marry them, or whether they were negotiating to entice you into bed. The Moonie's many brothers and sisters remain brothers and sisters pretty well whatever one does. Of course, Moonies can (and do) experience extreme discomfort by not coming up to scratch in certain particulars, but they *belong* – their primary identity is not being threatened. If they do not come up to scratch, they will be not be coming up to scratch *as* Moonies. (Only in rare cases will a member be asked to leave the movement.) Moreover, being in a *religious* community, the Moonie can always be secure in his or her relationship with God. He never ceases to love His children.

But recognition of one's identity is not solely dependent upon personal relationships. One can also hope to play a role within the community – to be a positive part of society by performing some task that contributes to the general weal, not just to exist as an interchangeable, disposable cog of the system. But this often presents a problem for the young person. There are few wars to be fought, and the causes that one might wish to espouse are either too intractable or too inaccessible for the young idealist. Frequently it takes a very long time to reach a position of responsibility in employment; the hope of changing the world by demos has been deflated since the 1960s. Even voluntary work, when found, may turn out to be excessively boring or unchallenging or doing little more than scratching at the surface of the problem. The welfare state might look after you, but can you be important to it?

Surely, the young person might argue, one is not achieving anything worthwhile by jumping on to the bandwagon of rat-race competition for individualistic materialism, and it is useless to hope to achieve anything through the hypocritical or apathetic religious institutions of the day. How would it be possible to assert a worthwhile identity in such a milieu? How could one do one's duty, fulfil one's responsibility, as a citizen, as an individual or as a person committed to fulfilling God's purpose? The values of orthodoxy (and Unification theology) imply that each individual has an important role to play in the history of mankind – there is a place for those who are willing to submit to God's will. The Unification Church offers its members the opportunity to make such a contribution. Moonies are builders of the Kingdom of Heaven.

The ideal revered in modern society of being an individual with control over one's life, making free choices and being responsible for the decisions that will affect one's own life is, it may appear, thwarted at every turn. 'They' are in charge – but even they are not in control. It is the inexorable workings of society, fate, science, Satan, or the wickednesses of man that have taken over. Traditional values have been lost, the world is being lost, and 'they' are incapable of doing anything about it.

Some of those who have imbibed the values of religious orthodoxy believe that if only we could return to the ancient truth with, perhaps, a new and unambiguous interpretation to lead us onward it might be possible to get back to control the future. While critics of the Unification Church see the members as abrogating personal responsibility and free will, the members themselves believe that they have made the momentous decision to commit themselves to God's work. They have, they believe, chosen to give up personal autonomy in certain unimportant areas, in the cause of making a difference in the most important areas of all. Were one just to follow one's own whims – even perhaps one's personal conscience or one's intuitive feeling, or if one were to work out the immediate consequences and thereby personally judge a short-term project, then the group would have no more strength than has the individual. By joining such a group, the helplessness and hopelessness of an aimless, lone identity has gone.

I have indicated that Unification Church members tend not to be drifters – they are people who seek clear definition and purpose – but may have felt themselves drifting, following the ambitions of their parents rather than pursuing their own desires or making any important decisions for themselves. By joining the Unification Church, Moonies can feel that they are asserting their identity. They have decided what they want to do, who they want to be. Their parents were unlikely to have ever chosen this for them. They have at least made a stand.

Some potentially negative consequences of making such a stand can be observed by comparing two kinds of apostates from the movement. Those who decide to leave of their own accord (over half the full-time members do so within two years) are likely to have faced some fairly agonizing self-appraisals. When they eventually leave, they are likely to have to face a further series of problems. They will probably feel that they had to admit to themselves, and to others, that they made a mistake in joining the movement – but however painful that admission may be, it will have been they who decided to do something about it. This, however, is not a luxury afforded to the ex-member who has been deprogrammed. The very concept implies that 'victims' were programmed in the first place. They became members only because they were brainwashed. For the entire period of their membership they will have had no true identity of their own. Because of this their parents were willing to sacrifice perhaps tens of thousands of dollars, and to take the risk of illegally kidnapping them. But those who have been 'successfully' deprogrammed (that is, who have renounced the movement) may suffer a severe identity crisis after the event. They are quite likely to have been persuaded that they neither joined nor left the Unification Church by choice; that other people had to take the law into their own hands to 'rescue' them. They may now find themselves with exactly the same problems that they were experiencing before becoming a Moonie, except that they have now lost confidence in their ability to decide their own future. One deprogrammee put it like this:

> 'I know the Family wasn't actually providing the answers I needed, but now I'm out, I realize just how badly all those questions are still bothering me. I feel so guilty about all the anxiety and trouble I've caused my parents. . . . I feel I have to go back to my studies just to make up for some of the hurt I've caused them – but I can't believe that this is what I'm really meant to be doing. I know I can't go back, but there's nowhere to go forward to.'

One way in which some of those who have been deprogrammed find that they can reintegrate themselves into the social space of society is to assist in the deprogramming of others. Once they have been on the active rather than the passive side of the process, they can start to feel in control, and begin once more to assert their own identities, not only to others, but also to themselves.

The final point that I wish to make has already been suggested at various places in the above discussion and does not need much elaboration here. It is that however much one may value one's identity, it is still necessary to believe that one's identity is held within a reasonably secure context – that the ground will not be pulled out from under one's feet, leaving one naked and alone – that, in other words, the symbolic social space within which one has located oneself will not dissolve away or drastically change.

Modern society is characterized by change. There is technological change; there are the changing balances of power; there are the cultural changes brought about through a mass communication system that both advertises and obscures ideas, and continually threatens to overturn established priorities of values. Yesterday's truth is today's old-fashioned ignorance. Today's economic structure, career structure, career opportunities will be gone tomorrow. Today's lover may be gone tomorrow too. The values of religious orthodoxy assert that there is an unchanging truth, and that there are unchanging values. The religious community provides a stable focus of self-identity and it provides a series of ascriptive, unchanging roles and relationships, while still providing the chance to achieve status through individual merit within certain, clearly circumscribed, areas and according to recognizable criteria. In relating to others, standards are standardized and the values of religious orthodoxy are respected. Good and bad, right and wrong do not shift according to vagaries of time and place, nor yet according to the particular individual to whom one is relating within the continuing community – the symbolic social space within which the individual is located has a reality that transcends the individual.

In this essay, it has been suggested that some individuals in society can subjectively experience a discovery and a security of identity within what appears to many to be a grossly unorthodox movement that denies its members any personal identity. It has, however, been argued that the Unification Church functions to provide an acceptable social space for its members because it meets certain values of orthodoxy through its beliefs and practices. It has, moreover, been suggested that it was the experiences that the members had had within the wider society that contributed to the potential resonance that such values would have for the individual in his or her search for a satisfactory identity – but that the practices and institutions of the society itself were apparently unable to provide an adequate basis for such an identity for such people.

Membership of the Unification Church is numerically very small in the West – perhaps three thousand full-time members in North America and a further two thousand in Europe. Obviously it would be foolhardy to try to generalize too widely from so small a minority. I certainly do not wish to suggest that the only way to find one's identity in modern society is through some sort of religious orthodoxy. Other options are available, and these can work perfectly satisfactorily. These options may, however, have certain curious overlaps with or be reactions to some kind of orthodoxy, and although many options may take a purely secular form, there do seem to be indications that religious forms have a tendency to re-assert themselves within the most secular of contexts. My suspicion is that either too much or too little socially-specific orthodoxy could allow or even facilitate the rise of new, unorthodox systems to re-present the traditional values of religious orthodoxy. It may well be that just as we seem to be moving furthest away from religious orthodoxy, we find that some of its values will be re-asserted from within what might appear to be the strangest of places.

Notes

1 I would like to thank the Social Science Research Council of Great Britain for awarding me the grant with which this research was carried out. Further details of the methodology and about the Unification Church can be found in Eileen Barker, *The Making of a Moonie: Brainwashing or Choice?*, Blackwell, Oxford, 1984.
2 Hans Mol, *Identity and the Sacred: A Sketch for a New Social-scientific*

Theory of Religion, Blackwell, Oxford, 1976.
3 *Divine Principle*, Holy Spirit Association for the Unification of World Christianity, Washington, 1973.
4 Matthew, Chapter 16, verse 24.
5 Mary Douglas, *Natural Symbols: Explorations in Cosmology*, Barrie & Rockcliff, London, 1970.
6 David Hay, *Exploring Inner Space*, Penguin, Harmondsworth, 1982.

Colonization and resistance

15

Franciscan missionaries in sixteenth-century Mexico

INGA CLENDINNEN

Missionaries are people committed to the notion of the portability of religion: they 'have Faith, will travel'. In what follows I want to explore the encounter between sixteenth-century Spanish Franciscan missionaries and the pagan Aztecs of Mexico, to see how viable that notion of portability is. First I will sketch the implicit model of religious change the Franciscans worked from, and then investigate the defects of that model through an analysis of what the missionaries actually achieved, and their confusions about it. Finally I want to draw out from this particular example some propositions of a more general kind about the relationship between the cluster of sentiments, actions and understandings touched by the sacred that we call 'religion', and the larger and more inclusive cluster of sentiments, actions and understandings we call 'society'.

Conditions of the particular historical encounter to be kept in mind are: that the Spanish attempt to convert the Indians followed on military conquest, the missionaries pursuing their activities alongside the vigorous exploitation of the native populations by their compatriots, and that the missionary campaigns were official, being initiated and supported by the Spanish Crown.

Franciscans dominated the field in priority, numbers and energy, the first official Franciscan mission, the famous 'Twelve Apostles to the Indies', arriving in Mexico four years after the fall of the Aztec capital. They were men drawn from the strenuously reformed province of San Gabriel, preaching a newly-purified and examined faith. They and those who came after them were ready for hardship, flexible in organization, unified in ideology and intrepid in the defence of 'their' Indians against the depredations of their compatriots. Nor were they naive, being made shrewd enough anthropologists by the professional eye they kept on their fellow-Spaniards' doings, and brought by the experience of their own training to a nice sense of the power of minute regulation to mould and elicit response. They were acute observers of the native world they were committed to change. The dimensions and indeed the nature of the task were novel, but the Franciscans had experience of missionary work in Spain, some ministering to the recently and forcibly 'converted' Moriscos, and more striving to animate the faith of the 'Old Christians' through their preaching circuits.

The Mexican mission was also to be accompanied by death. A native population estimated at 26 millions at contact in 1519 was reduced to 1¼ millions – that is, by 90 per cent – in less than a century.[1]

Faced with the massive undertaking of the Mexican conversion, the Franciscans did what missionaries typically do: they examined the 'Aztec religion' for points of similarity with their own. They found that the Aztecs of Mexico were, like Spanish Catholics, a people habituated to the forms of an institutionalized religion. They sustained a professional priesthood, distinguished from the laity by distinctive dress and demeanour, by sexual abstinence and severe self-mortification, by access to special knowledge and their role as intermediaries between ordinary people and the gods. Ceremonial was public and elaborate, following a complex ritual calendar, involving sacred locations both man-made and natural, the manipulation of sacred images and other ritual paraphernalia, the use of sacred chants and dance and the wearing of special garments. The laity were participants in the cycle of fasting through feasting, in auto-sacrifice and in the making of offerings to the images of the gods, although at a less strenuous level than that required of the priests. The priestly hierarchy penetrated down to the most local level of Aztec society, with priestly involvement in the rites of passage of the ordinary person. Both religious systems offered an array of divine persons, whether Aztec deities or Catholic saints, who specialized in particular human needs. And – as the missionary friars never tired of noting – the Aztecs practised rituals which looked very like baptism and confession, and on certain occasions ate sacred breads which were named the flesh of a god. If some friars were perturbed by the violence and suffering which announced the new Christian deity, the Aztecs were familiar with militant gods, and the prestige brought by victory. They had themselves required from those they conquered the recognition of the supremacy of their own tribal god, and the readiness with which some chiefs accepted baptism and offered worship to the Virgin Mary (the Spanish conquistadores' favourite image) even during the course of the conquest indicates their eagerness to ally themselves with a triumphant deity.

That kind of analysis, in which the (hopefully) recipient religion is described in the terms and categories of the incoming religion, has its uses. But it is, of course, highly selective, and that selectivity has sinister consequences. The very orientation of the description protects the missionary or the analyst from recognizing the native religion as a distinctive imaginative universe, another coherent way of making sense of the world. It rather presents itself to them as a bundle of discrete beliefs and bits of behaviour and dispositions – a habit of burning incense here, an inclination to self-mortification there, a belief in a rain-maker god yonder. It also feeds the assumption that meanings – at least in the case of the religion designated as inferior – can be detached from the objects or gestures or roles which act as their symbolic vehicles, which objects or gestures can then be used for new purposes.

This way of thinking opens the way to what I have called the 'trade-store model' of conversion or directed religious change. The trade store I have in mind is an invention of European colonialism. As part of the general civilizing mission, a store is set up in an interesting native area, and stocked with goods considered attractive to the natives. Their attraction lies in their similarity, yet superiority, to some native product. ('Why do you need to catch fish? See this fine tin of sardines!') With time and enough penetration of the market, 'undesirable' native products and preferences are displaced, to be replaced by European products and learnt European preferences. So the natives are benefited at once materially and morally.

Missionaries – and most analysis of missionary activity – often conceptualize 'conversion' in precisely the same way: as the displacement, by guile, persuasion or force, of undesirable elements in the native religion and their replacement by roughly homologous 'correct' beliefs and understandings from the new religion, until, with the insertion of enough new pieces, *voilà*! the conversion is effected. While it is not a simply cumulative notion of conversion – the assumption seems to be that at some point the new picture 'emerges' – it carries psychological benefits, as its stages are reassuringly easy to count.

In Mexican studies that trade-store model dominated early attempts by both historians and anthropologists to account for the vicissitudes of the conversion process, and to assess its outcome.[2] More important, the same implicit model controlled the thinking of the missionary friars themselves. Here I want to explore what the consequences of that control were for the missionary friars in the strategies they evolved to effect the conversion, and the criteria they invoked to evaluate their achievements.

The friars' first step was to exploit the context of coercion by gathering up the sons of Indian lords and isolating them in special schools, where they were instructed in the essentials of the

Christian faith. Those 'essentials' were defined for the missionaries (and for us) by the Indian catechism devised by one of the fathers. The *Doctrina Cristiana* of Alonso de Molina closely resembles the catechisms in use in the peninsula at the time. It consisted of the 4 essential prayers (the Credo, the Pater Noster, the Ave Maria, the Salve Regina); the 14 Articles of the Faith; the 10 Commandments of the Lord; the 5 Commandments of the Church; the 7 Sacraments, the 7 Virtues and the 7 Sins; the 14 works of mercy; the 7 gifts of the Holy Spirit; the 8 Beatitudes; the 3 powers of the soul and the 3 enemies of the soul; the formula of the general confession . . . and so on. The Indians also had to learn how to make the sign of the cross.

The Franciscans worked with a desperate sense of urgency, as Indians were dying around them unbaptized and so lost. Their ingenuity in teaching methods was magnificent. Having at first no knowledge of Nahuatl, the Aztec language, they borrowed from the Aztec tradition of pictographic writing and drew pictures of hell and of specially grievous sins, and even made sturdy attempts to represent the major prayers in picture-writing. They were initially unready (as so many missionaries have been) to translate those prayers into the Indian tongue, in part for fear of corrupting their meaning, and also because they believed those particular Latin syllables could open the way to God's grace, even if spoken with little understanding. So they chose to begin the process by giving their Indians little drawings representing certain Nahuatl words which happened to sound like the required Latin word, so the Indians would say the words while counting off syllables or phrases by shifting little stones from one heap to another. For example, for the Pater Noster the friars selected the simple Nahuatl word 'pantli' or flag for 'pater', and 'nochtli', the fruit of the tunal cactus or prickly pear, for 'noster'. So the Indians would mutter 'pan-tli noch-tli' and so on through the prayer until with time they would be brought to a correct pronunciation and a correct understanding.

It was slow work. Ingenious as they were, such methods could call forth only a halting and piecemeal response. The Franciscans' own religious life had ecstatic experience as its highest goal: to see that complex and vibrant faith reduced to a few clear truths enshrined in clear language, or the great burdened sign of the cross, so powerfully charged with significance, reduced to the awkward learned movement of a hand between forehead and breast and shoulder, must have been disquieting. (The trade-store model does not do violence only to the native religion.) The friars remembered the exuberant processions and festivals of Catholic

Spain: expressions of popular religiosity they had always viewed
with more benevolence than had more rigidly orthodox orders.
So they cast around for ways to engage the enthusiasm of the
Indians; to awaken in them some emotional response, to bring
some life to those rote-learnt prayers and compulsory observances.

That spontaneous response was to come, and the friar Toribio
de Motolinía, one of the original 'Twelve Apostles to the Indians',
recorded the stages of its growth with tender relish. Initially, he
recalled, the Indians fled from the friars:

> it was very distasteful to them to hear the word of God, and all
> the knowledge they wished was of how to give themselves over
> to vice and sin by taking part in sacrifices and festivals, eating,
> drinking, and becoming intoxicated at them, and offering to the
> idols their own blood, drawn from their ears, tongues, arms
> and other parts of their bodies . . . this land was a copy of hell,
> its inhabitants shouting at night, some calling on the devil,
> some singing and dancing.

The friars put a stop to those pagan performances by using the
young lads in their mission schools as a kind of Red Guard, the
boys going out in groups of up to a hundred, at first under the
direction of one or two friars but later independently, to break up
the ceremonies and deliver the delinquents for punishment to the
nearest monastery. But the turnabout in Indian attitudes came
only when the friars managed to involve the Indians directly and
actively in Christian worship. The strategy they hit on came
directly out of the trade-store model of conversion. One friar,
who knew how large a part chants and dance had played in the
pagan rituals, prepared for a Christmas festival by composing a
'solemn song' in the native tongue about the Virgin Mary and the
birth of Jesus, and gave his Indians permission to make special
costumes to dance in the ceremony. Success was immediate: so
many Indians came pouring in, some from distant places, that the
church and even the patio were filled to overflowing. Others
learnt from this experiment: Motolinía recalled the 'fire of
devotion' suddenly kindling in Indian hearts when they were
given prayers 'in their own tongue and set to music in a simple
and pleasing tune':

> they were so eager to learn, and there were so many of them,
> that they were fairly piled up in the courtyards of the churches
> and shrines and in their own section of the town, singing and
> learning prayers for three and four hours on end; and their haste
> was so great that wherever they went, by day or by night, one

could hear them on all sides singing and reciting the whole catechism.[3]

The time of enthusiasm had arrived. Weeping, moaning Indians begged for baptism, and despaired if the fathers demurred at their lack of preparation (not many Franciscans demurred). Eager Indians sought out friars to make their confessions, and begged for harsh penances. The friars, remembering the great Aztec ritual dramas, had devised little plays on Christian themes: they saw them seized on and elaborated beyond their best hopes and indeed their comprehension, as villagers jubilantly expended their meagre resources on grand processions, with musicians and circling, garlanded dancers, honouring the lavishly-decked image of their favourite saint. The village churches, so long neglected and empty save for their compulsory classes, were swept and decked with flowers and fresh pine branches, and their altars were heavy with offerings, while the Christian cross or shrines to the saints marked out the sacred places in a landscape which had once been mapped by devotions to the Aztec gods. Particular Christian festivals invoked great enthusiasm. All Souls' Night saw offerings made to the dead in every churchyard, and there was wild enthusiasm for self-scourging, which on Holy Thursday was so intense as to move watching Spaniards to tears, and even emulation.

Mastery of the catechism did not keep pace with popular enthusiasm for collective ritual performances, but the asymmetry did not worry the friars too deeply. Officially they were committed to testing the Indians' capacity to recite the whole catechism at baptism, marriage, and then at each prescribed yearly confession. But they were reconciled to the gap familiar in all education programmes between proclaimed official goals and realistic objectives. Perhaps the friars were able to teach the catechism in its entirety to the noble boys sequestered in their special schools, and part of it to the children of commoners, who were required to attend daily instruction, but as a programme of instruction for the mass of Indians it was clearly utopian, and in practice the friars (there were only about sixty active in all of Mexico in 1540) were ready to settle for very much less.

That 'much less' came down to the ability to make the sign of the cross, and to repeat the four basic prayers. Even that modest aim was not fully realized, to judge from the records of the Mexican Episcopal Inquisition of the late 1530s and early 1540s. Few of the baptized Indians who came into its nets could stammer their way through all four prayers, and made the sign of the cross only uncertainly. They were probably typical. Motolinía for one was scathing about those sticklers for intellectual tests – usually clerics fresh from Spain, as he acidly commented – who would refuse baptism to some poor Indian, who had perhaps made a special journey of two or three days, simply because the Indian through anxiety and natural timidity could not say the prayers. For Motolinía the Indians' passionate desire for baptism, their despair at its refusal, and above all their docility, their uncomplaining endurance of hardship and the absolute simplicity of their lives identified them as already worthy of the Kingdom of Heaven.

On the same grounds he would have admitted them freely to communion, but that was to remain a cautiously-granted privilege. The Indians had access to the sacraments of baptism and marriage, and if only rarely to extreme unction, there being too few priests, and too many dying Indians, the dead were buried in consecrated ground. Ideally Indians, like Spaniards, were to confess once a year, but, like Spaniards, often didn't. They were admitted to Holy Orders not at all.

Later missionaries, with more experience behind them, would have perhaps been made suspicious by the phenomena I have outlined, but the Franciscans, preaching the word of God to a previously undiscovered people, had Christ's mission as their only precedent. However committed they were to the 'corpus of beliefs' notion of Christianity as encapsulated in the Molina catechism, they were equally or more committed to the view that Christianity existed through its participatory rituals, and in a certain style of social and religious expressivity. They had themselves initiated and encouraged the efflorescence of that exuberant ceremonial life, selecting out of pre-contact practice the dispositions and bits of behaviour – an enthusiasm for dance and music, a taste for colour and costume – which they now saw incorporated into the Christian displays of the villages. Those displays, with their local processions, the transparent competitive pride in their particular saints, were profoundly gratifying to the friars, recalling as they did the spontaneous expressions of popular piety they had watched so affectionately in Spain.

The recognition of failure came later. To some, like Motolinía, who died in 1568, it came not at all. But by that year, nearly fifty years after the conquest, few friars were persuaded that the mission had been successful. Bernardino de Sahagún, the great Franciscan ethnographer of the Aztecs, unmatched and unchallenged in his knowledge of Indian life and Indian ways, had arrived in Mexico in 1529, only five years after that first official mission. He was to write at the end of a long life spent in the

Christian cause that there had been no conversion; that 'a darkness had been spread . . . to preserve the early fame of both baptizers and baptized', and that the whole heartbreaking task still remained to be done.[4] The elaborated ceremonies which had so delighted Motolinía were in Sahagún's view suffused with motifs and meanings of the old religion, and the Spaniards who watched them so complacently were being deceived under their very noses. The eager feasting of the dead on All Souls' Eve and the enthusiastic scourging of Holy Thursday he saw as acts of worship to the old gods, however gilded by dissimulation, and the bulk of his bulky writings was dedicated to bringing his fellow missionaries to recognize what they were looking at. Diego Durán, a Dominican who had grown up from early childhood in Mexico, and spoke Nahuatl 'like a native', concurred in Sahagún's bleak judgment. He believed that while the names of the Aztec gods had been forgotten, and Indians worshipped before Christian images with apparent devotion, they still lived according to the rhythm of the pagan calendar and understood the world in its terms. Heathenism, he thought, threaded through everything: in all their banquets and recreations; in their wakes and funerals, weddings and births; in all the activities of the everyday world: 'in sowing, in reaping, in storing grain, even in ploughing the earth'. The problem was to separate it out:

> The ancient beliefs are still so numerous, so complex, so similar to our own in many cases that one overlaps the other.
> Occasionally we suspect that they are playing, adoring idols, casting lots regarding future events in our very presence.[5]

What had gone wrong? Or, rather, what, if anything, had ever gone right? I think we are seeing, in the failure of the strategies, and in the friars' confusion over the diagnosis of the symptoms of that failure, the inescapable consequences of the application of that simple, commonsensical trade-store model of religious change. Consider first the strategy for the rote-learning of the Pater Noster. By setting their Indians to murmuring 'pantli nochtli' the friars were acting on two assumptions integral to the trade-store model: that words – Indian words at least – have only one simple and stable meaning, and further that words or any other vehicle for meanings for that matter, can be abducted from the web of understandings of which they were a part, and so made available to carry new meanings, or, in this particular case, to function as a convenient sequence of mere sounds. But meanings cannot be so casually sliced off. They are crucially and chronically context-dependent, taking their sense from their sustaining system, as increasing numbers of linguists, historians, anthropologists and philosophers keep demonstrating. 'Pantli' did indeed mean 'flag'. But it also signified the white banners of human sacrifice, while 'nochtli', the tunal fruit, was for the Aztecs the symbol of the excised human heart, the 'precious eagle cactus fruit' upon which the Sun and the other great gods fed. We can't know what the Indians made of muttering 'pantli nochtli' while they shifted their stones about, but we can know it could not have been what the friars intended.

The friars did not carry the notion that meanings can be stripped away from their material vehicles over to their own cultural expressions. There they saw the meanings as at once manifest and integral. For example, for them the wearing of the habit signified their poverty, humility, modesty, and their dramatic differentiation from their proud, exploitative, acquisitive and carnally-minded fellow-Spaniards. They had been impressed by the Aztec priests' austere devotion to their gods, and had approved their long black garments, 'like Dominicans', the Franciscans thought. They therefore expected the Indians would effortlessly 'read' the message contained in the wearing of the habit: that an ascetic priesthood is an ascetic priesthood. They were accordingly distressed and angered to discover a story abroad that the friars were in fact dead men, corpses, who wore their habits by day to conceal their rotting bodies, but who set them aside at night when they roamed to hell to seek out their women.

The missionaries put this dispiriting story down to deliberate malice. It probably had a more innocent genesis. Aztec priests wore swaddling garments, but only for some of the time. At other times they went naked, or decked in the regalias of the gods: on numbers of public occasions their bodies were displayed. Lay Spaniards rarely doffed their clothes, but their servants could testify to their normality, and their dress revealed the human contours of their bodies clearly enough. Only the friars went always muffled in body-concealing garments. And they dramatic-ally shunned women – at least in daylight hours. Indians were familiar enough with the notion of sexual abstinence before entry into the ritual zone, but they had no sense of celibacy as an active virtue, nor of the depth of Christian anxiety about the flesh. Therefore it would be a reasonable inference that friars concealed their bodies because those bodies were actually (not only metaphorically) vile, and avoided licit sexual relations because they sated themselves illicitly at night. A message mangled in translation.

Perhaps the most distressing legacy of their dependence on the trade-store model was exposed when the friars turned to evaluate the outcome of their efforts. They had acquiesced in the professional necessity that their own lived faith should be dismembered into portable, communicable forms. The problem was: how were they to recognize it when it was reconstituted in this alien place? What were its essential identifying features? It is here I think that their particular perplexities shed light on the large question of the relation of 'religion' to 'society'.

For Motolinía, the matter was simple enough. It did not matter if the Indians had minimal intellectual grasp of Christian doctrine, or if their popular devotions displayed continuities with the old ways. Indeed, some of those old ways he read as intimations of Christianity, as when he described the Aztec ritual of baptism:

> In many parts of this country they bathed new-born children on the eighth or tenth day and then, if the child was a boy, they put a tiny shield in his left hand and an arrow in his right hand; if it was a girl, they gave her a tiny broom. This ceremony seemed to be a sort of symbol of baptism and meant that the baptized were to fight against the enemies of the soul and to sweep and clean their souls and consciences so that, by baptism, Christ might enter.[6]

Why were the Indians so clearly Christian? Because of their social ethics and essentially because of their natures: their simplicity, their innocence, their contentment with little. Some old people, he thought, were almost saints already; even the Indians' compulsive drinking he attributed to their touching inability to manage the things of this world. His experiences in Mexico led him to question not the 'Christianity' of the Indians, but of some Spaniards.

Sahagún was not much more interested in the Indians' capacity to recite the catechism than was Motolinía, not because he considered the issue of intellectual understanding to be irrelevant, which was Motolinía's position, but because he knew words could deceive. Indians could recite their prayers, demonstrate their expertise in the dogmas, but that did not make them Christian. What mattered were the rhythms and patterns of action displayed in their religious practices, and those patterns and rhythms betrayed the continuation of traditional cosmological understandings of the person and the person's relationship with the seen and unseen world. Where Motolinía saw the joyful devotions of a 'naturally' devout people, Sahagún saw in those same devotions the terrible proof that the lived religion was pagan.

The Dominican Durán saw the least ambiguous continuity in the small rituals which casually speckled the ordinary daily routines of life. But did the Indians understand their import, or did they perform them as it were mechanically? In public ceremonies the continuities persisted, but he was still unsure how conscious the Indians were of them: he never tired of rehearsing the remarkable number of apparent parallels between the rituals of the two religions, which first promised to make conversion so easy, but which he now suspected were malicious devices of the Devil to impede the holy work. He thought the timidity of temperament noted by Motolinía was the consequence of the Indians' terrible afflictions; that their spirits had been so hurt and crippled that they dreaded novelty, and clung more in despair and fear than conviction to the old ways. But what puzzled him most was what he saw as a curious insubstantiality in the Catholicism even of those Indians who knew and indeed seemed to believe in the Christian doctrines. Why was their piety unpersuasive? It was not lack of instruction, for 'what people in the world have been preached to, indoctrinated and taught more than this nation?' It was not lack of capacity, for in actual understanding many Indians excelled Spanish peasants. It was, rather, the lightness with which they held the faith; they 'believed' the dogmas, but 'if a thousand dogmas were preached, they would believe them all'. And meanwhile, in the daily round of planting and harvesting, of giving birth and dying, they followed the ways of their ancestors.

That fatal inconstancy he contrasted with Spanish peasants:

> Let us consider that in Spain there are people as uncouth and coarse, or almost so, in some parts of Castile, . . . in corners of provinces where men's minds are extraordinarily brutish and rude (especially in matters of religious instruction), much more so than these natives. At least the latter are taught catechism every Sunday and holy day, and receive the Gospel. The former, though in many villages, never hear a sermon in their lives.

None the less, these coarse peasants were rock-solid in the faith, and would let themselves be torn to pieces 'defending a single article':

> If you ask [one], 'Why is God One and also a Trinity?' he will answer, 'Because that is the way it is.' And if you ask him, 'Why are there Three Persons in the Trinity and not four?' he will answer, 'Why not?' And these two answers, 'That is the way it is', and 'Why not?' satisfy all their doubts and questions

regarding the Faith, since they believe firmly what their parents taught them and what is believed and sustained by our Holy Mother the Church.[7]

That Durán was right in his estimation of the lack of theological sophistication of some Spanish peasants is confirmed by William Christian's fine study of village visionaries in sixteenth-century Spain. Men and women caught up in the investigation by the Church did no better than their Mexican Indian counterparts when it came to the recital of the four essential prayers. Christian introduces us to one male villager, whom we have no reason to regard as atypical, who did not know the Salve Regina or the Credo, although he could manage the Ave Maria and the Pater Noster. A woman questioned in 1523 was rather better instructed: she could say all four prayers, with only a few mistakes. But, as Durán over in Mexico knew well, inability to recite prayers did not mean lack of commitment to the faith. The man confessed each year, and while he could not recite the Ten Commandments or the other prescriptions of the Church, he had a lively if unorthodox understanding of what constituted 'sin'.

> Asked by his Reverence what it was he confessed, if he did not know the deadly sins or the Ten Commandments or the five senses, he said he confessed what he did know about. He was asked if pride or envy or lust or the killing of a man or insulting someone with offensive words was a sin, and to each of these he replied he did not know. He was asked if theft was a sin, and he said that, God preserve us, theft was a very great sin.

The woman who knew her four prayers knew no others – 'save one she said at night to "God the Father and to Saint Mary Mother and to the Holy Majesty [the Crucifixion] and to the flower that was in it [sic] and to Saint Bernard".' However much her homemade prayer grieved her inquisitors, she was in the estimation of her own parish priest a 'good Christian', attending mass regularly, fasting occasionally, and receiving communion every year. Above all, she was an eager participant in the devotions at the local shrines.[8]

We might well want to ask Durán at this point what was this quality about his Spanish peasants – who could not confidently recite the prayers, whose religious practices, while exuberant, were unconventional, and whose understanding of basic dogmas was at least unorthodox – which made them unequivocally Catholic, while Mexican Indians, who did pretty much the same things, were not. Durán's answer would be 'the Spaniards' firmness in the faith' – leaving aside just what constituted the faith – 'and their readiness to die for it'. But while particular Mexican Indians might have been easily unnerved in the presence of a Spanish priest, and would readily acquiesce in whatever proposition he happened to present, particular Indian communities were to be notably intransigent when authorities lay or ecclesiastical interfered in village devotions, by ordering the replacement of a specially cherished cross or the retirement of a specially beloved image. Then they rioted, and after punishment rioted again, with exemplary conviction.

To make sense of all these confusions we need an important distinction drawn by William Christian in his *Local Religion in Sixteenth Century Spain*, a work which merits a much wider readership than it seems to have received.

Christian's concern is not with religion as prescribed, but religion as practised. He discovered that in describing religion as it was practised by the Spanish laity in the later sixteenth century the distinctions conventionally drawn in studies of religion and society – urban/rural; popular/patrician; 'little' tradition/'great' tradition; traditional/modern – did nothing to illuminate the kind of religious practices he was encountering, which was at once 'rural and urban, lettered and unlettered, more or less modern, and even applied to the king'. What it was, he decided, was 'local': closely tied to a particular landscape and to the holy places where the divine could be contacted; following a sacred calendar of feasts, fasts and other observances; corporate; conservative. While 'the vast majority of sacred places and moments held meaning only for local citizens', all communities engaged in equivalent activities. Between the local and what he called the 'universal' religion there was a two-way process: 'while the Catholic Reformation was affirming the subordination of the former to the latter, communities continued, as they always had, to adopt and domesticate the symbols and discourse of the Church Universal for local votive use'.

That 'religion as practised', localistic, particularistic, partisan, conservative, he contrasts with a different vision of what religion is about. The paragraph deserves quoting in full:

> Certain kinds of people did not think in local terms, and their loyalties were only vestigially with their home place. Examples might include, for sixteenth century Spain, humanists and Erasmians in the first decades, perhaps some circulating monastics, the alumbrados, and mystics like Teresa of Avila. These were precisely the people, because they were least local,

because they were idea makers, literary as well as literate, who controlled the written culture and whose religiousness we know most about. After all, they are most like the translocal idea makers who write history. Our biases conforming with theirs, we systematically exclude information about the local, or look at it, from their view, as superstitious, whereas in fact the local-minded are by far in the majority in our culture as well as theirs.[9]

Christian provides an immediately persuasive example of the tension between localist experience and translocal orthodoxy when he talks of the village priests he encountered in the Spanish province in which he was working in 1976 and 1977. After noting the

fierce pride with which some brotherhoods or town authorities guard the books of miraculous images, even from the priest, [leaving] little doubt that whatever canon law may say, local religion is theirs,

he continues:

The priests are usually from different villages. They often speak of local devotions with a bemused tolerance, occasionally wondering out loud about 'pagan superstitions'. But when asked about the shrines of their home villages, the same priests speak with tenderness, excitement and pride. For them religion learned at home, embedded in the home landscape, transcends the doctrinal attitudes learned in the seminary, which they may apply elsewhere.[10]

Christian's distinction, between that chronically local 'religion as practised', and 'religion' as conceptualized by translocal men, provides the clue for the unravelling of the dilemmas and divisions which beset the Spanish missionary friars of the sixteenth century, and, I suspect, many missionaries since. The Mexican missionaries sustained within their 'Christianity' the same tension as do Christian's present-day village priests, but exacerbated painfully, as such tensions always are, by the exigencies of the colonial encounter, where notions usually left comfortably implicit must be made explicit. Above all, they were as missionaries committed to the 'translocal' position; to a refined-to-propositions Christianity as encapsulated in the Molina catechism, or as distilled and dramatized in the sacraments or other rituals, yet their own religion-as-practised was a product of the intensely local religiosity of Spain: a local religiosity firmly contexted within the home place, and a shared historical experience of the Reconquista and the whole drama of Christendom. It was that complex cluster of sentiments, actions and understandings – that specifically Spanish social experience, of which so much was not articulable – that would not 'travel'. Durán uneasily felt its loss, but thought the problem lay with the Indians' 'Catholicism', and not with the fact that they were 'Indian': that is, contexted in a quite different local experience. What this application of the Christian model suggests is that the problem of 'conversion' is a very general one, potentially existing everywhere in the gap between translocal preacher and locally oriented community. We are, however, much more likely to be made aware of it by anxieties revealed in our sources, when the 'preachers' are missionaries anxious about the efficacy of their mission and not able to take for granted the disquieting ways of their flocks.

This can be observed even in the differences between the Mexican Franciscan friars. Sahagún was a man of a notably translocal turn of mind. Confronted by any kind of 'religious behaviour', Spanish or Indian, he analysed, identified, classified, judged. Motolinía, despite the same pressures of training and profession towards a translocal position, remained a man of local religiosity, identifying with Indian expressive religious practices, and persuaded of their authenticity. But that 'authenticity' resided for him in the mode and style and confident localism of the expressions, not in the concepts informing them.

Men like Motolinía – and like many modern commentators – thought to demonstrate that 'conversion' had worked by pointing to the similarities between Indian and Spanish Catholicism: to the 'same' pilgrimages and processions; the 'same' enthusiasm for the village saints; the 'same' collective celebration of collective rites of passage. But what is similar here is not the cosmological understandings but the localism of the religiosity displayed. If we filmed the Indians at their devotions they would look – some exoticisms aside – 'Catholic'. If we asked them, they would say they are Catholic. That, in the most important sense, makes them so. But they did not and do not believe what are claimed by translocal men to be key propositions in Christian belief. For them notions of the centrality of individual salvation, and the linear movement of Christian time, in which a human drama of fatherhood, disobedience, punishment and reconciliation is played out in history as in each individual life, are alien.[11] As I would suggest might well be the case in a multitude of other 'Christian' communities.

Missionaries are translocal men *par excellence*, professionally committed to the view that a complex faith can be converted into portable form and reestablished in a new locality without serious deformation. Unsurprisingly, they find the horticultural metaphor irresistible – rooting out idolatries, preparing the ground, nurturing the tender plants of the faith – because that metaphor conveniently assumes that a faith, like a plant, is a living thing which can be moved through space and yet retain its distinctiveness and its viability, whatever the ground in which it is relocated, and will in time bring forth the old familiar fruit. My own view is that such plants are site-specific, and dependent on their precise habitat – although we can expect to find structurally similar species flourishing in similar ecological niches. For most people in most places 'religion' and 'society' interfuse: we, translocal people that we are, strive to separate them.

There is a related implication. There are no world religions, or world ideologies for that matter, save in the systematized abstractions of translocal individuals, who will typically find the practices of particular locals deplorably confused and lax. Yet if they attempt to preach the Pure Word to those locals, they risk being caught themselves in the 'missionary position'.

Notes

The original footnotes have been much reduced to meet necessary restrictions on space.

1   For the reforms and their influence in the New World, see J.L. Phelan, *The Millennial Kingdom of the Franciscans in the New World* (2nd ed. revised), Berkeley and Los Angeles, University of California Press, 1970, and for some unexpected outcomes Inga Clendinnen, 'Disciplining the Indians: Franciscan Ideology and Missionary Violence in Sixteenth Century Yucatan', *Past and Present*, 94, February 1982, pp.27–48. For the population loss, S. Cook and W. Borah, *The Aboriginal Population of Mexico on the Eve of the Spanish Conquest*, Berkeley and Los Angeles, University of California Press, 1963.

2   E.g. M. Edmonson (ed.), *Nativism and Syncretism*, New Orleans, Tulane University Press, 1960; S. Tax (ed.), *The Heritage of Conquest*, N.Y., Cooper Square Publishers, 1968; E. Wolf, *Sons of the Shaking Earth*, Chicago, University of Chicago Press, 1962, pp.166–75.

3   Fray Toribio de Motolinía, *Motolinía's History of the Indians of New Spain*, trans. and edited by E.A. Foster, Berkeley and California, The Cortes Society, 1950, pp.45, 52, 94; Fray Pedro de Gante to the Crown, n.d., *Cartas de Indias*, Ministerio de Fomento, Madrid, 1877, pp.42–7.

4   *Procesos de Indios Idólatras y Hechiceros*, Mexico, Publicaciónes de Archivo General de la Nación, III, 1912–13, *passim*.
5   Fray Bernardino de Sahagún, 'Psalmodia Christiana' (1583), in J. García Icazbalceta, *bibliografia Mexicana del siglo XVI*, Mexico, Fondo de Cultura Economica, 1954, XVI, p.82.
6   Motolinía, *op. cit.*, p.132.
7   Fray Diègo Durán, *The Book of the Gods and Rites and the Ancient Calendar*, trans. and ed. Fernando Horcasitas and Doris Heyden Norman, University of Oklahoma Press, 1971, pp.54–5.
8   W. Christian Jr, *Apparitions in Late Medieval and Renaissance Spain*, Princeton, 1981, pp.153–4, 167.
9   W. Christian Jr, *Local Religion in Sixteenth Century Spain*, Princeton, 1981, pp.177–81.
10   Christian, *ibid.*, p.20.
11   W. Madsen, 'Christo-Paganism: a study of Mexican religious syncretism', in M. Edmonson, *op. cit.*

Further reading

For moving (and theoretically – sophisticated) evocations of the dilemmas of missionaries, see G. Dening, *Islands and Beaches*, Hawaii, 1980, and J. Clifford, *Person and Myth: Maurice Leenhardt in the Melanesian World*, Berkeley, 1982.

16
Notes on the Devil's Cult among South Andean miners

TRISTAN PLATT

The Toucan asked me if I was new, yes sir, where are you from, from San Pedro sir, are your parents alive, they're in the harvest sir, you'll get used to the mine (I listened to him), the first days are difficult (I said nothing), we can tell a new one right away (I listened to him), later on you won't even want to go outside, yes sir, come over here then, sir?, come over here, I'll show you something. And that was when I really met him, a few steps from that moment. I'd already heard about him outside the mine and many things had been said about him. Before receiving my entry-order as a trucker from Head Office, I'd imagined him, feared and respected him, but I didn't know exactly how he was. . . . He was sitting in a hole in the bored rock, he had a cigarette-end hanging from his lips, his eyes were made of marbles, with impressive green, blue and red stripes, I was frightened and fascinated by his face – long, smooth, lead-and-copper-coloured – and by his pointed ears coming out of his oval-shaped head; he sat there naked and with his penis big, erect and thick. His arms were held close to his thin body, his feet were without toes, his neck was wrapped in many-coloured paper streamers, and around him were bottles – many of them medicine bottles – full of alcohol, and coca-leaves, cigarettes. . . . 'Uncle (*Tío*)' said the Toucan. 'Uncle', I repeated.

Khoya Loco (René Poppe 1979: 31–2)

Listening to some of the more doctrinaire prophets on the Bolivian Left, one sometimes gets the impression that miners and peasants are as different from each other as quartz is (supposedly) from peas, that the miners act as a monolithic political block due to their highly-developed 'class-consciousness' while the peasants are essentially petty-bourgeois tradesmen whose only interest is the state of the market for agricultural goods, that the miners have left the irrational superstition of the 'indian' peasants behind them and are now firmly on the road to assuming, once and for all, their position at the vanguard of the oppressed peoples of Bolivia. And there can be no doubt that many miners' leaders *do* nurse an almost unconscious sense of superiority towards the peasants: as one said to me once, 'when the peasants come to the mine they learn how to use toothpaste, they learn what a cinema is, they learn what *civilization* is.'

We need not waste too much time here on the 'civilization' claim ('cannibalism' is a rational and decorous way of disposing of the dead in comparison with 'Western civilization's' modern methods of killing), except to note the insidious, ethnocidic effects of an idea peddled by the wielders of power to justify their own supremacy: in Bolivia, 'civilization' was what nineteenth-century whites invoked (as twentieth-century whites still do) to justify their efforts to 'incorporate' South Andean indians into the newly 'enlightened' Republic (the 'favourite daughter of Bolivar' as some put it), and was part of a complex of ideas which we can dub 'liberal nationalism'. Let us quickly listen to the words of óne of these nineteenth-century patriarchs, to get the general tone of the white attitudes:

Of course, if the tribute and other impositions which weigh upon the indians were removed, leaving him in his isolation, leaving him with his hatred and resentment towards the other classes of society, and above all keeping him in that state of stupid apathy from which he looks with hatred and disdain on everything pertaining to culture and civilization, then we would be doing a great harm to society and to that very race which we are trying to lift up.

The indian would then be forced further into his laziness and dejection, and this would increase his hatred towards the whites and *mestizos*, he would work less, since his needs would be limited to his wretched subsistence, there would be no further trade between us and the natives, and so society would be deprived of all that wealth which is the product of the indians' labour. . . .

And yet this does not mean that we should prolong the head-tax, which is considered obsolete by economic science. . . . That would be equivalent to keeping the indians in that state of brutish subjection which they have suffered for three and a half centuries, and in which they will continue for many more centuries if we don't wrench them firmly from that shadowy path in which they at present walk overwhelmed and dejected, with never a beam of the shining light of civilization nor the consoling torch of the faith; it would be equivalent to maintaining injustice and evil, and flouting the holy law of God and Society: the Progress of Humanity. Until, finally some political cataclysm would come to wrench them from their apathetic idiocy: then they would shake their chains with terrible convulsions, they would throw themselves into battle guided by desperation, and their victory would be a catastrophe. Yes, it would be as catastrophic for America as was the invasion of the Northern Barbarians for Europe many centuries ago, – perhaps more so . . .: our indians, if once they triumphed over the other classes, would exterminate them completely, since only thus could they satisfy the thirst for vengeance built up in them for so many centuries.

(Dr Pedro Vargas, *La América Libre No. 7*, Potosí, 12/8/1864)

In other words, according to this Spanish American version of the 'White Man's Burden', we had better 'civilize' all the indians as quick as we can, or else they might kill us all off, thereby ruining God's plans for Human Progress. And (as other Bolivian patriarchs make clear) the best way of 'civilizing' them is to develop capitalism, create new markets, and mesh them into them as soon as possible, preferably destroying their 'subsistence ghettoes' in the process. The policy is as alive today as ever before, even though the role of 'God's plan' in the justification has been replaced by phrases like 'improving living-standards', 'diet' and 'hygiene' – and 'toothpaste and cinemas' of my mining leader friend.

Now, the question that arises is why phrases belonging to nineteenth-century racist rhetoric have been taken up by supposedly revolutionary miners' leaders, and applied in such a way as to establish a gulf between themselves and the peasants. After all, the Bolivian Mine-Owners Association, founded in 1924 to protect the tin-barons' interests, did not mince words when talking about the workers: this institution, a nest for classic laissez-faire liberalism, considered the mine-workers a bunch of lazy indians, inherently perverse and dedicated to drink and brutality, whose wages should be fixed as low as the labour-market permitted in order not to foment 'a parasitic way of life among the idle'. In other words, the Mine-Owners considered the indian mine-worker in exactly the same terms as the nineteenth-century liberal patriarchs used about the indian peasants. Why, then, do miners' leaders not embrace the cultural component in their social situation, and come forward in the name of the Andean Indian Workers in Town and Country of Bolivia? Why do they not take up what unites them with the peasants, rather than harping on what separates them from each other?

One, highly mechanical, explanation would be that only with the emergence of the wage-relation can truly lucid, and revolutionary, political views develop. And indeed no one would wish to deny the lucidity with which many mine-workers in Bolivia can discuss the nature of the world market and the terms of Bolivia's insertion into it. They are quite clear about the exploitative role assumed by the State bureaucracy in the Nationalized Mining Corporation (COMIBOL), and their own role as producers of surplus-value for State and Company. However, this political lucidity clouds somewhat when they have to deal with the peasants. Low prices for agricultural goods, for example, has been a traditional method used by the State for keeping down mining wages. The miners recently fell right into this trap when faced with a peasant strategy of widespread road-blocks in order to force a rise in the price of agricultural goods. They tried to persuade the peasants to abandon their action; and were deaf to the highly sophisticated peasant reply, namely, that the miners should instead declare indefinite strike in favour of higher wages with which to pay for the more expensive goods brought for sale by the peasants.

So we are forced to examine more carefully the origins of this curiously nineteenth-century component in the mining-leaders' ideology. Without going into the details here, we should observe that early twentieth-century leadership for the miners' revindications came principally from the petty-commercial sector of the mining camp, those small shopkeepers who could only expand their operations if a healthy volume of coin was in circulation. Since the majority of their customers were, in fact, the mining-workers themselves, it was obviously in the interests of these small tradesmen to support the workers' claims for higher wages, since this would immediately increase their own turnover. In Llallagua-Uncía (Siglo XX) in North Potosí, the most important of the early twentieth-century tin-mining camps, the tradesmen also shared with the workers a lucrative business in 'stolen' mineral: the mine-workers would bring choice pieces of ore and sell them in the local store, and the storekeepers would then resell them to the international metal-dealers who clustered round the nearest railway-station at Challapata. Here too, then, the interests of workers and tradesmen were linked.

Thus, in the local newspapers before the First World War, we sometimes find tradesmen and workers pressing for higher wages within a classic liberal framework of ideas: higher wages will lead to a greater volume of money in circulation, and thus to an expansion of trade. These terms are perfectly compatible with the 'liberal-nationalist' reference-points which, on other occasions (as we have seen), could also be mobilized against indian peasant culture, and I suspect that their origins can be traced back to eighteenth-century Colonial mercantilist thought. Inclusion of the racist component thus became, for many miners (or perhaps parts of the heads of many miners), a small price to pay for a place in the sun of Modern Nationhood: as a *class within Society* they could achieve a degree of recognition from on high which was denied them as a *culture outside Society*. And in addition they could assume the complacency of being 'civilized' and 'progressive' (whatever the tin-barons might say to the contrary), as opposed to the 'savage' and 'superstitious' indians left behind in the countryside. In the classic Bolivian phrase, they had been able to 'overcome themselves' (*superarse*).

This, then, was the somewhat shaky foundation upon which Union, and later Vanguardist, positions could be constructed. Since then the 'revolutionary superiority' of the miners over the peasants has rarely been questioned at a doctrinal level, in spite of practical convergences between both sectors at moments of political upheaval. But it is the convergences that I wish to emphasize here, particularly in relation to a shared tilth of religious ideas which constitute, for both miner and peasant, a common set of divine co-ordinates for social life and action. At this level, then, the so-called 'superstitions' which the mine-workers are supposed (according to the 'liberal revolutionary' reading of their situation) to have left behind with the llama-dung, reappear in their midst as a key area in which miners and peasants continue to share a common Culture. This common 'world-view' is less surprising when we remember that the mining work-force was in fact made up predominantly of rural migrants, whose culture, while naturally readapted to mining conditions, neverthe-less retained key elements of its rural expression. Although it is understandable why many eurocentric 'white revolutionaries' prefer to dismiss such 'ethnic' features of mining consciousness as 'primitive' and 'irrelevant', and limit themselves to preaching the doctrine of (unequal) alliance between classes on the European model, there can be no doubt that the notion of Cultural Defence, as a point of convergence for different sectors of the South Andean people, *could* provide a new, deep spring of imaginative motivations which would completely supersede the stale rhetoric of present-day Bolivian party-politics, while at the same time embracing the inter-sectorial importance of certain key economic revindications (higher farm prices together with higher wages, for example, or the need for subsistence reserves to face drought years such as 1983).

The fact that most miners participate in a Cult to the Devil, whose ritual expressions take place deep within the mine, has been commented on by anthropologist folklorists and writers both within and outside the country. Once again, this Cult has generally been considered as a uniquely mining phenomenon: an element in an industrial culture which represents a 'cultural enclave' in relation to the different rural culture which surrounds it (June Nash), a fetishistic image of capitalist and imperialist exploitation (Augusto Cespedes, Michael Taussig), a 'tradition' which should be supported by Management in the interests of harmonious labour relations (Alberto Guerra). . . . While the Devil's Cult does indeed receive special elaboration in the mining context, I consider that the isolation of the Devil's Cult from rural indian religion is just another expression – this time by the 'specialists' – of that reification of economic sectors whose origins I have just discussed. I therefore prefer to look at the different aspects of mining life, not just in relation to the chain of intermediaries that link the contract-worker at the face to the international metal market in London, but also (and no less importantly) in relation to the regional society of which it is a part.

In the case of the 'Devil' (or 'Uncle', as he is more generally known), he is a feature of both rural and mining belief-systems in North Potosí, and many peasants may have had contact with him before entering the mine. Mining and farming are two sides to a single productive coin – the earth as source of wealth – and the associated activities are presided over by a divine couple, the 'earth-father' ('uncle') and the 'earth-mother' (in very approximate translation). Peasants offer libations and prayers to both deities in various ceremonies throughout the year, and Andean dualistic thought would find it strange to contemplate one half of the couple alone, each being thought of as complementary to the other. Peasants have told me that the 'uncle earth-father' (*tiu pachatata*) holds in his power all the gold and silver of the Inka, which returned to the earth with the arrival of the priests. August (an interstitial month in the agricultural calendar) is called the 'month of the Devil', and during its first days the 'uncles' bring out all their buried wealth which burns in the frozen nights of the South Andean mid-winter. For, in fact, there are many 'uncles' – just as there can be many 'devils' in the Christian cosmology – and these may sometimes be met with by a peasant as he walks, in the shape of a serpent, a toad or a lizard: their appearance may herald a sudden stroke of good fortune for the peasant (finding a hidden treasure, for example). In the night, they may sometimes be seen through the shadows driving ghostly mule- or llama-trains laden with treasure, which they take into their mountain caves to 'stock up' the ore-shoots.

To see the overlapping of mining and farming belief-systems at its clearest, let us start with a little gold-and-antimony mine in North Potosí – at its biggest, it only employed 100 workers – which opens and closes according to fluctuations in world antimony prices, and whose workers are none other than the peasants from the surrounding indian communities, who put in seasonal labour when the mine is functioning so as to earn a little cash to cover their limited market needs. My information comes from an interview in 1981 with the mine's hereditary ritual specialist, don Benjamín Lima, who is responsible for preparing the ritual table for the ceremonies held at Carnaval and on 1 August.

According to don Benjamín, his mine's ritual patrons are 'like a human couple', and their names are 'uncle George earth-father' (*tiu jorge pachatata*) and 'aunt Asunta-Luisa earth-mother' (*tia asunta luisa pachamama*). During the ceremonies, their figures, modelled in clay, are placed at the head of a weaving laid on the ground (the 'table'), with a sprig of two contrasted shrubs 'planted' by each one. A bottle of wine is placed at the 'uncle's' side (the right-hand side from the perspective of the figures), and a bottle of grape alcohol on the 'aunt's' side, with a bowl of red-black maize placed before the wine, and a bowl of grey-and-white maize placed before the grape-alcohol. Six little clay dishes are then placed in line in front of each bowl of maize. After libations and coca-leaf have begun circulating, the contents of each maize-bowl is ground to flour on a grinding-stone, sprinkled with the crushed dust of other ritual elements (which we need not bother with here), mixed with wine or alcohol as appropriate, and thus turned into a pile of dough. A little of each mass of dough is then placed in each of the six little dishes corresponding to its side of the table, and modelled into 'six mountain-peaks' in each dish – a total of 36 for 'uncle George' and 36 for 'aunt Asunta-Luisa'. These dishes are later taken and buried as offerings in sacred places around the mine. Meanwhile the participants pass through the whole mine, pouring libations in every corner, placing coca-leaf, and smearing each work-post with the blood of a sacrificed llama or goat. The ceremony ends with music and dancing in the mouth of the mine.

Now, this ceremony is very similar to another ceremony carried out by each peasant household every three years in their own homes. Just as the mining ceremony is meant to ensure 'good luck' in the mine – safety from accidents and abundant high-grade ore-shoots – so the peasant ceremony is aimed at ensuring abundant crops and animal young. In the household ceremony of the Carvajal family, which I witnessed in 1974, the named 'uncle' and 'aunt' did not appear, only the general titles 'earth-father' and 'earth-mother'; moreover, the animal sacrificed was (appropriately enough, cf. Matthew 25: 32–3) a sheep rather than the 'diabolic' goat or llama. But in general the elements of the ritual table were the same, and the dishes were also buried (together with the head of a sacrificed animal) in the hills surrounding the hamlet. It seems, in fact, that the ore-shoots are thought of as plants, which can grow or wither according to the wishes of the 'uncle'; thus, what is essentially the same ceremony can be employed to ensure both agricultural and mining 'fecundity'.

Before turning to the Devil's Cult in the great tin-mine of Siglo XX, we should also note that many peasants may also indulge in mining activities on a casual, collecting basis, sometimes entering into workings, both abandoned and in use, in order to carry out 'stolen' metal and sell it to the small tradesmen, as at the beginning of the century. In these adventures, they will also recognize that the power which can give them success lies in the 'uncle', and many will tell stories of particularly dangerous 'uncles' which guard particularly rich deposits of mineral. This is important, as it means that the Devil is, once again, a living part of North Potosí religious beliefs, peasant no less than mining, and therefore those interpretations (like Michael Taussig's) which emphasize the relation between the Devil's Cult and the wage-relation within capitalism become far less convincing. The Devil is worshipped by all those who go underground in search of metal, even if they are peasants, simply because he is the divinity which guards the deposits, and regardless of the productive relations which accompany the extraction of metal. In fact, the Devil is a common feature in Bolivian urban literature as well, so the real question is why the Devil receives so much attention in Bolivia as a whole, rather than limiting his Cult to the capitalist mining sector. We will come back to this point later, when we ask what the Devil in fact represents beyond his anti-Christian appearance (which in fact is a Christian way of referring to, and thereby controlling to some extent, phenomena which are outside the Christian experience).

Meanwhile, let us take a quick look at the Devil's Cult in the great tin-mine at Llallagua-Uncía. The mine itself is divided into two Sectors, North and South, corresponding to the two rival mines which were finally centralized into a single company in 1924 by Simon Patiño, the Bolivian 'tin-king'. In each of these two Sectors we find a chapel dedicated to the Virgin of the Conception, whose image was also placed at the crossings in the Silver-Mountain of Potosí from the sixteenth century on. These chapels are located in the two main entry-tunnels, not far from the surface and the light of day, and the festival of the Virgin is celebrated on 8 December under the patronage of ritual sponsors from a different Work-Section each year within each Sector (except for one section which attends the chapel of Jesus' Heart on 1 May . . .). Now the Virgin was not present so explicitly in the little gold-and-antimony mine we looked at before: indeed, only in so far as peasants tend to identify the Virgin with the earth-mother was she present at all. This, then, is a first important difference between the little mine and the big mine of Siglo XX: the old Colonial patron introduced by Spanish priests to 'exorcise the Potosí silver-mines and 'baptize' mining-activities reappears in the tin-mines of the twentieth century, and, at the same time, takes up the role of major opponent, and thus to some extent religious partner, of the Devil who lurks further into the darkness.

There, in the main galleries, we find at last man-sized figures of the 'uncles', seated on stone benches as in the description at the beginning of this talk, deeply impressive for the newcomer who sees how they 'draw' on the cigarettes in their mouths as the air enters the cavity, or how the alcohol poured between their fang-like teeth reappears in a fountain coming out of their erect penises. The older miners laugh, and explain that there's a channel connecting the mouth with the genitals: like good Christians (as they conceive themselves to be) they don't confuse a plaster statue with the powerful reality it represents. . . . Small offerings of coca-leaf, alcohol and cigarettes are made every Tuesday and Friday – the 'Devil's Days' – and big celebrations are held at Carnaval and on 1 August. Here libations are poured for the 'uncles' of each work-section, the teams go and visit neighbouring sections to make offerings to other 'uncles', the cardinal points of the mine are invoked, the Sectors as well, and devotees recite the numbers of metres below the Glory Hole at the top of the mountain of all the levels and galleries: 650, 383, 355, 320, 285, 250, 205, 140, 90, 55, 0. . . . According to one informant, Paulino Yucra, the celebrations culminate in his section with all the miners going up in the cages through the 'Mystic Shaft' and splashing libations at every level they come to: for him, this meant that the miners were behaving like a 'root', or like 'ants that enter their house'. Thus the libation-pouring turned into a massive sacraliz-ation of every corner of the great underground city: 'cultural possession' was taken of them all, and they were all placed under the protection of the powers that control risk, danger and wealth in the heart of the mine.

Unfortunately, I have no information on the composition of the ritual 'tables' in Siglo XX, although sacrifices of llamas (above all) are performed: when the Management is feeling generous, it provides the animals, which are then taken in on the trucks splashing blood as they go along. But enough has been said to show the transformation and expansion of the Cult in comparison with the religious practices of the little mine looked at before, even though we can also see how everything that happens in Siglo XX is perfectly coherent with a 'world-view' which unites farming and mining activities within a single religious vision. The climax of the celebrations occurs when the miners, dressed them-selves as 'Devils' with brightly-painted horned masks and glittering teeth made from mirrors, pour forth to dance in the streets, leaping and roaring behind the sword of St Michael who leads them – as in Roman triumph, although it is not always clear who is triumphing over whom – to pay their respects to the Virgin. Religious 'decency' is thereby safeguarded outside the mine, although once back inside the Devil regains his unquestioned supremacy. . . .

Simon Patiño is said to have been a firm believer in the 'uncle', and certainly encouraged Management participation in the Cult. In fact, one informant at Siglo XX told me how engineers would carry out ceremonies beside the hydro-electric dam which provides the mine with electric energy, so that the divine patrons of thunder and lightning would also send the water necessary for the mine's operations. This suggests that we are dealing with a Company which, at the same time as it became a byword in world finance for technical efficiency and profitability, was also within the religious world of the Andean peoples, managing to reconcile Western technology with religion, 'science' with belief. Patiño used to attend the sacrifice of the animal provided by Management, and danced with the workers – at least in some miners' memories – during the festival in honour of the 'lord of metals'. At this time Patiño would also give a personal gift of clothing to each worker, while the workers reciprocated the gift with precious pieces of ore. This exchange should probably be interpreted as a mutual pledge between men and Management: if productivity rose, wages could rise also, would be Patiño's reading of the situation; whereas from the men's point of view the meaning was rather, improve our wages and we will produce more metal. . . .

With the Revolution of 1952, in the wake of which all Bolivia's major mines were nationalized and the State Mining Company (COMIBOL) set up, the miners' hopes seemed to have been realized. According to one miner interviewed by June Nash, such abundant libations were poured in the years shortly after the Revolution that the galleries seemed more like a pub – but this intensification of the Cult should probably be attributed to the workers' wish to increase production during the period of 'Workers' Control' (1952–6). With the military coup of René Barrientos in 1964, however, the ceremonies were formally prohibited as focuses of seditious meeting-places. This then was the time when the Devil's Cult took on a new role: regular ceremonies around the 'uncles' statues continued to take place in secret, and became precisely what Barrientos had feared, namely focuses of mining resistance in the face of the new technocratic militarism. Let us listen to the words of a miner from San José (Oruro), who expressed perfectly the new function of the Devil's Cult in a context of military repression:

'This tradition within the mine must be kept up, because there is no communication more intimate, sincere and beautiful than when the workers all chew coca-leaf together and offerings are made to the 'Uncle'. That's where we talk over our problems, our work-problems, and that's where a generation so revolutionary is born that the workers begin to think about structural change. This is our University. Our experience during the libation-pouring (*ch'alla*) is our greatest moment.'

(In June Nash 1979: 159)

Who, then, is the 'Devil', the great Devil that appears as Lucifer in the street-dancing, and whose multiple fragmentations appear as a whole hierarchy of lesser demons, from the 'uncles' of the galleries in Siglo XX and Oruro, to the little provincial goblins, like the patron of the gold-and-antimony mine we looked at? The Quechua and Aymore word for 'devil' is, in fact, *supay*, and in order to counteract the Christian overtones of the word 'Devil', we should begin by asking for the meaning of this word in a pre-Christian context. Fortunately, recent philological work by the Australian linguist Gerald Taylor has shed some light on this problem. Taylor has pointed out that *supay* seems originally to have meant 'soul of the dead' or 'ancestor', whose home (*supaywasi* = 'house of the dead') was probably located beneath the earth. Now for the Christian Church, the widespread Andean 'cult of the dead' was a particularly abominable piece of 'paganism': therefore, by what Taylor calls an 'ideological mutation', the ancestors – traditional focus of 'heresy' and 'superstition' – became equated with 'devils', and *supaywasi* became the Andean term for the Christian 'Hell'.

On one reading, therefore, the adoration of *supay*, the 'Devil', by indian miners both today and in Colonial times is perfectly coherent with Christian ideas that associate the Devil with riches and death. But on another reading, the *supay* is adored as the spirit of the dead, and his cult can be seen as a prolongation of a pre-Colombian 'cult of the ancestors'. Now it seems that being sent to work in the Colonial silver-mines was considered a virtual death-sentence by those indians whose turn had come round: thus, through their 'sacrifice' to the ancestors, the ancient guardians of prosperity, a pre-Colombian Andean religious formula involving human sacrifice to the dead was being acted out in terms that could also be 'read' as an expression of a very Christian belief in the Devil. It is the possibility of these 'double readings' of words like 'Devil' that makes the study of Andean religion so peculiarly complex.

A further clue to the identity of the great *supay* is offered by the myths which surround the Cult. These myths tell of a threatening 'ogre' called Wari, whose destructive advance on one mining city

(Oruro) was checked by the Virgin. Now Wari is the name of a very ancient Andean God, whose cult in the seventeenth century still flourished in the labyrinthical, underground temple of Chavín (built between 1000 and 800 years before Christ), where his voice could be heard by devotees, speaking through shamanic intermediaries. It may be significant that the iconography of this ancient temple is closely bound up with a God with a fanged, feline mouth, and that the modern masks used by the devil-dancing miners also emphasize fangs in a catlike mouth. . . . Perhaps, therefore, we should leave open the possibility that a deep-seated Andean religious complex is still partially extant, though in a transformed historical context, and continues to flourish in a labyrinthical, underground 'temple': the great tin-mines of modern Bolivia. The capacity for mobilization wielded by this God is still, as we have seen, considerable, and would probably be greater were it not for the snare of 'liberal progressivism' in which he has become enmeshed.

And the generalized presence of the 'Devil' in Bolivian culture, both urban and rural? As we have seen, a simple explanation in terms of the effects of the growth of capitalism is not acceptable, if only because the Devil is present in many social contexts which are not characterized by mining capital and the wage-relation. It is therefore preferable to attribute this generalized presence to the persistent weight of a down-trodden Andean culture, whose spiritual life still appears to those 'outside' it (like many urban and white middle-class sectors) as something dark, irrational and threatening which looms up from the infernal emotional depths of a civilization subordinated and despised – and yet inescapably present. We are dealing (I suggest) with the prolonged effects of a confrontation between civilizations, in which the eurocentric Spanish inheritance still struggles to neutralize an Andean alternative that refuses to die – or, perhaps, which achieves its most powerful emotional presence *through its death*. . . .

White 'liberal revolutionary' theoreticians of the 'National Problem', like their companions on the Right still tend to deny this ancient confrontation any modern relevance, carving up their indian enemy into a set of discrete (but more manageable) 'classes', which can then be analysed in terms of their capacity for 'alliance'. Popular collective memories, however, still insist on the importance of thinking through the history of that original sixteenth-century dualism; and while perfectly conscious of the sectorial strains and stresses that affect its different class-components in different ways, they reveal nevertheless that the analyses of the nineteenth century, in which the Andean-European opposition was recognized as the fundamental determinant of the Bolivian experience, are still essential to any serious understanding of the South Andean crisis.

Bibliographical note

This talk is a rapid resumé of arguments laid out more fully in a Spanish text to be published shortly in Bolivia and Perú.

Almaraz, Sergio, *El Poder y la Caida*, La Paz–Cochabamba, 1967.

Arzans de Orsúa y Vela, Bartolomé, *Historia de la Villa Imperial de Potosí*, edition by Lewis Hanke and Gunnar Mendoza, Rhode Island, 1965 (*c.*1735).

Berthelot, Jean, 'L'exploitation des Métaux Précieux au Temps des Incas', *Annales E.S.C.*, 33e Année – Nos 5–6, Paris, 1978.

Cespedes, Augusto, *El Metal del Diablo*, La Paz, 1969.

Duviols, Pierre, 'Huari y Llacuaz: agricultores y pastores. Un dualismo prehispánico de oposición y complementaridad', *Revista del Museo Nacional*, vol. XXXIX, Lima, 1973.

Fortún, Julia Elena, *La Danza de los Diablos*, La Paz, Ministerio de Educación y Bellas Artes, 1961.

Guerra, Alberto, 'Trayectoria de una Deidad Calumniada', Oruro, Instituto de Investigación Cultural para Educación Popular (INDICEP), Año VI, vol. 9, 1975.

Harris, Olivia and Albó, Javier, *Monteras y Guardatojos. Campesinos y Mineros en el Norte de Potosí*, La Paz, Cuadernos de Investigación CIPCA, 1975.

Lumbreras, Luis, 'Los estudios sobre Chavín', *Revista del Museo Nacional*, vol. XXXVIII, Lima, 1972.

Nash, June, *We Eat the Mines and the Mines Eat Us*, New York, 1979.

Platt, Tristan, *Estado Boliviano y Ayllu Andino*, Lima, 1982.

Poppe, René, *El Paraje del Tío y otros relatos mineros*, La Paz, 1979.

Taussig, Michael, *The Devil and Commodity Fetishism in South America*, Chapel Hill, 1980.

Taylor, Gerald, 'Supay', *Amerindia*, Paris, 1979.

17
Religion in the Zimbabwe guerilla war

TERENCE RANGER

Introduction

Until quite recently rural Africans were thought of as *tribesmen*. Their religion was held to be the expression of traditional social values. Its study was the preserve of the anthropologist. Many anthropologists were sympathetic to African systems of belief, revealing their inner logic and their function as sustaining ideologies. On the other hand, their studies neither showed tribal religion itself as capable of change and innovation nor were at all sympathetic to such obvious evidences of religious change as rural adherence to a 'folk' missionary Christianity or the formation of African prophetic churches. Anyone committed to social revolution who read the works of these anthropologists must necessary conclude that African religion itself was archaic and irrelevant to existing or hoped-for social change and that other rural religious manifestations were merely a manifestation of social breakdown rather than of social reconstruction.

Today rural Africans are usually thought of as *peasants*. This has the advantage of defining them in terms of their changing relationship to a wider society and thus opens the possibility of a more dynamic treatment of their consciousness and religious ideas. But as far as rural religion is concerned this possibility has not yet been realized. Social historians of Africa have begun to draw on the rich comparative literature on peasant societies in Europe and elsewhere; students of African peasant religion have been impressed by work on rural popular religion in Europe. From this they have drawn a model equally static but much less sympathetic than the model of tribal religion offered by the anthropologists. Stuart Clark's recent article in *Past and Present* admirably sums up the general picture of early modern European rural popular culture available to the Africanist:

> The early modern peasant, the argument runs, was a prisoner of a natural environment which was unintelligible to him and which he could not master. As a result of his ignorance of the natural processes governing the climate, the production of crops and his own health, and of his technical inadequacy he was the victim of unrelenting physical misfortune. . . . Physical and

mental insecurity gave rise to emotional trauma. Preoccupied with surviving in hostile, mysterious surroundings, lost in a world of which they had only imprecise knowledge, simple men became victims of severe, even psychotic anxiety . . . continually subject to the encroachments of the supernatural. . . . To real physical dangers were added imaginary dangers. Men were subject to terrors of fantasy about nature, their own bodies and the actions of spirit agents. . . . These various psychological tensions are said to have been reflected in the institutions, beliefs and ritual practices of the peasantry. . . . Among the 'imaginary' fears engendered by precarious living conditions and mental instability . . . were beliefs in the suffusion of 'supernature', in a vengeful deity and in omnipresent demonism, as well as reliance on an animistic scheme of causation.[1]

If this picture were to be taken as valid for African peasantries then one could only conclude that 'supernaturalism' is in itself one of the major oppressions from which rural Africans have to be delivered by means of an education in the true natural and societal causes of their poverty. And such a picture *is* powerfully sustained by one of the most influential sets of ideas animating African revolutionary movements. Franz Fanon, apostle of the revolutionary mission of the African peasantry, nevertheless drew them in their unawakened state as having withdrawn from the real world of colonial oppression into a world of supernaturalist fantasy:

A belief in fatality removes all blame from the oppressor; the cause of misfortunes and of poverty is attributed to God; He is Fate. In this way the individual accepts the disintegration ordained by God, bows down before the settler and his lot. . . . There are maleficent spirits which intervene every time a step is taken in the wrong direction, leopardmen, serpentmen, six-legged dogs, zombies – a whole series of tiny animals or giants which create around the native a world of prohibitions, of barriers and inhibitions far more terrifying than the world of the settler. . . . We no longer really need to fight against them since what counts is the frightening enemy created by myths. We perceive that is settled by a permanent confrontation on the phantasmic plane.[2]

Some Marxist commentators differ from Fanon in their dismissal of the revolutionary potential of the peasantry but share with him a notion of the escapist fantasy and unreality of peasant religion. For a radical scholar such as Catherine Coquery Vidrovitch, the essential repudiation of colonialism by African peasants can never find full or effective expression because of the constant eruption of rural religious ideas. Thus, Simon Kimbangu, the remarkable prophet of the early 1921s, 'realized the contradiction between the divine message and the application colonialism was making of it'; but in the event his 'non-syncretist Christian movement of betterment through religion minimized political conflict inasmuch as it implied both acceptance of western values and the will to modernize the Congo'. Matswanism in the Congo, 'while finding its strength in the rural masses' tradition of resistance' nevertheless 'aborted' protests 'of a more modernizing inspiration'. 'The movement, based originally on the idea of Congolese nationalism, had regressed in the form of a religious sect with an ethnic and rural appeal, which recovered . . . the millenarian accents of the beginnings of the century. These had drained it of its dynamic political content.' Modern nationalist movements have 'co-habited' with such rural protest. The result is a putatively modern style of politics 'grafted on . . . a chaotic combination of religious references, millenarianist and charismatic currents and techniques of the imaginary. This combination had to confront the immediate demand for change borne of that new consciousness of intense economic exploitation which had ended in profound social misery.'[3]

It can readily be appreciated, then, that African revolutionaries who wish to meet this demand for change, end this economic exploitation and alleviate this social misery, have seen in peasant religiosity one of the main obstacles to success. It can readily be understood also why radical academics, supportive of these movements of revolution, have drawn up a typology of African rural revolts in which the key transition from archaic to modern, from abortive to successful, is the passage from supernaturalism to secular self-awareness.

A main advocate of such a typology has been the distinguished chairman of the History Workshop panel, Basil Davidson, who is as much honoured for his unswerving commitment to African liberation as for his unceasing exploration of the significance of the African past. He sees Mau Mau as in itself transitional. It was 'a rebellion such as nobody in East Africa had seen before, whether in its force and drive, in its manner of organisation and leadership, or its aims. In all these respects it made a bridge between the past and the future.' But in the forests supernaturalism came to predominate:

In the early phases the Kikuyu *mundo mugo*, oracle spokesmen or diviners, had helped to enforce discipline and morale; now they began to undermine what they had helped to build, relapsing into magical explanations of reality, claiming to command operations by reference to their prophecies, spreading belief in the efficacy of charms. . . . In this situation the 'joints' between traditional and modernising ideas and forms evidently continued to collapse. . . . Superstition flourished. Discipline went by the board . . . fighters and commanders fell increasingly into actions of despair.[4]

The key variable, Davidson goes on to explain, is whether:

a leadership emerges that can really lead 'out of the past into the future'. Can the movement in question rise . . . above the bedrock of its rural culture, above utopian or messianic hopes, above magic or corresponding superstition?

What is necessary is 'a modernising elite' that can stay 'close to the movement of rebellion'. Mau Mau 'never possessed any modernizing leadership save what they could produce out of their own ranks'. In the guerilla movements of Lusophone Africa, on the other hand, a modernizing elite *did* emerge, stayed close to the peasants, and through the processes of a people's war helped to carry them from superstition to rationality:

Village volunteers never had much difficulty in learning to handle, fire and even repair rifles and light automatics: the difficulty came in accepting secular explanations of reality in place of religious explanations. It was one thing to learn to ambush the enemy, quite another that witches could not hurt you. This was the learning . . . which imposed the need for protracted war.[5]

Yoweri Museveni, from whom I took my Fanon quotations and who is now himself President of Uganda, having been a guerilla leader, has vividly described this process of revolutionary secularization as he saw it on a visit to northern Mozambique in 1968:

The peasants of Northern Mozambique have undergone the cleansing effect of revolution. . . . The peasant in Cabo Delgado has participated in killing the white man – the former 'demi-god'. . . . In the course of the revolution, the peasant is also liberated from parochialism. . . . The peasant gains much ideologically from the intellectual. . . . He becomes more scientific and discards most of the superstitions . . . and the whole magical superstructure that characterizes a frustrated colonial society. . . . The transformation of the peasant into a rational anti-imperialist fighter becomes a must.[6]

Now, into this clear and persuasive typology and sequence how can we fit the experience of the Zimbabwean guerilla war? There can be no doubt that it *was* a 'people's war' and a successful one. Unlike Mau Mau but like the war in Mozambique it won the political victory which is the aim of all such struggles. It came after the war in Mozambique and its most effective leaders were inspired by FRELIMO's ideology and practice. And yet the relationship of guerillas to peasant religion in Zimbabwe was completely different from anything that all the preceding analyses might have suggested. In Zimbabwe the war *intensified* rather than transcended peasant religious belief.

To my mind neither functionalist anthropology nor materialist analysis nor yet a social history which has absorbed the teleological assumptions of European studies of popular culture are adequate to the task of explaining this. All three involve a conde-scension towards the rural Africans who constitute the object of their study. African peasants are seen as incapable of comprehending their environment – whether the immediate natural environment and the technologies appropriate to its exploitation and manage-ment or the broader societal environment of colonial oppression and rapid change. They assume a reality which the scholar apprehends but the peasant does not: a reality which the scholar can express in analytical language to which the peasant has no access. Peasant religion is seen as 'false consciousness', more or less damaging depending upon whether we are asking what was its con-tribution to the functioning of small-scale rural societies or asking how it has related to effective opposition to colonial capitalism.

To my mind we have to start from the assumption that peasants had and have a privileged access to many – to most – of the realities of their own existence. They do not respond to or talk about these realities *only* in terms of religion, but African peasant religious discourse is nevertheless a privileged language in which reality is categorized and transformed and to which the scholar has to struggle to gain access. The Workshop preliminary statement affirms 'the centrality of religion to any study of society, culture or politics'. In the same way I shall argue that peasant religion in the Zimbabwean guerilla war is not an odd and embarrassing epi-phenomenon. The essential reality of that war cannot be comprehended until we begin to understand what peasant religion was saying within it.

Becoming peasants and developing peasant religion in Zimbabwe

It is possible to describe early modern European peasant societies as 'traditional' in the sense that they inherited very many assumptions and beliefs and practices from the generations of peasants who had preceded them. It is not possible to describe African peasants in Zimbabwe in the same sort of way. In some parts of Africa there had been pre-colonial peasantries – and in Senegal, for example, Islamic brotherhoods used their established influence over producers so as to organize a pre-colonial peasantry more efficiently for colonial production. But African cultivators in Zimbabwe *made themselves* into peasants as a response to colonialism.[7] Whites in Zimbabwe on the whole wanted Africans to be migrant labourers or subsistence farmers, or better, wanted the men to migrate to work and the women to maintain the family in the rural areas. Africans chose, where they could, to become peasants instead and to sell the surplus of family production. As I have argued in a recent series of lectures,[8] African cultivators could only make themselves into peasants through a whole series of innovations. They had to change the division of labour between men and women so that women worked even harder at cultivation but men also put a high proportion of their time and energy into farming as they had not done before. They had to move close to markets; to produce new crops; to learn how to break trader monopolies. They had to break away from the old concentrated patterns of settlement and to fan out in family homesteads scattered over a wide area. They had to break away where they could from the old obligations to provide labour and tribute in cereal or cattle to the headmen and chiefs: peasants needed all their labour-time and all their production. They aspired towards literacy; increasingly they aspired to the acquisition of ploughs and carts. Where Africans succeeded *en masse* in making themselves into peasants – as they did, for instance, in the district upon which I have especially focussed in my recent Zimbabwean research – rural appearances were deceptive. There were still chiefs, even if these were now dependent upon colonial appointment and raised revenue from official salaries rather than from the tribute of their people. Actual methods of cultivation did not change for a long time: much of pre-colonial 'custom' continued. Yet the people were no longer essentially tribesmen: they were essentially peasants and they were developing a peasant 'consciousness'.

All these changes had inevitable religious implications. Various missionary bodies were enabled to establish themselves and to acquire large followings largely because they met *peasant* needs. Missions offered literacy: some of them also preached 'the gospel of the plough' and regarded improved agriculture as next to godliness. But different missionary societies also offered different ideologies of labour and community, each appropriate to a particular level of peasant aspiration. In the Makoni district, where I carried out my field research, I found a rough fit between the three main mission societies and the three main layers of the African peasantry. The American Methodist missionaries aimed at economic transformation as well as spiritual regeneration.[9] Their star converts were peasant entrepreneurs, who combined an enthusiasm for the gospel of the plough with the energy to be derived from the American Methodist spiritual style of ardour under discipline.[10]

Anglicanism in Makoni, on the other hand, was the faith of the smaller surplus-marketing peasants, most of whom still used hoes for cultivation and drew upon 'traditional' communal labour gangs for harvesting. A network of Anglican schools and churches sprang up in the zones of small peasant production. As I have written elsewhere:

> The Anglican teacher-catechist ruled his flock with great dignity and honour and in return gave them access to literacy and to basic 'modernising' skills – village hygiene, the growth of groves of gum-trees, and so on. Village life focussed round the church, with its carved animal clan totems; villagers marched on high days to the mother church of St Faith's, carrying their totemic banners. Edgar Lloyd, for some thirty years the dominant influence on Makoni Anglicanism, accepted joyfully the village ministry. On leave in England he took a course in 'Peasant Pottery' at the Camberwell School of Arts and Crafts; his wife Elaine took a weaving course at the Peasants Art Guild.[11]

If Anglicanism was thus replacing the old network of tribesmen under chiefly discipline with a new network of surplus-producing peasants under churchly discipline, Catholicism in Makoni concentrated rather on producing a total Catholic community on the huge farms owned by the Church at Triashill and St Barbara's in the east of the district. On these farms the German priests evicted 'Pagans, polygamists and Protestants', creating a region of Catholic subsistence peasants. The Triashill area was remote and hilly, cut off from markets. The successive Catholic orders which ran the farm – Trappists, Mariannhill Fathers, Jesuits, Irish

Carmelites – agreed on the ideal of maintaining an organic peasant community.[12]

In this way there arose nuclei of 'folk Christianity' where the needs of a particular kind of peasantry coincided with the particular type of peasant religion offered by the missionaries. It was *folk* Christianity – that is to say that the African converts did not merely passively accept the doctrines and rituals of the churches. They developed peasant cults of their own within the churches and pressed in upon them for spiritual powers of healing and fertility. At American Methodist camp meetings witches confessed and demons were exorcised while missionaries were not looking; American Methodist African pastors made rain and healed barren women. Anglican peasants, going on pilgrimage to the shrine of the catechist Bernard Mizeki, who had been killed in the anti-colonial uprisings of 1896, were less impressed by the sermons on Christian unity than they were by the growing reputation of the shrine as a place of healing. Yet these *folk* elements in Makoni peasant Christianity were not survivals from the traditional past. They were in themselves innovations, attempts to displace the ancestral spirits and the spirits of the territory from their central role in the system of 'explanation, prediction and control', and to replace them with the power of the Holy Spirit. The radical Dutch anthropologist, Van Binsbergen, has argued that in western Zambia, a region of almost universal labour migration, the colonial period saw a great decline in the *ecological* concerns of religion: in western Zambia men looked for fortune away from the land. Zimbabwean peasants, by contrast, were *more* concerned with agricultural production than they had been in the past: their religion had to be ecological but in the mission church nuclei the peasants wanted it to be Christian as well. Perhaps, indeed, only the increased power available in the concept of the Holy Spirit in contrast to all lesser spirits seemed appropriate to the increased importance of agricultural success.

Thus peasant folk Christianity was neither irrational, in the sense of being an inappropriate response to the needs of their situation, nor was it evidence of the breakdown of coherent rural institutions. It was rather a major element in an evolving peasant consciousness and a major force in the transformation of 'tribal' institutions into peasant institutions. However, I don't wish to give the impression that only mission Christianity played an important constructive role in Makoni peasant society. The two other significant types of religion in twentieth-century Makoni also responded to change and to peasant needs.

This was certainly true of the independent African prophetic churches which began to spring up in the area in the 1930s. These constituted a criticism of the failures of the colonial economy; of the inadequacies of the peasant ideologies preached by the mission churches; but also of the bankruptcy of 'traditional' custom and religious ideas. The prophetic churches spoke to peasants who could find no market for their crops because of the Depression and who were only too well aware of the discriminatory treatment of their produce by the Rhodesian State. The prophets told their followers not to depend on production for the market and not to work for whites: agricultural surpluses were to be devoted to building up the church community. Missionary education and 'improved' agricultural techniques had proved valueless in this emergency and were to be abandoned. On the other hand, there was to be no return to veneration of the ancestral spirits or propitiation of the spirits of the land. Indeed, the prophets declared, the missionaries had failed because they had been half-hearted in their Christianization. In the prophetic churches all the old spirits were to be vanquished and driven out by the Holy Spirit. Witches would be healed. The purified peasant community would then live for itself alone.[13] I don't, of course, suggest that this ideal could be realized. As the market for peasant produce recovered so also did peasant confidence in the mission gifts of literacy and technology: Revivals within the mission churches, led by African Christians themselves, restated the mission peasant ideologies with renewed vigour. But the prophetic movements were no atavistic retreat: in a period when none of the urban political associations made any connection with peasant discontent, it was the prophetic churches which made the most effective and rigorous critique of the colonial system. Indeed, since so much of the structure of colonial rural society had been raised by and depended upon the Christian mission churches, the *theological* critique which the prophets launched at the missionaries was very much to the peasant point.

This debate of the 1930s was, then, a debate between Christians. But what of African religion itself? It is normal to say that it 'survived': the importance of the spirit mediums during the guerilla war, it is remarked, shows how effective its 'survival' was. Yet the term 'survival' gives altogether too passive a notion of what has been at stake, or of what was at stake in the guerilla war. Spirit mediums were not influential in the war because they represented the society of a hundred years ago: they were influential because they represented major peasant interests in the 1970s.

In fact the spirit mediums were bound to be deeply involved in any debate over the uses of land. In pre-colonial times they had given spiritual sanction to the tributary system of land use. As I have written in another paper:

> Pre-colonial religious observance was very much concerned with maintaining a proper relationship to the environment. . . . The key figures were spirit mediums, men or women believed to be possessed by the spirits of founders of chiefly dynasties or by the spirits of the land. Such mediums called upon the people, through the Chiefs, to make offerings for rain and fertility at the *rukoto* ceremony at the beginning of October and offerings in thanksgiving at the first fruits ceremony in February. The mediums and Chiefs controlled the agrarian cycle. They told people what crops could be grown and when planting would begin – and imposed penalties on anyone who planted a prohibited crop or who sowed seed too early. Before sowing, the people who lived near a major medium took their seed to a ceremony at his kraal; there the seeds were mixed with *divisi* medicine to ensure fertility. A mixture of seeds and *divisi* were sent by the medium to the Chief; people then brought their own seeds to the Chief to add to the mixture and a field at the Chief's kraal was cleared and planted before any other cultivation could commence. A special field was also maintained at every headman's kraal, the produce of which was sent to the Chief. Finally, the medium proclaimed and the Chief enforced rest days or *chisi* in honour of the spirit, on which no agricultural work was done. In this way the mediums administered a set of rules of land management and conservation. They also gave spiritual sanction to the tributary demands of the Chiefs.[14]

At first sight it would seem that the spirit mediums were bound to condemn the whole movement from tribesman to peasant. And in fact there *was* an inevitable hostility between the mediums and the thrusting American Methodist entrepreneurial peasant. Such an entrepreneur needed to take advantage of every local variation of soil and rainfall; to plant where he thought best and what he thought best and when he thought best; to ignore the *chisi* rest days; and to adopt new techniques of labour allocation and management which ran counter to some of the tradition communalities. But most peasants in Makoni were not like this. The small-surplus producing peasants sold their familiar grain crops, hoe-cultivated in the familiar way, made use of communal work-parties. As we have seen, they had made many other changes but they had not changed these fundamentals. So spirit mediums did *not* condemn the middling or small-scale peasant. It was true that even such peasants were failing to pay tribute to the chiefs and headmen, but as chiefs and headmen became increasingly the instruments of the colonial bureaucracy the spirit mediums took care to distance themselves from 'traditional' political authority.

The mediums objected not to the sale of surplus but to the increasing European intervention in agricultural production, the enforcement of agricultural rules and the levying of taxes and rates. Thus the pronouncements of the mediums often expressed the consciousness of the small surplus-producing and subsistence peasants, rather than the interests of the chiefs and headmen or of the new entrepreneurial elite:

> The spirit disapproves of certain developments introduced in modern days (runs one such pronouncement). For instance it does not care for contour ridging because it causes too much work and has introduced features that were not in the landscape in former days. His spirit declares that there is no pleasure in walking the fields or bush as the contours make movement difficult. This innovation makes the tribal spirit angry and as a result people are short of food. The tribal spirit . . . dislikes the rising rates levelled by the rural councils. . . . The spirit gave people soil on which to grow their crops . . . but nowadays they were being told to plough here and not there, only in particular places, unlike the instructions of the tribal spirit, which were merely to plant and water would be provided.

Nor was this the irrational expression of unregenerate peasant conservatism. It unerringly expressed opposition to the very factors which increasingly from the 1930s onwards made life hard for the small peasant – eviction from 'white' lands into over-crowded Reserves; followed by the official explanation of the poverty of these Reserves in terms of bad agricultural practice instead of in terms of the over-crowding; followed by demands that peasants give up scarce land and labour to build contour ridges. And the mediums also expressed small peasant hostility towards the entrepreneur:

> Very rarely do Africans die of starvation. They have enough. They can get help from others . . . relatives and friends. . . . If one brother needs help, another must come forward and help. . . . The sons of today expect something in return for what was given, but this is a European custom. Amongst the Shona there is no usury.[15]

All forms of religion in Makoni, then, adapted themselves to the realities of peasant society. The religious pluralism of the twentieth century fitted a differentiated peasantry. All the varying levels of religion allowed for a collective involvement as well as for the emergence of a local charismatic leadership; all allowed for innovation, whether through the development of formal education or through prophetic revelation. Of course, the fit between differentiated peasant experience and religion was not exact: even peasants were concerned with spiritual and material realities other than those of agricultural production; religious forms and ideas which emerged at one moment of crisis or opportunity for the peasant economy lived on into later periods to which their particular vision of reality seemed much less suited; a good many religious propositions and insights did not 'work', just as a good many secular propositions and insights did not assist the peasantry. (A striking example being the recurrent failure of the rational advice of agricultural experts.) Nevertheless, in ways obviously much more complex than I have been able to show here agrarian innovation and religious innovation in the rural areas of Zimbabwe were inextricably intertwined. Any movement seeking to reach the peasantry, to mobilize them, would have to seek to understand what it was that peasant religion had to say about reality and about aspiration.

The guerilla war and religion

The African nationalist movements of the late 1950s and early 1960s did try to reach and mobilize the peasantry. They did this pretty much from the outside, without understanding peasant 'techniques of the imaginary'. In effect they did not need to in order to achieve the type of mobilization which took place in the open mass nationalist period. Peasant opposition to land alienation and to enforced agricultural rules and the nationalist ability to provide peasants with occasionally effective legal or political aid were enough in themselves to bring about a working coalition. African nationalism had some things to say about religion but these were mainly cultural nationalist 'religion-in-the-head' propositions which made little connection with rural religion itself. Thus nationalist intellectuals glorified the most famous of the spirit mediums of the past as part of the whole process of appealing back to vanished black empires. This had little to do with the local role of the medium as a focus for peasant resistance. During the nationalist period, the most significant local religious consequences were the attacks made on the entrepreneurial mission churches and their members because these would not throw in their lot with the peasant nationalist solidarity.[16]

The guerilla war when it came was a very different matter. Then the guerillas really did need to mobilize the peasants into a literally life and death struggle: then they really did need to understand what peasants were thinking and saying; they really did need to know how to touch the deepest levels of peasant belief and aspiration. In Zimbabwe there was no time, no possibility and, I would argue, no necessity for the guerillas to attempt a secular transformation of peasant thought. In Zimbabwe there were no liberated zones in which the intellectuals of the liberation movements might set up schools or in which guerilla medics might demonstrate the superiority of scientific medicine. In Zimbabwe the night-time *pungwes*, or political education sessions, did not educate the peasantry in a materialist analysis: instead they repeated the story of how the whites had taken the land. From one perspective all this might seem an indictment of the inadequacies of people's war as it was waged in Zimbabwe. I do not see it in this way. To my mind the Zimbabwean war was a people's war in which the people made a great deal of the ideological as well as the practical running. To my mind the Zimbabwean peasantry already understood the reality of their oppression. Their understanding could usefully be generalized through political education, so that peasants understood that the processes of land alienation and state intervention had taken place on a national scale and could only be remedied by a seizure of the colonial state. But their understanding could not usefully be changed. To my mind, also, the religious modes in which the interaction between peasants and guerillas were routinely expressed represented a powerful condensed statement of reality and aspiration, the articulation of which was an advantage rather than a disaster for the anti-colonial struggle.

One can understand the use made of peasant religion during the guerilla war either in terms of guerilla needs or in terms of peasant needs. Guerillas above all needed legitimacy. It was a deliberate policy that the majority of guerillas operating in a particular district should not have originated from that district. In this way a guerilla could not be tempted to favour his own kin or to seek to settle old scores. But this meant, of course, that the great majority of guerillas were strangers to the peasant elders who had hitherto dominated radical rural politics. The guerillas entered a district bearing the fanciful 'Chimurenga names' they had chosen for themselves, so that today peasants vividly remember their first meeting with young men calling themselves 'Dracula' or 'Mao' or

'Uriah Heap'. At these first meetings guerillas often went out of their way to assure peasants that they were not the monsters of official propaganda – 'See, we have no tails.' But at the same time it was not possible to assert totemic or extended kin links with a young man known only as Dracula. Quite deliberately guerillas were *outside* peasant society.

Yet, of course, it was vitally necessary that they should also be inside it; recognized by it as possessing the right to enter the land, to operate out of the holy places. It was necessary, too, that they should be seen as linked with the past and its traditions of resistance to colonialism. The Rhodesia Front had tried to stop the guerillas obtaining such legitimacy by co-opting the rural past for itself. In the 1970s the policy of 'Indirect Rule' reached extraordinary heights of ingenious absurdity, as District Commissioners sought to find fully 'traditional' chiefs and even sought to recruit influential spirit mediums to the support of the regime. This government policy had had some success. In Makoni district, for example, the medium who claimed to be possessed by the greatest of all Shona spirits, Chaminuka, had placed himself and his network of subordinate mediums at the disposal of the government, who flew him about over the combat zone so that he could denounce the guerillas from the skies as spillers of blood and destroyers of the land.[17]

Two courses were open to the guerillas in these circumstances. They might have denounced the whole idea of 'tradition' and attacked all mediums as fraudulent; equally where the central authorities of the mission churches had denounced the guerillas, they might have assaulted Christianity as merely another form of exploitative superstition. The other course was to seek to find ways of linking themselves more closely to peasant religion – whether it took the form of respect for the mediums or the form of folk Christianity – than the Rhodesia Front had been able to do. Such a strategy meant finding popular mediums who had held aloof from the government and who were prepared to throw the whole legitimacy of the past behind the guerillas: it meant finding, in the core zones of peasant folk Christianity, grass-roots 'holy men', ready to bring folk Catholicism or Anglicanism over to the guerilla side. It was this second strategy which the guerillas chose.

Admittedly, the first military operation carried out by guerillas in western Makoni was the execution of the medium of Chaminuka and the rocketing of his spirit hut. But over the body of the medium, the guerillas informed the people that his death had proved his fraudulence: they also told the people that they fought in the name of the true spirits and were supported by all true spirit mediums.[18] Thereafter, whenever guerillas entered a new area in Makoni they brought with them the medium recognized as being possessed by the spirit 'owner' of the land; the medium carried out the ceremonies necessary for them to be received by the spirits of the land and allowed to operate out of the burial caves of the chiefs and headmen. In the core folk-Christian areas, on the other hand, the guerillas worked with the men who alone were recognized by the local peasant population as capable of conferring legitimacy. Around Triashill and St Barbara's the guerillas worked with two remarkable Irish priests who remained on their stations throughout the war. In the Anglican areas of Chiduku Reserve, the guerillas worked with leading Anglican laymen or with part-time Anglican clergy like the headmaster of Toriro school, Stephen Matewa.[19] Of course, there were no hard and fast boundaries: Christians throughout the core zones of folk Christianity came to sing the *Chimurenga* songs in honour of the great spirits. The effective collapse of central hierarchical authority freed the local churches to make their own new compromises and accommodations.

Two oral texts will give some idea of guerilla interactions with peasant religion in all their complexity. First from an interview which I carried out with George Bhongoghozo, intelligence officer for the guerilla groups in Makoni in 1978 and 1979:

'Of course we used to work with the mediums. The two near Matotwe used to foresee and then warn us of enemy attacks. A very young medium at Nyachibva hill, which was another of our bases, also used to help in the same way. Many of the guerillas were also themselves mediums. They had spirits helpful to war. It might be that one of their ancestors had been a great warrior and his spirit came to help. Or it might be that they had a *shave* (personal spirit) of fighting. These gave them courage and also impressed the people. Indeed, the masses used to believe that we moved supernaturally and not on our own feet. The enemy attacked where we had been and we were not there any more. They did not know that we had been warned by the mediums at Matotwe.'[20]

And next from the other side, so to speak, an interview with Archdeacon Alban Makoni, who when the war began was priest in charge of Matsika parish in Chiduku with 50 out-stations and 27 schools:

'The comrades arrived in Matsika early in 1976. I was then away visiting my children in England. . . . At this stage the comrades were very hostile to Christianity. "We don't want to hear about Jesus. Jesus can do nothing." In the crisis of the war they put emphasis on the spirits. In Chiduku Reserve the chief base for the comrades was Ruwombe mountain, the second most important base for them in the whole of Manicaland. Ruwombe was a holy mountain, on which offerings were made for rain. It became a major reception centre for comrades coming in from Mozambique and passing on through the district, at the rate of 50 a day. Ruwombe was attacked by the Army but no guerillas were killed – they said because of the protection of the spirits. In a similar way Muwona hill in Makoni, was the hill where the chiefs were buried. When I was a boy I used to be told never to point at Muwona, but indicate it if necessary with my fist clenched. Muwona became a firm stronghold for the guerillas after certain ceremonies had been carried out to make this possible.

'My father was a Christian teacher who taught me that herbalists and mediums were of the devil. But even before the war I began to know more about African religion and during the war even stout Christians were mixed up. The spirit mediums became very important.

'Anyway, I began to work with the guerillas and they began to change their minds about Christianity. I gave them the goods they had asked for and they gave me a receipt and reported back to Mozambique that St John's, Matsika, was working with the liberation. . . . Later I supplied them with medicines from our registered clinic. When the Bishop came to visit I told him of the needs of the comrades. He said: "On no account must you meet them or you will be in trouble." I said: "Bishop, we are in trouble already!"

'Then the comrades warned me that I was in danger from the Security Forces. The soldiers came and surrounded my house and pointed all their guns at me. So I left Matsika and moved into Rusape where I became Archdeacon. From there I used to go out to meet the comrades and through Christian Care, and more recently through the United Nations Commission for Refugees I was able to channel aid in ways the comrades approved. . . . During the war I discovered the importance of social work.

'When they saw that the Church was helping them and that so many people in Chiduku wanted to remain Christians, the comrades began to change their minds and to respect Christianity. Today Matsika parish is very poor. The people lost so much in the war that collections bring in nothing. We have had to hand out free food this year. But I was able to preach yesterday in Matsika church on the supreme power of God over all and any spirits. In my congregation there were many comrades. One of them said to me afterwards: "Now the war is over there begins the biggest war of all – inside us, between Jesus and the devil. And I can assure you that it feels inside me as though they are fighting with A.K. rifles!" '[21]

These two texts allow us to see the situation from the guerilla and from the clerical point of view. But what about the needs of the peasants? Guerillas needed legitimacy: the radical clerics needed to keep their flocks together in support of the guerillas. Peasants needed three things. They needed to retain those solidarities which religion had created: they needed to draw upon religious idioms which gave particularly effective expression to their own protest against the regime: and they needed to find some way of influencing the guerillas. By far the majority of Makoni peasants backed the guerillas but nearly all of them also wanted to obtain some purchase on these strange young men: to restrain the use they made of the gun. Within the folk Christian cores this need found Christian expression. At Triashill and St Barbara's it was the Irish priests who laid down the moral bye-laws which came to be observed by both peasants and guerillas.[22] Outside these core areas, however, these needs were met by means of the spirit mediums.

It is possible to show how the mediums articulated the peasant programme of resistance and how they imposed constraints upon the guerillas. As the war spread, so very many mediums distanced themselves still further from the chiefs. The anthropologist, David Lan, spent two years after the end of the war carrying out field work in the Zimbabwean north-east, focussing particularly on the mediums and their role in the 1970s. In a recent seminar paper Lan argues that in the north-east:

the centre of political authority has progressively shifted from the chiefs to the mediums to the guerillas and, finally, to the newly established ZANU (PF) political committees. . . . The interference of the white administration in the appointment of chiefs and in the operation of their traditional duties had the effect of delegitimising their 'ancestral' authority . . . willingly or otherwise the chiefs became intimately associated with the white government. The mediums rejected it and demonstrated their rejection by their 'ritual' avoidance. . . . Mediums may not ride in buses or cars. The smell of petrol is so dangerous that the medium of Mutota is said to have died of it. They may not enter shops or eat food produced by mechanical means. . . . It is inconceivable that a medium would accept employment from a white person. . . . Many mediums refuse to see whites at all . . . an acting out of avoidance of whites based on experience of them in the past. . . .

By accepting their lowly position in the government hierarchy, the chiefs had acquired the authority to receive a monthly salary, to collect taxes, to wear a flamboyant uniform, and to little else. Their followers were left with no authority but to do what the government required of them. The shift of 'traditional' political authority from the chiefs to the independent, nationalist *mhondoro* mediums provided the thousands of deeply discontented villagers in Dande with the authority to do what the ancestors required of them. They received the authority to resist.[23]

I found much the same in Makoni, where in addition the mediums above all expressed and sacralized the peasant claims to the 'lost lands'.

As for the role of the mediums as law-givers to the rural communities in war, I have cited the relevant Makoni evidence before and can do no better than to cite it again here. In February 1981 I interviewed the senior medium of the Tandi chiefship in Chiduku, and his acolyte described the spirit's dealings with the guerillas:

Akuchekwa told the boys he would protect them but that they must not do the things which the spirits disliked. The spirits refused to accept the shedding of innocent blood. If 'sell-outs' went to the boys and said, 'This one is a witch', 'this one is an informer', they were not just to kill them. The boys obeyed the spirits. Things were quite perfect then. And the spirits protected the boys.[24]

Amon Shonge, leader of a communal farm in the north of the district offered the same picture for an area of particularly radical peasant politics:

This use of mediums was the same everywhere. The comrades had to contact the spirit medium first to introduce themselves. Then they would be told what to do. They were told which were the holy places and given some sort of bye-laws to guide them. They were told that they must not kill innocent people. Nearly everyone started to feel that the mediums were very important people.[25]

Conclusion

I have shown that peasant religion in Zimbabwe was inevitably involved in that profound crisis for peasant society, the guerilla war. Indeed, I could have gone on to show yet more – how, for instance, the American Methodist tradition in Makoni was first mobilized by Bishop Muzorewa to provide the organizational and symbolic muscle for his African National Council, and then found itself after Muzorewa's entry into the Internal Settlement defined by the guerillas a main enemy. Hence the old American Methodist centre of Gandanzara, home of the peasant entrepreneurs, was regularly attacked by guerillas and defended by Muzorewa's auxiliaries in the nearest thing to pitched battles and the nearest thing to class-war that the conflict in Makoni was to produce. But instead of continuing to discuss the fascinating details – and I have said nothing about the role of the prophetic churches in the war, for example – I wish to conclude by making one last point.

I have been arguing in this paper that the Zimbabwe data compels some rethinking of the dominant typology. Basil Davidson, to whom I have attributed the clearest enunciation of that typology, was in the chair when this paper was given. His comment was that he thought we were arguing at two different levels. He did not dispute that peasants could be mobilized in the way I have described. But unless there developed within the liberation movement as a whole a more effective 'modern' ideology there could not after the war be an effective transformation of colonial society nor could the needs of the peasants be met. The regular appeal to the memory of the great mediums by ZANU politicians, which was one legacy of the role of religion in the war, did not seem to bode well for the emergence of an effective modernizing ideology. And as for the peasants, they were certainly able to participate very effectively in the war, at each local level, by drawing on the sort of ideologies I have been describing. But these did not allow them to demand and to produce the sort of state which could or would bring about a profound revolution in the rural economy. I think that maybe we are still arguing about something substantive. To my mind it is everywhere almost impossible for peasants, no matter how ideologically sophisticated, to be able to create for themselves a state which will act in their interests. There is an inevitable tension between peasantries and states, even revolutionary and liberationary states. To my mind, if peasant programmes are to be achieved this has to be done by means of constant peasant pressure upon the state. In Zimbabwe there has been, since the war, very effective peasant pressure, especially in the form of peasant 'squatting', the mass invasion of the lost lands. Peasants have continued to demand more land and less interference. And this demand is certainly still powered by religious ideologies, as spirit mediums continue to claim the land of the ancestors and as local folk Christian communities continue to exercise the autonomy from hierarchies which they won during the war.

Notes

1 Stuart Clark, 'French Historians and Early Modern Popular Culture', *Past and Present*, 100, August 1983, pp.69–71.

2 F. Fanon, *The Wretched of the Earth*, London, 1967, pp.42–3.

3 Catherine Coquery Vidrovitch, 'Peasant Unrest in Black Africa', *Agrarian Unrest in British and French Africa, British India and French Indo-China in the Nineteenth and Twentieth Century*, Past and Present Conference, Oxford, July 1982.

4 Basil Davidson, *The People's Cause. A History of Guerillas in Africa*, London, 1981, pp.92, 97.

5 Davidson, *op.cit.*, pp.113, 117, 124.

6 Y.T. Museveni, 'Fanon's Theory of Violence: Its Verification in Liberated Mozambique', in N.S. Shamuyarira (ed.), *Essays on the Liberation of Southern Africa*, Dar es Salaam, 1972, pp.14–15, 20, 21.

7 Jean Copans, 'From Senegambia to Senegal: The Evolution of Peasantries', in *Peasants in Africa*, edited M.A. Klein, London, 1980, pp.77–103. It has been argued for some districts in Zimbabwe that a peasantry emerged long before colonialism. Thus Dr H.K. Bhila argues that in the kingdom of Manyika, which adjoins Makoni district to the east, peasant production dated back at least as far as regular contact with Portuguese trading bases. H.K. Bhila, *Trade and Politics in a Shona Kingdom*, London, 1982.

8 The Smuts Commonwealth Lectures, Cambridge, February to March 1983. These lectures have been published under the title *Peasant Consciousness and Guerilla War in Zimbabwe: A Comparative Study*, London, 1985.

9 O'Farrell, 'Report', *Journal of the Rhodesian Annual Conference*, 1926, p.28. For a fuller treatment of the 'fit' between varying types of Christianity and varying peasant experiences see Terence Ranger, 'Poverty and Prophetism: Religious Movements in the Makoni District, 1929–1940', Henderson seminar, University of Zimbabwe, March 1981; 'Religions and Rural Protests: Makoni district, Zimbabwe, 1900 to 1980', in Janos Bak and G. Benecke (eds), *Religion and Rural Revolt*, Manchester, 1985.

10 *Rhodesian Annual Conference*, 1923, pp.67–8.

11   Terence Ranger, 'Religions and Rural Protests'.
12   'Religions and Rural Protests'.
13   Terence Ranger, 'Poverty and Prophetism'.
14   'Religions and Rural Protests'.
15   Michael Gelfand, *The Spiritual Beliefs of the Shona*, Gwelo, 1977, p.134.
16   For a detailed account of this in Makoni district see N.E. Thomas, 'Christianity, Politics and the Manyika', doctoral thesis, Boston, 1968.
17   Terence Ranger, 'The Death of Chaminuka: Spirit Mediums, Nationalism and the Guerilla War in Zimbabwe', *African Affairs*, 81, 324, July 1982.
18   *Ibid*.
19   Terence Ranger, 'The Church and War: Holy Men and Rural Communities in Zimbabwe, 1970–1980', in W.J. Sheils (ed.), *The Church and War*, Oxford, 1983.
20   Interview between Terence Ranger and George Bhongoghozo, Rusape, 16 February 1981.
21   Interview with Archdeacon Alban Makoni, Rusape, 2 February 1981.
22   Terence Ranger, 'The Death of Chaminuka'.
23   David Lan, 'Spirit Mediums and the Authority to Resist in the Struggle for Zimbabwe', Institute of Commonwealth Studies, London, January 1982. Lan has since published the fullest and most profound study of the role of mediums in the war, in *Guns and Rain*, London, 1985.
24   Interview with the acolyte of the Akuchekwa medium, Tandi, 27 February 1981.
25   Interview with Amon Shonge, Weya, 25 March 1981.

The Reformation

18

The Reformation in Edinburgh: The growth and growing pains of urban Protestantism

MICHAEL LYNCH

In 1566 John Knox tried to assess in the preface to Book IV of his *History of the Reformation of Religion within the Realm of Scotland* the remarkable progress the reformed church had made since the Reformation of 1559–60. His claims were characteristically uncompromising.

> Touching the doctrine taught by our ministers and . . . the administration of Sacraments used in our churches, we are bold to affirm that there is no realm this day upon the face of the earth that hath them in . . . the like purity. . . . And as concerning the suppressing of vice, yea, and of the abolishing of all such things as might nourish impiety within the realm, the acts and statutes of the principal towns reformed will yet testify.

There is much to be said in his support. Although the Reformation parliament of 1560 had only abolished papal jurisdiction, proscribed the mass and adopted a reformed Confession of Faith, there had been rapid progress in Scotland towards a godly Reformation, in many respects arguably more so in the early 1560s than in England: saints' days had been abolished along with the use of the organ and sign of the cross at baptism; ordinary bread was used at communion and private celebration of the sacraments forbidden.

The Protestant reformers of 1560 had singled out the larger burghs as the future growth-points of their spiritual Reformation without equivocation in the *First Book of Discipline*. There was even competition amongst the burghs to be the first to bring their respective Reformations to a satisfactory conclusion. Some towns, like St Andrews and Dundee, had anticipated the decisions of the Reformation parliament and set up a reformed congregation with preacher and kirk session in the course of the crisis of 1559–60. Edinburgh had had a slow start and civic prestige was at stake; a petition presented by the burgh's craftsmen to the town council in November 1560 suggested the steps necessary, including their own advancement, to make Edinburgh 'a mirrour and exempill to all the rest of this realme'.

Knox had been appointed as Edinburgh's first Protestant minister in July 1559. After two abortive attempts to take the town, the Lords of Congregation succeeded at a third attempt in April 1560 and the details of the Knoxian Reformation were quickly set in train. In May a newly installed loyalist council stopped paying the stipends of the burgh's chaplains and banned all other payments to chaplainries; in June the town took over the property and income of the friaries which lay within it; in August the vestments and treasures of the collegiate church of St Giles were auctioned off; by the end of the year Sunday markets had been abolished; by Easter 1561 attendance at the sermon was enforced and ex-priests and ex-religious who showed unwillingness to conform were threatened with expulsion from the burgh. By November 1562 the 'faithful brethren of Edinburgh', as they termed themselves in a subscription list for the building of a new poor hospital, comprised half of the burgh establishment. The barebones of Edinburgh's Reformation are well known and seemingly as uncompromising as Knox himself.

This seemingly largely straightforward pattern of rapid evangelization under the protective shield of a sympathetic and omnicompetent civil authority, backed usually by sympathizers among the neighbouring nobles and gentry, has been taken to be the norm not only in Edinburgh but most of the Scottish burghs. It is, however, a peculiarly durable orthodoxy since little detailed research has been done until very recently not only on the urban Reformation in Scotland but also on the specific workings of any of the sixteenth-century burghs. It has been assumed that burghs were governed by a town council which was virtually a closed oligarchy, able to re-elect itself from year to year. It has often been argued, as a consequence, that the closed doors of the council chamber were a significant aid to this seemingly rapid spread of Protestantism or, some would prefer, to the wholesale repression of Catholics. Yet both of these arguments probably exaggerate the actual power available to burgh magistrates or councillors. A town council held authority only in so far as it represented the views of the burgh establishment and it continued to protect the accumulated privileges and conventions which held burgh life together. A largely self-perpetuating oligarchy did run burgh affairs but its authority usually rested not on flagrant nepotism or machine politics but consent. The key to the progress of the Reformation in the larger Scottish towns lies in tracing the route to consensus. Protestantism in 1560 was, so far as it is possible to tell, a minority movement in most of them. It was certainly so in

Edinburgh, where the town's Protestants declined the offer of a religious referendum in the summer of 1559, maintaining that 'God's truth should not be subject to the voting of men'. By Easter 1561, eight months after the close of the Reformation parliament, only 1,300 – considerably less than a fifth of the burgh's adult population – took communion by the new rite. There was no magical mass conversion to the reformed church in 1560 or immediately after. In most of the Scottish towns, and certainly in Edinburgh, it is more important to describe the Reformation settlement which was set in motion in the years after 1560 than the tentative and stop-go pattern of growth of Protestantism before 1560.

In the bulk of the Scottish burghs Protestants did not gain power as the natural climax of a carefully orchestrated campaign against abuses and the mass; power was thrust into their hands by outside forces. But who were these new-found Protestants? In most cases they seem to have been the old urban establishment with a new set of clothes. A gentlemen's agreement was often reached between the Lords of the Congregation and the town council to conform and in some cases, as earnest of its good intent, the council decided to absorb a Protestant element within it. There were few purges of town councils; a key plank in the programme of the Congregation was, after all, the restoring of power into proper hands. In Edinburgh, however, there was not one purge in the course of the events of 1559–60 but two. A Protestant town council and its minister, Knox, were imposed on the town not once but twice during the crisis. The Reformation settlement was thus all the more slow to emerge there because a genuinely new regime had been installed. Its members were not all social *parvenus*; there was a hard core of about a third of them with both social respectability and experience of office. Yet it was difficult for them to shed the collective image of *arrivistes*. And this was the council – a body as much nervous as hawkish – which set in train purging Edinburgh of its 'dregs of papistry' in April 1560.

The task of Protestantizing Scottish urban society was not a straightforward one. In the capital there were also special difficulties. There was not one influential local noble but two, who pulled in starkly different directions. The earl of Morton, the protector of Douglas interests and a signatory of the First Bond of the Congregation in 1557, brooded menacingly a few miles to the south-west at Dalkeith; the resolutely Catholic house of Seton, which held land immediately both to the east and west of the town at Winchburgh and Seton, threatened reprisals when it was forced out of office as provost of the burgh in favour of a Douglas in 1559–60. Although the town did not have a university it was an intellectual and cultural metropolis as much as it was a trading one. It had two printing presses, which for a time between 1561 and 1562 exchanged verbal blows between Knox and the Catholic controversialist, Ninian Winzet. For much of the 1560s Edinburgh experienced two separate sets of intellectual stimuli: along with the twice-yearly visit of the party conference of the godly, meeting in the General Assembly, it had the virtually continuous presence of the court, the first genuine court milieu since the 1540s, with a strong dash of French evangelical humanism about it as well as Catholicism. George Buchanan, David Riccio, Thomas Randolph, the English ambassador, and Alexander Clark, the financial backer of an edition of Buchanan's *Psalms* printed in Edinburgh in 1564 and client of James Stewart, earl of Moray, had all known each other in Paris in the 1550s. The French connection was not confined to the court. Edinburgh had a large legal community and until 1600 all Scottish advocates went to French universities to qualify in both canon and civil law. Most of these lawyers had first studied at St Andrews, which was the natural university for Edinburgh burgess sons to attend. It would be mistaken to think of them all having drunk at the Protestant well of St Leonard's College; it should be remembered that by the late 1540s the fashionable college to attend was St Mary's, which was the centre of the Catholic intellectual reform movement. An Erasmian-tinged civic humanism was as important a barrier in the path of unfettered Protestant progress in Edinburgh as was a healthy civic Catholicism. The Protestant party discovered as much when it tried in 1562 to dismiss the master of the town's grammar school, who had persistently refused to take communion or even attend the sermon. He appeared unexpectedly before the council with twenty-two character witnesses, including substantial representation from the burgh's professional men, some of them at least nominally Protestants. Professional vested interests, combined with moderate Protestant opinion, was enough to see off the first attempt to dismiss him. Several more attempts were subsequently made but faltered before, first, the protection of Queen Mary and, more decisively, that of the law courts. The Edinburgh town council was taken to the Court of Session in 1569 during the explicitly Protestant regency of the earl of Moray and forced to reinstate its Catholic schoolmaster, who retained his position until he retired gracefully fifteen years later. It was relatively easy to be rid of Catholic relics; disposing of the contracts of Catholic office-holders proved more difficult.

There were two potential brakes on the pace and character of the urban Reformation in Scotland. One lay in the very structure of burgh society and its ingrained conventions and customs. The other proved to be the men who held power in each of the burghs. The case of the Edinburgh Catholic schoolmaster brought both sets of brakes into operation. One of his character witnesses was a merchant, John Marjoribanks – a magistrate on the very council which was trying to impose a religious test on office-holders. Here was a Protestant magistrate publicly defending a Catholic recusant or, to be precise, his contract. One of Marjoribank's colleagues on the same council was another leading merchant, James Watson. He was a Protestant of a different stamp, one of the original caucus brought to power by the Lords of Congregation in 1559, a man who remained consistently on the activist wing of Protestantism and was implicated in the Riccio murder. Yet this ultra-Protestant had a Catholic wife. She was one of a number of wives of prominent men prosecuted in 1563 for attending the mass in the Chapel Royal at Holyrood. It is as well to bear in mind that Scottish society, urban as well as rural, was firmly co-agnatic. A wife retained her own name after marriage, her own property and her own kinship network. Marriage was a contractual convenience but not a merging of kin. As a result a resolutely Protestant household, like that of James Watson, might often conceal a second household, resolutely Catholic, within it.

There are two ways to describe what happened to the Protestant caucus brought to power in 1560. One lies in the steady infiltration into their ranks over the course of the first half of the 1560s of the 'moderate tendency'. The landmarks lie in annual council elections; each election between 1561 and 1567 was a genuine contest, resulting in a shift, in one direction or another, in a struggle between the ultra-Protestants of 1560 and the more moderate-minded men. The original Protestant party of 1560 slipped almost imperceptibly into a Protestant coalition, irenic, socially conservative and Erastian by inclination. By 1566 this slippage of power away from the original caucus of 1560 had reduced its influence to a rump of three on a town council of nineteen. That was why so many of the men brought to power in 1560 became involved along with their two ministers, Knox and John Craig, in the desperate gamble of 9 March 1566 – the Riccio murder. By then the choice was quite stark – blood on their hands or political eclipse. Ironically the Riccio affair made little difference; the fall of Queen Mary fifteen months later did, though only for a time. It was not until the resolution in 1573 of a six-year-long civil war between queen's men and king's men, a far more bitter and divisive affair than the Reformation crisis, that Protestantism decisively regained the upper hand politically. By then, of course, John Knox was dead and the victory had taken a civil war which split the burgh establishment down the middle in its loyalties to do it.

The second process is more difficult to describe precisely. It took the form not of an obvious political struggle between two increasingly starkly-defined political factions. It was rather an increasingly open split within the Protestant mind – even in a mind such as that of James Watson, where the pull of a wife's kin clashed with party policy. Traditional habits, the still-important notion of the preservation of the town as a *corpus christianum*, neighbourliness, kin, civic humanism, caution and common sense – all combined to blunt the force and direction of the Protestant programme. And Erastianism – 'it is the king we have to do with' wrote an Edinburgh merchant in the 1580s in the midst of another bout of agonizing by Edinburgh's Protestant conscience – was exploited with increasing subtlety by the crown in the mid-1560s. Knox's *History*, with its dramatized irreconcilables – 'In religion there is na middis' – does not take account of any of these forces. It is, at times, quite deliberately misleading as well as uncompromising. In 1566 the queen produced a leet at the time of the annual council election; her nominees, Knox claimed, were 'papists, the rest not worthy'. Yet the leet included Edinburgh's two commissioners for that year to the General Assembly. One of them, John Preston, would wholeheartedly back the Melvillian party in its struggle with James VI eighteen years later in the crisis of 1584. It is at first glance an odd scenario – a man who withdrew support from John Knox but who backed Andrew Melville to the hilt – until one realizes that Knox did not enjoy popular support whereas the Melvillians did. There was a Protestant mob in Edinburgh in the 1580s; there was not one in the 1560s, only a Catholic mob to provoke. Knox had by 1565 overplayed a weak hand of cards; the Protestant revolution of 1560 had provoked a conservative backlash which had brought about a genuine crisis in the Protestant conscience as well as a shift in political factions. Erastianism by then produced apparent inconsistency of behaviour as well as mere compromise.

There were from the very beginning logistical difficulties in trying to convert a population of 12,500 in which there was considerable devolution of authority. The social structure of the Scottish towns had a dual aspect. There still existed a strong sense of the burgh community, reinforced by the fact that in Scotland all burghs were a single parish. In a very real sense the Scottish town was still a *corpus christianum* with its focus in its collegiate church under the overall patronage of the town council; it was important to both the reformers and their critics that the seamless robe should remain intact. In another sense burgh society was not one *corpus christianum* but many. The collegiate church of St Giles' had more than forty side altars and aisles dedicated to different saints; fourteen of them were administered and controlled by the town's fourteen incorporated craft guilds. The Reformation, as a result, could not engulf society like a tidal wave; it had to penetrate and flood each of these separate compartments. None of them had shown much in the way of early Protestant stirrings before 1560; a number remained as private Catholic churches in miniature for some time after 1560. There was not a great deal the council could do about this; it did not customarily interfere in the affairs of the guilds. So although the town sold off its own collection of religious vestments in the summer of 1560, the skinner craft prevaricated for a further two years. They were then bought by the craft's own deacon, but not as souvenirs of a bygone Catholic cult; the craft's chaplain was caught saying mass in his house in 1565. When the council did intervene to check too open a display of Catholic strength in the guilds it was not altogether successful. The hammermen were the town's second largest guild and, with an altar in St Giles' and a separate outside chapel staffed by two chaplains, had more to lose than most. In 1562 the council imposed a Protestant loyalist as head of the guild and tried to alter the balance of power within it by creating a number of new masters. The pressure worked for a time but by 1568 the Catholics were back in control where they remained until purged in 1573 at the end of the civil war. The Catholic counter-thrust came, it should be noted, during the supposedly Protestant regency of Moray. The guilds remained closed societies. Catholic councillors might be purged in 1559 and 1560 but Catholic craft deacons were a more difficult proposition. The kirk session and the guild would in time co-operate to implement godly discipline but not in the Reformation generation.

The *corpus christianum* of Edinburgh as a whole was an unwieldy body. The pre-Reformation establishment – with the forty-odd altars of St Giles', two further private collegiate churches, two friaries and fully two handfuls of private chapels – had comprised a veritable small army to minister to the spiritual needs of its inhabitants. The 'extras' were necessary. In 1592, by which time Edinburgh's population had increased, but not significantly so because of two serious outbreaks of plague in 1568 and 1585, the kirk session organized a census of parishioners. It had, it found, 8,000 communicants in the one parish of St Giles'; it recommended the splitting up of the old medieval parish into eight new parishes, each with about 1,000 communicants. This was exactly the reverse of what was happening in some English towns by the end of the sixteenth century. Exeter was trying to reduce its anachronistic plethora of nineteen parishes; Edinburgh was finally tackling the practical consequences of its own medieval past and the myth of the *corpus christianum* by splitting up its single parish.

It has recently been argued that the best indicator of the consolidation of Protestantism in Scotland after 1560 lies in charting the spread of a parish ministry. It is a thesis primarily addressed to rural Scotland. But what of the burghs, which were given highest priority by *The First Book of Discipline*? From 1562 until 1574 Edinburgh had two ministers and a reader to cater for a population in excess of 12,000. Dundee, with a population of about 5,000, was the only other burgh to appoint a second minister in the 1560s. The overworked vicar of the London parish of St Stephen's, Coleman Street, might well complain in 1630 that he could not possibly know all the 1,400 communicants in his flock personally. Yet Knox and his two colleagues in Edinburgh had each in theory about 2,500 communicants, assembling in three different parts of St Giles' and an overflow in Trinity College 300 yards away, to minister to. The numbers in their charge were probably nominal at best. Much of this is the hidden history of the Edinburgh Reformation because the kirk session records are only extant for an eighteen-month period in the mid-1570s. Yet there are possible indicators, such as the candlemaker, Henry Easton, who came before the session to admit that he had absented himself from communion for the past fourteen years. This was in 1575. Easton had probably never enjoyed what Knox called the most perfectly administered communion rite 'upon the face of the earth'. There were serious gaps in the implementation of discipline. Some were by choice – although the Church itself held the right of excommunication and was thus notionally more powerful even than in Calvin's Geneva it needed the co-operation of the civil magistrate to enforce banishment. That did not happen in Edinburgh until 1569. Some gaps stemmed from the structure of society itself. Easton belonged to a craft which was not incorporated and thus escaped the mutually reinforcing authority of town council, kirk session and guilt, which on the face of it was such a feature of the consolidation of urban Protestantism in Scotland. Thirty per cent of adult males fell within the network of privilege – whether of burgess-ship or incorporated guild; their households stretched the skein of godly discipline a little further, to their wives, children, apprentices and servants – at least in theory. It is difficult to believe that the system of communion tickets which evolved in the 1560s was any more effective in monitoring the behaviour of the remainder than it was in the case of Henry Easton. The exercise – the so-called privy kirk – which had emerged in the second half of the 1550s had perhaps promised the unprivileged masses an active stake in a godly future to come; there had been apprentices and journeymen elected to office as elders and deacons, a strange sight in a society so conscious of privilege and rank. They had disappeared from view after 1560.

This had happened when the privy kirk, as Knox put it, 'took on a public face' in 1560. Yet the evolution of the privy kirk into a burgh church is only the first instalment of the story. The second has yet to be evaluated by ecclesiastical historians of the Scottish Reformation, although it has been elsewhere. The various deficiencies of the new burgh church – not least of them in sheer lack of manpower – induced a retreat back into the Protestant household for the better part of a generation. This was all the more ironical since much the same happened, for different reasons, to the Catholic cult. The new burgh church was an impressive but rather hollow edifice. It is not surprising that there were no myths constructed – by propagandists of either side – of Knox's 'godly city'. It was not until 1580 that Edinburgh became, in the words of the nephew of Andrew Melville, the 'Zion' of the reformed Church.

It was finance and taxation, however, which constituted the most formidable obstacle for the new Church to surmount in the Scottish urban reformation. The first of the many compromises forced upon the Protestant regime swept to power in Edinburgh by the Lords of Congregation in 1560 was on taxation. The new regime tried in its first weeks in power to levy a forced loan to help the Congregation's siege of the French troops entrenched behind the formidable walls of the port of Leith, some two miles away. The tax assessors it appointed were understandably all Protestant loyalists, many of them from outside the traditional circles of power. The loan fell well short of target amidst complaints by some Catholic burgesses of punitive assessments. As was customary, a review and audit was held shortly afterwards. This was the point at which Edinburgh's counter-revolution began; the auditors were drawn from the conventional cross-section of the burgh establishment and duly allowed some of the complaints. The issue was not religious but constitutional:

if the business of tax assessment and audit was to continue it had to be conducted in a manner which enjoyed the confidence of the whole burgh community. So known Catholics continued, if not on the council, at least as the overseers of much of the town's financial business throughout the 1560s.

From 1562 most burgh ministers were paid by the compromise arrived at with the crown in the thirds of benefices. The thirds, however, only met the basic stipend of one minister in each burgh; his incidental expenses and the full costs of any other appointees had to be borne by the burgh itself. There were real difficulties in doing this. Burghs in Scotland were not accustomed to paying direct taxation for local needs; even national taxation did not become a regular occurrence until the 1580s. Burgh revenue was gathered from a bewildering number of indirect means, which varied in their details from town to town; Edinburgh had more than thirty sources. The solution offered by Knox was radical. In his tract of 1558, *A Letter addressed to the Commonalty of Scotland*, he had forecast that when the godly society was established rich and poor would both share in and contribute to it equally. The full consequences of Knox's manifesto did not become clear until five years later. The town council resorted to a compulsory household tax of four shillings a year on all inhabitants to pay for Knox's colleagues, John Craig, the second minister appointed in 1562, and a reader. The ministerial tax of 1563 broke a number of conventions and proved to be a disastrous failure. It was one of eight separate schemes devised in the course of the 1560s to pay for the programme of the kirk; some attempted to include poor relief and education alongside payment of the ministry and various degrees of coercion were used. All the schemes failed. The new religious establishment was not placed on a stable basis until at least the 1580s, perhaps not until an annuity tax was devised in 1635. Edinburgh had much the same difficulties as Norwich and a number of other English boroughs in meeting the price of a preaching ministry, the true mark of 'civility' in a godly civic commonwealth.

Poor relief proved much more difficult to settle in the Scottish towns than in England. There was no tradition in Scotland of merchant charity to fall back on and there proved to be substantial resistance, in Edinburgh and elsewhere, to a poor rate. In 1574 an act was passed by the Scottish parliament, probably at the prompting of Edinburgh, to enable town councils to raise a compulsory poor rate. The act was in frank imitation of the English parliamentary legislation of 1572. Yet there was a vital difference. The legislation of Elizabethan parliaments on poor relief built on relatively successful measures which had already been taken in certain towns like Norwich, where elaborate machinery designed to rationalize the treatment of its poor had come into effect in 1571. In England parliamentary legislation sought to extend a system already in existence. In Scotland the act of 1574 was designed to give added force to a system which had already been tried a number of times in Edinburgh and rejected. When implemented in Edinburgh the new compulsory poor rate ironically raised less than the old *ad hoc* system of voluntary donations at the church door on Sundays. It lasted less than two years, ending in acrimony between town council and kirk session, each blaming the other for the fact that the town had proved unwilling to accept direct taxation even to support its own poor.

The unwillingness of Edinburgh and the other Scottish burghs to meet the bill for the new godly society severely limited the expectations of the reformed Church. Historians of the Scottish Reformation have yet to come to terms with the fact that the full-scale establishment of Protestantism in the burghs required money but that money there, as elsewhere, was difficult to come by. The urban Reformation was as under-financed as the rest of the Scottish Reformation.

The Scottish urban Reformation is slowly being dissected. Research is under way on Perth, Dundee, St Andrews and Aberdeen and it is probably premature to anticipate the conclusions which will emerge in the next few years. It is safe to say, however, that there were at least three major variables at work, which may produce a picture of a series of local Reformations, each proceeding at its own pace and, to some extent, with its own distinctive problems. The first variable lay in the structure of the pre-Reformation ecclesiastical establishment, which varied significantly from burgh to burgh. Most of the large burghs were not bishops' seats so that the picture which has emerged from the only continuous kirk session record from 1559 onwards, in St Andrews, is likely to be untypical. The reformers deliberately tried to shift the focus of ecclesiastical organization towards burghs which were not the centre of the old dioceses – to Edinburgh, Dundee, Perth, to Aberdeen as distinct from Old Aberdeen. They were probably right to do so, but success did not come overnight. Reformation Protestantism was not really an urban movement in Scotland; reformed Protestantism along Melvillian lines clearly was by the 1580s. The second variable lay in the fact that the structure of urban institutions and the detailed workings of government varied from burgh to burgh; Edinburgh had fourteen incorporated guilds whereas other burghs had seven or less and there was no set list; in Edinburgh the medium of the head court had fallen into disuse earlier in the century whereas in Perth it was important enough in 1560 to be called to elect the burgh's commissioners to the Reformation parliament. Consensus was expressed differently in different burghs. Lastly, and perhaps most significantly for the future, relations between centre and localities were in a state of flux in the sixteenth century and this applied to the burghs as much as to elsewhere. Some burghs, like Perth, Stirling and Edinburgh, experienced repeated and direct intervention by the court in their affairs during the Reformation period; others, like Dundee and Aberdeen, which were at opposite poles from each other in their religious instincts, escaped with an occasional cursory inspection. The Scottish Reformation settlement in this respect seems to bear a good deal of similarity to the patchy and ambiguous pattern in the localities of the Elizabethan church settlement in England.

Bibliography

Cameron, J.K. (ed.), *The First Book of Discipline*, Edinburgh, 1972.

Cowan, I.B., *The Scottish Reformation: Church and Society in Sixteenth-Century Scotland*, London, 1982.

Dickinson, W.C. (ed.), *John Knox's History of the Reformation in Scotland*, 2 vols, Edinburgh, 1949.

Kirk, J., ' "The polities of the best reformed kirks": Scottish achievements and English aspirations in church government after the Reformation', *Scottish Historical Review*, 1980, vol. 59, pp.22–53.

Lynch, M., *Edinburgh and the Reformation*, Edinburgh, 1981.

Lynch, M., 'From privy kirk to burgh church: an alternative view of the process of protestantisation', in N. Macdougall (ed.), *Church and Society in Scotland, 1450–1929*, Edinburgh, 1983.

Makey, W.H., *The Church of the Covenant, 1637–1651: Revolution and Social Change in Scotland*, Edinburgh, 1979.

Marwick, J.D. (ed.), *Extracts from the Records of the Burgh of Edinburgh*, vol. 3 (1557–1571), Scottish Burgh Records Society, 1875.

Reid, W.S., 'The coming of the Reformation to Edinburgh', *Church History*, 1973, vol. 42, pp.27–44.

White, A., 'The impact of the Reformation on a burgh community: the case of Aberdeen', in M. Lynch (ed.), *The Early Modern Town in Scotland*, London, 1986.

19

Luther and women:
The death of two Marys

MERRY WIESNER

God has created men with broad chests and shoulders, not broad hips, so that men can understand wisdom. But the place where the filth flows out is small. With women it's the other way around. That's why they have lots of filth and little wisdom.[1]

Women are created for no other purpose than to serve men and be their helpers. If women grow weary or even die while bearing children, that doesn't harm anything. Let them bear children to death; they are created for that.[2]

There is nothing better on earth than a woman's love.[3]

Oh how passionately I yearned for my family as I lay at death's door in Schmalkald. I thought I would never see my wife and little children again. How much pain that distance and separation caused me! Since by God's grace I have recovered, I now love my dear wife and children all the more.[4]

From just these four statements, one can easily understand the tremendous variation in assessments of Luther's opinion of women. His champions, from the sixteenth century to the present, have seen his attack on celibacy and stress on the positive side of marriage as rescuing women from the depths of scholastic misogyny and denigration.[5] In the words of William Lazareth:

The union of Martin and Katie was not cursed with the birth of the Anti-Christ. Instead it was blessed by God with the birth of the Protestant parsonage and the rebirth of a genuinely Christian ethos in home and community. Luther's marriage remains to this day the central evangelical symbol of the Reformation's liberation and transformation of Christian daily life.[6]

Elizabeth Ahme agrees:

Luther's appraisal of women was basically determined through the realization that she was also created by God and saved through Christ. With this Luther overcame all obstacles that stood in the way of her fulfillment as a woman, and opened the way for a happy acceptance and affirmation of the role which God had given her.[7]

Luther's acceptance of male dominance and belittling of female ability is seen as simply a continuation of classical, Biblical, patristic, scholastic, and humanist misogyny, a tradition that even Luther couldn't break.

Those who emphasize Luther's negative views also range over centuries, from Counter-Reformation biographers to contemporary feminist observers. Sigmund Baronowski in 1913 cautiously noted:

> His judgment of women is not exactly as ideal as some would have us believe. . . . We hear nothing from Luther about the personal worth and dignity of women. . . . The brutal openness with which he thrusts women into the 'natural' law of sexual life, the shocking ruthlessness with which he portrays the burning and sinful lusts of consecrated virgins, not out of his own experience but with alleged Biblical proof – all of this degraded female honor and dignity much more than simple vulgar satires did.[8]

Martha Behrens, sixty years later, was much more harsh:

> His remarks indicate a basic, almost pagan and mythological fear of woman and her power. . . . Idealized by Luther, marriage was a masculine institution calling for complete self-abnegation by woman either as mother, wife or daughter. Rather than freeing her from the medieval ideal of celibacy, this idea chained her to a restrictive ideal of servitude. Moreover, Luther's teaching that God was pleased by this servitude served to spiritualize or hallow these biological roles, causing resistance against development in other areas.[9]

As usual with any area of Reformation scholarship, there are also those who take a middle view, pointing out the continuity between Luther's ideas and those of his predecessors, both humanist and scholastic. John Yost notes:

> The Renaissance humanists, civic and Christian alike, emphasized marriage and family life as the best means for all social relations. . . . God had established marriage and family life as the best means for providing spiritual and moral discipline in this world. . . . In this way, civic and Christian humanists enable us to see more clearly the larger context for the revolutionary change in domestic life brought about by the Protestant reformers.[10]

Kathleen Davies also finds more continuity than change in pre- and post-Reformation attitudes toward married life as reflected in English sermons, pamphlets and conduct books.[11]

Thus the range of opinions on Luther's ideas about the position of women, and the impact of those ideas, is very broad. There is ammunition enough in his writings to support any position. Rather than simply adding my own interpretation of *what* Luther said, I want instead to retreat from that battlefield somewhat and explore *how* he said what he did. In other words, what kind of language, images and metaphors did he use when speaking to and about women? How does he use the female and the feminine?

One of the most important contributions of feminism to all disciplines has been to make us aware of just this point – that *how* we say things, the implicit and sub- or unconscious message which comes through our choice of words, may be as or even more important than what we are actually saying. There is no such thing as 'just semantics'. Language is power. Language is both a reification of power relationships in any society, and a way of exerting power over others. It rises out of social, political and intellectual structures, and then in turn affects those structures. And no one recognized this more clearly than Luther. He chose his words, images and allusions carefully, because they would evoke a certain response.

Though the two are related, I think it will be useful if we make a distinction between the female and the feminine in Luther's writings. By female, I mean his descriptions and discussions of actual women or 'woman' in the abstract. By feminine I mean his use of imagery, particularly when referring to God or Christ or the Church, which stresses qualities which were then, and are still, felt to be more 'feminine' than 'masculine' – gentleness, nurturing, undemanding love, submissiveness and so on.

The female image that occurs most often in Luther's writings is his ideal, the wife and mother:

> What better and more useful thing can be taught in the church than the example of a godly mother of the household who prays, sighs, cries out, gives thanks, rules the house, performs the functions of sex and desires offspring with the greatest chastity, grace and godliness: What more should she do?[12]

The word that Luther uses again and again in his descriptions of this ideal woman is *natural*. It is natural for people to want to marry and have children, it is natural for women to be subject to the authority of men, it is natural for women to experience pain and even death in childbirth, and so on. What is 'natural' for

Luther comes both from what he views basic human nature to be, and from the order he feels God imposed on the world. Women's subjection to men is inherent in their very being and was present from creation – in this Luther essentially agrees with Aristotle and the classical tradition:

> The man has been given so much dominion over the woman, that she must name herself according to him. For that reason, a woman adopts her husband's names and not vice versa. This has happened because of God's gracious will so that she stays under her husband's rule, because she is too weak to rule herself.[13]

This subjection was made more brutal and harsh, however, because of Eve's responsibility for the fall – in this Luther agrees with patristic tradition,[14] though he repeatedly admonishes husbands to rule their wives reasonably and gently: 'The woman is a weak vessel and tool, and must be used carefully as you use other tools.'[15] Wives were to accept this rule unquestioningly no matter how severe, even from husbands who were not Christians.[16] Luther realized this might be difficult or unpleasant. 'Women are generally disinclined to put up with this burden and they naturally seek to gain what they have lost through sin.'[17] Challenging this was a sin, however:

> But if a woman forsakes her office and assumes authority over her husband, she is no longer doing her own work, for which she was created, but a work that comes from her own fault and from evil. For God did not create this sex for ruling, and therefore they never rule successfully.[18]

Obedience had replaced chastity as women's prime virtue:

> It is the highest, most valuable treasure that a woman can have to be subject to a man and certain that her works are pleasing to him. What could be happier for her? Therefore if she wants to be a Christian wife, she should think: I won't mind what kind of husband I have, whether he is a heathen or a Jew, pious or evil. I will think instead that God has put me in marriage and I will be subject and obedient to my husband. For all of her works are golden when she is obedient.[19]

Marriage and motherhood, instead of virginity, was now a woman's highest calling, as Luther repeats over and over again. God has established marriage in the Garden of Eden, which made marriage the only institution present before the fall, the 'order' on which all other 'orders' – the economic, the political, etc. – were based.[20] While Luther acknowledges that some women, because of physical ailments or a shortage of men, might be forced to act 'unnaturally', and not marry, in no case should a woman choose to do so.[21] Men choosing to remain celibate were going against their natural sexual drive, but Luther does allow that the ability to remain truly celibate, though rare, could be a gift from God. Women choosing to remain celibate, however, were not only fighting their natural sex drive, which Luther and everyone else in the sixteeth century felt to be much stronger than men's, but also the divinely imposed order which made woman subject to man. For Luther it was inconceivable that a woman would choose not to marry. He says at one point, when advising people how to console women in childbirth: 'Say, yes, dear lady, if you were not a wife, you would certainly wish to become one, so that you could do God's will by suffering and perhaps dying through these delicious pains.'[22] Marriage and motherhood was the only way for women to fulfil their God-given function.

Even a woman as prominent and respected as Margaretha Blarer, the sister of Ambrosius, was suspect because of her decision not to marry. Martin Bucer accused her of being 'masterless', to which she answered, 'Those who have Christ for a master are not masterless.' Her brother defended her decision by pointing out that she was very close to his family, and took care of the poor and plague victims; he compliments her by calling her 'Archdeaconess of our church'. Even Ambrosius limited his sister's role somewhat, however, for when Bucer encouraged her to learn Greek, he answered, 'I ask you not to encourage her, for she already pays too much attention to Latin. You know the ingenuity of women. They need to be reined in more than spurred on, so that they don't throw themselves into learning and neglect their more appropriate and worthy tasks.'[23] Even a woman who chose to remain unmarried was to be limited to appropriate, 'natural' female activities.[24]

Luther's supporters point to his idealization of the wife and mother as the best evidence for his positive view of women. The wife and mother was finally awarded her due place, and her labours in support of her husband and children appreciated. If we look more closely at some of the metaphors Luther uses to describe her, however, the view is not such a positive one:

> The woman is like a nail, driven into the wall. . . . She sits at home. The pagans have depicted Venus as seated on a seashell for just as the snail carries its house with it, so the wife should stay at home and look after the affairs of the household.[25]

She enjoys staying home, enjoys being in the kitchen . . . does not enjoy going out . . . does not enjoy speaking to others.[26]

How was she to best serve God? Yes, certainly by faith and prayer, but primarily by obedience to her husband and carrying out her normal household tasks without complaint:

When a woman is in the kitchen or when she is making a straw bed, this is an everyday thing. This does not bother the Holy Spirit. . . . A wife is appointed for things that are very ordinary in the judgment of the flesh but nevertheless extremely precious in the eyes of God.[27]

For Luther, the ideal woman in the home is Martha, seeing to the preparation of food and overseeing the servants, not Mary, trying to understand Christ's teachings better. He belittles his own wife's efforts to understand or learn: 'There is no dress that suits a woman as badly as trying to become wise.'[28]

This ideal bothered at least one woman. Katherina Zell, the wife of Matthias Zell and a tireless worker for the Reformation in Strasbourg, worried that she was too caught up 'with the cares and service of Martha'. Luckily for Katherina, 'My dear husband has given me place and time, and always encourages me to read, listen, pray or study, allowed this day or night, yes, it gave him great joy, even when it led to neglect of his needs or harm to his household.'[29] Luther could perhaps have learned something from Zell on this point.

Women other than the ideal wife and mother appear occasionally in Luther's writings, but are usually depicted in a negative or belittling manner. Eve, of course, is given the harshest treatment:

The rule by women has brought about nothing good from the beginning of the world. When God set Adam up as Lord over all creatures, everything was good and right, and everything ruled for the best. But the woman came and also wanted to have her hand in things and be wise; then everything collapsed and became a complete disorder. We've got you women to thank for that.[30]

Women have inherited from Eve their tendency to believe lies and nonsense.[31]

This is certainly nothing new, for many writers since Jerome had laid the responsibility for the fall on Eve alone, but Luther's de-emphasis of the role of Mary weakened one side of the standard best woman/worst woman dichotomy, and thus stressed the negative side of all women's 'nature'.

The female saints and martyrs also receive somewhat ambiguous treatment. Luther felt that celibacy was so difficult to maintain, that only their early deaths had sent them to heaven still virgins:

> God has not allowed many virgins to live long, but hurried
> them out of this world, as with Cecelia, Hagne, Lucia, Agatha
> and so on. He knows how precious their treasure (virginity) is
> and how difficult it is to maintain very long.[32]

Luther's opinion of the character and piety of most nuns and sisters is even harsher, as his scathing depictions of life in the convent point out.

Other than female religious and Biblical characters, prostitutes are the only kind of unmarried women that Luther refers to frequently. Most German cities, including Wittenberg, tolerated – and even licensed and taxed – some prostitution, provided women were discrete and lived either in city brothels or in certain quarters of the city. Luther saw prostitution as an abomination, and preached and spoke fervently against it, not because it was degrading and harmful to the women involved – though there are occasional cases of women in the sixteenth century even sold into prostitution to pay back their father's debts – but because the women corrupted and enticed his students. He describes them regularly as 'Stinking, syphilitic, scabby, seedy and nasty. Such a whore can poison 10, 20, 30, 100 children of good people, and is therefore to be considered a murderer, worse than a poisoner.'[33] They were the tools of the Devil, who had sent them to Wittenberg to bewitch his students. The power to bewitch men was not only held by prostitutes, however:

> All women know the art to catch and hold a man by crying,
> lying and persuasion, turning his head and perverting him . . .
> it is often more difficult for him to withstand such enticements
> than to resist his own lust.[34]

All women, therefore, share the qualities of a prostitute to some degree.

Luther also uses the image of the whore symbolically. As Donald Kelley notes, 'Feminine epithets (next to scatology) were among the commonest forms of abuse. The equation of simony with prostitution made Rome a "whore" to Luther and the Sorbonne the "Pope's whoring chamber".'[35] 'The devil's whore' is Luther's favourite epithet for human reason:

> Usury, drunkenness, adultery and murder can all be detected
> and understood by the world as sinful. But when the devil's

bride, reason, the petty prostitute, enters into the picture and wishes to be clever, what she says is accepted at once as if she were the voice of the Holy Ghost. . . . She is surely the Devil's chief whore.[36]

By extension, all women who attempt to act reasonably may also be seen as whores of the Devil.

Unmarried women in the abstract are almost never considered in his writings. When they are, it is as a problem to be dealt with, and Luther's solution is that which many cities adopted in the sixteenth-century – requiring them to live with a family, forbidding them to live on their own or with each other. They would thus fall under the 'natural' control of a male head of household.

This emphasis on marriage not only as the only ideal for women, but as their only natural vocation may have contributed to feelings of hostility toward unmarried women. This came at a time when the sex ratio in Europe was changing in favour of women, which meant fewer women could find a mate to carry out their 'natural' inclinations even if they wanted to. How much this contributed to witchcraft accusations, which were usually first directed at just such women, is difficult to say, but it certainly is a factor to be considered, as Erik Midelfort has pointed out.[37] Ian MacLean also noted recently, 'The prosecution of widows or single women as witches may be due to an unspoken fear of abandoning the traditional view of woman as a person married or destined for marriage.'[38]

Gerald Strauss has stressed the class bias in Luther's message, that it was 'pitched to the solid burger'. I would also emphasize its sexual bias. As Strauss comments, it did not appeal to 'the great multitude of men and *women*' (my emphasis).[39] Unmarried women certainly found little in Luther's message which was directed to them, and may have stayed with or gone back to their old, less formal beliefs and practices in which they did have a place, such as soothsaying and witchcraft.

Thus the image of the female which emerges from Luther's works is an ambiguous one. Yes, she was created by God, and yes, she could be saved through faith. Marriage was an order blessed by God, and a proper theatre for exhibiting Christian virtues. But as we have seen, the words used to describe even the woman who lived up to the ideal are hardly complimentary ones – a weak vessel, a nail, a tortoise – and those used to describe women who do not follow the ideal even harsher – burning with lust, stinking, tools of the Devil and so on. These are no harsher than those used by medieval theologians, but in Luther they are not balanced by praise of the Virgin. As has been often pointed out, the cult of Mary may have been detrimental to women's actual position, as it set up an ideal to which no normal woman could hope to attain, but it did describe at least one woman in totally positive terms. Luther does refer to Mary occasionally when defending women against satirists and vulgar writers – as in his answer to the author of 'The Stinking and Putrid Female Bodily Parts' – but even in this he weakens his praise by going on to say, 'One should just as easily accuse and hate the nose, as it is the latrine of the head.'[40]

Mary was a symbol of women's chief reason for being – motherhood – 'Even Christ himself wanted to be called the seed of a woman, not the seed of a man', but this, too, was qualified:

> Yet how great would the pride of the men have been if God had willed that Christ should be brought forth by a man. But this glory has been completely taken from the men and assigned to the women (who are nevertheless subject to the rule of the men) so that the men should not become vainglorious but be humble.[41]

Even the best woman was simply God's tool to teach men a lesson.

Along with a transformation and lessening in the role of Mary and a reduction of the female ideal from heavenly to housebound, one also finds a de-emphasis on what might be termed the feminine qualities of God and Christ.

Luther does use some maternal and nurturing images to describe Christ, particularly that of the brood-hen and her chicks: 'Look at the hen and her chickens and you will see Christ and yourself painted and depicted better than any painter could picture them.'[42] He also uses some emotional and ecstatic images to describe the believer's experience of faith, especially in the Magnificat: 'All the senses floating in God's love . . . saturated by divine sweetness.'[43]

The overwhelming image of both God and the believer in Luther's writings is a masculine one, however. True faith is energetic, active, steadfast, mighty, industrious, powerful – all archetypally masculine qualities in the sixteenth (or the twentieth) century.[44] God is Father, Son, Sovereign, King, Lord, Victor, Begetter, 'the slayer of sin and devourer of death' – all aggressive, martial and totally male images.[45] With the home now the centre of women's religious vocation, even the imagery of the Church becomes masculine, or at least paternal and fraternal. Instead of

'The Bride of Christ', we now have a brotherhood of believers, honouring divine paternity with the Lord's Supper. It was a supper, an *Abendmahl*, a domestic image, but no mother served the meal, not even 'Holy Mother Church'.

The late medieval period had been one rich in feminine images of God – Jesus our Mother who bears, comforts, revives, consoles, feeds and nurtures us. Not only Mary, but God as well offered unquestioning, accepting, 'feminine' love. St Anselm of Canterbury, Marguerite of Oingt, Julian of Norwich and numerous others use phrases like 'our tender Mother Jesus (who) feeds us with his blessed breast', or 'You on the bed of the Cross . . . gave birth in a single day to the whole world', or 'By your gentleness the badly frightened are comforted'.[46]

As Caroline Bynum has recently pointed out, these feminine images of God not only made the Divine appear more personal and imminent, but also allowed women to feel more Christ-like.[47] Female mystics, anchoresses, nuns or other holy women exemplified affectivity and love, i.e., the 'feminized' parts of God, and could gain authority and power through this. Their mystical union with or direct experience of 'Jesus our Mother', 'which was sometimes expressed in visions of themselves as priests, enabled them to serve as counselors, mediators, and channels to the sacraments – roles which the 13th century Church in some ways increasingly denied to women and the laity.'[48] 'The God of medieval piety was a Mother/Father, Sister/Brother, Lover/Child, a God of demanding *and* accepting love, a God who is born within each one of us and who bears us into life as a travailing mother.'[49] Women could thus not only identify with and emulate Mary, but could directly identify with the feminine side of God.

For Luther and most other Protestant theologians, this was impossible. God and Christ were male and transcendent, not androgynous and immanent. As Caroline Bynum notes:

> I would say that we can see Luther, and much of Calvin and some of Catholic Reformation theology as an attempt to recover the sense of God's glory that was characteristic of the early middle ages, i.e., as a reaction against the emotional piety of the late Middle Ages that made God human and comforting and accessible to those in all walks of life, but thereby undercut in some sense man's ability to believe that salvation was done for him by a power infinitely other than himself.[50]

It was through that emotional piety, however, that some late medieval women had forged a link to God which gave them authority and power as acceptable as that provided by the priestly office. 'Their spirituality sometimes even suggests that the combination of mystical authorization and a peculiarly female freedom from the power of office is a superior role (to the priestly role that theologians denied them).'[51]

Protestants also denied women a priestly role, and by stressing God's glory and power, archetypally male qualities, rather than God's accessibility and nurturing, made it more difficult for women to identify with God. 'One woman's proclamation that she was a female "Christ" was denounced as a "horrible thing" by the Protestants as much for its sexual impropriety as for its theological presumption.'[52] Christ was no longer 'Our Mother', so women could not be Christs for sexual as well as spiritual reasons.

Thus Luther established Martha, the obedient wife serving God through daily household tasks, as the ideal woman, belittling both Mary her sister who chose to devote herself to learning Christ's teaching, and Mary the Virgin Mother of Christ, who had almost become a female God in much late medieval Marian piety. By downplaying the feminine qualities of God and using paternal or fraternal imagery in describing the Church, he also placed religion clearly within the male sphere. The domestic, female realm was private, affective, immanent; the worldly, male realm, which included not only politics and education, but also religion, was public, rational and transcendent.

Luther was, of course, not the first or only one to differentiate sharply between male and female realms, to feel that woman's subjection to man was 'natural'. The Renaissance humanists had clearly felt this.[53] As Joan Kelley points out, women could never hope to achieve the Renaissance ideal of 'man', whereas they could achieve the medieval ideal of sanctity.[54]

On the level of popular opinion the matter may perhaps be summed up by saying that in the private world women represented the positive virtues of adornment, service and moral strength; in the public world they posed at best a threat to order and at worst a deformation of nature. In most ways, then the key to sixteenth-century social, religious and political structure – and change – was the principle of male domination.[55]

Luther added his voice, then, to widely accepted notions of the proper role of women, but the strength of that voice and the power of his language gave contemporaries and followers new ammunition. His metaphors and imagery were repeated for centuries; his words became Protestant dogma on the subject.

Women themselves have made various attempts to combat this, to reclaim the 'nurturing values in their religious heritage', from seventeenth-century pietists to the nineteenth-century women Ann Douglas describes in *The Feminization of American Culture*, to twentieth-century feminist theologians trying to go 'Beyond God the Father'.[56] So far, however, Luther's language has prevailed. Woman has become wife, the two Marys have been replaced by Martha. Luther did sanctify marriage – in this one may agree with his defenders – but by that sanctification feminized and domesticated women.

As Ian MacLean concluded, 'Marriage is an immovable obstacle to any improvement in the theoretical or real status of women in law, in theology, in moral and political philosophy.'[57] A woman fulfils her only God-given and natural function through marriage, but always remains, in Karl Barth's words, 'B, and therefore behind and subordinate to man'.[58] Barth is, of course, simply putting Luther in twentieth-century terms. The image is the same.

Notes

Abbreviations

Erl.:   *D. Martin Luthers sämmtiliche Werke*, Erlangen and Frankfurt, 1826–57.

WA: *D. Martin Luthers Werke.* Kritische Gesamtausgabe, Weimar, 1883–   .

WA, TR: *D. Martin Luthers Werke.* Tischreden, Weimar, 1912–21.

LW: *Luther's Works*, American edition, Philadelphia, 1955–

1 Erl. 61, 125.
2 Erl. 20, 84.
3 Erl. 61, 212.
4 WA, TR 4, 4786.
5 Karl Bücher, *Die Frauenfrage im Mittelalter*, Tübingen, 1910, pp.68ff; Walter Kamerau, *Die Reformation und die Ehe*, Verein für Reformationsgeschichte, 1892; Emmett W. Cocke, Jr, 'Luther's View of Marriage and Family', *Religion in Life*, 42 (Spring, 1973), 103–16.
6 William Lazareth, *Luther on the Christian Home*, Philadelphia: Muhlenberg Press, 1960, p.vii.
7 Elizabeth Ahme, 'Wertung und Bedeutung der Frau bei Martin Luther', *Luther*, vol. 35, pp.63–4.
8 Sigmund Baranowski, *Luthers Lehre von der Ehe*, Münster, 1913, pp.198–9.
9 Martha Behrens, 'Martin Luthers View of Women', MA Thesis, North Texas State, 1973, pp.34 and 95.

10   John Yost, 'Changing Attitudes toward Married Life in Civic and Christian Humanism', *ASRR Occasional Papers*, vol. 1 (Dec. 1977), 164. Similar ideas also in Yost, 'The Value of Married Life for the Social Order in the Early English Renaissance', *Societas*, VI/i (Winter, 1976), 25–37.

11   Kathleen Davies, 'Continuity and Change in Literary Advice on Marriage', in *Marriage and Society: Studies in the Social History of Marriage*, ed. R.B. Outhwaite, New York, 1981.

12   LW 5, 331.

13   Erl. 33, 112.

14   WA, TR 1, 1046; WA 15, 419; 16, 218.

15   Erl. 51, 431.

16   Erl. 51, 46–7.

17   LW 1, 203.

18   LW 15, 130.

19   Erl. 51, 428.

20   Olavi Lahteenmaki, *Sexus und Ehe bei Luther*, Schriften der Luther – Agricola Gesellschaft, nr 10, Turku, 1955. Lilly Zarncke, 'Die Naturhafte Eheanschauung Luthers', *Archiv für Kulturgeschichte*, 25 (1935), 281–305.

21   WA 20, 149.

22   WA 17, 1, 25.

23   Maria Heinsius, *Das unüberwindliche Wort: Frauen der Reformationszeit*, Munich, 1953, pp.45–57.

24   It is interesting to speculate on how much effect this ideal had on Catholic Counter-Reformation leaders. As Ruth Liebowitz has pointed out, women in the late sixteenth century wanted to form active orders, working out in the world (comparable to the Jesuits) but were generally blocked by the Church, which wanted them strictly cloistered: 'Virgins in the Service of Christ', in R.R. Reuther (ed.), *Women of Spirit*, New York, 1979, pp.132–52. Thus although Catholic women still had the option of remaining unmarried, they were to be cloistered in the convent in the same way that Lutheran women were to be cloistered in their own homes. The ideal woman in all religions became increasingly similar, a woman who was 'chaste, silent and obedient': Suzanne Hull, *Chaste, Silent and Obedient: English Books for Women 1475–1640*, San Marino, 1982.

25   LW 1, 202–3; WA 42, 151.

26   LW 29, 56; WA 25, 45.

27   WA 25, 46; LW 29, 56.

28   Ahme, p.67. Even Luther did not go as far as Henry VIII in this matter, however. He did encourage his wife to read the Bible, while an Act passed in England in 1543 forbade Bible reading by 'Women, artificers, prentices, journeymen, husbandmen and laborers . . . for

the advancement of the true religion. Noblemen, gentlemen and merchants might read the Bible in their own families: noblewomen and gentlewomen might read it privately, but not to others.' This Act was repealed in 1547 when Henry's more enlightened son assumed the kingship. Hull, p.xii.

29   Heinsius, pp.20 and 24.
30   WA, TR 1, 1046.
31   WA 1, 431–5.
32   WA 10, 1, 708.
33   Erl. 61, 272.
34   WA, Tr 4, 4786; LW 7, 76.
35   Donald Kelley, *The Beginning of Ideology*, Cambridge, 1981, p.75.
36   Er. 16, 142.
37   Erik Midelfort, *Witchhunting in Southwestern Germany 1562–1684*, Stanford, 1972, pp.184–6.
38   Ian MacLean, *The Renaissance Notion of Woman*, Cambridge, 1980, p.88.
39   Strauss, *Luther's House of Learning*, Johns Hopkins, 1978, p.307.
40   WA, TR, 3, 2807b.
41   LW 1, 256–7.
42   WA 10/1/1, 280.
43   WA 7, 547, 549, 550.
44   WA 10/3, 285; WA 42, 452.
45   Ian Siggins, *Martin Luther's Doctrine of Christ*, New Haven, 1970, *passim*.
46   Eleanor L. McLaughlin, 'Male and Female in the Christian Tradition', in *Male and Female: Christian Approaches to Sexuality*, ed. Ruth Tiffany Barnhouse and Urban T. Holmes III, New York, 1976, pp.43–4.
47   Caroline Bynum, *Jesus as Mother: Studies in the Spirituality of the High Middle Ages*. U. Cal. Press, 1982.
48   Bynum, p.185.
49   McLaughlin, *Male/Female*, p.46.
50   Bynum, p.185.
51   Bynum, p.255.
52   Donald Kelley, p.74.
53   Ian MacLean, *The Renaissance Notion of Woman*.
54   Joan Kelley, 'Early Feminist Theory and the Querelle des Femmes, 1400–1789', *SIGNS*, 8/1, Autumn 1982, p.8.
55   Donald Kelley, pp.75–6.
56   Mary Daly, *Beyond God the Father*, Boston, 1973. Quote is from Douglas, *Feminization*, New York, 1977, p.167.
57   MacLean, p.85.
58   Karl Barth, *Church Dogmatics: A Selection*, trans. and ed. G.W. Bromiley, New York, 1962, pp.218–20.

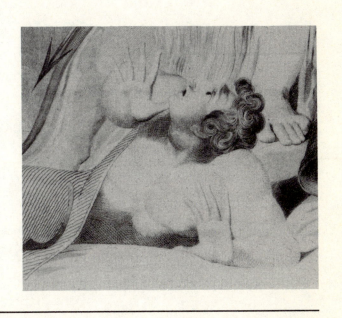

Revivalism

20

Revivalism and Welsh society in the nineteenth century

CHRISTOPHER B. TURNER

The unique Religious Census of 1851, despite its statistical shortcomings, demonstrated at least two irrefutable facts of comparison. The first was that Wales was a conspicuously religious nation relative to England. The second was that the distinction, in religious terms, between the industrial and the rural areas was much less apparent in Wales than in England or, indeed, than in many parts of western Europe.

In the report which accompanied publication of the Census returns its author Horace Mann estimated that, in order to be even minimally effective, the churches and chapels should make provision for 58.4 per cent of the total population in each registration district.[1] In England the overall provision rate was 51.4 per cent. In Wales this figure was 75.6 per cent. The registration districts throughout Wales generally exceeded Mann's base figure with comfort. Only in districts such as Merthyr Tydfil, with a rate of 66 per cent, did the figures display any cause for concern. In South Wales the overall provision rate was 73 per cent, while in the less industrialized northern counties of Wales the figure was 83 per cent.[2]

Even the situation in Merthyr was encouraging when compared with similar industrial regions in England. Despite rapid population growth denominational efforts to provide religious ministration were most creditable. The Aberdare sub-district alone had doubled its population from 9,322 in 1841 to 18,774 in 1851.[3] Actual attendance on census Sunday is difficult to gauge but the impression is that nonconformist chapels in Merthyr, and in Wales generally, were well attended. In fact, the Census merely confirmed what contemporaries already knew about the religious condition of Wales.

The half-century before the Census had witnessed a period of almost unrestricted growth among the Welsh denominations. One feature of this growth was the spectacular membership increases during years of revival. The main revivals occurred in 1805–9, 1817–22, 1828–9, 1831–2, 1839–42, 1849 and, perhaps the greatest of all revivals, that of 1859. The rather incomplete membership figures supplied by the denominations can be corroborated by an analysis of the frantic chapel building programmes to accommodate the tide of new members, particularly in Glamorgan and Monmouthshire.[4] The denominational histories also testified to the large membership increases generated by successive revivals.[5] Moreover, these revivals undoubtedly continued a tradition initiated by the Methodist leaders of the eighteenth century, such as Daniel Rowland and Howell Harris.

But the central question to be examined in this paper is not merely why Wales should continually nurture revivalism but why the industrial areas of Wales, particularly the so-called 'frontier' communities of the South Wales coalfield, should prove so receptive to an evangelistic religion. An outline of the main features of Welsh revivalism may help to determine this.

Contemporary descriptions of religious revivals in Wales varied according to the standpoint of the observer. An English traveller, B.H. Malkin, who happened to visit Merthyr at about the time it was experiencing its first recorded revival in 1803, commented that, 'Almost all the exclusively Welsh sects among the lower orders of the people have in truth degenerated into habits of the most pitiable lunacy in their devotion.'[6] Most English observers constantly highlighted the over-indulgence of Welsh revivals and cited as evidence the common practice of 'jumping'. Welsh preachers, though, defended such charges with vigour. The celebrated Baptist preacher Christmas Evans, for example, drew the obvious comparisons between the lifeless religion of England and the genuine emotionalism and attraction of Welsh religion. Evans maintained that this emotion and the sympathy of feeling which existed between the preacher and his congregation was the force that had sent the Gospel, '. . . into every nook of the mountains of Wales, as well as into the cities, towns and villages; while in England, with all the advantages of education, the Gospel, in a manner is hid in a corner. . . . Common preaching will not do to rouse sluggish districts from the heavy slumber into which they are sunk. Indeed, formal prayers and lifeless sermons are like bulwarks raised against these things in England.'[7]

Since the Methodist Revival of the eighteenth century the various religious groups in Wales had laid considerable stress on the efficacy of preaching directly to the people. They based their approach entirely on what they perceived as a fundamental truth, namely, that salvation was attainable by faith. In turn, faith was best instilled in the congregation by hearing the word preached with conviction. Sermons were therefore delivered with fervour, striking allegory but most of all with simplicity.[8] We should not be surprised at this simplistic approach. It is no exaggeration to say that in the early nineteenth century a humble upbringing greatly enhanced, or even justified, a minister's rise to prominence. Another English observer, in the pioneering newspaper *Morning Chronicle* wrote of religion in Merthyr that, 'many of the preachers are wholly uneducated men – that is to say their learning extends no further than to simple reading and writing . . . many of them were at the outset of life daily labourers, like the classes whom they now lead. There were more miners in the dissenting ministry than any other class of workmen.' He continued, 'The preacher who has himself been a labourer knows best the labourer's nature and adopts the most likely means of affecting and ruling it . . . they are, in consonance with the genius of the Welsh language, abundancy figurative.'[9] Examples from the vast store of denominational biographies or 'cofiannau' are numerous. The great Calvinistic Methodist preacher John Jones, Talsarn, had been a labourer repairing roads.[10] His mentor, Henry Rees, had spent much of his early life in farm service.[11] The historian of the Welsh Independents, Thomas Rees, a convert of the 1829 revival, had left his home in rural Carmarthenshire in 1835 and moved to Aberdare, where he worked for some years as a collier.[12] The Wesleyan preacher Thomas Aubrey had worked as a puddler at the furnaces both of Merthyr and Nantyglo.[13] In 1837 the Baptist John Jones, 'Mathetes', had removed from his native Cardiganshire to Dowlais where he worked as a miner. At that time he attended Caersalem Chapel and when he entered the ministry in 1846 he became an ardent temperance advocate. He was convinced that having witnessed the evil effects of drink among his fellow workmen temperance was essential if industrial society was to make any progress.[14]

Another feature of Welsh revivalism and no doubt a contributory factor in its emotionalism was the part played by external tensions within the wider society. Historians have debated the causes of revivals from many standpoints. While there is much disagreement over the precise role of social determinants, most would agree that such factors must have some effect, if only because preachers used social tension as a means of warning their congregations about the perils of divine retribution. On 17 August 1831 the steampacket *Rothsay Castle* went aground off the coast of Anglesey with the loss of over a hundred lives.[15] At the Calvinistic Methodist association held at Pwllheli in September John Elias drew a dismal picture of the religious and moral condition of Wales. In a direct reference to the disaster he claimed that wherever Gospel truths were absent, 'the enemies shall come in like a flood'.[16] The allusion was made all the more poignant by the fact that Elias himself had lost a number of personal acquaintances in the wreck.

He viewed the episode as divine judgment and he exhorted his hearers to ask God to cleanse them of spiritual pride and self-satisfaction.[17] Elias subsequently embarked upon a series of preaching engagements, and a visit by this fearful preacher was said to have hastened a revival throughout Caernarfonshire, where 2,000 new members were added to the Calvinistic Methodists alone.[18]

Similarly, in October 1859 the *Royal Charter* was wrecked in a storm off Anglesey, on this occasion with the loss of 400 lives.[19] The revival of that year had proceeded quickly through many parts of Wales but Anglesey before the *Royal Charter* tragedy had displayed little enthusiasm. However, this disaster, coupled with the visit of one of the leaders of the revival, David Morgan, suddenly aroused considerable revival activity throughout the island.[20] In the face of such tragic loss of life local people urgently sought an assurance of ultimate salvation. And as the preachers forcefully pointed out, there was a great need to placate God's anger by confession and prayer.

But to return to 1831, the influence of John Elias over the progress of the revival was completely overshadowed by the appearance of cholera. In the summer of 1831 a virulent strain of the malignant 'Asiatic Cholera' had appeared in the north of England. The apparently irresistible advance of the epidemic provoked a morbid fear among the ordinary people and the immediate reaction was a resort to salvationism. Cholera first appeared in Wales in the spring of 1832, when it arrived in Flint.[21] The imminence of 'y geri marwol' had been proclaimed for some time, especially in the denominational press. John Jones, Talsarn, had repeatedly warned his congregations in Caernarfonshire of the impending doom and he advised them to trust in God and seek His grace immediately.[22] In Flint the chapels were full at 5.00 a.m. for the duration of the epidemic.[23] It also spread quickly westwards and, when news reached the Anglesey villages of Tynygongl and Glasinfryn that cholera had been reported in Beaumaris, there were prolonged public prayers at the Calvinistic Methodist monthly meeting for the removal of the plague by the grace of the Holy Spirit.[24] There were reports of hundreds flocking to the chapels throughout Wales and the effect of the cholera had clearly been to capitalize on and extend Elias's earlier lead.

In 1849 it was South Wales that suffered the worst ravages of a second cholera epidemic. It struck Merthyr with particular ferocity and was said to have claimed over 1,500 lives.[25] Once again panic and understandable fear predated its actual arrival. At least one medical practitioner projected that it was fear which promoted the spread of cholera. Fear, he believed, creates, 'An epidemic state of mind which materially influences the propagation and spreading of epidemic diseases. . . . I believe no one circumstance is more calculated to disseminate epidemic and contagious disease than . . . going about prophesying woe, spreading ill news . . . so as to give their communications an intense interest of a sombre and disastrous character.'[26] He added that in his opinion religious belief 'exerts a preventive force against all diseases'. Such advice seemed well heeded, and the numbers seeking religious consolation were so great that special meetings were held daily in many chapels. *The Welshman* commented in August 1849 that cholera in Glamorgan, 'continues to generate fear and gloomy forebodings in the public mind, and we find in the proceedings of the various religious societies . . . a tolerably correct indication of the state of public feeling.'[27]

At Merthyr the clamour for spiritual consolation increased as the streets became, 'black with funerals and resounded all day with the hymns sung, according to immemorial usage amongst the Welsh, at the burial of friends and relatives.'[28] At Hermon Calvinistic Methodist Chapel, Dowlais, a leading deacon and twenty-eight members were claimed by cholera but many more were received into membership at the same time.

In reality, towns such as Merthyr harboured a number of endemic as well as epidemic diseases. Typhus, tuberculosis and relapsing fever were constant threats and must have contributed to the relatively high religiosity of these areas. It was basic insecurity that put religious excitement at a premium. Preachers, too, played their part in translating external stress into a quest for salvation involving chapel attendance and then full membership. Inevitably, cholera revivals resulted in considerable backsliding and falling off in attendance when the disease abated.[29] But such was the demand for the comfort offered by the chapels at the height of the revival that it is difficult to see what chapel leaders could have done to prevent this.

There were factors in Welsh industrial society that created a specifically religious interest even in what can be termed 'normal' times. The harsh realities of work underground meant that an ever-present fear of death or serious injury became an accepted fact of life. South Wales appeared particularly susceptible to colliery disasters and a feature of life underground – and this was especially true during revivals – were the numerous prayer meetings at the coal face with the objective of thanking God for sparing those present and entreating Him to continue His vigilance.[30] The same was true of the slate caverns of Bethesda and Blaenau Ffestiniog in the north.[31]

But these external pressures were omnipresent and cannot therefore fully explain intermittent bursts of religious revival. Generally, such factors merely escalated revival movements which already existed within the denominations themselves. It was Christmas Evans who warned solemnly that, 'The revival that begins in the Church, and proceeds from thence to the world and not that which commences outside of the Church, is more frequent, and more efficient in its converts, for the pangs of labor are to begin in Zion.'[32] In 1831–2 it was cholera that impelled the revival into a movement across Wales but it was only in the north, where Elias's influence was greatest, that lasting membership gains were made.

The revivals of 1839–42, which collectively were known as the 'temperance revival', were prompted initially by the general debate within the chapels concerning the translation into Welsh of the book, *Lectures on Revivals of Religion* by the American revivalist C.G. Finney.[33] Yet it was these same social strains, such as low wages and trade depression, that had generated the resort to Chartism and Rebecca, which also fortified the revival and attendant temperance crusade in the industrial communities. Finney's lectures also provided a useful handbook for less talented preachers. Successful exponents of revivalism such as Elias and John Jones, Talsarn, had instinctively followed Finney's advice long before his lectures were written. It should also be noted that the term 'revivalist' could never be applied to these Welsh preachers who would hardly have admitted the need for 'special means' in their approach. Contemporaries pointed to the similarities between the society of the American frontier and the Welsh industrial frontier as a reason for the success of Finney's lectures in Wales. The mobile populations of both societies were unsettled by the general instability of life. Lacking in basic institutions as they were they constituted ideal targets for an evangelistic, occasionally millenarian, message preached with fiery simplicity. Frontier religion has been described as an 'escapist' faith which justified social problems as divinely ordained and thus placed the exigencies of present circumstance into proper perspective.[34]

Yet the question still remains as to why a revivalistic response seemed so singularly appropriate in the newly industrialized areas of Wales, especially when other western European countries displayed a generous amount of anti-religious sentiment or at best indifference within the lower classes.[35] In order to explain the revivalist surge of industrial Wales we should perhaps look more closely at the origin of that society as much as to its volatile nature.

For the most part migration into the iron and coal towns of Glamorgan and Monmouthshire was short-distance. In 1851, of the total population aged twenty and over in the Merthyr Tydfil Registration district 18 per cent gave their place of birth as Carmarthenshire, 5 per cent hailed from Cardiganshire, 9 per cent from Breconshire and 6 per cent from Pembrokeshire.[36] In fact had previous censuses asked for similar information it is likely that these proportions would have been much higher. But heavy immigration into Merthyr in the first half of the nineteenth century was a reality. The Education Commissioners of 1847 noted that, 'The workmen, who are perpetually immigrating, live together very much in clans, eg: the Pembrokeshire men in one quarter, the Carmarthenshire men in another and so on.'[37] Immigration into the iron and coal towns naturally increased in times of economic prosperity. The Brecon road into Merthyr in the 1850s was regarded as a wages barometer, the in-coming pressure increasing as wages were high and employment plentiful.[38] A contemporary commentator, G.S. Kenrick of the Varteg Iron Works, stated that within the population of Pontypool and Merthyr, 'There are many who come from Cardiganshire to the ironworks for five or seven months in the winter season, live economically while here and take home £15 or £20 to their families, which pays the rent of their farm . . . and a few luxuries.' He also estimated that four-fifths of the houses in Trevethin were provided with Bibles and a hymn book or some other religious publication.[39] But evidence of this short-distance migration may be found in an earlier phase of industrial development and such evidence also revealed a distinctly religious significance. During the iron boom of the 1820s in the north Monmouthshire area there was a preponderance of Cardiganshire folk among the founders of chapels, especially among the Calvinistic Methodists. It was believed that it was their previous knowledge of chapel organization that equipped these people for leadership.

The 'Old Forge' chapel, later Penuel, at Ebbw Vale had been founded by people from the Blaenannerch/Aberporth district of Cardiganshire. The historian of this chapel also maintained that the cause was further nurtured by successive acquisitions from the same source throughout the nineteenth century. A central figure in the history of Calvinistic Methodism in Monmouthshire was Owen Enos whose stated ambition was to remove the religious atmosphere of his native Cardiganshire 'to the benighted hills of

Gwent'.[40] Chapels such as Carmel, Abertillery and Gobaith, Blaina, also had Cardiganshire people in their diaconates.[41]

The social upheaval experienced by immigrants arriving in the industrial areas might have been expected to cause a certain disinterest in continuing chapel memberhsip. But in Wales it appears that the first and overriding desire of the immigrant was to seek spiritual and social fellowship at a suitable meeting house or chapel, or even the chapel of another denomination if necessary. By the 1840s, when the migratory pattern was well established, rural chapels took action to ensure continued chapel attendance by prospective migrants. This was achieved by issuing departing members with a letter of recommendation or 'Llythyr Canmoliaeth'. This letter transferred pastoral care of that member to a church in the vicinity of the new home. This practice was especially prevalent among the Independents though it was also known among the Baptists and Calvinistic Methodists.[42] It was also possible that for other migrants such letters might have been replaced by verbal understandings, though many, it would have to be admitted, were forced to attend the chapel most accessible to them.

This system of transference had a further implication. One of the most active periods of growth of Ebenezer Independent Chapel, Trecynon, was between 1854 and 1861. At that time many Cardiganshire people came to work in the collieries of the district and the chapel history notes that many of these brought letters with them. But it was also significant that in 1857–8, when a bitter and protracted strike was in progress in the Aberdare valley, the numbers of immigrants fell considerably.[43] It was interesting too that at the very time when migration into these areas was not a viable alternative a most powerful religious revival was stirring in Cardiganshire.

Given the strength of the clear link between the new urban settlements and the rural districts it was not surprising to find that revivals themselves showed a similar topography. Welsh revivals appeared to spread along a well established network. Mainly, it was by preachers visiting individual chapels and also by means of large outdoor gatherings such as 'Association' meetings or 'Sasiynau'. Markets and fairs could provide ideal opportunities for the dissemination of the revival message and revival histories often record the activities of farmers who having heard of the revival at market returned to their distant localities full of spiritual fire.[44]

Almost all the revival movements of the early nineteenth century were initiated in non-urban areas. An example was the revival of 1828–9, which originated in Caio, Carmarthenshire, though it quickly spread to the neighbouring villages of Llanddeusant and Trelech.[45] From there the revival moved south to Swansea and the surrounding industrial districts. By January 1829 a group of 'revivalists' from Llansamlet came to Neath to assist at the opening of a newly erected Calvinistic Methodist Chapel.[46] The next district to come under revival influence was the Aberdare and Merthyr valleys. The scale of the revival clearly baffled contemporary commentators. The *Cambrian* newspaper was resigned to the opinion, 'that people evidently catch the sympathy from each other'. The paper also noted that the main protagonists were 'the lower orders and least educated part of the community, and very recently admitted members of these religious societies'.[47] Nevertheless, in order to respond to this revivalistic impulse the converted must have already been conversant with such concepts as hell and damnation, salvation, prayer and other elementary Christian terminology.

Perhaps the best example of the town and country link within Wales was demonstrated in the 1859 revival. Within months of the start of the revival at Tre'rddol, Cardiganshire, the industrial districts were exhibiting many instances of mass conversion. A Dowlais minister observed that, 'Hundreds in this place have friends and relatives in Cardiganshire on whose minds considerable effect was produced by hearing of their conversion.'[48] One history of the revival quotes a letter from John Edwards of Taliesin, a village at the heart of the Cardiganshire revival, to his brother Morgan of Aberaman, a coal mining village in the Aberdare valley, telling him of the wonderful events taking place and hoping for a similar revival in the valleys.[49] Nor was the link one-way. The members of Ebenezer Chapel, Trecynon, a chapel with a revival tradition, immediately sent two of its members, with family connections in Cardiganshire, to view the revival at close hand in Aberaeron. When they returned the congregation immediately responded and Ebenezer became the centre of the revival in Aberdare.[50] It was possible that the connection between town and country was strong enough to ensure that few religious men would wish to see their present churches in a state of spiritual deadness while the churches of their rural homes were receiving the full heat of revival fire.

Nonconformity in the industrial districts was reinforced in two ways. First, by the continued immigration from the same source and second, by the purposeful activity of those who remained in the rural environment. It must be remembered that the revival in Cardiganshire had a very specific effect. Contemporaries continually remarked that the Cardiganshire revival of 1859 came to full churches. In direct contrast to the mass influx into the chapels of the industrial areas the denominations in Aberystwyth, for example, actually became more cautious in the admission of new members during the revival.[51] The main emphasis was on a renewed spiritual feeling and gathering in the younger generation to protect the cause in future. For much of the nineteenth century the denominations were less concerned with recruiting the irreligious than with restoring and reviving existing hearers. It was noted that in Aberystwyth in 1859 the majority of the converted were 'hen wrandawyr' (old hearers).[52] In Bethesda in 1859 it was thought a remarkable fact that a man was brought into the fold not from heathenism but from the abject state of not having attended a place of worship for fifteen years.[53]

The concern for the future of the cause explains the pervading emphasis on family religion. During the revival of 1831 John Elias advised his congregations thus: 'O be careful that family religion is encouraged and supported among you. Be very particular on this head if you wish that the kingdom of Christ should be extended and established among you and your children.'[54] In Cardiganshire in 1859 it was believed that 'scarcely could there be found in it a family which was not a religious family, or a house that was not a house of prayer.'[55] This was no doubt an exaggeration but the continual impression given by the revival in the rural areas was that the majority of the converted were 'the regular attendants upon the means of grace'. Recruitment therefore was from the peripheral group of 'hearers' who in normal times occupied gallery and rear seats in the chapels and while they might come to hear the word and sing the hymns they did not participate in church ceremony or organization. This group also included the children of Christian parents, especially those in the Sunday schools.

It was little wonder that such a religiously integrated, basically rural, society should breed stability or at least the appearance of stability. The denominations fostered this perception by preaching the morality of a unified society in which concepts of class differentiation were unknown. In this way it was understandable why immigrants into the industrial districts should look back on traditional values with affection. The frontier communities of South Wales may have lacked their own traditions but the maintenance of close links with relatives in rural areas helped immigrants to adjust to their new environment where stability was largely absent. Chapel attendance and the fellowship which it engendered acted as a comfort and provided immigrants with a tenable identification with their immediate past. It was predictable that emigration would carry traditional practices and values into the new communities, but the desire to recreate rural religion in the industrial areas was also thought necessary for other reasons. Towns like Merthyr were known to accommodate the lowest strata of society, inhabiting the worst slums and displaying the least morality. Recently arrived country people perceived this and were anxious to set themselves apart by emphasizing the strength of their religious convictions, first in creating religious institutions and second, in ensuring that such institutions were continually revived.[56]

The comparative strength of nonconformity, and the relevance of religious revival, in these industrial communities was attributable in large measure to the immigration of, for the most part, a religiously instructed and Christianized people. This was precisely why Finney's lectures had been so successful in Wales. He was essentially a traditional revivalist who assumed that his audiences could relate to the fundamentals of Christian religion. It was only later in the century when the scale of non-Welsh immigration became irresistible that the affinity between the rural and urban districts was finally undermined. But it is a great tribute to the early Methodist leaders and to the other denominations that their work in the period before 1830 had been so effective in founding a strong religious interest which remained constant for so long. Indeed, despite the fading of the town/country nexus after 1860, it was still strong enough in 1904 to sustain one final revival which, although it originated in rural Cardiganshire, experienced its most expansionist and emotional results in the heart of industrial South Wales.

Notes

1   *Census of Great Britain, 1951. Religious Worship in England and Wales*, London, 1853, pp.ccxcii–ccxcv and pp.126–9.

2   This section is based on the introduction in I.G. Jones (ed.), *The Religious Census of 1851: A calendar of the Returns relating to Wales*, vol. I, Cardiff, 1981.

3   *UK Census, 1851: Enumeration and Birth places of the People*, London, 1853.

4   See, The Returns of Protestant Dissenting Meeting Houses, *Parliamentary Papers*, London, 1852–3, (156) LXXVIII, pp.81–2.

5   For example, H. Hughes, *Hanes Diwygiadau Crefyddol Cymru*, Caernarfon, 1906, *passim*, E. Parry, *Llawlyfr ar Hanes y Diwygiadau Crefyddol yng Nghymru*, Corwen, 1898, pp.116–40.

6 B.H. Malkin, *The Scenery, Antiquity and Biography of South Wales*, London, 1807, vol. I, p.262.

7 J. Cross, *Sermons of Christmas Evans*, Philadelphia, 1846, p.44.

8 See E. Griffiths, *The Presbyterian Church of Wales Historical Handbook, 1735–1905*, Wrexham, 1905, pp.130 *et seq.*

9 *Morning Chronicle*, 15 April 1850.

10 O. Thomas, *Cofiant . . . y Parchedig John Jones, Talsarn*, Wrexham, 1874, vol. I, pp.61–2.

11 A.M. Davies, *Life and Letters of Henry Rees*, Bangor, 1904, p.147.

12 J. Thomas, *Cofiant . . . Thomas Rees, D D, Abertawe*, Dolgellau, 1888, p.65.

13 S. Davies, *Cofiant . . . Thomas Aubrey*, vol. I, Bangor, 1884, p.xii.

14 J.V. Morgan, *Welsh Religious Leaders in the Victorian Era*, London, 1905, pp.174–80.

15 See J.H. Bransby, *A Narrative of the Dreadful Wreck of the Rothsay Castle*, London, 1832.

16 J.O. Jones, *Cofiant . . . Robert Ellis, Ysgoldy*, Caernarfon, 1883, p.239.

17 E. Morgan, *Valuable Letters, Essays and other papers of the late John Elias*, Caernarfon, 1847.

18 See H. Hughes, op. cit., p.338.

19 *North Wales Chronicle*, 26 November 1859 and T. Phillips, *The Welsh Revival: Its Origin and Development*, London, 1860, p.129.

20 *Carnarvon and Denbigh Herald*, 24 December 1859 and H. Hughes, op. cit., p.450.

21 The epidemic is well described in G.P. Jones, 'Cholera in Wales', *National Library of Wales Journal*, vol. 10, 1957–8, pp.281–300.

22 O. Thomas, op. cit., vol. I, p.219.

23 G.P. Jones, op. cit., p.286.

24 *Y Drysorfa*, May 1982, p.348.

25 *The Welshman*, 21 December 1849.

26 G. Bird, *Observations on Cholera*, Swansea, 1849, p.19.

27 *The Welshman*, 10 August 1849.

28 *Morning Chronicle*, 15 April 1850.

29 H. Hughes, op. cit., pp.331–4; *Carnarvon and Denbigh Herald*, 11 August 1949.

30 *Cambrian*, 9 July 1858; *Y Fwyell*, April 1894, pp.37–8.

31 J.J. Morgan, *Hanes Dafydd Morgan, Ysbyty a Diwygiad '59*, Mold, 1906, p.438; J. Venn, *The Revival in Wales*, London, 1860, p.161.

32 J. Cross, op. cit., p.48.

33 T. Rees, *Miscellaneous Papers relating to Wales*, London, *c.* 1866, p.93; the theme is fully discussed in R. Carwardine, 'The Welsh Evangelical Community and Finney's Revival', *Journal of Ecclesiastical History*, vol. 29, no. 4, October, 1978 especially pp.469–73.

34 See E.T. Davies, *Religion in the Industrial Revolution in South Wales*, Cardiff, 1965, p.60.

35 For an introduction to this subject see H. McLeod, *Religion and the People of Western Europe, 1789–1970*, Oxford, 1981.

36 *UK Census*, 1851.

37 *Report of the Commissioners of Inquiry into the State of Education in Wales*, 1847, I, p.304.

38 *Cambrian*, 30 June 1857 and 19 March 1858.

39 G.S. Kenrick, 'Statistics of the Population in the Parish of Trevethin', *Journal of the Royal Statistical Society*, 3, (1841), pp.370–2.

40 E. Price, *The History of Penuel Calvinistic Methodist Church, Ebbw Vale*, Wrexham, 1925, pp.22–3.

41 National Library of Wales (NLW), Calvinistic Methodist Archives, History of Calvinistic Methodism in Monmouthshire, 14,702, vol. I, f.77.

42 *Y Diwygwir*, April 1852, p.117; *Y Drysorfa*, August 1854, p.137; *Seren Gomer*, January 1857, p.6.

43 J. Treharne, *Hanes Eglwys Ebenezer, Aberdar*, Aberdare, 1898, p.22.

44 NLW Calvinistic Methodist Archives, 12,684, f.6.

45 NLW Ms. 8321E and *Evangelical Magazine*, August 1828, p.359.

46 *Cambrian*, 10 January 1829.

47 *Ibid*.

48 E. Davies, *Revivals in Wales*, London, 1859, p.39.

49 J.J. Morgan, op. cit., p.51.

50 J. Treharne, op. cit., p.35.

51 J. Venn, op. cit., p.4.

52 NLW Calvinistic Methodist Archives, 12,684, f.10.

53 E. Davies, op. cit., p.85.

54 E. Morgan, op. cit., p.181.

55 *The Revival*, 24 September 1859; 8 October 1859.

56 See, for example, *Baner ac Amserau Cymru*, 7 March 1860.

21

Primitive Methodists in the northern coalfields

ROBERT COLLS

On 25 May 1812 Felling Colliery exploded. The sound was heard for miles around; the force of the blast rained coaldust down over a wide area. Very soon the pithead was a throng of women and children anxious for news. Some bodies were recovered from the foot of the shaft but the rescuers were unable to penetrate into the workings. There they faced a dense wall of gas, 'choke damp', and beyond that, parts of the roadway and coalface were aflame.

The owners, Messrs Brandling, Henderson, and Grace, wanted to stop-up the shaft in order to extinguish the fire. The villagers argued that this would kill all hopes of survival for those who might be trapped. They and other pitmen who had come to help and advise recalled examples of survival against all the odds. The owners wanted to save their inflammable investment; the community was adamant that where there was oxygen there was hope. The owners had their way. Two days later the mine was sealed. At nearby Low Fell, the carpenters made and stacked ninety-two coffins.

Six weeks later the pit was re-entered. A massive crowd from all parts of the coalfield had gathered. Constables were stationed in case the crowd turned angry or hysterical. The corpses had putrefied and recoverers daubed their hands in oakum before picking them up. Forty-one widows were persuaded not to look nor to have the dead back in their homes. The last burials took place on 19 September, four months after the explosion.

The parish curate was Rev. John Hodgson – thirty-three years old and recently married to a stone merchant's daughter. Hodgson came from Westmoreland, of the 'statesman' farming class. After Bampton Grammar School and some school teaching, he had been ordained in 1805 and appointed to Tyneside the following year. His consuming passions were intellectual: geology, archaeology, theology and history. In 1813 he was to devote his life to his great antiquarian *History of Northumberland*. But Hodgson was also a dutiful priest. He knew Felling and was, we are told, 'at all times overflowing with kindness' for its pitmen. For Anglican priests this was remarkable enough but it did not stop there. He counselled the bereaved, buried the dead, started a fund, initiated scientific inquiries (leading to Humphrey Davy), and he publicized the causes and effects of the explosion ' "contrary to the feleings of the coal-owners" ' (letter of 1831, *J. Raine*, pp.92–3). For months the coalowners suffered his pamphlets with clenched ears. It was not until December 1812 that they made any response.

Yet, for all Hodgson's qualities he could not be more than an outsider. The labouring poor he saw as his flock, and flocks are not the same species as shepherds. His sympathy was for common, sinful, burdened Humanity, his charge was to the needy – the dispensations and ministry of the Church, as a duty, to those beneath. On the day of the explosion, when the mining community had gathered to pool its long experience of pits and their owners, Hodgson was scornful. Their experience could not be valid, it was only self-delusion and 'wicked industry' (*J. Raine*, p.103). The next day, when pitmen from all parts met to discuss what was to be done, Hodgson could only dismiss their skills as so much conceit: 'Everyone had some example to relate of successful attempts. . . . Their reasonings and assertions seemed indeed to be a mixture of those prejudices . . . which cleave to workmen whose experience has afforded a partial insight . . . and not to be grounded on any memory of facts, or to result from a knowledge of the connection between causes and effects' (*J. Hodgson*, p.23). For Hodgson, the 'insane sport' of hope went on over the weeks of incarceration. His flock were foolish and their experience was wanting. As a priest and intellectual he was groomed for these kinds of perception.

In the pit lay the body of John Thompson, class leader of the Felling Methodists. Fixated by knowledge of his own salvation, in torment with an evocation of Sin all around and within, and much given to weeping in worship, Thompson's religion was a world apart from Hodgson's. One wonders what the curate would have made of the theological 'partial insight' of the class leader? The class leader lacked the curate's status, his learning, his reasoning, his philanthropy – for Thompson's world did not easily engender such bounties. Thompson's Methodism may have been self-deluding, it was certainly prejudiced; it could have been a partial insight at best, or an 'insane sport' at worst, but the man had died as he had lived, alongside his people. And this the good curate, or his Church, could never do. And what was true of Felling was true of the coalfield. The pit villages found themselves bereft of Anglicanism not just for all the conventional reasons – church building, absenteeism, class rituals and the like – but also because compared to the Methodists, and the Primitive Methodists in particular, the Anglican Church chose to stand aside from the experiences of most of the people whose name it bore.

The first Primitive Methodist preachers entered the North East from their Yorkshire circuits in June 1820. They represented a sect barely nine years old but preached a salvation self-consciously 'primitive'. Their first successes were small: a sowing of tiny societies around Darlington, in the Dales, and in and around Shields, Newcastle and Sunderland.

The exhilarations of revival did not come until February 1822 in a wave which first rose in Teesdale, surged across into Weardale, and came down the valleys into Tyneside and Wearside. From the bolstered, exuberant, societies of Shields, Stockton and Sunderland the coalfield was systematically missioned in the summer and autumn of 1823. By October there were as many Primitives in its coaly hinterland as in Sunderland itself. From the 1820s to the 1840s they registered their presence, their reputation, and their organization. In general they grew, routinely, with falls here and there. There were three phases of stagnation and three of revival, interspersed, in an upward curve. The first stagnation came in

1829–31, the epic years of Tommy Hepburn's union, its first strike and victory. The second came in 1833 and lasted through the middle 1830s after Hepburn's defeat and the eviction, blacklisting, and penury which followed it. The third came in similar fashion, after the defeat of the great strike of 1844, lasting through the middle 1840s. The revivals came in between: in 1831–2, as the coalfield sat in the grip of lock-out, troops, and cholera; in 1841–3, coincident with the demise of Chartism but the return of trade unionism; and in the late 1840s, with a modest recovery from the settlement disruptions of the mid-1840s.

All of this happened amidst unprecedented economic development. The period saw two bursts of frenzied investment in the coalfield, one for railways and one, linked, for coal. Between 1836 and 1843 sixty-one new collieries were sunk. This brought a lot of moving about. Although most of the new workforce were recruited from the existing mining districts – themselves prolific – the community was increasingly on the move as new excavations promised better wages and new villages promised better houses.

But in an age when 'settlement' was a moral as well as a geographical expression, the migratory, unstable inhabitants of the new collieries were seen as depraved, even as dangerous. The first threats to order had been perceived as urban threats, and structures for the mass control of the poor had come out of the late eighteenth- and early nineteenth-century town. But as the concern for order increased, heightened by coalfield migration and by trade unionism and popular politics, the mining community became *the* main focus of the fears of the dominant classes in the North East. During the 1830s and 1840s the pit villages are described as by turns idle, deceitful, ignorant, vicious, drunken, shameless, irreligious and dangerous. Of course, what we have here are perceptions of a class as well as perceptions of a community.

It was into this expanding, dislocating, ideologically-dividing coalfield that the Primitive Methodist preachers had walked. By the 1840s they were considered to have made their mark. On the one hand they were blamed for their zeal, producing a particular kind of working-class confidence; on the other hand, they were praised for their order, producing a kind of control which other agencies could not achieve. Both judgments were essentially correct – an apparent paradox which has confused historians ever since. To understand the men and women they produced one has to go beyond piecemeal contemporary observations and look at their psychology of religious belonging.

In 1791 Thomas Curry, a Tyneside keelman, sat expectantly in a Methodist service:

No sooner was the text pronounced, 'Arise, shine, for thy light is come, and the glory of the Lord is risen upon thee', than he was filled with joy unspeakable. . . . To use his own simple language, 'his heart was like to jump out of his body'. For long after, whenever he mentioned this, his bursting heart found relief alone in a torrent of tears. (C.N. Wawn)

After this Curry gave up his life to Jesus. His psychological and religious experience beats at the heart of Methodism. Not that there is much notion of 'psychology', however understood, in the contemporary accounts. Then, and right into the twentieth century, revivals and conversions were attested as a natural phenomenon, divinely inspired. Like volcanoes, they just erupt: they are 'breakings out', 'mighty movings', 'seasons of grace' and 'seasons of power'.

For the coalfield it is possible to see both 'external' and 'internal' factors in the work of revival. Externally, one can list economic development and migration; the crisis of class and culture; the contingency of death – of infants, or by cholera, or accident; the community's own inherent propensities – for superstition, for direct action, for millenarianism; and the village itself – a tightly-built local community. Internally, one can see the Methodists themselves trying to initiate, or to ride, and then to harness, revival forces externally conditioned. This meant first appropriating the external factors, and then trying to internalize them according to their own lights. The result was an effective organizational discipline which was laid upon members after conversion or attendance; a powerful sense of group identity and expectation; a democratic impulse for self-expression and self-made meaning in a world which largely denied it; and finally, a carefully prized freedom to associate. This freedom permitted a tenure which was not granted, say, to Dissenters after 1689 or to trade unionists for most of the nineteenth century. They valued this liberty, and in a revolutionary epoch they were right to do so, even though they were not granted it for the best libertarian reasons.

Probably the most notable aspect of external and internal factors was the way in which, during the formative years, they impinged upon each other. Wesley was an autocrat but even he, especially in the early years, was constantly forced to shift his views by the contagion of numbers which pressed upon him. Methodism did not 'come' to save anybody trailing clouds of glory; rather, it was made by people.

We forget this at our peril. In the heated moment of revival, and in the cold tempering of the human personality through the organization thereafter, a reactive exchange took place. The historical result was an intermittent fusion between that which grew to be called 'Methodism', and the needs and culture of the poor. In the coalfield this reactive exchange could happen at the casual level: in using village bellmen to raise a congregation; in class meetings held in pubs because there were no halls or they were too poor to rent them; in preachers who exploited the vernacular; in pinching popular tunes for dignified verses. Or the exchange could happen at the deepest meanings of life and death: in the zeal for a righteous death from a community whose traditional funeral rites were meticulous; in the capacity for mutuality of a class who had little else to offer each other; in the taste for a sudden salvation from a people whose lives were always a lottery and the translation from nothing to enough, illness to health, life to death was often arbitrary. When the middle-class came to watch they could not comprehend. As they cultivated the controlled, what could they make of a religion which espoused discipline but also heard by its passions and saw by its visions?

John Wesley himself felt these contradictions. After experiencing his 'heart strangely warmed' (*Journal*, 24 May 1738), he heeded Peter Böhler's advice and tried not to let his intellect tie up his feelings. He submitted to Whitefield's style:

> I could scarce reconcile myself to this strange way of preaching in the fields . . . having been all my life (till very lately) so tenacious on every point relating to decency and order, that I should have thought the saving of souls almost a sin, if it had not been done in a Church. . . . At four in the afternoon, I submitted to be more vile. (quoted in R.E. Davies, p.69)

Wesley did not leap the class gulf, he jumped in. In a grotesquely unequal society where the exotic few could tolerate no sign of street-contact or human relationship lest their charade of differentness be broken, Wesley broke every rule. On the streets and in the fields he declared his common humanity, his equal sin, the equal opportunity of grace; he did this shoulder to shoulder, fustian to broadcloth, cheek to jowl, and his rod broke forth a torrent. At times its force embarrassed and humiliated him, but he accepted its witness: 'And oh how dreadful, yet pleasing, was the sight! All this time many were crying for mercy' (*Journal*, August 1771).

But Wesley could not privilege feelings above all else. Faith as the pure gift of God came first. Faith was 'the eye . . . the ear . . . the palate . . . the feeling of the soul' (J. Wesley, *Earnest Appeal* . . ., pp.4–5), Faith was 'the evidence of things not seen' (p.15). However, faith needed the stiffening of reason and Scripture, for to have faith was 'to believe the Holy Scriptures and the articles of our Faith are true' (J. Wesley, *The Principles* . . ., p.8):

> There are many, it is confess'd (particularly those who are stiled mystick divines) that utterly decry the use of reason . . . in

religion. . . . But we can in no wise agree with this. We find no authority for it in holy writ. (*Earnest Appeal . . .*, p.14)

Once established, the closed circuit of Faith-Scripture-Reason conferred their own truths upon each other. Constantly searching for balance, Wesley valued Faith as the greatest gift but at the same time refused to admit its preponderance. When the Final Judgment was given, the plain, rational, Scriptural Christian who has tried hard, repented, and sought Sanctification *without* the favour of *Justification* by Faith, need not be afraid:

> . . . it is allowed that Entire Sanctification goes before our Justification of the Last Day.
> It is allowed also that Repentance and *Fruits meet for Repentance* go before Faith. . . . By Repentance, I mean, Conviction of Sin, producing Real Desires and sincere Resolutions of Amendment: and by *Fruits . . .*, Forgiving our Brother, ceasing from Evil, doing Good, using the Ordinances of God. . . . But these, I cannot as yet, term *Good Works*. (J. Wesley, *A Farther Appeal . . .*, p.4)

There is a certain woolliness here which Wesley was criticized for, but his movement forced him to seek compromise and balance. Intellectually, he balanced Puritanism and Arminianism, Faith and Works; devotionally, he balanced law and spirit, the formal and informal; organizationally, he balanced space for the personal with need for the cohesive. The Methodist economy he built, bit by bit, reflected all this. The missioning blew where it listeth, saved souls where it could, and yet Wesley had to determine 'by the grace of God, not to strike one stroke in any place where I cannot follow the blow' (R. Southey, vol. i, p.421). The result was a crusade for all the people which developed as a system which produced its own 'seminaries and their hierarchy, their own regulations, their own manners, their own literature . . . a distinct people, an *imperium in imperio*' (R. Southey, p.1).

The personal had to be managed: scripture was chosen with specific persons in mind; worship was collective, but it was also 'a means of grace' for the individual. Wesleyan hymns are often in the first-person pronoun but the 1780 hymnal was published to regulate the old 'lining-out' with the written advice to 'Sing all. . . . Sing lustily. . . . Sing modestly. . . . Sing in Time. . . . Sing Spiritually' (J. Telford, pp.9–10). For women, the more the movement swayed to the managed and away from the personal the more their position deteriorated. Men dominated the organizational routines but when the Spirit blew hard and free then women came up in gusts with the right to know and to speak. Wesley at first resisted this, and then half retracted. The 1803 conference advised against women preachers but recognized extraordinary calls which were permitted, for female hearers only, in exceptional circumstances. By the time of Bunting extraordinary calls were just every fanatic's licence. Against this, the Primitives (and the Bible Christians) – more bound to the personal in their early years – positively welcomed the spiritual, scriptural, and organizational validity of women preachers. Although their calling was worth only half the wage of a man's and their administrative role was limited, their right to be itinerant preachers was fully recognized. However, as the Primitives entrenched their management and also came to regulate the personal, women itinerants dropped out. After 1841 they were barred.

Wesley struggled to hold the balance of forces he had helped to unleash. After his death the problems became acute. Conference tried hard to uphold his spirit; in its 1806 Articles of Religion we find doctrine, followed by 'Scripture proofs', followed by 'Testimonies from the Writings of Mr Wesley'. However, it was Jabez Bunting who led Methodism into its next, distinctive, phase. Bunting stopped the balancing act. Under him, a movement was turned into an ecclesiastical structure. The Wesleyans built their church at the price of expulsion and secession. The battle lines were drawn and redrawn in the period from Ludd and Sidmouth to the Flysheets controversy of 1846–9, but the general struggle was between the connexional and the provincial, the scholastic and the personal, men and women. Once the ecclesiastical structure was erected, it was enclosed; it could brook no rivals, it considered its own adversarial ranks as ' "little men, and selfish men, and jealous men and crafty men, and sneaks, and slanderers, and all that tribe" ' (W.R. Ward, *Early Victorian Methodism*, p.xvii).

The 'Wesleyan' circuits suffered the secessions and expulsions, and the frustrations, of a hardening institutional structure. The North Shields Wesleyan Joseph Peart called upon the Primitives to come and preach in 1822 without even knowing who they were – their name 'Ranters' was good enough for him (H.B. Kendall, ii, p.169). The Primitives arrived in Allendale in 1821 but they had been preceded there by the 'Bochimites', founded in 1814 by Francis Swindle. The Bochimites ceased to meet after Swindle died but like him they had found new religion by losing old – 'Swindle's sermons seem to have consisted principally of tirades against Wesleyanism' (G. *Dickinson*, pp.113–14).

Hugh Bourne's *Bochim* (Judges 2:5) was at Harriseahead, in Staffordshire. There, this moorland carpenter formed his own society and built its own chapel in 1800. The Tunstall Circuit put up with him until 1808 when he was expelled for field preaching, a mode of preaching which the Wesleyan establishment regarded as by turns emotional, sexual and potentially seditious. In 1811 he joined with William Clowes's Burslem followers to form the Primitive Methodists. The sect grew, joltingly, from Waterloo to Peterloo and in 1820 the Hull and Hutton Rudby Circuits reached Durham. Such was their confidence that within twenty-five years the coalfield circuits were preparing to mission France and New Zealand.

Bourne and Clowes had been attracted by American revivalist techniques, particularly the English tour of Lorenzo Dow in 1805–7. The emotional manipulations of the field and 'camp' meeting left a lot of room for the distortion of Wesley's difficult balance between feelings and scriptural theology. Wesley had made no doctrinal break with the Church of England but in the excitement of the emotional moment, the controlling ballast of scriptural theology could be jettisoned for an outright stress on the personal – that Justification, New Birth, Sanctification, Revelation and Perfection came all at once, in the writhings of the convert.

The criticisms once levelled at Wesley were now heaped upon Ranter heads. Bourne was seen as a Lord of Misrule presiding over a religious parody by the ignorant and foolish. This was unfair; after 1824 Bourne made strenuous efforts to regulate the preachers and what they said. Nevertheless, like all the rituals of misrule the Primitives' alleged inversions depended for their impact on the rigidity of what they were seen to parody. Bunting's Wesleyanism provided all the ossification necessary. Even at the time of the Primitive rupture the Wesleyans were still being criticized for their emphasis on the personal, with Lord Sidmouth very interested in gagging it. Wesleyan preachers were typically charged as unchecked self-servers: wilful, greedy, and carnal. What was said of the Wesleyan preacher was even more true of the Primitive: '"His two longest things are his nails and his prayers. . . . He is in the broad way for public preferment, and in the SIDE PATH FOR PRIVATE GRATIFICATION"' (*A Professor*, p.iii, p.viii). This 1810 satire takes the form of a Methodist tract, 'the CONFESSIONIST'. The attack is exclusively upon the first-person self-testimony of the preacher. It denies the experiential as too often the rationalization of self-interest, and presents self-interest as greedy and ignorant. As Kierkegaard said of Luther so it could be said of Wesley when Böhler counselled simple trust over intellectual complexity – the scholar '"closes his books and says, 'No it is not knowledge that matters,'"' but what when it is the ignorant who shun the books they have never read and say the same? (*J. Kent*, pp.149–50). Here the problem was to do with Protestantism's mass application of Paul's or Luther's (or Wesley's) personal experience. And the problem was human before it was theological.

This 1810 satire takes the form of a Methodist tract, 'the

CONFESSIONIST'. The attack is exclusively upon the first-person self-testimony of the preacher. It denies the experiential as too often a mere rationalisation of self-interest.

The problem was human before it was theological. No tract of Wesley's could have solved it. In the revival meeting, in a matter of minutes, an entire Protestant theological system could be demonstrated with stunning clarity. Premised by the Adamic Law and The Fall, the concepts of New Birth, Justification, Sanctification, faith by Revelation, and the beginnings of Perfection and Assurance could all tumble out as necessitous and simultaneous experiences. Within a human struggle there waged a cosmic drama. Wesley's theology did not cast these concepts as phased processes but as mutually conferring events given by God and accepted by humans, if need be, in a moment. After this, of course, was the long march to Holiness, but the march began here.

And it was *here* that the Primitive preachers found themselves in a radically different position from, say, Anglican priests. Their persona mattered more, and it was fixed. Pulled taut between the poles of Bible and Faith, and tested daily in the community, there was no place for detachment or irony or understatement. The community knew what to expect and the preachers knew what was expected. Unlike priestly dispensations the preachers were bound to an intimate assault on their people in the hope of winning something out of them. Sometimes they did better than others but what was necessary was a performance which had to be given extemporarily if they were to win through. And it was the nature of the extemporary more than the personal which raised the alarm. The ruling class were horrified, Bunting, and even Bourne, tried to regulate it, but given the conditions, it was built in to the Methodist economy.

What we now have is an oral history; years of extemporary verbal performances – intonations, rhythms, dialects, anecdotes, addresses, prayers, the third dimension of music – which the historian can hardly know. It represents a buzz of words and music over our history, not audible through the written record. Its power must have come through a constant reinforcement of Epic and Naturalist modes of discourse. The Epic came from God. In high language, Bible and Hymnal raised the proceedings to the pitch of verse. Verse was the medium of monologue between Maker and made. Monologue transcended ordinary reality: it put mythology beyond anecdote, explanation beyond experience, Divine before human. Woven into this, the extemporary came to express the natural, personal, and everyday. It denied artifice; the language was conversational. It introduced dialogue; knowledge of God was glimpsed and shared by brothers and sisters. It avoided analysis; analysis dissolved into description

– a description of experience, living between the Divine and the everyday. Between them both was born wonder. And it was the sense of wonder which made 'Galilee and Canaan, Moab and Kedron' (D.H. Lawrence, 'Hymns . . .'), and Jesus, real and resurrected in the dirty streets of England.

Once justified, by whatever means, the organization would bind you to it and your new life would be guided by new images. Being saved was what you did. The new life was precariously grappled with above the vortex. Above, lay life and righteousness; below, lay death and sin. This perpetual consciousness of life-struggle produced a different sort of person. At best they enjoyed the confidence and incorruptibility of the self-made. The men trickled into trade unionism and politics as a working-class vanguard. The women ran the home and taught the family to overcome the poverty and illness and filth which engulfed them. Chapel was their ground of being; 'life' was where it was practised.

What we see in Primitive Methodism is a politics of religion: the production of men and women who are Christian, and can be Christians, in society. Wesley and Bourne knew about this, and this was their greatest contribution.

In the coalfield the Methodist contribution to trade unionism, Liberalism, and the Labour Party was not so much a contribution of ideology as a direct giving of persons of a new kind. It lasted for nearly a hundred years. As late as 1927 we find William Straker, general secretary of the Northumberland miners, swapping texts as blows with the Rector of Morpeth:

> 'I would recommend John J. Davies to borrow a copy of the New Testament and turn up the 23rd Chapter of the gospel according to Saint Matthew.. . . Anything our principal speaker said was mild indeed compared to the above condemnation of a class. We also have to remember that the Scribes and Pharisees . . . when they listened to this . . . that they, like this man Davies would regard it as "pernicious nonsense".' (J. Davison, p.226)

The charge of 'pernicious nonsense', of the right of the poor to make themselves to know themselves, was where we began with Rev. Hodgson. The Methodist part in the making of the English working-class made that charge harder to stick.

Select bibliography

A Professor (pseud.), *Confessions of a Methodist*, London, 1810.
Children's Employment Commission, Appendix to First Report, Mines, Part 1. Parliamentary Papers, 1842.

R.E. Davies, *Methodism*, London, 1964.

R.E. Davies and E.G. Rupp, *A History of the Methodist Church in Great Britain*, London, 2 vols, 1965, 1978.

J. Davison, *Northumberland Miners 1919–1939*, Newcastle, 1973.

G. Dickinson, *Allendale and Whitfield*, 2nd edn, Newcastle, 1903.

R. Fynes, *The Miners of Northumberland and Durham*, 1873, reprint Wakefield, 1971.

J.F.C. Harrison, *The Second Coming. Popular Millennarianism 1780–1850*, London, 1979.

J. Hodgson, *An Account of the Explosion . . .*, Newcastle, 1813.

H.B. Kendall, *Origin and History of the Primitive Methodist Church*, London, 2 vols, 1905.

J. Kent, *Holding the Fort. Studies in Victorian Revivalism*, London, 1978.

D.H. Lawrence, 'Hymns in a Man's Life', in W. Roberts and H.T. Moore (eds), *Phoenix II*, London, 1968.

T. Lessey (ed.), *Short Account of the Life and Christian Experience of John Thompson*, Newcastle, 1812.

R. Moore, *Pitmen, Preachers, and Politics*, Cambridge, 1974.

J. Obelkevich, *Religion and Rural Society*, Oxford, 1976.

W.M. Patterson, *Northern Primitive Methodism*, London, 1909.

Philotheos, *A letter to the People called Methodists, on their unscriptural mode of addressing God at their Prayer Meetings, with brief remarks on females speaking and praying in public*, Manchester, 1826.

J. Raine, *A Memoir of the Rev. John Hodgson*, London, 2 vols, 1857, 1858.

I. Rivers, 'John Wesley and the Language of Scripture, Reason and Experience', *Prose Studies*, 4, 1981.

B. Semmel, *The Methodist Revolution*, London, 1974.

R. Southey, *The Life of Wesley*, London, 2 vols, 1820, 3rd ed. 1846.

W.F. Swift, 'Women Itinerant Preachers of Early Methodism', *Proceedings of the Wesley Historical Society*, vols xxviii, xxix, 1952, 1953.

J. Telford, *The Methodist Hymn-Book Illustrated*, London, 1906.

E.P. Thompson, *The Making of the English Working Class*, London, 1968.

V. Ward, *A Miniature of Methodism*, 5th edn, London, 1829.

W.R. Ward, *Early Victorian Methodism. Correspondence of Jabez Bunting 1830–58*, Oxford, 1976.

W.R. Ward, *Religion and Society in England 1790–1850*, London, 1972.

C.N. Wawn, *Thomas Curry, The Pious Keelman*, Newcastle, 1822.

Wesley Historical Society, *Articles of Religion 1806*, Publications, London, 1897.

J. Wesley, *The Journal*, ed. N. Curnock, London, 8 vols, 1909–16, reprint 1938.

J. Wesley, *An Earnest Appeal to men of Reason & Religion*, Bristol, 1771, 6th ed.

J. Wesley, *A Farther Appeal to men of Reason & Religion*, London, 1778, 5th ed.

J. Wesley, *The Principles of a Methodist*, London, 1796.

The Catholic parish

22
Catholicism and the
New York Irish 1880–1910

HUGH McLEOD

The parish of Sacred Heart, on the traditionally Irish, now substantially Puerto Rican, West Side of Manhattan, recently celebrated its centenary. As is usual, they published a parish history. These are often disappointingly uninformative, the all-too-brief text being scattered among letters of congratulation from the Pope, the Archbishop and the Mayor, and advertisements for local Catholic-owned businesses. This history was something more for at least two reasons: the author was a leading church historian, Henry J. Browne, and his work was partly based on a questionnaire which some thirty long-standing parishioners completed. One of the replies, that of a telephonist, now in her seventies, who was the daughter of an Irish-born janitor, included a striking sentence: 'The immigrants,' she wrote, 'of the years 1914 etc. were insecure, unknowledgable, frightened, and the only thing that kept them going was their faith which they passed on to the next generation.'[1]

This quotation from an immigrant's daughter reads just like a sentence out of Oscar Handlin's *The Uprooted*: was Handlin's interpretation of immigrant religion right after all, in spite of the apparently devastating criticism his famous book has received?[2] In Europe, peasants who had migrated to the working-class suburbs of the cities were deserting the churches of their birth, and often joining militantly secularist political parties: why did this not happen among the Irish of New York? How exactly *did* Catholicism help the Irish immigrant to cope with the traumas of migration across the ocean, and their children to endure the poverty that so often remained their lot? These are the questions I shall try to answer.

In 1898 New York attained its present boundaries, following the merger of the old New York (henceforth Manhattan and Bronx boroughs) with Brooklyn, and the annexation of Staten Island and of various smaller towns and rural areas on Long Island. With some 3 million inhabitants, Greater New York ranked second to London among the world's cities. In spite of the growing pace of Italian and East European immigration, the Germans and Irish still predominated as they had done for over half a century. In 1900 persons of Irish stock made up 22 per cent of the greater city's population. The chief strength of the Irish lay in control over New York's dominant Democratic Party. This meant that they were well represented in all areas of public employment, and that there was a small, but very powerful Irish elite of politicians, lawyers and contractors. But a quarter of the occupied males of Irish stock in Manhattan and Bronx boroughs were still in unskilled jobs, and three quarters were manual workers. This paper is primarily concerned with the working-class majority at a time when Irish New Yorkers were typically employed as labourers, teamsters, policemen, building craftsmen, domestic servants.

In the early twentieth century about 90 per cent of New York's Irish-born population were Roman Catholics.[3] Nor was this merely a nominal affiliation. Few, if any, aspects of Irish-American life were more prominent than their religion.

For one thing, devout and indifferent alike lived surrounded by the symbols of their Catholicism. Irish districts, like the Middle West Side of Manhattan, were thickly filled with churches, some fitting neatly into the rows of tenements, others towering above the adjoining buildings. On the West Side in 1901 there were eleven Catholic churches in the two miles from 23rd Street to 60th Street, one every three or four streets. And a study, published in 1905, of West Side working-class life claimed that all the Irish Catholic homes visited by the author were decorated with pictures of Christ and the saints.[4]

Surveys around 1900 showed that about 90 per cent of Irish-born Catholics claimed membership of a specific parish. Levels of church attendance were lower, but still, by comparison with European cities during the same period, very high: the count of church attendance in Manhattan borough in 1902 showed that about 50 per cent of adult Roman Catholics went to mass on the Sunday of the census.[5] This average included non-Irish Catholics, notably Germans and Italians; the figure for those of Irish descent was probably higher. The clergy tried to draw this enormous population of those accepting some sort of Catholic identity into an all-embracing 'parish life' (termed by the church reformers of the 1960s 'the Catholic ghetto'), which was intended to protect them from the contamination of a Protestant or pagan environment. A history of the Catholic church in New York, published in 1905, described the great network of organizations that characterized the modern parish, and which was 'aimed to meet every need of the parishioner and to deal with every condition'.[6] And a recent study of New York priests, partly based on interviews with those ordained in the 1920s, referred to the

'Catholic culture' still flourishing at that time, in which the priest was 'cult leader, confessor, teacher, counsellor, social director, administrator . . ., recreation director for young and old, and social worker', and where 'hundreds went to mass each week, went to confession every Saturday, were members of parish organizations, . . . enjoyed the parish dances, plays, card parties and athletic teams, packed the parish mission for weeks as the children did the parochial school or Sunday School of religion, were attended at baptisms and marriages, in illness and death.'[7] In the later nineteenth century, priests in many parts of Europe were making similar attempts to enclose their parishioners within the ghetto; in the United States they were unusually successful, because sectarian exclusiveness was reinforced by ethnic exclusiveness. In fact, it was probably in the inter-war years that the grip of this subculture was firmest, as by then the long and painful process of building an alternative system of Roman Catholic education was more or less complete, and the ghetto had not yet been undermined by mass migration to religiously mixed suburbs, and by the revival of Catholic liberalism.

I shall look next at two superficially attractive yet inadequate ways of interpreting the strength of Catholicism and its influence on Irish-American life. One solution has been to posit some archetypal 'immigrant experience', of which religion was an essential part. Another approach would be to see Irish-American religion primarily as a means of coping with and compensating for poverty. The classic statement of the former view is Oscar Handlin's:

> The more thorough the separation from the other aspects of the old life, the greater was the hold of the religion that alone survived the transfer. Struggling against heavy odds to save something from the old ways, the immigrants directed into their faith the whole weight of their longing to be connected with the past.

Timothy Smith, in an article that synthesized more recent research, called in question most of Handlin's subsequent arguments. Yet in one important respect his assumptions remained the same: in analysing the relationship between religion and ethnicity within a wide range of immigrant groups, he overlooked the possibility that the actual importance of religion was much greater in the history of some immigrations than others.[8]

Yet it seems to me that the differences between the religious histories of the various immigrant groups in turn-of-the-century

America are at least as significant as the similarities. The role and nature of formal religion varied, for instance, according to the degree of religious homogeneity within the group; according to the relationship between national identity and the dominant religion; and according to the degree to which political radicals or secular nationalists had succeeded in challenging the moral authority of the clergy. Statistics collected by New York Protestants at the start of the twentieth century showed that the great majority of the city's population had some kind of sectarian allegiance; but the degree to which the members of the various ethnic groups joined a church or attended services varied widely. The Irish and Poles generally showed the highest figures, Germans and Scandinavians some of the lowest. To explain these contrasting patterns, account has to be taken not only of the effects of migration as such, but of the specific collective experiences of each group, and the position of its members in the economic and political structure of New York.

In explaining the unusually important role of the Church in Irish New York life, I would stress the cumulative effect of a series of factors. The most fundamental was the strength of Catholicism in Ireland as the main source of identity for three-quarters of the population. But the chances for survival of this inherited link between Catholicism and Irish identity were greatly enhanced by the fact that so little seemed to have changed in New York. The Irish Catholics who settled there in large numbers from the 1830s onwards found a city where anti-Catholic and anti-Irish attitudes were rife at all social levels. Manifestations ranged from discrimination in the hiring of labour to the Protestant bias in the teaching of the city schools. By the early 1840s, Irish Catholics were being organized (successfully) to oppose Protestant control of the city's schools, and (unsuccessfully) to demand public money for Catholic schools; they were forming guards to protect their churches from nativist gangs; and the Irish vote was already a potent factor in city elections. During the following decades, Irish Catholics gradually established a dominant position in city politics; but the economic elite continued to be strongly Protestant, as were many of the city's leading newspapers, and the New York legislature. In the late nineteenth century many of the Irish still kept bitter memories of the days when 'No Irish needed apply', even if it was now newer immigrants from Italy and eastern Europe who bore the main brunt of America's scorn.

Two further facets of this situation seem relevant: the dominant position within the Archdiocese of New York that the Irish enjoyed in the second half of the nineteenth century, and the mutually supportive relationship between the church and the Democratic Party. Hughes, who became Bishop in 1842 and Archbishop in 1850, was the first of a long line of Archbishops of Irish descent, continuing to the present day. In a city where every area of life had an ethnic dimension, the unmistakable Irishness of the church contributed to the strength of Irish loyalty. Moreover, at the parish level, the Irish did not have to contend, as Catholics of other nationalities so often did, with a hostile pastor doggedly trying to impose an alien form of Catholicism. The relationship with the Democratic Party meant that the Church was a powerful as well as a popular institution. The power and status of Catholic priests and Democratic politicians was mutually reinforcing. The clergy would in emergencies offer the faithful explicit advice on how to vote – during the 1894 state elections, for instance, the clergy of Sacred Heart were said to have 'entreated, almost commanded' their congregation 'to vote the straight Democratic ticket'.[9] More generally, they offered respectability to a profession who were easy targets for moralists, and the clergy in turn extended their own powers of patronage by using their political connections to gain favours for parishioners.

In this situation, Catholic churches and priests were important symbols. On 12 July 1870, when a body of Irish Catholics attacked an Orange family picnic, killing several people, the attack was said to have been provoked by the rumour that the Orangemen had fired on a Catholic church while en route to the picnic site. Similarly with the clergy: Irish-Americans were proud of their priests, and especially of those that used their churches to support the Irish national cause, though they were also a bit resentful of the clergy's frequent demands for money, and of the other controls they attempted to exercise. This feeling, that in the reputation of their clergy the good name of the whole community was at stake, was reflected in the lack of any Irish tradition of jokes about clerical sex-lives. The Federal Writers' Project in the 1930s collected stories and jokes current within the various ethnic groups in New York. Their chief source of Slovak stories was an elderly woman, who had been brought up in rural Slovakia: she told a series of jokes in many of which priests were prominent, their overriding concerns always being money and seduction. Priests also appear prominently in the Irish stories – both those set in Ireland, and those set in New York, where the two chief protagonists are a pair of 'typical Irishmen' called Casey and Finnegan. But the relationship between priests and people that these stories present is much less clear-cut. Priests appear as rather unworldly in some respects, yet with a propensity for mild forms of sharp practice; as dedicated men, but with a taste for the good things of life. The people regard their priests with respect, and recognize all their religious obligations, at least in principle; but they realize that the norms prescribed by the Church may at times conflict with the standard practice of everyday life. In a typical story, Casey is a traffic policeman, and sees a car trying to jump the lights at a busy Midtown intersection. He whistles to the driver to pull in, and then unleashes a flood of bad language, before asking to see his licence – only to discover that he is the Reverend Father Callaghan. For a moment Casey is non-plussed, but then he says: 'I'm sorry, Father, I didn't know you were a priest, what with your coat-collar turned up and all. But let me tell you this. You're lucky it was me who stopped you. Because if the Protestant cop at the next crossing had seen you, he'd have given you the chair.'[10]

I am now going to look at the relationship between their Catholicism and the poverty and chronic sickness which were the lot of so many Irish immigrants and their children in the New York of eighty years ago. At first sight the New York Irish would seem to provide a classic illustration of the thesis that the main function of religious movements is to compensate for physical or psychic deprivation,[11] and that, in Marx's famous words, religion is 'the heart of a heartless world, the spirit of spiritless conditions, the opium of the people'.

In spite of the political power of the Irish community, the poverty of many of its members was reflected in high rates of death, pauperism and crime. The 1890 census showed that across the United States as a whole natives of Ireland had a far higher rate of pauperism than any other immigrant group, and that they ranked second to the Italians in the proportion who were in jail. In 1889–90 the white death rate in New York was at 26.3 per 1000, the second highest among American cities, and at most ages those of Irish stock were the most vulnerable. Their rate of accidental death was even higher than that of the blacks, and comparison between those of Irish and German stock showed that, with the exception of cancer and suicide, nearly every form of death claimed Irish victims at a faster rate than German.[12] The 'widow-woman' was a very familiar figure in Irish neighbourhoods.

In this situation Irish New Yorkers sought the direct help of their saints. The city was riddled with shrines, where a sacred picture, statue or relic attracted the anxious and afflicted in ones and twos, in regular congregations or in vast crowds. Quack doctors and chemists partly took the place of the hospitals the poor feared, and the qualified medical practitioners whom they could not afford. But the affection and gratitude that these could not inspire, Catholics lavished on their saints. Herzfeld's invaluable study of twenty-four West Side families gives many examples of the big role of accident and illness in their lives, and notes the frequency with which the saints were called in aid to provide cures and to protect against such disasters.[13]

In less tangible ways, the Catholic faith offered many hard-pressed tenement dwellers the assurance that their sufferings had some meaning and value, and that, if they stuck to their tedious duties, they would be rewarded. Men often found release from the drudgery of work, and from a noisy, smelly home, in saloons and pool-rooms. Women, after the brief freedom of adolescence, were for much of their adult life tied to the kitchen by young children. As the children grew older they often found that the task of bringing them up fell mainly on their own shoulders, and that their husbands offered little support. For many women in this situation a few hours spent in church each week offered almost the only relief, and a valued source of continuing strength. This was the theme of several replies to the Sacred Heart questionnaire. One old woman, for instance, wrote: 'I've only been an occasional church-goer. Only when the load got too heavy to bear did I share it with God.' And a younger and more strictly observant parishioner, wrote: 'Sacred Heart has been, and always will be a place of miracles for me. I draw whatever strength I need from it – it isn't just a place of worship, it's Sacred Heart – full of wonder, hope, faith, mystery & yes, miracles.'

But any theory that attempts to link the religiosity of Irish-Americans with their sufferings must take account of the alternative focuses of community life, and must note the strains, as well as the strengths, in the relationship between Church and people. It appeared, in fact, to be precisely the poorest who were most likely to be estranged from the Church.

By comparison with the poor Catholics of many European cities, the Irish of New York appeared remarkably pious. But their pastors were more aware of the fact that many Irish-Americans had given up the practice of their faith. And poverty seemed to lie at the heart of the problem. Typical were the reports by the Paulist fathers, who ran parish missions with a special stress on temperance. At St Veronica's, Greenwich Village, in 1894, they admitted that the improvement in the quality of Catholic life that they had hoped for after their last mission had only been partly realized: 'For, given the same conditions, poverty, desultory and irregular work, a superabundance of saloons, and other occasions of sin, it would take a miracle, or the most unremitting manifestations of zeal to work any notable change.' And the response to the mission in their own parish of St Paul's on the West Side in 1879 inspired an analysis of the connection between poverty and religious apathy. They saw this relationship as having several dimensions: poverty tempted some to seek escape by routes that the Church condemned, including crime and prostitution; the enforced idleness caused by unemployment sucked others into the saloon subculture, which in practice was one of the Church's strongest rivals; the poor found it difficult to achieve the standards of respectability expected of churchgoers; and frequent moves led to a 'lack of attachment to any particular church or priest'.[14] Each of these points gains some corroboration from other sources.[15]

In so far as poverty led to the strengthening of ties between neighbours, it could contribute to the base of community feeling on which an institution like the Church could build. But some poor families were continually moving in search of work; sheer exhaustion left some with no surplus energy for anything but the struggle to bring up a family and the release offered by an occasional drinking spree; and the very poorest families seldom or never had the spare resources that would enable them to enter a network of borrowing and lending. It was in such socially isolated families that the ties of sectarian loyalty sometimes broke altogether. The case-files of the Charity Organization Society are an interesting indicator here. The summary sheets stated the religion of the adult members of families applying for aid. But the C.O.S. often found it hard to determine what that religion was. Many of the applicants had no settled allegiance, but would make use of whatever benefits a church had to offer. The Roman Catholic Church was particularly vulnerable to counter-attractions offered by the greater resources and probably less stringent requirements of the Protestants.[16]

For the many people who remained emphatically Catholics, but who normally lived on the margins of parish life, the high point of religious enthusiasm was the parish mission, held every three or four years, when hell-fire sermons would pack the church for several nights running, thousands of confessions would be heard, hundreds of pledges administered. This was the occasion when they could affirm their continuing Catholic identity, their acceptance in principle of official doctrine, and their loyalty to their priests. The missioners sometimes found the ethos of the congregations amassed on these occasions somewhat uncongenial. At St Bernard's in 1900 the Paulists reported that many came who had not received the sacraments for years, and that they got 'a regular "mixed ale" crowd'; at St Patrick's, Brooklyn, the year before, they had suggested that the women attending included a 'too large contingent of the careless beer-drinking type – missing mass and the sacraments all too much'.[17] Some of these partly involved Catholics might have fitted the stereotype exemplified by Charles Booth's assertion concerning the London Irish that they were 'as a rule devout . . . but at the same they are great beggars, as well as heavy drinkers, and there is no sign that the form that practical religion takes in their case helps to make them in these respects either more self-reliant or more self-restrained.' But if we look at the hard core of parish stalwarts the prevalent ethos is very different – and indeed remarkably similar to that of the 'respectable Methodists', as described in Moore's study of Durham miners.[18]

The Sacred Heart questionnaire is interesting here, as the parish lay in the much-abused Hell's Kitchen district. The daughter, born in 1904, of a Sanitation Department worker, remembers that her parents had 'a nice home', though they had to be careful; they and all their friends were 'all very hard-working, religious, trying to give their neighbours, their church, all they could'. Like many of the others, she ridiculed the 'Hell's Kitchen' tag. The daughter, born 1906, of a trolley-car conductor objected 'furiously' to this name. Hers was a poor, but emphatically self-sufficient family: 'We never needed financial help – nor did we think the Church was over-demanding in asking our financial help.' Another woman, whose father drove a trolley-car, and who grew up in the parish in the 1920s and 30s, insists: 'we lived in a good neighborhood. If there were toughness around we did not know it or see it, we were brought up in our home not on the street. No one stole or hurt anyone that I ever knew. All my friends grew up very nice. . . . There were five children in our family. My parents worked hard to bring them up. They never had to accept charity from any one or any place. . . . They always supported their church and school. Then if there was money left over they bought a well needed pair of shoes.'

The West Side described here is very different from that suggested by Pauline Goldmark and her colleagues at the New York School of Philanthropy. In a study published in 1914, they referred to the 'dullness of these West Side streets', 'the traditional apathy', the 'decades of lawlessness and neglect', the street fights and drunken brawls, and the prevalence of 'every villainy'.[19] When this was written, the oldest of the respondents to the Sacred Heart questionnaire would have been at parochial school, and presumably, in Goldmark's eyes, on the threshold of a career of delinquency. The apathy, the passive resignation, not to mention the lawlessness or the life of the streets described by Goldmark and her colleagues, were the very opposite of the values they associated with their Irish working-class parents. Granted a tendency towards the patronizing and the melodramatic on Goldmark's part, it seems fair to interpret the militant respectability of these Catholics as a means of protecting their families from aspects of local life that were unpleasantly prominent. Their Catholicism looks less like the famous 'opium' than a stimulus to and sanctification of values that offered a basis for pride in a situation of suffering and humiliation, and some defence against its effects.

The survival strategy that the Church implicitly endorsed had several dimensions. At the individual and family level, it included hard work, independence, strict standards of 'decent' behaviour, and subordination of individual desires to the apparent needs of the family. At the neighbourhood and parish level it included an ethos of mutual support and solidarity, and various forms of collective action in defence of sectional interests, notably work for the Democratic Party.[20]

Democratic politicians often seem to have come from a strongly Catholic background, and they saw it as good politics to remain on close terms with the Church. Some conservative Protestants have recently suggested that a good Christian has to be a Republican: a much older tradition decrees that a successful Democrat must be a good Catholic. Even in 1976 Governor Brown of California was being advised by aides, worried by his slipping image, to 'hit the communion rail'. At the beginning of this century such prominent exponents of New York machine politics as Charles F. Murphy, leader of Tammany Hall from 1902 to 1924, and George Washington Plunkitt, originator of the concept of 'honest graft', were well known as assiduous attenders at Catholic services and liberal benefactors of Catholic parishes. Certainly, being seen at mass was, as Plunkitt would have put it, 'a good business proposition'. But there is reason to think that the piety of many of these hard-bitten local politicians was as much conviction as calculation, and that the Catholic parish was a particularly effective breeding-ground for the city bosses of this period. A characteristic figure was Murphy, known to his intimates as 'Mr Murphy' or, behind his back, as 'Silent Charlie'. The son of Irish immigrants, he began his career driving a bus, but made a fortune first by owning a chain of saloons, and then through politics, where he established cordial relationships with various contractors. Accessibility was one of the foundations of his power, and it was significant that he lived all his life in his native Gas House district, even after he had a suburban estate and several automobiles. Another was a reputation for generosity, based on numerous small gifts to those in need and large donations to charity committees. While these qualities ensured his popularity, his highly respectable, and indeed puritanical, public persona also added to his reputation, and helped to secure the approval of the clergy. According to a hostile journalist: 'He had none of the ordinary vices: he drank liquor occasionally, but his drinks were sparse and the time far separated. In smoking he did not indulge, neither did he swear, nor gamble at cards, although he was not a stranger to stock market speculations.'[21] Murphy, and those like him, had no talents for oratory, and made no claim ever to have had an idea. Their genius lay in human relations: getting to know, and learning how to organize, manipulate and satisfy large numbers of individuals both within the party machine and among their constituents. Absolute essentials for politics of this kind were hard work, meticulous concern for detail, and above all a reputation for loyalty. It was precisely qualities of this kind that were most esteemed by the Catholic church in New York. It was appropriate that Tammany Hall's most famous son, Al Smith, should also have been a devout Catholic, and Handlin, in his biography of Smith, draws a direct parallel between his attitude to the Church and his attitude to the party.[22] Similarly, the autobiography of a New York priest, who was assistant in a downtown parish in the 1920s, shows how the diocese looked above all for good 'organization men': the good assistant priest was one who sunk himself so completely in parish routine that the archbishop heard nothing about him, either good or bad; to ecclesiastical superiors the only possible response was obedience, while in dealing with parishioners he had to combine firmness with a willingness to devote limitless time to those who needed it.[23]

It would be quite wrong, then, to suggest that the religiosity of Irish New Yorkers made them passively accepting of their lot. More plausibly, it could be argued that Catholicism narrowed their options, and predisposed them to working within the existing system. However, the neat equation, Irish-Catholic-Democrat, was continually being challenged by a vocal minority committed to revolution in Ireland and/or labour militancy in America, and enjoying a good deal of sympathy, though only seldom active support from their Tammany-voting church-going neighbours. The alliance between the Church and Tammany Hall faced its greatest test in 1886, when Henry George ran for mayor on the United Labor Party ticket, and came fairly close to defeating the Tammany nominee. George's most powerful advocate was Fr Edward McGlynn, pastor of St Stephen's on East 28th Street, already widely popular as a speaker for the Irish Land League, and already in conflict with Archbishop Corrigan, leader of the conservative faction in the bitterly divided American hierarchy. When McGlynn refused to keep out of George's campaign, Corrigan suspended him; and when he refused to go to Rome to explain himself, he was excommunicated. From the moment that McGlynn was suspended a large movement in his support grew up among New York Catholics. Some boycotted their parish church, or refused to pay for the support of their priest. An estimated 75,000 marched through St Stephen's parish in solidarity with its pastor. Some Catholics left the Church altogether. Many tried to remain within the Church, while still supporting McGlynn's Anti-Poverty Society, which the Arch-bishop proscribed. Eventually in 1892, under the influence of a new Apostolic Delegate and of more liberal members of the hierarchy, McGlynn was re-admitted to the Church – but shunted off to an obscure upstate parish.[24]

This is the kind of episode that acted as a catalyst for the estrangement of Church and workers in many parts of Europe. In New York this never quite happened. Several factors can be mentioned in explaining the ability of the Catholic church in New York to survive this greatest crisis in its history with relatively little long-term loss of popular support. Some have already been mentioned: for instance, the depth of Catholic identity among the majority of Irish New Yorkers, including those only marginally involved in parish life, and the great prestige enjoyed by the clergy as a body. It is significant that the leader in the brief revolt against Archbishop Corrigan and Tammany Hall was himself a priest, and thus offered the working-class Irish voter the best of both worlds: an attractive programme, delivered in familiar language, with the authority attaching to his office. It is also noteworthy that McGlynn and his supporters made no attempt to form a breakaway church: their hopes were focussed on reinstatement by the Roman Catholic authorities. Two other points seem relevant to the Church's ability to retain a large working-class base in New York. The first is that whereas there certainly were wide differences of social status within New York Catholic congregations, there was seldom the clear-cut division of interest that was apparent in, for instance, many areas of France and Spain, where the clergy had close ties with large employers. At the turn of the century, wealthy Irish New Yorkers were typically lawyers, doctors, politicians, saloon-keepers. Large employers and financiers tended to belong to the Protestant denominations of British origin. Second, the United Labor Party's near success in 1886 proved a flash in the pan. Thereafter, the great majority of Irish voters returned to their older Democratic loyalty, and the rise of the Socialist Party in the early twentieth century left Irish neighbourhoods largely untouched. In a New York dominated by inter-ethnic competition, a tight network of common interests bound Irish workers, businessmen, politicians and priests together, in spite of the strains inherent in their relationship.

Notes

I want to thank the British Academy and the Social Science Research Council for financial help, Owen Dudley Edwards for critical comments, and Jay Dolan and the late Harry Browne for help in getting access to sources.

1 Questionnaire on history of Sacred Heart parish, reply by Mary Fitzgerald (kept at Sacred Heart rectory, New York City); H.J. Browne, *One Stop above Hell's Kitchen: Sacred Heart Parish in Clinton*, New York, 1977, p.35.

2 O. Handlin, *The Uprooted*, 2nd edn, Boston, 1973, ch. 5. Two studies which, without directly criticizing Handlin, present very different versions of immigrant religion from his, are R. Vecoli, 'Prelates and Peasants: Italian Immigrants and the Church', *Journal of Social History*, 1969, vol. 11, pp.217–68; T.L. Smith, 'Lay Initiative in American Religious Life', T. Hareven (ed.), *Anonymous Americans*, Englewood Cliffs, 1971, pp.214–49.

3 See the surveys of religious affiliation in the Protestant journal *Federation*, published between 1900 and 1906.

4 E. Herzfeld, *Family Monographs*, New York, 1905, pp.45–6.

5 Church attendance figures taken from *New York Times*, 24 November 1902.

6 J.T. Smith, *The Catholic Church in the Archdiocese of New York*, 2 vols, New York, 1905, II, p.470.

7 P. Murnion, 'Towards Theopolitan Ministry: The Changing Structure of the Pastoral Ministry, New York, 1920–1970', Ph.D. thesis, Columbia University, 1972, p.128.

8 Handlin, op.cit., pp.105–6; T. Smith, 'Religion and Ethnicity in America', *American Historical Review*, 1978, vol. 83, pp.1155–85.

9 *New York Times*, 5 November 1894.

10 W.P.A. Collection on New York City Folklore, May Swenson and

Augustine Fitzgibbon folder (Folk Music Division, Library of Congress, Washingon, D.C.).

11   The American sociologists, Glock and Stark, have written extensively in support of this view. See for instance C. Glock (ed.), *Religion in Sociological Perspective*, Belmont, 1973, pp.217–18.

12   J.S. Billings, *Vital Statistics of New York and Brooklyn*, Washington, 1893, pp.3, 9, 22, 51.

13   Herzfeld, op.cit., pp.19, 27–31.

14   Mission Chronicles, 9–23 December 1894; 30 November–18 December 1879 (Archives of Paulist Fathers, St Paul's rectory, New York City).

15   See especially Herzfeld, op.cit., p.24.

16   Case-files R-127, 130, 133, 136, 138 (Archives of Community Service Society, New York City).

17   Mission Chronicles, March–April 1900; 26 November–24 December 1899.

18   C. Booth, *Life and Labour of the People in London*, 17 vols, London, 1902–3, 3rd series, vol. 7, p.401; R. Moore, *Pit-men, Politics and Preachers*, London, 1974, ch. 6.

19   *Boyhood and Lawlessness*, pp.8–9, 21–2, in P. Goldmark (ed.), *West Side Studies*, 2 vols, New York, 1914.

20   Articles in the *Calendar* of St Paul's parish often cover issues of this kind: for instance, 'Heroism in Family Life' (March 1898), 'Fair Treatment' for the worker (September 1898), articles criticizing rich Catholics (October 1907) and recommending total abstinence (November 1907), 'Be Neighborly' (January 1908), 'The Home' (January 1908), 'Be Proud You're Irish', 'Help the Poor' and 'Strive to Improve yourself, Young Men' (March 1908), 'Boys who need the Rod' (April 1908), 'Socialist Ignorance' (May 1908), articles attacking graft, and demanding action to raise wages, improve housing and cut unemployment (October 1910). (Archives of Paulist Fathers hold a complete run from 1886.)

21   G. Myers, *The History of Tammany Hall*, New York, 1917, pp.302–3. See also N.J. Weiss, *Charles Francis Murphy: Respectability and Responsibility in Tammany Politics*, Northampton, Mass., 1968, pp.18–22, 32–5.

22   O. Handlin, *Al Smith and his America*, Boston, 1958, pp.19–20.

23   E.R. Moore, *Roman Collar*, New York, 1950.

24   The most recent account is R.E. Curran, 'The McGlynn Affair and the Shaping of the New Conservatism in American Catholicism', *Catholic Historical Review*, 1980, vol. 66, pp.184–204.

23
Popular anticlericalism in nineteenth-century rural France

ROGER MAGRAW

The textbook myth that nineteenth-century peasant France remained fervently Catholic is not without some foundation. The roots of the Counter-Revolution in the 1790s lay in the hostility of Catholic peasants to an urban-based, apparently irreligious, revolution. The weakening of the power of the rural curé, the unilateral imposition of the Civil Constitution of the Clergy, the anticlerical excesses of the *armées révolutionnaires* which drank communion wine or melted church bells down for cannon balls all produced resentment in rural France. Although historians such as Bois and Tilly have focussed on peasant hatred of land-grabbing urban bourgeois as the key to counter-revolution, Tackett has argued that the hold of a numerous, well-trained and strongly-rooted clergy on the countryside of western France explains geographical location of population resistance to the Revolution. Half a century later France's first universal (male) suffrage elections, in April 1848, appeared to confirm the power of the rural clergy who led parishioners direct from Easter mass to elect Catholic-royalist *grands notables*.

And yet if this myth retains some plausibility, particularly for the Vendée, much of Brittany, the Massif Central and Flanders, where church attendances of 90 per cent were still the norm in 1900, it requires, none the less, very careful qualification. By May 1849 over one-third of rural departments were voting heavily for radical, frequently anti-clerical, '*Dem-Soc*' candidates. From 1876 onwards universal (male) suffrage, in a France where the peasantry remained the largest single category of voters consistently produced anticlerical Republican majorities. Gambetta defeated the royalist 'Moral Order' by proclaiming as his battle-cry: 'clericalism, there is the enemy!' Ferry secularized the public sector of education, Combes ended the Concordat.

Such anticlerical parliamentary majorities reflected two important realities of rural France. First, large areas of 'dechristianization', of low religious practice, of indifference or overt hostility to the clergy had emerged in the Paris basin, central France, the Limousin, Burgundy, the Rhone valley, Provence, Lower Languedoc, the central Loire valley and much of the South-West. Marcilhacy's studies of the Orléans diocese disclosed male church attendance to be below 4 per cent in 1850. Round Montargis, a forest region sympathetic to the Left, male practice was below 2 per cent. Mgr Dupanloup's clergy, asked to fill in questionnaires for his diocesan enquiry, portrayed themselves as isolated and powerless amidst an indifferent population. In the village of Chanteau there was not a single church confirmation between 1793 and 1863! Energetic bishops like Mgr Bonnet of Bordeaux struggled for decades to improve the quality of their clergy, to stem the tide of 'dechristianization', only to express a sense of failure in their last years. Lazarist missionaries struggling to evangelize the dioceses round Paris in the 1850s estimated overall male practice there as below 5 per cent. The Bishop of Tours lamented in 1874 that his diocese was 'cold, apathetic', 'we can no longer recruit priests here.' Second, there were now regions such as the Vosges or the Tarn where, although religious practice remained high, and although scepticism had little intellectual appeal to the peasantry, nevertheless hostility to the pretensions of the clergy had grown to the point where 'Catholic' rural voters were willing to vote repeatedly for anticlerical republican politicians.

It is obviously impossible to 'explain' rural anticlericalism and 'dechristianization' simply in terms of the behaviour of nineteenth-century priests or changes in the rural economy. Inevitably many of the idiosyncrasies of particular dioceses or individual villages were moulded by previous history. Rival villages, 'counter revolutionary' or 'revolutionary' in 1793, can sometimes be found in opposite camps during the sixteenth-century wars of religion. Some areas which were Catholic bastions in the nineteenth century, such as the Pas-de-Calais (diocese of Arras), had been effectively evangelized during the Counter Reformation. The Ancien Regime had maintained a façade of specious unanimity in religious matters which cracked once state enforcement of conformity was relaxed. Parts of the Charentes, where religious practice collapsed rapidly after 1789, had been forcibly reconverted from Protestantism a century earlier. Anticlerical areas round Cluny in Beaujolais or in the mid-Loire valley correlate with the presence of monastic houses in the eighteenth century which had been widely hated because they had been dominated by nobles and had collected the tithes. In the Aude in the 1870s hatred of the monastery of Frontfroide, where until 1789 seven monks had shared an income of 63,000 livres per annum, remained alive in local popular consciousness. Conversely in the West in the 1780s a lower percentage of the tithes went to monastic houses, much more to the parish clergy. Possibly, therefore, the tithes were less resented in the West. In parts of the Midi nineteenth-century Republicans became adept in manipulating the regionalist myth of the Albigensians, portrayed as heroic defenders of the Midi against the centralizing, 'northern' monarchy, the bishops and the Inquisition. In general Ancien Regime clergy seem to have been more popular when, as in the West, recruited from rural areas than, as in the Centre, when seen as urban intruders.

The upheavals of 1789–1815 also left indelible marks on priest/peasant relations in subsequent decades. Some villagers were left without a priest for thirty years. Others had to make do with Spanish or Italian priests, often of indifferent quality. 'A poor region – bad priests have lost us the countryside,' lamented Mgr Bonnet of his Bordeaux diocese. The Jacobin *'décadi'* encouraged the habit of Sunday work in the fields. In Binas (diocese of Blois), as in many other parishes, the church itself was used for several years as a barn by local landed *notables*. Inevitably the delay between birth and baptism had frequently lengthened. Civil marriages appeared. After 1815 many dioceses still suffered from a shortage of priests – the Yonne had 180 vacant parishes. Years of squabbles between juror and non-juror priests often deepened conflicts within villages.

Explanations for anticlericalism in rural France can usefully be sought in three areas – in the effects of socio-economic change in the countryside, in assaults on the clergy by their ideological enemies and, third, in the behaviour and attitudes of the clergy themselves. Although it will return to the first two explanations later, this paper will essentially concentrate on the third, for a case can be made that the clergy contributed substantially to their own unpopularity.

The role of the nineteenth-century village clergy was broad and varied. They acted as confidants, advisers and witchdoctors. They visited the old and sick, had a charity-role in the *bureau de bienfaisance*, helped supervise the village school, gave catechism classes, raised funding for upkeep of the church and came to organize *syndicats agricoles*, co-operatives, sports clubs. Many diocesan studies emphasize that a reasonable proportion of priests stayed for long periods in the same village without provoking serious conflicts. Many became respected as local historians and folklorists.

Yet 1789 had seriously weakened their position. They now faced in mayors and municipal councils rivals for village hegemony. The loss of church land and tithes deprived them of independent sources of wealth, making them dependent for their salary on regimes (such as those of 1830–48 or 1876–1914) which might view them with suspicion. Though recruitment, which had plunged alarmingly after 1798, rose rapidly from 1815 until the 1860s, this increase in vocations cannot obscure fundamental weaknesses. Increasingly priests were recruited from 'Catholic' regions (West, Massif Central) which were forced to 'export' priests to less devout regions. Seminarists were drawn from strata of the upper peasantry, artisanate and the petty-bourgeoisie. Frequently the choice of vocation was made not by the young man concerned but by his parents in alliance with the local curé, for (until 1905) the priesthood offered a safe, modestly lucrative career for sons of modest (rarely very poor) and large families. While Stendhal's portrait, in *Scarlet and Black*, of crude ambitious, ignorant seminarists attracted to their career only by its salary may appear to be the distortions of a fervent anticlerical, it is largely confirmed by Marcilhacy's study of the Orléans diocese. Mgr Dupanloup's efforts to improve seminary training to produce competent parish clergy had little success. The intellectual level remained poor. One answered the question in his circulated enquiry on whether marriages were always blessed in church by replying, 'Always – however there are some which are not.' Others got the local teacher to fill in the form for them. After a decade in his post, Dupanloup was still issuing orders to his priests not to 'cough, spit or wipe noses during Holy Mass, except during the singing of hymns'. His efforts failed to check the 'dechristianization' of the diocese. His priests remained out of touch with intellectual and political changes of the century, out of sympathy with the aspirations of their peasant parishioners for social improvement and education. Their seminary education provided them with little science, philosophy or modern history. Too often they viewed schools, roads, cafés and improved food as signs of the curse of 'materialism' rather than as 'progress'.

In the Restoration the bishop of Soissons expressed pleasure at the rise in clerical recruitment, but only with the qualification that he preferred to have 'the Lord's vineyard ploughed by donkeys rather than to leave it fallow'. All too often the clergy of nineteenth-century France appear bigoted, high-handed, puritanical and semi-educated. Faced with a range of new, tricky problems they lacked elementary tact and ability to compromise. Faced with undeferential mayors and villagers they became bellicose, obstinate. Singer emphasizes the vehemence of their letters to ecclesiastical or departmental authorities. Such verbal violence stemmed from resentment at the relative decline in their authority since 1789, mixed with a gnawing sense of intellectual inadequacy. They had a Manichean vision, dismissing their opponents as agents of the

Revolution or the Devil. One Vendomois curé in the 1860s argued that his rival, the mayor, called the Apocalypse a myth, 'speaks of the Virgin as a whore . . . says the Sun is his Father and the Moon his Mother,' in short, 'he serves the interests of Hell.' Verbal violence spilled over easily into physical assault, as in St Georges-des-Landes (Limousin) in 1862 when the curé attempted to strangle the mayor! Frequently village opponents were denied funerals or First Communion for their children.

Increasingly many curés behaved in a paranoid fashion induced by that growing sense of isolation captured in the novels of Bernanos or Hervé Bazin. Their erratic behaviour stemmed, in part, from a decline in church attendance, which it then accelerated. In the 1880s the secretary to the antisemitic propagandist Drumont, who blamed the Church's decline on pernicious Jewish influence, was a Loiret curé whose empty pews allowed him the free time to travel regularly to Paris. The virulent Catholic antisemitism of the 1880–90s stemmed from an attempt to avoid serious analysis of dechristianization by blaming it on a Jewish conspiracy which began with Christ's crucifixion. The mood of despair is reflected in the letter of one Saône-et-Loire priest in 1900: 'It is hard for a priest to live amongst a population which wishes to hear nothing of religious things. It is hard to see the church empty on Sunday, to find oneself spurned by the dying, rarely to give confession.'

Yet, faced with growing problems, the clergy exacerbated the situation by refusing to attempt any real self-critique. In 1850 clergy were blaming *cabarets*, evil books, Voltairean doctors for anticlericalism. By the 1890s they had added the Jews to their list. Few stopped to enquire if they themselves bore a share of the blame. In 1882 *Semaine Religieuse* of Albi was still claiming that 'in the priest there is something that is superior to man. To venerate the priest is to approach God.' Yet in this same decade Tarn peasants who shared little of the militant atheism of the socialist miners of Carmaux began to vote solidly for Ferry's laic Republic. For the clergy the whole world was out of step except themselves.

Undoubtedly the clergy's politics incited rural anticlericalism. The ties between Catholicism and royalism meant that religion became the ally of a political party and was recognized as such by its opponents, so that anticlericalism became a key element in the political consciousness of social groups who supported Republicanism. Conflicts engendered by resentment at the Legitimism of local curés served to politicize villages well before Eugen Weber's watershed decade of the 1870s when 'politics' allegedly came at last to the French countryside. Certainly it was then that

Gambetta swept the peasantry into the Republican camp by convincing them that royalism meant clericalism, a return to the horrors of feudalism and tithes. Yet the appeal of Bonapartism, particularly in central and south-western France, had rested on astute manipulation of similar rhetoric. During the *veillée* in Zola's *Earth*, a Bonapartist pamphlet is read aloud which portrays Louis Napoleon as guarding them against a feudal/clerical reaction. In 1867 in Bonapartist Dordogne there were riots protesting against the return of 'seigneurial' insignia on church pews. Conversely in the 1869 elections Dauphiné peasants refused to vote for Bonapartist candidates who had Legitimist-clerical family traditions.

This strand in peasant mentality was a constant factor in many regions across the century. In Avesnois (Pas-de-Calais) peasants who had acquired church lands provided a nucleus of village anticlericals who feared that a clerical-royalist regime might overturn the revolutionary land-settlement. In Haute-Saône in 1845 there were riots when clergy claimed rights to wood from the local forests. Fear of the tithes was exacerbated during the Restoration when the moral 'duty' to pay the tithe was smuggled into diocesan catechisms by returning émigré bishops. The fact that, as in the Isère in the Second Empire, some curés continued to pressure their parishioners into paying tithes kept alive old memories and fears which the Republicans exploited so effectively in 1876. In Treilles (Orléans) a report of the 1850s affirmed that 'people mistrust the priest whom they suppose to be dreaming of the tithes'.

The loyalty of village clergy to Legitimism derived in part from conviction, in part from financial dependence on royalist *notables*. This theme was endlessly reiterated by anticlerical writers from Stendhal to Zola. Julien Sorel in *Scarlet and Black* is advised by abbé Chelan to flatter the *chatelains* to further his ecclesiastical career. Though peasant small-holding and high religiosity did sometimes coincide, in general one could argue that religious practice *tended* to be lower in regions like the Limousin lacking a resident class of rural *notables* than in areas like the Sologne (Loiret) where landed aristocrats continued to pressure dependent sharecroppers and farm-servants. Clergy in Lower Languedoc were forced to rely increasingly for financing of schools and charities on a declining Legitimist élite – a dependence which increased their unpopularity in a region with left-wing sympathies. One frequent flash-point for local conflicts was denial by royalist clergy of 'rites of passage' to their opponents. Denial of church funerals to ex-Jacobins, *biens nationaux* purchasers, or to those who had undergone civil marriage ceremonies during the revolutionary years was commonplace. Agulhon has emphasized that in Provence such actions by the clergy against liberal lawyers active in defence of villagers' communal rights generated intense anger among populations who had a 'cult of the dead' and believed that even freethinkers had a 'right' to a 'proper' burial. At Barjols (Var) in 1847 a crowd of 200 forced open church doors and conducted their own funeral service. Similar disputes occurred in the Chartres diocese in the 1820s.

It is difficult to draw up a precise chronology of such disputes. Already by the 1820s there was a popular backlash against revivalist missions which combined religious evangelism with pro-Bourbon propaganda. Satirical pamphlets against these missions circulated widely in central dioceses. Since the missions had coincided with severe hailstorms which had destroyed peasants' crops, one rumour which circulated was that the missions were agents for insurance companies who 'send them into our countryside to terrify us and force us to take out insurance policies' against crop failure! During the revolutionary upheavals of 1830 mission crosses were torn down, clergy dared not appear in public in their *soutanes*, and many fled from their parishes. A glance at the archives of the July Monarchy suffices to show that many clergy refused to accept the verdict of '1830'. In the Vaucluse one curé physically assaulted a musician who played the *Marseillaise* at a village fete. In the Perpignan diocese Rosset found disputes in 48 villages as curés refused to accept the new regime, while mayors took revenge for clerical arrogance during the Restoration by denouncing priests as 'Carlists'. One curé, booed during mass, lifted his *soutane* to expose his backside to the congregation and then had his house stoned in the evening. Many villages petitioned the government in protest at curés who used the pulpit to denounce '1830'. The seminaries, said one Allier mayor, were 'spewing out fanatics'. In the Orléanais villages supported a movement led by the abbé Clavel which protested at the clergy's Legitimism, calling for tolerant priests in line with the 'needs of the century' and the 'liberal institutions of France'.

The prominence of religious rhetoric in the politics of reaction during 1849–51 forced the left into direct confrontation with organized religion. (However, for an analysis stressing the religiosity and populist egalitarian christianity of the left's own discourse see Ed. Berenson – *Populist Religion and Left Wing Politics in France 1830–52* (1984).) Undoubtedly most regions sympathetic to the '*Dem-Soc*' movement were already areas of declining religious practice, yet both Marcilhacy and Cholvy argue that it was the Second Republic which administered the *coup de grace* to what remained of clerical popularity in radical departments such as the Loiret or the Hérault. Cholvy interviewed a woman in the 1950s who explained that neither she nor her parents or grandparents had entered church since 1851 when the village curé betrayed her ancestor to the Bonapartist police! In the forested Gâtinais the breach widened between a rural clergy which preached acceptance of the *status quo* and woodmen, agricultural labourers and peasants who had been converted to 'socialism'. Local curés claimed that church attendances, already low, virtually collapsed. Significantly the one local curé in sympathy with left-wing ideas was moved from his parish by Mgr Dupanloup.

For a decade the clergy then revelled in their alliance with authoritarian Bonapartism, exploiting the Falloux Law to control rural education. Yet even in the 1850s the Bonapartist regime, aware of the need to maintain its image as defender of the peasant gains of 1789, was wary of too close identification with rampant clericalism, and at the village level anticlerical gestures were the one form of public protest allowed to defeated 'reds'. The Italian question after 1859 swung the pendulum against the clergy whose opposition to French intervention was highly unpopular. In Dauphiné churches emptied in protest at sermons defending the Pope's Temporal Power. In the still-Catholic Tarn in 1863 peasants voted for a (Jewish) Bonapartist candidate who promised local railway construction against a pro-Papal candidate backed by the clergy. In 1869, when Bonapartism tried to rebuild its relations with the Catholics to form an anti-socialist bloc, the damage had been done. The term 'anticlericalism' first came into general usage in the 1869 election campaign, with peasants voting for Republicans rather than for Bonapartist candidates suspected of clericalism.

The final clerical crusade came during the Moral Order years (1871–6) when the clergy, including 'liberals' like Mgr Dupanloup who had been sceptical of the wisdom of the *Syllabus of Errors* (1864), attempted to secure a royalist restoration. Their mood was militant. It was the culmination of two decades of clericalism marked by attempts to impose Catholic schools on reluctant municipalities, demands for money for village churches, manipulation of emotions aroused by 'miracles' like La Salette for royalist purposes and the crusade for the Temporal Power (T. Kselman, *Miracles and Prophecies in 19th-century France* (1983)). The clergy had, however, overplayed their hand. Many Frenchmen, traumatized by the Franco-Prussian war, viewed the clergy's obsessions with Rome as 'unpatriotic'. Gambetta's triumphs ended the threat of a royalist restoration. During 1876–80 countless village Republicans gleefully savoured their revenge. Republican municipalities banned religious processions, tore crucifixes from school walls, 'de-baptized' streets, erected statues of Marianne. In Pertuis (Vaucluse) '*Liberté, Égalité, Fraternité*' was engraved on the church door.

Nevertheless it would be misleading to claim that village anticlericalism was totally 'political'. One fundamental cause of friction between priests and villagers was the attempt by the clergy to purge religious practice of those 'pagan', 'superstitious' accretions with which it was tainted. The village priest derived much of his traditional authority from his role as magician. He was expected to ring church-bells to ward off thunderstorms, to bless livestock, lead processions to holy fountains to ensure good weather, to permit women to tie garters to bell-ropes to achieve fertility, to promote cults of local saints like St Roch who protected the community from disease. Villagers felt closer to 'their' local saints than to the God of the official church. Traditionally the clergy had pandered to such feelings. A diocesan enquiry in Blois (1840) found 39 village priests claiming that local *saints guérisseurs* had achieved miracle cures.

Peasant support for such 'natural' religiosity could coincide with religious ignorance, mediocre church attendance and latent anticlericalism. In the Gâtinais forest respect for the curé as 'sorcerer' and fear of werewolves coexisted with violent anti-clericalism and radical political sympathies. In the Narbonnais women prayed, 'St Salvare, give me a lover or I'll punch you on the nose.' Effigies of local saints were smashed if they had failed to 'deliver' good weather. By purging religious practice of such 'superstitions' the clergy, in Weber's apt metaphor, became engaged in chopping off the branch of the tree on which they themselves were perched. The impure collusion of religion, superstition and clerical venality in such practices aroused the derision of petty-bourgeois critics, vets, café-owners, teachers, village artisans. Yet the 'purification' of religious practice failed to appease such critics, who found in the *Syllabus of Errors*, Marian piety or the ultramontane cult of miracles ample evidence that the clergy were still in the vanguard of obscurantism. Yet many peasants were left confused, disorientated. In Mortemart (Haute-Vienne) there were riots in 1843 when the curé tried to remove the statue of a now-dubious local saint.

In 1866 a crowd of 4000 from 20 parishes gathered at Le Mouge to celebrate the feat of St Eutrope despite the refusal of local clergy to participate. At Bugnac (Haute-Vienne) in 1874, where the priest's refusal to participate in a procession to pray for good harvest weather had been followed by a violent hailstorm, the angry crowd which assaulted the *presbytère* shouted, 'Is it possible that priests who preach religion are seeking to abolish it?' In the Blois diocese in the 1840s clergy expressed regret that saints' *fêtes* attracted big crowds, for this led to drinking and 'debauchery', and applauded their demise. One curé wrote, of the cult of St Genou, 'I am the unhappy witness to a great superstition mixed up with, or to be more precise, which ends up in continuous dancing with all its scandalous consequences. I would, with all my heart, like to abolish it.' At Cordes (Tarn) in 1890 when the clergy boycotted processions for similar reasons, these were organized by the Republican municipality – a splendid example of shrewd anticlerical opportunism. By 1900, after decades of clerical indifference, the Creuse still had 100 'good fountains' to which villagers remained obstinately loyal.

It is dangerous to generalize on these issues. The Breton clergy acquiesced prudently to traditional practices to avoid alienating their parishioners, indeed often became the defenders of Breton language and traditions against the alien French. (Possibly 'folk Catholicism', already suspect in the eighteenth century, enjoyed a revival in the 1790s among counterrevolutionary peasants deprived, temporarily, of clerical control by the absence of priests? See O. Hufton 'The Reconstruction of the Church 1746–1801' in G. Lewis and C. Lucas (eds), *Beyond the Terror*, Cambridge University Press, 1983.) As the century developed clergy came to find unexpected virtues in local folklore as a barrier against French language and culture which came to appear the vehicles of Republican anticlericalism and materialism. Possibly the strength of clericalism in Basque, Breton and Flemish areas stem from the ability of the clergy to masquerade as champions of threatened regionalist traditions. By the last decades of the century Midi bishops like Mgr de Cabrières in Montpellier attempted to hold back the tide of dechristianization by encouraging 'patois' culture. Yet in much of Provence and Lower Languedoc this strategy came rather too late, for, earlier in the century, bishops in the Midi had been critical of popular religiosity, hostile to 'patois' catechisms. The archbishop of Marseilles in the 1860s had banned his clergy from preaching sermons in Provençal. De Cabrière's predecessors had been austere northerners, out of sympathy with the boisterous 'excesses' of the *confréries* whose sociability lay at the heart of southern culture. Attempts to stamp out drinking and dancing which accompanied the *confréries'* celebration of religious festivals weakened the hold of the church on male parishioners in the Midi. Subsequent attempts by clergy to erect new religious practices based on the cult of the Virgin, ultramontane piety and the organization of *Enfants de Marie* groups appealed largely to women. This 'feminization' of rural religion was by no means confined to the Midi. Mgr Dupanloup's enquiry into his Orléans diocese discovered that 67 per cent of girls attended mass, 20 per cent of married women, 3.8 per cent of adult males.

Many clergy ascribed this collapse of male religiosity to '*respect humain*'. In the Orléanais men refused to attend confession because 'the curé would dominate them, and they don't wish to be dominated in any way'. For young men First Communion was a 'necessary permit to enter the adult world' – and the last time they entered a church. Peasants 'regarded as slaves' sharecroppers of the big estates compelled by the *notables* to go to mass. In 1899 a correspondent to a Tarn newspaper wrote 'what a contemptible sight to see on a Sunday those men gathered in the village church under the vigilant eyes of their wives whom they have not been able to resist!' Anticlericalism may be viewed as an expression of *machismo*. Not only was churchgoing seen as diminishing manhood and independence, but the priest was viewed with suspicion as a rival to the husband, as a threat to a man's control over his womenfolk. In particular men resented the use of the confessional to ban birth-control, widely practised in the countryside to avoid subdivision of peasant landholding. The birth-rate in 'Catholic' Britanny remained high, while in 'dechristianized' Lower Languedoc it fell markedly. This raises a difficult chicken-and-egg problem. Did Midi *vignerons* become anticlerical because they practised birth-control against the wishes of the clergy, or did they feel free to practise birth-control *because* the hold of the clergy had already been weakened? It is clear, however, that clergy complained that confession declined because 'husbands raise objection to it'. One Carcassone diocese priest lamented in 1877 that 'this region produces wine in abundance, but is sterile in children'. The 'detestable practice of onanism' was a curse of the countryside. Complaining of the independence of his winegrower parishioners in Gaillac (Tarn), one priest denounced their habit of Sunday work and the 'greed' which 'pushes them to have only a single heir'. In the Orléanais there were reports in the 1850s of peasants beating their wives for going to confession, arguing that the priests used it 'to dominate the conscience of the commune'.

Attempts by the clergy to regulate sexual behaviour were symptomatic of a wider puritanical meddling with social life, though older complaints that clergy were hedonistic *bon viveurs* still surfaced. The bishop of Tulle (1862) claimed that some of his priests were 'drunkards and gamblers'. In 1902 one Breton teacher expressed belief that the curé's ceaseless war against local rabbits left him no energy to attack the laic school! Yet undoubtedly in the nineteenth century the balance shifted the other way. A standard ploy of anticlerical writers, from P.L. Courier in the Restoration to E. le Roy, the Périgord regional novelist, via the *Dem-Soc* propagandist Pierre Joigneaux in 1848, was to express nostalgia for the '*bon vieux curé*' of times gone by rather as socialists lament the demise of the 'good old Toryism' of Rab Butler! This paragon had been, at least in retrospect, wise, tolerant, flexible. Too often the younger, post-1815 clergy appeared puritanical, intolerant, meddling. The tone of seminary training was frequently 'Jansenist', negative, morose. Seminarists were taught to distrust pleasure, see the world as a vale of tears, dismiss earthly things as irrelevant. Since the world was corrupt, it was the priest's duty to preserve his flock from contact with it by creating a Christian ghetto.

The most spectacular outcome of clerical 'neo-Jansenism' was the crusade against village dances. During the Restoration P.L. Courier claimed that this was responsible for a 75 per cent fall in churchgoing in some villages. Whereas once the curé had not only tolerated but even inaugurated village dances, claimed the curé of St-Denis-en-Val (Loiret) in 1859, after 1815 attitudes had changed. The notorious curé d'Ars viewed dancing as the 'rope with which the Devil leads the most souls to Hell'. Priests in the Albi diocese were condemning dances in the diocesan enquiries of both 1835 and 1900. Even 'traditional' group dances became suspect because danced in the evening *veillées* which were unsupervised mixed-sex gatherings likely to release the pent-up animal sexuality of the young. However, particular venom was reserved for new 'erotic' dances. The Restoration Missions were already denouncing the waltz in 1820. With the 'truly satanic' polka, argued Père Marie-Antoine of Albi 'evil becomes absolute'. Female dancers were singled out for denunciation, for, according to this clerical killjoy, 'all (a woman's) life ought to be summed up in four words – pray, work, keep quiet and suffer.' In Aussac (Tarn) an irate curé bolted church doors to stop villagers using church benches at the local ball. Musicians and dancers were excluded from the sacraments. Villagers, who regarded dancing as a natural part of sociability and an integral stage in courtship, were bemused by the clergy's attitudes. When Saturday-night dances in rural *bourgs* became commonplace, priests preached against women who rode bikes to attend them. The ensuing peasant resentments had important consequences, providing one explanation for why the still-

Catholic peasantry of the Lavour region (Tarn) came to vote Republican, for, with all its faults, the Republican ethos accepted dancing as 'natural'.

Clerical puritanism caused villagers to derive glee from the clergy's own sexual misdemeanours. The idea, expressed in Zola's *Faute de l'abbé Mouret*, that the priest was outwardly ascetic but inwardly frustrated and obsessed with sex was widely shared. From the pamphlets of P.L. Courier onwards one can see a fascination with sexual offences committed by the clergy. Many men accused priests of deriving vicarious sexual gratification from their probings, during confession, into details of wives' sexual lives. Although diocesan archives are generally uninformative about sexual scandals involving the clergy, cloaking them in a veil of hazy rhetoric, spectacular cases often emerged for public scrutiny, as in the Saône-et-Loire in 1900 when a 'dirty pig' of a curé allegedly exposed himself before catechism pupils. In the Orléanais in the 1850s 'people go on repeating that the priest doesn't believe a word of what he teaches, and in preaching every Sunday he is simply doing his job and earning his money. As for morals, people are not afraid to say that if the priest succeeds in keeping to these in public, being a man he has the same passions as all other men, and seeks, like them, but secretly, to satisfy them. That is the opinion of the clergy held in the countryside.'

Nor was it merely dancing and sex which clergy denounced. Carnivals were treated with suspicion after their utilization by the 'reds' in 1848–51 as vehicles for mockery of ecclesiastical and bureaucratic dignitaries. In Pyrénées-Orientales, religious festivals were 'captured' and parodied by radical villagers during the Second Republic. The café, too, was suspect as a *contre-église* where peasants spent Sunday mornings discussing politics instead of attending mass. At Blandinières (Pyrénées-Orientales) in 1832 a Legitimist priest who tried to shut cafés and ban bowls was hounded from the village by a *charivari*. Many clergy in 1848–51 echoed Montalembert's demand for rural *cabarets* to be banned – an issue shrewdly publicized by the socialist *Feuille du Village* which accused priests of seeking to deprive the toiling peasant of his one chance in the week to have a drink, a smoke, a chat with his fellows. As the number of rural cafés grew, increasing by 23 per cent between 1873 and 1900, the laments of the clergy grew louder. Many priests accused mayors of supporting cafés to curry favour with their constituents rather than doing their 'duty' by enforcing sobriety.

Indeed the conflict of mayor and curé, immortalized in *Clochemerle*, lay at the heart of rural politics. The establishment of municipal councils and mayors challenged the hegemony of the curé who had hitherto kept local official records and acted as intermediary with the outside world. The mayor became *the* local figure of authority. His contacts with the sub-prefect made him an important distributor of official patronage, a pork-barrel wheeler-dealer able to secure the rural vote by adroit offers of recommendations for minor official jobs, café licences, hunting permits or by promises to build local roads. In Provence mayors clashed with village priests because they claimed the right to control local charity (the *bureau du bienfaisance*).

If much of the friction between mayor and curé resulted from petty squabbling over village hegemony, their conflict could acquire ideological overtones. The steady decline in the numbers of aristocratic mayors deprived the clergy of allies at the *mairie*. Orleanist mayors in the 1830s, Bonapartists in the 1860s or Republicans after 1876 could all be political rivals of Legitimist curés. Protests from mayors were responsible for many of the 3,500 displacements of parish priests in 1837 alone. Studies in the Vendômois and the Dauphiné have emphasized the extraordinary frequency of bitter battles over church-building repairs or the choice of school. Curés, regarding a restored parish church as a symbol of their prestige, sought to humiliate municipal councils by undertaking unauthorized repairs. Mayors, responsible for the payment of building contractors, in turn appealed to the penny-pinching avarice of their constituents. In extreme cases pro-mayor villagers tore down newly-finished church repairs. Each side would try to mobilize support from bishop, prefect and public opinion. Parish councils – chosen by prefect, mayor and curé – were often deeply divided. Paradoxically, as Zola suggests in *Earth*, anticlerical villagers who resented paying for the church frequently felt that their village would be slighted if the church were closed or the curé withdrawn, as some bishops threatened to do.

As market agriculture spread, and peasant appreciation of the uses of literacy grew, so mayors won support by suggesting that money would be more usefully spent on a school than on the church, and by hinting that a lay teacher would be better qualified to import useful knowledge and skills than were nuns and *frères*. Frequently mayors chose lay teachers because they feared that congregational teachers would be allies of the curé, while the *instituteur* would be the mayor's protégé who could save money by doubling as town-clerk.

The turning point in this long-running saga came in 1860. During the 1850s the clergy, revelling in the support of the regime, used their power to get mayors dismissed. The Italian issue allowed municipalities to fight back. *Elected* municipal councils, arguing that *they* represented village opinion, acted as schools of local democracy which helped to raise levels of political consciousness, hence paving the way for the 1876 Republican election triumph. At least one-third of the 108 villages in the Vendômois had conflicts between mayors, municipalities and villagers on one side and curés and Catholic notables on the other. Such conflicts appeared individually petty to the prefectoral authorities – but cumulatively they posed a threat to rural 'order'.

The 1876–1914 period marked the apogee of the hegemony of *Monsieur le Maire* – agent of the laic Republic, symbol of 'progress' and 'democracy' in the countryside, patron of the laic school, organizer of the 14 July festivities and of a network of laic school and sports associations.

Many of the disputes described above were triggered by quarrels over expenditure. Financial matters played a wider role in sustaining rural anticlericalism. Fear of the return of the tithes had already been discussed. Accusations that clergy overcharged for funerals and marriages were widespread. A proverb in south-western France suggested that the sound of the church-bells (*Donne! Donne! Donne!*) meant '*Give! Give! Give!*' Priests had no children, a large *presbytère*, and were obviously better-off than most villagers. The role of curés as moneylenders in the Limousin scarcely improved their reputation in a region where 'usurers' were detested by the peasantry. Peasants in the Loiret regarded the priesthood as a lucrative *métier*. One local priest argued that 'in the countryside, one is suspicious, jealous. The material well-being of the priest excites the envy of a poverty-stricken population which lives from day-to-day and eats black bread soaked in pools of sweat.' Pamphlets, such as *La Religion d'argent*, denouncing clerical avarice circulated in villages which, according to one priest, were 'ravaged by the most disastrous slander which Hell ever vomited onto Earth'. Disputes over funeral costs multiplied during the 1846–51 agrarian depression – as at Chalus where the priest scandalized the village by insisting on a widow's straw mattress as payment. Part of the implicit subversive appeal of Courbet's masterpiece *Burial at Ornans* stems, Tim Clark argues, from the painting's portrait of a well fed, red-faced curé presiding over a rural burial. Zola suggested, too, that villagers resented the speed with which priests hurtled through services for poor families. Many priests clung on to their control of charity in order to preserve their power over the old, the sick, the poor. The peasant farmers of the corn-growing Beauce, politically moderate and socially conservative, made pragmatic use of the 1848 revolution to demand cuts in church fees.

Thus attitudes and behaviour of the clergy were of fundamental importance in inciting or deepening rural anticlericalism. However, the clergy themselves cited socio-economic change and the attacks of their ideological enemies as explanation for their own declining influence. Many priests expressed relief that their villages were remote, with poor communications with the wide world of towns, markets, railways. Most local studies agree that a correlation *can* be made between low religious practice and areas of economic change and market-agriculture. In the Orléans diocese isolated, swampy, aristocrat-dominated Sologne retained high church attendance, whereas the commercial corngrowers of the Beauce, the winegrowers and boatmen of the Val de Loire were all more detached from the clergy. In the Tarn anticlerical winegrowing Gaillac contrasted with the Catholic Castres uplands. In Lower Languedoc the wine-plains experienced a rapid 'de-christianization' not shared by the uplands. In the Hérault wine areas practice was actually higher in towns like Montpellier than in the countryside. Undoubtedly in the Midi the rapid expansion of wine-monoculture was a crucial factor in changing mentalities. It brought *vignerons* into contact with towns like Béziers with their cafés, billiards, brothels and their politically radical strata of coopers and barrelmakers. The big wine-estates experienced absentee ownership and employed migrant labourers whose *déracinement* contributed to the decline in religious conformity. 'Since wine began to furnish them with so much cash, men no longer attend services, frequent cafés increasingly, and trips to towns, postponed till Sundays in order to avoid losing working hours during weekdays, contribute considerably to the "de-moralisation" of the countryside' lamented the curé of Angeliers (Aude). Round Béziers, where church attendance fell below 10 per cent and religious vocations slumped from 20 per thousand to 2.3 per thousand between 1826–46 and 1867–86, there was a local proverb, 'If our Saviour returned to Earth, it is the people of the Biterrois who would crucify him again.' The boom-slump economy of wine monoculture produced periodic economic crises (1846–51, 1875–90, 1900–10) which nurtured the radical political tradition of the Midi. Bishops were booed during episcopal visitations, 'anti-superstitious' Good Friday banquets were organized, *charivaris* mocked village priests and one lucky baby was 'baptized' Lucifer Blanqui Vercingetorix!

Among other regions of endemic anticlericalism were forest areas of central France where clergy found the *frondeur* spirit of lumbermen, charcoal-burners and wood-floaters impossible to control. Seasonal migration to building work in the cities eroded clerical influence in the remote Limousin. Corbin is cautious about 'blaming' the migrants for Limousin dechristianization, arguing that the clergy's obsession with their pernicious influence obscures other factors such as the weak presence of Catholic *notables*. Yet undoubtedly the migrants *did* help spread 'insubordination', birth-control practices and radicalism. Distaste for the suppression of the Commune, in which many peasant-masons were killed, dramatically reduced already weak religious practice after 1871, with some curés finding only the sacristan present during Mass, and 'systematic and reasoned impiety' stalking their villages.

How 'systematic and reasoned' was rural anticlericalism? Clearly much anticlericalism stemmed from pragmatic peasant resistance to specific clerical attitudes and frequently co-existed with residual Catholic belief. How important, then, were those ideological dangers which the clergy themselves denounced as major sources of their woes? Did freemasons, freethinkers, 'bad' books and newspapers, sceptical local *notables*, play a major role in disseminating anticlericalism? In the Orléanais in the 1830s one curé attributed the 'Voltaireanism which is sweeping our villages' to the 'authority, words, example of the big tenant-farmers, educated people, JPs, lawyers, doctors . . . which come to the aid of murderous doctrines.' Others blamed the flooding of the countryside by cheap editions of anticlerical pamphlets sold by *colporteurs*. In the Var radical ideas spread down to the peasantry via the 'cultural brokerage' of small town bourgeois. Such explanations are more plausible for the concentrated habitat of Provence than for the isolated villages of Limousin or the Tarn. Although masonic lodges and free-thought groups existed in the Tarn in the 1880s, they recruited largely petty-bourgeois and their wider influence was confined to artisans and to the miners and glassworkers of Carmaux. Their impact on the peasantry was small. On the other hand, in Burgundy *vignerons* were among the members of the numerous *libre-pensée* groups, while in Saône-et-Loire Goujon has described a whole network of Republican societies in the villages such as laic-school groups and sports groups sponsored by anticlerical *notables*. Macé's anticlerical educational pressure group, *Ligue de l'Enseignement* had considerable rural support for its lectures in the Yonne. In the Vaucluse masonic lodges helped shield the reviving Republic movement in the 1860s. During the 3rd Republic anticlerical regional newspapers (*Dépêche de Toulouse*; *Petit Méridional*) had wide circulation in the southern countryside.

It is difficult to assess the importance of the village *instituteur* in undermining clerical hegemony. Possibly the legendary teacher-curé rivalry may have been exaggerated. The conservative atmosphere of the *Écoles Normales* of the July Monarchy produced conformist teachers deferential to the clergy. In the 1840s in the Côte d'Or 94 per cent doubled as choirmasters. After a brief hiatus in 1848–51 when village teachers *were* active in the *Dem-Soc* movement, the Falloux Law purged radicals from the teaching corps and, as Flaubert observed in the scene of the humiliation of the village schoolteacher in *Bouvard et Pécuchet*, the teachers of the 1850s were frequently cowed and deferential. Mgr Dupanloup's clergy voiced few complaints about anticlerical teachers in these years. Even during the 3rd Republic many played little part in any direct assault on religion. In 'Catholic' upland areas of Lower Languedoc teachers tended to adapt to local mores, to conform to Catholic *rites de passage* to avoid giving offence. There is little evidence that the advent of the laic school led, *per se*, to a decline in religious practice.

Yet this is not the entire story. In an enquiry sponsored by the Bonapartist education bureaucracy in 1861 teachers expressed deeply-felt grievances against the interference of the clergy in village education. As the Bonapartist–Catholic split widened during the 1860s a spate of conflicts erupted in which teachers, often with support from villagers and with the tacit sympathy of *Université* inspectors, sought to stem the tide of clerical take-overs of schools and to ride the wave of peasant interest in 'useful' education, for, as improved transport opened up possibilities for commercial farming, schools could offer literacy to help peasants keep accounts while the chance of careers as postmen, rail-clerks, etc., began to expand for literate peasants. Teachers gradually supplanted the curé even in Catholic Brittany, not through any openly Republican/anticlerical propaganda but because they made themselves *useful* in the villages as scribes, tax-advisers, organizers of *syndicats agricoles*, and by getting their pupils to gain school-leaving certificates which offered career prospects. In so far as the clergy resisted these developments their prestige suffered. Many of Mgr Dupanloup's clergy, while endlessly complaining of the ignorance and brutality of their parishioners, feared education for, as one curé observed, 'the less they read, the less they will read bad books'. 'Our best people', another claimed, 'are those who know neither how to read nor write.' Many clergy suspected a correlation between literacy and irreligion, although religious sociologists have insisted that literacy was higher in Catholic Doubs or Flanders than in anticlerical Corréze or Allier.

However, school attendance *does* in general appear to have been higher before 1881 in 'blue', Protestant or anticlerical areas in the three departments recently studied by R. Gildea – Ile-et-Vilaine, Gard and Nord (R. Gildea *Education in Provincial France*, Oxford, 1983, pp.213–14). Yet already in the 1850s the farmers of the Beauce saw 'catechism [as] a waste of time', and argued that 'it is more worthwhile to learn to read, write and calculate'. In his memoirs of early twentieth-century Brittany Hélias recounts that his father nearly hit the local curé who pressured his wife to stop sending their son to the laic school.

In short, it was through gradual work in the countryside – rather than through anticlerical outbursts such as that of the teacher at Fitou (Aude) who in 1877 celebrated the Republicans' victory by smashing the school crucifix and throwing it in the latrine – that clerical influence was eroded. In the Tarn in the early 1880s there were conflicts in 80 villages as priests resisted the Ferry Laws. Fifty priests had their salaries suspended for electoral interference, some staged public burnings of laic textbooks. Yet all this clerical agitation failed to destroy the local peasantry's Republicanism.

Conclusion

What was the overall significance of rural anticlericalism? Initially it played a genuinely 'progressive' role. By undermining the power of the village curé, it weakened the power of reactionary royalist *notables*. Bitter disputes involving mayors, villagers and clergy in the 1850–76 period helped to sharpen the peasantry's political awareness. In time clerical/royalism was driven back into its bastions in parts of Brittany, the Vendée and the Massif Central. Too often, however, the beneficiaries of anticlericalism were simply the new bourgeois/Republican élites who were able to manipulate anticlericalism, as the old elites had manipulated religion, for their own ends. Bonapartism won peasant support by its shrewd awareness of peasant fears of a return to the Ancien Regime. Then anticlericalism became the semi-official ideology of the Republic, providing a *revolution à bon marché*, a useful rhetoric to persuade peasants to support 'progressive' bourgeois *notables* – often grain or wine-merchants, moneylenders – who offered the peasantry little social or economic reform during the agrarian depression of the 1880s. Republican *notables* sponsored a decorous village 'official' culture built upon laic school groups which took over from the clergy-dominated choral societies of the 1850s. Many departments in the central Loire valley, and in the south of the Parish basin 'red' in 1849, became simply moderate Republican in their politics, with politicians offering a spurious radicalism consisting largely of anticlerical rhetoric. Mesland's study of the *bourg* of Pertuis (Vaucluse) illustrates how mastery of anticlerical gestures kept bourgeois Radicals in control until the 1900s, despite the ravages of phylloxera on the local economy. In Loir-et-Cher socialists in the countryside retained loyalty to the Republic because of its anticlerical policies despite the fact that local Republicanism was dominated by businessmen and socially-conservative lawyers. In Lower Languedoc, hit by successive wine crises, anticlericalism proved a continued populist vote-winner which allowed Radicals to preserve their progressive credentials despite their ties with rural capitalism and big wine-merchants.

Thus if religion had once been the opium of the rural masses, anticlericalism could, in its turn, become the socialism of fools. Significantly, perhaps, in rural areas which became socialist bastions it was socio-economic not religious quarrels which now provided the focus for village politics. Anticlericalism, though strong, was now largely latent – a 'given' fact rather than the issue over which men fought. In the Var, as Tony Judt shows, the clergy were treated simply with 'absolute and almost disdainful indifference'.

Bibliography

Agulhon, M. (1982), *The Republic in the Village*, Cambridge University Press.

Bée, M. *et al.* (1976), *Mentalités religieuses dans la France de L'Ouest au XIXe et XXe siècles*, Caen, Annales de Normandie.

Cholvy, G. (1973), 'Religion et Société au XIXe siècle: le diocèse de Montpellier', *Information Historique*, 35, pp.225–31.

Cholvy, G. (1976), 'Indifference religieuse et anticléricalisme dans le Narbonnais au XIXe siècle', *Fédération Historique de Languedoc-Médit et du Roussillon*.

Corbin, A. (1975), *Archaisme et Modernité en Limousin au XIX siècle 1845–80*, Paris, M. Rivière.

Faury, J. (1980), *Cléricalisme et Anticléricalisme dans le Tarn 1848–1900*, Toulouse, Université de Toulouse-le-Mirail.

Gargan, E.T. (1978), 'Recruitment to the clergy in 19th-century France', *Journal of Interdisciplinary History*, no. 9, pp.275–95.

Hilaire, Y. (1963), 'La pratique religieuse en France 1815–78', *Information Historique*, no. 2, pp.57–69.

Hilaire, Y. (1977), *Une Chrétienté au XIX siècle? Le diocèse d'Arras 1849–1914*, Paris, Université de Lille.

Le Meur, M.V. (1973–4), 'Le culte des saintes dans le diocèse de Blois 1840', *Cahiers de l'Institut de la Presse et de l'Opinion*.

Marcilhacy, C. (1958), 'L'anticléricalisme dans le Loiret (1820–50s)', *Archives de Sociologie des Religions*, no. 6, pp.91–103.

Marcilhacy, C. (1963), *Le diocèse d'Orléans sous l'épiscopat de Mgr Dupanloup 1849–78*, Paris, Plon.

Marcilhacy, C. (1964), *Le diocèse d'Orléans au milieu du XIXᵉ siècle*, Paris (?), Sirey.

Mesliand, C. (1960), 'L'anticléricalisme à Pertuis', *Archives de Sociologie des Religions*, no. 10, pp.49–62.

Rosset, P. (1982), 'L'agitation anticléricale dans le diocèse de Perpignon au début de la Monarchie de Juillet', *Revue Historique*, no. 543, pp.185–204.

Silver, J. (1980), 'French peasant demands for popular leadership in the Vendomois (1850–90)', *Journal of Social History*, no. 14, pp.277–90.

Singer, B. (1983), *Village Notables in Nineteenth-Century France: Priests, Mayors and Schoolteachers*, Albany, State University of New York Press.

Tackett, J. (1982), 'The West in France in 1789; the religious factor in the origins of counterrevolution', *Journal of Modern History*, vol. 54, no. 4, pp.715–45.

Weber, E. (1979 edn), *Peasants into Frenchmen*, London, Chatto & Windus.

Zeldin, T. (1970), *Conflicts in French Society*, London, Allen & Unwin.

24
'Mary the Messiah': Polish immigrant heresy and the malleable ideology of the Roman Catholic Church in America, 1880–1930*

JOHN BUKOWCZYK

Roman Catholicism enjoyed far weaker ties to America's Polish immigrants than stereotypes have depicted. If the Poles' reputation for religiosity survived, it was not the persistence of pre-migration rural culture alone, but the success of a range of church strategies which reinforced – imposed and extended – habits of religious devotion among them. The creation of national (i.e., ethnic) parishes, the erection of a system of parochial schools, the introduction of Polish teaching nuns, and the spread of Marian mysticism all sought to counter unbelief. Such strategies and devices, however, were far less successful in combatting those who did not abandon religion tradition in favour of secularism, but instead opted for heresy. Against the latter, immigrant churchmen used the malleability of Roman Catholic Marian symbols as a means of keeping their immigrant co-nationals safely within the fold. Out of Marian mysticism they created what can be called 'Marian messianism'.

Two major heresies fractured the unity of Polish Roman Catholicism during the period of the partitions. The first grew up in the 1830s as Polish nationalists came to blows with the Roman Church hierarchy over the thorny 'Polish question'. During that time, Rome's recognition of the Polish partitions inspired nationalist partisans like Poland's great Romantic poet, Adam Mickiewicz, to create a Romantic, radical Polish nationalist tradition, still distinctly Christian but, after the fashion of French liberal Catholic Hugues-Felicité-Robert de Lamennais (1782–1854), decidedly anticlerical. Called Polish messianism, Mickiewicz's heretical religious nationalism endowed the Polish nation with the mission of a chosen people whose tribulations and sufferings would redeem Poland and earn its resurrection. The resurrected Poland would herald the moral regeneration of the Universe and thus become the 'Christ of Nations' (DeChantal, 1974, pp.6, 9; Brock, 1960, pp.148, 157; Losskii, 1936, pp.20–1; Gardner, 1941, p.326).

Polish messianism passed out of vogue between the positivist 1860s and 1880s, but was revived by nationalist publicists late in the century. In an atmosphere of renewed nationalist ferment, it comes as no surprise that Polish messianic writings found a receptive audience among Poles who migrated to the United States during this period. Polish immigrants voraciously read Mickiewicz, Julius Słowacki, and other messianic poets whose works appeared excerpted on fraternal benevolent association calendars and almanacs and filled Polish language libraries. Polish messianism raised the nationalist ardour of working-class immigrants, but parenthetically also offered them a compelling alternative to the ideology of orthodox Roman Catholicism and to the domination of the clergy. Positing a mystical, visionary link between Poles and their God, Polish messianism resembled the

Marian mysticism espoused by the Polish sisterhoods. Indeed, Mary held a prominent place in the Polish messianists' devotions (Peterkiewicz, 1975, pp.64–5). But because Mary so much symbolized long suffering, docility, patience, humility, and above all obedience to the Church, the message of Marian mysticism was other-worldly, passive, and escapist – in short, hardly a suitable inspiration for a broader religious or political activism (Lewy, 1974, pp.253–4). The Polish messianists' mysticism therefore highlighted Jesus Christ, the Redeemer. Crucified or resurrected, Christ symbolized a religious involvement that was politicized and active. Polish messianism thus added a terrestrial purpose to orthodox Roman Catholic mysticism: Polish national liberation.

Between the 1850s and the 1880s, the church in Poland increasingly had absorbed some of the messianists' concerns – e.g., opposition to the partitioners – while some Polish clerics, principally from the Galician lower clergy, began to echo the messianists' calls for social justice (Wandycz, 1974, pp.136, 196, 226, 234). Doctrinally, however, Poland's church remained very conservative and, as noted, developed a pronounced Marian devotionalism – derisively termed 'Mariolatry' – which became a dual prop of the first and second estates – the clergy and the aristocracy (Winowska, 1956, passim). Polish churchmen remained thus preoccupied when the Western European church – in such varied countries as France, England, Italy, Germany, and Austria – was subsequently gripped by the diverse and eclectic movement for reform which came to be known as modernism. Peaking around 1900, Church modernists challenged ecclesiastical authority as centred in Rome, stressed the importance of revelation over dogma, sympathized with efforts at social reform, supported scientific research free from dogmatic constraints, and sought to have the Church come to grips with the undeniable facts of the modern rational world. Deeply absorbed in their own national religious affairs, Poles seem to have escaped these modernist influences during this period (Heaney, 1967, pp.991–5; Aubert, 1978, pp.186–203; Stefan, 1939, passim; Ranchetti, 1969, pp.9–67; Vidler, 1934, p.213; Reardon, 1970, pp.9–67). Yet despite the country's reputed theological retardation, it seems likely that some Polish clerics had to have been familiar with modernist ideas, given Poland's intellectual proximity to France and its geographical proximity to Germany. Immigrant priests might have been similarly exposed because of the English influences on Christianity in America (Daim, 1970, p.81; Vidler, 1934, pp.143–81; Vidler, 1970, pp.109–33). Meanwhile, social and economic change in Poland became an independent source for modernist-sounding thought.

Though difficult to characterize, the period's second major Polish heresy, the Mariavite movement, blended together conservative Marian devotional themes with reformist tendencies which in the West might have been termed modernist. At the outset, the religious revival that coalesced into the Mariavite movement differed little from other outcroppings of Marianism in nineteenth-century Poland. In 1888, a pious young Pole named Feliksa Kozłowska founded a small religious community, not unlike other female religious congregations which were spawned in post-insurrectionary Poland. By 1893, however, Kozłowska claimed to have had a series of revelations in which God showed her 'the universal corruption of the world . . . [and] the laxity of morals among the clergy and the sins committed by priests.' The doomed world's last chance for rescue was 'in the Veneration of the Most Holy Sacrament and in Mary's help'. To spread this doctrine God reportedly directed Kozłowska to help organize a congregation of priests aptly called the 'Mariavites' after their Marian devotionalism. God allegedly made Kozłowska the 'mistress and mother' of the Mariavite congregation. In good Marian fashion – viz., the Annunciation (Luke 1:26–38) – she replied, 'Behold! the handmaid of the Lord; be it unto me according to thy word' (Peterkiewicz, 1975, pp.10ff.; Appolis, 1965, pp.51–67; Stasiewski, 1967, pp.217–18).

The sect that Feliksa Kozłowska and Rev. Jan Maria Michał Kowalski, her later collaborator, founded was piously Marian, but it also explored themes that paralleled some of the modernists' concerns. Responding to contemporary social issues, the Mariavites challenged the authority of Rome, questioned the doctrine of papal infallibility, and criticized the clergy. They advocated a kind of religious democracy, replaced Latin with Polish in the liturgy, and – as they watched Poland changing around them – promoted new social service functions for a changing church that would cushion ordinary people from the shocks of Poland's social and economic transformation, e.g., mutual aid and savings associations, schools, commercial and agricultural co-operatives. Finally, they espoused a personal revelatory mysticism that shook dogmatic certitude. Whereas some modernists had reasoned that revelation was a more immediate, direct religious experience than dogma or other intellectual formulations of the faith, the Mariavites practised what they preached and lived the living faith. Because of the Mariavites' disobedience to episcopal authority and their mystical tendencies (but probably also because of their alleged sexual aberrations), Kozłowska and the Mariavite priests were excommunicated in 1906. Thereupon they opted for schism. At their peak, around 1911, the Mariavites gathered in as many as 200,000 adherents. If they were not clearly 'modernist' in orientation, in some ways they certainly could claim to be 'modern'. More a popular movement than an intellectual heresy as was Western European modernism, the socially active Mariavites showed particular strength in industrial centres of Poland like the coal-mining region of Silesia and the textiles city of Łódź, the 'Polish Manchester' (Peterkiewicz, 1975, pp.12–13, 35–7, 61, 119; Appolis, 1965, p.53; Aubert, 1978, p.193; Ranchetti, 1969, pp.157–8; Vidler, 1934, p.142; Stasiewski, 1967, pp.217–18).

No record of direct Mariavite involvement in the United States has surfaced; perhaps there was none. Yet a third heresy did arise among the Polish immigrants in the United States which shared a number of elements in common with the Mariavites, the modernists, and the Polish messianists. That heresy, the Polish National Catholic movement, emerged during the 1890s and early 1900s in the heavily Polish anthracite region of eastern Pennsylvania to produce the only major schism ever to split the Roman Catholic church in the United States.

The roots of schism in eastern Pennsylvania ran as deeply as the region's coal veins. Throughout the 1880s and 1890s, Polish demands for control of parish property and Polish-speaking priests had sparked intermittent local conflicts with Roman Catholic pastors and bishops throughout America, but because so many conservative urban bishops favoured an accommodation with the immigrant Catholics, most of these early fights did not result in the formation of schismatic churches, but in the founding of new Roman Catholic parishes led by the dissidents (Abel, 1924, p.19). In 1896, however, Poles in Scranton, Pennsylvania, who sought parishioner representation in the management of parish affairs, were sharply rebuked by their pastor and reprimanded by the local Irish bishop. With tensions mounting, dissidents asked Rev. Francis Hodur, pastor of a nearby Polish parish, for aid, and he advised them to build their own church. When the bishop refused to consecrate the new church unless they turned over the deed to the property, the insurgent Poles invited Hodur to defy episcopal authority and establish a dissenting parish. Therewith Scranton's working-class Polish immigrants passed the point of no return. In 1904, the conflict finally climaxed when what had formerly been an 'independent' or 'people's' church consolidated the ever-growing number of breakaway parishes in the region into the Polish National Catholic church, with Hodur himself eventually serving as bishop (Andrews, 1953, pp.17–20, 26–29, 31; Wlodarski, 1974, pp.21–3, 25, 181; Greene, 1975, pp.98, 113; Fox, 1961, p.28).

If Polish National Catholicism articulated working-class immigrant concerns, its success or failure ultimately would depend upon other more practical matters. The Polish National Catholics' insurgency was able to take root and spread because it circumvented the single greatest obstacle that often had thwarted Polish religious dissent, the Poles' religious tradition of sacerdotalism. The defection of legally ordained Polish Roman Catholic priests to the Polish National Catholic church and, more importantly, the legal consecration of Hodur as an Old Catholic bishop (which thus made him a part of the apostolic succession and empowered him to ordain new priests) now enabled excommunicated schismatics to acquire sacramental mediators who were religiously as valid as Roman Catholic clerics. The structure of the schismatic Polish National Catholic church thus fortuitously accommodated Polish religious tradition and produced a system of authority that conformed to the Poles' religious expectations. As for the underlying religious ideology that could legitimize the antecedent act of schism, Bishop Hodur sought a doctrine which would connect schismatic clerics directly to God, sidestep their episcopal or papal superiors, and command wide popular appeal. In fact, a suitable ideology was not hard to find, for only one such tradition of extra-institutional religious dissent had made a serious mark on nineteenth-century Poland and Polish America – Polish messianism. As a young seminarian in Cracow, Hodur had read all of Adam Mickiewicz's mystical poetry. With the founding of the schismatic church, he now built an institutional home for the heresy of Polish messianism (Wlodarski, 1974, p.39).

Three major messianic themes formed the centrepiece of Polish National Catholic doctrine. The first theme was a pointed anticlericalism. 'The Roman bishops,' Hodur wrote in 1928, 'greedy for power and domination over the whole world, withdrew from the people and ceased working the way the Apostles worked.' In the Polish National Catholic church, Hodur believed, 'Our measure of religion is our personal relationship to Jesus Christ, to the Holy Teacher.' 'The duty of every priest of the national church' is not self-aggrandizement, but 'to aspire to a surplus of justice' for the people (Hodur, 1928, pp.3–4). The Polish National Catholic priest still retained special authority in the spiritual and moral affairs of the parish and, accordingly, significant influence in its temporal affairs as well. But given the fact that intense struggle between parishioners and their priests had helped spark the schism, that temporal influence was deliberately curtailed. Management and administration of Polish National Catholic parishes passed largely into the hands of laymen, who also had a voice in clergy assignments. Church procedure abolished pew collections and required clerics to perform all sacramental services free of charge 'according to Jesus' injunction', unlike their Roman Catholic counterparts. Adult parishioners also were freed from the symbolically submissive act of individual confessions to particular priests, but instead could publicly confess their sins in a group at mass. Finally, the Polish National Catholic church denounced the Roman Catholic dogma of papal infallibility and instead expounded religious law at meetings of the General Synod of the church (Fox, 1961, pp.24, 82, 117; Andrews, 1953, pp.39, 42, 48, 69–70; Wlodarski, 1974, pp.109, 177, 188).

The schismatics' belief that the Roman Catholic clergy oppressed Polish working people revealed a second Polish messianic theme carried over into Polish National Catholic doctrine: progressive social politics. Hodur's political consciousness had been influenced by 1890s Galician populism, a radical agrarian movement which had inherited democratic traditions popularized by Polish Romantic nationalists in the 1830s. During the schismatic ferment in eastern Pennsylvania, the Polish National Catholic church shaped these progressive social concerns around the needs of Polish anthracite miners and incorporated them into church docrine. Polish National Catholicism sought to become a working-class religion, to provide an active social ministry to Polish labouring people, and 'to defend the interests of the oppressed and down-trodden' (Wlodarski, 1974, pp.40–1, 50). Church doctrine thus embraced egalitarianism. In it, Christ was 'the leader, teacher and friend of the poor, spurned disinherited . . . masses of the nation'. Indeed, the poor formed an integral part of the religion (Hodur, 1966, p.13). The Polish National Catholic church's liturgical calendar featured a Feast of the Poor Shepherds, which 'signifies, through the visit of the shepherds to the infant Christ, the part played by poor and homeless people . . . in helping to make known God's love to mankind' (Andrews, 1953, p.60). Not surprisingly, the church also promoted the interests of the downtrodden through temporal activities. For example, unlike the local Roman Catholic parishes, the church sided with Polish working people after the 1897 Lattimer Massacre and during the 1900 and 1902 anthracite strikes (Greene, 1968, pp.141, 155, 183; Buczek, 1974, p.154; Wieczerzak, 1983, pp.5–35).

However central anticlericalism and social progressivism were in Polish National Catholic ideology, a third theme became the wellspring of legitimacy for the schismatic religion. That theme was messianic Polish nationalism. Like its messianic forebears, the Polish National Catholic movement inverted Roman Catholic symbolism. It shifted symbolic focus away from the crucified Christ or the merciful Mary, with their passive, long-suffering connotations; and it discarded religious devices like pilgrimages, indulgences, relics, and Marian scapular medals which the Roman Catholic church had used to control the faithful (Wlodarski, 1974, pp.187–8; Fox, 1961, p.49). Instead, Polish National Catholics emphasized Christ resurrected and ascendant. By further shifting emphasis to Christ's glorious Second Coming, the apocalyptic Millennium contained in the Book of Revelation, the Polish National Catholic church transformed the text that Roman Catholic theologians had used to promote belief in the Immaculate Conception of Mary into a tract with revolutionary political implications for the Christian person and the Polish people (Lewy, 1974, pp.39–41). Drawing on the religious legacy of Roman Catholic mysticism, the Polish National Catholic church envisioned that spiritually reawakened individuals would come 'nearer to God' in a personal, direct, unmediated way (Hodur, 1966, pp.7–9). But by focussing on Jesus the Messiah, the risen Christ, the Polish National Catholic church, unlike its Roman Catholic counterpart, counselled not passivity, but action; not obedience, but initiative; not denial, but affirmation.

The resurrection allegory and apocalyptic promise contained in Polish National Catholic ideology pointedly applied to Poland, for Polish National Catholicism tried to become the messianic religion of the oppressed Polish nation (Fox, 1961, p.90; Hodur, 1966, p.13). Practice throughout the church stressed Polish nationalism. One of Hodur's first acts when he broke completely with Rome in 1900 was to replace Latin with Polish as the language of the mass. In 1904, the church opened a seminary which it named Bartosz Głowacki House, in honour of the Polish peasant hero who fought under Kościuszko at the celebrated Battle of Racławice. In 1914, the Polish National Catholic church synod added a feast to the liturgy, the Feast of the Polish Homeland. Among the Polish national heroes that church holidays honoured were the three Polish messianists – Zygmunt Krasinski, Julius Słowacki, and Adam Mickiewicz – and the Polish Romantic nationalist poet, Marja Konopnicka (Wlodarski, 1974, pp.71–2, 90, 103; Andrews, 1953, pp.60, 74).

Though the Polish National Catholics adopted a religious

organization that had a distinctly congregational look, it seems that contact with American Protestantism and exposure to American political institutions exerted little if any influence on this Polish religious and social movement (Smith, 1971, pp.214–49). To the contrary, Polish National Catholicism arose from the circumstances and conditions Polish immigrants faced in industrial America and drew upon intellectual and ideological traditions indigenous to the Polish group. The Polish National Catholics' ties to Polish messianism are palpable. Hodur's theology, however, also evoked some of the concerns of the Roman Catholic modernists – viz., opposition to the doctrine of papal infallibility, commitment to social reform, criticism of the clergy. Moreover, some of the intellectual antecedents of both movements were similar. Both were linked to the French reformer Lamennais, modernism indirectly through liberal Catholicism, Polish National Catholicism directly through the Polish messianists. Also, Hodur had formal ties and the modernists informal connections with the anti-papal Old Catholic church (Vidler, 1934, pp.22–3, 235–6; Schroeder, 1969, pp.13–46). Still, despite these points of concourse with modernism, Polish National Catholicism in the United States shared more in common with Poland's Mariavite movement. Reflecting late nineteenth-century social change, both movements democratized religious practice, attacked papal authority and Roman Catholic dogma, invoked Polish messianic symbols, promoted social service, and drew their strength in industrial areas (Appolis, 1965, p.58). Perhaps it comes as no surprise, then, that the Polish National Catholics and the Mariavites developed some institutional links, however transitory. The Mariavites briefly co-operated with the Polish National Catholics, until a quarrel between Mariavite leader Jan Michał Kowalski and Hodur drove them apart. One Mariavite priest, Szczepan Żebrowski, broke with the sect and emigrated to the United States where he reportedly was consecrated as a Polish National Catholic bishop. Finally, it should be recalled, both Hodur and Kowalski themselves were consecrated bishops by Old Catholic bishops in Utrecht (Peterkiewicz, 1975, pp.39, 44–5; Appolis, 1965, pp.53, 59; Greene, 1975, p.113).

It is impossible to gauge how quickly – or deeply – adherents to the new church embraced these doctrinal innovations. In terms of sheer numbers, however, the church's partisan stance paid off during the World War period, when Poland was 'resurrected'. The rising tide of left-wing Polish nationalism boosted church membership in the United States to between 60,000 and 85,000 members by 1925–6 (Wlodarski, 1974, p.117; Fox, 1961, pp.62–3;

Kubiak, 1970, p.134). Even so, the success of Polish National Catholicism fell far short of the leaders' more sanguine expectations, for it never became the official church of Poland nor the majority religion in Polish America. In part this resulted from the church's own institutional limitations. In part, however, it also resulted from popular religious conservatism. Tradition dies hard, and given the nature of Polish peasant religiosity – the centrality of magic, sensualism, and ritual in Polish rural religious practice and the longstanding association between Roman Catholicism and Polish national identity – there are reasons why the Polish National Catholic church might have had only modest appeal despite its attempts to attract working-class communicants (Piwowarski, 1971, passim).

But Polish National Catholicism also found that it had to reckon with a determined Roman Catholic opposition which likened the heretical Polish nationalist challenge to assorted secular threats it had faced and took decisive steps to outmanoeuvre it during those turbulent years. Polish Roman Catholic priests branded the nationalist schismatics 'pagans', 'heathens', 'atheists', 'revolutionaries', 'lawbreakers', and 'heretics' (*Nowy Świat*, 21 September, 19 October 1922). Moreover, given the nature of patronage and clientage networks in immigrant settlements, National Catholic dissenters also faced economic and social sanctions because of their religious secession. But Polish National Catholicism threatened the Roman Catholic church, it should be noted, because it made a persuasive and compelling ideological argument. The Roman Catholic church therefore also met the schismatics' thrust with an artful ideological parry.

Though Polish National Catholicism attacked the authority of the entire American church hierarchy, it fell to Polish-American priests, who held day-to-day responsibility for Polish immigrant religious affairs, to counter the schismatic insurgency touched off by their immigrant co-nationals. Many Polish priests themselves had participated in Polish nationalist politics. Shunning heresy but none the less attempting to bend Roman Catholic orthodoxy to fit Polish political requirements, they succeeded in fashioning an ideology with such wide appeal in Polish America that it stole the schismatics' rhetorical thunder. Cleverly merging formerly incompatible iconographies, they took the messianic elements of the Polish Romantic nationalist tradition and harnessed them to the Roman Catholic church's hegemonic symbol system, Marianism. The resulting fusion might be called 'Marian messianism'.

In the history of the Church, there was another side to the docile, long-suffering Mary. Mary was a splendidly malleable symbol who elicited submission to the Church, but also invoked resistance against its foes. Nowhere was Mary's dual nature more pronounced than in Poland. During the Middle Ages, Polish knights sang a hymn to the Blessed Virgin Mary before battle, and Mary's miraculous martial role recurred frequently thereafter. Poles defending the monastery at Jasna Góra against an invading Swedish Protestant Army in 1655 raised the icon-like image of Our Lady of Częstochowa before the enemy force and, it was claimed, saw the siege miraculously lifted (Bilda, 1948, pp.17–18, 20, 22–3, 25–6, 123–4; Slowiak, 1950, p.63; Helm-Pirgo, 1966, p.27; Stefan, 1939, pp.100–1; Dabrowska, 1946, p.129). After that victory, Poland's King John Casimir named the Blessed Virgin Mary as Queen of the Polish Crown. Henceforth, too, the Galician town of Częstochowa became a popular pilgrimage site and patriotic Poles forevermore would associate a feminine Poland with her patron, the Blessed Mother. Marian martial usages thus continued. At the Polish relief of Vienna in 1683, the battle cry of Jan Sobieski's forces as they charged the Turkish host was Marian, 'In the name of Mary, help us, Lord God!' (Winowska, 1956, p.696). A century later Poles who joined Kościuszko's insurrectionary army to fight for Polish freedom in the 1790s reputedly wore Marian scapular medals, given to them by wives, sisters, mothers (Bilda, 1948, p.58; *Dziennik Chicagoski*, 4 April 1894). By the period of the partitions, Mary clearly had become Poland's foremost nationalist emblem.

In all of these instances, perhaps Mary merely functioned as any mother would, protecting her imperilled children. But the Cult of Mary contained elements that went beyond the Blessed Mother's traditional protective, maternal, nurturing role. It contained elements that imputed redemptive attributes directly to her. This occurred as early as the Middle Ages when Mary was identified with Jesus through such devices as the doctrine of Mary's compassionate martyrdom and the 'Cult of Sorrows' to which it gave rise. In it, Mary was believed to have felt all the suffering from the tortures that Jesus was to experience (Warner, 1976, p.218). The image of Mary promulgated by the 'cult of sorrows' it spawned thus featured many of the same elements attributed to Christ's martyrdom – pierced heart, bloody tears, crown of thorns – and Mary became a redemptive figure in her own right.

The Blessed Virgin Mary's 'co-operation with Jesus in redeeming mankind' came to be known as the doctrine of 'coredemption'. In it, Mary became a coredeemer, wholly dependent upon Christ, but in perfect spiritual union with him. 'By her compassion,' Roman Catholic theologians granted, 'Mary comerited for man all that Christ merited by His Passion' (Horak, 1967, pp.323–4). The Polish Resurrectionist Fathers, who dominated immigrant religious affairs in Chicago, embraced the mystery of coredemption in the devotional life of their congregation. Poland's Mariavite sect also celebrated the doctrine of coredemption but carried it to the point of heresy, when the sect's foundress, Feliksa Kozłowska, lost herself in revelatory mysticism, when her followers styled her a second Virgin Mary or Mary reincarnate, and when the Mariavites defied the authority of the Roman pontiff (Winowska, 1956, p.704; Appolis, 1965, pp.57, 59).

Significantly, when Roman Catholic churchmen and their lay partisans plunged into Polish nationalist politics in the late nineteenth century, they too drew upon the doctrine of co-redemption and the symbolism of the Cult of Sorrows: a Mary-like Poland compassionately suffered a Christ-like martyrdom. A long address delivered at a Chicago Polish nationalist demonstration in 1895 typified this new ideological genre. Poland, one speaker intoned, is 'nailed to a cross'; 'its hands and feet tied', it 'cannot shed its fetters'.

> You, our beloved mother, be glorified the more through your poverty, martyrdom and defamation, for all these will help make a crown [viz., of thorns] for your glorious head.
> (*Dziennik Chicagoski*, 2 December 1895)

The Chicago speech once again made it abundantly clear that Marianism could be readily changed from a submissive doctrine into an ideological weapon. Marianism thus became messianic, as Mary shed part of her meekness and acquired active, mystical redemptive powers, similar to Christ's but virtually independent of his. Like the Marianism of the Mariavites, this bordered on heresy. But like the Marianism of the Resurrectionists and the various Polish sisterhoods – that is to say, like orthodox Marianism – it stayed safely on this side of the invisible, indelible line that defined the bounds of acceptable religious belief and practice. Marian messianism, however mystical, did not challenge the authority of the Pope or his bishops, did not undercut the institutional church. To the contrary, Mary the Messiah enabled the church to bridge the gap between piety and modernity. A political redeemer but not a religious one, she allowed the church to extend its ideological influence into the relatively alien sphere of aggressive Polish nationalist politics.

As this turn widened the secular political influence of Polish Roman Catholic churchmen, it also placed them on a collision course with the schismatic Polish National Catholics. With war impending in Europe, in December 1912, Polish immigrant factions patriotically resolved to close ranks in a Committee for National Defence (Komitet Obrony Narodowej, abbreviated K.O.N.). While the Polish Roman Catholic clerical leadership pushed to give this body a Roman Catholic cast, Polish National Catholic leaders insisted on an equal role, for not to have done so would have belied the purpose of their schismatic movement. Clearly, K.O.N. could not contain two Polish churches with equal ambitions yet diametrically opposed claims to legitimacy and political programmes. When a vote for seating the schismatic Polish National Catholics split evenly, the resolution was moved that representatives of the Roman Catholic Alliance of Polish Priests also be excluded. Incensed, the Roman Catholic clerical faction bolted from the meeting and formed its own organization, the Polish National Council (Polska Rada Narodowa) (Stefan, 1939, pp.58, 63–4, 100; Buczek, 1974, p.48; Renkiewicz, 1973, p.16; Galush, 1974, pp.111, 211–12; Pliska, 1955, p.82; Buczek, 1976, p.55). Thus engaged, Polish Roman Catholic prelates and their proclericalist partisans also raised the tempo of ideological warfare against their leftist and schismatic opponents. At their disposal was the entire Marian messianic symbology.

During the next ten years, a messianic Mary became the central ideological symbol of Polish Roman Catholics involved at home and abroad in Polish nationalist politics. A Polish political poster published for a Polish-American convention in Buffalo, New York, in 1914 solidified the image of the 1895 Chicago speech by depicting a seated woman, chained and crowned with thorns, who represented the shackled, martyred, Mary-like Poland (Waldo, 1974, p.184). In the Polish Army's training camp at Niagara-on-the-Lake, Canada, at the start of the First World War Polish immigrant troops sang the Polish anthem, 'Boże Coś Polskę' (God Who Helped Poland), beneath a flag that bore an image of the Blessed Virgin Mary (Stefan, 1939, pp.138–9; Waldo, 1953, p.187). Donors to the campaign to raise money for the Polish Army in France, a fund drive conducted by the immigrants' proclerical, conservative leadership, received prints of Ladislaus Benda's painting in which the Blessed Virgin of Częstochowa united the three Polish partitions – redeemed them – and blessed Polish-American troops speeding to battle (Pliska, 1955, p.248).

In Poland, too, messianic Marian symbols filled Polish Roman Catholics' ideological arsenal. A huge nationalist demonstration in Cracow in 1910, commemorating the five-hundredth anniversary of the victory over the Teutonic Knights at the Battle of

Grünwald, featured the mass singing of the medieval hymn to the Blessed Virgin Mary, 'Bogu Rodzica' (Mother of God) (Stefan, 1939, pp.100–1). But the best example occurred ten years later when General Piłsudski, an anticlericalist and moderate socialist, defeated an invading Bolshevik army on the outskirts of Warsaw on the banks of the Vistula River. The battle took place on 15 August 1920, the Roman Catholic Feast of the Assumption of the Blessed Virgin Mary; to counter Bolshevik antireligious propaganda and to neutralize Piłsudski's political gain from the victory, Polish rightists, noting the date, ascribed victory to Mary's miraculous intervention and dubbed the triumph '*Cud Wisły*', 'the miracle on the Vistula' (Wandycz, 1969, p.241). The Pope soon followed suit. By designating 3 May as the Feast of the Queen of Poland, the Pope shrewdly turned the anniversary of Poland's revolutionary Constitution of the Third of May (1791) into a Polish national holiday to honour Mary, Poland's Saviour (Bilda, 1948, pp.58, 131).

Thereafter, Roman Catholic churchmen – both immigrant and American-born – alternated Marian themes according to circumstances and situation. As the political excitement of the early 1920s subsided, Marian messianism easily yielded to the Roman Catholic church's time-honoured ideological mainstay, Marian mysticism, which continued to serve a hegemonic function. Here, the highlights of devotional life in one Roman Catholic parish in New York are instructive. In the early 1920s, the Vincentian Fathers, a missionary order devoted to Marian mystical doctrine, assumed control of Brooklyn's Saint Stanislaus Kostka parish. In 1926, the new pastor returned from a visit to Rome with a relic of Saint Theresa of the Infant Jesus, a recently canonized nun, and instituted regular devotions to this Marian figure. With the outbreak of the Depression and amidst the rising tide of Marianism, in autumn of 1920 the parish celebrated the hundredth anniversary of the apparitions of Our Lady of the Miraculous Medal to Catherine Labouré, a Daughter of Charity, while the same year a Saint Theresa Society was formed there. In 1934, as the Depression deepened, Marian mystical devotions reached a new height when the parish received a gift painting of the popular Saint Theresa from artist Tadeusz Styka (*Saint Stanislaus Kostka*, pp.42–3, 84). Needless to say, Marianism was not confined to this one parish during the period. Since 1931, New York Poles also encountered Marian radio broadcasts, as Father Justin Figas of Buffalo, New York, began his syndicated 'Rosary Hour' (Buczek, 1974, p.111; Figas, 1934–44–46).

As Marian mysticism helped contain popular ferment in the

1920s and 1930s, Marian messianism once again helped mobilize Polish Roman Catholics during the following decade. In September 1939, over four decades after the female image of a martyred Poland had gained ideological currency in the United States during the Polish nationalist agitation in the 1890s, Poland once again endured an hour of national crisis. As Nazi and Soviet armies overran their homeland, Poles in America rallied anew behind familiar ideological banners – messianic and implicitly Marian. In one newspaper advertisement printed in November 1939, a thorn-crowned, shackled woman, dressed in royal robes bearing a Polish coat-of-arms, sat beside a thorn-framed visionary panorama depicting the devastated Polish countryside (*Czas*, 24 November 1939). A political cartoon of similar vintage was even more striking. The cartoon showed a blood-stained sword bearing swastika and hammer-and-sickle markings, plunged into a Polish city's smoking ruins. A peasant woman, labelled 'Poland', hung from the hilt of the sword: the woman was crucified (Waldo, 1953, p.242).

In the nineteenth and early twentieth centuries, Roman Catholic churchmen had tried a variety of approaches to hold on to communicants whose faith they could no longer take for granted. Lacking the support of a devout landed gentry that had sustained it in Europe, the Roman Catholic church still had to seek for new secular allies that could bolster it against the strains of a modern American society locked in the throes of industrial growth and urban change during the period. At the diocesan level, native-born bishops made overtures to industrialists and they in turn reciprocated, recognizing, as William Howard Taft remarked, that the church formed 'one of the bulwarks against socialism and anarchy in this country'. At the parochial level, immigrant pastors courted local factory managers and eventually worked out a modus operandi with middle-class parishioners who became pillars of their communities and mainstays of the ethnic parishes (Cross, 1967, pp.34–5; Bukowczyk, 1980, pp.239–56, 270–7).

But despite these secular props, in American factory districts religious practice simply could no longer be coerced as in manorial Europe. To be sure, religion could still serve a powerful function in working-class lives, but in order to do so that religion necessarily had to change to accommodate the needs of men and women who had entered the urban, industrial world. Meanwhile, changing pastoral and clerical style also tried to conform to the changing sensitivities and identities of working-class parishioners (Buczek, 1982, pp.20–36). The changing composition of the clergy also fitted working-class parishes more closely, as peasant, working-class, and lower middle-class sons began to enter the priesthood on both sides of the Atlantic (Bukowczyk, 1982, pp.45–6; Ciupak, 1965, p.401). Yet perhaps most important were the political moves that churchmen undertook to keep the allegiance of working-class immigrants. The malleable Marian symbols which they used fired immigrant hearts, excited their minds, and preserved their souls in the bargain. Marian ideology operated as a mechanism of control. But it also worked as a militant engine. In both roles, it powerfully countered erosive secular ideologies and dangerous heresies wielded by anticlericalists of all political persuasions.

Notes

* Abridged version reprinted from the *Journal of American Ethnic History* 4 (Spring, 1985). Permission of the editor is gratefully acknowledged.

Versions of this article were presented at the 1980 meeting of the Organization of American Historians in San Francisco and the History Workshop on Religion and Society, held during July 1983, in London. I wish to thank Ronald Bayor, Stanley Blejwas, Christa Walck, Christopher Clark, Stephan Thernstrom, Mark Stolarik, Victor Greene, Christopher Johnson, Daniel Buczek, and the members of the conference panels for their helpful discussion, suggestions, and comments at various stages in its preparation. I would also like to thank Veronica Plewa for typing the abridged manuscript.

Abel, T.F. (1924), 'The Poles in New York: A Study of the Polish Communities in Greater New York', M.A. thesis, Columbia University.

Andrews, T. (1953), *The Polish National Catholic Church in America and Poland*, London, SPCK.

Appolis, E. (1965), 'Une Église des Derniers Temps: L'Église Mariavite', *Archives de Sociologie des Religions*, vol. 10, pp.51–67.

Aubert, R. (1978), *The Church in a Secularized Society*, tr. J. Sondheimer, New York, Paulist Press.

Bilda, H.L. (1948), 'The Influence of Częstochowa on Polish Nationalism', M.A. thesis, St John's University.

Brock, P. (1960), 'The Socialists of the Polish "Great Emigration"', in A. Briggs and J. Saville, eds, *Essays in Labour History in Memory of G.D.H. Cole 25 September 1889–14 January 1959*, New York and London, MacMillan and St Martin's Press.

Buczek, D. (1974), *Immigrant Pastor: The Life of the Right Reverend Monsignor Lucyan Bójnowski of New Britain, Connecticut* (1974), Waterbury, Conn., Heminway Corp.

Buczek, D. (1976), 'Polish-Americans and the Roman Catholic Church', *Polish Review*, vol. 21, pp.39–61.

Buczek, D. (1982), 'Three Generations of the Polish Immigrant Church: Changing Styles of Pastoral Leadership', in S. Blejwas and M.B. Biskupski, eds, *Pastor of the Poles: Polish American Essays*, New Britain, Conn., Polish Studies Program Monographs, No. 1, Central Connecticut State College, pp.20–36.

Bukowczyk, J.J. (1980), 'Steeples and Smokestacks: Class, Religion, and Ideology in the Polish Immigrant Settlements in Greenpoint and Williamsburg, Brooklyn, 1880–1929', Ph.D. diss., Harvard University.

Bukowczyk, J.J. (1982), 'Factionalism and the Composition of the Polish Immigrant Clergy', in S. Blejwas and M.B. Biskupski, eds, *Pastor of the Poles: Polish American Essays*, New Britain, Conn., Polish Studies Program Monographs, No. 1, Central Connecticut State College, pp.37–47.

Ciupak, E. (1965), *Kult Religijny i Jego Spoleczne Podłoże: Studia nad Katolicyzmem Polskim*, Warsaw, Ludowa Społdzielnia Wydawnicza.

Cross, R.D. (1967), *The Emergence of Liberal Catholicism in America*, Cambridge, Mass., Harvard University Press.

Czas (Brooklyn, N.Y.), 24 November 1939.

Dabrowska, M.A. (1946), 'A History and Survey of the Polish Community in Brooklyn', M.A. thesis, Fordham University.

Daim, W. (1970), *The Vatican and Eastern Europe*, A. Gode, tr., New York, Frederick Unger.

DeChantal, Sr M. (1974), *Out of Nazareth: A Centenary of the Holy Family of Nazareth in the Service of the Church*, New York, Exposition Press.

Dziennik Chicagoski (Chicago), 4 April 1894, Reel 56, III, B3a, IIH, IG, Chicago Foreign Language Press Survey.

Dziennik Chicagoski (Chicago), 2 December 1895, Reel 56, III, B3a, Chicago Foreign Language Press Survey.

[Figas], Justyn [M.]. (1934–1947), *Mowy Radiowe, 1931–34 – 1944–1946*, 8 vols, Milwaukee, Wis., Nowiny Pol.

Fox, P. (1961), *The Polish National Catholic Church*, Scranton, Pa., School of Christian Living.

Galush, W. (1974), 'American Poles and the New Poland: An Example of Change in Ethnic Orientation', *Ethnicity*, vol. 1, pp.209–21.

Gardner, M. (1941), 'The Great Emigration and Polish Romanticism', in W.F. Reddaway *et al.*, eds, *Cambridge History of Poland*, 2 vols, New York and London, Cambridge University Press, vol. 2, pp.324–5.

Greene, V.R. (1968), *Slavic Community on Strike: Immigrant Labor in Pennsylvania Anthracite*, Notre Dame, Ind., Notre Dame University Press.

Greene, V. (1975), *For God and Country: The Rise of Polish and Lithuanian Ethnic Consciousness in America, 1890–1910*, Madison, Wis., State Historical Society of Wisconsin.

Heaney, J.J. (1967), 'Modernism', in *New Catholic Encyclopedia*, New York, McGraw Hill, vol. 9, pp.991–5.

Helm-Pirgo, M. (1966), *Virgin Mary Queen of Poland (Historical Essay)*, New York, Polish Institute of Arts and Sciences in America.

Hodur, F. (1928), 'Doctrines of Faith of the National Church', lecture given at the Warsaw Synod, typewritten translation.

Hodur, F (1966), *Our Faith*, T.L. Zawistowski and J.C. Zawistowski, tr., mimeographed paper.

Horak, M.J. (1967), 'Coredemption', in *New Catholic Encyclopedia*, New York, McGraw-Hill, vol. 4, pp.323–4.

Kubiak, H. (1970), *Polski Narodowy Kościół Katolicki W Stanach Zjednoczonych Ameryki W Latach 1897–1965; Jego Społeczne Uwarunkowania i Społeczne Funkcje*, Cracow, Polska Akademia Nauk.

Lewy, G. (1974), *Religion and Revolution*, New York, Oxford University Press.

Losskii, N.O. (1936), *Three Chapters from the History of Polish Messianism*, Prague, International Philosophical Library Periodical Publication, vol. 2, no. 9.

Nowy Świat (New York), 21 September 1922, 19 October 1922.

Peterkiewicz, J. (1975), *The Third Adam*, London, Oxford University Press.

Piwowarski, W. (1971), *Religijność Wiejska W Warunkach Urbanizacji: Studium Socjologiczne*, Warsaw, Biblioteka i 'Więzi'.

Pliska, S.R. (1955), 'Polish Independence and the Polish Americans', Ed.D. diss., Columbia University.

Ranchetti, M. (1969), *The Catholic Modernists: A Study of the Religious Reform Movement, 1864–1907*, I. Quigly, tr., London, Oxford University Press.

Reardon, B.M.G., ed. (1970), *Roman Catholic Modernism*, Stanford, Calif., Stanford University Press.

Renkiewicz, F. (1973), *The Poles in America, 1608–1972: Chronology and Fact Book*, Dobbs Ferry, N.Y., Oceana Publications.

St Stanislaus Kostka, Brooklyn/Greenpoint-New York, 1896–1971 (n.d.), South Hackensack, N.J.

Schroeder, O. (1969), *Aufbruch und Misverständnis: Zur Geschichte der Reformkatholischen Bewegung*, Vienna, Verlag Styria.

Slowiak, W.J. (1950), 'A Comparative Study of the Social Organization of the Family in Poland and the Polish Immigrant Family in Chicago', M.A. thesis, Loyola University.

Smith, T.L. (1971), 'Lay Initiative in the Religious Life of American Immigrants, 1880–1950', in T. Hareven, ed., *Anonymous Americans*, Englewood Cliffs, N.J., Prentice-Hall.

Stasiewski, B. (1967), 'Mariavites', *New Catholic Encyclopedia*, McGraw-Hill, New York, vol. 9, pp.217–18.

Stefan, S.B. (1939), 'The Preparation of the American Poles for Polish Independence, 1880–1918', M.A. thesis, University of Detroit.

Vidler, A.R. (1934), *The Modernist Movement in the Roman Church: Its Origins and Outcome*, Cambridge, Cambridge University Press.

Vidler, A.R. (1970), *A Variety of Catholic Modernists*, Cambridge, Cambridge University Press.

Waldo, A.L. (1953–74), *Sokolstwo, Przednia Straż Narodu: Dzieje Idei i Organizacji w Ameryce*, 4 vols, Pittsburgh, Sokolstwa Polskiego Ameryce.

Wandycz, P.S. (1969), *Soviet-Polish Relations, 1917–1921*, Cambridge, Mass., Harvard University Press.

Wandycz, P.S. (1974), *The Lands of Partitioned Poland, 1795–1918*, Seattle, Wash., University of Washington Press.

Warner, M. (1976), *Alone of All Her Sex: The Myth and Cult of the Virgin Mary*, New York, Alfred A. Knopf.

Wieczerzak, J.W. (1983), 'Bishop Francis Hodur and the Socialists: Associations and Disassociations', *Polish American Studies*, vol. 40, pp.5–35.

Winowska, M. (1956), 'Le Culte Marial en Pologne', *Maria: Etudes sur la Sainte Vierge*, H. du Manoir, ed., 7 vols, Paris, Beauchesnes.

Wlodarski, Rev. S. (1974), *The Origins and Growth of the Polish National Catholic Church*, Scranton, Pa., Polish National Catholic Church.

Religion and radicalism

25
God and the
English Revolution

CHRISTOPHER HILL

From way back in the nineteenth century, and still when I was at school, the seventeenth-century English Revolution used to be known as the Puritan Revolution. This name lost favour after Marx, Weber, Tawney and others taught us that religion was not a self-sufficient motivating factor, but was mixed up with economic and social matters, with the rise of capitalism. Yet even Marxists have been known to speak of Puritanism as the ideology of the English revolutionaries. God still has a role in the English Revolution. I want to look at the effects of God on this revolution, and its effects on God.

God was not only on the side of the Parliamentarians. There seem indeed to have been three gods – a trinity – at work during the Revolution. First there was the God who blessed the established order, any established order, but especially that of England. Kings and bishops ruled by divine right, the clergy had a divine right to collect 10 per cent of their parishioners' income as tithes – so conservatives said. The existing hierarchical structure of society, the great chain of being which ran through nature and society and which Shakespeare stated – probably ironically – in *Troilus and Cressida*, was God-given and must be preserved. All change was bad and dangerous, because the mass of mankind was sinful, had been irredeemably sinful since the Fall of Adam. The State exists to prevent the horrors which sinful humanity – and especially the lower orders – would perpetrate if not held in by law and power.

The second God, the God of the Parliamentarians, was also in favour of order; but he stressed justice rather than mere existence *de facto*. The Hebrew prophets in the Bible denounced the injustices of rulers and called for reformation. But only certain kinds of change were permissible: reformation should go back to Biblical models, to the primitive church of the New Testament. The Bible was used as litmus paper to test existing institutions. Were bishops to be found in the New Testament? If not, they should be abolished. This was a dangerously wide-ranging principle. Colonel Rainborough in 1647 found nothing in the Bible to justify the 40/- freeholder Parliamentary franchise. This did not lead him to reject Parliaments, but to call for manhood suffrage. Others, more conscious of the risks of uncritical application of the Bible to sinful seventeenth-century society, thought that change, however desirable, could be justified only if supported by the authority of the magistrate. Lesser magistrates might take the initiative if the sovereign did not, Dutch and French Calvinists thought. So they authorized revolt if supported by the respectable classes. Calvinists also found the protestant ethic in the Bible – thrift, sobriety, frugality, disciplined hard work, monogamy: a discipline which was especially necessary for the labouring classes, and which it was the duty of the magistrate to enforce lest social chaos should result.

But in the course of the Revolution some people found a third God, a God who – like the Holy Ghost – was to be found in every believer. And since it was difficult to ascertain who were true believers, this came to mean that God could be found in every man (and sometimes in every woman too). The full horrors of this doctrine were plumbed only in the 1640s; but worshippers of the second, Calvinist, God were aware of the existence of this third deity, and from the first tried to safeguard against his emergence. The Bible after all said many very remarkable things, and untutored readers of it might draw very remarkable conclusions. Arise Evans, a Welshman, tells us of the impact that coming to London made on his thinking. 'Afore I looked upon the Scripture as a history of things that passed in other countries, pertaining to other persons; but now I looked upon it as a mystery to be opened at this time, belonging also to us.' In *Amos* and *Revelation* he found descriptions of what was happening in revolutionary England. In *Amos* 9.1 the Lord said 'smite the lintel of the door, that the posts may shake': Evans thought this could only refer to Speaker Lenthall.[1] But others used Biblical texts for more consciously subversive purposes.

The God within sometimes looked like a god of pure anarchy: there might be as many gods as there were men, Gerrard Winstanley came to recognize.[2] But this is something which developed fully only after the breakdown of all authority in the 1640s, when lower-class sects of every heretical kind could meet and discuss freely: I shall return to it later.

There is of course nothing surprising in this many-facedness of God. Any state religion which survives for any length of time has to perform a multiplicity of roles: it has to console the down-trodden as well as to maintain the mighty in their seats. It has to persuade the rich to be charitable as well as the poor to be patient. Usually orthodox Christianity had interpreted the consolatory passages in the Scriptures as referring to an after-life. But this is sometimes difficult to square with the Biblical text. As the Bible became available in English after the Reformation, and as literacy sank down the social scale, so men and women began to take literally the more subversive texts of the Bible which their betters preferred to read allegorically.

But in the century before 1640 there had been some sort of consensus, at least among those who were able to express their views in print. John Foxe in his best-selling *Book of Martyrs* taught a view of history as a cosmic struggle between Christ and Antichrist, with God's Englishmen firmly on the side of right. England was a chosen nation, which God continually intervened to protect. In 1588 he blew with his winds and the Spanish Armada was scattered; a century later the protestant wind wafted William of Orange safely over to England to replace the papist James II. Even the revolutionary Great Seal of the English Republic claimed that freedom had been 'by God's blessing restored'.

God punished individuals and societies for their misdeeds, 'The cause of plagues is sin', declared a preacher in 1577; 'and the cause of sin are plays. Therefore the cause of plagues are plays.'[3] God's wrath would be visited on sinful societies. One reason for emigration to America in the 1620s and 30s, to which historians perhaps do not attach sufficient importance, was a desire to escape from the wrath to come. Thomas Cooper in 1615, dedicating a sermon to the Lord Mayor, Aldermen and Sheriffs of London and the Commissioners for Plantations in Ireland and Virginia, reminded them of the need 'to provide some retiring place for yourselves if so be the Lord for our unthankfulness should spew us out'.[4] Fourteen years later John Winthrop, first Governor of Massachusetts, was 'verily persuaded God will bring some heavy affliction upon this land, and that speedily'. 'As sure as God is God,' said Thomas Hooker in 1631, 'God is going from England.'[5] When Mrs Anne Hutchinson saw the barren in-hospitality of New England, she tells us, her heart would have shaken if she 'had not a sure word that England should be destroyed'.[6]

One of the ways in which Parliaments of the 1620s had expressed implied criticism of Charles I's government was by calling for a fast in order to propitiate the God who was angry with his people's sins. During the civil war Fast Sermons preached to Parliament were used to whip up support for the Cause. So God regularly showed his approval and disapproval of human actions, particularly those of rulers. The problem was how to interpret the signs. For many, success seemed evidence of God's support, and failure witnessed to divine disapproval: though sometimes, confusingly, it was left to a tiny remnant of the faithful to preserve the truth in secret. Arguments of this type were naturally used when convenient by both sides as the fortunes of civil war swayed backwards and forwards between 1642 and 1645. But in retrospect Parliamentarians came to claim that it was God, not man, who called the Long Parliament in 1640; that God, not man created the New Model Army and brought about the trial and execution of Charles I in 1649. The Fifth Monarchists Thomas Harrison and John Carew, the Quaker Isaac Pennington, all saw 'the finger of God' in England's deliverances; 'The Lord hath appeared in our days to do great things,' declared the republican Edmund Ludlow. 'The God of the Parliament . . . hath gone with you,' the Independent divine John Owen told Parliament in a sermon of June 1649, preached to celebrate the defeat of the Levellers. Oliver Cromwell believed that the Army had been 'called by God', and fiercely defended 'the revolutions of Christ himself', God's 'working of things from one period to another'. 'God hath done great and honourable things' by the agency of the Long Parliament, the Quaker Edward Burrough admitted; the Bristol Baptist Robert Purnell, the Fifth Monarchist John Tillinghast, the Independents Thomas Goodwin and John Cook, the Quaker George Bishop, all agreed.[7]

William Sedgwick, famous Army preacher, in December 1648 denounced the Army's intervention in politics, since it prevented a peaceful settlement with the King which he had hoped would reunite the country. But a few months later he completely reversed his position. The trial and execution of the King, the establishment of the republic, the abolition of the House of Lords – these events overwhelmed him by their sheer magnitude. *Because* the Army's actions had been unique, unprecedented, they must have been inspired by God. The only problem as Sedgwick saw it, was to bring this fact home to the generals so as to make them live up to their responsibility now that God 'is upon motion, marching us out of Egyptian darkness and bondage into a Canaan of rest and happiness'.[8] We may compare Marvell's sense of Cromwell as 'the force of angry heaven's flame', which ''Tis Madness to resist or blame'.[9]

The ultimate in divine intervention of course was the Second Coming, the end of the world, ushering in the millennium. Prophecies in *Daniel* and *Revelation* established that a great conflagration will mark the end of the world. Any Christian who takes these prophecies seriously must be anxious to ascertain when this holocaust will take place. I believe many Middle Western

American Christians are today looking forward with relish to helping to expedite it by means of nuclear warfare.[10] In the late sixteenth and early seventeenth centuries there seemed to be good reasons for supposing that the end of the world was imminent. Interpreting the Biblical prophecies was not left to cranks; it attracted the attention of serious historians, chronologists and mathematicians, from John Napier (inventor of logarithms, which speeded up his calculations of 666, the number of the Beast) to Sir Isaac Newton. By the early seventeenth century a certain agreement had been reached by these scholars, fixing on either the 1650s or the 1690s as the likely date for the end of the world. This was accepted by perfectly serious and sober people with no axes to grind. Thus when John Milton in 1641 spoke of Christ as 'shortly-expected King', he was probably thinking of the 1650s, though he may have extended the possibilities a decade or two.

For Milton the important thing about the Second Coming was that it would put 'an end to all earthly tyrannies', including that of Charles I. It involved political revolution. Here we come to a great divide. The orthodox view was that after the destruction of the world a new heaven and a new earth would be created, in which the elect would henceforth lead blissful and quite different lives: it was a totally other-worldly concept. Millenarians, however, interpreted the Biblical prophecies to mean that after Christ's Second Coming he would rule on *earth* for a thousand years (the millennium). Whether Christ would rule in person or through his saints was a question: the radicals tended to foresee a rule of the saints (i.e. themselves). One can see how such widely-held ideas could turn into theories justifying a dictatorship of the godly minority. 'The godly' indeed became almost a technical term, which sectaries applied to themselves and their enemies sometimes applied to them ironically. A train-band colonel in 1647, defending London from an expected attack by sectaries, was surprised to be ordered to fight against all 'malignants, sects and sectaries and all gody persons that shall come to oppose the City'. He protested that he hoped he was godly himself.[11]

Millenarian ideas could lead to rejection of régimes which seemed to be excluding Jesus Christ from his proper authority. For many – like William Sedgwick – the execution of Charles I only made sense if it cleared the way for King Jesus. When the Army went to conquer Scotland in 1650 its watchword was 'No King but Jesus'. But only three years later the Fifth Monarchist Vavasor Powell had to tell his congregation to ask God 'Wilt thou have Oliver Cromwell or Jesus Christ to rule over us?'[12]

Millenarian ideas could also turn into a sort of revolutionary internationalism. Hugh Peter told Parliament in December 1648 that 'this Army must root up monarchy, not only here but in France and other kingdoms round about'. Marvell foresaw Cromwell in this liberating role:

> As Caesar he ere long to Gaul,
> To Italy an Hannibal,
> And to all states not free
> Shall climacteric be.

In 1651 Admiral Blake, commanding the strongest fleet in the world, said on Spanish territory that monarchy was on the way out in France as well as England. He gave it ten years in Spain, a slower-moving country.[13] John Rogers the Fifth Monarchist declared in 1653 'We are bound by the law of God to help our neighbours as well as ourselves, and so to aid the subjects of other princes that are either persecuted for true religion or oppressed under tyranny.' Part of the English Army should be sent to France or Holland, to conduct a revolutionary war. George Fox, founder of the Quakers, in 1659 rebuked the Army for not going to Spain, to overthrow the Inquisition. 'Never set up your standard until you come to Rome', he urged, in words that show he was not yet a pacifist.[14]

But God could also speak direct to private individuals. Lady Eleanor Davies, a slightly eccentric person, in 1633 prophesied that Charles would come to a violent end. She was sent to Bedlam, but was taken more seriously after the King's execution.[15] In the political freedom of the 1640s and 50s quite humble men and women could be entrusted by God with political messages. Gerrard Winstanley in the winter of 1648 heard a voice telling him to set up the communist colony whose necessity to solve England's economic problems he had long been working out.[16] Three years later John Reeve was appointed one of God's Two Last Witnesses on earth, and he went on to found the sect later known as the Muggletonians, which lasted until 1979.[17] God dictated reams of rather mediocre verse to Anna Trapnel. George Fox and John Bunyan received messages, as did innumerable less well-known characters.

The point I am making is that it was *natural* for perfectly normal people to hear God speaking to them: it was not, as it would be to-day, *prima facie* evidence of insanity. This followed indeed from what I earlier described as the third manifestation of God, the theological assumption that God dwells in all his saints, perhaps in all men and women. The Quakers became the best-known exponents of this theology, but it was widespread during the revolutionary decades. Gerrard Winstanley believed that God was the same thing as Reason; indeed he preferred the word Reason to God, because he had 'been held under darkness' by the word God.[18] Reason, Winstanley thought, dictated that men and women should help one another, should co-operate, should indeed form communist communities for this purpose. So when Winstanley spoke of Christ rising in sons and daughters, he meant that he expected the spirit of Reason – i.e. co-operation – to rise in everybody and make them see the rationality of a communist society. The Second Coming was not Jesus Christ descending from the clouds but Reason rising in sons and daughters; and, Winstanley added, that was the only Second Coming there would ever be.[19] So the logic of protestant heresy led to secularism.

Politics was invariably expressed in religious language and imagery. Winstanley used the stories of Cain and Abel, Esau and Jacob, to express his class analysis of society; the younger brother would overcome his oppressing elder brother. David and Goliath, Samson and the Philistines, were symbols of revolt against tyranny. Existing corrupt society was designated as Sodom, Egypt, Babylon. The Pope had been Antichrist for Foxe and most protestants, as he had been for Lollard heretics earlier. Winthrop hoped that New England would become a 'bulwark against the kingdom of Antichrist'.[20] The Parliamentarian revolutionaries saw their royalist adversaries as 'the Antichristian faction'. The great Puritan preacher, Stephen Marshall, in a famous sermon preached to the House of Commons in February 1642, declared that 'many of the nobles, magistrates, knights and gentlemen, and persons of great quality, are arrant traitors and rebels against God'. What more desperate incitement to class war than that? 'The question in England', he said in 1644, 'is whether Christ or Antichrist shall be lord or king.' In the same year some Parliamentarian soldiers claimed that they 'took up arms against Antichrist and popery'. They believed that 'the people, the multitude' would pull down the Whore of Babylon; 'we are the men that must help to pull her down.'[21] Christopher Feake in 1646 saw 'in monarchy and aristocracy an enmity against Christ'.[22] So of course they should be abolished if opportunity arose.

But soon Parliament itself was being called Antichristian, and the adjective was applied to Presbyterians in the 1640s, to Cromwell in the 1650s. Any national church was naturally Antichristian, many sectaries asserted. Cromwell himself said it was Antichristian to distinguish between clergy and laity. Richard Overton and Henry Denne thought intolerance Antichristian: Baptists said the same of infant baptism. Bunyan put the social point more subtly by describing Antichrist as a gentleman.[23] For Winstanley covetousness, buying and selling, were Antichristian; property was the devil, Christ community. Jesus Christ was 'the true and faithful Leveller'.[24] There was a whole code of Biblical shorthand on which (among many others) Winstanley and Milton drew with great effect. Winstanley argued that all the Scripture prophecies 'concerning the calling of the Jews, the restoration of Israel and making of that people the inheritors of the whole earth' foretold 'this work of making the earth a common treasury' which the Diggers were carrying on.[25] Milton could not attack monarchy directly in *Paradise Lost*, since he was a marked man who had been lucky to escape execution in 1660; instead he merely recalled that monarchy had been founded by a rebel 'of proud ambitious heart', who

> not content
> With fair equality, fraternal state,
> Will arrogate dominion undeserved
> Over his brethren.[26]

Milton did not even need to name Nimrod, whom Charles I had spoken of with approval: he could rely on his readers' Biblical knowledge.

During the Revolution God said unusually revolutionary things to and through his saints. Abiezer Coppe the Ranter, for instance, announced that God, 'that mighty Leveller' would 'overturn, overturn, overturn'. 'The neck of horrid pride must be chopped off' so that 'parity, equality, community' might establish 'universal love, universal peace and perfect freedom'. 'Thou hast many bags of money, and behold I (the Lord) come as a thief in the night, with my sword drawn in my hand, and like a thief as I am – I say deliver your purse, deliver sirrah! deliver or I'll cut thy throat. . . . Deliver my money . . . to rogues, thieves, whores and cutpurses, who are flesh of thy flesh and every whit as good as thyself in mine eyes. . . . The plague of God is in your purses, barns, houses, horses, murrain will take your hogs (O ye fat swine of the earth) who shall shortly go to the knife. . . . Have all things common, or else the plague of God will rot and consume all that you have.'[27]

George Foster had a vision of a man on a white horse who cut down those higher than the middle sort and raised up those that were lower, crying 'Equality, equality, equality. . . . I, the Lord of Hosts have done this. . . . I will . . . make the low and poor equal with the rich. . . . O rich men, . . . I will utterly destroy you.' For Foster as for Coppe and Winstanley God was 'that mighty Leveller'.[28] Lawrence Clarkson preached a new permissive morality. 'There is no such act as drunkennes, adultery and theft in God. . . . Sin hath its conception only in the imagination. . . . What act soever is done by thee in light and love, is light and lovely, though it be that act called adultery. . . . No matter what Scripture, saints or churches say, if that within thee do not condemn thee, thou shalt not be condemned.' 'Till you can lie with all women as one woman, and not judge it sin, you can do nothing but sin.' Coppe had a similar libertine theology. 'External kisses have been made the fiery chariot to mount me unto the bosom of . . . the King of Glory. . . . I can kiss and hug ladies, and love my neighbour's wife as myself, without sin.'[29]

Radicals like Clement Wrighter and the Quaker Samuel Fisher argued that the Bible was not the infallible Word of God but a historical document to be studied and interpreted like any other. Some radicals rejected the immortality of the soul, heaven and hell. 'When men are gazing up to heaven,' Winstanley argued, 'imagining a happiness or fearing a hell after they are dead, their eyes are put out, that they see not . . . what is to be done by them here on earth while they are living.'[30]

One can understand that conservatives began to feel that freedom could go too far, that it was time to stop God communicating through the common people, or at least prevent his words being freely discussed, verbally and in print. Hence the restoration of the censorship in the 1650s, the suppression of Levellers, Diggers, Ranters and Fifth Monarchists. Hence the move to restore authority to the state church. Alderman Violet made the point succinctly in May 1650, reporting on the economic crisis to the Committee of the Mint: 'I propose as remedies, first, to settle able and godly ministers in all churches throughout the nation, that will teach the people to fear God, to obey their superiors and to live peaceably with each other – with a competent maintenance for all such ministers.'[31] He had got his priorities right. Ten years later Richard Baxter justified the restoration of episcopacy in the interests of discipline.[32]

One can see too why in the 1650s men desperately searched for certainty. There were so many rival accounts of God's wishes, so many differing interpretations of the Bible, that men sought either an infallible interpreter of God's will, or some other way of replacing the old certainties with a new consensus. The Church of England had collapsed, and no single church took its place. An infallible prophet or the infallible inner light were possible answers. But prophets died, and the inner light said different things to different people.

A more promising alternative was to look for secular solutions, for a science of politics which would guide human actions. Thomas Hobbes in *Leviathan* (1651) argued that a ruler could claim the allegiance of his subjects only in so far as he could protect them. When Charles I was defeated in the civil war, he could no longer do this, and so subjects had a *duty* to switch their allegiance to the *de facto* power of the Commonwealth. Political obligation had nothing to do with claims by divine right; it was a question of fact; could the sovereign do his job of protecting his subjects? Hobbes similarly destroyed claims by any group to rule because God favoured them: the restoration of monarchy in 1660 in any case made nonsense of such arguments by Parliamentarians. So Hobbes undermined all theories of obligation based on the will of God. It is the beginning of modern secular political theory. Every individual has a right to his own ideas; no subject and no church can claim a right in God's name to subvert the *de facto* sovereign.

Five years later the republican James Harrington advanced his own science of politics – the idea that political structures depend on economic structures, that when the economic base changes the political superstructure (Harrington's word) must change too. The English Revolution, he argued, had witnessed a transfer of power to those who had amassed landed property in the century before 1640; no government could be stable which did not recognize their right to rule. The events of 1660–88 appeared to confirm Harrington's analysis, and hammered another nail into the coffin of religious theories of political obligation and resistance. 'A commonwealth is not made by man but by God,' declared Harrington piously; but God acted through secondary causes, through the balance of property.[33]

The return of Charles II in 1660 ended the Revolution by restoring monarchy to preside over the rule of the propertied. When men took stock, these secular theories seemed to make sense. Charles was proclaimed King by the grace of God, but everybody knew that God had needed earthly agents to get Charles restored. During the interregnum each party had claimed God on its side in the hour of victory; but each side had also had to rethink its position in the years of defeat. Either God was very unstable and erratic, or his ways were incomprehensible to mere human intelligence: better to leave him out of account altogether. This sceptical trend was strengthened by the alarm which the third God had caused, the God who existed within the consciousness of lower-class sectaries. So the keynote of upper-class thinking after 1660 is opposition to 'fanaticism', 'enthusiasm', to claims to inspiration, whether in literature or in religion and politics. The royalist Sir William Davenant described 'inspiration' as 'a dangerous word'.[34] Milton continued to be visited nightly by his Muse, but claims to literary inspiration fell out of fashion until they revived with romanticism after the French Revolution.

For those Parliamentarians who believed they had been fighting for God's Cause, the total defeat which the restoration implied was a shattering blow. 'The Lord had spit in their faces,' Major-General Fleetwood wailed.[35] A condemned regicide found it difficult to answer the question, 'Have you not hard thoughts of God for this his strange providence towards you?'[36] Men had to stress the justice of an avenging God rather than his mercy. Clarkson heard men say that God was a devil and a tyrant.[37] 'God did seem to be more cruel than men,' Lodowick Muggleton admitted. Milton was thus only one of a large number who found it necessary to justify the ways of God to men, to account for the apparent triumph of evil over good.[38] Unless the freedom of man's will could be established, Milton believed, there would be 'an outcry against divine justice'.[39] God was on trial, for Traherne, Bunyan, Rochester and Dryden as well as in *Paradise Lost* and *Samson Agonistes*.[40]

It is a turning point in human thought. After 30 January 1649 kings never forgot that they had a joint in their necks. And God was never quite the same again after he had been put on trial in popular discussion. He withdrew into the Newtonian stratosphere. *The Decline of Hell* which Mr Walker has traced in the seventeenth century proceeded apace.[41] Fasts and fast sermons faded out in the 1650s; an MP was laughed at for excessive quotation from the Bible.

After 1660 the restored Church of England was taken over by 'Latitudinarians', mostly former Puritans, who abandoned divine-right claims for bishops and tithes, and based them on the law of the land. The Latitudinarians played a prominent part in the newly-founded Royal Society, whose scientists also did much to talk down 'fanaticism' and 'enthusiasm' with their rejection of 'extremes', their stress on moderation, common sense, the English genius for compromise, etc., etc. But here too the intellectual climate favoured a secular science of politics, an empirical probabilism. Common sense of course led to intellectual muddles. Fellows of the Royal Society proclaimed a belief in witchcraft, based on the evidence of their senses and the authority of the Bible. 'No spirits, no God,' said Henry More, later FRS.[42] It was too bad that safeguarding the existence of God meant death for many lonely old women.

In the early 1650s the Ranters had abolished sin. But history abolished the Ranters, and sin came back in strength after 1660. The Quakers, who had denounced the state clergy for preaching up sin, found a place for it in their post-restoration theology. The sinfulness of the mass of humanity had always been used to explain the wickedness of change. Even Milton, in *Paradise Lost*, explained the defeat of the Revolution by the sinfulness of the English people, who had failed to live up to the high ideals and aspirations put before them.

Dissenters, excluded from the state church, now formed a separate nation, huddled into their self-supported congregations, desperately concerned with survival in a hostile world. They were cut off from national political life and the national universities. Most of the sects followed the Quakers into pacifism and abstention from politics. Their God now presided over a provincial, stunted culture; he was no longer capable of transforming nations. The sects accepted that religion should not concern itself with high politics; the emphasis henceforth fell more on questions of conduct and personal morality, such as arose in the confusing growth of capitalist society with its new standards. The sects adapted themselves to this new world, becoming – to adapt Lenin's phrase – schools of capitalism. The nonconformist conscience was to revive as a political force only after the internalization of the work ethic had led many dissenters to prosper: but that was far ahead in 1660.

For those whose lack of property put them below the line which marked off 'the political nation', restoration of the familiar, consoling rituals of the traditional church may have been acceptable. Others no doubt just opted out. The strenuous virtue which Milton expected of the English people was no longer demanded. They lapsed into the traditional assumption that politics was for their betters: church and state, king and country, the royal touch to heal scrofula, monarchy as a spectacle now safely controlled by the propertied class.

1640 was the last national revolution whose driving ideology was religious. Milton left behind him a theological *summa*, the *De Doctrina Christiana*, which was so heretical that it could not be published, even in Latin. When his literary executor tried after his death to publish it in the Netherlands, all the power of English diplomacy was exerted to prevent it. The confiscated manuscript lay among the State Papers until 1823. When it was published – on the orders of a King, translated by a bishop – the dynamite of the 1660s had become a damp squib. Since the American and French Revolutions revolutionary doctrines were no longer expressed in religious idiom; they did not need God.

What remained after 1660 was a secularized version of the myth of the chosen people, which Charles II still proclaimed.[43] From the days of Richard Hakluyt British imperialist expansion had neatly combined the glory of God with the profits of those who organized the expansion. 'Look westward then,' cried Thomas Thorowgood in 1650; 'there you may behold a rising sun of glory with riches and much honour, and not only for yourselves but for Christ.'[44] The conversion of the natives loomed large in company prospectuses, but never came to much when it was found to conflict with commercial profit.

The millenarian Thomas Goodwin wanted England to be 'the top of nations'.[45] Fifth Monarchists supported commercial war against the Dutch. The republican James Harrington had advocated 'a commonwealth for increase'. 'The late appearances of God unto you' were not 'altogether for yourselves'. If 'called in by an oppressed people' (Scotland? Ireland? France?) England had a duty to respond. 'If you add unto the propagation of civil liberty . . . the propagation of liberty of conscience, this empire, this patronage of the world, is the kingdom of Christ.'[46] Marvell had similar ideas, and Dryden in *Annus Mirabilis* put forward pseudo-millenarian predictions of a glorious imperial and trading future for London and England, with no religious overtones at all. This became common form.[47]

Ireland – the first English colony – was a case in which the Cause of God got hopelessly mixed up with economic and strategic considerations. Most of the English revolutionaries believed that Charles I and Laud had been part of, or at least had connived at, an international Roman Catholic plot for the conquest of England and the subversion of protestantism. In this plot Ireland's role was crucial. It was the open back-door to foreign Catholic invasion. Spanish troops had landed there in the 1590s, French troops landed there in the 1690s in an attempt to restore James II to the English throne. The Revolution of 1640 unleashed the Irish rebellion of 1641, which was soon headed by a Papal Nuncio. So the Cromwellian reconquest of Ireland seemed a necessary blow against Antichrist, to prevent the restoration of monarchy by invasion through Ireland. The radicals, fiercely attacking Cromwell on internal matters, offered no real opposition to the conquest and enslavement of Ireland with a few notable exceptions, such as the Leveller, William Walwyn. The English republic, in Karl Marx's pregnant words, 'met shipwreck in Ireland'. 'The English reaction in England had its roots . . . in the subjugation of Ireland.'[48] If ever God showed himself a conservative it was in thus using religion to mislead the radical revolutionaries.

So God played many parts in the English Revolution. First came the landslide of 1640–1, when suddenly the apparently all-powerful government of Charles and Laud found itself unable any longer to persecute the saints: and when by overwhelming majorities in Parliament the repressive machinery of the prerogative courts was swept away. When the King tried to resist, God raised up an army against him; when stalemate seemed likely to occur, God and Oliver Cromwell created the New Model Army. After the second great revolution of 1648–9 God continued his favour by permitting the conquest of Ireland and Scotland, the Navigation Act of 1651 and the consequent aggressive commercial foreign policy – Dutch War, Spanish War, Dunkirk seized, piracy brought under control. In turn the events of 1660 came to seem as providential as the events of 1640–1 and 1648–9. But with a difference. In 1649 the Army had acted positively as God's instrument, had brutally but effectively shattered the image hitherto worshipped as divine; in 1660 it was the return of the traditional rulers that seemed providential.

Neither man's power nor policy had place; . . .
The astonished world saw 'twas the mighty work of heaven,[49]

sang Sir Francis Fane. God had changed sides and was now overwhelmingly on the side of the establishment, as he had previously been on the side of shocking innovation: the restoration came in spite of rather than because of the royalists. Those who had been the instruments of the omnipotent God in 1648–9 were now revealed as impotent mortals, for whom the God of history had no more use.[50]

The Glorious Revolution of 1688 was an additional providence, another landslide like those of 1640 and 1660, another reassertion of the predetermined social order. It confirmed England's historical right to rule the world. Further confirmation came from the Industrial Revolution, another unplanned gift from heaven. The secular millenarian interpretation of England's manifest destiny was validated by these providential social transformations.

So where are we? In the 1640s the belief that men were fighting for God's Cause was a tremendous stimulus to morale. A popular slogan in the North said that 'God is a better lord than the Earl of Derby'. The theoretical duty of a feudal lord was to protect his underlings; what impressed them more was his ever-present power. If you lived in Lancashire or the Isle of Man it was difficult to think that there could be a greater power than the Earl of Derby. In the 1640s confidence in God's overlordship gave the Puritan citizens of Lancashire towns courage to resist even the Earl of Derby, who ultimately in 1651 was executed for 'treason and rebellion . . . in a town of his own', Bolton.[51] Yet in 1660 his son reappeared in Lancashire to wield his father's old authority: in the long run God had proved a weaker lord.

After 1660 a new ruling-class consensus formed, when God again presided over the established order. God = history = success = what happens. One conclusion we may perhaps draw is that any religion can serve any social purpose, because of the ambiguity of its basic texts. We should not think of protestantism as causing the rise of capitalism, but rather of protestantism and Puritanism being moulded by capitalist society to suit its needs. After 1660 God continued to offer consolation in the after life to those who were unhappy on earth. But between 1640 and 1660 God had also stimulated protest, rejection of an unjust society and its laws; he had legitimized movements for change. 'True religion and undefiled', said Winstanley, 'is to let everyone quietly have earth to manure, that they may live in peace and freedom in their labour.'[52] Land for all might have been the basis for a different consensus.

How much of the radical tradition survived underground we do not know, for the censorship closed down again after 1660, and victors write history. At the end of *Samson Agonistes* Milton envisaged God's Cause as an undying phoenix; 'and though her body die, her fame survives,/ A secular bird, ages of lives.'[53] I do not myself think that ideas like those of the radicals get totally forgotten: men were discussing Winstanley's writings in a Welsh valley in the 1790s[54] – an interesting time and an interesting place. But God the great Leveller, who wanted everything overturned, a God active today in Latin America, seems to have left England after the seventeenth-century Revolution; and not to have returned.

Notes

1 Evans, *A Voice from Heaven to the Commonwealth of England* (1652), pp.26–7, 33, 45, 74–5; *An Eccho to the Voice from Heaven* (1653), p.17, quoted in my *Change and Continuity in Seventeenth-Century England*, London, 1974, pp.59–60.

2 'No man shall be troubled for his judgment or practice in the things of his God', Winstanley, *The Law of Freedom and Other Writings*, Cambridge, 1983, p.379.

3 E.K. Chambers, *The Elizabethan Stage*, Oxford, 1923, IV, p.197; cf.

R. Sibbes, *Complete Works*, Edinburgh, 1862–4, VI, pp.153–4.

4   Thomas Cooper, *The Blessing of Japheth, Proving the Gathering in of the Gentiles and Finall Conversion of the Jewes* (1615), Sig. A 2–3.

5   P. Collinson, *The Religion of Protestants: The Church in English Society 1559–1625*, Oxford, 1982, p.283; E.S. Morgan, *The Puritan Dilemma: the Story of John Winthrop*, Boston, 1958, p.40.

6   Ed. D.D. Hall, *The Antinomian Controversy, 1636–1638*, Middletown, CT, 1968, p.338.

7   I give evidence in my *The Experience of Defeat: Milton and Some Contemporaries* , London, 1984, pp.171–3, 319–21; ed. W.C. Abbott, *Writings and Speeches of Oliver Cromwell*, Cambridge, MA, 1937–47, I, pp.696–8, III, pp.590–3.

8   *The Experience of Defeat*, pp.102–5.

9   Marvell, *An Horatian Ode upon Cromwels Return from Ireland*.

10 See a forthcoming article by Richard H. Popkin, 'The Triumphant Apocalypse and the Catastrophic Apocalypse' in *Nuclear Weapons and the Future of Humanity*, eds Avner Cohen and Steven Lee, New York, 1986.

11 Quoted in M.A. Gibb, *John Lilburne, the Leveller*, London 1947, p.183.

12 Quoted in my *Antichrist in Seventeenth-Century England*, Oxford, 1971, pp.108, 158.

13 Quoted in my *Puritanism and Revolution*, London, Panther ed., 1969, pp.133–4.

14 *Ibid.*, pp.140, 146.

15 *Change and Continuity in Seventeenth-Century England*, p.54.

16 See my *The Religion of Gerrard Winstanley, Past and Present Supplement*, No. 5, 1978, pp.20–3.

17 C. Hill, B. Reay and W. Lamont, *The World of the Muggletonians*, London, 1983, pp.23, 64.

18 *The Religion of Gerrard Winstanley*, p.8.

19 *Ibid.*, pp.29–32, 48; see also a debate on *The Religion of Gerrard Winstanley* in *Past and Present*, No. 89, 1980, pp.144–51.

20 Morgan, *op. cit.*, p.40.

21 *Antichrist in Seventeenth-Century England*, pp.79–82, 86.

22 T. Edwards, *Gangraena* (1646), III, p.148.

23 *Antichrist in Seventeenth-Century England*, pp.93–6, 108, 110, 121–3; Bunyan, *Works*, ed. G. Offor, Glasgow, Edinburgh and London, 1860, II, p.54.

24 *The Religion of Gerrard Winstanley*, pp.35, 37.

25 Winstanley, *The Law of Freedom and Other Writings*, p.88.

26 Milton, *Paradise Lost*, XII, 24–37.

27 See my *The World Turned Upside Down*, Penguin ed., Harmondsworth, 1975, pp.210–11.

28 *Ibid.*, pp.223–4.
29 *Ibid.*, pp.215, 315.
30 *Ibid.*, pp.259–68; Winstanley, *The Law of Freedom and Other Writings*, p.353.
31 *Calendar of State Papers, Domestic, 1650*, p.180.
32 R. Baxter, *A Sermon of Repentance, Preached before the . . . House of Commons . . . April 30, 1660*, p.45.
33 *The Experience of Defeat*, pp.193–7.
34 Davenant, *Godibert*, 1651, ed. D.F. Gladish, Oxford, 1971, p.22.
35 *Clarke Papers*, ed. C.H. Firth, Camden Soc., IV, p.220.
36 H.G. Tibbutt, *Colonel John Okey, 1606–1662*, Bedfordshire Historical Record Soc., XXXV, 1955, p.154.
37 Clarkson, *Look about You* (1659), pp.29–30.
38 *The Experience of Defeat*, pp.307–9.
39 Milton, *Complete Prose Works*, Yale ed., New Haven, CT, 1953–82, VI, pp.397–8.
40 *The Experience of Defeat*, p.309; my *Milton and the English Revolution* (1977), pp.351–2, 58–60.
41 D.P. Walker, *The Decline of Hell: Seventeenth-Century Discussions of Eternal Torment*, Chicago, 1964, *passim*.
42 H. More, *An Antidote to Atheism* (1653), p.164.
43 *The Experience of Defeat*, p.248.
44 Thomas Thorowgood, *Jewes in America* (1650), Sig. c 3v.
45 *The Experience of Defeat*, p.181.
46 *Ibid.*, p.199; Harrington, *Political Works*, ed. J.G.A. Pocock, Cambridge, 1977, pp.329–33.
47 M. McKeon, *Politics and Religion in Restoration England*, Cambridge, MA, 1975, pp.63, 153, 174–5, 249, 268–81.
48 Karl Marx and Friedrich Engels, *Correspondence, 1846–1895: A Selection*, ed. Dona Torr, 1934, pp.279, 281; cf. p.264.
49 Quoted by J. Sutherland, *English Literature in the Late Seventeenth Century*, Oxford, 1969, p.3.
50 *The Experience of Defeat*, pp.321–3.
51 Edward Hyde, Earl of Clarendon, *History of the Rebellion and Civil Wars in England*, ed. W.D. Macray, Oxford, 1888, V, p.184.
52 *The Religion of Gerrard Winstanley*, p.28.
53 Milton, *Samson Agonistes*, lines 1706–7.
54 *The Experience of Defeat*, p.42.

26
Chartist religious belief and the theology of liberation

EILEEN YEO

In an article on 'Christianity in Chartist Struggle, 1838–1842', I explored the religious dimension to the Chartist fight for parliamentary democracy.[1] Although I had discovered a cluster of religious beliefs in sources like sermons, speeches and banners, I did little with them. I had wanted to locate them in some tradition, so I turned naturally, as all historians of Britain do, to look back at the beliefs of the plebeian Puritans during the seventeenth-century Revolution. Although there were some shared emphases, like the concentration on the promise of Genesis, the stress of the spirit of God within human beings and also the relentless reading of the Signs of the Times, I was disappointed by the comparison. It was only recently when I started reading the theology of liberation that is being developed, preached, practised and died for in Latin America today, that I felt I was penetrating more deeply into the Chartist cast of mind.

In this paper I want to draw out some of the striking parallels and point to some differences by comparing the writing and preaching of three figures. I shall use the work of the Peruvian priest, Gustavo Gutierrez, *A Theology of Liberation: History, Politics and Salvation* (1971)[2] which has been called the 'best known and most comprehensive presentation of the new theological thought in Latin America'. For Chartist belief, I shall focus on the Rev. William Hill, the Swedenborgian minister who was once a handloom weaver and also active in the Factory Movement, who looked after his congregation in Hull while at the same time editing the main Chartist newspaper, the *Northern Star*. I will pay special attention to a sermon he preached at the Hyde Working Men's Institution which was reported in the *Star* on 4 September 1839, not long after the failure of the Chartist General Strike and during a period of widespread arrests and heavy repression. Also, I want to consider the Rev. Joseph Rayner Stephens who seceded from the Wesleyans and established the breakaway Stephensite Methodists, which became a plebeian sect and, by 1839, could boast ten preaching stations and thirty-one preachers in the Ashton circuit alone. He is a more contentious choice because by August 1839 he was repudiating the Charter and saying that all he had ever supported was 'The Bible, the whole Bible and nothing but the Bible'. None the less before this point, Chartists had revered him as the exemplary minister of religion, who preached that the ministry must stand 'as a moral breakwater against the swelling surge of pride and oppression' and who lived the part. The sermon I particularly want to consider is *The Political Preacher, an Appeal from the Pulpit on Behalf of the Poor*, which was delivered on 6 January 1839,[3] less than a week after he had been arrested and charged with seditious conspiracy.

Clearly there are problems about comparing a systematic and sustained work of theology with single sermons which are fragments of a mind, preached at specific moments in the heat of battle. My short discussion will do an injustice to Gutierrez, whose argument is complex and builds in a carefully architected way over some 300 pages. Also unfairly, the beliefs of Hill and Stephens will be made to seem underdeveloped by comparison since their purpose was to preach and to stir action, while Gutierrez's is to clarify – to undertake 'critical reflection on Christian praxis in the light of the Word' (p.13). I shall focus on three themes of common concern – God in history, Bondage, Liberation – and then on one absent theme, Women's Liberation.

God in history

Central to all three is the belief that God acts and saves, not in some separate spiritual or metaphysical realm, but in material human history. For Gutierrez, the account of creation in Genesis is significant not so much to explain the origins of the world or to satisfy a curiosity about beginnings. Creation is significant as the start of human history and the sign that God intends salvation to be worked out within the material world. The coupling or fusion of God the Creator and God the Redeemer is frequent in the Bible.[4] The beginning has an end from the start: but it is through human labour that the approach to this end will be achieved. Gutierrez cites Genesis 1:28, 'God said unto them, Be fruitful and multiply and replenish the earth, and subdue it: and have dominion over the fish of the sea, and over the fowl of the air, and over every living thing.' This text signifies that 'man is the crown and centre of the work of creation and is called to continue it through his labour.' Stephens also made frequent use of this text, seeing in it a promise of plenty to be realized through human effort.

Since God works in history, it is important to explore the historical and social dimensions of the Bible, not dismiss them as a carnal veil concealing a deeper spiritual truth. Stephens agreed with Hill's determination not to seek 'mystical meanings, or occult senses, or spiritual interpretations or allegorical similitudes' and also with Hill's insistence that the Bible's historical episodes

> contain great and imperishable principles, whence we may reason by analogy, and which we may apply with certainty to the conduct of all men, at all times, in all places, and under all circumstances.[5]

For Gutierrez, inhabiting a post-Hegelian world, a dialectical understanding of the same history is essential for grappling with liberation and eschatology. The Bible contains the most direct, though still partial, statement of God's Promise to human kind: 'The Promise unfolds, – becoming richer and more definite – in the *promises* made by God throughout history.' The Covenant and the Exodus, the Kingdom of Israel and, decisively, the New Testament proclamation of the gift of the kingdom of God on earth are all concrete and increasingly enlarged views of the Promise. Still

> The Promise is not exhausted by these promises nor by their fulfillment; it goes beyond them, explains them, and gives them their ultimate meaning. But at the same time, the Promise is announced and is partially and progressively fulfilled in them. There exists a dialectical relationship between the Promise and its partial fulfillments. (p.161)

Christ's arrival is the greatest fulfilment and extension of the promise so far. That he came to earth as a human being decisively confirms God's plan for salvation to take place in the human world – not in any afterlife or disengaged spiritual interior. Christ has universalized the promise, extending it from the Jewish people to all men, and unified it, bringing together political liberation, salvific history and communion with God. For Gutierrez, Christ's own being demonstrates that every man is the temple of God which is concrete Good News about the way to love and have communion with God. This is through acts of love and justice to our neighbour who is also the temple of God: 'the love of God is unavoidably expressed *through* love of one's neighbour' (p.200). This attitude to our neighbour will unblock the way for the development of his full potential or for his salvation which, to Gutierrez, is the same as his liberation into full humanity. For Stephens and Hill too, practical love of our neighbour is the central teaching of Christianity 'whose first and last and only law on earth is that we should love our neighbour as ourself – doing unto others as we would they should do unto us'.[6]

But the theology of the neighbour needs development: the neighbour is not simply an individual with whom we come into personal contact:

> the neighbor is not only man viewed individually. The term refers also to man considered in the fabric of social relationships, to man situated in his economic, social, cultural, and racial coordinates. It likewise refers to the exploited social class, the dominated people, and the marginated race. The masses are also our neighbor, as Chenu asserts. This point of view leads us far beyond the individualistic language of the I-Thou relationship. Charity is today a 'political charity', according to the phrase of Pius XII. (p.202)

Our neighbour is a collective entity as well as an individual person. Sin and salvation must have a collective, as well as an individual, dimension.

Bondage

'Bondage' or 'oppression' are key concepts for describing social sin. Oppression or bondage denote social relations which are the negation of love between neighbours because the powerful deprive the weaker of material subsistence, human dignity and social justice. 'Sin,' writes Gutierrez, 'is evident in oppressive structures, in the exploitation of man by man, in the domination and slavery of peoples, races and social classes' (p.175). The nineteenth-century preachers also recognized that sinful relations were part of ongoing social institutions and could be created and sustained by law: 'the laws and institutions of England', thundered Stephens, 'are laws of violence and institutions of blood.' The eradication of sin involves fearless analysis and, if necessary, prophetic denunciation of social structures, a practice for which the nineteenth-century radicals were attacked as are their counterparts today. 'It has been my practice – and has been charged upon me as a crime', asserted Stephens –

> to apply the rules of God's commandments to various institutions of the social system, in my own immediate neighbourhood, and in the country at large – to bring the principles and operations of the manufactures, the commerce and the legislation of this professedly Christian land to the standard of God's Holy Word.[7]

The litmus test for the good or sinful nation is how it treats the weakest collective neighbour. Gutierrez identifies the most vulnerable as 'the most exploited social class' but also joins with Hill and Stephens in singling out the poor, widows, orphans and strangers. The nineteenth-century preachers were fond of choosing texts which dealt with this theme: Hill preached Jeremiah 7:3–7, including the words,

> if ye thoroughly execute judgment between a man and his neighbour; If ye oppress not the stranger, the fatherless, and the widow, and shed not innocent blood in this place, neither walk after other gods to your hurt, then will I cause you to dwell in this place, in the land that I gave to your fathers, for ever and ever.[8]

To do justice is to know God and his promise. Any breach in love or justice for the defenceless is not only a breach with men but a rupture in communion with God.

The Book of Exodus, which tells of the Jews in slavery in Egypt and then of their liberation has a paradigm quality. First, it is an exemplary evocation of bondage and oppression and, second, it is a clear sign that political and social liberation is God's overriding will, which needs the active consent of human agents to be accomplished. Third, it provides a permanent language for liberation struggles wherever they might occur. Not only did Stephens meticulously explore each link in the chains of bondage under Pharaoh, but he compared Egypt with England and found the English worse off. The English

> groan being burdened with a heavier and far more bitter yoke. We are no where told that in Egypt the men were worked so hard or had to work so long as our fellow countrymen have – nor that little children were driven to work at all as children and women are every where forced to do in the corn fields, the coal pits and the cotton mills of christian England. There is nothing said of hunger or nakedness, or roaming houseless abroad – of filth, rags, starvation and misery, such as is at this hour the hapless lot of millions of our fellow country men. Nor was the 'Law' to strangle and drown every male child half so inhuman, half so horrible a mode of 'legislating for the independence and comfort' of the people 'lest they should multiply' too fast and become too many for the security of the estates of their representatives, as the plan adopted and carried out by christian statesmen in our own country under the provisions of the 'Poor Law Amendment Act'. The Israelites had still their home and their hearth – their wife and such of their children as did not come under the 'provisions of the act'. They 'dealt' mercifully

as well as 'wisely' with them in comparison with the 'dealings' of the 'Poor Law Commissioners for England and Wales' who break up every poor man's cottage, take away every poor man's wife, lay their bloody hands on every poor man's child, imprisoning, starving and destroying without mercy and without measure all the Poor of England 'lest they should multiply', and replenish the earth.[9]

For both Gutierrez and Stephens, the Exodus underlines the need for a partnership between God and human beings to bring about liberation. For Gutierrez, the Exodus gives deep organizing significance both to the past and to the future: it confirms and clarifies the picture in Genesis of the role human activity must play in the salvific process:

> By working, transforming the world, breaking out of servitude, building a just society, and assuming his destiny in history, man forges himself. In Egypt, work is alienated and, far from building a just society, contributes rather to increasing injustice and to widening the gap between exploiters and exploited.
>
> To dominate the earth as Genesis prescribed, to continue creation, is worth nothing if it is not done for the good of man, if it does not contribute to his liberation in solidarity with all, in history. The liberating initiative of Yahweh responds to this need by stirring up Moses' vocation. Only the *mediation of this self-creation* – first revealed by the liberation from Egypt – allows us to rise above poetic expressions and general categories and to understand in a profound and synthesizing way the relationship between creation and salvation so vigorously proclaimed by the Bible. (pp.158–9)

Stephens holds out the Promise of the covenant to galvanize us into action: 'Be prepared', he counselled, 'no matter what sacrifices we are called upon to make, to be fellow workers together with God in bringing our brethren out of a house of social bondage, into a land, whose wiser laws, and more righteous institutions cause "milk and honey", peace and plenty, to abound for a happy and contented people' (p.37). Here are the elements of an enduringly resonant vocabulary to convey present oppression, to give a vision of future liberation and to underscore the need for human effort, in co-operation with God, to bring about the transition.

Liberation

What will the land of milk and honey look like? Israel under the
Covenant provides a partial vision of right-living under the
critical eye of a vengeful God: the words of the prophets, the life
of Christ and the acts of the primitive Christians make further,
but for Gutierrez still incomplete, disclosures. Bliss, to Hill, was
very mundane. The institutions of property had to allow for
independence, security, benevolence and to prevent oppressive
inequalities of power from developing. Hill highlighted the
Biblical example of how the Israelites distributed land by lot
according to family need and how they periodically restored
alienated property so that 'every man had property of his own,
upon which, by the produce of his own labour, to sustain his own
family, and have something left for the exercise of hospitality to
strangers'. Underlying all institutions and actions there had to be a
feeling of brotherhood according to Christ's instructions, 'let him
that hath two coats give one to him that hath none; receive not
honour from each other for one is your Master and Father, and ye
are brethren'. The Chartist movement, with its practice of
political democracy and its land plan for a vast increase in peasant
proprietors, was an appropriate instrument for realizing God's
promise.

Gutierrez, even more than Hill, follows the precepts of social
love and justice far beyond the limits of existing property and
power relations. Not only is it necessary to remake the
exploitative relations inside South American countries, but the
international oppression of imperialism must be undone. With
eyes fully open, he faces up to the actual revolutionary
movement in Latin America – often Marxist, usually violent – and
sides with it, summoning prophetic denunciation of injustice to its
aid.[10] But he also reserves space for the specifically Christian
concern with utopia and with faith: with the creation of a new
humanity through the construction of a more just and brotherly
society and with the liberation from sin and communion with
God and all men. Christian construction can start now. The
Church can make a witness of poverty which means making itself
poor as an expression of love for the poor and solidarity in the
struggle against poverty. It can also adopt an attitude of 'spiritual
poverty' or openness to the future promised by God. Where the
struggle will end cannot be foreseen, especially as the oppressed
gain in confidence and reveal new human possibilities. Christian
hope keeps us from any confusion of the Kingdom with any one
historical stage, from any idolatry toward unavoidably ambiguous

human achievement, from any absolutizing of revolution. In this way hope makes us radically free to commit ourselves to social praxis, motivated by a liberating utopia and with the means which the scientific analysis of reality provides for us. And our hope not only frees us for this commitment; it simultaneously demands and judges it (p.238).

Stephens's attitude to social transformation is hard to label. No democrat or socialist, he accepts the existence of rulers in various areas of social life but only on condition that they love and protect the weak. At the same time, he totally abhors oppression and feels that it is built into specific institutions and laws: the New Poor Law, the Factory System, etc. He enjoins England to turn from her wicked path, he demands that levels of the social structure be dismantled, he urges political and religious rulers to attend to the real duties of their social roles before it is too late:

> Would the clergy of England, even now, at the eleventh hour, in God's name, and in God's behalf, 'judge the fatherless and plead for the widow', less than twelve months might change this wilderness into a broad field of fertility and beauty. Should they, on the other hand, unhappily hold their peace, when they behold the wickedness that is committed in the land, join hands with the lay-man in grinding the faces of the Poor, less than twelve months may seal the doom of both and bring down upon all, our cup already all but running over, the righteous vengeance our sins have merited. . . . He will consume us with the fire of His wrath; our own way will He recompense upon our heads, saith the Lord God. (p.30)

To call Stephens a Tory is not helpful. He is an Old Testament prophet unleashing harsh denunciation, forceful analysis and violent imagery which could take people far beyond any particular political position he might hold.

Women's liberation

So far, I have gone out of my way to use the language they do: Man, Mankind, His as the personal pronoun for Yahweh, fraternal, brotherhood, fruits of *Man*'s work, *his* destiny. It is clear that this language unreflectively subsumes women under men. Women are similarly subsumed into family relations: in Biblical Israel, they feature as widows to be protected and as wives to be given security within marriage. Neither Hill, Gutierrez nor Stephens raise any questions about whether patriarchal gender relations can be as inhibiting as unequal social relations, whether they can decisively obstruct women from achieving true dignity and from assuming their own destiny in conformity with God's salvific plan. Nor is there concern with the pervasiveness of male words in the theological language.

To modern theologians and philosophers of women's liberation these are cardinal omissions. Rosemary Ruether sees the continuing religious subordination of women as one of the deepest betrayals of the heart of the gospel which began in the earliest Church with the unwillingness to work at realizing the last part of the promise that 'in Christ there is neither Jew nor Greek, slave nor free, male nor female'.[11] Mary Daly finds the whole discourse of theology so saturated with excluding and oppressive male imagery, that she refuses to call herself a theologian and is intent on creating a new vocabulary, which will shake us out of our common sense into an awareness of new possibilities. 'The sisterhood of man' is one of her constructions, giving a generic status to terms associated with males *and* females. In the light of the writing coming from the women's movement, the writers I have been discussing seem strikingly gender-blind in a way that helps to maintain the subordination of women. I will now try to situate Stephens at least in the context of his time, and see if the same judgment is as obviously true.

The Garden of Eden episode in the Bible is, of course, the touchstone for arguments about women's nature. I shall compare Stephens's treatment with two others more extreme. Far out on the edge even of the socialist movement, Goodwyn and Catherine Barmby saw the fall as the separation of the hermaphrodite into Adam and Eve or 'the disunion of the man-power and the woman-power imaged by the separation of the man and the woman bodies'. For the Barmbys' liberation involved not only a struggle against social subordination but also against psycho-sexual alienation. To be a true communist, 'the man must possess the woman-power as well as the man-power, and the woman must possess the man-power as well as the woman-power. Both must be equilibriated beings.'[12]

At the other extreme of the spectrum, the Rev. Francis Close, 'the Pope of Cheltenham', expounded an exemplary Evangelical position. In *A Sermon, Addressed to the Female Chartists of Cheltenham, Sunday, August 25, 1839*, he read them the theological riot act.[13] He told them that because Eve had sinned in tempting Adam to eat of the apple, all women had to suffer a threefold curse. First, they were given a nature that would magnify suffering because of 'the very constitution of their bodies, the delicacy of their nerves and the excitability of their feelings'. Second, they were to suffer in childbirth and third, suffer by being subject to their husbands. This was the state of play until God chose a woman, Mary, to be the vessel of salvation. 'The condition of the female sex' was then 'wholly changed' and woman was 'restored in a measure to her paradisical level'. Instead of being forced into submission, she could now, in her proper domestic sphere, voluntarily and cheerfully submit to it!

> the centre of all your virtues, and the fountain of all your influence in society, *is your home* – your own fire-side – it is amongst your children, it is in the bosom of your family, and in the little circle of friends with whom you are more immediately connected, there your legitimate influence must be exercised; there you are born to shine. . . . Be the pious mother; be the obedient wife; yield that voluntary and cheerful submission to the wishes of your husband, which was extorted from you, till Christ removed the curse.

The public sphere emphatically belonged to men who had a different nature. Close mustered all the damning imagery in the arsenal to attack Chartist women who strayed into the sphere of politics. Like Eve, they were temptresses and witches 'inciting rather than allaying bad passions'. They were unfeminine, destitute 'of female decorum, of female modesty and diffidence'. They were unEnglish, akin to their French sisters, who 'glutted themselves with blood; and danced like maniacs amidst the most fearful scenes of the Reign of Terror!' Biblical and political demonology converged to discredit women in a political role.

Stephens stood closer to Close than to the Barmbys. None the less his emphasis was different.[14] He did not linger on woman's sin but on the fact that God brought Jesus into the world through the body of a woman. Like Close he assumed that women had a different nature from men, but just because of this, his emphasis was on men's duty to protect women rather than on women's to obey men:

> woman, as she is declared to be the weaker vessel, so is she the most specially chosen vessel of God – chosen for that sacred office; and if chosen of God for that sacred office, then is she, by man, her fellow, by man, her mate, by man, whose is the wisdom, as hers is the love, by man, whose is the strength and power, as hers is the gentleness and the kindness of the milk of nature, so is she, by man, most of all God's gifts, to be cherished, protected, and defended.

The conditions of women's happiness were: companionate marriage, comfortable subsistence and many children ('above all to have sons'). To the ears of women today, this is not exactly a message of women's liberation or a message detaching our human potential from our fertility. But this was a message about women's protection, which spoke to the deepest concerns of many working-class women at the time. In many industries, change was disrupting the sexual division of labour as well as the balance of authority in the family; the hated New Poor Law, with its segregated workhouse, which kept women from men and children from parents, was destroying the family altogether. Since women's wages were so low, women on their own had a hard time surviving, particularly if they had to support a family. In this situation, it was realistic for women to support Stephens, which they did in large numbers, however attractive the socialist vision of future liberation might be.

The nineteenth-century English Chartist preachers and the twentieth-century Latin American exponents of the theology of liberation lived in widely different times and places. None the less, they responded to the same prophetic hope and tension within Christianity. They rejoiced in the Christian promise of a kingdom of God on earth to be created by human beings, whose full humanity would be liberated in the process. This promise exists in permanent, dynamic tension with the actual state of the world and works 'constantly to delegitimize the actuality of these historical communities in order to stir them again into a new exodus in search of that liberated community that is the mandate for their existence'.[15]

A language and symbolism is provided for a continuous and legitimate liberation struggle: oppression, promise or covenant, exodus, liberation. These terms are not some newly invented instrumental vocabulary but are signs already embedded in the experience, the common sense and the feelings of the oppressed people in both times and in both places. Nevertheless, on one crucial area, the tensions are stilled and the dynamics are stalled. In the writings of Stephens, Hill and Gutierrez, women are not being propelled by the promise into a totally liberated future. There is little forward momentum being generated by the tension between being and becoming. If anything the process seems to be going into reverse: being is to be brought more into conformity with past being than with future becoming.

Notes

1 *Past and Present*, no. 91, 1981.
2 *A Theology of Liberation. History, Politics, Salvation*, Sister Caridada Inda and J. Eagleson trans. and eds, London, 1974; 1st edn, Lima, 1971.
3 London, Whittaker, 1839.
4 p.154. He points especially to the Second Isaiah 'the best theologian among the old testament writers'; p.158 for Genesis 1:28 which Stephens used in many sermons and speeches, drawing loud cheers.
5 Stephens, op. cit., pp.13, 16, 38.
6 *Ibid.*, p.13. Hill, like Gutierrez, cites Matthew 25:31ff. and the parable of the Good Samaritan to indicate the need for active love.
7 p.13, also p.38 where he argues that the Bible provides a model for conduct 'in heart and life where our own deeds and feelings are individually concerned, and in the principle of all law, the structure of all society and the administration of the power of all government, where the well-being of nations is affected; in all things regulate our proceedings, public as well as private, according to the directions of God's most Holy Word.'
8 Stephens preached Ezekiel 22:29–30 and cited Isaiah 1; for similar texts, Gutierrez, op. cit., pp.194–6.
9 p.36. Gutierrez makes a similar list of oppressive conditions, op. cit., p.156.
10 pp.88–92, 114–15, 301–2.
11 R. Ruether and E.C. Bianchi, *From Machismo to Mutuality. Essays on Sexism and Woman–Man Liberation*, New York, 1976, p.137; Mary Daly, *Beyond God the Father. Towards a Philosophy of Women's Liberation*, Boston, 1977, pp.4, 6–7, 9, 22. For a good picture of feminist theology, which appeared after my essay was written, cf. Letty Russell (ed.), *Feminist Interpretation of the Bible* (Oxford, 1985).
12 Barbara Taylor, *Eve and the New Jerusalem*, London, 1983, pp.178–9.
13 London, 1839, pp.3–4, 8, 14–15, 17.
14 Sermon delivered at Stalybridge, in *Northern Star*, 2 March 1839.
15 Reuther, op. cit., p.137.

27
'Get Up, Stand Up':
The rastafarian movement

E. ELLIS CASHMORE

We're sick and tired of your easing, kissing game
to die and go to heaven in Jesus' name.
We know and understand
Almighty God is a living man
>   (*Get Up, Stand Up,* Bob Marley and Peter Tosh,
>   Tuff Gong Music, 1973)

I'm from Africa, but I was born in the West Indies.
>   (Ras Anthony, London 1977)

Introduction

It is a time in history when many people feel things are
approaching an end. The growing threat of nuclear annihilation,
the accelerating depletion of natural resources, the toxification of
the atmosphere; these give concrete historical substance to the
sense of *fin de siècle*. The conviction is growing amongst certain
groups that many other things are ending too. And these groups
have no substance to their prediction – it is based simply on a faith
in a deity, Haile Selassie, and a myth of a golden age that is
shortly to be restored. Members of the modern day rastafarian
movement believe that the whole social cosmos is shortly to be
overturned by their messiah; after the transformation, the whites'
material control over blacks will be broken and black people will
be returned to Africa to live harmoniously and self-sufficiently.

Like many religious movements, Ras Tafari draws strength and
sustenance from the myth of a golden age in the past – in this
case, a united continent called 'Ethiopia' untouched by European
colonizers. But this is no retreatist movement, patiently waiting
for a return to a distant utopia. Ras Tafari embraces a political
vision and a political theory that marks it off as a forward-
looking, radical movement.

Since the mid-1970s, the movement has grown staggeringly
amongst the black ghetto youths of England's inner cities. Tens of
thousands of blacks have been drawn to the rastafarian image of a
reunited Africa. It is unquestionably the fastest growing black
movement in the world, attracting adherents from the USA,

Australia, parts of Europe and the Caribbean where it first emerged in the 1930s. In fact, the best way to understand the attraction of the movement is to begin in that period.

Origins: Garvey and the black king.

The rastafarian yearning to go to Africa draws its inspiration from the philosophies of Marcus Mosiah Garvey, who, in the 1920s, created the Universal Negro Improvement Association (UNIA). This organization had one simple aim: to unite black people with what Garvey considered their rightful homeland, Africa. Garvey contended that as all black people in the Western world were descended from Africans, they should rightfully return there. The European colonizers had fragmented the African continent and dispersed its population throughout the world. Divided as they were, blacks were not able to organize themselves politically, nor indeed express themselves culturally or intellectually.

For Garvey, blacks in the Americas had not only been repressed physically but their minds had been affected by years of being subordinated to the whites. Slavery had demoralized them to the point where they actually regarded themselves as inferior. So programmes aimed at the gradual integration of blacks into white society were meaningless for Garvey. His alternative was to restore the lost dignity of blacks by breaking totally with the white world. As he expressed it:

> We shall organize the four hundred million Negroes of the
> world into a vast organization to plant the banner of freedom
> on the great continent of Africa. . . . If Europe is for the
> Europeans, then Africa is for the black peoples of the world.
> (*New York Times*, 3 August 1920)

Throughout the 1920s, Garvey travelled in the USA and the Caribbean in what was ultimately a vain attempt to enact a grand mass migration. He even bought a steamship line for this purpose. The UNIA's flag of red, black and green (Ethiopia's national colours) symbolized its affinity with Africa. It is difficult to assess the membership of the organization and the actual figures are less important than the general impact Garvey made on black consciousness. He called for a 'second emancipation – an emancipation of the minds and thoughts' (*Daily Gleaner*, 2 August 1929).

By 1938, Garvey had gone through several encounters with the police, both in the USA and Jamaica, his birthplace. His popularity declined and he left for England where he died in 1940, his dream of reunited Africa unfulfilled. Yet the myth surrounding Garvey was to grow immeasurably bigger than the man himsel and the disparity between the two was bridged by the attribution of a single, undocumented phrase: 'Look to Africa when a black king shall be crowned for the day of deliverance is near.' Around this prophecy, rastafarian philosophy was created.

Garvey's 'back-to-Africa' imperative was clearly the influence behind one of the rastafarian concepts. But the influences behind the other main concepts are more obscure, for Garvey at no stage endorsed the view that Ras Tafari, or Haile Selassie I as he was called after his ascension as Emperor of Ethiopia, was the messiah of black people. Far from foretelling the coming of Haile Selassie as a redeemer, Garvey lambasted him as a 'great coward' and 'the ruler of a country where black men are chained and flogged' (quoted in Cronon, 1974: 162).

Garvey certainly generated interest in Ethiopia by publishing articles on Ethiopian history in his journal *The Black Man*. He also couched many of his speeches in an apocalyptic idiom, referring particularly to the Book of Revelation: 'Weep not: behold the Lion that is of the tribe of Judah, the Root of David, hath overcome, to open the book and the seven seals thereof' (5:5–6). Perhaps more importantly in this context, he augmented his organization with what he called the African Orthodox Church. The church leader, Reverend George Alexander McGuire, instructed his members to tear up pictures of white Christs and Madonnas and replace them with black versions (*New York Times*, 6 August 1924). Garvey justified this:

> Our God has no colour, yet it is human to see everything
> through one's own spectacles, and since white people have seen
> their God through white spectacles we have only now started to
> see our own God through our own spectacles . . . we Negroes
> believe in the God of Ethiopia, the everlasting God (Garvey,
> 1967, vol. 1: 33–5).

While never acknowledging Haile Selassie, Garvey most certainly primed his followers' interest in Ethiopia and stirred them with the 'look to Africa' directive. Yet a recent theory claims that it was an associate of Garvey's, the Reverend James Morris Webb, who actually uttered the influential words and developed a basis for rastafarian thought in a publication called *A Black Man Will Be The Coming Universal King*, first published in 1919 (White, 1983: 9).

The theory traces the influences to another publication, *The Black Man's Bible* compiled by a certain Robert Athyli Rogers between the years 1913 and 1917. This became the foundation for a black supremacist sect called the Afro-Athlican Constructive Church which filtered its way into Jamaica in 1925. It seems that at least some of Garvey's followers found *The Black Man's Bible* plausible, particularly the chapter that spelled out the black man's glorious destiny beyond Armageddon. There was a certain complementarity between the 'bible' and Garvey's teachings and, while Garvey himself staunchly denied any connection, many others blended the two to produce a fascinating vision of a new social order.

The event that precipitated the growth of a coherent rastafarian movement came in 1930: the coronation of Haile Selassie brought together Garvey's 'black king', the day of deliverance and the 'God of Ethiopia'. Three central characters, it seems, were responsible for formulating the doctrine in which all blacks would be dramatically returned to Africa ('Ethiopia') in a cataclysmic change to be organized and executed by the redeemer and rasta deity Haile Selassie. Leonard Howell, H. Archibald Dunkley and Nathaniel Hibbert are generally credited with founding the movement in Jamaica and transforming it into an invigorated millenarian movement unshakeably committed to the consummation of history Garvey had pointed to: 'No one knows when the hour of Africa's redemption cometh. It is in the wind. It is coming. One day, like a storm, it will be here' (Garvey, 1967, vol. 1:9).

The three new prophets, in the early 1930s, attracted adherents, at the same time introducing new restrictions. Hair was to be grown in accordance with Leviticus, 21:5: 'They shall not make baldness upon their head.' So rastas, as the followers became known, coiled their hair into long, ropey 'dreadlocks'. Diets were to be 'ital', meaning natural and clean, no meat (especially pork), shellfish, scavenger seafish, etc. Ganja, or 'herb', a form of marijuana, was given religious significance and its smoking as a religious rite urged, rastas referring to Psalms 104:14: 'He causeth the grass to grow for the cattle, and herb for the service of man.'

In the years that followed, the rastafarian movement developed spasmodically in Jamaica. Its followers on occasion gathered at ports to await the arrival of Haile Selassie's ships – which, of course, never came. Sometimes frustrated at the seeming lack of progress, rastas mounted armed raids as if to assist the expected millennium. During the 1960s rastas essayed into Jamaican party politics – with a conspicuous lack of success – in efforts to relate the movement to practical matters. Yet despite the failure of the transformation to materialize and the enormous criticism heaped upon it by Jamaican authorities, the movement continued and grew more vigorous in its insistence on political change. The concept of the redemption ceded place to more immediate short-term goals, as blacks on the island called for improvements in their material lives. 'The phrase now current among them (rastas) is "Liberation before repatriation",' one writer observed of the contemporary members in the 1970s (Barrett 1977: 172).

The rastafarian image underwent something of a change in the 1970s: whereas in the 1960s they were what one writer described as 'the cult of outcastes' (O. Patterson, 1964), in the 1970s they became more of a positive cultural force, contributing to Jamaica's art and especially music, principally through the medium of reggae music. In the late 1970s one reggae musician emerged who was to symbolize rasta values and beliefs. But more than this, he played a catalytic role in the rastafarian movement's growth throughout the world. His popularity ensured a wide audience for rasta messages and concepts. His music captured the thrust of rasta themes to perfection. His name was Robert Nesta Marley.

The rastaman cometh

Marley epitomized rasta. In appearance, he cut the image of the archetypal rastaman with his head of long, coiled dreadlocks. His music was not just rasta-inspired, much of it was hymnal in quality. He wrote and sang of Ras Tafari, the return to Africa and, perhaps more pertinently, the inequalities of Babylon, that white-dominated system of control which keeps blacks suppressed and whites in power.

Between 1976, the year of the release of his influential *Rastaman Vibration* album, and 1981, when he died of cancer, Marley took the rastafarian message to the USA, Canada, parts of Europe, Africa and Australasia. It seemed Marley had relevance virtually everywhere there were black people who found a substantial gap between their own material positions and those of whites; where they experienced oppression and perceived injustice; where they felt the need to respond and recognized in the rastafarian movement a mode of response. Marley provided a personal focus for them. He came across as someone in whom the rasta deity had vested special powers; someone possessing what rastas call 'insight' – the wisdom that comes through lengthy consultations with other rastas ('reasoning') combined with a god-given gift of knowledge. Through his songs, the prophetic Marley warned in his metaphorical description of the white-dominated world: 'Slave driver the table is turn/catch a fire so you gonna get burn' ('Slave

Driver', Copyright Control, 1973). He issued a message to all other religions that were based on the concept of salvation in an after-life: 'We're sick and tired of your easing kissing game, to die and go to heaven in Jesus' name, we know and understand almighty God is a living man' ('Get Up, Stand Up', Tuff Gong Music, 1973). In one song, 'Exodus' (music BVI/Rondor music, 1977), he confidently asserted: 'We know where we're going, we know where we're from, we're leaving Babylon, going to our Father's land.'

Marley was without doubt the single biggest influence on the movement's world-wide growth although, obviously, his reception was caught up in a general emancipatory mood among black audiences. In the 1970s and 1980s, with the demise of Black Power philosophies in the Western world, young blacks were leaderless and without direction. Discontented with their conditions, they were open to the influences of Marley and inspired by his rastafarian interpretation of the world.

Babylon

Yet interestingly, Marley was only ten years old when the rastafarian movement was first sighted in England. The United Afro-West Indian Brotherhood was a rastafarian-oriented organization that surfaced briefly in London in 1955 (S. Patterson, 1963: 360). Then: 'Early in 1958 a group of bearded and rather conspicuously dressed young men were noted in the Brixton area. Several local informants confirmed that these were Ras Tafarians' (S. Patterson, 1963: 354n). It seems that many migrants from Jamaica brought their beliefs and commitments with them. Little evidence on the movement in the UK in this period is available. It seems reasonable to suggest that it remained small and insignificant, attracting only a hardcore following.

There were developments in the 1960s and 70s with the formation of rasta organizations such as the Universal Black Improvement Organization, the Twelve Tribes of Israel and the Ethiopian World Federation (which, though not totally rastafarian, attracted a strong rasta membership). These groups were successful in a limited way, establishing organizations and creating interest in the rastafarian movement, but without seizing the hearts and minds of young blacks. Yet the movement was able to take off precisely because it had no genuine central organization – as is the case with many sectarian movements. There was never any single leader with the authority to impose an unambiguous interpretation of doctrine (and therefore heresy) on the membership. One of the underlying tenets of rastafarian philosophy had always been that no person has any privilege or power over another: all are equal in 'human truths and rights'. The expression 'I and I' captures this; it means that dualities such as 'you and I' are absurd and that all people are equal and bound by the spirit of 'jah' or god.

There are a complex of reasons behind the enormous upsurge of interest in rastafarian ideas and images in the late 1970s and early 1980s. In my book *Rastaman* (1983), I have attempted to unravel some of them. But, in this context, let me state briefly that the growth of the movement is attributable to the material conditions of black youths coupled with the increasingly widespread availability of rastafarian messages through the medium of reggae music generally and the work of Bob Marley in particular. It was a powerful combination and one which set many thousands of youths along what I have called 'the journey to jah'. This involved a series of sometimes spontaneous (sometimes organized) reasoning sessions at which literally any topic could be discussed and debated at length, but always using an interpretive matrix derived from rastafarian philosophy.

This theory informed rastas' reasoning and provided a comprehensive model for interpreting any event, no matter how large or small the scale. Basically it held that, since the sixteenth century, white Europeans have sought to dominate blacks materially, culturally and intellectually. In slave days they did so through conquest and physical control. Since the late nineteenth century and the advent of legal emancipation, whites have developed other mechanisms to maintain white supremacy: education designed to maintain blacks' ignorance and religions manufactured to sedate blacks' consciousness. Garvey had recognized this when he spoke of 'a second emancipation'. For Garvey, blacks were their own worst enemies in the sense that they had for centuries accepted the white man's definition of them: inferior in every sense. This was a vestige of slavery but was being kept alive by blacks themselves. Once revealed, the captivity could be broken; Babylon, the whole system of domination, could be destroyed. As Marley urged his followers: 'Get up, stand up/don't give up the fight/it's not all that glitters is gold/half the story has never been told' ('Get Up, Stand Up', Tuff Gong Music, 1973).

The appeal of the Babylonian captivity theory lay in its simplicity and its encyclopaedic nature. Yet like other eschatologies, rasta theory has to grapple with daily life, global events and even, on the face of it, the unassimilable – such as, for example, the death of Haile Selassie in 1975 (shortly before the rasta take-off period in the UK). Ethiopia had been trouble by civil discontent since before 1973 when a failure of the annual rains resulted in an acute famine in many areas. The Emperor's authority cracked under the pressure of malcontents in 1974 and he was confined to barracks after a Co-ordinating Committee of Armed Forces seized power. After a prostate gland illness, Haile Selassie was returned to Addis Ababa for surgery which was ultimately unsuccessful. The illness was the official cause of his death on 27 August 1975. Many rastas regarded the death as inconsequential: for them, the deity had merely assumed another form and his presence remained within them. But the vast majority of rastas inferred from the reports of his death another example of the Babylonians trying to debilitate blacks. Haile Selassie had not died at all: he had 'disappeared', probably captured by the imperial forces of the West, but powerful enough to escape whenever he wished. Newspaper reports detailing Haile Selassie's death were dismissed as 'imperial propaganda' or 'the lies of the West'.

More potent, perhaps, for the growth of rasta sentiment in England were a range of experiences locally – for example, the police harassment of young blacks. The replacement of the 'sus' laws (Vagrancy Act 1824) with the Criminal Attempts Act in 1981 was an aspect of the Babylonian connivance: it gave the impression that a law that harshly affected blacks was being removed, yet it was replaced by an equally repressive set of legislation.

As more and more black youths became involved in the movement, the theory of the Babylonian captivity gained currency. So telling was the theory when applied to the life experiences of black youth that it was not necessary to accept the whole package of rastafarian beliefs. Babylon was the reality of black youths, regardless of whether they accepted the divinity of Haile Selassie and the inevitability of a return to Africa.

By 1983, the rastafarian presence was established in virtually every English city. The conviction that Babylon was a reality grew with every round of black school leavers who found their way into unemployment queues. Disillusioned at a society they believed denied them opportunities and discriminated against them, blacks found in the movement a coherent theory that offered not only an explanation of their present circumstances but an historical interpretation of why this was so, plus a vision of the future in which those circumstances could be transformed (Cashmore and Troyna, 1982: 72–86). Nowadays, there is a widespread but selective adoption of rastafarian concepts and the lines of membership have become increasingly blurred. Perhaps the only meaningful way of determining whether one is a believer is his or her acceptance of Haile Selassie. Even so, many rastas are ambivalent about the role of the deity in the movement. The upsurges of black youths in English cities in 1981 and 1985 indicate that the feeling that something must be done to effect change is growing. A god detached and unrelated to material circumstances is of little use to black youths. Their god is a motivating force within them; so if they go rioting in the streets, then this is still the will of god, for the spirit of jah lives in them. Although early critics complained that the movement was too contemplative, the 1981 and 1985 disturbances have, at least, disclosed a potential for action in the movement (Cashmore, 1981).

The rastafarian movement in England continues to attract adherents from the ranks of black youths, both male and female. The patrifocal features of its early years have receded and women now play a more active part in the movement, involving themselves in the many arts and crafts projects, bookshops, workshops, etc. that rastas have developed in recent years. The very fluidity of the membership makes an estimate of numbers impossible, but tens of thousands of young blacks are engaged in rasta activities of some kind – if only by attending rastafarian functions. The movement's rapid growth has caused some consternation, even panic in the 'outside' world; to rastas, this is evidence of the impercipience of the Babylonians or their dread of the coming crisis in the West.

It would be misleading to depict the movement only as a religion. As one rasta put it, 'it is a way of life.' Elements of worship, ritual and liturgy it has, but there is a critical anti-colonialist force guiding the movement. It is not anti-white, but anti-system – the system rastas call Babylon. Its impact on the believer, therefore, is total rather than segmental. Being a rasta does not mean setting aside one day a week for worship: it means immersing oneself in a different conception of the world, accepting a new religious order, a new interpretation of the past and future and a new political critique of society. To many, the rastafarian movement may pose a threat but to others it has brought an invigorating force in the form of a critical impulse to the black community. To the rasta, the movement is restoring confidence and providing the theoretical equipment with which to comprehend and criticize a social system that has, for over 400 years, anchored black people at the foot of society. It is 400 years too long for rastas; now is the time to 'get up, stand up'.

References

Barrett, L. (1977), *The Rastafarians*, London.
Cashmore, E. (1981), 'After the Rastas', *New Community*, vol. 9, no. 2, pp.173–81.
Cashmore, E. (1983), *Rastaman*, London.
Cashmore, E. and Troyna, B. eds (1982), *Black Youth in Crisis*, London.
Cronon, E. (1974), *Black Moses: The Story of Marcus Garvey*, London.
Garvey, M. (1967), *Philosophy and Opinions*, 3 vols, London.
Patterson, O. (1964), 'Ras Tafari: the cult of outcastes', *New Society*, vol. 4, 111, pp.15–17.
Patterson, S. (1963), *Dark Strangers*, London.
White, T. (1983), *Catch a Fire: The Life of Bob Marley*, London.

Socialism and religion

28
The Christian Left and the beginnings of Christian–Marxist dialogue, 1935–45

DAVID ORMROD

Until approximately 1931, Christian Socialism in Britain was most successful in reinvigorating the life of the churches and calling them back to the 'social question'. In October 1928 however, a contributor to the first issue of the new *Socialist Christian*, the Rev. Marcus Donovan, commented,

> There are signs that we are losing the fervour of the earlier years of the century. The Christian Social Union and the Church Socialist League were twenty years or more ago the inspiration of many of us. I am inclined to think there were more men ordained about that time than ever before. The social crusade caught us up, and we felt that we were doing a man's work in the slum parishes to which we were sent. And undoubtedly the movement had an influence out of all proportion to its numbers. If we didn't bring one working man to church, we brought the church nearer to the working man, and the Archbishop's Committee's Fifth Report (1918) represents the high water mark of the official church opinions on social questions. Yet now we are conscious of a decline.
> (*The Socialist Christian*, 1(1), p.15)

A similarly pessimistic assessment of Christian Socialism for the 1930s and 40s is followed by Dr Edward Norman in his largely polemical study, *Church and Society in England, 1770–1970*, which in more general terms attempts to discredit the liberal or radical views held by sections of the Anglican establishment during the last century. By concentrating his attention mainly on the Christian Social Union stream of Christian Socialism, on the career and writings of William Temple, and on the evidence of episcopal charges and other statements, Dr Norman ignores and hence misrepresents the strength and authentically socialist character of the Christian Socialist movement of the 1930s and 40s. Furthermore he fails to acknowledge the activities of its proliferating organizations and the breadth of its publications during this period, shown in the diagram (Figure 28.1).

After the Labour defeat of 1931, Christian Socialists increasingly worked for socialism within the Labour Party, as a critical voice

435

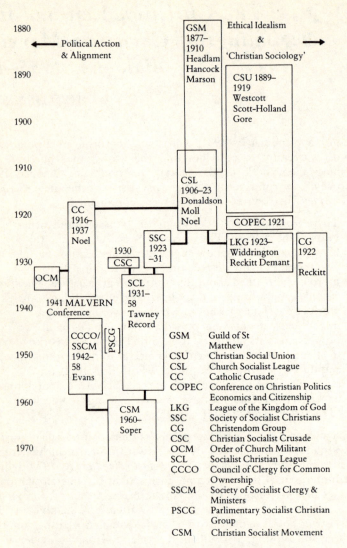

1880
← Political Action & Alignment

GSM 1877–1910 Headlam Hancock Marson

Ethical Idealism & 'Christian Sociology' →

1890

CSU 1889–1919 Westcott Scott-Holland Gore

1900

1910

CSL 1906–23 Donaldson Moll Noel

1920

CC 1916–1937 Noel

COPEC 1921

SSC 1923 –31

1930

CSC

LKG 1923– Widdrington Reckitt Demant

CG 1922– Reckitt

OCM

SCL 1931–58 Tawney Record

1941 MALVERN Conference

1950

CCCO/ SSCM 1942–58 Evans

PSCG

1960

CSM 1960– Soper

1970

GSM	Guild of St Matthew
CSU	Christian Social Union
CSL	Church Socialist League
CC	Catholic Crusade
COPEC	Conference on Christian Politics Economics and Citizenship
LKG	League of the Kingdom of God
SSC	Society of Socialist Christians
CG	Christendom Group
CSC	Christian Socialist Crusade
OCM	Order of Church Militant
SCL	Socialist Christian League
CCCO	Council of Clergy for Common Ownership
SSCM	Society of Socialist Clergy & Ministers
PSCG	Parlimentary Socialist Christian Group
CSM	Christian Socialist Movement

The depth of the boxes showes the periods during which the organisations flourished.

The width of the boxes indicates, roughly, the relative sizes of the organisations. Thus the CSU was a more broadly based and larger organisation than, for example, the Catholic Crusade.

Some organisations were formed as splinter groups from others and are therefore connected by a line.

FIGURE 28.1   Christian Socialist organizations.

within the party. R.H. Tawney, A.D. Lindsay, and Stafford Cripps played major roles in expressing a visionary but radical and practicable socialism during the 1930s, largely through the vehicle of the Labour Party (Crossman, 1960, pp.311–12, 816–18; Terrill). Their objectives can be loosely summarized as a belief in the real possibility of constructing an 'ethical state', a state, that is, which would accept responsibility for providing equal educational opportunities, a certain level of housing provision, minimum rates of pay, acceptable working conditions, and so on. The duties of *Christian citizenship* formed a theme which ran through much of Temple's writing especially, which spelt out the need for an inter-locking relationship between Church and State (Temple; Baker).

During the late 1930s, however, and in the early years of the war when discontent with the coalition government mounted, Christian Socialism underwent a substantial politicization. Popular pressure for an 'ethical socialism' developed drawing together Christians and socialists, both marxist and non-marxist. Its most well-known manifestation was the Common Wealth movement and party led by Sir Richard Acland. But the extent of Christian-Marxist dialogue in this period remains largely forgotten, reported especially in the pages of *Left News* from June 1941 onwards, and to a small extent in the *New Statesman*. Like Tom Wintringham's proposals for an alternative defence strategy, this literature awaits rediscovery and further exploration by socialist historians (Fernbach, pp.82–3). This essay will suggest that the threat of fascism during the 1930s transformed the objective of Christian Socialist thinking (the Kingdom) from the 'ethical state' to the internationalist 'moral community'. In the process, a new theology was created, the foundations of which were laid by John Macmurray and popularized by Kenneth Ingram.

In 1933, Gollancz published a volume of thirty-three short essays to mark the centenary of 'perhaps the chief Christian triumph in history', Wilberforce's Emancipation Act and Shaftesbury's Factory Act of 1833, referred to by contemporaries as the defeat of 'the Black Slavery and the White Slavery' (Dearmer, p.9). *Christianity and the Crisis* attempted to relate the Christian social movement to the crisis of the 1930s. The contributors, mainly Anglican clergy and laymen, wrote of 'chaos and confusion' in intellectual and moral life, in literature, international relations, and in the social and economic order. They included William Temple, Charles Raven, Maurice Reckitt, P.T. Kirk, Albert Mansbridge and Hewlett Johnson, but there was no common perspective to hold the book together, still less to provide a programme of reform. Temple's conclusion argued that it was only through 'individual repentance on the part of a sufficient proportion of men (who) control policy, commerce, and industry' that political and industrial problems could be cured (Dearmer, p.608). Socialist solutions and marxist ideas were not considered, and the inclusion of Berdiaeff's polemic against 'communist secularism' which emphasized the 'militant atheism' of communism 'directed to ends completely anti-Christian', signified marked hostility (Dearmer, p.582).

It was precisely to challenge reductionist views of communism – the idea that communism professed a mechanistic determinism and reduced all phenomena to physical and chemical factors – that a small group of Christians, marxists and other socialists conceived a new symposium which would make some identification between marxian socialism and certain elements of Christian belief (Lewis, 1935, p.13). *Christianity and the Social Revolution* was planned in the weeks following the appearance of *Christianity and the Crisis*, although publication was delayed until 1935. Gollancz's communist assistant, John Lewis, edited the collection with assistance from Karl Polanyi, Donald Kitchin, Joseph Needham, Charles Raven, and John Macmurray; other contributors included Conrad Noel, W.H. Auden, Gilbert Binyon, John Cornford, A.L. Morton and Reinhold Niebuhr. Raven provided the only link between the two volumes, and contributed the introduction to the second, which maintained:

> the cast-iron closed system which rightly or wrongly we have associated with marxism has been rendered elastic and transformable . . . what matters is that the original theory which logically left no room for personality or spiritual quality has been drastically reshaped; that materialistic concepts, in the strict sense of the words, are now anathema; and that by assimilation to Spinoza, Hegel, and the idealists a fresh and synthetic scheme of thought is being constructed. (Lewis, 1935, p.24)

An optimistic statement perhaps, but the collection included two essays by John Macmurray which moved towards a synthesis of Christianity and Communism via Marx's early thought, through his understanding of Hegel and Feuerbach and the release of the human content of Christianity from its religious forms, from the organized churches. 'What Christian Socialist, however optimistic,' Macmurray asked, 'has ever dreamt of claiming that he had the church behind him?' (Lewis, 1935, p.511). At this stage Kenneth Ingram was regarded by Lewis as a crude reductionist (Lewis, 1935, p.12), and Hewlett Johnson had not yet been converted to the cause of Soviet Communism (Johnson, 1968, p.142). The 'Christian Left' hardly existed in 1935, but the publication of *Christianity and the Social Revolution* marked a complete break in Christian Socialist thinking and the real beginnings of Christian-Marxist dialogue in England. It opened up the possibility of the existence of a new generation of Christian Communists, committed to the disappearance of idealistic religion whilst referring that ideal to the world of material reality.

It was during 1937 and 1938 that a loose association or tendency known as the Christian Left developed, independent of any of the existing Christian Socialist organizations. As was the case with many non-religious socialists, it was the Spanish Civil War which exercised a strongly radicalizing influence on significant numbers of Christians. In April 1937 a religious delegation was invited to Spain by the legitimate Spanish government, because nationalist propaganda had alleged widespread republican atrocities against the Church. Stories circulated of the burning of churches and the shooting of priests and many felt that the 'fate of Spain was bound up largely with Christian opinion throughout the world'. Nine representatives of the major denominations therefore visited Spain, including the Dean of Canterbury, Hewlett Johnson, Professor John Macmurray, and Kenneth Ingram. After an arduous, dangerous and distressing visit, the delegation issued statements in Paris and London which emphasized that there were no signs of a republican attack on religion, 'but an intense religious life which is part and parcel of the struggle for the defence of the Republic' (Johnson, 1937). Large sections of the British press and members of the Anglican hierarchy attacked the delegation's authentic observations, and Hewlett Johnson was accused of intervening 'on the side of unadulterated communism' (Johnson, 1968, p.148). This episode served to draw together the nucleus of the Christian Left at a time when large numbers of ordinary Christians were becoming aware of the horrors of fascism.

Later in the year a Left Book Club edition of *Christianity and the Social Revolution* was published with a preface by John Lewis which appealed for a united front against fascism, an alliance between socialists and Christians. This gave rise to a large correspondence and was followed up by a conference for religious leaders on Christianity and socialism. 'It was more successful than we dared hope', Lewis commented later, 'and we at once suggested to the (Left Book Club) groups that they should invite members of the churches to work with them whenever suitable subjects arose' (Lewis, 1970, p.49). Hewlett Johnson had meanwhile decided to turn his attention to the Soviet Union, following his experiences in Spain and his gradual disillusionment with the Social Credit Movement, and visited the country with his friend A.T. D'Eye, a WEA lecturer. D'Eye had lived in the Soviet Union in 1934 and had an easy familiarity with the literature of marxism, which he imparted to the Dean. More than anything else, it was D'Eye's influence and their joint visit which converted Hewlett Johnson to communism (Johnson, 1968, pp.149–54; D'Eye). On their return, they planned the writing of *The Socialist Sixth of the World* which appeared two years later in December 1939. Gollancz and Lewis encouraged Johnson as a writer and a speaker at Left Book Club gatherings, although Gollancz later ridiculed his public meetings and tried to distance himself from those powerful communist influences which had sustained the Left Book Club (Gollancz, 1953, pp.358–63).

The ground was thus prepared for a fruitful alliance between socialist and Christian opinion, ranging from philosophical and theological discourse to mild propaganda. In July 1938, Lewis and Gollancz launched a Christian Book Club, with the publication of *The Struggle for Religious Freedom in Germany* by A.S. Duncan-Jones, Dean of Chichester. Hewlett Johnson was general editor. Just under one thousand members enrolled, and the editors of *Left News* commented, 'The mobilisation of that thousand means, in effect, the mobilisation of tens of thousands of the Christian public', since the bulk of the membership consisted of clergymen (*Left News*, 27, July 1938, p.872). Several local Christian Book Club groups sprang up on the model of the Left Book Club groups, and by October, seventeen such groups existed. (The number of local LBC groups then stood at around 880.) If the Spanish Civil War had mobilized more socialists than Christians, then the Nazi persecution of the churches, described in the Dean of Chichester's book, demanded a specifically Christian commitment to the struggle against fascism. *The Struggle for Religious Freedom in Germany* pointed out that fascism was not merely a political system but was also a religion, a form of radical mysticism sustained by apocalyptic conceptions, and that in the last resort, nazism would be faced with 'the one opponent that violence cannot subdue', the Christian faith. It went on to describe the growth of fascist paganism within the 'German Christian' movement led by Bishop Hossenfelder and the heroic opposition of the Confessional Church, where the English-speaking world came to believe the 'true soul' of Germany was to be found. At this stage, John Lewis believed 'there is an immense opportunity . . . in rallying the churches against fascism' since the only open resistance to Hitler within Germany now came from the Christian opposition (*Left News*, 30, October 1938).

As a response to the spread of fascism in Europe, the growth of the Christian Left necessarily proceeded in directions quite different from those followed by the earlier Christian Socialist organizations. In the first place, it developed as a contribution *within* a spectrum of socialist and communist debate, whereas the earlier Christian Socialist organizations had frequently been isolated, addressing only their own membership. At the Left Book Club Summer School of 1938 for example, a section on Christianity and Socialism with Needham, Polanyi, Lewis and Ingram as principal speakers was included amongst sections on philosophy, the economic crisis, international and home affairs, current political problems, and the Soviet Union, involving a galaxy of left intellectuals (*Left News*, 25, May 1938). In the second place, just as German fascism used a quasi-mystical language and attempted to develop a new religion, albeit a form of crude paganism, the spokesmen of the Christian Left tended to see themselves as innovators in the religious sphere, propelled by an upward thrust in the course of evolution. Thus, Ingram suggested in 1939:

> At this particular stage in world development, the Divine Will is driving mankind forward towards a higher stage in social evolution. If this is resisted, then there can only be a regression to barbarism . . . man must choose whether he goes forwards to socialism or backwards to fascism . . . (fascism) cannot be defeated by anything merely negative, only by progress. (*Left News*, 33, January 1939)

Later, writing in *Left News* towards the end of 1941, Ingram claimed that the columns of that periodical might serve as 'a laboratory where the religion of the new age can be tested and hammered into shape . . . from the world-upheaval must come the evolution of a new type of Christianity if Christianity is to survive' (*Left News*, 66, December 1941). In the third place, the Christian Left inevitably gave much attention to the persecution of the Jews, the historic role of the Jewish religion, and the unity of Judeo-Christian thought as materialism. Macmurray believed that fascism depended upon the Jewish consciousness which it opposed: that it had annexed the negative side of that consciousness, that is, the purely racial side by which it claimed the German people as the chosen race, and was inevitably driven to reject the positive reality and outcome of Judaism, which was Christianity.

This was expressed in *The Clue to History* published at the end of 1938 (Macmurray, 1938, pp.225–9).

It is at this point that we can perceive something of the sympathy and common understanding linking the two principal spokesmen of *Left News* and the Christian Left, respectively Gollancz and Macmurray. The connection is important because although Macmurray produced a short-lived periodical entitled *Christian Left*, it was through *Left News* that the tendency made a broader impact. Victor Gollancz, as a Jewish publisher with an exceptional breadth of religious knowledge and experience, was in a unique position to communicate the course of events in Germany. He regarded himself as a 'Jew at heart' – his parents were orthodox – who was nevertheless a follower of Christ, believing in 'the World's desperate need of Christianity' (Gollancz, 1952, p.433). With Macmurray, he shared not only a firm grasp of the dialectical unity or complementarity between Judaism and Christianity in the historical process, but also a belief in the unavoidable necessity governing the realization of the divine intention within that process – summarized in Macmurray's assertion that 'human intentions which are opposed to the intention of God for men are necessarily self-frustrating'. This passage from Gollancz's autobiography might equally well come from *The Clue to History*:

> We must fulfil our own natures, and help God, by healing the breach between religion and politics, between the sacred and profane – thus realising the intention of Judaism: and how, when it comes to it, we cannot help doing so. (Gollancz, 1952, p.433–4)

Although Macmurray followed an academic career – he held a chair of philosophy at University College, London, in the 1930s and at Edinburgh in the post-war period – he is one of a small number of philosophers to have written autobiographically. It was his experiences during the Great War which caused him to view the churches as the 'various national religions of Europe' and to regard the purpose of his own philosophizing as the eradication of war (Conford, p.16). He therefore turned towards marxism in the 1920s, especially the early writings, and accepted Marx's criticism of nineteenth-century Christianity as unreal, idealist, and sentimental. The reality of Christianity, Macmurray discovered, lay in its Jewishness, in the nature of the Hebrew consciousness which could not accept a dualistic separation between religious activity and other departments of life, between thought and action. Hebrew religion viewed God as a worker, he maintained, unlike dualistic religions which viewed God as an aristocrat (Macmurray, 1938, p.33).

From an emphasis on the intensely religious character of Judaism, Macmurray went on to expound a method by which religion might interpret evolution. Those few marxist writers and theologians who have attempted to trace interconnections between Christian and marxist thought have generally done so by following through humanistic Hegelian concerns and categories within marxism, particularly the question of alienation – such as Meszaros and, more recently, Lash (Lash, chapter 14). Macmurray, it is true, had much to say about the form of the personal: that creative action was experienced most fully in personal relations, and that consciousness could not be understood in isolation from society. But his contribution, especially in the late 1930s, was directed towards a more *scientific* understanding of the way in which the religious impulse transformed society than might be expected from a Hegelian marxist. (In the 1960s, he described himself, in a letter to T.R. Sayers, as a 'kind of Lukacs marxist'.) The inevitability of socialist transformation, he believed, derived less from any economic determinism than from the essential nature of human personality, most fully disclosed in the ministry of Jesus. Psychology and anthropology were as important to Macmurray's marxism as economics.

Macmurray, in fact, viewed Jesus not as an ethical idealist, laying down a specific code of behaviour, but as a prophet with a concrete understanding of 'the way in which the world worked', of the pattern of evolution. The dialectical processes underlying the evolution of human society, Macmurray argued, involved two sets of contradictions: the first between the intentions of men and the will of God, and the second between the historic facts of the Jewish diaspora and the state-building tendency of Christianity (Macmurray, 1938, pp.42–120). In this 'divine' interpretation of evolution, a secular vocabulary corresponds to the Christian one in Macmurray's scheme, so:

God as Creator	=	workmanship
the action of God in history	=	historical process
the purpose of God	=	the creation of a personal community of free and equal persons

As far as the first contradiction is concerned, Macmurray wrote:

History has to be thought both as the act of God in the world, and as the act of Man in the world . . . (however) The intentions of man not only do not coincide with the intention of

God, but are often in active opposition to it. The principle through which Jesus achieves this unification is fundamentally simple, though its applications and expressions are manifold. It is that human intentions which are opposed to the intention of God for man are necessarily self-frustrating. . . . If (man's) intention is the opposite of the divine intention, then they necessarily achieve, not what they intended, but its opposite. This principle is not an 'act of faith'; it is a discovery of reason. Its necessity is a logical necessity. There is no need for an 'intervention' of God to frustrate the purposes of men who are in opposition to him, since they cannot be in opposition to him without being in opposition to themselves. (Macmurray, 1938, pp.94–5)

The same law of self-frustration was also seen to operate at the level of whole societies, as a second type of contradiction or dialectic. On the one hand, the Jewish religion and the historical phenomenon of the Jewish diaspora rejected nationalism as the basis for human society, but tended towards the idea of racial superiority; on the other, Christianity ostensibly aimed at the creation of a community of free and equal persons, but in its prevalent dualist forms tended to towards state-building and extreme nationalism. In Macmurray's view, fascism represented the purely negative side of the dialectical relationship between Judaism and Christianity, as an attempt to provide a racial basis to the European conception of nationality. On the positive side, a fully integrated Judeo-Christianity would produce an internationalist moral community, but in 1938, this was the remotest of possibilities. In its opposition to the Jewish consciousness, Macmurray believed that fascism would only universalize that consciousness, hence, somewhat ambitiously, 'it is the inevitable destiny of fascism to create what it intends to prevent – a socialist commonwealth of the world' (Macmurray, 1938, p.237).

This, briefly stated, was the political theology of the Christian Left. The style and terse language of Macmurray's books made for difficult reading, however, and some of his ideas, particularly those focussing on the primacy of the personal were presented in a more accessible form by the Anglo-Catholic lawyer, Kenneth Ingram. Ingram's *Christianity – Right or Left?* (1937) and *Towards Christianity* (1939) avoided any discussion of Macmurray's attempts at a Christian-Marxist synthesis, but elaborated a radical Christian Socialism which attacked dualism, laboured the distinction between idealist and realist Christianity, and suggested that the latter should on no account develop its own social programme (as the Christendom Group had attempted, associated with Maurice Reckitt and 'Christian Sociology') but throw its full weight behind the left (Ingram, 1937, pp.149–50). Ingram's speeches at Christian Book Club and Left Book Club conferences, meetings and summer schools evidently drew their main inspiration from Macmurray, for example:

> (fascism) cannot be defeated by anything merely negative, only by progress. Since the aim of Christianity is the building of a Kingdom of persons' in which there is an equal opportunity for all, the Church must identify itself with the movement towards socialism. (*Left News*, 33, January 1939)

The aspirations of the Christian Left were primarily inter-nationalist, in which the vision of an international moral community transcended that of the 'ethical state' of progressive Anglicanism. To the socialist morality thus implied, Ingram added his own hopes for a sexually liberated society, contrasting the bogus sex-obsessed morality of idealist Christianity with the deeper social morality of realist Christianity. He was convinced that the main source of antagonism towards the Church lay in the area of sexual morality, and advocated a new sexual morality for the 'new age'. Ingram was strongly influenced by Edward Carpenter, was himself homosexual, and regarded male comrade-ship as the highest relationship and the only way to bridge the gulf between social classes (Hilliard, pp.203–4). If the main drive behind Macmurray's work was a loathing of nationalistic violence and militarism, it seems that Ingram was driven by the need to integrate his sexuality with his religious beliefs. During the 1940s he argued that the morality of sexual behaviour was determined only by the presence or absence of love (Ingram, 1933, pp.67–70).

The outbreak of war naturally produced something of a hiatus in these discussions, but by 1941, an important shift had occurred in their direction. Rather than presenting a united front against fascism, the purpose of an alliance between Christians and socialists was envisaged as the equally urgent one of determining the priorities and principles upon which a new postwar society might be built, based on an 'ethical socialism'. From the Christian side, the new elements in the situation demanded, first, a greater flexibility in the thinking of the Christian Left. Macmurray's socialist thought became self-consciously less scientific, less inevitablist, as he came to doubt the usefulness of dialectical theory in explaining the Nazi phenomenon. As a Christian, Macmurray believed that human reality was superorganic, but that this would not invalidate the use of dialectics for the interpretation of history because,

> the historical process is organic in type so long as social development is not planned as a whole, but is the unplanned resultant of human activity which all aim at something less or something other than the control of the social process itself. This, it now seems (in 1941), was too optimistic. I did not believe in the possibility of the success of the Nazi effort, even in the short run, to control its own social process in resistance to socialism. The Nazis have succeeded in asserting a rational control of society as a whole. I do not think that they can be successful, in the long run, but they have introduced an element of planning and therefore of rational calculation into the social process which makes the dialectical interpretation no longer fully adequate. The appearance of this dispute about ethics and socialism is a direct and necessary result of this. (*Left News*, 59, May 1941)

The 'dispute' to which Macmurray referred was a long-running debate on 'Socialism and Ethics' in the columns of *Left News* from March–June 1941 which preceded and in a sense gave birth to the regular monthly feature, 'From the Christian Left', which continued for two years. This new insistence on the moral element in socialism involving a 'passionate love of humanity' coincided with a loss of faith in social systems which rested merely on rational planning. Gollancz advocated a return to the 'evangelical spirit of socialism' characteristic of the early days of the ILP: a socialism not primarily more efficient than capitalism, nor the inevitable next stage in historical development, but the 'embodiment of goodness in organised social life' (*Left News*, 60, June 1941). In the second place this change in direction meant that the marxist-inclined and internationalist thinking of the Christian Left could draw closer to the earlier concerns of orthodox Christian Socialists embodied in the idea of the 'ethical state'. In January 1941, William Temple had chaired and convened the Malvern Conference, a group of two hundred Anglican clergy and laity which met to consider the 'ordering of the new society' from an Anglican point of view. Its proceedings were theological rather than practical but widespread interest was aroused by the passing of an anti-capitalist resolution proposed by Sir Richard Acland, stating that private ownership of the principal resources could be a 'stumbling block' to the Christian life (*Malvern, 1941*; Baker, pp.32–4). The Malvern Conference aroused the expectations of progressive Anglicans and provided a meeting-ground for the older CSU stream of reformist Christian Socialism (represented during the 1930s by the Industrial Christian Fellowship) with the small but influential Christian Left. Kenneth Ingram, Mervyn Stockwood and Alan Ecclestone participated from the Christian Left and Richard Acland's persuasive interventions presented the case for common ownership. Two pamphlets containing the Malvern findings had a joint circulation of over a million, and from a more detached position, Professor Joad saw clear evidence of a growing minority of practising Christians eager to 'align themselves with the revolutionary tendencies stirring in the matrix of the times' (Dark; Joad). Mervyn Stockwood wrote to the editor of *Tribune* to announce that 'the Church is more socialist than you' (*Tribune* 2.v.41, quoted Calder, p.37). In the Christian Left columns of *Left News*, a widening circle of radical Christian Socialists – including John Collins, Mervyn Stockwood, Sidney Dark and Richard Acland as well as the core of the original Christian Left, Macmurray, Ingram, and Gollancz – attempted to extend the limits of 'Malvernization' and appealed to socialists to 'release themselves from servitude to an outworn nineteenth-century anti-Christian materialism' (*Left News*, 63, September 1941). Important contributions came from Macmurray on religion in the Soviet Union, Tillich on Marxism and Christian Socialism, and Laski on religion, morality and policy.

It was Acland's Common Wealth movement and party which, from 1942, served as the main political channel through which the claims of an 'ethical socialism' were to be pressed. Gollancz regarded Acland, in preference to Stafford Cripps, as the 'only prominent politician of our day who has consistently and uncompromisingly made the Christian and socialist appeal' (Gollancz, 1952, p.275). Acland's well-known books, *Unser Kampf* (1940), *The Forward March* (1941), *How it can be done* (1943), and his pamphlet of 1941, 'It Must be Christianity', set out the case for common ownerhip and the renunciation of empire based on moral rather than material premises. One of Acland's numerous correspondents wrote, after reading *Unser Kampf*, 'I welcome your book because it sets up a moral standard for society based directly on the Christian ethic, and then dares to indicate the practical political and economic consequences of this moral standard' (Calder, p.25). Several prominent Christian Socialists were associated with the Common Wealth movement and the two informal groupings from which it was formed, Forward March and the 1941 Committee, including Ingram, Macmurray, A.D. Lindsay, the Bishop of Bradford, as well as fellow-travellers Gollancz and Joad. Tom Driberg, an Anglo-Catholic socialist, was one of three Common Wealth candidates to be elected to Parliament in the Maldon by-election of 1942 (Driberg, pp.180–5).

In concrete political terms, the Common Wealth party made only a limited impact. But it was only one of a number of political responses to the build-up of pressure for an 'ethical socialism' during the war years. Another was the formation of the 1945 Parliamentary Socialist Christian Group with a membership of over one hundred Labour MPs, which exercised a powerful influence in maintaining the post-war Labour government's commitment to a socialist programme (Skeffington-Lodge; *Faith and Hope*). The history of the Christian Left may appear as one of the lost causes of history but the influence of a body of ideas or a climate of opinion can rarely be specified in an exact and predictable way. Indeed, it was Macmurray's special insight to suggest that creative action often proceeds through a process of *negative* contradictions, rather than through the translation of human intentions into actuality. The Christian Left never attempted to present a concrete political programme of its own, but to challenge existing ideologies, secular and ecclesiastical, and to create conditions of mutual understanding between Christians and Communists. In 1954, Kenneth Ingram described it as a school of thought which 'is largely an expression of the conviction not merely that Christianity demands social thinking and action, but that social thinking and action themselves create a radical development in religious understanding.' If this comment seems to hark back to his earlier aspirations towards 'hammering into shape the religion of the new age' during the early years of the war, it also anticipates the insights of modern liberation theology (Ingram, 1954, p.207).

In two respects at least, it can be said that the 'dialectical religion' of the Christian Left produced significant effects. Its impact in terms of realizing the international obligations of a 'moral community' was felt through widespread Christian support for a number of international agencies formed in the late 1940s and 50s, particularly Christian Action (founded by Collins in 1947) and War on Want (founded mainly by Gollancz in 1952), but also the Movement for Colonial Freedom (1954) and the Campaign for Nuclear Disarmament (1959) which were partially organized by Christian Left sympathizers (Acland, 1976). And then Macmurray's efforts to explore the interconnections between Marxism and Christianity remain as landmarks in the history of Christian-Marxist dialogue. Their neglect may be partly explained by the fact that Macmurray's first priority was an understanding of German fascism rather than a less historically specific phenomenon such as colonialism. But his insights into the Hebrew consciousness and the sources of Christian dualism survive as reminders of the creative potential of the religious impulse in societies which have largely abandoned organized religion. In this respect, the relevance of his thought to improved East-West understanding is clear.

Items referred to in the text (in the order in which they are used)

The Socialist Christian (ed. F. Hughes), October 1928, 1(1).

R.H.S. Crossman, 'An Anthology of Tawney', *New Statesman*, 26 November 1960.

R.H.S. Crossman, 'G.D.H. Cole and Socialism', *New Statesman*, 3 September 1960.

R. Terrill, *R.H. Tawney and his Times*, 1973.

W. Temple, *Citizen and Churchman*, 1941.

E. Baker, *William Temple and his Message*, 1946.

D. Fernbach, 'Tom Wintringham and Socialist Defence Strategy', *History Workshop*, 14, 1982.

P. Dearmer (ed.), *Christianity and the Crisis*, 1933.

J. Lewis (ed.), *Christianity and the Social Revolution*, 1935.

H. Johnson, *Searching for Light*, 1968.

H. Johnson, *Report of a Religious Delegation to Spain*, 1937.

J. Lewis, *The Left Book Club: an Historical Record*, 1970.

A.T. D'Eye, *Russia Revisited: with the Dean of Canterbury through the USSR*, 1945.

V. Gollancz, *My Dear Timothy, an Autobiographical Letter to his Grandson*, 1952.

V. Gollancz, *More for Timothy, being the second instalment of an Autobiographical Letter to his Grandson*, 1953.

Left News.

J. Macmurray, *The Clue to History*, 1938.

P. Conford, 'John Macmurray, a Neglected Philosopher', *Radical Philosophy*, Spring, 1977.

N. Lash, *A Matter of Hope. A Theologian's Reflections on the Thought of Karl Marx*, 1981.

K. Ingram, *Christianity, Right or Left?*, 1937.

D. Hilliard, 'UnEnglish and Unmanly; Anglo-Catholicism and Homosexuality', *Victorian Studies*, 25(2), 1982.

K. Ingram, *Modern Thought on Trial*, 1933.

Malvern 1941; the Life of the Church and the Order of Society, being the Proceedings of the Archbishop of York's Conference, 1941.

S. Dark, 'Alternative for Christianity', *New Statesman*, XXIV (602), 5 September 1942.

C.E.M. Joad, 'Prospect for Religion', *New Statesman*, XXIV (601), 29 August 1942.

A. Calder, 'Commonwealth', University of Sussex PhD thesis, 1977.

T. Driberg, *The Best of Both Worlds*, 1953.

T.C. Skeffington-Lodge, 'The Socialist Christian League', *The Christian Socialist*, 100, 1980.

Parliamentary Christian Socialist Group, *Faith and Hope and 1950*, 1949.

K. Ingram, 'The Church and Social Thinking' in S.G. Evans (ed.), *Return to Reality*, 1954.

R. Acland, 'Matters of Politics' in I. Henderson (ed.), *Man of Christian Action: Canon John Collins – the Man and his Work*, 1976.

29
The God-builders in pre-revolutionary Russia: Social democracy as a religion

CHRIS READ

The idea of socialism as a religion did not begin in Russia nor was it confined to that country. In England, for example, socialism had many intimate ties with organized religion and, like humanism, some of its varieties themselves took on the form of a church even to the extent of there being socialist rites and services. In France Saint-Simon had long ago proclaimed socialism to be *Le Nouveau Christianism*. This tradition, however, had no influence on Russian socialism. One of the first people who did have an influence on Russia and pointed out that socialism was a religion, was the self-taught philosopher, Joseph Dietzgen, whose main work in this field was *Die Religion der Sozialdemokratie*, published in 1891. His admirers considered him to be the supreme example of the common man who, naturally from his experience of and reflection on his work and on society, had undergone a development parallel to that of Marx and had arrived at a dialectical materialist conception of the world which had a great deal in common with that of Marx and Engels. (Both Lenin and

Engels thought highly of Dietzgen.) But perhaps more than any external influence, the main reason that Russian socialism had a religious interpretation lay in the Russian intellectual tradition and the place of religion in that tradition. For example, A.V. Lunacharsky (1875–1933), who wrote the most important and thorough treatise on the religious roots of socialism at this time, and Berdyaev, both recorded that in their early development religion played an important role as a phenomenon that had to be faced and explained.

These and other Russian social democratic thinkers, the so-called God-builders (*Bogostroiteli*) did not form a coherent movement and each member emphasized different features of a common pool of sources, which included Christ, Marx and Nietzsche. It was built up partly as a response to idealist taunts that socialism ignored philosophical questions and partly because the general religious atmosphere of the time spilled over into this quarter. In any case a movement which pretended to intellectual respectability and popularity in Russia had to come to terms with religious questions because they were so much part of the way of thinking of the Russian people. In addition, the peculiar position of religion in the state structure of the autocracy gave it a special significance, far greater than in any major western European country.

The central work of the God-builders was, without doubt, Lunacharsky's two-volume work *Religiya i sotsializm* (*Religion and Socialism*) – the fruit, he wrote, of a long-standing interest in the phenomenon of religion. The fundamental notions of the book, said Lunacharsky, had been fermenting in his mind for ten years.

> The basic ideas – the essence of religion in general, the meaning and direction of the development of religiousness, the connection between scientific socialism and the cherished expectations of mankind as expressed in religious myths and dogmas and the replacement of them by metaphysical systems, the central position of 'labour' in the net outlook – all [these ideas] arose at an early date in the author's mind and were not changed in essence, but were only clarified and consolidated in proportion to his deeper acquaintanceship with the history of religion and philosophy and with scientific socialism (Lunacharsky, 1908, vol. 1, p.7).

The root of his interest in religion and in idealism may well have lain in his deeply humanistic openness to all aspects of human experience and to his respect for the artistic and cultural achievements of mankind. He was aware of the appeal of religious ideals to man, but for him Marxism was attractive because it was a richer tradition, and as a companion work to his book on religion, he hoped to write another which would disclose 'the great treasury of ideals concealed within Marxism, a treasury before which all the enthusiasms and highly scientific fabrications of the idealists pale' (Lunacharsky, 1908, p.18). Thus for Lunacharsky religion had been a creative factor in human history and the argument of his book was that the creative and archetypal aspects of it were of value to the socialists and that socialism, particularly as it shared with the best of religion a thirst for justice and equality, had grown out of a religious–socialist tradition going back at least to Moses.

Lunacharsky's view of religion derived in its entirety from nineteenth-century German criticism of religion and theology. Lunacharsky was quite clear about the provenance of his ideas and in his chapter 'What is religion?' he showed how, step by step, transcendental religion had been replaced by humanist religion. The first and most important contribution was that of Feuerbach, whose work, according to Lunacharsky, resulted in the raising of anthropology to the status of theology. 'After Feuerbach, the philosophical religion of God is dead,' he proclaimed (Lunacharsky, 1908, p.31). Thus Feuerbach substituted 'man' for 'God' and the religious problem was solved.

For Lunacharsky, as for Plekhanov and many other socialists, the root of the old religion lay in fear of natural forces arising from ignorance of their causes. Primitive man, aware of his own consciousness, attributed a similar consciousness to the natural forces which threatened him – hence the myths by which man explained the phenomena of the natural world. In his anthropological 'biological' definition of religion, Lunacharsky said that 'religion is that thinking about the world and that feeling of the world which psychologically resolves the contrast between the laws of life and the laws of nature' (Lunacharsky, 1908, p.40). This rather obscure formulation was amplified elsewhere to show that by it Lunacharsky meant that primitive religion served to explain the mysteries of nature in a partial way and only with the fullness of scientific knowledge which was not available before Marx, could the religious conception of the world, as opposed to the scientific one, be shown to be false. 'Scientific socialism' on the other hand 'resolves these contradictions puts forward the idea of the victory of life, of the subjugation of the elements to reason by means of knowledge and labour, science and technology' (Lunacharsky, 1908, p.42).

But this was only the negative side of the socialist attitude to religion as it developed in nineteenth-century Germany. There was a feeling not simply that the religious era was over but that socialism, in some way, was destined to replace it in human life. In this period Joseph Dietzgen was one of the most influential of the writers who developed this theme and he devoted a major work to *Die Religion der Sozialdemokratie*. Lunacharsky quoted from this volume with enthusiasm:

> Dear fellow citizens – *in the idea of social democracy is contained a new religion* which, as distinct from all existing ones, aspires to be accepted not only by the heart but also by the mind. Social democracy differs from other ordinary objects of mental labour because it is a revelation of the human heart in the form of a special religion. *The aim of religion*, strictly speaking, *is to give relief from the sorrows of earthly life to the worn out human heart*. Up to the present, however, this had only been achieved in an idealist way, by resorting to dreams and allegories, invisible gods and promises of life after death. As for the Gospel, it genuinely promises to finally transform our vale of sorrow and grief by the most real, most actual and tangible methods.

'This,' said Lunacharsky, 'is a categorical and splendid expression to which we subscribe joyfully' (Lunacharsky, 1908, p.33; Dietzgen's words were taken from his *Die Religion der Sozial-demokratie*, p.1). Thus socialism attempted to construct on earth what was formerly thought could exist only in heaven. Like the apocalyptic thinkers such as Merezhkovsky and Vyacheslav Ivanov and even Berdyaev and Bulgakov, Lunacharsky asserted that the kingdom of God, the utopia, could be built on earth and that man and earthly society were perfectible.

The second element which Lunacharsky drew from Dietzgen was also analogous to a Russian religious concept, that of *sobornost'*, of the superiority of collectivism to individualism. The religion of socialism, said Dietzgen, rejected the possibility of the separated self attaining perfection. It could only reach perfection through social organization, so the objective of social democracy was the perfection of social organization, which would allow the individual to achieve his fulfilment. This, he continued, could be achieved only through love, about which religion only dreamt. In conclusion, for Dietzgen the social democrat believed not in God and spirit, but in the social democratic structure of society (Lunacharsky, 1908, p.33). Dietzgen's argument was thus, said Lunacharsky, based on the thesis that 'man must have a system' (Lunacharsky, 1908, p.36). A similar point was made by Liebknecht. Lunacharsky quoted one of Liebknecht's statements in the Reichstag to the effect that the devotion of social democratic people to each other and to their cause was like a religious love of one's neighbour. Liebknecht said, 'this is *a religion*, not the religion of the popes but *the religion of humanity*. It is a faith in the victory of good and of the idea (Lunacharsky, 1908, p.37).

With Nietzsche, Lunacharsky concluded that, 'Man: your business is not to seek meaning in the world but to give meaning to the world' (Lunacharsky, 1908, p.46). 'The new religion,' said Lunacharsky, 'the religion of humanity, the religion of labour, gives no guarantees. But I maintain that even without God and without guarantees – the masks of that same God – it is still a religion' (Lunacharsky, 1908, p.49).

Lunacharsky's own contribution to this debate was to elaborate a view of mankind evolving from primitive animism to socialism – the religion of labour. He saw five main stages in this process of development. The first one was cosmism which represented primitive man's fearful view of nature, followed by Hellenism, reaching its height in Platonism, which he put below Judaism, the third stage, because although Judaism was the religion of 'the slave-man' it was, even in this lowest form, the first 'purely humanist religion' (Lunacharsky, 1908, pp.136–7). The fourth stage was Christianity, which combined the previous two, its history being intertwined with the struggle of the fifth stage, the religion of labour, to emerge. In Lunacharsky's own words:

> *Ancient cosmism* says: I bow down before the world and its laws.
> *Plato* says: I do not accept the world, I build another better world in dreams, I worship them, I repudiate life for the sake of dreams, I proclaim them the sole reality.
> *Israel* says: I do not accept the laws of the world. Over the world there must rule a mighty, living will similar to the human, leading it to enlightenment and to justice. We note at this point that *Christianity* combined the last two theses to the great detriment of both and then stopped to extricate itself from its unbearable contradictions.
> *The religion of labour* says: I recognise the world as material requiring to be re-worked, we accept the ideal as a plan of the recreation. Freedom and justice or the rule of organised humanity, while it does not yet exist, is born only in suffering (Lunacharsky, 1908, pp.223–4).

It was the later stages of this process which occupied the greater part of Lunacharsky's attention. He was especially interested in Christianity because he saw it as the result of a fusion of

Platonism and Judaism. Thus, for Lunacharsky, religious development and philosophical development were very closely allied. Each movement – cosmism, Platonism, Judaism, Christianity, pantheism, deism, idealism, materialism, socialism – grew organically from its predecessor, so that he traced a direct line from primitive religion through Plato, Christ, Augustine, Spinoza, Kant and Hegel to Marx and from Marx to the greatest Marxist philosopher, Bogdanov. From this vast canvas, the present study can only isolate and consider three aspects, which will be dealt with in turn: first, the relationship between Christianity and communism as it developed in history; second, the view that Marx's philosophy was religious; and third, the view that Bogdanov represented, as it were, the most advanced point of this process. In all these aspects the ideas of religion and revolution were closely interwoven.

The communist, socialist element in Christianity was, said Lunacharsky, present from the beginning and was indeed dominant at that period. Despite these errors, the early Christians were characterized by their 'beautiful tenderness and beautiful sense of brotherhood' (Lunacharsky, 1911, p.59). Christianity in Rome and in Palestine was based on the idea of the brotherhood of man and was a proletarian movement containing communistic strains or 'the Christianity of earthly hope' in Lunacharsky's words (Lunacharsky, 1911, pp.61–3). This 'semi-revolutionary Christianity' was best expressed by Tertullian who 'preceded Rousseau in the radicalness of his revolutionary denial of all cultural values. He resolutely protested against the state and the fatherland and spread anti-militarist propaganda' (Lunacharsky, 1911, p.66). This tradition, however, began to decay, so that, as a result of gnostic influences there were at least two struggling tendencies within Christianity. On the one hand the 'Christian communist proletariat' which was 'in significant measure penetrated by the collectivist spirit' and on the other, the teaching that 'each individual soul must seek its own salvation' which caused Christian communism to decay and endeavoured to replace it by individualism (Lunacharsky, 1911, p.101). The final blow to the democratic structure and independence of Christian communism came from the developing hierarchy which began to turn the Church into an administrative and defensive organ and produced the hierarchy which (and here Lunacharsky quoted Kautsky) became a ruling class to oppress the masses (Lunacharsky, 1911, p.115). The early Church structure, according to Harnack, came to reflect the imperial state structure – its popes were its emperors, Peter and Paul were its Romulus and Remus, the archbishops and bishops were its proconsuls, the monks and priests its legions. Finally, the praetorian guard of the new Church were the Jesuits (who, according to this account, were already performing mischief some ten centuries before the birth of their founder!) (Lunacharsky, 1911, p.121). In Augustine, the Church achieved its full self-consciousness. It turned, said Lunacharsky, to the Pauline doctrine of grace which minimized the merits of individual attempts to achieve salvation and maximized the role of the Church as owner and manager of indivisible saving grace. Christ had guaranteed the survival of the Church but outside the Church there could be no salvation (Lunacharsky, 1911, p.134). In Augustine,

> the Church reached its peak. It changed from being a religious philosophy of the poor and created a new position saving its class ideology from pernicious aridity. The democratic Christian spirit and common sense demanded a struggle against the terrible, oppressive and stately building of Catholicism (Lunacharsky, 1911, p.138).

Thus, in this period Christianity, according to Lunacharsky, performed the rather impressive feat, in Marxist terms, of being the ideology of no fewer than four conflicting social classes: first, the proletarians; second, the traders; third, the aristocracy; and fourth, the new class of the hierarchy created by Christianity itself (Lunacharsky, 1911, p.60). The emergence of the hierarchy did not end the struggle entirely and the socialist element kept reappearing at later dates, he continued, the most recent being the contemporary Russian Christian socialism of Merezhkovsky who tried to unite popular God-seeking and the religious philosophy of Gogol, Dostoevsky and Solov'ev with the political principles of Bakunin, Chernyshevsky and Herzen (Lunacharsky, 1911, p.178).

Exactly what Lunacharsky's views have to offer to an historian of the Church is not our concern at this moment, nor is the question of what he owed to various sources such as Kautsky, whose book on the origin of Christianity appeared in 1908. What is significant in the present context is that Lunacharsky saw the existence of a natural communism expressed in Christianity which was suppressed by the ruling class. For Lunacharsky it was the function of Marx, among others, to show that the communist elements were the true and enduring ones while the ecclesiastical structure and doctrine had been used by the ruling class to suppress the legitimate hopes of the oppressed. Unlike others in the field, said Lunacharsky,

> I dare to say that this philosophy [of Marx] is a *religious philosophy*, that it has its source in the religious quest of the past, engendered by the economic growth of mankind, and that it gives the brightest, most real, most active solution to the 'cursed questions' of human self-consciousness, which were resolved in an illusory way by the old religious systems (Lunacharsky, 1911, p.326).

The fundamental tenet of the new creed was the statement that thinking was determined by the social environment (Lunacharsky, 1911, p.326).

According to Lunacharsky, it was Bogdanov who continued the tradition of Marx

> In our opinion Bogdanov is the only Marxist philosopher continuing the pure philosophical tradition of Marx . . . In reality empiriomonism is for the most part a return to Marx, to genuine unvulgarized, unplekhanovized Marx. For the rest it marks a step forward, I would say, in a straight geometrical line in the direction projected by Marx (Lunacharsky, 1911, p.371).

Lunacharsky's conception of socialism as the fifth religion, the religion of labour, found its philosophical equivalent in Bogdanov who was, as Lunacharsky went on to say, concerned with the questions of existence and consciousness, which were central elements in the new religion, and of the reconciliation of individual and collective through the medium of an ideology which expressed collective consciousness. In Lunacharsky's own words:

> The fundamental question faced by Bogdanov and all Marxist philosophers is the relationship between existence and consciousness. For Marxism this is not primarily a question of the relationship between physical and psychological . . . but of the relationship between *social existence*, that is of *co-operation* with society, and individual *consciousness* in the form of *ideology* (Lunacharsky, 1911, pp.371–2).

Bogdanov's views were important to Lunacharsky's conception because despite differences of terminology and sometimes of ideas themselves, we find in his [Bogdanov's] outlook – in his brilliant construction on the firm foundation of genuine Marxism – splendid soil for the growth of the socialist religious consciousness (Lunacharsky, 1911, p.372).

A clear hint as to what Lunacharsky hoped to gain by

considering socialism as a religion was given in the final stages of his work. 'I am of the opinion,' he said,

> that the singling out and understanding of these ideals, as realistic religious principles within proletarian socialism, must powerfully facilitate the development among the proletariat of the mighty rudiments of psychological collectivism (Lunacharsky, 1911, p.385).

Although he did not emphasize it here, it was obvious that in a country such as Russia, where the Church and religion had perhaps a stronger appeal to the masses on whom the socialists were relying than among the relatively Godless townspeople and working men of France, Germany or England, an appeal in the form of religion might, as Lunacharsky suggested, help a great deal in the spread of the socialist ideal. Maksim Gorky, who had always expressed a deep love for the ordinary people of Russia, emphasizes this aspect of the transformation of the natural religious characteristics of the Russian people into natural socialist ones in the novel *Ispoved'* (*The Confession*) which was one of the most straightforward expositions of the God-building ideal. In it the central character, Matvei, was searching for God and found his God in the people 'which is the only God that works miracles', and, continued Matvei, it was the people who created religious consciousness.

This novel was in many ways a remarkable diversion from Gorky's other works of the period and was, in fact, treated by Soviet critics and by Gorky himself later on, as an aberration brought about by the reactionary influences of this most difficult period for the revolutionary movement. In the early stages of the book. Matvei was under the influence of various conventional ecclesiastical conceptions of God presented to him by simple believers or by decadent aristocratic monks. None of these was satisfactory. He was driven from one to another by an irresistible inner drive.

> The stars flicker restlessly to show their full beauty at the rising of the sun, love and sleep caress and intoxicate you and a bright ray of hope darts flame-like through your soul. There is, somewhere or another, a glorious God!
>
> 'Seek and ye shall find Him.' How beautiful are those words – words that must never be forgotten, for they are, in truth, worthy of human reason (Gorky, vol. 8, p.323).

While acting under this impulse, Matvei encountered the worker and political organizer Yonash who began to direct him to a more satisfying view of God. Yonash told him:

It is the people that creates gods – innumerable people of the world! Holy martyrs greater than those whom the Church honours. That is the God that works miracles. I believe in the spirit of the people – the immortal people whose might I acknowledge (Gorky, vol. 8, p.331).

Was it, asked Matvei, the peasantry who created God? Yonash replied:

I spoke of the working classes of the world, of their united strength, the one and eternal source of deification. . . . Even now many are seeking the means of fusing all the forces on earth into one, and creating out of it a splendid and beautiful God who shall embrace the universe (Gorky, vol. 8, p.332).

The chief enemy standing between man and the fulfilment of this collective destiny was individualism. The present deplorable human condition originated on the day

when the first human individual tore himself adrift from the miraculous power of the people, from the parent mass, and from the dread of isolation and its own impotence, it transformed itself into a wicked skein of petty desires – a skein which was christened 'I'. This 'I' is man's worst enemy. For the sake of its self-defence and self-assertion on earth, it has fruitlessly killed all the intellectual forces and all the great faculties for creating spiritual wealth in mankind (Gorky, vol. 8, p.344).

Matvei's lingering doubts were resolved when, in one image, Gorky showed that the people could literally perform miracles when they, with the assistance of the icon of Our Lady of Kazan, restored an epileptic girl to health. Matvei underwent at that moment a mystical conversion which transfigured his perception of the world. 'I stood on the summit of experience,' he said

and beheld the world as a fiery stream of living forces that strove to unite all in a single force, the goal of which was hidden from my sight. Nevertheless I joyfully recognized that ignorance of that goal was to me the source of infinite spiritual development and vast earthly beauty, and that in this infinity lay unbounded bliss for the living soul of man. . . . The earth stood before me in her luxuriant flowery garment of autumn, a

> field of emeralds for the great games of men, for the battle for
> the freedom of these games, a holy place of pilgrimage at the
> festival of Beauty and Truth (Gorky, vol. 8, p.378).

Matvei was moved to pray to the immortal people – 'You are my
God, and the creator of all gods which you have formed from the
beauties of your spirit in the labour and rebellion of your search.
And the world shall have no other God that works miracles. This
is my confession and my belief' (Gorky, vol. 8, p.378).

Such was the essence of Gorky's extraordinary and untypical
novel, a far cry from realism and a great concession to the
mysticism and idealism of the decadents who might have agreed
wth Gorky's view that life was 'games' played 'at the festival of
Beauty and Truth'. This was an echo of the Gorky who in 1900
remarked in a letter to Chekhov, 'Solov'ev, I am reading him
again. How clever and subtle' (Letter to Chekhov, October 1900,
in Gorky, vol. 28, p.135). He was, however, and remained, an
unrelenting opponent of the idealist group as represented by
Struve, Berdyaev and Bulgakov and he worked hard to set up the
socialist publishing venture *Znanie* as a direct counter to the
idealists' *Voprosy zhizni* (*Novyi put'*) (Gorky, vol. 28, p.323).

In *Ispoved'* Gorky saw in the religious phenomenon a powerful
metaphor and analogue, although in distorted form, of the spirit
of human brotherhood which inspired his socialism. But not only
did Gorky use religious images to explain the essence of his
humanist socialism in a very simple fashion which would be
immediately familiar to his audience, he also suggested the
conversion of the emotional energy generated by religious
experience into that required to build socialism. This was one of
the most attractive features of religion for the God-builders. It
enabled them to fulfil the fundamental desires of the individual for
truth and for immortality in a secular way and fulfilled the desire
of each man for a satisfying faith which was deeper and more
human than the philistine platitudes of the positivists. Only
religion could provide a universal view to match Gorky's and
Lunacharsky's love for all humanity and for all its achievement.

Be that as it may, another aspect of Gorky's novel was the fact
that it was steeped in the spirit of God-seeking which was to be
found in many quarters among the intelligentsia of this period.
There is a tendency, perhaps stemming in part from the similarity
of the terms in Russian, to mention God-building and God-
seeking in the same breath. But whereas God-building might, as
in Gorky's case, incorporate elements of God-seeking, none of the
other God-seeking tendencies had much in common with God-

building. God-building was strictly a Marxist heresy while many of the God-seekers were not in any sense Marxists. While both to some extent reflected and embodied the religious and socialist mood of the period, they moved in different spheres. For Berdyaev, Lunacharsky was a man 'from the other world', the world of political organization, demonstrations, strikes, not that of the ivory tower of Vyacheslav Ivanov's Wednesday salons near the Tauride Palace (Berdyaev, pp.8–9). For Lunacharsky, Berdyaev was a man who, from similar presuppositions to his own, had developed in a very different direction. In the introduction to *Religiya i sotsializm* Lunacharsky recalled a day in Kiev ten years previously when the idea of writing the book had been forming in his mind. On that day in 1898 he had read a paper on 'Idealism and Marxism' which contained the kernel of his ideas. On that occasion one of his opponents had been a social democrat who shared his preoccupation with and interest in such problems, N. Berdyaev. 'But,' said Lunacharsky, 'what a difference in the results!' (Lunacharsky, 1908, p.7). This initial contact was continued in exile in Vologda but neither Berdyaev nor Lunacharsky mentioned to what extent they exchanged ideas. Despite the coolness and the disagreement between them, Lunacharsky said that Berdyaev understood the tasks facing Marxism in the intellectual sphere better than the Marxists themselves because he was concerned not only with the sociological necessity of Marxism but also with truth. He also agreed with Berdyaev that a teaching which ignored the force of subjective ideals in the struggle with reality was a false one (Lunacharsky, 1908, p.7).

The question of the relationship between God-building and God-seeking was one which interested members of both groups and discussion of it attracted attention in 1908–9. Socialists who rejected God-building naturally rejected God-seeking too and tended to fail to distinguish between the two schools, but the God-builders themselves took up the issue. In particular Bazarov dealt thoroughly with the topic in a series of articles, which were all reprinted in *Na dva fronta* (*On Two Fronts*), and in a lecture at the St Petersburg Literary Society.

Bazarov's fundamental disagreement with the God-seekers lay in their false conception of individualism. 'God-seeking is one of the symptoms of the very slow but very deep cultural crisis, the crisis of individualism,' he said in his lecture. He then went on to explain that

It is not positivism which turns science from being the revelation of truth into a means of comfort, but it is individualism which cuts humanity off from its capacity to understand the objective value of scientific and of artistic creativity. Individualism corrupts, devalues and reduces to the level of a comfortable pastime, to *je m'en fichisme*, that great culture which it itself created. This is an evident symptom that the cultural content of individualism is already exhausted, that its mission is already fulfilled, that it is time for the Moor to retire (Bazarov, 1909, pp.362–3).

Elsewhere he supplemented this by saying that the attraction of individualism was that it made it possible to believe that individual liberation could be achieved independently, but the revolutionary movement and the working class could not succumb to this delusion. Freedom could come only as a result of struggle by the progressive class as a whole.

Not the conscious communist, not even the most implacable enemy of the bourgeoisie can be fully liberated from the bourgeois psychology as long as bourgeois relations exist in reality. The new consciousness cannot be created by separate individuals or by groups of individuals, nor by religious sects, nor by political parties. It can only be the affair of all humanity once it has done away with the material bases of its bourgeois 'prehistorical' existence (Bazarov, 1908, p.239).

Thus, even for this Marxist, salvation could only be universal, not individual. Indeed he was relying on a central theme of Marxism in this, which went back to the very roots of Marxism, because Marx's criticism of Proudhon and the utopian socialists rested to a large degree on Marx's belief that the reform of consciousness preached by these people was not sufficient to change society.

Bazarov was, as he said, fighting on two fronts, on the one hand against bourgeois individualists like Merezhkovsky and on the other against socialist dogmatists like Plekhanov and Lenin. Each side accused him of belonging to the other and his refusal to identify in any way with either resulted in powerful attacks by him on both. These attacks were returned, particularly by Plekhanov and Lenin and his associates. Though their views showed many differences at this time, they both agreed that the various attempts at a new start for the intelligentsia in this period, represented by the new religious consciousness, the God-builders and *Vekhi*, were part and parcel of one and the same retreat into religion and mysticism as a result of the setbacks to the revolutionary movement. Both treated the movement with complete contempt and worked energetically to reestablish 'orthodox' Marxism (though this meant different things to each of them) and 'orthodox' materialism.

The main thrust of Plekhanov's attack on 'the so-called religious-seeking in Russia' was aimed at Lunacharsky, Merezhkovsky and Gorky. His disagreement with Lunacharsky rested on the latter's assertion that religion was that conception of the world which resolved the contradiction between the laws of life and the laws of nature (Lunacharsky, 1908, p.40). Plekhanov's own definition of religion was quite different.

> *Religion* can be defined as *a more or less structured system of notions, moods and actions*. The notions form the *mythological element* of religion, mood is related to the sphere of *religious feeling*, and actions to the spheres of *religious worship*, or, to put it another way, *of cult* (Plekhanov, 1909, no. 9, p.184).

The remainder of the first article of this series of three was devoted to expanding this conception in anthropological terms with particular reference to the emergence of religion from nature and the environment, in accordance with Marx's conception that consciousness was determined by environment.

Turning from this hazy prehistory to the contemporary 'religious seekers' in Russia, Plekhanov showed that their conceptions were far from new. Marx himself devoted a great deal of attention to those socialists of his time and earlier who had seen socialism as a religion, for example, the utopian socialists, Saint-Simon, Fourier and Leroux, who all had religious elements in their outlook. Thus for Plekhanov the debate was ended by Marx himself and to continue proposing ideas specifically rejected by Marx proved the unmarxist nature of Lunacharsky's book. By invoking the highest authority and repeating his scorn, Plekhanov attempted to cut the God-builders off from the socialists. Gorky also fell under Plekhanov's anathema even though he was, according to Plekhanov, a wonderful artist, but

> even great geniuses are frequently helpless in the field of theory. One does not have to go very far to find examples: Gogol, Dostoevsky and Tolstoy are giants in the field of artistic creativity, but they displayed the feebleness of a child whenever they considered a fundamental question (Plekhanov, 1909, no. 10, p.188).

Finally, he turned to the decadents, in particular Merezhkovsky and Minsky. They were suffering from the symptoms of a disease – individualism. Gippius complained in the introduction to her collected poems that 'up to the present we have not found the

Universal God nor have we caught that which we are striving for. Until that time our prayers – our verses, alive for each one of us will be misunderstood by, and will be unnecessary for, some' (Gippins, p.vi). Plekhanov offered an explanation of why the verses of the symbolists 'live for each one of us' should be unnecessary and misunderstood.

> It is simply because they are the outcome of extreme individualism. When the human world surrounding him is not necessary to and not understood by the poet, the poet himself becomes unnecessary and is misunderstood by the surrounding human world (Plekhanov, 1909, no. 12, p.197).

They also provided a distinction between the God-seekers and the God-builders and Plekhanov did not confuse them. Such fine distinctions, however, were far beyond Lenin, for whom, as was pointed out in the previous chapter, philosophy and propaganda went hand in hand. For him, Lunacharsky and other 'destroyers of dialectical materialism proceed fearlessly to downright fideism' (Lenin, vol. 18, p.10). Writing to Gorky in November 1913, Lenin said,

> God-seeking differs from god-building or god-creating or god-making etc. no more than a yellow devil differs from a blue devil. To talk about god-seeking, not in order to declare against all devils and gods, against every ideological necrophily (all worship of a divinity is necrophily, be it the cleanest, most ideal, not sought-out but built-up divinity, it's all the same), but to prefer a blue devil to a yellow one, is a hundred times worse than not saying anything about it at all (Lenin, vol. 48, p.226).

Lenin was concerned only with the inroads God-building had made in the party and sought to attack its influence. For him God-building, God-seeking, 'otzovism' and 'ultimatism' were used interchangeably, but only to refer to Bogdanov and his followers. God-seeking as a phenomenon outside the party never provoked a response from him.

Lenin's views on religion at this time were formulated in his article on 'The attitude of the workers' party to religion', published in *Proletarii* in May 1909. Like Marx and Engels, Lenin's views existed on two levels, the theoretical and the practical, which were not always in step with each other so that while on the one hand he said that Marxism was 'a materialism which is absolutely atheistic and positively hostile to all religion' (Lenin, vol. 17, p.415) and that 'we must combat religion – that is the

ABC of *all* materialism' (Lenin, vol. 17, p.418), on the other hand he added, 'we must not only admit into the Social Democratic Party workers who preserve their belief in God, but must deliberately set out to recruit them. We are absolutely opposed to giving the slightest offence to their religious convictions' (Lenin, vol. 17, p.422). For Lenin militant atheism could only play into the hands of the bourgeoisie. 'An anarchist who preached war against God at all costs would in effect be helping the priest and the bourgeoisie (as the anarchists always do help the bourgeoisie *in practice*)' (Lenin, vol. 17, p.421). Lenin attempted to steer a course between this anti-religious mania and on the other hand the 'opportunism' of German social democracy which extended the principle of religion as the private affair of the individual, with which Lenin agreed, into religion as a private matter for the party, which he opposed. On the contrary, he said, 'the party must have a firm stand on the religious question' (Lenin, vol. 17, p.417).

Lenin's own definition of religion differed from the others considered in this chapter in that it related only to the social form and functions of religion and not to its supernatural or philosophical claims. He said that Marx's dictum that religion was the opium of the people was 'the cornerstone of the whole Marxist outlook on religion' (Lenin, vol. 17, p.416). 'Marxism has always regarded all modern religious organisations,' he continued, 'as instruments of bourgeois reaction that serve to defend exploitation and to befuddle the working class' (Lenin, vol. 17, p.416). Far from taking into account Lunacharsky's view that religion contained great ideals which should not be lost sight of, Lenin saw nothing in religion beyond its social form and roots.

> In modern capitalist countries these roots are mainly *social*. The deepest root of religion today is the socially downtrodden condition of the working masses and their apparently complete helplessness in the face of the blind forces of capitalism which every day and every hour inflicts upon ordinary working people the most horrible suffering and the most savage torment, a thousand times more severe than that inflicted by extraordinary events, such as wars, earthquakes etc. 'Fear made the gods.' Fear of the blind force of capital, blind because it cannot be foreseen by the masses of the people, a force which at every step in the life of the proletarian and small proprietor threatens to inflict and does inflict 'sudden', 'unexpected', 'accidental' ruin, destruction, pauperism, prostitution and death from starvation. Such is the *root* of modern religion which the

materialist must bear in mind if he does not want to remain an infant-school materialist (Lenin, vol. 17, p.419).

The social democrat consequently should fight religion as part of the general class struggle against capitalism. To eradicate the roots of religion was to eradicate capitalism itself (Lenin, vol. 17, p.419). Thus for Lenin religion was nothing more than an ideological arm of capitalism, an intellectual tool used for the mental suppression of the working class. The questions examined in the previous chapters of this study and in the earlier part of this chapter completely escaped his attention, even when he was confronted by them within his own party and his own faction in the form of Lunacharsky and Gorky. The philosophical issues for which the God-builders stood were completely integrated, in Lenin's mind, with the general question of the political struggle against Bogdanov.

The people dealt with in this chapter provide another variation on our basic themes. Bulgakov, Berdyaev, Lunacharsky and Gorky were all religious collectivists, the first two explicitly idealist, the latter two, at least according to their critics, were crypto-idealists. This distinguished them from religious individualists like Merezhkovsky, Rozanov and the liberal philosophers. It also distinguished them from the materialist collectivists, such as Plekhanov and Lenin.

The central theme of these disputes was still idealism or materialism, individualism or collectivism, and it was on their attitudes towards these that the intellectual, and often political, position of the participants was based. The second part of this study will attempt to show how the theoretical positions defined above were related to the political divisions of the day and in particular the attitude of the intelligentsia to the central question of revolution.

For further information on this subject, see Christopher Read's *Religion, Revolution and the Russian Intelligentsia 1900–1912. The Vekhi Debate and its Intellectual Background*, London 1979, from which this chapter is taken.

Bibliography

Bazarov, V. (1908), 'Lichnost' i lyubov' v svete "novogo religioznogo soznaniya', *Literaturnyi raspad. Kriticheskii sbornik*, vol. 1, pp.221–40, Petersburg.

Bazarov, V. (1909), 'Bogoiskatel'stvo i bogostroitel'stvo', *Vershiny,*

Literaturnokriticheskii i filosofsko-publitsisticheskii sbornik, pp.331–64, Petersburg.

Bazarov, V. (1910). *Na dva fronta*, Petersburg.

Berdyaev, N.A. (1935), 'Russkii dukhovnyi renessans nachala XX-go v. i zhurnal *Put'* (k desyatiletiyu *Puti*), *Put'*, no. 49, pp.3–23, Paris.

Dietzgen, J. (1891), *Die Religion der Sozialdemokratie*.

Gippius, Z. (1904), *Sobranie stikhov* (1899–1903), Moscow.

Gorky, M. (1949–55), *Sobranie sochinenii v tridtsati tomakh*, Moscow.

Lenin, V.I. (1958–65), *Polnoe sobranie sochinenii*, 55 vols, 5th edn, Moscow.

Lunacharsky, A. (1908), *Religiya i sotsializm*, vol. 1, Petersburg.

Lunacharsky, A. (1911), *Religiya i sotsializm*, vol. 2, Petersburg.

Plekhanov, G.V. (1909), 'O tak nazyvaemykh religioznykh iskaniyakh v Rossii', *Sovremennyi mir*, no. 9, pp.182–216; no. 10, pp.164–200 and no. 12, pp.167–201.

30
Socialist propaganda in the Italian countryside

FRANCO RIZZI

In 1895, the Socialist deputy Valdino Morgari published an article in the newspaper *La Lotta di classe* (Class Struggle) suggesting how to conduct propaganda. The article, later reprinted in the collection *Il manuale del socialista* (The Socialist's Manual),[1] provides clear examples of the methods by which a socialist could spread the message. For the more talented propagandists, public means of spreading socialist ideas were recommended: holding a lecture or giving a speech in order to reach a large number of workers. The rest were advised to pursue the individual approach, a less sensational style of propaganda, yet one which would still be useful, especially if it were spread 'within domestic walls, in small workshops, at the table in cafés or pubs'.

Debate was the crucial element in this second type of propaganda. By speaking to people informally (so Morgari believed) the people canvassed would feel more able to express their doubts, and give their full attention to the simple, penetrating explanations of the meaning of socialism. 'The person who has been disagreeing' we read in 'Arte della propaganda ("The Art of Propaganda")', and 'who has been losing the argument at every point is filled with wonder when he hears such beautiful ideas for the first time. He meditates and the ideas enter his head.'[2] One constant element in this kind of proselytizing, reminiscent of the rhetoric of Catholic mission, is the ease with which the socialist idea (imagined as if it had a concrete shape and weight) is supposed to enter the head of the worker, like a nail driven in to a wall.

But the efficiency of this penetration depends on the ability of the propagandist to pick the right people. He must be like the wise farmer who 'because he cannot till a vast field with his own two hands alone, encloses a few pieces with hedges, and cultivates them carefully, so that he is sure of a good harvest.'[3] Every propagandist had to learn to ignore the 'fearful and feeble' so as to concentrate on the courageous ones, those from whose ranks the 'good soldiers' and the 'powerful agitators' for the socialist word would be drawn. The suggested methods of initiating a discussion with someone quite ignorant of socialism presuppose that the propagandist is trying to bring about a kind of socialist revelation. Thus we find Morgari suggesting that 'when people are talking about public or private calamities, the conditions of work, their misery or family troubles, the propagandist ought to exclaim "There is one remedy for this, and one alone – socialism." Everyone turns their heads to listen, and he sets out the ideas.'[4]

There are two keys to success in this work. The first is to touch the questioner's heart – he must be offered reading which will stir his emotions. Perhaps *Socialism* or *Social Morals* by Benoit Malon, writings whose vivid and realistic descriptions force the reader to reflect on social injustice. Here we see the beginnings of the sentimental and humanitarian vein in Italian socialism – a theme to which we shall return. The second key to success as a propagandist follows on from the first. So, we read in 'The Art of Propaganda': 'Once they have been attracted by the honey placed on the rim of the cup they will sip at the scientific theories.'[5] Here we have another feature of Italian socialism, its eclecticism.[6] This aspect is related to the positivist strand in Italian socialism: the conviction that there could be precise knowledge of the laws that govern society, a knowledge that socialism alone could provide.

The most suitable instrument for conveying these truths was the book (or the more elementary pamphlet). These would stimulate 'the neophyte to meditation'. So the propagandist had to have material of this kind to hand, ready to give those who were becoming in their words, 'converted' to socialism. This was a public which could read. Individuals would be given an issue of the socialist paper as the first step to getting them to subscribe. Parallels to Christian conversion are evident throughout: the propagandist was usually represented as the good pastor who takes care of his flock, who leads the neophytes to the socialist circle, who puts them in touch with other socialists, takes them to meetings, gets them to do recruiting work, getting subscriptions etc. . . . These are the early stages of the journey which will conclude with their taking out membership of the socialist party.

But how was the typical propagandist trained – or rather, what would the party have wished the training to be like? For those who had a certain amount of education, 'The Art of Propaganda' recommended that they read:

> Above all, any summary of the theories of Darwin and Spencer, which will inform the student of the trends in modern scientific thought. Marx will complete the formidable triad with his celebrated and indispensable *Capital*, the gospel of contemporary socialists. In the recent volume of Ferri, *Socialism and Positive Science*, the student will see how the three giants, Darwin-Spencer-Marx, complement one another. Benedetto Malon's *Complete Socialism* will provide a complete over-view of the past, the present, and even a little of the future of our movement; and there is a good resume of this work now published in Italian with the title *Socialism*. We must not forget *The Essence of Socialism* by Schäffle, a book which is very favourable to us, . . . written by an opponent of our ideas. Also read *Looking Backward* by Bellamy – it is a novel and you can't swear to all of it, but it sheds a ray of light on the dark paths of our future, and it admirably presents the moral side of socialism.[7]

This quotation is a classic example of the highly eclectic character of the cultural model offered to party militants.[8] Yet we need to ask what sort of audience this advice was aimed at. Morgari's was an image of the ideal propagandist, certainly someone of urban origin. In real life, however, and especially in the country, the main means of dissemination would have been the traditional forms of sociability, like the eating house, the work gang, or the fireside circle. Those were the places where people would have been most likely to have read or discussed the pamphlets produced by some leading party members. But these pamphlets dealt with the election issues, taxes, or religion – not Ferri's work on *Socialism and Positive Science*. In addition we ought to remember that in spite of the drive to systematization evident in propaganda compiled by Morgari, the Italian Socialist Party's ambition to create what Maria Grazia Rosado has termed 'a culture co-ordinated at the level of the party' was a failure.[9]

We need rather to reconstruct the cultural politics of the Italian Socialist Party at the turn of the century from the fragments of debate which remain. Here, the party's preoccupation with reaching the masses coloured its entire discussion of the propaganda question and its assessment of what was required. Simple, accessible educational material was its first priority, and *Critica Sociale* itself intended to create a library of booklets which could meet the need. In 1896 a prize was offered for the work which best succeeded in

> a congenial exposition of the principles of socialism, a polemic, a novel which will deal in popular form with some problems or particular arguments (taxation, universal suffrage, social legislation and so forth), or even a brief dramatic work adapted to the popular socialist theatres which are springing up here and there.[10]

Works like this were the foundation of socialist propaganda. In one such book, Eugenio Ciacchi's *To the Peasants*, the author starts by explaining the economic oppression practised by the capitalists, and then sets out the socialist alternative. He is anxious to stress, however, that all this is only an introduction to socialism: 'Pay attention, oh my peasant friends, what you have learned today is not socialism, it is just a step towards socialism. It's actually just a crumb of elementary socialism.'[11] The pamphlet writers, usually party leaders and products of an urban socialist education and culture, were only aiming to provide a basic framework for oral propaganda to build on and to make it easy for people to understand basic socialist themes by providing vivid examples.

In the early 1890s, the Socialist Party began a campaign to penetrate the countryside. The party believed that the only way to conquer the rural masses was to engage in propaganda, using pamphlets as the major tool. In one article which appeared in *Critica sociale* in 1893, the advantages of socialist work with the peasants were set out:

> In fact, the relative virginity of peasant thought, which has remained immune from the influences and delusions of political parties, is what makes it likely that they could make the leap from that coarse, semi-pagan religious thinking to a more elevated social thinking. Their meagre needs, the natural

austerity of their lives, far from the temptations or vain resentments which sometimes give an unhealthy colouring to the proletarian agitations in the city . . . all this and more clears the path for propaganda in the countryside.[12]

The world described in this article is one which seems to have no history. It is a land still to be conquered, where all traces of previous struggle – for instance, the agrarian strikes of the 1880s – have been obliterated. Even the leagues, the associations, the work of Socialist Catholics amongst the rural masses have been forgotten in the enthusiasm with which *Critica Sociale* imagines the impending socialist conquest of the countryside. And this kind of naive optimism, often quite incapable of grasping the actual class divisions in the countryside, was to remain a distinctive feature of the production of propagandist pamphlets even much later, when the debate between reformism and maximalism swept the party.

The pamphlets dealt with a limited range of topics. Above all, they aimed to explain in simple terms the kind of exploitation which field workers, temporary agricultural labourers and small peasants were subjected to. There were pamphlets which dealt with specific issues, or were directed to particular sectors such as child or women labourers. Most often, they were written in the form of a dialogue: between a socialist and a peasant, a priest and a socialist, a bigot and a socialist, or a worker and a socialist and so on. Sometimes the pamphlets resorted to parables, as in Prampolini's *The Mountain*; or to fables or poetry. Usually, their theme was the misery of the rural masses.

The pathos which pervades these stories is no different from the pietistic, sentimental atmosphere which characterizes all the literature and art of that epoch. Hunger, disease, and death, for example, were the focus of series of sketches published by socialist almanacs. The rounded shoulders of the rice-weeder were recurrent motifs in the pictures of Angelo Morbelli, who gave up landscape painting to draw attention to the plight of these workers. And it was in this climate of pathos, 'of Zola-esque images of society's down and out', that the socialist dreams of 'the redemption of all humanity' were cultivated.[13] However, one can also discern an oscillation between this 'radical pathos' and the exaltation 'of the patient resignation, the courage to work, the virtues of the ideal peasant', which finds its most convincing pictorial expression in Jean François Millet's painting *The Angelus*.[14]

Religion was a major preoccupation of the pamphlet writers.

Whether directed at children or mothers, peasants or workers, there was always a reference to the Catholic religion as if it were a kind of disease which infects the people. The images used by Angelo Cabrini were typical:

> There is a vast crowd of poor folk in this world today whom civilization has never given a crumb, nor has it ever let them smile; a crowd of semi-brutes, from whom the misery of centuries and the Catholic pus of centuries has extinguished any sense of consciousness or rebellion.[15]

Warnings against a religion that supports the bosses' order were linked with an increasingly elaborate anti-Catholic socialist polemic. This anti-Catholicism was gaining ground, especially in the early years of the twentieth century, when alliances were being created between the Catholic and conservative forces in Italy, and Catholic, anti-socialist organizations were beginning to spread. To an extent, therefore, such polemics can be explained by the climate of political conflict. But the roots of anticlericalism in Italian socialism lie much deeper, springing from both the liberal Mazzini Risorgimento tradition and the radical anarchist worker tradition which played such a large role in the workers' movement. As we shall see, however, the various party exponents took up rather different positions on the issue of religion. Indeed, there was a gulf between the official position of the party, which had adopted the Erfurt formula (1891) according to which religion was a private matter; and the propagandist literature, which was full of anti-Catholic polemic.[16]

In fact, the propagandists tried to distinguish between primitive Christianity and church Christianity as if they were two separate and opposed things. This was expressed most powerfully in Camillo Prampolini's pamphlet, *The Christmas Sermon*, where Christ's preaching is contrasted with that of the church. Taking Christ's sayings about equality and human brotherhood, Prampolini insists that all the rest – parish priests, bishops, cardinals and popes – are superfluous to being Christian. He calls on the workers to join together and to put into practice that form of social justice from which 'the Kingdom of God' will be born.

This pamphlet provoked a vigorous polemical debate. The Catholic journals attacked Prampolini, accusing him of having distorted and falsified Christian doctrine; while the socialists replied with other writings such as the anonymous *The Doctrine of Christ and the Doctrine of the Priests*. *The Christmas Sermon* must have been very successful, if we can judge by the figures reported in *La Guistizia*, the socialist periodical in which Prampolini's writings appeared: it was estimated to have sold 60,000 copies. Other socialist periodicals reprinted the piece as well, and it was even being translated for Belgian and American audiences.

However, Prampolini's position on religion, which amounted to 'drawing primitive Christianity's theme of equality into the socialist ambit',[17] was not shared by all other socialist writers. In a pamphlet called *Socialism and Religion*, the author Bertesi tried to argue that because socialism is positivist, it must be neutral on the subject of religion. Its aim must be to abolish the divisions between the exploiters and the exploited. 'By its very nature it must gather all the workers together, whatever their faith, whatever their cult.'[18] This was clearly different from Prampolini's position, even though both writers engaged in a polemic against the church and both condemned the Catholic political organizations (the Christian democrats) which opposed the emancipation of the workers.

Prampolini's was an extremely hostile assessment of religion, and attitudes like his led the socialists to exploit every opportunity of attacking priests, bishops and popes. In the socialist almanac of 1902 for example, we find a long chronology with the ominous title 'The delinquent popes'. It begins with Pasquale I (817–824) and provides a list of his misdeeds; and it finishes with Leo XII (1901), described as the pope who had used his 'moral authority in the Jesuit inspired encyclical Rerum Novarum' to sell 'the rights of the humble to the powerful on earth, in violation of the dictates of the law of Christ who died for the humble on the cross – and purely for the sake of worldly motives and monetary gain.'[19]

At the same time, however, the recurrence of themes drawn from the works of Christ and the church constitute a significant feature of all these socialist productions. And as they adopted literary models drawn from populist or Catholic traditions, they strengthened the tendency to present socialism as the religion of modern man.

However, as the discussion developed, religion and socialism increasingly tended to be counterposed to one another. This was achieved by setting out a series of propositions designed to lay bare the hypocrisy of what the clergy were saying and demonstrate the justice of what the socialists said. The dogmatic assertions of the church would be countered with the scientific assertions of socialism, as affirmed by E. Belfort Bax and H. Quelch in their *New Socialist Catechism*, published by Nerbini in 1904.[20] But it was not only science that could open the eyes of those who had not yet learnt to see – the daily life of suffering itself was a fertile ground on which the socialist word could fail. In the words of a poem called 'The Seed':

And Christ said,/Germs of peace/ the humble seed which I sow
in the earth / in my sack I have no better seed. . . . But those to
whom the guardianship of the field has been entrusted/ are the
sort of labourers/ who disturb the earth/, scatter to the winds/
the seeds of peace which belong to us all/ and sow war. . . .
Now we are sick of the guardians/, oh good Jesus, who sow the
germs of your seed to the wind/ and now, gentle Jesus, we
want to manage without them;/ for with these dread ones, you
sow but we never reap.[21]

In this way, by repeatedly focussing on the worker's plight – on
hunger, disgrace, on the deaths through poverty of infants and
children – the pamphlets were to be used to champion the
workers' cause. At the same time, they were explicitly designed to
tackle the church on its own ground. So we find:

In the catholic catechism	In the socialist catechism
'Give food to the poor and hungry'	'Abolish the oppressors and the oppressed'
'Clothe the naked'	'Help the ragged: get them fur coats'
'Bury the dead'	'Abolish the living tombs of the quarries, of the sulphur mines, of all the horrible tombs where people work'
'Counsel the doubters'	'Give courage to the oppressed who tremble with fear'
'Admonish sinners'	'Raise your voice against exploiters of every kind'
'Pray to God for the living and the dead'	'Leave the Lord God, the living and the dead in peace'[22]

The project of presenting socialism as both science and faith, as
at once religion or faith in human kindness and as the heir to the
humanitarian tradition, can seem a trifle incongruous. But it was
also the source of the propaganda's strength.

These pamphlets certainly succeeded in training the socialist
militants. Moreover, they established the socialists with a
distinctive image: socialism was defined by the priests as
irreligious, by the bourgeoisie as subversive, and by the
proletarians as a kind of new religion. At national level, it was the
pamphlets' diffusion which, together with the struggles and the

agrarian strikes, accelerated the rural masses' identification with some kind of socialist project, vague as this was. The Sicilian Fasci are a typical example. Egalitarianism, brotherhood, the abolition of oppression, common ownership – all seemed possible, as Hobsbawm wrote, quoting the words of a Sicilian peasant, thanks to those 'angels come down from heaven'.[23]

It is this widely felt longing for liberation among the peasant masses which is the key to interpreting socialist success in the countryside. It was the socialist' response to this need which won out, at least in the early years. But socialist success was also due to the fact that its propagandists were not above presenting socialism as a religion and faith. None of this, of course, can account for the party's ambivalence, both in programme and in political action, when it was confronted with the radicalism of workers' and peasants' struggles at the end of the century. But it does explain its recourse to models for spreading socialism like the catechism, or the commandments. And it accounts for its persistent use of language shaped by Christian traditions; or explains why, for instance, a festival like the First of May should be termed 'the Easter of the Resurrection of the Oppressed'. Morover, these were the models with which the peasants themselves identified. So, during movement of the Sicilian Fasci, a peasant woman from Palermo told a journalist:

> 'Jesus was a true Socialist and he wanted precisely what the Fasci are asking for, but the priests do not represent him well, especially when they are usurers. When the Fascio was founded our priests were against it and in the confessional they said that the Socialists are excommunicated. But we answered that they were mistaken, and in June we protested against the war they made upon the Fascio, none of us went to the procession of the Corpus Domini. That was the first time such a thing ever happened.'[24]

(Translated by Anne Farmer Meservey, Guy Boanas and Lyndal Roper)

Notes

1   G. Messina, *Il manuale del socialista*, Florence, 1901, pp.313ff.
2   *Ibid.*, p.314.
3   *Ibid.*, p.315.
4   *Ibid.*, p.315.
5   *Ibid.*, p.316.

6   See G. Turi, 'Aspetti dell'ideologia del PSI (1890–1910)' in *Studi Storici*, 1980, no. 1, pp.61–94; pp.71ff.

7   G. Messina, *Il manuale del socialista*, pp.314–15.

8   Eclecticism is not just a feature of Italian socialism alone, but characterizes European socialism in general. See E.J. Hobsbawm, 'La diffusione del marzismo (1890–1905)', *Studi Storici*, 1974, no. 2, pp.241–9.

9   M.G. Rosado, 'Biblioteche popolari e politica culturale del PSI tra ottocento e novecento', *Movimento operaio e socialista*, XXIII, 1977, pp.259–88.

10 F. Turati, 'Il legato di Eduardo Mattia per la propaganda socialista', *Critica Sociale*, 1 January 1896.

11 E. Ciacchi, *Ai contadini*, Florence, 1900, p.9.

12 'La conquista delle campagne', *Critica Sociale*, 1 April 1893.

13 See R. Bossaglia, 'Dal realismo sociale al simbolismo populista', in the exhibition catalogue, *Arte e socilalità in Italia dal realismo al simbolismo*, Milan, 1979.

14 J.C. Chamboredon, 'Peinture des rapports sociaux et invention de l'éternel paysan: les deux manières de Jean François Millet', *Actes de la recherche en sciences sociales*, nos 17–18, 1977, pp.7–28; F.J. Clark, *The Absolute Bourgeois: Artist and Politics in France 1848–1851*, London, 1973.

15 A. Cabrini, 'La vita delle risaiuole', *Critica Sociale*, 20, August 1891.

16 G. Verucci, *L'Italia laica prima e dopo l'unità*, Bari, 1981, pp.350ff.

17 G. Turi, 'Aspetti dell'ideologia del PSI'.

18 A. Bertesi, *Socialismo e religione*, Rome, 1901.

19 *Almanacco Socialista Italiano*, 1902.

20 G. Turi, 'Aspetti dell'ideologia del PSI', pp.89ff; A. Nesti, '*Gesù socialista*'. *Una tradizione popolare italiana (1880–1920)*, Turin, 1974.

21 *Almanacco Socialista Italiano*, 1902.

22 *Almanacco Socialista Italiano*, 1898.

23 E.J. Hobsbawm, *Primitive Rebels*, Manchester, 1959, p.99.

24 *Ibid.*, p.183.

Religion and nationalism

31

Pearse's sacrifice: Christ and Cuchulain crucified and risen in the Easter Rising, 1916

SHERIDAN GILLEY

The idea of sacrifice occurs in Christian cultures in realms remote from high theology, and the invocation of the soldier's sacrifice in war became highly topical, in 1982, when even sensitive Anglican bishops defended the British onslaught in the Falklands with the text 'Greater love hath no man than this, that a man lay down his life for his friends.' The pacifist might reply that the Scripture does not say that a man should kill for his friends; yet it has needed only this little war to remind us of the power of sacrifice even in modern language, in the ambiguous willingness to give up one's own life while taking the lives of others. It was this understanding of sacrifice in war, while invoking the model of the passion of Christ, which inspired and justified the first ultimately successful 'anti-colonial' revolution of the twentieth century, the Irish Rising of Easter 1916; and the speeches and poetry of the leaders of the Rising, of Joseph Mary Plunkett and Thomas MacDonagh, and more especially of Padraic Pearse, drew upon the sacrificial Christ of a prayerful Irish Catholicism.

The Easter reference in the Rising has always attracted attention. As James Stephens declared at the time, on Easter Sunday in Dublin they cried 'Christ has risen' in the churches; they cried 'Ireland has risen' on Easter Monday (Augustine Martin, 1966, p.38). 'Elsewhere Easter is celebrated as the Feast of the Resurrection,' remarks Terence de Vere White. 'In Dublin it is celebrated as the Feast of the Insurrection' (O'Brien, 1973, p.308). The resurrection of Ireland at Easter derives its power from a long tradition: the identification of Ireland and the Irish people with Jesus, as the suffering Christ of the nations martyred by the British, runs deep through nineteenth-century Irish Catholic culture. Yet in the wider European setting, the metaphor of suffering like Christ was so far from revolutionary violence as to incur the Marxist indictment of religion for offering an other-worldly justification for present suffering, and certainly the political conservatism of the court of Rome, in its century of warfare with revolutionary Italian nationalism, discouraged even Irish Catholics from developing the case for a just war into an argument for armed rebellion. There *were* Catholic revolutions in the nineteenth century, in Poland and Belgium, as well as a strong movement of Catholic civil disobedience in Prussia and the German Empire; and in Ireland there was a minority of revolutionary priests, from the 'croppy' clerics of Wexford in 1798 to the irrepressible neo-Fenian Father Patrick Lavelle. But the Church in general opposed the Irish rebellions of 1798, 1848 and 1867, supporting instead the non-violent nationalism of O'Connell and later Home Rule (Lyons, 1971; Norman, 1965). Archbishop Paul Cullen, later a cardinal, as ruler of the Irish Church for more than a quarter of a century from 1850, earned the undying hatred of the revolutionary Fenians by refusing them the sacraments (Norman, 1965), yet deep-seated anticlericalism failed to develop (McCartney, 1967; Newsinger, 1979), and the bridges with constitutionalist, not violent, nationalism were mended by Cullen's episcopal successors. Despite the survival of an underground insurrectionary tradition in the tiny Irish Republican Brotherhood, founded and funded from America, the victory of the constitutionalist school seemed complete by 1900, through an alliance between the priesthood and the parliamentary politicians (Larkin, 1975, 1978, 1979; Miller, 1973; Tierney, 1976). To the outward eye, the non-violent character of Irish Catholicism seemed secure until the very eve of the Rising, which satisfied none of the Church's conditions for a just rebellion (Horgan, 1948, p.285; Shaw, 1972, p.118): so that Pearse and his fellow rebels were in revolt not only against the British, but against the explicit teaching and the dominant element in Irish Catholicism itself.

Yet the Rising was overwhelmingly the work of Catholics; only one of the 1916 leaders, Tom Clarke, an old Fenian and sometime convict in England, remained true to the Fenian past by dying without the last rites, and the principal Protestant connected with the Rising, Roger Casement, was received into the Church before his execution. Some other nationalists like Maud Gonne had already taken a nationalist path to Rome (Levenson, 1977, p.94). Catholicism had baptized revolution: and that by means of an understanding of Christ which carried revolution into the heart of Catholicism.

The revolutionary ideal was no more exclusively Catholic or even Christian in origin than Irish nationalism itself. Irish constitutionalism was partly a product of English Utilitarian influence, and revolution came to Ireland from republican France, firing the imagination of the rebels of Protestant background if not Protestant conviction, like Robert Emmet and Wolfe Tone.

The Irish nationalist pantheon was always an ecumenical one, and Catholic nationalists were never narrow sectarians, but readily accepted Protestant leaders like Isaac Butt and Parnell. Yet from the 1820s, the great majority of Presbyterians and Church of Ireland Protestants became militantly Unionist and often No Popery Evangelical, and so Irish Nationalism became Catholic in it mass membership, as the expression of the wrongs of an impoverished and persecuted people. This trend was enhanced in the second half of the nineteenth century as the ardours of Italianate devotion (Larkin, 1972) warmed nationalist feeling (O'Farrell, 1971), and as the language revivalists set to work to rescue the dying tongue and culture of the Gael. Here again, in the revival of Gaelic culture, the leaders were often Protestants opposed by the great mass of their co-religionists: many of the professional Gaelic scholars were Catholics, some were priests, but Douglas Hyde, the famous President of the Gaelic League, and Standish O'Grady, whose histories of heroic pagan Ireland so stirred the emotions of the young Padraic Pearse, were both sons of Church of Ireland Rectors. The greatest writers of the literary revival, Yeats and Synge, were also Protestants by birth, while another, non-Catholic, element came into the revolutionary tradition through James Connolly (Owen Dudley Edwards, 1971), a curious Catholic Marxist who might be said, like many of the early Socialists, to have believed in a devout Christianity all his own (Ransom, 1980, pp.29, 94).

Yet the fires of 1916 burnt out the foreign matter in Catholic nationalism. The idealism of literary nationalism was accepted, but not its ventures towards the wild romantic realism of J.M. Synge's depiction of the peasantry. As Pearse's lieutenant in the Dublin Post Office, Connolly, crippled by British bullets, made his confession and was anointed by a Capuchin friar to die a Christian hero, and his Socialism never came to mean anything to the great mass of Irishmen. O'Grady's semi-pagan heroism and a Jacobin republicanism purged of anti-Catholicism and anti-clericalism became part of the spiritual endowment of the most Catholic state in Europe, a state which was the creation of a Catholic revolution.

Pearse's life and thought lie at the heart of that transition, the translation of ideals not specific to Catholicism into language seemingly Catholic. Like many other an Irish rebel, Tone, Emmet, Davis and Mitchel (Horgan, 1948, p.9), he was of mixed English-Irish ancestry, his father being an Englishman, a successful ecclesiastical sculptor of radical London and Birmingham Unitarian background, converted with his English wife to

Catholicism in Dublin (Ruth Dudley Edwards, 1977). His second wife, Padraic's mother, was an Irish Catholic, and from his Irish great aunt the boy got his taste for Irish folk culture. His Gaelic was an acquired tongue which he never spoke with the fluency of a native, and his schooling, by the Christian Brothers, though much more nationalist than most Irish education, was wholly geared to a Gradgrind English examination system which he later described as a 'Murder Machine'.

Pearse qualified as a barrister, but his one notable appearance in court, if an oratorical triumph, was a legal failure. His early work was as a teacher and Secretary of the Gaelic League's Publications Committee, and in both his educational and linguistic endeavours he showed an efficiency and wisdom out of sorts with his literary reputation as a dreamy idealist. As editor of a famous Gaelic journal from 1903, he was responsible for encouraging many practical good works. After 1908, he founded two schools, St Enda's for boys and St Ita's for girls, in which a wide-ranging curriculum emancipated students from the examination treadmill (and from coercion and corporal punishment), while under an honours system drawing its inspiration from the 'fosterage' practised in the courts of Irish kings, the students enjoyed considerable freedom from authority as a 'Child Republic' with its own elected officers (Ryan, 1919, p.80). Pearse is a clear exception to the rule that no man is a hero to his pupils, who seem almost without exception to have loved their school. Like the Gaelic League itself, St Enda's did not seek to be monolingually Irish, but was based on a bilingualism taken from Catholic Belgium. It is true that the pupils sometimes 'ran wild' (Thornley, 1971, p.343) and that the schools were in chronic financial difficulties, and because Pearse's programmes for expansion and building outran his meagre income, St Ita's had to close. Yet here again, as F.S.L. Lyons declares in his Introduction to Séamas Ó Buachalla's collection of Pearse's letters (1980), Pearse was a man 'meticulous and systematic' (Ó Buachalla, 1980, p.xvii) in his business arrangements, and, except perhaps in his own eyes, was by no means a worldly failure when he took the path to hopeless revolution.

But the first paradox of Pearse's nationalism was that spiritual success was the reward of worldly failure. 'The Gael is not like other men,' he wrote in a famous early address, 'the spade, and the loom, and the sword are not for him. But a destiny more glorious than that of Rome, more glorious than that of Britain awaits him: to become the saviour of idealism in modern intellectual and social life, the regenerator and rejuvenator of the literature of the world, the instructor of the nations, the preacher of the gospel of nature-worship, hero-worship, God-worship' (Pearse, 1924, p.221). The passage might have been written by a Deist nationalist enthusiast like Mazzini on behalf of Young Italy; it is notable, moreover, for the uncompromising, superhuman standards which it sets for Irish nationhood. Pearse's idealist refusal of the decadent realism of contemporary European literature is just as absolute, for the Gaelic race is the only one possessing 'a literature natural and uncontaminated . . . as different from the unnatural literature of to-day as the pure radiance of the sun is different from the hideous glare of the electric light' (Pearse, 1924, p.225). Though he was later to change his mind on the value of the realism of Synge, the young Pearse was a passionate believer in the purity and perfection of Irishness, and that made him no moderate Home Ruler, but an exponent of separatism from the very first. Yet the lesson here – 'the spade, and the loom, and the sword are not for him' – is one of conquest by the spirit not the sword, by the weapons appropriate to the school-teacher and Gaelic Leaguer. Indeed the lecture concludes with Newman's vision of an international Catholic University in Dublin, and Pearse's early political intransigence remained firmly rooted in the realm of absolute ideas.

Pearse was, however, offering as severely censored a reading of the Gaelic inheritance as of foreign literature, a Puritan Victorian understanding of heroic Ireland common to the Gaelic movement as a whole. The considerable traditional elements of bawdy and eroticism (Connolly, 1982, pp.192–4) were strained out in the translation in the interests of an Ireland pure and holy; not so the violence, which it was impossible to purge, and which is so grandiloquently idealized as Christian chivalry in the rhetorical volumes of O'Grady (1878 and 1880). The hall of King Concobar Mac Nessa of the Red Branch of Ulster is hung with 'the naked forms of great men clear against the dark dome, having the cords of their slaughter around their necks and their white limbs splashed with blood' (O'Grady, no date, pp.3–4); and Concobar's court is the setting for the coming of the young Cuchulain whom Pearse was to make 'an important if invisible member of the staff' of St Enda's (Pearse, 1917b, p.90). 'A.E.', the mystic George William Russell, describes Cuchulain in his tribute to O'Grady, as *'that incarnation of Gaelic chivalry, (of) the fire and gentleness, the beauty and heroic ardour'* displayed in a hundred gory battles against overwhelming odds (O'Grady, no date, p.xiii). Cuchulain's ending is like Christ's, 'strapped to a post and shedding his life's blood in the defence of his people' (Owen Dudley Edwards and Fergus Pyle, 1968, p.45). Pearse declared that 'the story of Cuchulainn (sic) symbolises the redemption of man by a sinless God' (Pearse, 1924, p.156), and wanted an Ireland 'teeming with Cuchulains . . . a Cuchulain baptised' (Thompson, 1967, pp.76–7), and the mingled of Christian and pagan elements appears in his ideal for St Enda's:

> the knightly tradition of the macradh of Eamhain Macha, dead at the Ford 'in the beauty of their boyhood,' the high tradition of Cuchulainn, 'better is short life with honour than long life with dishonour,' 'I care not though I were to live but one day and one night, if only my fame and my deeds live after me;' the noble tradition of the Fianna, 'we, the Fianna, never told a lie, falsehood was never imputed to us,' 'strength in our hands, truth on our lips, and cleanness in our hearts;' the Christ-like tradition of Colm Cille (sic), 'if I die, it shall be from the excess of the love I bear the Gael.' (Pearse, 1917b, p.7)

This famous 'non-Christian' saying of Colum Cille, St Columba, inscribed on the walls of St Enda's, with Cuchulain's 'better short life with honour' comes from a late and suspect source (Shaw, 1972, p.134); but even in a different idiom, the same mingling of warlike sentiment and patriotism with Christianity could be also found in schools in England, in the years before the First World War (Marrin, 1974, pp.127–8). There is, however, an easy transition in Pearse's work from the blood of Cuchulain to the blood of Christ, and from there to the blood of the Irish political martyrs, and so to a more explicit enunciation of the underlying doctrine that the shedding of blood makes men holy.

The full statement of this position belongs to the last years of Pearse's short life: as late as 1912, he welcomed the Home Rule Bill as a first step to separation, while warning 'that if we are again betrayed there shall be red war throughout Ireland' (Ruth Dudley Edwards, 1977, p.159). There was, therefore, a significant turning of a minority of nationalists in this year to the physical force school (Martin and Byrne, 1973, p.108), out of disillusionment with the power of the moderates to win Home Rule; and it was also in 1912 that Pearse published his canonization of non-Catholic rebels in a ferocious litany intended in no sense of blasphemy, but in deadly reverence:

> In the name of God,
> By Christ His only Son,

By Mary His gentle Mother,
By Patrick the Apostle of the Irish,
By the loyalty of Colm Cille,
By the glory of our race,
By the blood of our ancestors,
By the murder of Red Hugh,
By the sad death of Hugh O'Neill,
By the tragic death of Owen Roe,
By the dying wish of Sarsfield,
By the anguished sigh of Fitzgerald,
By the bloody wounds of Tone,
By the noble blood of Emmet,
By the Famine corpses,
By the tears of Irish exiles,
We swear the oaths our ancestors swore,
That we will free our race from bondage,
Or that we will fall fighting hand to hand.
                                    Amen.
          (Ruth Dudley Edwards, 1977, pp.161–2)

So Pearse saw no incongruity in proclaiming at the grave of Wolfe Tone, who had loathed Catholicism (Shaw, 1972, pp.128–9): 'We have come to the holiest place in Ireland; holier to us even than the place where Patrick sleeps in Down. Patrick brought us life, but this man died for us. . . . He was the greatest of Irish Nationalists; I believe he was the greatest of Irish men . . . it must be that the holiest sod of a nation's soil is the sod where the greatest of her dead lies buried' (Pearse, 1922, pp.53–4). So too, Pearse on Davis, a Protestant: 'The highest form of genius is the genius for sanctity, the genius for noble life and thought. That genius was Davis's' (Pearse, 1922, p.328). Last, there is the ringing peroration to Pearse's elegy over the grave of the Fenian O'Donovan Rossa:

This is a place of peace, sacred to the dead, where men should speak with all charity . . . but I hold it a Christian thing, as O'Donovan Rossa held it, to hate evil, to hate untruth, to hate oppression, and, hating them, to strive to overthrow them. Our foes are strong and wise and wary; but . . . they cannot undo the miracles of God who ripens in the hearts of young men the seeds sown by the young men of a former generation. And the seeds sown by the young men of '65 and '67 are coming to their miraculous ripening to-day. . . . Life springs from death; and from the graves of patriot men and women

spring living nations. The Defenders of this Realm have
worked well in secret and in the open. They think that they
have pacified Ireland. . . . They think that they have foreseen
everything, think that they have provided against everything;
but the fools, the fools, the fools! – they have left us our Fenian
dead, and while Ireland holds these graves, Ireland unfree shall
never be at peace. (Pearse, 1922, pp.136–7)

The theme of resurrection is a law of nature, as well as God's.
'It is murder and death that make possible the terrible beautiful
thing we call physical life. Life springs from death, life lives on
death', and death can give birth to life (Pearse, 1917b, p.61).
Pearse found the roots of his identification of Ireland's cause
with God's in some of the seventeenth-century poetry (but see
Shaw, 1972, pp.141–2) mourning over Cromwell's Ireland, which
Pearse had translated from the Irish, as in 'Prophecy':

'Victory shall be to the host of the Gael
Over Calvin's clan – the trickster, the thief, the liar;
Their nobles shall triumph over heretics,
And shout at the routing of Clan Luther.. . .

'I pray God, if He deign to hear me,
I pray Jesus Who seeth all this,
And the Holy Ghost again with one will,
Mother Mary and Patrick White-Tooth,

'Kindly Colum and Holy Brigid,
That they may weld the Gael together,
And that thus they may compass this deed:
The banishment of the Gall and the freeing of Ireland.'
(Pearse, 1924, pp.69, 71)

The Irishman's proper emotion is hatred of the Gall. 'Just as in
early Irish manuscripts,' writes Pearse, 'Irish love of nature or of
nature's God so frequently bursts out in fugitive quatrains of great
beauty, so in the seventeenth and eighteenth century manuscripts
we find Irish hate of the English (a scarcely less holy passion)
expressing itself suddenly and splendidly' (Pearse, 1924, pp.34–5).
If love of Ireland was holy, then so was hating England.
Yet Pearse's ferocity was directed against abstractions, not
individuals. No man of violence himself, but a radical deeply
opposed to capital punishment, he would 'weep over a dead
kitten, and once stopped gardening for a whole day because he
had killed a worm by accident' (Ryan, 1919, p.126). His plays and
stories about women and children have a tenderness verging on

the lachrymose: of the dying Old Matthias, who loved children, and was rewarded with a vision of Iosagan, 'Jesus-kin', the Christ child, to fetch him a priest, though Matthias had frequented neither clergy nor mass: of the Virgin and Child's visit to a barren woman, who later conceives; of the Christ-devotion of Mary Magdalene:

> O woman, of the snowy side,
> Many a lover hath lain with thee,
> Yet left thee sad at the morning tide;
> But thy lover Christ shall comfort thee . . .
>
> O woman that no lover's kiss
> (Tho' many a kiss was given thee)
> Could slake thy love, is it not for this
> The hero Christ shall die for thee?
>
> (Pearse, 1917a, p.80)

'God loves the women better than the men', remarks Pearse with the voice of the narrator. 'It's to them He sends the greatest sorrows, and it's on them He bestows the greatest joy' (Pearse, 1917a, p.135). Pearse's psychology is a passionate intensity of extremes, and his ferocity is near neighbour to tenderness; great hate is born of great love, hate of the Gall, love of the Gael.

A hostile critic roundly declares that these direct emotions arise from Pearse's immaturity of vision, which places children before adults, and favours the rustic culture of the peasantry over urban sophistication, primitivism over civilization, and an ideal moral and literary simplicity over realist complexity (Thompson, 1967, pp.58–82). All the favoured qualities, however, are also those of Irish Catholic devotion, whether in the joyous tenderness of Iosagan and his mother, or in the reiterated theme of the *mater dolorosa*, the sorrowing mother, who becomes the mother of Christ, and is also Mother Ireland. The Keening Woman cries for twenty years for her dead son killed by the British: the story ends with prayer for the soul of the son, and the saying of the Rosary. Mother Ireland bears Cuchulain to her glory, and traitors to her shame. In the three Mother poems written just before his execution, Pearse addressed his own mother on the dolorosa theme:

> My gift to you hath been the gift of sorrow,
> My one return for your rich gifts to me, . . .
>
> (Ó Buachalla, 1980, p.382)

'The Mother' offers Pearse and his gentle brother Willie, the ecclesiastical sculptor who died with him, to God:

> I do not grudge them: Lord, I do not grudge
> My two strong sons that I have seen go out
> To break their strength and die, they and a few,
> In bloody protest for a glorious thing,
> They shall be spoken of among their people,
> The generations shall remember them,
> And call them blessed; . . .
>
> (Pearse, 1917a, p.333)

These last lines recall the Magnificat. Willie Pearse's statue of the 'Mater Dolorosa' still stands in a Dublin chapel, and 'A Mother Speaks' is an address to the sorrowing Virgin, and was taken by the Capuchin Father Aloysius to Mrs Pearse on the day of Padraic's death:

> Dear Mary, that didst see thy first-born Son
> Go forth to die amid the scorn of men
> For whom He died,
> Receive my first-born into thy arms,
> Who also hath gone out to die for men,
> And keep him by thee till I come to him.
> Dear Mary, I have shared thy sorrow,
> And soon shall share thy joy.
>
> (Ó Buachalla, 1980, p.383)

Pearse's identification of his mother with Mary is also an identification of himself with the Christ of the Passion, a preoccupation which originally arose out of his brilliant Passion Play in Irish, performed by his family, friends and pupils on the stage of the famous Abbey Theatre in 1911, with the blessing of Yeats, and with women keeners to provide an Irish setting: 'the Irish medium', recalled Pearse's pupil Desmond Ryan, 'had not veiled but intensified the meaning and pathos of the story. Some of us, too, thought, though to many it may seem an irreverence, that our national and individual struggle was in ways a faint reflection of the Great One just enacted. Is it not so? The Man is crucified as the Nation' (Pearse, 1917b, p.108). This theme is made explicit in Pearse's morality 'The King', again, enacted by his schoolboys, in which a sinless child-king from a monastic school takes the place of his sinful monarch to die in battle for the freedom of the people. 'Do you think', asks his teacher Abbot, 'I would grudge the dearest of these little boys, to death calling with that terrible, beautiful voice?' (Pearse, 1917a, p.55). There is, then, an identity between the nation, Christ, the victim who dies for it and Pearse. 'The people who wept in Gethsemane, who trod the sorrowful way, who died naked on a cross, who went down into hell, will rise again glorious and immortal, will sit on the right hand of God, and will come in the end to give judgment, a judge just and terrible' (Pearse, 1922, p.345). These themes all come together in the hero of his play *The Singer*, the revolutionary schoolteacher MacDara, who loses his faith, but refinds it in the Passion of the people: 'The people, Maoilsheachlainn, the dumb, suffering people: reviled and outcast, yet pure and splendid and faithful. In them I saw, or seemed to see again, the Face of God. Ah, it is a tear-stained face, blood-stained, defiled with ordure, but it is the Holy Face!' (Pearse, 1917a, pp.34–5). And as the people are as Veronica's Veil to Christ, so MacDara is again the son of Mary 'on the Dolorous Way', and is Christ in his triumphant conclusion: 'One man can free a people as one Man redeemed the world. I will take no pike, I will go into the battle with bare hands. I will stand up before the Gall as Christ hung naked before men on the tree!' (Pearse, 1917a, pp.24, 44). Or as Pearse said in his last address to his pupils at St Enda's: 'It had taken the blood of the Son of God to redeem the world. It would take the blood of the sons of Ireland to redeem Ireland' (Pearse, 1917b, p.98).

The means, then, to this salvation is by the shedding of blood. Pearse wrote of the carnage of the first years of the war that 'Heroism has come back to the earth. . . . The old heart of the earth needed to be warmed with the red wine of the battlefields' (Pearse, 1922, p.216). Or, as he declared in anticipation of his own coming revolution, 'We may make mistakes in the beginning and shoot the wrong people; but bloodshed is a cleansing and a sanctifying thing, and the nation which regards it as the final horror has lost its manhood' (Pearse, 1922, pp.98–9). This doctrine is not, again, specifically Catholic in origin, though it occurs in the popular novels of the Catholic Canon Sheehan (Lyons, 1979, p.91). Rather, it derives from Cuchulain and from the favourite Nationalist image of Ireland as the rose which needed to be watered with blood, as immortalized by Pearse's exchange with Connolly in Yeats's famous poem:

> There's nothing but our own red blood
> Can make a right Rose Tree.
>
> (Yeats, 1950, p.206)

The rose, however, has its relation to the Passion, as in Joseph Mary Plunkett's 'I see His blood upon the rose' (Plunkett, 1916, p.50); and even Connolly, no conventional Catholic, had been impelled to give the idea a religious cast: 'of us, as of mankind before Calvary', he wrote, 'it may truly be said "without the shedding of blood there is no redemption"' (Lyons, 1979, p.90).

In less dramatic form, the same idea existed in Protestant Britain in the generalized notion that the First World War would purge sin and selfishness through the redemptive shedding of blood (Wilkinson, 1978, p.188; Thornley, 1971, p.342). Some Irish Catholics also gave the war a religious justification, like the Irish MP Tom Kettle, who died on the battlefield, one of the half a million soldiers of Irish ancestry to fight in the British and Dominion armies:

> Know that we fools, now with the foolish dead,
> Died not for flag, nor King, nor Emperor,
> But for a dream, born in a herdsman's shed,
> And for the secret Scripture of the poor.
> (F.X. Martin, 1967b, p.63; Owen Dudley Edwards and
> Fergus Pyle, 1968, p.100)

But here again, there are links with Pearse: Kettle dies for the dream of the poor, not for the king, while as in the theme of the sacrifice of the fool, the connexion between the planned Rising and the Passion is completed by the boast of their holy foolishness. The Rising was a theatrical gesture, an act of imagination, rather than a serious military affair (F.X. Martin, 1967b, p.127; F.X. Martin, 1968, pp.110–12). It was the work of a tiny conspiracy within the wider separatist movement: Sinn Féin had no part in it, though Sinn Féiners were to reap the reward, Casement's German mission had failed, and the leaders of the Irish Republican Brotherhood had also failed in their attempt to trick the mass of Professor Eoin MacNeill's Volunteers to join them. They took on the British Empire knowing that they must be beaten: yet for that Pearse was already prepared. 'I speak that am only a fool . . .' he had written:

> I have squandered the splendid years that
> the Lord God gave to my youth
> In attempting impossible things, deeming
> them alone worth the toil.

The impossibility of the Rising is part of its attraction, for the consummate Christian hero is the fool:

> Was it folly or grace? Not men shall
> judge me, but God . . .

Sacrifice of self is the chief message of the Gospel:

> For this I have heard in my heart, that a
> man shall scatter, not hoard,
> Shall do the deed of to-day, nor take thought
> of to-morrow's teen,
> Shall not bargain or huxter with God; or
> was it a jest of Christ's
> And is this my sin before men, to have
> taken Him at His word?
> The lawyers have sat in council, the men
> with the keen, long faces,
> And said, 'This man is a fool,' and others
> have said, 'He blasphemeth;'
> And the wise have pitied the fool that hath
> striven to give a life
> In the world of time and space among the
> bulks of actual things,
> To a dream that was dreamed in the heart,
> and that only the heart could hold.
>
> (Pearse, 1917a, pp.334–5)

The lawyers in council, declaring 'He blasphemeth', are the Sanhedrin, and respectable Society; they are also the enemy, with political economy, of Christianity, as well as the British legal system which Pearse the barrister had forsaken (Pearse, 1917b, p.81; McCay, 1966, p.45). They all stand for the judgment of the world on Christ, which forgets that he triumphed through failure. Pearse's final act – recalling MacDara's nakedness, – is one of total sacrificial 'Renunciation':

> Naked I saw thee,
> O beauty of beauty,
> And I blinded my eyes
> For fear I should fail . . .
>
> I turned my back
> On the vision I had shaped,
> And to this road before me
> I turned my face.
>
> I have turned my face
> To this road before me,
> To the deed that I see
> And the death I shall die.
>
> (Pearse, 1917a, pp.324–5)

Pearse foresaw and chose this destiny, even to the final

dereliction of rejection by his people. The image arose from this
dream about one of his pupils of St Enda's about to die for a
cause, confronted by a silent indifferent crowd. Pearse applies it to
himself in the person of MacDara: 'I seemed to see myself brought
to die before a great crowd that stood cold and silent; and there
were some that cursed me in their hearts for having brought death
into their houses' (Pearse, 1917a, p.25). Again, Pearse was to
experience this himself, in reading the Proclamation of the Irish
Republic to indifferent bystanders on the steps of the Post Office,
and in enduring the more actively hostile jeers of Dubliners
outraged by the destruction of their city. Yet the initial hostility of
both Church and Nation to Pearse was to pass, as British bullets
immortalized him as hero. '"Kings with plumes may adorn their
hearse," ran a popular tribute . . . "but angels meet the soul of
Patrick Pearse"' (Ryan, 1919, pp.1–2). And so the religious
imagination made true the sub-title of Ruth Dudley Edwards
brilliant life of Pearse – 'The Triumph of Failure', turning fine
rhetoric and indifferent poetry into a nation's creed.

It was Yeats, of course, who saw that these mildly comic fools,
poets and school masters, had been transformed by the power of
their sacrifice into something deadly serious:

> Being certain that they and I
> But lived where motley is worn:
> All changed, changed utterly:
> A terrible beauty is born.
>
> (Yeats, 1950, p.203)

The final immortal oxymoron is almost a quotation from
Pearse: the Abbot's 'terrible, beautiful voice' of death. Yeats
concludes on the theme of love and death:

> And what if excess of love
> Bewildered them till they died?
> I write it out in a verse –
> MacDonagh and MacBride
> And Connolly and Pearse
> Now and in time to be,
> Wherever green is worn,
> Are changed, changed utterly:
> A terrible beauty is born.
>
> (Yeats, 1950, pp.204–5)

Pearse was not the finest poet of the Rising: that was Thomas
MacDonagh. The dying tubercular Joseph Mary Plunkett, with

his bejewelled fingers and bejewelled verses and eve-of-execution marriage is also a more complex and interesting writer than Pearse, as he places Ireland's resurrection and Christ's against a background of cosmic imagery drawn from the mystic St John of the Cross (Ryan, 1963). Yet Pearse was arguably 'the most influential thinker, the most inspirational personality of the Rising' (Augustine Martin, 1966, p.39). One of his many brilliant and grateful pupils writes of him and his companions, with no sense of irony, that 'we are now living the dream they died for' – that is, modern Ireland (Reddin, 1943, p.241).

There was of course more to the Catholicism of the Rising than Pearse. The confessionals crammed on Easter Saturday with men and boys, 'the striking fact that the rank and file of the Volunteers, almost to a man, prepared for the rising by going to confession and holy communion' (F.X. Martin, 1967b, p.20); the steady pace of the Rosary through the British bombardment; the O'Rahilly kneeling for a final blessing; even, in lighter vein, the impression of a modern writer 'that a few hundred British soldiers, dressed as priests, could have walked into the Post Office unhampered and put a sudden end to the entire rebellion', and the anxiety of combatants confronted with Friday chicken, until their chaplain, Father Flanagan, had taken his fork to the bird (Coffey, 1971, pp.126, 202). For these men, the religious legitimation of the Rising, even in the face of clergymen whom they had often defied, was of desperate importance, and Pearse provided that legitimation through the very symbols of the Faith. The consequences for Ireland were of course disastrous. Foolish talk costs lives, and as some Irish historians now recognize, the rebellion discredited the constitutionalist tradition and permanently alienated the Protestants of Northern Ireland from Irish nationhood. The passionate purity of the young firebombers of Belfast is Pearse's legacy, and an increasing number of Irish Catholics, like the splendid Jesuit Professor Francis Shaw, in his posthumously published challenge to the canon of Irish history (Shaw, 1972), have dared to say that Pearse's ideals were hardly Christian.

It has been for some of the novelists and poets to reject Pearse most unambiguously: Sean O'Casey's prostitute sourly remarking of the Nationalists, 'they're all in a holy mood to-night' (Augustine Martin, 1966, p.40); Joyce creating a deliberately bourgeois anti-hero and sure that 'heroism is, and always was, a damned lie' (Watson, 1979, p.221); Yeats withdrawing into the tower of his old-age poetry from the Catholic nation he had helped to make:

> Did that play of mine send out
> Certain men the English shot?
>
> (Yeats, 1950, p.393)

or in another concluding oxymoron which occurs in Pearse:

> A revolutionary soldier kneeling to be blessed;
> An Abbot or Archbishop with an upraised hand
> Blessing the Tricolour. 'This is not', I say,
> 'The dead Ireland of my youth, but an Ireland
> The poets have imagined, terrible and gay.'
>
> (Yeats, 1950, p.368)

Yet it was an Ireland dreamed of by the young poet Yeats, who had lived in fascinated horror to disown his dream. 'Too long a sacrifice can make a stone of the heart', and for Yeats that stone was the heart of Catholic Ireland:

> Out of Ireland have we come.
> Great hatred, little room,
> Maimed us at the start.
> I carry from my mother's womb
> A fanatic heart.
>
> (Yeats, 1950, p.288)

In that sense, of turning the heart to the stone of a fanatic hate, it must be said of Pearse's sacrifice that it was magnificent, but hardly Christianity. Perhaps there is a lesson here for the liberation theologies of our time, which can be so free with the blood of the oppressor. Yet I had written this conclusion when I heard an army chaplain in Falklands cathedral telling his men that war had changed them utterly, with a deeper knowledge of God and of themselves. How far is it from that to the doctrine that blood purifies? The crucified Christ has many contradictory faces in the history of the Church, and the true Christ is difficult to find. It is too hard a saying that even this Irish Christ-modelled sacrifice of a Christian man and nation should be accounted wholly wrong.

There is also the uncomfortable consideration that Pearse's sacrifice, like Christ's, succeeded by its failure:

O wise men, riddle me this: What if the dream come true?
What if the dream come true? and if millions unborn shall dwell
In the house that I shaped in my heart . . .?

> (Pearse, 1917a, p.336)

Certainly in Northern Ireland, Pearse's vision retains its power.

The existence of his set of Roman Catholic devotional images which offer a sanction to revolutionary activity does not, of course, in itself provide an explanation of the violence of the para-militaries in Ulster. This has a far more complex explanation in the social ghettoization of the Protestant and Catholic communities, in the long years in which Catholics suffered discrimination and disability, even in the weakening authority of the priesthood in the 1970s to keep communal violence within bounds: the Bishop of Down and Connor met very different reactions from his flock when he opposed barricade-building in 1970 and 1974. Yet in so far as the Irish state was itself a creation of a Catholic revolution, there is undoubtedly an Irish Catholic imagery which speaks at a deeper level than self-interest, an imagery of sacrifice and suffering as in the pictures which appeared on Belfast and Derry walls during the H-Block hunger strikes. Surely there have been few stranger applications of the Beatitudes than the ascription of the text 'Blessed are they who hunger for justice's sake', in a tenement mural, to the martyrdom of Bobby Sands. The heart of the matter is this: the English historian of the working class Raphael Samuel has spoken of the way in which Englishmen sympathetic to revolution cannot but be influenced by the anti-revolutionary bias of English culture. For an intellectual Marxist reared on *A Tale of Two Cities*, 'revolution' can still call up Dickens's ghastly vision of *tricoteuses* and tumbrils. It is on this level, of the image which enshrines the whole experience of a culture, that Irish Catholicism retains its revolutionary character: needing, as in Ulster, only the time and favourable harsh circumstance to leap from the past back into life.

References

Coffey, Thomas M. (1971), *Agony at Easter: The 1916 Irish Uprising*, London: Penguin.

Connolly, S.J. (1982), *Priests and People in Pre-Famine Ireland 1780–1845*, New York: Gill and Macmillan.

Dangerfield, George (1977), *The Damnable Question: A Study in Anglo-Irish Relations*, London, Constable.

Edwards, Owen Dudley and Pyle, Fergus (1968), *1916: The Easter Rising*, London: MacGibbon & Kee.

Edwards, Owen Dudley (1971), *The Mind of an Activist – James Connolly*, Dublin: Gill and Macmillan.

Edwards, Ruth Dudley (1977), *Patrick Pearse: The Triumph of Failure*, London: Victor Gollancz.

Egan, Desmond (1966), 'Attitudes to Catholicism in the Modern Irish Novel', MA thesis, University College, Dublin.

Horgan, John J. (1948), *Parnell to Pearse: Some Recollections and Reflections*, Dublin: Browne & Nolan.

Larkin, Emmet (1972), 'The Devotional Revolution in Ireland, 1850–75', *American Historical Review*, 77, pp.625–52.

Larkin, Emmet (1975), *The Roman Catholic Church and the Creation of the Modern Irish State, 1878–1886*, Philadelphia: American Philosophical Society.

Larkin, Emmet (1978), *The Roman Catholic Church and the Plan of Campaign in Ireland, 1886–1888*, Cork: University Press.

Larkin, Emmet (1979), *The Roman Catholic Church in Ireland and the Fall of Parnell, 1888–1891*, Liverpool: University Press.

Levenson, Samuel (1977), *Maud Gonne*, London: Cassell.

Lyons, F.S.L. (1971), *Ireland since the Famine*, London: Wiedenfeld & Nicolson.

Lyons, F.S.L. (1979), *Culture and Anarchy in Ireland 1890–1939*, Oxford: Clarendon Press.

McCartney, Donal (1967), 'The Church and the Fenians', *University Review*, iv, pp.203–15.

McCay, Hedley (1966), *Padraic Pearse: A New Biography*, Cork: The Mercier Press.

Marrin, Albert (1974), *The Last Crusade: The Church of England in the First World War*, Durham, North Carolina: Duke University Press.

Martin, Augustine (1966), 'To Make a Right Rose Tree', *Studies: An Irish Quarterly Review*, pp.38–50.

Martin, F.X., OSA (ed.) (1967a), *Leaders and Men of the Easter Rising: Dublin 1916*, London, Methuen.

Martin, F.X. (1967b), '1916 – Myth, Fact and Mystery', *Studia Hibernica*, 7, pp.7–126.

Martin, F.X. (1968), 'The 1916 Rising – A *Coup d'État* or a "Bloody Protest"?' *Studia Hibernica*, 8, pp.106–37.

Martin, F.X. and Byrne, F.J. (eds) (1973), *The Scholar Revolutionary: Eoin MacNeill, 1867–1945, and the Making of the New Ireland*, Shannon: Irish University Press.

Miller, David W. (1973), *Church, State and Nation in Ireland, 1898–1921*, Dublin, Gill & Macmillan.

Newsinger, John (1979), 'Revolution and Catholicism in Ireland, 1848–1923', *European Studies Review*, 9, pp.457–80.

Norman, E.R. (1965), *The Catholic Church and Ireland in the Age of Rebellion, 1859–1873*, London, Longmans.

O'Brien, Conor Cruise (1973), *States of Ireland*, London: Hutchinson.

Ó Buachalla, Séamas (ed.) (1980), *The Letters of P.H. Pearse*, Gerrards Cross, Colin Smythe.

O'Farrell, Patrick (1971), *Ireland's English Question: Anglo-Irish Relations, 1534–1970*, London: Batsford.

O'Grady, Standish (no date), *The Coming of Cuculain*, Dublin: The Talbot Press.

O'Grady, Standish James (1878 and 1880), *History of Ireland: The Heroic Period*, 2 vols, London, Sampson Low. Republished (1979), New York, Lemma.

Pearse, P.H. (1916), *The Separatist Idea*, Dublin: Whelan & Son.

Pearse, P.H. (1917a), *Collected Works of Padraic H. Pearse: Plays Stories Poems*, Dublin and London: Maunsel.

Pearse, P.H. (1917b), *The Story of a Success: Being a Record of St Enda's College September 1908 to Easter 1916*, Desmond Ryan (ed.), Dublin and London, Maunsel.

Pearse, P.H. (1922), *Collected Works of Padraic H. Pearse: Political Writings and Speeches*, Dublin and London, Maunsel & Roberts.

Pearse, P.H. (1924), *Collected Works of Padraic H. Pearse: Songs of the Irish Rebels and Specimens from an Irish Anthology: Some Aspects of Irish Literature; Three Lectures on Gaelic Topics*, Dublin, Cork, Belfast, The Phoenix Publishing Co.

Plunkett, Joseph Mary (1916), *The Poems of Joseph Mary Plunkett*, Dublin, The Talbot Press.

Ransom, Bernard (1980), *Connolly's Marxism*, London, Pluto Press.

Reddin, Kenneth (1943), 'A Man called Pearse', *Studies: An Irish Quarterly Review*, pp.241–51.

Ryan, Desmond (1919), *The Man called Pearse*, Dublin and London, Maunsel.

Ryan, Desmond (1934), *Remembering Sion*, London, Arthur Barker.

Ryan, Desmond (ed.) (1963), *The 1916 Poets*, Dublin, Allen Figgis.

Shaw, Rev. Professor Francis, S.J. (1972), 'The Canon of Irish History – A Challenge', *Studies: An Irish Quarterly Review*, LXI, pp.113–53.

Thompson, William Irwin (1967), *The Imagination of an Insurrection Dublin, Easter 1916: A Study of an Ideological Movement*, New York: Oxford University Press.

Thornley, David (1971), 'Patrick Pearse and the Pearse Family', *Studies: An Irish Quarterly Review*, LX, pp.332–46.

Tierney, Mark (1976), *Croke of Cashel: The Life of Archbishop Thomas William Croke, 1823–1902*, Dublin, Gill & Macmillan.

Watson, G.J. (1979), *Irish Identity and the Literary Revival Synge, Yeats, Joyce and O'Casey*, London, Croom Helm.

Wilkinson, Alan (1978), *The Church of England and the First World War*, London, SPCK.

Yeats, W.B. (1950), *The Collected Poems of W.B. Yeats*, London, Macmillan.

Religion and fascism

32

'A marriage of convenience': The Vatican and the Fascist regime in Italy

JOHN POLLARD

'You shepherds it was the Evangelist had in mind when she that sitteth upon the waters was seen by him committing fornication with the kings . . .'

Dante, *Inferno*, Canto XIX

Background: the consequences of the 'Roman Question'

The role of the Catholic Church in Italian politics, and in a longer historical perspective its contribution to the overall political development of the Italian peninsula, has always been determined by a factor missing in every other Catholic country – the presence of the Papacy. Given that presence, the Catholic Church in Italy speaks with a greater and more direct authority than elsewhere, for its head is no mere cardinal primate, but the Bishop of Rome, the Vicar of Christ himself, and as the infallible head of the Catholic Church throughout the World, the Pope is able to make use of the enormous international prestige and influence which goes with the office in his dealings with the Italian State.

This lesson was learnt the hard way by Cavour and the Moderate Liberals who unified Italy in the middle of the nineteenth century. Like their fellows in other European countries, the Italian Liberals in their attempt to modernize Italy came into conflict with the Church, whose property, legal privileges and social influence they restricted by means of legislation.[1] But the Church and State conflict which developed during the Italian *Risorgimento* had a dimension which sharply differentiated it from similar disputes elsewhere, for the Italian Liberals had to contend with the fact that the popes exercised 'temporal power', that is territorial sovereignty over the Papal States of central Italy. When United Italy was finally created, it was necessarily at the expense of these states with the result that Pope Pius IX (1846–78) refused to recognize the new state and excommunicated its rulers. And when the last remnant of his 'temporal power' was extinguished by the Italian occupation of Rome in September 1870, the Pope withdrew into the Vatican: thus was born the 'Roman Question', which was to complicate Italy's foreign relations and poison her internal politics for close on sixty years.[2]

The popes quickly learnt to do without their 'temporal power', and indeed were thankful to be relieved of its burdensome responsibilities, but they never renounced their claim to its restitution in some form nor did they abandon their demands for the repeal of the anti-church legislation. At the mercy of a strongly anti-clerical and masonic ruling class, the Church in late nineteenth-century Italy was obliged to endure further restrictive measures and even the occasional outburst of anticlerical violence. And though there is evidence of a religious revival in Italy at this time, the dominance of secular and anticlerical values contributed to the 'dechristianization', as Catholic observers described it, of Italian society. The memory of injustices, real and imaginary, which the Church had suffered at the hands of the Liberal State was to be a powerful motive determining the Vatican's response to the rise of Fascism in the 1920s.

The Vatican's most effective weapon in its struggles with the Liberal State after 1870 was its ability to mobilize the support of 'obedient' Italian Catholics both in the organization of the Catholic Movement and in its boycott of Italian politics. In an effort to insulate the Catholic masses from the secular values of Liberal Italy, they were organized into a kind of subcultural 'ghetto', a network of recreational, cultural and leisure organizations complete with their own newspapers.[3] A further impetus to the development of the Catholic Movement came with the publication in 1891 of the great social encyclical *Rerum Novarum* of Pope Leo XIII (1878–1903). In response to his call for Catholics to combat Socialism by actively helping to meet the material and spiritual needs of the working classes, Catholic associationalism in Italy and elsewhere spread rapidly into the fields of banking, agricultural co-operatives and trade unionism. But the Catholic Movement in Italy differed somewhat from its counterparts in Germany, France, etc., by reason of its absolute dependence upon the Papacy, a fact which was demonstrated by the banning of the Christian Democrats, the first autonomous, political grouping to emerge inside the movement and the removal of its leaders from positions of power in the Catholic organizations. This incident was an ominous portent of the future, for in the 1920s the Vatican was to treat the Catholic Partito Popolare Italiano in much the same way and Italian Catholics in general were forced out of obedience to the Papacy to accept policies that were to contribute to the downfall of democracy.

The strength of Italian Catholic obedience to papal directives in this period is also borne out by the success in enforcing the 'Non Expedit', the papal decree of 1864 barring Catholics from taking part in Italian politics; it was not until the general election of 1904 that the ban was relaxed at a national level. Even the re-entry of Catholics into national politics was a carefully controlled experiment on the part of the Vatican and Italian hierarchy. It was inspired by the alarm of the new pope St Pius X (1903–14) at the growing strength of the Extreme Left in Italy and in particular that of the emerging working-class Partito Socialista Italiano. To counter this, Catholic voters were mobilized on behalf of candidates endorsed by the Liberal prime minister Giovanni Giolitti or in support of a handful of Catholic candidates.[4] Such was the success of this policy that in the general election of 1913 the Catholic electorate effectively saved Giolitti's parliamentary majority. This unofficial alliance between the Vatican and the Liberal ruling class helped take much of the bitterness out of the 'Roman Question'. By the beginning of the First World War Italian Catholics were back firmly in the political arena, and as a result of their support for the Italian cause, at the war's end relations between the Vatican and the Italian State had improved out of all recognition, permitting the first, albeit unsuccessful, negotiations to settle the 'Roman Question'.[5]

The anticlericalism of the early Fascist movement

In 1919 it seemed most unlikely that a close relationship would develop between the Vatican and Italian Fascism. The Fascist movement which Mussolini founded in March of that year comprised some of the most violently anticlerical elements in Italian politics – futurists, revolutionary syndicalists and ex-Socialists – and this showed through in the programme of the movement which called, amongst other things, for the confiscation of all Church property.[6] Mussolini himself never ceased to attack Christianity, the Church and clergy in both his speeches and his writings, the most notorious of the latter being a semi-pornographic novelette entitled *The Cardinal's Mistress*. Yet suddenly, in 1920, Mussolini saw the light and in a letter to the Nationalist hero Gabriele D'Annunzio he declared, 'I believe Catholicism can be used as one of the greatest national forces for the expansion of Italy in the World.'[7]

With the same cynical opportunism that motivated his other shifts to the right during his rise to power, that is his abandonment of socialism and republicanism, Mussolini made overtures to the Vatican. In his maiden speech to Parliament in

May 1921 he brazenly announced, 'Fascism neither practices nor preaches anticlericalism', and he went on to praise the patriotic, conservative values of Catholicism, offering the Church improvements in its material position if it would abandon its 'temporalistic dreams'.[8] Mussolini's change of heart was entirely political, there is absolutely no evidence that he had renounced his life-long atheism or his anticlerical instincts. He had set out to win the Vatican's approval for his movements and thus outflank one of his major political competitors, the Partito Popolare.

Pius XI and the Fascist rise to power, 1919–26

The Vatican was originally as hostile to Fascism as Fascism was to the Vatican, and during the early years of the movement's existence the Vatican newspaper, *L'Osservatore Romano*, regularly condemned the Fascists for their anticlericalism and for their systematic use of violence against their political enemies. From 1921 onwards, however, partly as a result of the calculated respect with which Mussolini, in public at least, was treating the Church, and partly because of the support that some Catholics in the northern and central countryside were beginning to give to the Fascist movement, the Vatican newspaper began to treat Fascism with less hostility.[9] This trend was accentuated by the election of Pius XI (1922–39): the key elements in the new pontiff's attitude towards Italy was a deep-seated fear of the revolutionary threat that appeared to hang over the country coupled with a burning desire to bring about a 'Christian restoration' of Italian society, the starting point for which would be a settlement of the 'Roman Question'. It was not that the new pope's objectives differed substantially from those of his predecessor Benedict XV (1914–22), but that Pius XI pursued them with greater tenacity, single-mindedness and opportunistic skill.[10]

The other factor determining the development of the Vatican's attitude towards Fascism was the role played by the Partito Popolare in Italian politics at this time. Founded by Fr Luigi Sturzo, a former leader of the pre-war Christian Democrats, the party quickly won the adherence of the whole Italian Catholic movement, including the sitting Catholic MPs and the Catholic press.[11] But from the start, relations with the Vatican were uncomfortable: the Partito Popolare was regarded with suspicion not only because of the socialistic tendencies of its left wing but also because as an avowedly 'aconfessional' party, it placed a settlement of the 'Roman Question' low down on its list of priorities. The party's response to the Socialist challenge during the 'Red Two Years', when Italy was racked by a wave of strikes, demonstrations, occupations of the land and factories was equally disappointing to the Vatican, for the Partito Popolare refused to enter into pre-war-style alliances with the Liberals, and other forces of the Right, against the Socialists in the local elections of 1920 or in the parliamentary elections of 1921. And in Parliament, where the Partito Popolare was absolutely vital to the formation of any administration, the party's intransigent tactics during the long-drawn-out political crisis of the summer and the autumn of 1922 only seemed to render Italy more ungovernable.

By October 1922, in both the Vatican and right-wing, Catholic political circles there was deep disillusionment with the Partito Popolare; on the other hand, in these same circles and in Italian conservative circles generally Fascism was increasingly viewed with sympathy and respect. In common with other sections of the Italian establishment, the Court, the Armed Forces and right-wing Liberal politicians, the Vatican saw Fascism as a barrier to revolution and as a safe, stopgap solution to the country's chronic political crisis. It therefore breathed a sigh of relief at the eventual outcome of the crisis, when, after the threatened Fascist 'March on Rome', the King capitulated and appointed Mussolini as Prime Minister. The Vatican had particular reason to rejoice for one of his first acts of government was to announce a package of measures beneficial to the Church in Italy, the most important of which being the re-introduction of religious instruction into state primary schools, the placing of crucifixes in public buildings, and an increase in the salaries of those clergy paid by the state.

It is important to grasp the significance of Mussolini's gesture and the impact which it had upon Catholic opinion at the time. In taking these measures, by actively and materially helping the Church in Italy, the Fascist leader was doing something which none of his Liberal predecessors had dared to do, chained as they were by the anticlerical traditions of the Liberal State. To use Pius XI's own phrase, Mussolini had abandoned the 'anticlerical fetishism' of the Liberal ruling class. In this context, therefore, it would be absurd to suggest, as one Italian historian has, that there was a substantial continuity in the religious policy of Italian governments, Liberal and Fascist, after the end of the First World War.[12] Mussolini's ecclesiastical measures of November 1922 were a logical development of his radical change in attitude towards the Church which dates back to 1920, and it was precisely because they constituted a decisive break with the religious policy of Liberal governments that they won such favour with the Pope.

The measures were certainly very successful in consolidating support for Fascism in the Vatican, and among right-wing, Catholic politicians (later to be given the name 'Clerico-fascists' by Luigi Sturzo) whose activities undermined the ability of the Partito Popolare to oppose Mussolini's electoral 'reform' bill in the summer of 1923, and helped him win a crushing victory in the general elections of 1924.[13] The Vatican also played a crucial role in these events. Much of Mussolini's success in pushing the bill through Parliament was due to the direct intervention of the Vatican in the affairs of the Partito Popolare: on the insistence of Mussolini, it ordered Luigi Sturzo to resign as a Secretary-General, thus depriving the party of its ablest and most committed anti-fascist leader. And in the summer of 1924, when the abduction and murder of the Socialist leader Matteotti by Fascist thugs had created such a public outcry that it brought Mussolini's government to its knees, the Vatican's veto on a proposed alliance between the Partito Popolare and the reformist Socialists killed stone dead the only credible, alternative anti-fascist government. The Vatican had made its choice, it preferred the certainties of a tarnished Fascist government to the uncertainties of an anti-fascist alternative: it must, therefore, along with the other conservative forces in Italian society, accept responsibility for the establishment of the Fascist dictatorship which Mussolini announced in his historic speech of 3 January 1925.

Pius XI's abandonment of the Partito Popolare marked a return to the traditional policy of the Vatican which preferred an obedient, disciplined Catholic movement to an autonomous, Catholic political party. With the demise of the Partito Popolare in 1926 the Vatican became free once again to conduct its relations with the Italian State at the highest level without the embarrassing complications caused by the presence of a Catholic party in Parliament. The abandonment of the Partito Popolare was paralleled by increased Vatican attention to the needs of the core of the Catholic movement – Catholic Action. This network of groups of Catholic, lay activists was reorganized and strengthened in the period 1923–26. Pius XI was convinced of the efficacy and necessity of Catholic Action in all Catholic countries, but Italian Catholic Action had a particular role to play in his grand design, it was to spearhead his campaign to bring about a Christian revival in Italy. And, of course, by 1925 Pius XI along with right-wing, Catholic, lay politicians, was convinced that there was a better chance of bringing about such a revival under an authoritarian Fascist regime than under the Liberal democratic state; that not only was Fascism more likely to achieve a solution of the 'Roman Question', but that under its aegis it would be possible to bring about the restoration of that Christian, confessional state that had existed before the French Revolution.

The Lateran Pacts of 1929

The dictatorial regime which Mussolini constructed in the late 1920s involved not only the creation of a one-party, police state, but also the destruction or 'fascistization' of all trade union, cultural, sporting and recreational organizations in Italy as part of the Fascist design for a 'totalitarian' society – which Mussolini himself defined as being 'Everything inside the State, nothing outside the State and nothing against the State'.[14] Whilst the Vatican did not mourn the passing of the Partito Popolare and it even acquiesced, however reluctantly, in the dissolution of the Catholic trade unions, it became seriously alarmed when the Fascists began to lay violent hands on other branches of the Catholic movement – the Catholic newspapers, the sporting and recreational associations, and above all the youth organizations of Catholic Action.

Pius XI realized that in these new circumstances, only concrete, juridical guarantees – in other words a concordat between the Vatican and Italy – could protect the Catholic organizations from a complete Fascist take-over, and that such an agreement could only be obtained from Mussolini in return for the historical glory of having resolved the 'Roman Question'. The Pope also perceived that the nature of the new regime greatly increased the chances of successful negotiations: the anticlerical influence of the 'Fascists of the First Hour' had been much diminished since the fusion of the Fascists with the more conservative Nationalist Party in 1923. And Mussolini's own authority was enormously stronger in the new set-up. He was seen to possess an ability to negotiate and enforce agreements which had been denied to his Liberal predecessors.

At this stage of the game it was Pius XI who was forced to do all the running: throughout the spring and the summer of 1926 the Vatican wooed the Duce of Fascism with the subtlety and tenacity of a courtesan until in August the official representatives finally met, and after two and a half years of difficult and secret negotiations they succeeded in resolving the 'Roman Question'.[15]

By the Terms of the Lateran Treaty signed on 11 February 1929 the Papacy regained a tiny fraction of its former 'temporal power', the establishment of the one-hundred acre Vatican 'City' as a sovereign, independent and neutral state.[16] Even more valuable from the Vatican's point of view was the Concordat which brought about the partial restoration of the Church's property and privileges which had been taken away by Cavour and the Moderate Liberals. By means of the Corcordat the Church in Italy gained a position of influence in educational and matrimonial matters unequalled in any other country. For Pius XI the signing of the Lateran Pacts, or the *Conciliazione* as Italians called the event, was the crowning achievement of his reign: for him, 'God had been given back to Italy, and Italy back to God', by Mussolini, 'The man whom Providence has sent us.'

Fascism made its gains too: it took all the credit for healing the great spiritual wound in the Italian *Risorgimento* when in fact much of the progress in this direction had already been made by previous Liberal governments, and Mussolini's prestige was greatly increased both at home and abroad by his achievements as chief negotiator. The most immediate and valuable 'pay-off' for Fascism came in the form of Vatican instructions to Catholic electors to vote for the Fascist list in the 'Plebiscite' of March 1929: it was thus instrumental in massively consolidating the consensus on which Mussolini's regime was built.

The crisis of 1931

Despite the jubilation on both sides in 1929, the Lateran Pacts did not bring about the long-awaited peace between the Church and State: on the contrary, in the three years that followed the *Conciliazione* there was to be more conflict between the Vatican and Fascism than in any other period of their relationship. In the period 1929–32 relations between them were characterized by acrimonious diplomatic disputes, polemics between the Catholic and Fascist press and intransigent public statements on the part of both the Pope and the Duce culminating in a full-blooded crisis in 1931. What had gone wrong?

The disputes of 1929–32 were in large measure due to exaggerated and unrealistic expectations on both sides. Mussolini for his part was determined to use Vatican diplomatic influence to further Italian foreign policy aims in the Balkans, in the Mediterranean and in the Middle East, but the Vatican skilfully eluded these manoeuvres.[17] Palmiro Togliatti, Italian Communist Party leader-in-exile and an acute observer of Italo-Vatican relations, had predicted Mussolini's attempts to manipulate the new relationship with the Vatican. He also foresaw their inevitable failure:

The Fascists count on being able to exploit certain advantages in the international sphere, useful for the furtherance of the imperialistic designs of the Italian bourgeoisie, but they will not be very great or of long duration for the Church will take great care not to lose its universal character.[18]

Togliatti understood what Mussolini seemed incapable of understanding, that the Vatican, even a Vatican establishment that was thoroughly Italian in national origin from the Pope downwards, would go to any lengths to preserve its reputation for neutrality and impartiality in international affairs. By 1931 Mussolini seems to have learnt his lesson, but the experience left him with a deep sense of disappointment which contributed in no small way to the bitterness of the 1931 crisis.

In his turn, Pius XI was under the illusion that the Lateran Pacts provided the basis for the transformation of Fascist Italy into a clerical, confessional state. But between 1929 and 1932 the Regime vigorously resisted this aim of the Vatican and especially its attempt to use the Fascist State as its 'secular arm' in the battle against increasing Protestant propaganda and proselytism in Italy. If the Vatican was not willing to be associated with the foreign policy of Fascist Italy, then neither did Mussolini desire to be seen by his Anglo-Saxon admirers especially as the supine tool of Roman Catholicism. As he complained to his brother Arnaldo at the height of the 1931 crisis, 'We expected the Church to become the pillar of the Regime, we never intended for a moment that the Regime should become the servant of the Church!'[19]

An even more serious problem than disappointed expectations was the residual hostility towards the Lateran Pacts among rank and file Fascists and Catholics alike. During the debates in Parliament on the ratification of the Pacts in May 1929, Mussolini had tried to disguise the extent of his concessions to the Church by recourse to a little brutal, bellicose, anticlerical rhetoric, reassuring his listeners that 'within the State the Church is not only not sovereign, it is not even free'.[20] But this failed to convince some Fascist anticlericals. After 1929 resentment of clerical pretensions, and in particular the very public activities of Catholic Action, became increasingly common in Fascist circles. By 1930 Mussolini was forced to take heed of these feelings, his answer being to put in charge of the Fascist Party and its youth organizations two men, Giurati and Scorza, who were determined to complete the process of 'totalitarianization' of education and youth which had been halted by the signing of the Lateran Pacts. Such a change of policy on the part of the Regime made a conflict with the Vatican inevitable.

As the results of the 1929 'Plebiscite' showed, Catholic opposition to the Lateran Pacts was widespread, especially in the strongly Catholic or 'white' provinces of northern and eastern Italy.[21] Though the close relationship between the Vatican and Fascism made life difficult for Catholic anti-fascists, it had by no means defeated them.[22] Catholic anti-fascism was very much alive and kicking, its particular stronghold being the organizations of Catholic Action which, despite their supposedly non-political character, still harboured large numbers of *ex-popolari* amongst both the leadership and the rank and file. Catholic Action was, in any case, an object of real Fascist suspicion on account of its growing memberhsip and increasing activism, thus constituting in itself a major cause of tension between the Vatican and the Regime.

All of these problems were exacerbated by the 'great Depression' whose effects were only really beginning to be seriously felt in Italy in late 1930 and early 1931.[23] The recession created an upsurge of popular distress accompanied by a wave of anti-fascist agitation – Catholic included. Apart from the activities of the *ex-popolari* inside and outside of Catholic Action two clandestine groups, the Alleanza Nazionale and the Movimento Guelfo d'Azione won support in Catholic circles.[24] It was in order to reassert the authority of his regime against these forces that Mussolini gave orders for the dissolution of the Catholic youth organizations in May 1931.

The gravity of the crisis which followed this drastic action may be gauged from the fact that in his encyclical *Non Abbiamo Bisogno*, Pius XI came perilously close to condemning Fascism completely,[25] and that by way of reply to this document, the Fascist foreign minister Grandi urged Mussolini to denounce the Concordat unilaterally. But both sides had too much to lose from a continuation of the conflict and in September 1931 they eventually arrived at a compromise whereby Catholic Action survived with its youth and labour groups intact, but with some curtailment of its activities and a ban on *ex-popolari* from holding office in the organization.

Some Italian historians have interpreted the September agreement as a defeat for the Vatican but this is rather to misread the situation.[26] As another very perceptive contemporary observer has pointed out:

> The obvious restrictions on the activities of Catholic Action
> have tended to obscure the fact that what was at stake was the
> existence of Catholic Action and its independence of the secular

power, and on both these points the Pope obtained satisfaction.[27]

The survival of Catholic Action and its dependent organizations meant the defeat yet again of Fascist attempts to set up a truly totalitarian state in Italy, for despite the difficulties and restrictions under which it was forced to operate in the 1930s, Catholic Action was most emphatically not 'inside the State'. It was in fact inside the 'island of separateness' constituted by its youth organizations that the cadres of the post-1945 Catholic ruling class were formed during the 1930s and early 1940s.[28] A political regime which permitted the existence in its midst of an alien body like Catholic Action cannot really be called totalitarian. One need look no further than Nazi Germany, where the Concordat of 1938 was brutally ignored and the once powerful network of Catholic associations was almost completely destroyed, to see the fate of the Catholic Church in a genuinely totalitarian state.

The 'idyllic years', 1931–8

The September agreement of 1931 turned out to be a remarkably enduring document, guaranteeing relative harmony between the Vatican and Fascism for the next seven years, indeed, the great ecclesiastical historian Jemolo very aptly described them as the 'idyllic years'.[29] The two sides had at last learned what were the limits of their relationship and had agreed to respect them. On this basis, they managed to achieve a remarkable degree of convergence, a sort of 'ideological solidarity', in areas of economic and social policy and in the field of international affairs.

In his encyclical *Quadragesimo Anno* of May 1931, Pius XI had expressed reservations about the monopolistic, coercive nature of the single, Fascist trade union system established in 1926,[30] but there was, nevertheless, general approval in the Vatican for the Fascist 'Corporate State'. This much-vaunted system of mixed corporations of employers' and employees' representatives, which was in reality a façade for the repressive control of the labour force, fitted in well with the corporatist tendencies in Catholic social thought. As such, it received the enthusiastic support of intellectuals at the Catholic University of Milan, who also gave their uncritical assent to Fascist imperialism and racialism.[31] And Catholic Action also gave its approval to the 'Corporate State', though in a much more guarded fashion, hedging its bets by maintaining a small presence of its own in the labour field.

Fascist economic and social politics had the overall effect of retarding modernization, of 'freezing' the existing balance between town and country, industry and agriculture. Indeed, the Fascists actively propagated the concept of 'ruralization', glorifying 'honest', traditional rural values and culture whilst deprecating the corrupt, 'subversive' values of urban life. This suited the Church's book perfectly, of course, because it was in the countryside of northern and eastern Italy that Italian Catholicism had its deepest roots and greatest strength. Not surprisingly, the rural bishops and parochial clergy took part willingly in the activities connected with the 'Battle for Grain', which was an essential element in Fascism's campaign to achieve economic self-sufficiency.

Another major area of co-operation between the Vatican and Fascism was that of 'public morality', where Fascism had very quickly adopted a conservative policy, which was at odds with the libertarian attitudes of its original supporters among the Futurists and ex-revolutionary Left, by coming out publicly against divorce in 1923. Thereafter, the Vatican increasingly turned to the Fascist government to ensure a strict censorship of the theatre and cinema and to enforce the laws against pornography, indecency and blasphemy – Mussolini was even the president of the National Anti-Blasphemy League, a fact which gave rise to much hilarity in Fascist circles because the Duce was notoriously prone to the vice himself! The Regime was also at one with the Church in its repressive attitude towards women, an attitude plainly evident in the Rocco Criminal Code of 1931 which, for example, punished the adultress but not the adulterer. Needless to say, the Regime's 'Demographic Battle', with its encouragements to parenthood and its tax on bachelors was wholeheartedly and publicly supported by all Catholic authorities in Italy.

In the 1920s the Vatican had looked to Fascism to save Italy from the internal Bolshevik menace, and in the 1930s it sought the aid of the Regime to fight atheistic Communism on the international plane. The Vatican's preoccupation with Communism reached its height in the Spanish Civil War where Italian intervention was regarded as little short of a crusade. But by the mid-1930s Pius XI had come to the conclusion that Nazi neo-paganism in Germany was almost as much of a threat to the Church as Communism: in 1937, in his encyclical *Mit Brennender Sorge*, he unleashed against Hitler the condemnation which he had spared Mussolini. Fascist Italy therefore became of greater importance in the Vatican's overall international strategy, being cast in the role of leader of a 'third force' of Catholic neutral states – Austria, Hungary and potentially Poland – between Nazi Germany and Soviet Russia.

In the midst of the turbulent, tormented world of the 1930s, Fascist Italy appeared as a haven of peace, order and tranquillity to the men in the Vatican. Small wonder then that Vatican diplomacy during the Italo-Abyssinian War was directed towards assisting in the achievement of an honourable, satisfactory settlement between Britain and France and Italy.[32] The Vatican feared that a military or diplomatic defeat for Mussolini would lead to the collapse of Fascism and a communist take-over in Italy, or to Fascist Italy being driven into the arms of Nazi Germany.

'Divorce': the crisis of 1938

The fears of the Vatican on the latter score were, of course, to be entirely realized, and the relationship which developed between Mussolini and Hitler in the aftermath of the Abyssinian crisis was to prove fatal to the 'marriage of convenience' between the Vatican and Fascism. As the Rome-Berlin Axis developed between 1936 and 1938 the Vatican newspaper did not fail to express its anxiety, but the full impact of the 'brutal friendship' did not begin to make itself felt in Italy until 1938. March saw the Duce's abject acquiescence in the Nazi occupation of Catholic Austria, an event which shook the Vatican to its foundations, and May the Führer's visit to the 'Eternal City' which Pius XI ostentatiously boycotted. The worst came in July when Mussolini announced the introduction of racial legislation into Italy.

The Pope's response to the espousal of anti-semitism by the Regime – 'Spiritually we are all Jews', was his comment on the Duce's latest lunacy[33] – sparked off a wave of criticism from other Catholic quarters and a consequent rapid deterioration in relations between the Vatican and the Regime. Though there had always been a lively anti-semitic tradition in certain sections of the Italian Church, notably among the Jesuits, Catholic criticism of the Racial Laws was founded on principle. But the Vatican also had an immediate and specific reason for opposing the laws, for the clause forbidding marriages between Jews and Gentiles was in flat contravention of the Concordat of 1929.[34] The dispute between Pius XI and Mussolini over the Racial Laws was exacerbated by a parallel conflict over Catholic Action whose renewed growth was once more causing alarm and resentment in Fascist circles. The crisis of 1938 was resolved, if that is the right word, because the Vatican backed down over both the Racial Laws and Catholic Action, but also because Pius XI, 'That obstinate old man', as Mussolini described him, died in January 1939. His successor, Pius XII was more conciliatory towards both Italian Fascism and

German Nazism, but it is doubtful whether he would have been able to appease Mussolini in the long term for the Duce was rapidly returning to the rednecked anticlericalism of his political childhood and adolescence.[35] In all probability, only the outbreak of the Second World War prevented the renewal of conflict between the Vatican and the Regime.

What is certain is that Italy's entry into the war on the side of Nazi Germany in June 1940, which Pius XII tried desperately to prevent,[36] made 'absolute' the divorce brought about by the crisis of 1938. From this point onwards, the Vatican increasingly took its distance from Italian Fascism, the process of disengagement being already virtually complete when Fascism was overthrown in July 1943.

Conclusions

A leading Catholic historian in Italy has said of the relationship between the Vatican and Fascism:

> The Church was always 'different' from Fascism. The Church – be it at its highest levels or at its base – represented a different world from Fascism, and it would therefore not be correct to talk about a Fascist 'Church'.[37]

This is undoubtedly true: moreover, despite the existence of areas of 'ideological solidarity', there was in the final analysis a fundamental incompatibility between Catholicism and Italian Fascism which made itself felt, and was made explicit in public pronouncements on both sides, whenever relations between them reached a low ebb, as in 1929, 1931 and 1938. As the relationship between the Vatican and the Regime took shape, Pius XI became aware that Fascism was not the suggestible, permeable, conservative political force which he, and for that matter the rest of the Italian Establishment, had thought it to be. For the Fascists, as they constructed their Regime between 1922 and 1929, elaborated on the core of fundamental ideas which were already implicit in their early policy statements, and these proved to be as much if not more in conflict with the guiding principles of Catholicism as those of nineteenth-century liberalism had been.

The Fascist doctrine which was central to this conflict was totalitarianism, as the disputes over Catholic Action and its youth organizations demonstrate, but the Pope also found himself obliged to condemn other aspects of Fascist ideology such as its aggressive nationalism and its cult of violence, not to mention racial anti-semitism. And by the mid-1930s Fascism in its rallies and rituals, in its litanies to the Fascist martyrs and in its 'Decalogues', and above all in its idolatrous cult of the Duce, was emerging as a pagan rival to the Catholic religion. Only the most blatant compromising of principles on both sides made it possible to cover over this incompatibility and permitted the Vatican and Italian Fascism to live together, albeit uneasily and with difficulty, in a 'marriage of convenience'. For if Mussolini has frequently and rightly been stigmatized as an opportunist, then Pius XI cannot escape the same judgment.

In the long term it was obviously the Vatican which derived most of the benefits from its relationship with Italian Fascism. Despite the predictions of observers as diverse as Togliatti and Binchy that the price of the Vatican's collaboration with Fascism would be an anticlerical backlash, the Church rode out the fall of Fascism with comparative ease. Indeed, after that collapse and the abolition of the Monarchy in 1946, the Church emerged as the strongest surviving national institution in Italy, a phenomenon which the historian Chabod appropriately compared to the situation following the fall of the Roman Empire.[38] And it may be added that the role played by Catholic Action members, and the parochial clergy and laity generally in Armed Resistance from 1943 to 1945 also helped to restore the tarnished image of Italian Catholicism.

The Lateran Pacts also survived the fall of Fascism, and in 1947 they became a part of the new constitution, thanks to the support of Togliatti and the Italian Communist Party. Recognizing the enormously strengthened position of the Vatican, Togliatti was anxious to avoid burdening the infant Italian Republic with the kind of Church-State conflict that had been so damaging to the united Italian Kingdom; in his own words, 'The Republic is worth a mass.'[39] As a result of this confirmation of the Church's gains under Fascism, and of the emergence of the Christian Democrats as the dominant force in post-war Italian politics, the Vatican was able to achieve under the democratic Republic what it failed to obtain under the Fascist Regime, the transformation of Italy into a thoroughgoing clerical, confessional state in the 1940s and 1950s; what has been described as 'The Papal State of the Twentieth Century'.[40] This was the legacy of the relationship between the Vatican and Italian Fascism.

Notes

1   See A.C. Jemolo, *Church and State in Italy, 1850–1950*, Oxford, 1960, ch. I.

2   See C. Seton-Watson, *Italy from Liberalism to Fascism, 1870–1925*, London, 1967, chs I and 6.

3   Richard A. Webster, *The Cross and the Fasces: Christian Democracy and Fascism in Italy*, Stanford, 1960, chs I and 2.

4   C. Seton-Watson, op.cit., pp.272–81.

5   For an account of the talks between the Italian Premier, Orlando, and Mons. Cerretti of the Vatican in 1919, see *ibid.*, p.515.

6   A translation of the text is to be found in C. Delzell (ed.), *Mediterranean Fascism, 1919–1945*, New York, 1970, pp.12–14.

7   Author's translation of text as quoted in F. Margiotta-Broglio (ed.), *L'Italia e la Santa Sede dalla Grande Guerra alla Conciliazione*, Bari, 1966, p.82.

8   Author's translation of the text as quoted in P. Scoppola (ed.), *La Chiesa e il Fascismo: documenti e interpretazioni*, Bari, 1971, pp.52–4.

9   A.C. O'Brien, 'L'Osservatore Romano and Fascism: the beginning of a new era', in *Journal of Church and State*, Spring, 1971.

10 C. Falconi, *The Popes in the Twentieth Century: From Pius X to John XIII* (trans. by Muriel Grindrod), London, 1967, pp.151–234.

11 For a history of the *Partito Popolare*, see J.N. Molony, *The Emergence of Political Catholicism in Italy*, London, 1977.

12 F. Margiotta-Broglio, 'Fascism and the Church, 1922–25', in R. Sarti (ed.), *The Ax Within: Italian Fascism in Action*, New York, 1974, pp.33–40.

13 J.F. Pollard, 'The Italian Clerico-Fascists', in *Fascists and Conservatives in Europe*, M. Blinkhorn (ed.), London, 1987.

14 As quoted in C. Delzell, op.cit., p.94.

15 For an account of the negotiations see D.A. Binchy, *Church and State in Fascist Italy*, 2nd impression, Oxford, 1970, ch. VI.

16 The texts of the Lateran Treaty and the Concordat (but not the accompanying Financial Convention) are to be found in C. Delzell, op.cit., pp.156–64.

17 The only study of the diplomatic dimension of the relationship between the Vatican and Italian Fascism is Peter C. Kent, *The Pope and the Duce: The International Impact of the Lateran Agreements*, London, 1981.

18 Author's translation from article, 'La fine della Questione Romana', in *Stato Operaio*, February 1929.

19 Author's translation from transcription of intercepted telephone call as quoted in U. Guspini, *L'Orrecchio del Regime*, Milan, 1973, p.108.

20 Author's translation from the *Opera Omnia di Benito Mussolini*, Florence, 1951–63, vol. XXIV, p.44.

21 J.F. Pollard, *The Vatican and Italian Fascism, 1929–1932: A Study in Conflict*, Cambridge and London, 1985, pp.59–60.

22 *Ibid.*, pp.74–88.

23 R. De Felice, *Mussolini il Duce*, vol. I, *Gli anni del consenso*, Turin, 1974, pp.58–63.

24 J.F. Pollard, *The Vatican and Italian Fascism*, op. cit., pp.150–3.

25 For the text of the encyclical, see C. Delzell, op.cit., pp.169–74.

26 See, for example, R. De Felice, op.cit., p.271.

27 D.A. Binchy, op.cit., p.539; Richard A. Webster, op.cit., p.112 is of the same opinion.

28 *Ibid.*, ch. 10.

29 As quoted in P. Scoppola, 'State and Church in the Fascist Period', unpublished lecture given at Cambridgeshire College of Arts and Technology, November 1979.

30 The text of the encyclical is in C. Delzell, op.cit., pp.167–9.

31 Richard A. Webster, op.cit., ch. 12.

32 George W. Baer, *Test Case: Italy, Ethiopia and the League of Nations*, Stanford, 1976, pp.138–40.

33 As quoted in C. Delzell, op.cit., p.176.

34 Article 34 of the Concordat gave Church courts jurisdiction over Italian marriage law.

35 *Ciano's Diary (1939–45)*, ed. with an introduction by M. Muggeridge, London and Toronto, 1947, pp.26, 39–40, 186 and 248–9.

36 C. Delzell, op.cit., p.213.

37 P. Scoppola, 'State and Church in the Fascist Period', etc.

38 F. Chabod, *L'Italia Contemporanea (1918–1948)*, Turin, 1961, p.125.

39 J.F. Pollard, 'State, Church and Society in Italy Today', in *Journal of the Association of Teachers of Italian*, Spring, 1980, p.63.

40 Richard A. Webster, op.cit., p.214.

33

The Catholic church and the Estado Novo of Portugal★

TOM GALLAGHER

A religious land and an unpopular church

Thanks to avoiding the Reformation and failing to experience an industrial revolution, Portugal remained in key respects a traditional country where the Catholic church avoided many of the challenges faced by its counterparts elsewhere in Europe. Portugal was the only country in the western half of the continent in which not a single case of Protestant activity was reported in the Reformation period and where mass parties of the Left only began to emerge in the second half of the twentieth century. But the Church was not immune from the anticlerical attacks which the Catholic religious establishment faced after the seventeenth-century age of the Enlightenment. Indeed the early timing and subsequent scale of the challenge of secularism would appear to make Portugal noteworthy compared even to countries like Spain and France. The absence of parallel challenges to other bastions of the traditional order should also be taken into account.

Portugal's long era of Church–State conflict began with the onslaught on clerical power and influence mounted by the Marquis of Pombal, a modernizing despot who ruled Portugal as chief minister from 1750 to 1777. Pombal suppressed the Jesuits, curtailed the Inquisition and lessened the influence of the Church at court and in the colonies. He was able effectively to limit clerical influence because the Church had overreached itself in a number of ways. Especially crucial was its long-standing campaign against the converted jews known as 'New Christians', who were strongly represented in mercantile ranks as well as its own wealth and size: the landed wealth of the Church was proportionately even greater than that of its Iberian neighbour, and in Portugal more clergy were to be found per inhabitant than anywhere else in Europe.[1]

Pombal's assault on the Jesuits was emulated by the crowns of France and Spain and it represents one of the few occasions where Portugal has given a radical lead in politics to its European neighbours. By this time key traits in Church–State conflict were already beginning to emerge which would hold good for subsequent phases right up to and including the twentieth century: the religious orders bore the brunt of hostility because of their wealth, influence at court and propensity for setting norms in secular society; anticlericalism was far more common than anti-Catholicism; and attacks on the Church attracted opportunistic elements hoping to benefit from a redistribution of its wealth.

The Portuguese *ancien régime* began to be attacked in earnest after the French revolution and the Napoleonic occupation of Portugal. In the 1820s the Church found itself enmeshed in the quarrels between absolutism and various exponents of liberalism, which culminated in the 1832–4 civil war between two royal brothers around whom the partisans of tradition and reform assembled. Having backed the reactionary *Miguelistas*, the Church paid dearly when the victorious liberals seized its property and estates in the south. This was a backlash from which Portuguese Catholicism has never recovered in the province of the Alentejo where religious devotion fell disastrously in the remainder of the nineteenth century.[2] In this underpopulated region, parish structures were weak and it was the religious orders who ministered to the population. Meanwhile in the north, where the bulk of Portuguese were – and are – to be found, diocesan clergy were far more numerous and the *paroco* or parish priest was an integral part of most local communities.

Here the landholding system had a profound and lasting effect on social relations. The prevalence of *minifundia* or extreme smallholding meant that the gulf between wealth and poverty, noticeable in the south, was less wide north of the Tagus river which flows across the centre of Portugal and is the key geographic dividing line. Ownership of some land, however meagre, predisposed the peasantry against challenging the traditional system and, in an atmosphere of social cohesion, the Church flourished in many areas of the north.[3]

'Hanging the last kind with the intestines of the last priest'[4]

In the absence of its northern redoubt, the Portuguese church would have been ill-equipped to resist the third and greatest challenge to its authority, mounted by urban middle-class republicans who toppled the monarchy in 1910 and gave Portugal a republican constitution in 1911. Portugal's petit-bourgeois jacobins were profoundly influenced by French norms and cultural values, and five years after the effective separation of Church and State in France, Portugal's anticlerical rulers followed suit. But the State's restrictions on the Church imposed in a lightning series of decrees during 1911 were far more sweeping and indeed amounted to persecution.[4] All church property was nationalized, the faculty of theology at the University of Coimbra was abolished, holy days were made normal working ones, and the number of seminaries were reduced to five and put under government control.[5] There were several restrictions on worshipping after sunset, bell-ringing, religious processions and clerical freedom of movement. The Jesuits were once more sent packing, all foreign and foreign-trained priests barred, and ecclesiastical pronouncements censored. Divorce was introduced, the marriage ceremony was made civil and religious teaching was disallowed in schools. When these laws were introduced, the majority of bishops were expelled or else went into exile and diplomatic relations with the Holy See were later broken off in 1913.

The Church attracted the ire of republicans because of its pro-royalism and conservatism; of the various vested interests, like the military and the landed oligarchy in the south, it was by far the easiest to attack. It was also the only obvious target the republicans had to hand since they were not so radical that they wished to reconstruct the economic order. Portuguese jacobinism was socially radical but economically conservative and the anticlerical campaign was pitched to suit the tastes of the urban lower middle class who provided the bulk of the regime's support. Afonso Costa, the leading politician of the 1910–26 parliamentary republic even forecast an end to Roman Catholicism in several generations when speaking in Braga, the religious seat of Portugal, during 1911.[6] But if this is what Costa really hoped for, Republicanism was too flimsy a movement to bring about this objective and the regime would soon be preoccupied with internal power struggles and with staving off challenges from right-wing forces which would eventually overwhelm it in the 1920s.

Academic christian democracy and the coming of the new State

The anticlericalism which ran its course from 1910 to 1914 was largely an intellectual or middle-class affair where mass participation was signally absent. Popular anticlericalism manifesting itself in the church-burning of neighbouring Spain was absent and there was no grassroots backlash from ordinary Catholics in the north that could compare with the Cristeros movement in Mexico after its 1910 revolution. But faced with what seemed like a drive against organized religion itself rather than just clerical authority, a politically involved Catholic intelligentsia began to emerge during the early years of the republic.

In 1912, a Catholic student group known as the Academic Centre for Christian Democracy (CADC) was revived by Catholic students at the University of Coimbra, who also began editing their own newspaper, *Imparcial*. Located in the small-holding north, the university town of Coimbra would become the headquarters of young right-wingers radicalized by the excesses and chronic instability of the republic. Manuel Gonçalves Cerejeira (1888–1977) and António de Oliveira Salazar (1889–1970) were the key figures behind this Catholic nucleus, both men being destined to play major roles in Portuguese life during the next half century, Cerejeira, a future cardinal, carried a Mauser pistol during times when republican and conservative students were engaged in street battles. By 1914, the conservatives, with the Catholics at the forefront, had gained the upper hand in Coimbra, the first Catholic victory against republican secularism.

'Piety, Study, Action' was the motto of the CADC and after 1915, Salazar, its most gifted intellectual, was a lecturer in economics at Coimbra University. Both he and Cerejeira were careful to avoid identification with the standard right-wing causes, monarchical restoration being at the top of the list. In 1914, with the republic still looking fairly secure, Salazar declared 'democracy to be a historic phenomenon and by now irresistible'.[7] Almost a decade later (and probably much earlier), he had changed his tune and was confidently predicting that 'we are drawing near to that moment in political and social evolution in which a political party based on the individual, the citizen or the elector will no longer have sufficient reason for existence'.[8] By now, well into the twilight years of the republic, the spirit of the age was ceasing in Portugal to be liberal and secular. With democracy characterized by massive electoral abstentionism because of the misrule of bourgeois politicians, the Right was winning the battle of ideas. Former radicals like the anarchist Alfredo de Pimenta or the student leader Fernando Bissaia Barreto turned rightwards as students and young members of the upper classes fell under the influence of the French reactionary Charles Maurras whose *Action Française* was emulated by a Portuguese movement known as Lusitanian Integralism founded in 1914. This body had a greater initial impact than the CADC, largely because the lay Catholic movement was starting from a much weaker base-line after 150 years of anticlerical propaganda that was not without influence, even among conservative groups.

Despite the strength of devotionalism in the north, a mass Catholic party failed to emerge in Portugal as it would do in other countries such as Germany, Italy and Spain marked by Church–

State conflict. If the mainly illiterate peasantry had not been deprived of the franchise, it might have been a different story. Absent also was a strong Catholic social movement sponsoring friendly societies, co-operatives and labour associations. The Church had neglected the social sphere before 1910 and afterwards it was too embattled to give much time to cultivating the variety of lay vocational groups emerging under clerical direction in other countries. So cadres for a strong Catholic political movement were usually lacking but nevertheless, a Catholic party known as the Portuguese Catholic Centre (CCP) did emerge in 1917 and enjoyed success in the provinces of Minho and Beira in the north and in the Atlantic islands.[9]

Salazar was elected CCP deputy for Guimaraes in 1921 (only to resign his seat after one trip to the Lisbon parliament) and he was a candidate for Arganil in 1925.[10] Also in 1921, Jose Maria Braga da Cruz was elected CCP deputy for Braga, having received more votes than any other political candidate in the country.[11] He was an energetic and moderate politician who condemned dictatorship and stood aside from right-wing coup attempts. So the response of Catholics in politics to the crisis of liberalism was not uniform. Perhaps overestimating the strength of liberal republicanism because of the punishment it had received from that quarter, the Catholic movement refused to get involved in the pre-1926 conspiracies against the faltering parliamentary regime. This earned it the enmity of more explicit reactionaries who were also not amused when the CADC and the CCP remained neutral on the republic-versus-monarchy issue. This controversy weakened the Right and may have given the discredited 1910–26 regime a stay of execution of a few years but seems not to have caused *serious* divisions within the small lay Catholic movement. Interestingly, compared to Catholic lay movements abroad, little clerical control was exercised over it mainly because the Church was so disorganized and weakened by confrontation; so men like Salazar, Lino Neto, Mario de Figueiredo, and Diniz de Fonseca acquired a certain freedom of action which, in Salazar's case, may have been an indispensable preparation for when he came to exercise power in his own right.

Given its defensive and traditional character, it was appropriately in the spiritual and devotional realm and not in the political or social sphere that circumstances enabled the Church to organize its fight back. A popular revival in faith can be traced from the Miracle of Fatima which most Catholics believe to have occurred in the small central Portuguese hamlet of Fatima on 13 May 1917. Between May and October of that year, the Virgin Mary is supposed to have appeared six times to three peasant children. Prophecies were disclosed to the oldest one and soon throngs of peasants from all over northern and central Portugal were visiting the site of the apparition. Fatima became a shrine, from which the Church was able to mobilize part of the laity and launch a spiritual revival. In 1920, Leiria, the capital of the district where Fatima was located, became an episcopal seat and in 1930 the local bishop was able to announce that the cult of Fatima had the authorization of the Vatican.

The rise of Salazar

Appropriately it was from Braga, the religious capital of Portugal known as Portugal's Rome, that the revolution which swept away the parliamentary republic was launched on 28 May 1926. This was a wholly military affair but the army was ill-equipped to tackle the desperate economic crisis inherited from the bourgeois politicians. Civilian help was quickly enlisted and a watershed in the evolving authoritarian regime was reached in 1928 when Dr Salazar, the CADC leader from Coimbra University, was appointed minister of finance with sweeping powers. Able to veto expenditure in all government departments, he was financial dictator of the country virtually from the day he took office.

To some officers, he was a *deus ex machina* whose providential emergence prevented the country slipping back to party chaos but, on the civilian Right, he was not an unknown figure. In 1922, he had established himself as the leading political theoretician in the Catholic movement on delivering the keynote address at the 2nd conference of the CCP.[12] He was also a member of a conservative study group known as the Crusade of Nun Alvares Pereira which, since its foundation in 1918, had drawn together monarchists, integralists, conservative republicans, Catholics and other representatives of the growing Portuguese Right. By no means was he the scholarly recluse who emerged from obscurity to rescue the country, an oft-repeated legend in years to come. But the rise to power of a Catholic spokesman in a land where, under the constitutional monarchy and its republican successor there seemed little scope for Catholic politics, was truly striking.

Bourgeois liberals were unable to make effective propaganda against Salazar's elevation because they lacked credibility and were hampered by censorship. Prejudice against the Church had diminished among their political clientele, the urban lower middle classes and a modest religious revival may even have occurred in urban Portugal during the 1920s. Moreover Salazar was a useful compromise figure able to unite rather than fragment the Right. If a committed monarchist had taken charge of the dictatorship, the shaky ruling coalition might have quickly disintegrated; as for conservative republicans whose exemplar was the popular Francisco Cunha Leal, they were tarnished by their connection with the previous regime; and the army was quite unable to produce an effective or charismatic leader. But as for the Catholic wing of the counter-revolutionary movement, it was small and there was tacit acknowledgment that the Catholics did not have the means or the support to transform the country in a theocratic direction. However, the leading financial technocrat of the Right was found in its ranks and this was the clinching factor since the main danger to the 1926 revolution was undoubtedly presented by an ailing economy. When Salazar balanced the budget and staved off bankruptcy by using fiscal means which included rigid control of the money supply, he emerged as the undisputed civilian strongman of what had been a largely military regime and he was on the way to being dictator in his own right, a goal he finally attained on being appointed prime minister in July 1932.

'Politique d'abord': Salazar's relationship with the Church 1930–4

Some of Salazar's colleagues in the CADC had also gone far. In 1929, at the age of 41, Fr Manuel Gonçalves Cerejeira, who had once shared student digs in Coimbra with Salazar, became archbishop of Lisbon and the youngest cardinal in Europe. One year earlier, Mário de Figueiredo, with whom Salazar had once prepared for holy orders in a northern seminary, became minister of justice. But he resigned in June 1929 when a religious dispute involving the bishop of Evora and the officer who was the town's civil governor reached the cabinet. The officer objected to the ringing of church bells in the town at what he regarded an incessant rate and his stand was endorsed by the premier and a majority of the cabinet.[13] Their obduracy over such an apparently trivial matter may have been connected with the fact that President Carmona had recently given permission for an assault on the Lisbon headquarters of the freemasons. As over so much of southern Europe the freemasons and the Catholic authorities had been implacable foes since the beginning of the nineteenth century and many officers, including conservative ones, were affiliated to lodges. Although any masonic officers apprehended in the raid were set free, unlike civilian members, it was opposed by certain members of the *ditadura* (dictatorship), including cabinet ministers, so the bell-ringing affair was part of a wider dispute. The upshot was that Salazar and Figueiredo submitted their resignations; the government itself then resigned and President Carmona (who was effectively head of the *ditadura* despite his titular post) swore in a new cabinet with a different military premier but with the same finance minister: Salazar.

The fact that Salazar stayed on even though the clerical line in the bells controversy was overruled caused controversy in some Catholic circles. But Salazar was determined to show that he was not the prisoner or the mouthpiece of any one group and he felt that he should be regarded as far more than the chief representative in government of the Catholic lobby. Already by the late 1920s, he was creating his own power-base within the dictatorship and drafting in supporters to government positions whose political backgrounds varied although they shared Salazar's deeply conservative ethos. They were more likely to have a university background in common than membership of the CADC or the CCP, though many young Salazarists had belonged to these bodies. Salazar's increasing detachment from the Catholic movement meant that relations with Cardinal Cerejeira suffered. Those who later alluded to a 'Salazar-Cerejeira dictatorship' were wide of the mark.[14] Possibly relations between the two men were never as close again after Cerejeira had made a written plea for a wideranging political amnesty in 1930.[15] Salazar reacted angrily to this private clerical initiative and once it was made clear that the regime (which from 1930 began to style itself the New State) was all about creating an authoritarian order, there is no evidence that Cerejeira repeated his call for liberalization.

In explaining the ideological roots of the *Estado Novo* (New State), Salazar sought inspiration not only from traditional Catholic theorists or from those papal encyclicals which addressed themselves to social affairs. He was also influenced by Lusitanian Integralism whose views were largely based on the doctrines of George Sorel and Charles Maurras of Action Française. Maurras's doctrine of *politique d'abord* was condemned by the Vatican in 1926 and 'the Portuguese church solemnly informed Portuguese Catholics, among whom such doctrines were influential in the 1920s, that the condemnation of such errors was not confined to France alone'.[16] Many of Maurras's Portuguese adherents had been the sons of Alentejan landowners or 'latifundists' whose wealth had originally been acquired through benefiting from the sale of Church estates back in the 1830s. But lacking ideological ballast and faced with a middle class tired of radical experimentation, the Integralists, and a short-lived successor-movement known as the Blueshirts or National Syndicalists, had faded away by the mid-1930s.[17]

Keen to establish his total primacy on the Right by absorbing or closing down all movements which did not owe their origins to the Estado Novo, Salazar advised the CADC and the CCP to dissolve themselves. He persisted even after the Portuguese bishops issued an official note in November 1933 affirming the view that the CCP should remain in being in order to defend the Church in the secular sphere.[18] But by May 1934, both organizations had disbanded and many adherents joined the Uniao Nacional (National Union), the official political movement of the Estado Novo, the keynotes of which were authoritarianism, corporativism, and nationalism.

Catholics and Salazar's political elite

During the Salazar era, which would extend to 1968, no fewer than ten cabinet ministers were drawn from the Catholic student movement, the CADC.[19] Having never been a large-scale movement, this indicates the narrow elite base from which Salazar was drawing support. Most came from the northern rural middle class and, at least in the first decade of the Estado Novo, Catholic ministers automatically linked up with the more traditional and reactionary wing of the political establishment, often known as the *duros* (hardliners). Salazar himself belonged to the Right rather than to the Centre or Left within the spectrum of Estado Novo politics. Catholic and monarchist ministers made up a strong right-wing bloc in the political elite up to the 1950s. Mário de Figueiredo, education minister from 1940 to 1944, would have been a Catholic before being a monarchist in terms of the group he identified most closely with, while Fernando dos Santos Costa and Joao Pinto da Costa Leite, both two of Salazar's longest-serving ministers would have stressed their royalist affiliations.[20]

Given the importance of the education question in Catholic circles, it is not surprising that members of the Catholic lobby were in charge of education in the 1930s and 1940s. Usually politicians representing Catholic interests were relatively un-contentious. It was still the monarchist–republican cleavage which was most evident at ministerial level until, in the 1950s, cabinets became increasingly technocratic at a time when the republican, monarchist, and Catholic factions were losing much of their immediacy. By now, a few Catholic ministers like Manuel Cavaleiro Ferreira and Joao Antunes Varelo were reaching high office, having first come to notice in the bureaucracy or teaching at university rather than in any of the Catholic movements. Being non-partisan technocrats, they resembled the ministers Franco drew from the Spanish Opus Dei movement after 1957 but it is significant that clerical pressure groups such as Catholic Action or Portuguese Opus Dei were never as powerful enough in Portugal to provide a strong stream of recruits into the political elite. At least one important politician, Marcelo Caetano, who would be Salazar's successor, drifted away from the Catholic lobby in the 1930s perhaps because it was unable to provide a strong enough launching pad for this ambitious figure.

Possibly aware that a section of the Estado Novo's supporters in the cities were still influenced by anticlerical republican propaganda (which had been a work of generations), Salazar kept some distance from Catholic interests. The Church did not receive endowments or special concessions from government that might only have resuscitated anticlerical feeling. The Concordat of 1940, regulating the relationship between the Holy See, the Portuguese church, and the State, is a good case in point. It was only agreed after protracted negotiations between the various parties. Salazar drove such a hard bargain that negotiations almost fell through and it was only a last-minute ultimatum to Rome requesting that government terms be accepted or the Concordat would be shelved, which caused it to be promulgated on 7 May 1940.[21]

Under the Concordat, the Church was recognized as a privileged institution with a very large role in society but Church and State remained separate and some basic laws from Republican days were not overturned: religious teaching in schools remained voluntary, civil marriage and civil divorce were retained, and church property seized after 1910 by the state remained sequestered. Article 10 stipulated that the Holy See must, before nominating a bishop, communicate the name to the Portuguese government in order to determine whether there was any objection of a political nature.[22] By way of a contrast, churches and seminaries were to be exempt from taxation and the State was prepared to partly finance the building of churches but, given Salazar's Catholic formation, it is surprising that the 1940 settlement was not more favourable to the Church.

The Concordat was finalized in the midst of celebrations marking the 800th anniversary of the formation of Portugal and at a time when much of the rest of continental Europe was embroiled in war. The Portuguese church was not indifferent to the conflict and Cardinal Cerejeira was to take a pro-Allied position.[23] He had been influenced, among other things, by the Nazi seizure of Catholic Poland and by reports of religious persecution in Nazi Germany. But Catholic Portugal's attitude to the war was not uniform. Pro-German feeling within the Estado Novo was mirrored to a lesser extent in Catholic circles. Dr Alfredo Pimenta, a contributor to the Catholic press and 'the head of a small ultra-nationalist coterie of intellectuals who make no secret of their pro-German and anti-British views' clashed with Cardinal Cerejeira in 1943.[24] Pimenta 'sneered . . . at the Pope's injunction to pray for the return of the Russian people to the fold of the Church' and he disputed 'His Holiness's statement regarding the existence of religious persecution in Germany'.[25] Cerejeira replied by depriving Pimenta of the title of 'Catholic writer' in an official statement which referred to his influence having 'become the cause of scandal among the faithful'.[26]

Interestingly, this official rebuke was carried by *A Voz*, the Catholic Royalist newspaper which, in the past, had given its backing to tyrannies far and near in the name of Catholic principles. Founded in the 1920s when provincial Catholic newspapers were appearing in various parts of the north as part of the national Catholic revival occurring in the twilight years of the republic, *A Voz* was a reactionary daily which, in the 1930s had been inciting attacks on crypto-Jews in the north.[27] The opening of a synagogue in Oporto as well as the return to full Judaism of a number of crypto-Jews (they were the descendants of sixteenth-century Jews who had fled the Lisbon Inquisition by disappearing into the countryside where they retained important vestiges of their faith) appear to have occasioned the anti-semitic press campaign. By contrast, *Novidades*, the official daily newspaper of the Catholic church, which existed from 1923 to 1974, was less extremist.

The Portuguese church may still have been imbued with a counter-Reformation tradition, but it did not generally use its press outlets to harass other religions. Unlike Franco's Spain, Protestants were not generally harassed, the one exception being the Jehovah's Witnesses who were persecuted in the 1960s. Having been left undisturbed since they appeared in Portugal during the late 1920s, the authorities began to harass them in 1961 in the belief that Witness missionaries in Angola had helped to foment the 1961 rebellion there which marked the start of the 13-year colonial wars in Portuguese Africa.[28] So it would seem to have been state suspicion and intolerance rather than clerical pressure which lay behind this episode. But the Church *was* prepared to become involved in politics even at the risk of being branded an arch-collaborator of the Estado Novo.

The Church compromised? Fatima and government propaganda

Salazar's political philosophy was based on a distillation of traditionalist, nationalist and religious themes and it would have been strange if the Church in turn had not wanted to promote many of these. Certainly, in many parts of the north, the regime could rely on a sympathetic Church to socialize rural Portuguese in a conservative direction. The clergy had, of course, been exercising this role long before the onset of Salazar's corporative state. However, with a counter-revolution in full swing by the 1930s, the scope of the Church's lay activities widened considerably. In some of the most backward areas, especially in the north, the priest exercised the same role on behalf of the regime as did the party chief in the more developed authoritarian regimes. Parish priests in country towns and provincial villages acted as dispensers of official propaganda and agents of social conformity and political vigilance. Just to give one example: in 1950, the authorities in Braga got priests in every electoral ward to identify parishioners liable to support the opposition candidate, General Delgado, in the state-managed presidential elections, so that they could then be removed from the voting lists.[29]

Until Cardinal Cerejeira resigned as primate in 1971, the Church maintained a total silence on human rights and their violation.[30] It has been claimed that the PIDE (the secret police) were even given clerical authorization to carry out surveillance in seminaries[31] and few official ceremonies of importance took place at which no bishops were present. Officially the Church claimed that it did not mix in politics at all. This may have been true in relation to internal Estado Novo politics but a wealth of evidence would suggest that through its actions, it was enlisting itself under the Estado Novo banner.

It is no coincidence that the only ongoing manifestation approaching a mass propaganda effort in Portugal was the cult of Fatima. Making a great impact on the popular consciousness outside the main urban centres, it took off in the 1930s and represented a vigorous counter-attack on the part of a national church confronted by urban rejection, a previously hostile state, and a social base already crumbling in some rural parts not just in the south. The revival in mystical religious worship constituted a boon for a regime embarking on a process of national depoliticization. Salazar was promoted by some of the clerical promoters of the Fatima cult as the 'messiah' that Our Lady during her visitation of 1917 had promised would soon come to rescue

Portugal. Such a characterization impressed superstitious rustics confronted with the knowledge that their national leader had been approved by heaven as well as by the 'big shots' of Lisbon. In the rural Portuguese milieu, such crude parallels may have been as effective as the mass propaganda employed by the more ideological and modern dictatorships: in a country where over half the population was illiterate in 1930, more sophisticated propaganda coming from a Mussolini or a Goebbels would probably not have registered so easily.[32]

Safe for traditionalism: the Portuguese church 1945–74

Although a boost for the Church, the cult of Fatima did not revive the influence of the Church in secular fields. Catholic Action, the lay arm of the Church, was formed in Portugal during 1933 but it was a feeble and unadventurous movement even within the restricted ambit of conservative Catholicism. A review of its activities published in 1937 largely consisted of conference proceedings and the atmosphere of self-congratulation still hangs heavy over its 443 pages.[33]

Portuguese Catholic Action was comprised of separate men and women's organizations with their youth wings but significantly there was no mention of a Catholic workers' movement of equal rank. To play an active role in improving the lives of ordinary Catholics and bringing lapsed members back to the faith by championing their interests would have been to challenge some of the key tenets of the Estado Novo. This both lay and clerical Catholics were not prepared to do during most of Salazar's lifetime. Except in material terms, there was no transformation in the character of the Church during the four decades of the Estado Novo. New churches were built, a Catholic university in Lisbon was eventually opened in 1971. A rise took place in the number of young people becoming priests and nuns during the 1940s and 1950s but this influx was short-lived and vocations began to tail off markedly in the 1960s.[34]

Lisbon was always one of the weakest links of the Church. In the 1930s, a diocesan population of one and a half million was being served by only 320 priests, many of them 'old and worn-out' clergy.[35] On 8 December 1935, a pastoral issued by Cardinal Cerejeira painted an especially dismal picture:

> Black Africa of the Pagans is at the very gates of Lisbon – the mother church of so many Christian churches in Africa, Asia, Oceania. Should things continue thus, the time will not be long

coming when our Christian land will be turned completely into a cemetery of glorious Catholic and apostolic tradition like those brilliant dead churches in north Africa that were once illuminated by the genius of St Augustine.[36]

Priests were not equally spread over the country in the 1930s or later. In 1931, the northern city of Braga had three times as many priests as Lisbon, while a small rural diocese like Vila Real had almost as many again. On the whole, the position of the Church was far healthier in the north, as an opinion poll published during the last years of the Estado Novo made graphically clear in 1972. While between 15 and 35 per cent of all Roman Catholics regularly attended church on Sunday, there was over 90 per cent attendance in the north, less than 20 per cent in the centre, and only 5–10 per cent in the south.[37] In the north, there were nearly 2 priests per thousand Catholics, in the centre one priest for approximately 4,500, while in the south a priest might theoretically have as many as 12,000 people to look after.

If the Church wished to revive its credibility with communities which had virtually become dechristianized, it would have had to adopt a far more socially progressive outlook, one that would sooner or later have brought it into conflict with the State. This the religious hierarchy steadfastly refused to do during the forty-two years Cerejeira was Patriarch of Lisbon (1929–71). Priests who raised their voices against the widespread poverty and oppression of the Salazar era were removed from their parishes and cloistered in religious institutions. In 1958, when the bishop of Oporto, Antonio Ferreira Gomes, publicly criticized the appalling conditions of life which he had witnessed in his diocese, he received no support from his fellow bishops. This was the most serious episcopal challenge to Salazar during the lifetime of the Estado Novo and it came from a previously conservative bishop. It was followed up in 1959 by an attempted coup in which Manuel Serra, a leader of the youth wing of Catholic Action, was implicated but this was a relatively isolated event and did not betoken the rise of a radical Catholic movement as some observers hoped.[38] In 1959, Ferreira Gomes was forced out of Portugal and he would be under close watch from the PIDE as his voluminous file in the secret police archives makes clear until allowed to return in 1969.[39] While in exile, he was ostracized by other bishops at a meeting of the Second Vatican Council in Rome during 1963 and he was forced to seek lodgings with South American bishops.[40] Nevertheless even with its bishop in exile, it was Oporto more than any other diocese that reflected the more modern outlook of the post Vatican II church. Before the collapse of the Estado Novo in 1974, a progressive weekly Catholic paper had been founded in Oporto, pastoral activities were stepped up and a Council of Justice and Peace criticized existing social conditions and provided a forum for limited political action.[41]

Ferreira Gomes also had several counterparts in Portuguese Africa. Monsignor Sebastiao Resende, Bishop of Beira from 1943 to 1947, frequently denounced the excesses of the Estado Novo in the tropics while, in the 1950s, it is true that other colonial bishops did take a stand against forced labour. Much later, Bishop Manuel Vieira Pinto of Nampula (also in Mozambique) declared in the early 1970s that 'we prefer a Church that is persecuted but alive to a Church that is generously subsidised but at the price of a damaging connivance at the behaviour of the temporal powers.'[42] Bishop Pinto openly favoured a political rather than a military solution to the wars in Africa and he was expelled from Mozambique on the very eve of the 1974 revolution. His stand would have been anathema to Francisco Maria de Silva, the archbishop of Braga, known as 'the holy city of the national revolution', who stood at the opposite end of the spectrum and who openly condoned Portugal's presence in Africa.

Strangely, religious progressives got little backing from the Holy See even in the wake of Vatican II. Conservative papal nuncios were sent to Lisbon, where they bolstered the position of the reactionary clerical establishment by nominating conservative bishops. In Madrid, during the late Franco era, the papal nuncio was vital in promoting reform in the Spanish church but Rome seemed to prefer a static Portuguese church and made no effort to really aid Catholics who got into trouble under Salazar for attempting to implement the directives and encyclicals of Vatican II. In 1965, the government censored several Conciliar documents and forbade the study in schools of the encyclicals *Pacem in Terris* and *Mater et Magistra*.[43] Pope Paul VI still came to Portugal in May 1967 on the 50th anniversary of the Fatima apparition, even though he must have known that the visit would be exploited for political purposes. Later in 1970, he deeply angered the Portuguese authorities by granting a private audience to the leaders of the guerilla movements waging a struggle against Portuguese rule in her African colonies.

Cardinal Cerejeira was influential in Rome over many years and even in the progressive 1960s, he may have been too entrenched a figure to dislodge from his allegiance to a repressive dictatorship. During the Second World War, there had been a persistent rumour in Rome that, 'in the event of his being seized by the

Nazis, Pius XII had given precise directions and authority to Cardinal Cerejeira, Archbishop of Lisbon to take command of the Church.'[44] Monsignor Montini, later Pope Paul VI, was in 1951 even prepared to extend an invitation to Salazar that he visit Rome. 'We will have to bring the Prime Minister here' were his words to Jose Nosolini, a close friend of Salazar's but he showed no anxiety to go.[45] Doubtless other curious incidents still remain to be unearthed that can shed light on Salazar's relationship with the Vatican, one that had repercussions on domestic politics.

Conclusion

Never leaving the country or rarely mixing with his people, Salazar ruled not in the manner of Hitler and Mussolini but in the style of the Dalai Lama or the nineteenth-century ultramontane popes.[46] But his was no theocratic or confessional state as observers taking a lazy look at the Estado Novo often assumed. Salazar was not a lay dictator at the service of the Church. He may have shared the lifestyle of a priest and his statecraft can be described as jesuitical but he stood up to the Church in key matters and did not brook its regular interference in politics. Still the Portuguese church was prepared, at various levels, to offer practical help to the Estado Novo. Without its backing at local level, especially in the north, Salazar might have had to devise a more elaborate political infrastructure.

Ultimately intimate association with an unpopular government lost the Church the respect of an increasing number of Portuguese. In some ways, the Catholic church may have benefited more from the hostile parliamentary republic since at least its actions made people more willing to come to its defence when under attack. Under Salazar the Church was protected and some of its interests were advanced but a definite revival in its fortunes could have come about only if it had realized the drawbacks of being too intimately associated with a dictatorship of the privileged and had acted accordingly. However, there was no chance of this happening while the generation which, like Salazar, had spent its formative years resisting state anticlericalism, remained at the religious helm. Portuguese bishops possessed the same world view of many Estado Novo leaders, not least Salazar himself. They were united in their anti-communism, belief in hierarchy and in their desire to resuscitate the old and resist the new. This being the case, there was no need to formally unite Church and State. Indeed in Salazar the Church had a political leader who gave them much security while not conceding all their demands.

Notes

*   Research for this paper was carried out at different times with the help of the British Academy and the 27 Foundation.

1   Stanley Payne, *A History of Spain and Portugal* (vol. 2), University of Wisconsin Press, Wisconsin, 1973, p.410.

2   For religious conditions in the Alentejo during the mid-twentieth century, see Jose Cutileiro, *A Portuguese Rural Society*, Clarendon Press, Oxford, 1971, pp.249–70.

3   Tom Gallagher, 'Peasant Conservatism in an Agrarian Setting: Portugal 1900–75', *Journal of Iberian Studies*, 6, 2, Autumn 1977, p.60.

4   Antonio Jose Telo, *Decadenciz e Queda da I Republica Portuguesa*, A Regra do Jogo, Lisbon, 1980, p.81.

5   Richard Robinson, 'The Religious Question and the Catholic Revival in Portugal 1900–30', *Journal of Contemporary History*, 12, 1977, pp.352–3; Thomas C. Bruneau, 'Church and State in Portugal: Crisis of Cross and Sword', *Journal of Church and State*, 18, 3, Autumn 1976, pp.466–7.

6   Douglas L. Wheeler, *Republican Portugal: A Political History 1910–26*, University of Wisconsin Press, Madison, Wisconsin, 1978, p.69.

7   Hugh Kay, *Salazar and Modern Portugal*, Eyre & Spottiswoode, London, 1970, p.24.

8   Philippe C. Schmitter, 'The impact and meaning of "non-competitive, non-free, and non-significant" elections in authoritarian Portugal 1933–74', in Guy Hermet (ed.), *Elections without Choice*, Macmillan, London, 1978, p.150.

9   Telo, op. cit., p.90 has the CCP emerging in 1919 while the much likelier date of 1917 is given by Manuel Braga da Cruz, in his *As origens da democracia crista e salazarismo*, Editorial Presenca/Gabinete de Investigacoes Sociais, Lisbon, 1980, p.264.

10   Braga da Cruz, op. cit., p.16.

11   *Ibid.*, p.282.

12   1922 would seem to mark the beginning of Salazar's definite rise in national politics. See Telo, op. cit., pp.92–3; and Cecilia Barreira, 'A Ascencao de Salazar comecou em 1922', *Historia*, 31 May 1981, pp.70–8.

13   A.H. de Oliveira Marques, *Historia de Portugal* (vol. 2), Palas Editores, Lisbon, 1976 edition, p.340.

14   This phrase was sometimes used by Portuguese communists and their sympathizers.

15   Franco Nogueira, *Salazar, Volume 2: Os Tempos Aureos (1928–36)*, Atlantida Editora, Coimbra, 1977, pp.93–7.

16   Robinson, op. cit., p.357.

17   For the Blueshirts, see Joao Medina, *Salazar e os Fascistas*, Livraria

Bertrand, Lisbon, 1978, *passim*.

18   Siles Cerqueira, 'L'Eglise Catholique et la dictature corporatiste portugaise', *Revue Française de Science Politique*, 23, 3, June 1975, p.479.

19   Tom Gallagher, 'Os oitenta e sete ministros do Estado Novo de Salazar', *Historia*, 28, February 1981, pp.11–12.

20   *Ibid.*, pp.10–12.

21   Franco Nogueira, *Historia de Portugal, 1933–74*, Editor Barcelos, Oporto, 1981, p.184.

22   Bruneau, op. cit., p.471.

23   British Public Records Office, F.O. 371, 34844, Report from British embassy in Lisbon: 4 August 1943.

24   *Ibid.*

25   *Ibid.*

26   *Ibid.*

27   British Public Records Office, F.O. 371, Report from British embassy in Lisbon: 12 April 1938.

28   *1983 Yearbook of Jehovah's Witnesses*, Watchtower, New York, 1983, pp.176–216.

29   Cerqueira, op. cit., p.496.

30   Gerhard Grohs, 'The Church in Portugal after the Coup of 1974', *Journal of Iberian Studies*, 5, 1, 1976, p.36.

31   Jean Nicholas, 'Portugal after Salazar – the View from France', *Studies*, Spring 1969, p.26.

32   Tom Gallagher, *Portugal: A Twentieth Century Interpretation*, Manchester University Press, Manchester, 1983, p.94.

33   Jose Marie Felix, *A Accao Catolica Portuguesa, Nascimento e Primeiro Passos*, Sousa e Irmao, Familicao, 1937.

34   Joao Canico, 'The Church in Portugal', *Pro Mundi Vita: Dossiers*, Brussels, 1981, p.13.

35   Rev. Richard S. Devane, SJ, 'The plight of religion in the patriarchate of Lisbon', *Irish Ecclesiastical Record*, July 1937, p.40.

36   *Ibid.*, p.39.

37   Eugene K. Keefe, *Area Handbook for Portugal*, Foreign Area Studies, American University, Washington DC, 1977, p.154.

38   One observer who thought that a catholic-socialist opposition focus would have greater chance of success than the republican-communist one was Herminio Martins in his 'Opposition in Portugal', *Government and Opposition*, 4, 2, Spring 1969, pp.250–63.

39   Bishop Antonio Ferreira Gomes dossiers, 2878/58 SR and 3953-CI, PIDE/DGS archive, Fortress prison, Caxias, Portugal. The bishop's dossier consists of two bulky files and the PIDE had a concise list of his pastorals, homilies, conference addresses, etc. from 1950 onwards. His private mail was also being opened right up until 1973.

40   Keefe, op. cit., p.52.
41   Bruneau, op. cit., pp.480–1.
42   Keefe, op. cit., p.52.
43   Grohs, op. cit., p.36.
44   Carlo Falconi, *The Silence of Pius XII*, Faber, London, 1970, p.86.
45   Franco Nogueira, *Salazar, Volume 4: O Ataque (1945–58)*, Atlantida Editora, Coimbra, 1980, p.238.
46   Tom Gallagher, 'Dictatorial Portugal: A Bibliographical Essay', *Journal of Iberian Studies*, 9, 1, Spring 1980, p.11.

Art and music

34
The image and the Reformation

BOB SCRIBNER

Of the many misconceptions about the Reformation that should be expelled from popular understanding of that period the most striking is that about the relationship between art and the Reformation. It is certainly mistaken to believe that the Reformation, in Germany at least, destroyed art. This is at best a poor half-truth. It is related to a second misconception, encapsulated in an oft-cited tag from Lawrence Stone, that the Reformation was a shift 'from an image culture to a word culture'. This kind of judgment rests on an over-estimation of the role of printing in the Reformation, as well as on a confusion about printing's impact on 'ways of seeing' in the sixteenth century. I do not intend to go into either of these two points at any length here. Carl Christensen has already shown convincingly the fallacy of the first view in several articles and in his *Art and the Reformation in Germany* (1979). The second belongs to a wider debate about printing and the Reformation which I have no time to discuss further here. I should like in this paper to concentrate on two themes: first, the nature of iconoclasm in the German Reformation, which has been the source of some of these misconceptions; second the functions of the image in the sixteenth and seventeenth centuries, in the age of Protestant confessionalism.

1 Iconoclasm

Iconoclasm was certainly a feature of the Reformation in Germany, but it was not a principal characteristic of the Reformation. That the two have been so closely associated is in many ways a result of the reformers' own successful propaganda against the use of images in pre-Reformation religion. I do not want to dwell here on the theological debates about images between Luther and Karlstadt, or the differences between Luther and Zwingli – others have already treated these adequately (Christensen, 1979; Garside, 1966; Stirm, 1977). Rather I want to concentrate on *behaviour*, and to try to distinguish some rather different types of behaviour associated with hostility to images during the Reformation. (Here I think it is also important to distinguish between *iconomachy*, or hostility to the use of images, and *iconoclasm*, or smashing of images.) I want to mention seven different kinds of phenomena (admittedly they sometimes overlap), although there are also several others I might have pursued in addition to these.

(i) Dismantling of images

Here I am thinking of the removal of images (altars, statues) as the result of official policy, undertaken under control of the authorities, sometimes behind locked doors, away from public gaze. Here image-breaking was often not involved. Sometimes, as occurred in Nuremberg (see Christensen, 1979), not all images were removed, only those held to be the most objectionable because of their links with Catholic cults. The official attitude often taken on such occasions was that it was a matter of clearing space for evangelical worship. There were certain occasions when the dismantling of images got out of hand – often when private individuals tried to preempt official action, or when the scale of the removal made the dismantling a large-scale public event, for example removing images from the outside of buildings, walls or city gates.

(ii) Removal of images

This often went along with dismantling, and took the form of the original donors, or at least their families or heirs, being allowed to take away what they had paid to erect in the first place. Images were here regarded as personal property, if nothing else because they were often objects of some value, decorated with gold leaf or encrusted with jewels. They represented wealth as well as piety, and it is not surprising that donors should have wished to reclaim them, if only to reclaim the valuable material. Even in Zurich, which took the most radical attitude to the dismantling of images, donors were allowed to retrieve their property in this way, as they were in Strasbourg in 1530. What happened to those taken away privately in this way is a matter of speculation – whether they were destroyed or kept as private images. We know that the latter did sometimes occur, since some Protestant authorities acted to prohibit the keeping of private images after their public use had been abolished.

(iii) Formal destruction of images

There were many occasions in which dismantling of images involved the destruction of images, but the term still covers a very wide spectrum of behaviour. Sometimes it was impossible to remove an image without destroying it, as in the case of an image carved on a wall or gate. Sometimes workmen removing images showed 'excessive zeal' at their work, dropping and smashing what they removed. In many cases there was officially approved destruction as part of the dismantling. Perhaps the first act of this kind occurred in Wittenberg in 1522, when the Augustinians themselves removed the altars, paintings and statues from their chapel, smashing and burning what they could. Sometimes popular action preempted an official removal, as occurred in February 1522 in Wittenberg, when a crowd broke into the parish church and removed and destroyed the images there. Sometimes the destruction formed part of a 'ritual of rebellion' against civic authority, as occurred in Basel in 1529 (Scribner, 1978).

(iv) Mockery of images
This phenomenon appears several times during the Reformation, and may prove to have been more frequent than supposed if more evidence were gathered. Here images were mocked or degraded, rather than being destroyed. In Zwickau in 1524, an image of St Francis wearing asses' ears was set up on the town fountain, while an image of St Francis was placed in the stocks in Königsberg in 1524. This has overtones of the contemporary custom of the *Schandbild*, the scurrilous picture in which one attacked the honour of an enemy by dishonouring his image. Most frequently, an image of the enemy in question was hung upside down from a gallows to show that he deserved to be hung. It was a device used often in Reformation propaganda (Scribner, 1981: 78–81). An exact parallel is found in the case of an image of St John, which was hung upside down in Wolkenstein in Saxony in 1525. Such incidents were often close to the next category.

(v) Defilement and mutilation of images
Sometimes the defilement of images was carried out surreptitiously, as occurred in Augsburg in 1524, when a crucifix was smeared with cow's blood at night. It could also occur in public, however, such as the case of the man in Ulm in 1531, who defecated into the mouth of a crucifix which had just been removed from one of the city gates. Defilement of images – mostly smearing with dung – is found perhaps less often than mutilation, by chopping off limbs or beheading, or in the case of an image of St Peter in the south German abbey of Irrsee, which in 1525 had its stomach slit open before being hung upside down. Martin Warnke, in discussing attacks on images in Münster in 1534, pointed out the similarity between such mutilations and forms of judicial punishment, as if the image were being punished (Warnke, 1973). As well as hanging and disembowelment, the slitting of cheeks,

gouging out of eyes, and amputation of limbs were common punishments for convicted felons, and it is often as though the images were regarded in the same way. In Ulm in 1530, an image was taken away from the churchyard by a number of people, who then tortured it in private, in imitation of a judicial interrogation. Questions were put to it, and it was maltreated when it did not reply, having its hand cut off. It was challenged to prove its inherent personality, being asked, 'If you are Paul [sic! although it was a Christ-image], then help yourself.' In Basel in 1529, the Great Crucifix was taken from the Cathedral by a great crowd of people, who later burned it on the market square. As they went, they also addressed the image: 'If you are God, then help yourself; if you are man, then bleed.'

(vi) Iconoclasm as anti-liturgy

Most discussions of iconoclasm hitherto have largely ignored the link between hostility towards images, and their role in the liturgy of the pre-Reformation church. They featured prominently in 'folklorized ritual', that is, popular dramatized performances of liturgical action intended to make the liturgy's meaning plain to lay people. For example, on Ascension Thursday the ascent of Christ into heaven was dramatized by drawing up through a hole in the church roof a figure of Christ, and afterwards a rag doll coated with pitch was tossed down through the hole to represent the defeat of the Devil. Similarly on Whitsun, a dove was lowered from the roof to symbolize the descent of the Holy Spirit. Crucifixes featured prominently in the liturgy, as well as the *Ölberg*, strictly speaking a representation of Christ's passion in the garden of Gethsemane, often formed from statuary and set up outdoors in the churchyard. To this was sometimes added a Holy Sepulchre, used in the Easter liturgy, and a Calvary scene (Scribner, 1984).

Attacks on the images in the *Ölberg* occurred fairly frequently, and we could see them as attacks on the liturgy with which it was associated. In the same way, attacks on the crucifix were also attacks on the doctrine of the real presence of Christ in the Eucharist. The crucifix was closely associated with this doctrine because of the way it was used in the liturgy in the place of the consecrated host. In popular belief, it was also associated with the host miracles held to confirm the doctrine of the real presence, usually in the form of bleeding crucifixes. This reveals an important dimension to the words addressed to the Great Crucifix in Basel in 1529, 'If you are God, then help yourself; if you are man, then bleed.' Beside invoking the twofold nature of Christ, it challenged the crucifix to prove the real presence (for further on these points, Scribner 1984 and 1985).

(vii) Social conflict and iconoclasm

There were undoubtedly elements of social conflict involved in some acts of iconoclasm. This was suggested by Thomas Brady in his 1978 study of Strasbourg, pointing to the enormous value of images as 'symbolic capital' expressing the wealth and prestige of the donor or his/her family. Brady suggested that attacks on images in Strasbourg may have been an expression of class hatred, provoking from some reviewers the narrow-minded comment that such a view was reductionist and ignored religious elements. Yet we know that images *were* used as signs of social prestige. As Michael Baxandall (1980) pointed out, there was a marked trend at the beginning of the sixteenth century for altars in churches to be considered not public but private property, and to be named not after the patron saints, but after the donor family. Social hostility directed at such displays of prestige certainly need not exclude religious feeling. That the rich were able to purchase paradise through their works in this way may well have aroused a sense of religious injustice tempered with class hatred. The same comment could be applied to such altars as Luther applied to confraternities, that they pursued only the selfish interests of their members, instead of thinking of the salvation of the community as a whole.

To show how complex a mixture of religious zeal and social conflict was to be found in a single act of iconoclasm, let me cite one instance in detail, a case which also serves to illustrate some of my other categories above. It occurred in 1533 in Augsburg, at St Moritz's church, where the strongly Catholic Fugger family were the leading patrons. The churchwarden Marx Ehem, from another leading patrician family, was just as fervently Lutheran. On 1 February 1533 Ehem and his two assistants sought to prohibit celebration of Mass by locking the sacristy and preventing access to mass vestments and vessels. The Fuggers countered this by supplying at their own expense new vestments, a chalice, an altar cloth, candlesticks and candles. For Good Friday (11 April), Ehem made sure that he prevented the ceremony of 'laying Christ in the Grave' (usually done with a crucifix or life-size Christ figure) by having the Holy Sepulchre sealed up. Similarly, he had spirited away all the things necessary for the Ascension Day ceremony – the flags, incense, vessels, monstrance and especially the image of Christ seated on a rainbow, accompanied by angels and the Holy Spirit, which was drawn up through the hole in the roof. Antonius Fugger, however, secretly had a new figure made, more elaborate than the first, whereupon Ehem went to the church, and had the hole through which the figure was drawn sealed up with timbers and iron fastenings.

On Ascension Day (22 May) the Fuggers by some stratagem got their works-foreman into the church and had the hole reopened. They arrived to a packed church, and the ceremony took place in its traditional form. Ehem meanwhile went to the city mayor, who empowered him to go to the church at once, and if the figure had not been raised, to command that it remain on the floor. But if the 'ascension' had already taken place, Ehem was advised to go home quietly. Ehem went with his supporters to the church, arriving too late to prevent the raising of the figure, but he stood beneath it in the centre of the church and tried to disrupt what remained of the service. He soundly abused the sexton for opening the church doors, while his supporters scattered the vicars and the choir from their places. With his brother Jeremias, Ehem then began to lower the figure from the roof, until it was about twenty feet from the ground, when it was let fall, smashing to pieces on the floor. Jeremias Ehem claimed that the rope had slipped.

The town council tried to balance between two powerful families. It allowed Ehem to keep the church closed for three hours that day, but then had it reopened for Catholic worship. It then summoned Antonius Fugger before it, lectured him sternly on causing disturbance (sic!), and sentenced him to a token night in the tower. The fissures that criss-crossed this little drama were several. Besides that between Catholic and Lutheran over the role of images in church ceremonies, there was also a confrontation between Catholic champion and leading Lutheran zealot. Here it became a contest between proud patricians, with social face at issue as much as religious belief. There was also a conflict between church patron (Fugger) and elected church warden (Ehem). A Catholic reporter claimed that the Fuggers had more rights over the church than Ehem, for whereas the latter was elected for only three years, the Fuggers as founders were patrons in perpetuity.

Christensen (1979: 103–9) has pointed to the need to set iconoclasm in the wider context of popular support for reform, and official policy about its speed and extent. It has implications for our understanding of reception of Reformation ideas, the degree of 'protestantization' possible within a given community, and the extent of reform of worship. We can see from the examples I have given that there is a very great deal of work still to be done before we can appreciate more fully how the

Reformation dealt with the question of images. We need to explore how different kinds of iconoclasm reflect differing attitudes or mentalities, and different forms of behaviour, whether official or popular. We should set it in the context of social conflict, social status, community politics, popular belief and popular folklore. We do not yet have even the most basic of tools, a map charting the geography of iconoclasm in the German lands, or its phases. It seems likely that iconoclasm was spread throughout the German lands, from the Baltic to the Alps, from the Rhine to Saxony. But we need to superimpose on such a map another showing the extent of removal or suppression of images, for the degree to which this was done (most radically, it seems, in Zurich; perhaps least so in Lutheran Saxony) will tell us much about the nature of the Reformation in the different regions.

2 Functions of the image

The society created by Protestant confessionalism did not dispense with either the social, political or religious functions of images. There was certainly a decline in the production of works of art, though we must see this in the perspective of a very considerable boom in the previous century. Wealth undoubtedly played a part: we should not forget the growth of inflation and the decline of towns. It was the growing wealth of princes that made them the major patrons of art. It has recently been suggested that the decline in the number of books published after 1525 might not reflect the waning of religious enthusiasm, merely growing economic difficulties in the printing trade (Edwards, 1983: 215). There is no reason why the same argument should not be applied to the decline in art production. It is true that many artists, convinced of evangelical belief, gave up painting religious subjects – Niklaus Manuel Deutsch of Berne is a notable example. Many others, however, continued with them, and other forms of art began to replace the altarpiece, which did experience a decline. It was largely replaced by the Protestant epitaph, and there was to be a flourishing Protestant 'image culture' throughout the early modern period (Haebler, 1957; Lieske, 1973; Scharfe, 1968). In order to illustrate this 'image culture', I want to mention briefly seven different functions of the image.

(i) Polemical
We have just begun to explore the importance of imagery in Reformation polemics, despite some pioneering work by Coupe (1966) and Stopp (1965). This begins in 1520 and lasts well into

the seventeenth century (see also Scribner, 1981 and Kastner 1982). It could be said that these propaganda images had a *revelatory* effect, designed to expose the metaphysical origins of the Papacy as the seat of Antichrist, and of Protestantism as 'true religion'. They also aimed to arouse religious *solidarity* among fellow evangelical believers, raising their morale and encouraging them to stand firm. Finally, they were intended to have an *agitatory* effect, to incite their viewers to act on their Reformation belief.

(ii) Instructional

Luther believed as much as pre-Reformation teachers that images were valuable means of instruction. As he put it in 1522: 'children and simple folk . . . are more easily moved by pictures and images to recall divine history than through mere words or doctrines.' Thus he favoured the use of illustrated Bibles and Catechisms, and other illustrated religious books: only that the pictures should be consistent with right evangelical belief and the Word of God. Others continued to see the value of the use of images in liturgy. When the Elector of Brandenburg introduced the Reformation in his territories in 1540, he retained all of the popular visual elements – the figure on Ascension Day, etc. – that we have described above. He saw these as important means of teaching the young about religion, and they remained part of the Lutheran liturgy in Brandenburg until the beginning of the seventeenth century, when they were removed by 'Calvinization'.

(iii) Commemorative

The Catholic use of images to recall the lives of the saints did not cease with the Reformation. The image of Luther played an important part in the expression of evangelical fervour during the early years of the Reformation (Scribner, 1981), and this did not wane with the establishment of a confessional Protestantism. In many ways, it actually increased, especially after Luther's death in 1546, when there developed what can only be called a cult of Luther, expressed through Luther's image depicting him as a holy man, prophet and saint (Scribner, 1983). Some of these images were even credited with miraculous power: one sweated as a sign of imminent disaster, another was incombustible. In the eighteenth century, the validity of these miraculous images was attested by no less than the Dean of the Wittenberg Faculty of Theology, and the cult of the Luther image lasted well into the twentieth century (Scribner, 1986; Scharfe, 1968).

Nothing comparable developed with regard to other reformers, such as Zwingli or Calvin, but there did emerge a tradition of commemorative images of the major reformers, soberly produced but none the less intended to serve much the same function as Catholic 'holy pictures'. The first collection of these was published in 1580 by Theodore Bèze, Calvin's successor in Geneva, presenting the *icones* or 'true images' of famous and pious men who had contributed to the cause of the Reformation. Bèze's justification for producing such a work came close to the kind of explanation offered by Catholics for their use of images of the saints: 'I can say for myself that not only in reading the books of such great men, but also in looking on their likenesses, I am moved, I am as drawn to holy thoughts as if I were in their very presence.'

(iv) Images for piety

The use of images as an aid to prayer and contemplation, as an aid to piety was hinted at in Bèze's justification, and this function of images certainly found a role under Protestantism. Some were supplied with a hymn text or the text of a prayer. Depictions of Luther were often accompanied by a short life of the reformer and a prayer. There were also attempts to depict visually Protestant doctrines, although with little success initially. The most successful up to the middle of the sixteenth century was the contrast between Law and Gospel, developed by Lucas Cranach (Scribner, 1981). But there were other themes as well: Christ blessing the children, intended to refute Anabaptist views on infant baptism; or the Last Supper, perhaps aimed in some cases against a Zwinglian interpretation of the Lord's Supper. The most successful visual representation of the central Reformation doctrine of justification, God's freely given gift of grace, did not appear until the seventeenth century, when Rembrandt developed a number of biblical scenes to serve as typologies of Grace: the calling of Matthew, the Raising of Lazarus, the Prodigal Son and the Conversion of Paul, to list the most important. These themes often began their development with German Protestant artists of the sixteenth century (Halewood, 1982).

(v) Symbolizing power of the image

It could be said that Reformation art turned its images into biblical typologies, and certainly the success of Rembrandt's depictions depended on this. However we can also speak of Reformation art creating, as did Catholic art before and after the reform, images of considerable signifying power, intended to embody an entire concept or doctrine in a single symbol. The crucifix served this function in Lutheranism, symbolizing the saving death of Christ. It became a point of dispute with Calvinism, where there were attempts to 'Calvinize' Lutheran territories during the 'second Reformation'. The Calvinizers sought to remove the crucifix as idolatrous. There was considerable continuity, certainly, between the Lutheran use of the crucifix and the Catholic. Pre-Reformation devotion had placed the suffering and crucified Christ at the centre of popular piety, and it has been suggested recently that this may have helped shape Luther's own distinctive doctrines (Koepplin, 1983). In any case, the crucifix continued as a pious symbol for Lutherans. It was 'reformed' in a number of ways, not least by removing the figures of Mary and St John from the foot of the cross, standing as intercessors. Instead the representation of the risen Christ triumphing over Death and the Devil was added, which was clearly felt to be altogether more biblical. Some versions, however, only 'secularized' this scene, by placing in the position of the former Catholic saints either Luther or a secular protector of the Reformation, such as Frederick the Wise of Saxony. In some depictions, the saving blood of Christ was shown as the saving water of Baptism, in one depiction of the Cranach school flowing into a font, as if a fountain of life.

(vi) Glorification of patrons

In this use of images, religion and social status became as intermingled as under Catholicism. There was not just the development of the Protestant epitaph, which celebrated departed individuals as true and faithful Protestants. There were also 'martyr' pictures, to commemorate those who had suffered in the cause of the Gospel, such as the Elector of Saxony John Frederick, imprisoned after the Protestant defeat in the Schmalkaldic War in 1547. In some Protestant altars, the princely protectors were set in the presence of the holy, for example, as witnesses at the Baptism of Christ; or depicted as apostles at the Last Supper (alongside the major reformers: sometimes these reformer-apostles were also given haloes!).

(vii) Political imagery

This is suggested by our last category, and here we are close to crossing the boundary between religious and secular art. However, if we accept that there was a religiously inspired 'evangelical politics' in the sixteenth and seventeenth centuries, then we must accept that the images of that period glorifying the struggles to 'defend Protestantism' had a religious dimension as well. These could take the form of depicting an armed Protestant prince as the complete 'Christian soldier' (Scribner, 1981: 77). During the Thirty Years War, there were broadsheet depictions of the 'three incomparable heroes' who fought for the Protestant cause: Gustavus Adolphus, his ally the Elector of Saxony John George, and Luther. Such depictions were frequent in the literature of the Thirty Years War (Kastner, 1982; Coupe, 1966).

I hope to have shown here, albeit in a very sketchy way, that there is good cause to revise our attitudes about the Reformation's use of images. There was far more continuity with the pre-Reformation period than has been recognized in the past (doubtless a result of the attempt of confessional historiography to depict the break with the old as being as radical and drastic as possible). We can even find Protestant images which were perhaps used as magical amulets. One at least provided a Lutheran form of the pious saint's life, a hollowed-out coin from the seventeenth century, which was filled with a tiny pictorial biography of Luther (Scribner, 1983). I think we can safely conclude that there was no such dramatic passing away of an 'image culture' as is commonly supposed. There certainly were important changes in the 'ways of seeing', in the modes of visual perception. These have yet to be properly explored – here there is certainly a field of endeavour for art historians, social historians and historians of popular culture.

Bibliography and references

Baxandall, M. (1980), *The Limewood Sculptors of Renaissance Germany*, New Haven.

Bèze, T. (1580), *Icones id est verae imagines virorum doctrina simul et pietate illustrium*, Geneva.

Brady, T.A. (1978), *Ruling Class, Regime and Reformation at Strasbourg 1520–1555*, Leiden.

Christensen, C.C. (1979), *Art and the Reformation in Germany*, Athens, Ohio.

Coupe, W.A. (1966), *The German Illustrated Broadsheet in the Seventeenth Century*, Baden-Baden.

Edwards, M.U. (1983), *Luther's Last Battles. Politics and Polemics 1531–46*, Leiden.

Garside, C. (1966), *Zwingli and the Arts*, New Haven.

Haebler, H.C. (1957), *Das Bild in der evangelischen Kirche*, Berlin.

Halewood, W.H. (1982), *Six Subjects of Reformation Art: A Preface to Rembrandt*, Toronto.

Kastner, R. (1982), *Geistlicher Rauffhandel. Form und Funktion der illustrierten Flugblätter zum Reformationsjubiläum 1617*, Frankfurt-am-Main.

Koepplin, D. (1983), 'Reformation der Glaubensbilder: Das Erlösungswerk Christi auf Bildern des Spätmittelalters und der Reformationszeit', in *Martin Luther und die Reformation in Deutschland. Ausstellung zum 500. Geburtstag Martin Luthers*, veranstaltet vom Germanischen National-museum Nürnberg, Nuremberg.

Lieske, R. (1973), *Protestantische Frömmigkeit im Spiegel der kirchlichen Kunst des Herzogtums Württemberg*, Munich.

Scharfe, M. (1968), *Evangelische Andachtsbilder*, Stuttgart.

Scribner, R.W. (1978), 'Reformation, Carnival and the World turned Upside Down', *Social History*, 3.

Scribner, R.W. (1981), *For the Sake of Simple Folk. Popular Propaganda for the German Reformation*, Cambridge.

Scribner, R.W. (1983), 'The Reformer as Prophet and Saint', *History Today*, 33.

Scribner, R.W. (1984), 'Ritual and Popular Religion in Catholic Germany at the Time of the Reformation', *Journal of Ecclesiastical History*, 35.

Scribner, R.W. (1985), 'Volkskultur und Volksreligion: zur Rezeption evangelischer Ideen', in *Zwingli und Europa*, ed. P. Blickle, Zürich.

Scribner, R.W. (1986), 'Incombustible Luther: the Image of the Reformer in early modern Germany', *Past and Present*, 110.

Stirm, M. (1977), *Die Bilderfrage in der Reformation*, Gütershoh.

Stopp, F.J. (1965), 'Der religiös-polemische Einblattdruck "Ecclesia Militans" (1563)', *Deutsche Vierteljahrsschrift für Lituraturwissenschaft*, 39.

Warnke, M. (1973), 'Durchbrochene Geschichte? Die Bilderstürme der Wiedertäufer in Munster 1534/1535', in *Bildersturm: Die Zerstörung des Kunstwerks*, ed. M. Warnke, Frankfurt-am-Main.

35
Music and religion in the nineteenth century

JIM OBELKEVICH

Where there is religion, there is usually music: indeed, worship and ritual have been more closely and more consistently allied with music than with any of the other arts. In Christianity, its role has been a privileged one from the very beginning, and not only in worship, where it is virtually indispensable, but also in the realm of myth and imagination. After the last trumpet sounds there will be music – but no other art – in heaven.

Here on earth, to be sure, the churches' attitudes have been more ambivalent. If music can aid devotion, it can also stir up lust and vice; too often the devil has the best tunes. The church fathers, associating musical instruments with dancing and 'im-morality', actually banned their use in worship; the Reformers, condemning late medieval polyphony for distracting worshippers instead of edifying them, showed that church music itself had its dangers. While supporting and subsidizing music, the churches have often also been anxious to regulate it, to keep the 'handmaid' of religion in its place.

At any rate, as patrons of music – for many centuries the chief patrons – the churches have had a major influence on its development. Until the seventeenth and eighteenth centuries the history of music in the West is largely a history of religious music: in masses, motets and other sacred settings the composer's art found its highest expression. Eventually, of course, music escaped the churches' control. Secular forms emerged – opera, the symphony, the concerto – as demanding and serious as anything written for the church; by the nineteenth century most of what we would regard as the masterpieces of music were independent of Christianity, the products of a secular and autonomous art. Music and religion, it would appear, now went their separate ways.

Yet the matter was not so simple. In England, religious music lost none of its prestige; in Germany, secular music itself came to be invested with religious significance. Throughout Europe political ideologies with religious pretensions allied themselves with music. Instead of a divorce between religion and music, the ties between them were actually strengthened; the sacred powers of music were honoured, and exploited, by Christians, sceptics and socialists alike.

Music and Victorian Protestantism

Judged by continental standards, the musical life of the Victorians was inevitably found wanting; without a national opera, reputable orchestras or major composers, England was dismissed by the Germans as the 'land without music'. Yet if English music did not fit the continental pattern, it was vigorous enough in its own terms. With choral societies instead of orchestras, oratorio instead of opera, England was the only country in Western Europe where religious music still took precedence over secular. It would be no exaggeration to speak of a Victorian religion of religious music.

Within the churches, moreover, music gained a prominence and prestige in worship it had never previously known. While the spoken portions of the service contracted – the sermon shrank in the course of the century from an hour to 30 minutes or less – the musical portions grew steadily longer. Victorian church music, with the familiar combination of organs, choirs and hymns as its nucleus, was itself a product of the period; crystallizing first in the Church of England, it quickly became the norm in all the main Protestant denominations, and still survives as 'traditional' church music in the present day.

It is best studied in its Anglican version – the most elaborate, the most influential, and for all its undoubted popularity, the most revealingly controversial. It replaced an older, mainly rural pattern of church music, based on 'folk psalmody' and the west gallery bands, which was swept away, not without protest, by 'reforming' parsons in the 1830s and 40s. Yet the new style, more cultivated and genteel, an adaptation of cathedral music for middle-class urban parishes, also excited a certain unease.[1]

Organs, for example, had long been considered unsuitable for parish worship, and when they eventually became standard equipment, in the second half of the century, the doubts did not entirely go away. Powerful modern instruments, flooding churches with sound, too often submerged the words of the hymns; even during private prayer they churned away in the background, with every pause in the service tempting organists into 'vulgar display'. When affluent congregations replaced their organ three or four times in the course of the century, with each new model larger, louder and more expensive than the one before, a music instrument was turning into a status symbol, even a cult object. New organs were opened with special services that amounted to a consecration; placed ostentatiously in the chancel or transept, dominating the eye as well as the ear, these oversize pieces of machinery not only accompanied worship but invited it. Organ recitals, usually including secular works, even transcriptions from opera, only underlined the problem. A servant's role in worship was always a limiting and unlikely one for the 'king of instruments'.

Choirs, the second element in the new church music, were no nineteenth-century innovation, but their status was upgraded, and they were even awarded a better place in the church seating plan. Previously in the west gallery, they were now in the chancel, the most sacred part of the church; choristers wore surplices, like the priest, and had the privilege of making their way to their places in a separate procession of their own. (In town churches, at least, Anglican choirs usually consisted of male voices only; high churchmen were anxious to preserve the chancel from 'violation' by women and scorned the 'cock and hen' choirs of Dissent.) Improved singing, often approaching professional standards, made possible that high church pride and joy, the 'fully choral' service, in which nearly every item was set to music and the choir was in action throughout. An Evangelical complained after such a service that even the notices were sung.

Good singing, it was generally agreed, attracted congregations, but, as critics complained, they were rather passive ones, and the better the choir the more silent they were likely to be. Though congregational singing was encouraged both by Evangelicals and by Tractarians, their efforts came to little; there was resistance not least from the organists, some of whom deliberately made their hymn accompaniments so complicated that the congregation could not make out the tune, thus keeping the singing for the choir. Fashionable congregations in any case regarded singing as ungenteel and the choir as servants hired to perform the task for them; the custom of remaining seated until the choir had sung the first line of the hymn made the point clear. Many churchgoers were content simply to listen, as at a concert.

For Nonconformists, these new developments had too many Anglican, even high church, associations to arouse anything other than mixed feelings. If chapel people now followed the Anglican lead – having been innovators themselves a century earlier in introducing hymns – they did so at a careful distance; charges of 'churchifying' and 'Romanizing' were always liable to greet those who imitated Anglican fashion too closely. Nonconformists dissolved their instrumental bands and installed organs, but they also remained true to their traditions in keeping their mixed choirs, their hearty congregational singing and their focus on the sermon; only the most middle-class chapels went all the way to a chanted liturgy and choral service. (There had been trouble even over attempts to introduce organs, and there would be protests later when the Amen after a hymn was sung instead of spoken.) But at the end of the century, when Nonconformists lifted the ban on vocal solos in church and introduced secular 'musical services' (with gramophone 'recitals' in the 1920s), they went further in relaxing their musical puritanism even than the Anglicans. Music, a Methodist minister observed in 1910, was a 'divine art', and in an age of 'suffused pantheism' all music, 'at any rate all instrumental music', was 'sacred'.

Where Dissenters and Anglicans could agree was on the indispensability of hymns, the third ingredient in the new music and to most churchgoers the most important. Long established in Nonconformity, a surprisingly late arrival in the Church of England (only becoming legal in 1820), they now enjoyed, in quantitative terms at least, their golden age: in the 1850s and 60s, the peak decades, more than 400 collections appeared in England alone. They were produced for individual congregations; for entire churches (including the *Labour Church Hymn Book* (1895)); for a wide range of institutions with their own religious services (e.g., the *Public School Hymn Book* (1903)); for every shading of theology; and for every level of taste, including the highbrows who wanted poetry set to madrigals and the lowbrows who preferred 'doggerel set to jingles': there were hymns for everyone.

So popular were they that they were sung outside churches as well as within them; some virtually became folk songs. Families who sang them at church came home and sang them again round the piano:

> . . . the old Sunday evenings at home, with
>   winter outside
> And hymns in the cozy parlour, the tinkling piano
>   our guide

were recalled by ex-Congregationalist D.H. Lawrence.[2] Taught in the board schools as well as in church and Sunday schools, hymns were known to many working-class people who rarely attended a place of worship. They were sung on Whit walks and (to different words) in the trenches during the Great War; 'Abide with Me' was part of the festivities at the F.A. Cup Final. If there has been a 'common religion' in England in the last hundred years it has been based not on doctrine but on the popular hymns.

The search for their meanings can begin with the hymn texts themselves – though we will want to go further than Lawrence, for whom all that mattered was the exotic place names that aroused his sense of 'wonder'. In Sankey's *Sacred Songs and Solos*, the classic American revivalist collection, John Kent has found echoes of the family dramas of the uprooted lower middle classes: stern fathers, errant children far from home, reconciliation only in heaven. More conventionally conservative, as Stephen Wilson has shown, are the social and political themes of *Hymns Ancient and Modern* (1889 edition), the main Anglican collection. With God represented as a remote, powerful, sometimes martial figure, a father, king, lord or judge, the cardinal virtues are a childlike submissiveness and obedience. The hymns legitimate existing political authority and the social hierarchy; they recommend charity rather than justice and they defer the rewards of the righteous poor to the afterlife. Though portraying the relationship between man and God in erotic terms, they reject sexuality and reveal a masochistic streak, as if to justify pain and suffering.[3] What Wilson's perceptive but rather static analysis misses is that in the course of the nineteenth century hymns underwent a considerable degree of liberalization. Old shockers like 'There is a fountain filled with blood' were eased out; 'when my eyestrings break in death', in 'Rock of Ages', was replaced by 'when my eyelids close'; the 'worms'-ridden older hymns were treated with disinfectant. In contrast with the hardline Calvinism of some of the eighteenth-century hymns, those of the Victorians positively glory in human worth and activity.

The importance of the words, however, can be easily exaggerated: it was the music, after all, that made hymns popular. And it is the music in which Victorian religiosity – the emotional base, as distinguished from the doctrinal superstructure – most fully reveals itself. The best approach is through the many controversies over hymn music; though criticism of hymns fastened on the musical failings, their emotional style was usually the real target.

As many of the critics were both cultivated musicians and Anglicans, their complaints are to some extent predictable. The lively Methodist tunes of the eighteenth century, borrowed in many instances from dance music, were condemned as 'outrageously boisterous and vulgar'. American revivalist hymns and choruses of the Sankey type – 'Hold the fort for I am coming', 'Tell me the old, old story' – gave offence to sophisticates in every denomination. More surprising is the abuse – 'depressing', 'degenerate', 'hysterical', 'insincere', 'effeminate', etc. – dealt out to the Anglican standards of Dykes and Barnby. Harmonic mannerisms such as diminished seventh chords and dominant sevenths in cadences were dismissed as 'sickly sweet' and 'nauseating'. Yet for all their bias and excesses, the critics were often right. Even when the words of the hymn speak of humility, the music sounds pleased with itself; discords are resolved smoothly, even mechanically. (Similar criticisms would be made of pop music, both from the classical and the rock camps, generations later.) Earnest, self-absorbed, incurably sentimental, the hymn tunes reveal the soft centre at the core of Victorian Protestantism.

A second criticism of the hymn tunes was that instead of serving the texts, they were becoming an end in themselves,

enjoyed for their own sake – indeed that the words were being
sacrificed and subordinated to the music. Either the words were
'mangled together' to fit the 'procrustean bed' of the tune, or
syllables were repeated to make up the numbers (in one example,
admittedly apocryphal: 'Oh for a man-, Oh for a man-, Oh for a
mansion in the sky'). Sometimes the composer virtually disregarded the words, making no attempt to render their meaning,
mood or rhythm; performers similarly were criticized for an
'indifference to the words of hymns that is really terrifying'. The
subjection of words to music shifted attention not only to the
tunes but to the harmonies, increasingly a source of pleasure in
their own right. Before the nineteenth century, as Temperley
points out, each syllable of text (in music for congregational
singing) had been accompanied by a separate chord; but in
Victorian hymns the harmonies often changed independently of
the words, taking on a life and interest of their own.[4] The 'juicy'
harmonies familiar in Victorian part songs were used in hymns as
well, sometimes by the same composers: Barnby, for example,
was equally known for 'Sweet and Low' and for 'Lord of our life
and God of our salvation'. Thus the words no longer determined
either the tune or the harmony; with choir and organ going full
blast, they were reduced to just one strand, not necessarily the
most important one, in a larger, richer musical texture. The
specifically Christian element was in danger of being lost in the
pleasures of the music.

The significance of the new church music was as much social
and cultural as religious. Drawing its technique and style from the
respectable composers of contemporary art music, it had turned
its back on the rough and ready efforts of the west gallery bands;
at the same time its sleek, richly coloured style matched the self-
confidence and sentimentality of its audience. As a religious
phenomenon, the 'musicalization' of worship was both a product
of Victorian Protestantism and a symptom of its decline. At a
time when orthodox beliefs on such matters as eternal punishment
were causing doubt and dismay, beautiful music came as a
welcome diversion, papering over the doctrinal cracks. (Ritualism
had a similar effect, but was limited to a minority even of
Anglican churches; some version of the new music, by contrast,
was adopted in virtually every Anglican and Nonconformist
church in the country.) Music rekindled the spirit of worship just
as the traditional object of worship was becoming problematic.

The close ties between music and religion did not end at the
church door. Oratorio – dignified, sometimes boring, but highly
acceptable to the churchgoing public – dominated the wider

musical scene in England to the end of the century and beyond; *Messiah*, it was said, was the first article in England's musical constitution. That pride of place was not given to opera, as elsewhere, was primarily for religious reasons: opera fell foul of the Puritan and Evangelican ban on the theatre, but to attend an oratorio, as Wagner observed, was 'almost as good as going to church'. He might have added that musically, it was almost as good as going to the opera itself. Soloists, choruses and orchestras were common to both; when oratorios were performed at the leading festivals, singers who had made their names in opera were the star attractions. (In a similar way, oratorio circumvented religious prejudice against opera in America as well.)

Victorian religiosity ensured oratorio's cultural preeminence: it also provided it with the performers and audiences who formed its surprisingly broad social constituency. In most performances of oratorio the choruses were made up not of professionals but of amateurs from the choral societies, whose membership, particularly in the northern industrial districts, was by no means exclusively middle-class. Large numbers of working men and women learned to read music by the tonic sol-fa method, sang in chapel and church choirs, then progressed to the choral societies; for them as for their middle-class colleagues, singing oratorios was the peak of their musical aspirations.[5] (In Wales, by contrast, choirs were mostly male voice rather than mixed, and sang a limited repertoire; many of their members could not read music and, to the shock of their English counterparts, had never sung *Messiah*!) The choral societies grew rapidly after 1830 – the best known, in Huddersfield, was founded in 1836 – and had their heartland in industrial Lancashire and Yorkshire, themselves rivals for the distinction of 'musical capital' of England; the great northern town halls – their concert rooms, equipped with massive organs, dwarfed the municipal offices – were a tribute not only to civic pride but also to the cult of oratorio and choral singing. At their best the choral societies achieved remarkably high musical standards; European visitors like Berlioz were impressed, and a long line of disbelieving London music critics made the journey north only to be astonished by the artistry of mill girls and artisans. In their dedication to oratorio, their musical excellence and their broad social appeal, the northern choral societies were at the heart of Victorian musical life.

Even more than the hymns, oratorio transcended the tribal warfare between Protestant and Catholic, Anglican and Non-conformist which marked the Victorian religious scene. No doubt composers avoided subjects which might offend; at any rate, their own denominational (and national) origins were disregarded by a Protestant audience which listened with little complaint to works by agnostics like Sullivan and Stanford and by Catholics like Liszt, Gounod, Dvořák and Elgar – *The Dream of Gerontius* was set to a text by Cardinal Newman. Like hymns, oratorios owed their success or failure not to their doctrine but to their music, and as with hymns, the domination of music over text in the second half of the century steadily increased; with the influence of Liszt (*Christus*, 1867) and Wagner at its height, the tendency was for composers like Stanford to 'write an oratorio as a symphony and give voices a part in it'.[6] But as oratorios became less voice and text-based, their Christian content could easily be lost in a welter of orchestral effects; if they preserved a religious character it lay in the depth and intensity of expression in the music itself.

The fortunes of oratorio had always been tied to those of the churches; when the decline eventually set in – not till after 1900 – it was less because of competition from music halls or cinema than because the churches and chapels which had sustained the oratorio culture were themselves declining. The consequence was a major reorientation of English musical life: from the oratorio to the symphony, from the amateur to the professional, and from the provinces to London, where musical activity was more secular, more commercialized and more class-stratified.

Music and the 'secular religions'

Not all the religious music of the period was intended for Christians. For sceptics, socialists and other converts to new ideologies there was a small but significant body of post-Christian works – still religious in spirit even if no longer orthodox in content. Religion changed, sometimes drastically, but the links with music were preserved.

In England, where the reaction against Christianity tended to be a reluctant, cautious affair, it brought with it music of similar character. Indeed, many of those who had abandoned Christian doctrines would still attend church occasionally for the sake of the hymns and anthems. And when the organized rationalist groups held services of their own, they were content with adaptations of existing church music: in the West London Ethical Society in 1913 there were hymns, anthems and a chanted liturgy. But if the tunes were borrowed from the opposition – in the *Secular Song and Hymn Book* (1876), edited by Annie Besant, most came from *Hymns Ancient and Modern* – the texts reflected the freethinkers' own cultivated literary taste. *Hymns of Modern Thought* (1900), in an edition sponsored by the Hampstead Ethical Institute, offered contributions by Blake, Longfellow and George Eliot; guaranteed to be free of all 'theological dogma' – 'even the name of "God" . . . has been avoided' – they affirmed 'a growing faith in the capacities for good hidden within human nature'.

Where 'modern thought' inspired a music of its own was rather in large choral works, by composers who themselves had drifted away from Christianity. Vaughan Williams, agnostic son of an Anglican parson, with a 'personal mythology' of Bunyan, Blake and Whitman, wrote *Toward the Unknown Region* (1905) to a text by Whitman, while *Dona nobis pacem* (1936) draws upon the Bible, Whitman and John Bright's 'Angel of Death' speech. Delius, another infidel, was the son of German Protestant parents in Bradford and had been confirmed in the Church of England; arguing that English music would never amount to anything till it rid itself of Christianity, he wrote his *Mass of Life* (1905) to Nietzsche's *Zarathustra*.

In France, by contrast, where the break with Christianity came early and decisively, the musical and religious consequences were more radical. For what the Enlightenment sought to put in place of Christianity was a deism intended not merely as a private creed but as a civil religion – one which after 1789 was taken up and politicized by the Revolution itself. The musical result – the new militant faith was as incomplete with music as any traditional religion – was a new genre, religio-revolutionary in character, celebrating the ideals, heroes and holidays of the revolutionary movement. These works, written by some of the leading French composers and designed particularly for the great outdoor festivals of 1791–94, comprised 'hymns' to Voltaire, to Liberty, to Agriculture, and so on, as well as devotional music for the cults of Reason and the Supreme Being. Though derived in part from traditional church music, these works employed larger forces – massed outdoor choirs and bands – and were simpler and broader in style;[7] they envisioned not separate congregations but an entire nation, united through music in allegiance to Reason and Revolution. Yet as in the churches, music not only warmed the hearts of the faithful, it in some sense actually realized or embodied the ideals it celebrated.

Music had served church and king: it now served the will of the people. Could it not also serve the wishes of the politicians? Of the Revolution's legacies to the nineteenth century, political mobilization through music was one of the most attractive; as the common people entered the political arena, leaders would win their support with songs and anthems. The model only worked, however, when conditions were favourable. Liberalism, the first of the new creeds, had been set to music during the Revolution when its character was civic and religious; in the nineteenth century, as it became more individualistic, more rationalist and (on the Continent at least) more anti-religious, it tended to lose its musical backing. Nationalism, by contrast, more communal in outlook and often a surrogate for religion, was steeped in music. It was linked with the rediscovery of folk music, with composers like Grieg in Norway and Dvořák in Bohemia, and with the adoption of national anthems. Mazzini, inspired by the festivals of the 1789 Revolution, argued that nations divided by history could be reunited by music.

In utopian socialism the alliance between music and religion was closer still. The Owenites founded their American community at New Harmony and published a collection of *Social Hymns* (1938) as well as a *Social Bible*. Saint-Simon, presenting the final version of his system in *Le nouveau Christianisme* (1825), assigned to 'artists' (including musicians) the high moral and spiritual role traditionally performed by the priesthood; his views attracted the interest of Berlioz and Liszt as well as inspiring a number of works by the minor composer Félicien David. But of all these thinkers it is Fourier for whom music counts most. Building the new society he compared to a musician playing chords on a piano; harmony, the name he gave to the system as a whole and recurring constantly in its details, is his master metaphor. Not that live music was neglected. Anyone wishing to join the phalanxes, the basic units of the new society, would have to have a good ear for music and take part in community singing; attending performances of opera would be a 'semi-religious exercise' for all the 'children of Harmony'.[8]

Later, the analogy between musical and social harmony would weaken, if only because there were ever fewer concords and more dissonances in the music composers actually wrote. But the general links between religion, socialism and music remained. In England, at the end of the century, it was above all the 'religion of socialism' which won converts, and as before it was music – whether in the choirs of the Clarion Vocal Union, in William Morris's *Chants for Socialists* (1884), or in Holst's musical programmes for the Hammersmith Socialist Society – which best expressed their hopes for the 'good times coming'. In the Soviet Union, however, where socialist religion has turned conservative, socialist music, produced in huge quantities, has become merely functional or manipulative, if anthems like A.D. Kastalsky's 'Lenin' and 'To the Proletariat' are any indication.

The religion of music

As England, with its strong churches and mediocre composers, had created a religion of religious music, so Germany, with weak churches and great composers, created a religion of secular music. Primarily the work of the German Romantics, this involved not only a shift of religious feeling from Christianity to music but a new philosophical discourse on music, and indeed a redrawing of the entire cultural map.[9]

The first move, in effect, was to dissolve the old boundary between religion and art: for the Romantics, all art was religious. They then overturned both the artistic hierarchy, replacing poetry, its traditional head, with music, and the hierarchy within music, replacing vocal works with instrumental. The result, at least in its original form, was a religion not so much of music in general as of instrumental music – and one with a definite Protestant flavour. For Wackenroder, a Protestant like most of his fellow Romantics, instrumental music was 'the one true art, a heaven to be gained by the renunciation of reality'. (The very notion of 'absolute' music, in alluding to idealist philosophy, also bore traces of a secularized Protestantism.) As Luther had exalted the spirit above the letter, so the Romantics exalted music above poetry; innerworldly asceticism led to a Protestant aestheticism. Music, freed from the 'externals' of words and doctrines, was now the authentic language of the soul.

It was above all the music of Beethoven, unprecedented in its rendering of the inner life, both in struggle and in serenity, that the Romantics treasured for its religious qualities. Symphonies, sonatas, quartets – all were lauded as sources of spiritual insight, indeed of a new spiritual dispensation; his music, a later admirer claimed, 'opens up horizons beyond Church or creed'. Beethoven himself was saluted not just as a composer but as a culture hero, the supreme figure in the artistic pantheon. Hailed for his 'godlike' powers during his own lifetime and undergoing an 'apotheosis' after his death, he combined the qualities of God, Christ and Prometheus – a titanic, revolutionary creator who was yet a suffering one, whose very deafness was believed to have released the spirit within. In the educated classes, where music was compensating for the loss of Christian orthodoxy, Beethoven-worship was rampant. An English example is Sir George Grove: the son of Evangelical parents in the Clapham Sect and while still a believer the main contributor to a *Dictionary of the Bible* (1860–5), he lost his faith, turned increasingly to music, and besides editing the great *Dictionary of Music and Musicians*

(1878–89) wrote a standard work on Beethoven's symphonies, which he found 'as truly religious as any oratorio'. In America a similar path was followed by the New England Transcendentalists, some of whom left the ministry to pursue their musical studies; eventually abandoning Christianity altogether, they were devoted to music and 'revered' Beethoven.

Yet there was more to the Romantic cult of music than a transplanted religious vocabulary. From Schopenhauer it received a closely argued philosophical formulation which has underpinned attitudes toward music down to the present day. While the other arts merely imitate our ideas of the external world, music, according to Schopenhauer, presents the unconscious Will, the primal force in life. Wagner was deeply influenced by these views, and it is Wagner, both in his operas and in his writings, who gives the religion of music its most grandiose expression. When discussing Beethoven he turns constantly to Christian themes and texts, interpreting the Pastoral Symphony as 'Today shalt thou be with me in Paradise' and the finale of the Ninth as the 'Chorale of the new communion'; Beethoven himself was a 'Luther in his rage against the Pope'. If traditional religion had become 'artificial', music was a more than adequate replacement: it offered the 'essence of Religion free from all dogmatic fictions'! By 'teaching redemption-starved mankind a second speech in which the Infinite can voice itself', music would give modern civilization a 'soul', a 'new religion'. The composer, whether Beethoven or Wagner himself, was 'holy', a 'tone-poet seer' who 'reveals to us the inexpressible', his 'suffering' being his 'penalty for the state of inspiration'. For Wagner, prophet as well as musician, the aim was not only to entertain his audiences but to save their souls, the message (drawn from Christianity, Buddhism and Schopenhauer) being one of love and self-renunciation: 'My kingdom is not of this world.'[10] Wagner and his music soon became the object of a cult which provides one of the best examples of a religion of art. (Wagnerites often spoke of their 'pilgrimages' to Bayreuth, where the performances indeed had a 'liturgical' quality.) Yet what mattered to the devotees may not have been quite what Wagner intended: less the morality or the mythology than the music itself, with its uncanny power to evoke the strivings and sufferings of the inner life. In an age when art and religion alike were grounded in feeling, music was the most religious of the arts, and Wagnerian music the most religious of all.

By the late nineteenth century the supremacy of music was generally acknowledged. For the French symbolists, Wagnerites to a man, the call was for 'de la musique avant toute chose'; for

Pater, 'all art aspires to the condition of music'; for Shaw (in *The Perfect Wagnerite*, 1898), 'after the symphonies of Beethoven it was certain that the poetry that lies too deep for words does not lie too deep for music'. Painters, poets and novelists strove to give their works the rhythmic and non-mimetic qualities of music, and something too of its aura and mystique. Music, sharing its sacred power with the lesser arts, made possible the religion of art in general.

Music did not just entertain. It inspired, it comforted, it touched the soul. Formerly a 'beautiful art standing over against life', it was becoming a 'vehicle for some of the deepest and most obscure feelings of humanity'. No longer the handmaid of religion, subordinate to the churches, it was now independent, 'mistress in the house'. But in gaining its independence just as the churches were losing their hold, it filled the emotional gap left by their decline, taking on a religious character of its own.

Conclusion: the religion of music today

Romanticism has long since fallen from favour. But its essentially religious attitude towards music has had a deeper influence on us than we may like to admit. Even now, the hushed, reverential atmosphere at a classical concert is notoriously churchlike, and a Paul Tortelier can say that each time he plays Bach he 'kneels before the angels'.

What is new is that the religious dimensions of music have become apparent outside the classical scene, in jazz, rock and reggae as well. Rock has its deities (to his fans Eric Clapton is 'God') and its martyrs, like Jim Morrison and Janis Joplin, each with their cult following; we can hardly make sense of the Elvis cult, the biggest of them all, without reference to religion. 1960s rock, which its devotees liked to believe would bring a new heaven and a new earth, had something of the character of a radical religious movement of an earlier age.

For even in a 'secular' society, as Thomas Luckmann has argued, we need some sort of religion, however private or 'invisible' it may be; he only fails to add that it is likely to be audible – a religion we invent for ourselves in our music. At any rate the benefits of music and those of more traditional forms of religion seem remarkably similar. When we experience music as absolute, powerful, mysterious and ineffable, we single out the qualities conventionally attributed to the sacred, the numinous, or to God. Similarly the elation and exaltation produced by music are the nearest thing to the ecstasy of mystical religion. As for myth, though it may be losing credibility in church, it can still speak to us powerfully in the opera house; when Lévi-Strauss salutes Wagner as 'that God', it is for having elevated myth into religion by means of music. (In *The Raw and the Cooked*, dedicated to 'Music', Lévi-Strauss presents some of his own analysis of myth under (pre-Wagnerian) headings like 'Sonata' and 'Theme and Variations'.) If music does little to teach morality – not a universal function of religion in any case – the Victorians were not alone in supposing that 'good' music must have a moral effect on those who listen to it. (Operatic villains and film scores apart, music is even less adept at representing evil, though Mick Jagger's 'Sympathy for the Devil', performed at Altamont in 1969 for an appreciative audience which included Hell's Angels, is a well known exception.)

Where music has most successfully rivalled traditional religion is in answering the needs and longings of our inner life. There is music for every mood, comforting us, challenging us, raising our spirit; music, like God, is our friend – sometimes, we feel with gratitude, our saviour. When we are truly touched by music, it becomes part of us, an aspect of our identity; the story of our music, consequently, is the story of our lives, a spiritual autobiography revealing more about us (as 'Desert Island Discs' often demonstrates) than anything we put into words.

It would be easy to conclude that music, with its ability to soothe and console, also resembles Christianity in having a mainly conservative, stabilizing influence on society. If Saturday-night fever now counts for more than Sunday-morning fervour, the effect seems much the same; anyone seeking the 'heart of a heartless world' or the 'opiate of the people' can find it just as easily in music as in traditional Christianity.

Yet music can still play an emancipatory role – not only because it is used in political movements, but, more fundamentally, because our 'ordinary' experience of it can be such a powerful one. For as Ernst Bloch argued – like the Romantics and Utopians before him – our pleasure in music is no merely private or ephemeral affair. Through music, we come alive, we are made whole again, body and soul reunited; and at the same time we are freed from the constraints of society as it actually exists and taken outside ourselves into a kind of ideal realm – into what might once have been called a state of grace. Music, then, does more than delight us. It prefigures an alternative world, a higher order of human existence, a paradise temporarily regained; that makes it the most prophetic, even eschatological, of the arts, the 'central art', as Bloch reminds us, of the 'utopian consciousness'.[11] It has the power to liberate not in spite of but because of its religious character – a heretical faith, to be sure, of good without evil, rewards without punishments, where the only morality is that of the pleasure principle. Music does not describe that better world but provides us with what is perhaps more important, its inward reality – a world of which we have already tasted the first fruits, and which we may one day possess and know as our own. There is heaven in music.

Notes

1   Vic Gammon, '"Babylonian Performances": the Rise and Suppression of Popular Church Music, 1660–1870', in Eileen and Stephen Yeo (eds), *Popular Culture and Class Conflict 1590–1914* (Brighton, 1981); more generally, Nicholas Temperley, *The Music of the English Parish Church* (Cambridge, 1979), vol. 1, chs 6–9.

2   D.H. Lawrence, 'Piano', in *Collected Poems of D.H. Lawrence*, eds Vivian de Sola Pinto and Warren Roberts (London, 1964), vol. 1, p.148.

3   D.H. Lawrence, 'Hymns in a Man's Life', in *Phoenix II*, eds Warren Roberts and Harry T. Moore (London, 1968), pp.598–600; J. Kent, *Holding the Fort: Studies in Victorian Revivalism* (London, 1978), ch. 6; S. Wilson, 'Religious and Social Attitudes in "Hymns Ancient and Modern" (1889)', *Social Compass*, 22 (1975), pp.211–36.

4   Temperley, pp.305–7.

5   Dave Russell, 'The Popular Musical Societies of the Yorkshire Textile District, 1850–1914', Ph.D. thesis, University of York, 1979, ch. 3.

6   Arthur Hutchings, *Church Music in the Nineteenth Century* (London, 1967), p.111.

7   Adelheid Coy, *Die Musik der Französischen Revolution* (Salzburg, 1978), pp.6, 7, 55.

8   C. Fourier, 'Théorie de l'unité universelle', in *Oeuvres complètes* (Paris, 1966), vol. 5, p.6.

9   H.G. Koenigsberger, 'Music and Religion in Modern European History', in J.H. Elliott and H.G. Koenigsberger (eds), *The Diversity of History: Essays in Honour of Sir Herbert Butterfield* (London, 1970), pp.62–72; Carl Dahlhaus, *Die Musik des 19. Jahrhunderts* (Wiesbaden, 1980), pp.73–9.

10 R. Wagner, 'Beethoven' (1870), in *Prose Works*, trans. W.A. Ellis (London, 1892), vol. 5, pp.72, 77, 92, 102, 120, 123; 'Religion and Art' (1880), vol. 6, pp.249, 250.

11 E. Bloch, from an essay of 1939, quoted and translated by George Steiner, *TLS* (4 October 1985), p.1088.

Index